육사 | 해사 | 공사 | 국군간호

사관학교
기출문제

영 어

2024~2015

10
개년

연차별 동형
기출문제

2025
사관학교 기출문제
영어
10개년
총·정·리
2024~2015학년도

인쇄일 2023년 10월 1일 9판 1쇄 인쇄
발행일 2023년 10월 5일 9판 1쇄 발행
등 록 제17-269호
판 권 시스컴2023

발행처 시스컴 출판사
발행인 송인식
지은이 사관학교입시연구회

ISBN 979-11-6941-204-9 13740
정 가 22,000원

주소 서울시 금천구 가산디지털1로 225, 514호(가산포휴) | **홈페이지** www.nadoogong.com
E-mail siscombooks@naver.com | **전화** 02)866-9311 | **Fax** 02)866-9312

발간 이후 발견된 정오 사항은 나두공 홈페이지 도서정오표에서 알려드립니다.(나두공 홈페이지 → 자격증 → 도서정오표)

머리말

육군사관학교, 해군사관학교, 공군사관학교, 국군간호사관학교의 4개의 특수대학은 군 장교 양성을 위한 4년제 군사학교로, 졸업 후 군의 간부로서의 장래를 보장받을 수 있습니다. 즉, 졸업과 동시에 취업이 보장된다는 상당히 매력적인 점으로 인해 매년 높은 경쟁률을 보여 오고 있습니다. 사관학교는 이처럼 경쟁률이 높은데다 남녀 모집 인원이 정해져 있고 체력시험을 치러야 하는 등 전형 방법이 일반 대학과 다르기 때문에 상당한 준비가 필요합니다. 따라서 미리 자신이 원하는 대학의 모집요강을 숙지하고 각 대학에 맞는 입시전략을 세워야 합니다.

그렇다면 사관학교 입시에서 무엇이 가장 중요할까요?

당연한 말이지만 바로 1차 필기시험입니다. 왜냐하면 1차 시험에서 일정 배수 안에 들어야 2차 시험에 응시할 수 있는 기회가 주어지기 때문입니다. 각 사관학교는 같은 날 1차 시험을 치르기 때문에 복수지원이 불가능하다는 점 역시 잊지 말아야 합니다. 1차 시험을 잘 보기 위해서는 무엇보다도 기출문제를 꼼꼼히 파악하고 풀어보는 것이 중요합니다. 그래야 실제 시험에서 긴장하지 않고 실수를 최소화할 수 있기 때문입니다.

이에 본서는 사관학교 입시에 필수적인 과년도 최신 기출문제를 실어 연도별로 기출문제를 풀어볼 수 있도록 구성하여 연도별 출제 경향을 알 수 있도록 하였고, 책 속의 책 – 정답 및 해설에서 알기 쉽고 자세하게 풀이하였습니다.

본서는 여러분의 합격을 응원합니다!

사관학교 입학 전형

육군사관학교

※모집요강은 2024학년도에 기반한 것으로, 추후 변경될 수 있으니 반드시 육군사관학교 홈페이지에서 확인하시기 바랍니다.

▌ 모집 정원 : 330명(모집 정원 내 여자 42명 포함)
- 남자 : 인문계열 45%(130명), 자연계열 55%(158명)
- 여자 : 인문계열 60%(25명), 자연계열 40%(17명)

▌ 수업 연한 : 4년

▌ 지원 자격
- 2003년 1월 2일부터 2007년 1월 1일 사이에 출생한 대한민국 국적을 가진 신체 건강하고 사상이 건전한 미혼 남녀
- 고등학교 졸업자, 2024년 2월 졸업예정자 또는 교육부 장관이 이와 동등 이상의 학력이 있다고 인정한 자 (2023년 9월 4일 이전 검정고시 합격자)
- 「군 인사법」 제10조 2항에 의한 결격사유에 해당되지 않는 자
- 대한민국 국적과 외국 국적을 함께 가지고 있지 않은 자
- 법령에 의하여 형사처분을 받지 않은 자(재판계류 중인 자는 판결결과에 따라 합격을 취소될 수 있음)
- 재외국민자녀 : 부모와 함께 동반하여 외국에서 수학한 대한민국 단일국적자 중 수학능력 및 리더십이 우수한 지원자에게 입학의 기회 부여(7개국 언어 지원자 중 5명 이내 선발, 적격자 없을 시 미선발)

▌ 선발방법 및 전형기준

구 분	1차 시험	2차 시험	종합선발
전형 기준	■ 국어/영어/수학 　– 공통수학 : 수학Ⅰ, 수학Ⅱ 　– 인문계열 : (선택) 확률과 통계, 미적분, 기하 중 택1 　– 자연계열 : (선택) 미적분, 기하 중 택1	■ 면접시험 ■ 체력검정 ■ 신체검사	■ 1차 시험(50점) ■ 2차 시험(250점) ■ 고등학교 내신(100점) ■ 대학수학능력시험(600점)
비고	※모집정원 기준 남자 5배수, 여자 8배수 계열별/성별 구분하여 선발 ※대학수학능력시험과 유사한 형식으로 과목별 30문항(단, 영어는 듣기평가 없음)	※사전 AI면접 실시 후 면접분야에서 참고자료로 활용 ※한국사능력검정시험 가산점(우선선발 및 특별전형 합격자 선발 시에만 적용)	※성별, 계열별 총점 순에 의해 선발

해군사관학교

※모집요강은 2024학년도에 기반한 것으로, 추후 변경될 수 있으니 반드시 해군사관학교 홈페이지에서 확인하시기 바랍니다.

▌모집 정원 : 170명(모집 정원 내에서 여생도 26명)
– 남자 : 인문계열 65명, 자연계열 79명
– 여자 : 인문계열 13명, 자연계열 13명

▌수업 연한 : 4년

▌지원 자격
– 2003년 1월 2일부터 2007년 1월 1일 사이에 출생하여 대한민국 국적을 가진 미혼 남녀
– 고등학교 졸업자, 2024년 2월 졸업예정자 또는 교육부 장관이 이와 동등 이상의 학력이 있다고 인정한 자 (2023년 9월 1일 이전 검정고시 합격자)
– 「군 인사법」 제10조 1항의 임용자격이 있는 자
– 「군 인사법」 제10조 2항에 의한 결격사유에 해당되지 않는 자
– 재외국민자녀 : 외국에서 고교 1년을 포함하여 연속 3년 이상 수학한 자로서 고교졸업자 또는 졸업 예정 자(부모와 별도로 자녀 단독으로 유학한 경우는 지원할 수 없음)

▌선발방법 및 전형기준

구 분	1차 시험	2차 시험	종합선발
전형 기준	▪국어/영어/수학 – 공통수학 : 수학Ⅰ, 수학Ⅱ – 인문계열 : (선택) 확률과 통계, 미적분, 기하 중 택1 – 자연계열 : (선택) 미적분, 기하 중 택1	▪신체검사 ▪체력검정 ▪대면면접 ▪AI면접	▪2차 시험 성적(300점) ▪학생부 성적(50점) ▪대학수학능력시험(650점)
비고	※남자는 모집 정원의 4배수, 여자는 8배수를 남·여 및 문·이과 구분 선발 ※국어 30문항, 영어 30문항(듣기평가 없음), 수학 30문항	※체력분야 가산점 최대 3점 ※사전 AI면접 실시 후 면접분야에서 참고자료로 활용	※대학수학능력시험 선택과목 시 계열별로 해당하는 과목 선택하여 응시 필요. 계열별 해당하지 않는 과목을 응시하는 경우 선발 대상에서 제외

공군사관학교

※ 모집요강은 2024학년도에 기반한 것으로, 추후 변경될 수 있으므로 반드시 공군사관학교 홈페이지에서 확인하시기 바랍니다.

▌ 모집 정원 : 235명(남자 199명, 여자 36명 내외)

- 남자 : 인문계열 60명 내외, 자연계열 139명 내외
- 여자 : 인문계열 16명 내외, 자연계열 20명 내외

▌ 수업 연한 : 4년

▌ 지원 자격

- 대한민국 국적을 가진 미혼 남 · 여로서 신체가 건강하고, 사관생도로서 적합한 사상과 가치관을 가진 자
- 2003년 1월 2일부터 2007년 1월 1일까지 출생한 자
- 고등학교 졸업자 및 2024년 2월 졸업예정자 또는 법령에 의하여 이와 동등한 학력이 있다고 인정된 자
- 「군 인사법」 제10조 2항의 규정에 의한 결격사유에 해당되지 않는 자
   ※ 단, 복수국적자는 지원 가능하나, 가입학 등록일 전까지 외국 국적을 포기하여야만 입학 가능함
- 법령에 의하여 형사처벌을 받지 아니한 자(기소유예 포함)
   ※ 재판계류 중인 자는 판결결과에 따라 합격이 취소될 수 있음

▌ 선발방법 및 전형기준

구 분	1차 시험	2차 시험	종합선발

전형
기준
	■ 국어/영어/수학
	  - 공통수학 : 수학 I, 수학 II
	  - 인문계열 : (선택) 확률과 통계, 미적분, 기하 중 택1
	  - 자연계열 : (선택) 미적분, 기하 중 택1
		■ 신체검사(당일 합/불 판정)
		■ 체력검정(150점)
		■ 면접(330점)
			■ 1차 시험 성적(400점)
			■ 2차 시험 성적(480점)
			■ 학생부 성적(100점)
			■ 한국사능력검정시험(20점)

비고	※ 과목별 원점수 60점 미만이면서 표준점수 하위 40% 미만인 자는 불합격
	  - 남자 : 인문계열 4배수, 자연계열 6배수
	  - 여자 : 인문계열 8배수, 자연계열 10배수
		※ 개인별 1박 2일 소요
		※ 사전 AI면접 실시 후 면접분야에서 참고자료로 활용
			※ 한국사능력검정시험
			  가산점 부여방식 : 중급 이상
			  (제47회 이후 : 심화 이상)
			  취득점수×0.1+10

특별전형

재외국민자녀전형

- 선발인원 : 2명 이내 선발
- 지원 자격(다음 각 호를 모두 만족할 경우 자격 충족)
  1. 외국에서 고교 1년을 포함하여 연속 3년 이상 수학한 자(부 · 모와 별도로 자녀만 단독으로 해외 유학한 경우 재외국민자녀에서 제외)
  2. 주재국 고교성적 평균 B 이상인 자
  3. 각 외국어별 어학능력시험 최저기준 이상인 자

독립유공자 (외)손/자 · 녀, 국가유공자 자녀전형

- 선발인원 : 총 3명 이내(유공자별 최대 2명)
- 지원 자격 :「독립유공자예우에 관한 법률」제4조 제1호 및 제2호에 해당되는 순국선열과 애국지사의 독립유공자 (외)손/자녀,「국가유공자 등 예우 및 지원에 관한 법률」제4조에 해당되는 국가유공자의 자녀
- 종합성적 기준 지원분야 모집정원 1.5배수 이내 해당자에 대해 심의를 거쳐 선발

고른기회전형

- 농 · 어촌 학생
  1. 선발인원 : 5명 이내(남자 4명, 여자 1명 / 고교별 최대 2명)
  2. 지원 자격 :「지방자치법」제3조에 의한 읍 · 면 지역 또는 「도서 · 벽지 교육진흥법」제2조에 따른 도서 · 벽지 지역 소재 중 · 고등학교에서 전 교육과정을 이수하고 지원자와 부 · 모 모두가 중학교 입학 시부터 고등학교 졸업 시까지 6년 동안 읍 · 면 또는 도서 · 벽지 지역에 거주한 자 또는 지원자 본인이 초등학교 입학 시부터 고등학교 졸업 시까지 읍 · 면 지역 또는 도서 · 벽지 지역에 거주한 자
- 기초생활 수급자 · 차상위 계층
  1. 선발인원 : 5명 이내(남자 4명, 여자 1명)
  2. 지원자격 :「국민기초생활보장법」제2조제2호에 따른 수급자 또는 「국민기초생활보장법」제2조 제10호에 따른 차상위계층

국군간호사관학교

※ 모집요강은 2024학년도에 기반한 것으로, 추후 변경될 수 있으므로 반드시 국군간호사관학교 홈페이지에서 확인하시기 바랍니다.

▌모집 정원 : 90명(남자 14명, 여자 76명)

– 남자 : 인문계열 6명, 자연계열 8명
– 여자 : 인문계열 31명, 자연계열 45명

▌수업 연한 : 4년

▌지원 자격

– 2003년 1월 2일부터 2007년 1월 1일 사이에 출생한 대한민국 국적을 가진 미혼 남녀로서 신체 건강하고 사관생도로서 적합한 가치관을 가진 사람
– 고등학교 졸업자 또는 2024년 2월 졸업예정자와 이와 동등 이상의 학력이 있다고 교육부 장관이 인정한 사람
– 「군 인사법」 제10조 2항에 의한 결격사유에 해당되지 않는 자
– 국군간호사관학교 생도신체검사 예규에서 정하는 기준에 적합한 자

▌선발방법 및 전형기준

구 분	1차 시험	2차 시험	종합선발
전형 기준	■ 국어(듣기 제외) ■ 영어(듣기 제외) ■ 수학 – 공통수학 : 수학Ⅰ, 수학Ⅱ – 인문계열 : (선택) 확률과 통계, 미적분, 기하 중 택1 – 자연계열 : (선택) 미적분, 기하 중 택1	■ 인성검사 ■ 신체검사 ■ 체력검정 ■ 면접	■ 대학수학능력시험(700점) ■ 학생부(100점) – 교과(90점), 비교과(10점) ■ 2차 시험(200점) – 면접시험(150점), 체력검정(50점) ■ 한국사능력검정시험(가산점 α)
비고	※ 대학수학능력시험과 유사 ※ 모집 정원 기준 – 남자 인문 4배수, 자연 8배수 – 여자 4배수	※ 사전 AI면접 실시 후 면접분야에서 참고자료로 활용	※ 학생부 반영 방법 : 교과성적(90점), 비교과 성적(10점 : 결석일수 × 0.3점 감점) ※ 동점자 발생 시 선발 우선 순위 : 면접 〉 체력검정 〉 학생부 〉 수능 성적순

 모집 요강은 추후 변동될 수 있으므로 반드시 사관학교 홈페이지에서 확인하시기 바랍니다.

사관학교 Q&A

Q1 육군사관학교 2차 시험의 면접은 어떤 분야가 실시되나요?

2차 시험의 면접은 AI역량검사, 구술면접, 학교생활, 자기소개, 외적자세, 심리검사, 종합판정 등 총 7개 분야가 실시됩니다. 또한 사전 AI 면접을 실시하여 일부 면접 분야에서 참고자료로 활용됩니다. 면접시험의 구성은 당해연도 2차 시험 계획에 따라 일부 변경될 수 있습니다.

Q2 수시 제한에 해군사관학교도 포함이 되나요?

해군사관학교는 특별법에 의해 설치된 대학으로서, 대학(산업대학 및 교육대학/전문대학 포함)과 특별법에 의해 설치된 대학(전문대학 포함)/각종 학교 간에는 복수지원과 이중등록 금지원칙을 적용하지 않는다는 원칙에 따라 수시 제한과 관계없이 지원 가능합니다.

Q3 공군사관학교 지원 시 동아리활동에 대한 가산점이 있나요?

학교생활기록부 성적반영은 교과과목인 국어, 영어, 수학, 사회(인문)/과학(자연)에 대해서만 반영하며 비교과 과목(봉사활동, 독서활동, 동아리활동, 수상경력 등)은 점수에 직접 반영하지 않지만 면접 시 참고자료로 활용될 수 있습니다.

Q4 국군간호사관학교 입학하고 싶은데, 내신등급이 높아야 합격 가능성이 높은가요?

종합 선발 기준은 2차 시험 200점, 학생부 100점, 대학수학능력시험 700점을 총 합산한 최종성적 순으로 선발하기 때문에 비중이 높은 수능성적이 높을 경우 가능성이 있을 것으로 예상됩니다.

사관학교 졸업 후 진로

육군사관학교

육군사관학교 졸업생들은 졸업과 동시에 문학사, 이학사, 공학사 및 군사학사의 2개 학위를 취득하며 육군 소위로 임관합니다. 임관 후에는 계급별 군사교육을 수료하고, 야전부대에서 각급제대 지휘관 및 참모직책을 수행하며 주요 정책부서에서 군사전문가로 활동하기도 합니다. 본인 희망에 따라 국내 · 외 대학원에서 석 · 박사과정 위탁교육을 받을 수 있습니다. 졸업 후 의무복무기간은 10년이며, 본인 희망에 따라 5년차에 전역할 수 있습니다.

공군사관학교

공군사관학교 졸업과 동시에 공군 장교로 임관하며, 항공작전 및 기타 지원 분야에서 업무를 수행하게 됩니다.

– 항공작전분야 : 전투기, 수송기, 헬리콥터 조종과 항공작전 및 전략개발을 담당하는 분야입니다. 비행훈련은 4학년 2학기부터 실시되며, 비행교육입문과정, 기본과정 및 고등과정을 수료하면 정식 조종사가 됩니다.

– 지원분야 : 공중근무를 직 · 간접적으로 지원하는 임무를 수행하는 분야로, 조종, 항공통제, 방공포병, 기상, 정보통신, 군수, 시설, 재정, 인사행정, 정훈, 교육, 정보, 헌병, 법무, 군종, 의무 분야 등이 있습니다.

– 자기계발을 위한 전문교육 : 임무수행에 필요한 체계적인 군사 전문교육 기회를 제공받습니다.

– 석사 및 박사과정 교육 : 해당 분야 전문성 증진을 위해 국비로 국내 · 외 유명 대학에서 석사 및 박사과정 교육기회를 제공합니다. 대다수의 졸업생은 석사 이상의 학위를 취득한 후 공군의 다양한 전문분야에서 국가안보를 위해 헌신하고 있습니다.

– 사회의 다양한 분야로 진출 : 비행훈련을 마치는 조종사는 정부 공인 민간 항공기 조종사 면허증을 받으며, 전역 후 민간 항공에 취업할 수 있어 현재 많은 공사 출신 조종사들이 활동하고 있습니다. 지원분야에 근무하는 장교는 사관학교의 수준 높은 교육과 전문성을 토대로 사회 각 분야로 활발히 진출하고 있습니다.

해군사관학교

해군사관학교 졸업 후 진로는 다음과 같이 다양하게 선택할 수 있습니다.

− 해군 장교(소위)로 임관하여 대양해군 시대의 주역으로 진출

− 해병대 장교 등 자신의 적성에 맞는 다양한 병과 선택 가능

− 졸업 후 국내 · 외 대학원에서 석 · 박사 학위 취득 가능(국비 지원)

− 선택한 병과에 따라 항해사, 기관사 및 항공기 조종사 등의 면허취득 가능

− 국내 · 외의 다양한 유학 및 연수 기회 부여

− 졸업 후 5년째 되는 해에 전역(사회진출) 기회 부여

− 20년 이상 근속 후 퇴직(전역) 시 평생 연금 혜택 부여

국군간호사관학교

국군간호사관학교 생도들은 4년간 교육 후 「간호사 국가고시」를 거쳐 간호사 면허증을 취득하게 되며, 졸업과 동시에 간호학사 학위를 수여받고, 영예로운 육 · 해 · 공군 간호장교 소위로 임관하여 전국의 국군병원에서 간호전문인으로서 그 능력을 발휘하며 경험을 쌓게 됩니다. 군 병원 임상에서 간호전문인으로서 직책을 수행하는 것 이외에도 군의 교육기관, 정책부서 등에도 그 능력을 발휘하고 있으며 임관 후에도 국비로 석 · 박사 학위를 취득하여 국간사 교수 등으로 성장할 수 있도록 지원하고, 또한 국 · 내외에서 간호분야별(수술, 중환자, 응급, 마취, 인공신장, 정신) 주특기 교육을 받아 적성에 맞는 간호영역에서 근무할 수 있으며, 이러한 교육과 경험은 퇴역 후 사회 진출 시에도 귀중한 자산이 되어 민간의 각 기관에서 환영받게 됩니다. 또한 해외에 파견되어 세계평화유지를 위한 국군의료지원단(PKO)의 일원으로 국위선양에 기여할 수 있습니다.

졸업 후 6년간의 의무복무기간을 마치고 사회로 진출할 수 있으며 복무연장근무(임관 후 평균 10년), 또는 장기 근무자의 경우 영관장교 이상의 진출 기회가 주어집니다. 퇴역한 후 사회로 진출한 동문 중에는 민간병원, 간호정책 기관, 대학교수, 각급 학교 보건교사, 기타 보건관련기관 등 다양한 직종에서 그 능력을 발휘하며, 여성 지도자로서 각계각층에서 자리매김하고 있습니다.

이 책의 구성과 특징

사관학교 연도별 최신 10개년 기출문제

■ 사관학교 1차 시험 영어영역의 기출문제를 2024학년도부터 2015학년도까지 연도별로 정리하여 수록함으로써
연도별 기출 경향과 출제 방향을 파악할 수 있도록 구성하였습니다.

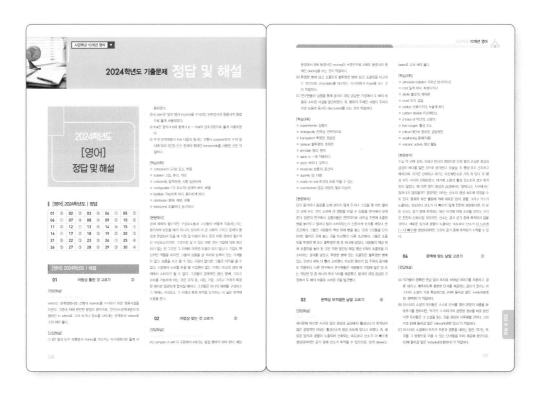

정답 및 해설

- **정답해설** : 각 문항별로 자세하고 알기 쉽게 풀이하여 수험생들이 쉽게 이해할 수 있도록 구성하였습니다.

- **오답해설** : 정답을 아는 것에서 나아가 오답이 오답인 이유를 명백히 이해할 수 있도록 오답에 대한 해설도 함께 수록하였습니다.

- **핵심어휘** : 본문에 제시된 주요 어휘를 정리하여 단어를 쉽게 익힐 수 있도록 구성하였습니다.

- **본문해석** : 본문 해석을 함께 수록하여 문제를 좀 더 쉽게 이해할 수 있도록 구성하였습니다.

목차

기출문제

정답 및 해설

사관학교 스터디 플랜

날 짜	연 도	과 목	내 용	학습시간
Day 1~3	2024학년도	• 영어영역 기출문제		
Day 4~6	2023학년도	• 영어영역 기출문제		
Day 7~9	2022학년도	• 영어영역 기출문제		
Day 10~12	2021학년도	• 영어영역 기출문제		
Day 13~15	2020학년도	• 영어영역 기출문제		
Day 16~18	2019학년도	• 영어영역 기출문제		
Day 19~21	2018학년도	• 영어영역 기출문제		
Day 22~24	2017학년도	• 영어영역 기출문제		
Day 25~27	2016학년도	• 영어영역 기출문제		
Day 28~30	2015학년도	• 영어영역 기출문제		

2025
사관학교
10개년 영어

2024학년도 기출문제
영어영역(공통)

01 글의 밑줄 친 부분 중, 어법상 틀린 것은? [3점]

The essential components of an economic system and how they function are best understood when they are seen not in isolation, but rather as they are connected to a larger social and cultural environment. Money is an essential component of any economy, but it serves no purpose by itself unless there is something produced by businesses that one could buy with ① it. Businesses also play a key role, but they cannot make profits unless there are households willing and able to buy their goods, and there are markets ② which the goods can be bought and sold. Households cannot be consumers in the U.S. economic system without a source of income ③ to earn money to spend in the marketplace. It is only when money, markets, businesses, and households are brought coherently together into a specific configuration ④ that they facilitate economic production, distribution, and consumption. Together they comprise a system and that system serves a broader purpose that ⑤ transcends the specific purposes of the components themselves.

* configuration: (각 요소의) 상대적 배치

02 (A), (B), (C)의 각 네모 안에서 어법에 맞는 표현으로 가장 적절한 것은? [4점]

Research shows that just placing food or drink out of sight or moving it a few feet away can have a big effect on consumption. In a series of studies, experimenters strategically placed jars of chocolates around an office and carefully counted how many were consumed. In one condition, they compared (A) placing / to place the jars on people's desks with moving them just six feet away. In another, they placed the chocolates in either transparent or opaque jars. Placing the chocolates on people's desks resulted in the staff's consuming an average of six more chocolates per person each day, and the chocolates in transparent jars were eaten 46 percent more quickly than (B) that / those in opaque jars. A similar principle applies to food around the house. In another study, researchers stocked people's homes with either large or moderate quantities of ready-to-eat meals and (C) discovered / were discovered that the food was eaten at twice the rate in the overstocked homes.

* opaque: 불투명한

	(A)	(B)	(C)
①	placing	…… that	…… discovered
②	placing	…… those	…… discovered
③	placing	…… those	…… were discovered
④	to place	…… that	…… were discovered
⑤	to place	…… that	…… discovered

03 다음 글의 밑줄 친 부분 중, 문맥상 낱말의 쓰임이 적절하지 <u>않은</u> 것은? [4점]

Over billions of years, the loss of water through the effects of ultraviolet radiation is thought to have ① <u>cost</u> Mars and Venus their oceans. Today, both are dry and sterile, their crusts oxidized and their atmospheres filled with carbon dioxide. Both planets oxidized slowly, and never accumulated more than a trace of free oxygen in their ② <u>atmospheres</u>. Why did this happen on Mars and Venus, but not on Earth? The critical difference may have been the ③ <u>rate</u> of oxygen formation. If oxygen is formed slowly, no faster than the rate at which new rocks, minerals and gases are ④ <u>exposed</u> by weathering and volcanic activity, then all this oxygen will be consumed by the crust instead of accumulating in the air. The crust will slowly oxidize, but oxygen will never accumulate in the air. Only if oxygen is generated ⑤ <u>slower</u> than the rate at which new rocks and minerals are exposed can it begin to accumulate in the air.

* sterile: 불모의 ** crust: 지각

04 (A), (B), (C)의 각 네모 안에서 문맥에 맞는 낱말로 가장 적절한 것은? [3점]

There are times when authors want us to determine certain messages and provide us with sufficient clues to lead us in the right direction without ever explicitly stating it. The genre of writing where this is possibly most (A) evident / unseen is in mystery novels. The author creates a web of clues that allows the reader to make inference after inference, conclusion after conclusion, and prediction after prediction. Imagine how boring it would be to read a mystery story if the author was immediately forthcoming with the most (B) relevant / irrelevant information. It would take all of the fun out of it. As savvy readers, we want to look for clues and piece the text-puzzle together in our minds. There is nothing more satisfying to a reader than figuring out the solution to a problem that a character is unable to identify or knowing the outcome of a situation before it unfolds. Remember, reading is an ongoing conversation. That means that, while the reader is

making inferences and conclusions, the author has (C) included / excluded clues that can lead the reader in that direction.

*savvy: 잘 아는, 박식한

	(A)		(B)		(C)
①	evident	……	relevant	……	included
②	unseen	……	relevant	……	included
③	evident	……	irrelevant	……	excluded
④	unseen	……	irrelevant	……	excluded
⑤	evident	……	irrelevant	……	included

[05~06] 다음 글의 요지로 가장 적절한 것을 고르시오.

05

Habits often prove to be quite fragile when changes appear predictably or unpredictably in our lives. How many times have you heard someone complaining or regretting their 'good hobbies' before marriage when they 'had the time'? I have heard it dozens of times and people always try to find excuses for lack of continuity. That's what we do. We find excuses. But if we just spent some time thinking and trying to understand how we function and how habits function, then we might see that habits need training to strengthen them, just like a muscle does, and the more they depend on some external factors or your disposition and mood to be maintained, the more vulnerable they are to interruption. Build your habits strong right from the beginning. If you want to start jogging, do it when it is sunny, do it when it is windy or rainy, do it when you feel happy and do it, by all means, when you feel sad. It is about connecting with a zone of enjoyment per se that goes beyond meeting a bunch of conditions to be carried out. [3점]

* vulnerable: 취약한 ** per se: 그 자체로

① 예기치 않은 상황에서는 침착한 태도를 유지하는 것이 중요하다.
② 습관을 꾸준히 유지하려면 훈련을 통해 처음부터 강화해야 한다.
③ 나쁜 습관을 없애는 데는 지속적인 자기 보상이 효과적이다.
④ 자신의 성격에 맞는 취미를 고르면 오랫동안 즐길 수 있다.
⑤ 건강한 생활 습관 형성을 위해서는 휴식과 회복이 필요하다.

06

People commonly think that the best way to attain happiness is to change their environment —their house, their clothes, their car, their job, their circle of friends. But those who have thought carefully about desire have unanimously drawn

the conclusion that the *best way — indeed, perhaps the only way — to attain lasting happiness is not to change the world around us or our place in it but to change ourselves.* In particular, if we can convince ourselves to want what we already have, we can dramatically enhance our happiness without any change in our circumstances. It simply does not occur to the typical person that satisfaction can best be gained not by working to satisfy the desires we find within us but by selectively suppressing or eradicating our desires. Throughout the ages and across cultures, thoughtful people have argued that the best way to attain happiness is to master our desires, but throughout the ages and across cultures, ordinary people have ignored this advice. [3점]

* unanimously: 이의 없이 ** eradicate: 없애다

① Many easily dismiss the idea that controlling desire can make us happy.

② Contrary to common belief, mastering our desires is nearly impossible.

③ Happiness is rarely achieved without the support of loved ones.

④ It is within our surroundings that our desires are bred.

⑤ If we don't desire anything, we won't gain anything.

07 밑줄 친 stand before the long green table 이 다음 글에서 의미하는 바로 가장 적절한 것은? [4점]

Serving in the military, I relied heavily on this saying to guide my actions. Whenever I had a difficult decision to make, I would ask myself, "Can you stand before the long green table?" Since WWII, the conference tables used in military boardrooms had been constructed of long, narrow pieces of furniture covered in green felt. Whenever a formal proceeding took place that required multiple officers to adjudicate an issue, the officers would gather around the table. The point of the saying was simple. If you couldn't make a good case to the officers sitting around the long green table, then you should reconsider your actions. Every time I was about to make an important decision, I asked myself, "Can I stand before the long green table and be satisfied that I took all the right actions?" It is one of the most fundamental questions a leader must ask themselves —and the old saying helped me remember what steps to take.

* felt: 펠트(모직이나 털을 압축해서 만든 천)
** adjudicate: 판결하다

① adapt your strategy to constantly changing field conditions

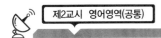

② request assistance in your task from those more knowledgeable

③ courageously carry out your plan without the approval of peers

④ convincingly justify your actions to a group of authority figures

⑤ persuade your peers that their campaign strategy is not realistic

08 다음 글에서 전체 흐름과 관계 <u>없는</u> 문장은?

[3점]

Consider a person looking at Picasso's powerful painting *Guernica* for the first time. Anyone can see the technical mastery and highly emotional content in the painting. ① But say we told the first-time viewer of *Guernica* that it is named after a girl who dumped Picasso when he was eighteen years old. ② That viewer's feelings about the painting might range toward puzzlement or confusion—given the scale and content of the work, it would seem to be a bit of an overreaction. ③ Then we tell the viewer that in reality it was painted as a memorial to the small Basque town that was heavily air-bombed in April 1937 by the combined Fascist forces of Germany and Italy, at the request of the Spanish Nationalists under the direction of Franco. ④ Even in his later years, Picasso continued to shift his interests, experimenting with new styles and techniques. ⑤ Presumably, the feelings of the viewer would change and more reflect those that Picasso intended any viewer of the painting to have.

[09~10] 다음 글의 제목으로 가장 적절한 것을 고르시오.

09

Perhaps there is something fundamentally bad about war, which is slowly becoming clear to us as a species. Perhaps aversion to war, even a recognition that it is wrong, lies deep within the human condition. There is some support for this idea in evolutionary anthropology. The change in body composition and face shape from the higher apes to *Homo sapiens* —to softer skin, blunter teeth and claws, lower brow-ridges—may have been part of an evolution away from violence. As we got better and better at cooperating in sophisticated ways to hunt, gather, build shelter, and raise children, the success of individuals became bound up with the success of the group. The groups that succeeded were those that weeded out the violent and disruptive. Social

2024 기출문제

and biological evolution thus intertwined, ensuring the success of the gentler ones who remained. [3점]

* aversion: 혐오

① Primitive Human Gentleness: An Anthropological Myth
② The Gentler Humans: Victors of the Evolutionary War
③ Violent Human Nature Revealed by Fossil Evidence
④ Staging a Successful War Campaign: A Fine Art
⑤ What Are Obstacles to Ending Human Conflict?

10

The rise of the anti-thrift culture would not have been possible without a widespread willingness to take on personal debt, and such willingness would not have emerged without the development of the credit card. Between 1958 and 1970, 100 million credit cards were distributed across the United States in what turned out to be a profound shift not only in purchasing patterns, but in how Americans began to experience themselves and their desires. The credit card ushered in an ease of use in a new age in which hard cash was not necessary to back up purchases, consequently leading to the widespread desire and expectation for instant gratification among consumers. This ease came in contrast to the social, natural, and economic environments which had historically regulated instant gratification by providing obstacles to it. Over the past century, then, our culture has shifted to one in which there are often very few behavioral obstacles to immediately getting what we want, resulting in the elevation of impulsive consuming instincts over the careful evaluation of the wisdom of such consumption. [3점]

* usher: 안내하다
** gratification: (욕구의) 충족

① Credit Cards: A Seed of Social Instability
② The Imported Origin of American Bankruptcy
③ Sound Credit: A Path to Financial Well-Being
④ Explosion of Credit Cards Boosting Individualism
⑤ Credit Cards Fostering an Instant Consumption Culture

11 다음 글의 주제로 가장 적절한 것은? [4점]

By the early 2000s, corporations began to realize they were facing new risks arising from globalization. Powerful global brands, it turned out, could be a source of vulnerability as well as profit. While corporations that owned such brands often imagined that they were engaging in arms-length transactions with foreign suppliers, consumers held them responsible for labor and environmental conditions throughout their supply chains, many links and many miles distant from the head office. Outsourcing production of athletic shoes to a factory in Indonesia or buying cocoa grown in Ghana through a trading company in Switzerland did not relieve footwear and confectionary companies of responsibility for working conditions and environmental impacts at their suppliers. Even companies that did not deal directly with consumers, such as ship lines and plastics manufacturers, found that their business customers harbored similar expectations. In the internet age, a company's brand could easily be tarnished by allegations of unethical conduct at firms that top executives may never have heard of, and such reputational damage was hard to undo.

* confectionary: 제과의 ** tarnish: 손상하다
*** allegation: (증거 없는) 주장

① difficulties in managing working conditions in overseas factories
② extended ethical responsibilities as a risk for global businesses
③ declining impact of brand reputation on purchasing decisions
④ growing risk of resource shortages for global manufacturing
⑤ risk management strategies employed by global businesses

12 다음 글의 목적으로 가장 적절한 것은? [3점]

Thank you for choosing ABC Toy Company as your trusted source of fun and entertainment for children. We appreciate your continued support and loyalty to our brand. However, we regret to inform you of a safety issue that has come to our attention. We have recently discovered that our Bunny-Mini dolls may cause skin rashes due to the paint used. The safety and well-being of our customers are of utmost importance to us, and we take this matter very seriously. As a precautionary measure, we are recalling all Bunny-Mini products from the market. If you have purchased any of these toys, we request that you bring the product to one of our stores to obtain a refund. We understand the disappointment

this may cause, especially to the children who love our toys. We assure you that we are taking all necessary steps to fix the situation promptly.

① 제품의 회수 및 환불 조치에 관해 알리려고
② 새로운 상품의 예약 구매 방법을 안내하려고
③ 인기 장난감의 빠른 품절에 대해 사과하려고
④ 변경된 환불 및 제품 보증 정책을 공지하려고
⑤ 판매 실적에 따른 고객 감사 행사를 홍보하려고

13 다음 글에서 필자가 주장하는 바로 가장 적절한 것은? [3점]

A lot of people make the mistake of treating their dog as a baby. This isn't a problem as long as you acknowledge that there is more to your dog than this. You have to first honour the animal, then the dog, then the breed and finally your individual pet. If you can do this, one-to-one close communication is the next step. Recognize that your dog isn't just a small furry person, she's much more than that. As an animal she has all her intuitions and instincts intact, unlike humans. She has senses of smell and hearing that are far more sensitive than yours, and as such she's much more aware of the natural world than you are. This means that most of the time your dog exists in a different world from you, so you have to respect her extra abilities and tune back into as many of your own instincts and intuitions as you can, if you really want to communicate with her. We still have these abilities. They're just buried beneath our civilized veneer.

* veneer: 베니어(얇은 판자)

① 반려견을 입양하기 전에 가족 구성원의 동의를 구해야 한다.
② 반려견의 건강한 삶을 위해 함께 활동하는 시간을 늘려야 한다.
③ 반려견의 개별적 특성을 고려하여 행동 교정 훈련을 해야 한다.
④ 반려견이 자연과 교감할 수 있도록 다양한 기회를 제공해야 한다.
⑤ 반려견과의 진정한 소통을 위해 그들의 본능과 직감을 존중해야 한다.

14 Florence Finch에 관한 다음 글의 내용과 일치하지 않는 것은? [3점]

Florence Finch was born in 1915, in the Philippines as a daughter of a Filipino mother and an American father. Prior to the Japanese invasion,

Finch was working at the U.S. Army in Manila. After Manila fell to the Japanese in 1942, Finch disguised her American connections and got a job with the Japanese-controlled Philippine Liquid Fuel Distributing Union. Working closely with the Philippine Underground, she diverted fuel supplies to the resistance and secretly got food to starving American prisoners of war. In 1944, she was arrested by the Japanese army and interrogated but refused to reveal any information. After she was liberated by American forces in 1945, she moved to the United States, became a citizen and joined the U.S. Coast Guard. In 1947, she was awarded the Medal of Freedom for saving American prisoners and performing other acts of resistance in the Philippines. She passed away in 2016 at the age of 101 in Ithaca, New York, and received a military funeral with full honors.

① 필리핀에서 태어나 마닐라에 주둔한 U.S. Army에서 근무했다.

② Philippine Liquid Fuel Distributing Union에서 직업을 구했다.

③ 연료를 저항군에게 빼돌리고 미군 포로에게 음식을 몰래 제공했다.

④ 1945년에 미군에 의해 풀려난 후 필리핀에 남아 여생을 마쳤다.

⑤ 필리핀에서의 공적을 인정받아 Medal of Freedom을 받았다.

[15~19] 다음 빈칸에 들어갈 말로 가장 적절한 것을 고르시오.

15

Positiveness, or more precisely, maintaining it well balanced at all times, is in itself a fundamental goal—one that never leaves the scene. As a baby, you would never think that such a possibility, as not trying to stand up again after falling on your bottom dozens of times exists. Falling is so naturally integrated as part of the process of trying to stand up that no one would think "The poor baby, he failed so much at standing!" We are born with persistence and the right mindset already —never giving up, always exploring, always believing we can do it— but somehow we 'manage' to lose them on the way. So, what we are doing in fact when trying to learn how to be successful is, to a great extent, an act of re-learning or remembering the first set of skills given to us at birth. Our aim to become more productive becomes, in a way, our aim to become more _____.

[3점]

① natural

② sociable

③ intelligent

④ resourceful

⑤ trustworthy

16

The part of the brain that controls our feelings _____. It is this disconnection that makes putting our feelings into words so hard. We have trouble, for example, explaining why we married the person we married. We struggle to put into words the real reasons why we love them, so we talk around it or rationalize it. "She's funny, she's smart," we start. But there are lots of funny and smart people in the world, but we don't love them and we don't want to marry them. There is obviously more to falling in love than just personality and competence. Rationally, we know our explanation isn't the real reason. It is how our loved ones make us feel, but those feelings are really hard to put into words. So when pushed, we start to talk around it. We may even say things that don't make any rational sense. "She completes me," we might say, for example. What does that mean and how do you look for someone who does that so you can marry them? That's the problem with love we only know when we've found it because it "just feels right." [3점]

① has no capacity for language

② obstructs our motor functions

③ operates independently of memory

④ doesn't make any moral judgments

⑤ is disconnected from decision-making

17

One obvious survival advantage to being able to _____ is that it helps a group of animals to know whether to defend their territory against an attack or to retreat. If there are more defenders than attackers, it might make sense for the defenders to stay and fight if there are more attackers, the wisest strategy might be to make a bolt for it. This suggestion was put to the test a few years ago by Karen McComb and her colleagues. They played tape recordings of roaring lions to small groups of female lions in Serengeti National Park in Tanzania. When the number of different roars exceeded the number of lions in the group, the females retreated but when there were more females, they stood their ground and prepared to attack the intruders. They seemed able to compare numbers across two different senses: the number of roars they heard versus the number of lionesses they observed, a task that seems to require a fairly abstract number sense. [3점]

* intruder: 침입자

① efficiently communicate with pack members

② compare numbers of objects in collections

③ identify the direction of moving objects

④ blend into surroundings as a disguise

⑤ mimic the calls of other species

18

It can happen that people who used to be part of our lives gradually lose their former faculties. Many aspects of this process bring suffering but do not threaten dignity. Going blind or deaf, being paralysed or having a tremor, having to deal with pain, anxiety or dizziness that are so severe that one can no longer leave the house: all of this is horrible and sometimes unbearable, but it is not already in and of itself something that threatens dignity. All of this involves a loss of autonomy, as well as various experiences of dependence, and sometimes this dependence is also experienced as powerlessness. Yet we have the power to support the people who go through this in such a way that their powerlessness does not become humiliation and threaten their dignity. We are still engaged in committed encounters with them, and our intellectual and emotional entanglements uphold the intimacy of our relationship. The loss of their faculties _____.

[4점]

* faculty: (신체 또는 정신의) 기능 ** tremor: 떨림

① forces them to endure humiliation

② will not demand others' assistance

③ does not alter how we relate to them

④ diminishes their resilience to depression

⑤ dramatically changes what they value in life

19

Imagine yourself as a predator, perhaps a hawk. From on high, you spot what appears to be a tasty snake. If you hesitate for even a few seconds, your meal might be gone. Time is of the essence, and you must act quickly. But there's a twist—a major one. If you mistake a venomous coral snake for a non-venomous king snake, it will cost your life. In the tradeoff between a meal and your life, the choice is obvious. For a predator, natural selection has shaped this decision-making process to favor the conservative choice—long-term benefits of survival over short-term benefits of a single meal. Thus, there is no need for the king snake to be a perfect mimic of the coral snake's colors to win this round of the evolutionary arms race. The same logic applies when you're deciding whether or not to eat a wild mushroom. If you are not absolutely sure, _____.
The cost of your life would be too heavy a price to pay. [4점]

* venomous: 독이 있는

① save as much food as you can now for desperate times

② don't let yourself fall prey to thoughts of tasty reward

③ dare to challenge yourself in the name of survival

④ don't forget that one's poison is

another's pleasure

⑤ be on the look out for predators hunting you

[20~21] 주어진 글 다음에 이어질 글의 순서로 가장 적절한 것을 고르시오.

20

Compare the way these two ideas—HDTV and the online video sharing platform — changed the basic rules of engagement for their respective media platforms.

(A) With just a few easy keystrokes, you could take a clip running on someone else's site, and drop a copy of it onto your own site. The technology allowed ordinary enthusiasts to effectively program their own private television networks, stitching together video clips from all across the planet.

(B) Going from analog television to HDTV is a change in degree, not in kind: there are more pixels the sound is more immersive the colors are sharper. But consumers watch HDTV the exact same way they watched old-fashioned analog TV. They choose a channel, and sit back and watch.

(C) The online video sharing platform,

on the other hand, radically altered the basic rules of the medium. For starters, it made watching video on the Web a mass phenomenon. But with the online video sharing platform you weren't limited to sitting and watching a show, television-style you could also upload your own clips, recommend or rate other clips, get into a conversation about them. [3점]

* HDTV: 고화질 텔레비전

① (A) - (C) - (B)   ② (B) - (A) - (C)

③ (B) - (C) - (A)   ④ (C) - (A) - (B)

⑤ (C) - (B) - (A)

21

Non-human animals are individuals with their own perspectives on life, who form relations with human and non-human others. In current human legal and political systems, and in many cultural practices, they are seen and used as objects.

(A) This movement from ethical consideration to political participation shifts questions about non-human animals from how they should be treated to how more insight can be gained into the ways they want to live

their lives, what types of relationships they desire with one another and with humans, and how we can and should share the planet that we all live on.

(B) Drawing on these views, and on insights provided by social justice movements that focus on democratic inclusion, recent work in political philosophy proposes to view non-human animals as political groups, and some of these as members of shared interspecies communities.

(C) Animal rights theorists have challenged this since the 1970s, arguing that non-human animals are sentient beings, who are similar to humans in morally relevant aspects and who should therefore be seen as part of our moral communities. [4점]

* sentient: 지각(력)이 있는

① (A) − (C) − (B) ② (B) − (A) − (C)

③ (B) − (C) − (A) ④ (C) − (A) − (B)

⑤ (C) − (B) − (A)

[22~23] 글의 흐름으로 보아, 주어진 문장이 들어가기에 가장 적절한 곳을 고르시오.

22

Experts, on the other hand, sorted their problems on the basis of deep-feature similarity that were related to the major physics principles governing the solution of each problem.

One of the best examples of the important role that similarity plays in problem-solving concerns the role of similarity and expertise in physics. In an influential paper, researchers asked physics PhD students (experts) and undergraduate students (novices) to sort 24 physics problems into groups and then explain the reasons for their groupings. (①) Novices generally sorted the problems on the basis of surface-feature similarity. (②) That is, they grouped problems according to the literal physics terms mentioned in the problem and the physical configuration described in the problem. (③) This suggests that experts accessed existing schemata and they used their knowledge of physics to create a solution-oriented sorting. (④) Since the problems were sorted according to these categories, it also suggests that these categories would likely be accessed when deciding how to solve a problem.

(⑤) That is, experts are likely to rely on similarity among problems to help them solve the problems quickly and efficiently. [3점]

* schemata: 선험적 도식

should operate are disrupted. (⑤) Such a person should be motivated to interact with others as a means of helping to confirm or disconfirm beliefs about the self and reconstructing assumptions about the world. [4점]

* visceral: 뱃속으로부터의 ** assimilate: 적응시키다

23

> If the disruption is intense enough, it may challenge a person's basic assumptions about the self and the world.

Beyond describing the different motives for people revealing their emotional experiences to others, researchers have offered deeper explanations concerning why people do this. (①) One explanation stems from the cognitive−motor view of expression. (②) According to this view, critical parts of one's experiences are encoded or retained at a nonverbal level in the form of mental images, bodily movements, and affect−related visceral changes (such as a twisting stomach or racing heart). (③) These nonverbal forms remain the focus of attention until they can be assimilated and put into words, particularly when the experiences are more emotionally intense. (④) Another idea is that people experience emotion when their anticipations of how the world

24 다음 글의 내용을 한 문장으로 요약하고자 한다. 빈칸 (A), (B)에 들어갈 말로 가장 적절한 것은? [3점]

> To make an aircraft fly is a constant struggle against physics. An airliner traveling six hundred miles per hour at thirty thousand feet is not something that happens naturally. It's not a fail-safe act, meaning the default is to crash—it's up to our ingenuity and decision-making to prevent it from happening. It's a unique environment that's highly unforgiving. Whereas a loss of power in a car typically results in a few hours on the side of a road, a loss of power in the air is often disastrous. Even in business, bet-the-company decisions are rare, and when encountered, only a fraction of the employees take part in them. Aviation, however, relies on everyone working at an optimum level *just* to keep the aircraft flying. It's an unstable system where even a single person forgetting to do their

job, or doing it improperly, can lead to catastrophic results.

Because it (A) the laws of physics, aviation involves a high-stakes environment in which each member's (B) performance is required to ensure safety.

	(A)		(B)
①	challenges	……	flawless
②	challenges	……	brave
③	redefines	……	unique
④	redefines	……	conservative
⑤	supports	……	responsive

[25~26] 다음 글을 읽고, 물음에 답하시오.

We are surrounded every day by products that don't work well, services that slow us down, and setups that are just plain wrong: the website that requires ten clicks to accomplish what should take only one or two the projector that stubbornly resists linking up with your laptop the machine at the parking garage that makes paying so difficult. Noticing that something is broken is an essential prerequisite for coming up with a creative solution to fix it. Making "bug lists" can help you to see more opportunities to apply creativity. Whether you use a piece of paper in your pocket or record ideas on your smartphone, keeping track of opportunities for improvement can help you engage with the world around you in a more proactive way. The running list can serve as a useful source of ideas when you're looking for a new project to tackle. Or you can make a bug list on the spot.

Write down the things that bug you, and you'll start _____. It may seem like you're focusing on the negatives, but the point is to notice more opportunities to do things better. And while many of the items on your bug list may be things you won't be able to fix, if you add to it regularly, you'll stumble onto issues you can influence and problems you can help solve. Almost every annoyance, every point of friction, hides a design opportunity. Instead of just complaining, ask yourself, "How might I improve this situation?"

* prerequisite: 선행 조건

25 윗글의 제목으로 가장 적절한 것은?

① Does Ignoring Bugs Let Them Multiply?

② Innovative Design: Easier Said Than Done

③ Forget the Broken, Appreciate the Beautiful

④ A Bug List: A Trigger for Creative Solutions

⑤ Self-Criticism: A Powerful Tool for Improvement

26 윗글의 빈칸에 들어갈 말로 가장 적절한 것은? [4점]

① taking routines for granted

② behaving yourself in public

③ being more mindful of them

④ being less reliant on technology

⑤ recognizing your own weaknesses

[27~28] 다음 글을 읽고, 물음에 답하시오.

Morality is changeable and culture-dependent and expresses socially desirable behavior. But even if morality is changeable, it is by no means arbitrary, especially since the change process itself takes a relatively (a) long time (measured in years rather than weeks). This is also because a social value framework—and thus morality—provides an important orientation function: Since time immemorial, people have been thinking about moral issues and dealing with them. This makes it clear that (b) consistent values, norms, and moral concepts always play a major role when people organize themselves in social communities. Ultimately, this also results in answers to questions of justice, solidarity, and care as well as the distribution of goods and resources.

Morality acts here as the (c) common lowest denominator for a given society. The (d) advantage is based on the fact that the values underlying morality

convey a socially accepted basic understanding and provide orientation in concrete decision-making situations. This makes morality functional and efficient for social groups: In order to be accepted in a community, the individual will strive not to act against this community. Conversely, this means that the behavior of the individual and the social group is ultimately (e) unpredictable. As a result, uncertainty about behavior is reduced and trust is built up.

* arbitrary: 임의적인 ** denominator: 분모

27 윗글의 주제로 가장 적절한 것은?

① disregard of morality found in extreme conditions

② justice and solidarity as basic elements of morality

③ fundamental role of morality in human communities

④ development of morality through cultural exchanges

⑤ punishment of moral code violations across societies

28 밑줄 친 (a)~(e) 중에서 문맥상 낱말의 쓰임이 적절하지 않은 것은? [3점]

① (a)　　② (b)

③ (c)　　④ (d)

⑤ (e)

[29~30] 다음 글을 읽고, 물음에 답하시오.

(A)

A long time ago, there was a poor village at the base of the Himalayan mountains. In the center of town, there was a huge clay statue of the Buddha. No one knew who had built it. One day, while sweeping snow off the statue with a broom, a young monk noticed a small crack in the clay. As the sun rose, he could see something glinting from deep inside. (a)He ran to the head monk, telling him that the Buddha was broken and something shiny was within it.

* glinting: 반짝이는 반짝임

(B)

The head monk was looked upon to give a final word. He turned to the boy who had found the crack and asked him what he thought. With all the villagers' eyes on him, (b)the boy spoke. "I think the monks who built this Buddha must have known what they were doing. No one would want to steal or destroy an ordinary clay statue. But one made of precious gold would be the object of everyone's desire." The monk nodded, and he said, "Let's not break open the statue. Maybe each of us is meant to learn that, underneath our ordinary exterior, there is gold at our core."

(C)

The head monk said, "That statue has been here for generations. There are many cracks in it. Leave me alone. I am very busy." The young monk went back to his sweeping. But (c)he couldn't keep himself from peeking into the crack. Sure enough, there was something shining in there. He called to his father, who was curious about his son's discovery. The father was surprised to see the glinting. (d)He had passed by the statue for years but had never noticed the glinting.

(D)

The father ran and told the villagers what (e)his son had found. Soon, everyone from the village gathered around the statue. The head monk chipped carefully with a chisel around the crack. The glinting increased. No one could deny that under the outer layer of clay, there was a gold statue waiting to be revealed. The villagers argued late into the night. Should they destroy the clay Buddha and never have to worry again about money or leave it as it had always been?

* chip: (조금씩) 깎다 ** chisel: 끌

29 주어진 글 (A)에 이어질 내용을 순서에 맞게 배열한 것으로 가장 적절한 것은? [3점]

① (B) − (D) − (C)   ② (C) − (B) − (D)

③ (C) − (D) − (B)   ④ (D) − (B) − (C)

⑤ (D) − (C) − (B)

30 밑줄 친 (a)~(e) 중에서 가리키는 대상이 나머지 넷과 <u>다른</u> 것은? [3점]

① (a)　　　　　② (b)

③ (c)　　　　　④ (d)

⑤ (e)

A discovery is said to be an accident meeting a prepared mind.
발견은 준비된 사람이 맞딱뜨린 우연이다.

– 알버트 센트 디외르디(Albert Szent–Gyorgyi)

2025
사관학교

10개년 영어

2023학년도 기출문제
영어영역(공통)

01 다음 글의 밑줄 친 부분 중, 어법상 틀린 것은?

Magellan and his crew were lucky in their weather. During the whole three months and twenty days during which they sailed about twelve thousand miles through open ocean, they had not a single storm. ① Misled by this one experience, they named it the Pacific. ② Had Magellan not been a master of the winds, he would never have made it across the Pacific. Leaving the straits, he did not go directly northwest to reach his desired Spice Islands, but first ③ sailed north along the west coast of South America. His purpose must have been to catch the prevailing northeasterly trade winds there that would carry him not to the Moluccas, ④ which the Portuguese were rumored to be in control, but to other spice islands still open for Spanish taking. Whatever his motive then, the course he chose is the ⑤ one still recommended by United States Government Pilot Charts for sailing from Cape Horn to Honolulu in that season.

02 (A), (B), (C)의 각 네모 안에서 어법에 맞는 표현으로 가장 적절한 것은?

We should not have to give up rights simply because we increasingly need to use the Internet to participate in society-to access bank accounts and medical records, for example. We should expect privacy protections for these services. However, choosing to participate in something like social media can (A) see / be seen as analogous to a person choosing to run for public office. When you decide to campaign, you knowingly sacrifice anonymity and some privacy, much as those who opt in to posting on Instagram, Twitter, or Facebook (B) are / do to varying degrees. We're all running for election in our social media feeds, and with that comes a tacit acceptance (and a legal one, in the small print) that the platforms will analyze our information and feed us ads to support their business models. We should do everything possible to safeguard our rights and protect our fellow cyber citizens from harm-but perhaps we should look beyond just crafting new sets of rules for individuals and

businesses collecting and trading our information and more closely (C) investigate / investigated the science of data collecting itself. [4점]

* analogous to: ~과 유사한
** anonymity: 익명성
*** tacit: 암묵적인

	(A)		(B)		(C)
①	see	……	are	……	investigate
②	see	……	do	……	investigated
③	be seen	……	are	……	investigate
④	be seen	……	do	……	investigate
⑤	be seen	……	are	……	investigated

03 다음 글의 밑줄 친 부분 중, 문맥상 낱말의 쓰임이 적절하지 <u>않은</u> 것은?

One feature of production−related sustainability innovation is the ① <u>prevalence</u> of 'hard' technology−based improvements over 'soft' cultural change. For many manufacturers, being innovative means 'adding' technology to a problem, particularly when it is to try to ameliorate the negative impacts of existing technology. Favouring technological fixes over softer, behavioural and cultural ones is perhaps ② <u>inevitable</u> in an industry like textiles that since the Industrial Revolution in the 18th century has been processing materials faster and cheaper by improving technology. However, the result is a tendency to ③ <u>neglect</u> the very substantial effect that behaviour has on determining a product's overall environmental impact. It also overlooks the ④ <u>significant</u> role of softer change in bringing sustainability improvements, and sidelines the contribution of non−technologists, like designers and consumers. Relying on technology to 'fix' all our problems can also have the more subtle and insidious effect of ⑤ <u>reducing</u> our tendency to avoid accountability for our choices and behaviour.

* ameliorate: 개선하다
** insidious: 서서히 퍼지는

04 (A), (B), (C)의 각 네모 안에서 문맥에 맞는 낱말로 가장 적절한 것은?

For manufacturers, a product that is thrown away after being used, forcing the customer to keep coming back for more, creates endless profit potential; a potential first discovered in the years after World War I, when there was a great need to find new uses for the (A) abundance / lack of materials produced for the war piled high in warehouses. For example, an absorbent material made from celluloid that had been used for military bandages and gas mask filters later gained a new use as the disposable Kotex sanitary napkin.

Manufacturers also had to figure out how to transform the wartime ethic of thrift and reuse-darning socks, keeping odd pieces of string, using tea leaves to clean carpets, and sewing rags into rugs-into a culture that embraced "throwaway habits" and the (B) hesitation / willingness to spend money on new "stuff." During the war, the U.S. government produced posters declaring "Waste Not, Want Not." By late 1917, the government was giving shops across the country signs to display in their windows reading, "Beware of Thrift and Unwise Economy" to help (C) encourage / restrain repetitive consumption. [4점]

* darn: 깁다, 꿰매다

	(A)	(B)	(C)
①	abundance	hesitation	encourage
②	abundance	willingness	restrain
③	abundance	willingness	encourage
④	lack	hesitation	restrain
⑤	lack	willingness	encourage

05 다음 글에서 전체 흐름과 관계 <u>없는</u> 문장은?

Smart machines have been a fantasy of humanity for millennia. ① Early references to mechanical and artificial beings appear in Greek myths, starting with Hephaestus, the Greek god of blacksmiths, carpenters, craftsmen, artisans and sculptors, who created his golden robots. ② In the Middle Ages, mystical or alchemical means of creating artificial forms of life continued. ③ The Muslim chemist Jabir ibn Hayyan's stated goal was Takwin, which refers to the creation of synthetic life in the laboratory, up to and including human life. ④ At one time, Jews and Muslims lived side by side, worked together, studied together and even today, there are many similarities when Islam and Judaism are observed from a religious perspective. ⑤ Rabbi Judah Loew, widely known to scholars of Judaism as the Maharal of Prague, told the story of Golem —an animated being that is created entirely from inanimate matter (usually clay or mud)—which has now become folklore.

06 다음 글의 요지로 가장 적절한 것은?

Michalko says that creative thinking has much in common with evolution by natural selection. The basis of evolution is variation, because without variation there is nothing to select from. In a similar manner, creative people are good at

generating a wide variety of ideas about a problem before choosing the one to proceed with. He exemplifies this way of thinking with Leonardo da Vinci, who is known to repeatedly have restructured his problems to see them from different angles. He thought that the first approach was too biased towards his usual way of seeing things. With each new perspective he would deepen his understanding of the problem and begin to see its essence. He called this method *saper vedere*-knowing how to see. At first sight this way of thinking may seem wasteful as most of the ideas will never come to any direct use. The point is that, by repeatedly seeking different approaches, we gradually move from our common way of thinking to new ways. Once in a while this process will result in a truly new and useful idea, which makes the whole effort worthwhile.

① 논리적인 설득만으로는 상대방의 편견을 바꾸기 어렵다.
② 여러 사람의 지혜를 모으면 더 빨리 문제를 해결할 수 있다.
③ 한 분야에서 성공했던 방식은 다양한 분야에 적용될 수 있다.
④ 문제에 다각적으로 접근하면 새롭고 유용한 생각에 이를 수 있다.
⑤ 창의적 사고력을 기르려면 문제의 원인을 파악하는 것이 필요하다.

07 밑줄 친 make 'a stone a stone again'이 다음 글에서 의미하는 바로 가장 적절한 것은?

The criterion of strangeness, if valid, would belong under the criterion of novelty. In his famous article on art as device, Victor Shklovsky asserts that defamiliarization is the criterion that makes literature art. In everyday life, we tend to take things for granted, not really perceiving them, and when talking about them in everyday speech, we economize expression by using well-known words and sayings —clichés —which the receiver understands immediately. By using unfamiliar, strange words and constructions, art tries to prolong and deautomatize the process of perception in order to make 'a stone a stone again'—make it as if you were seeing it for the first time. Defamiliarization draws the reader's attention to aspects of reality he is otherwise inclined to overlook. Shklovsky does not distinguish between the different levels of the communication process and gives examples of defamiliarization in the text, mental model and action. Defamiliarization may consist in whatever deviates from the usual. For instance,in a period where rhyme is common, rhymeless poetry becomes strange, and vice versa. On the level of the message, defamiliarization would mean that the action would somehow force the reader to think differently. [4점]

① replace symbols with ordinary words

② make ordinary things unordinary

③ turn a word into an image

④ define a thing more precisely

⑤ make readers read between the lines

[08~09] 다음 글의 제목으로 가장 적절한 것을 고르시오.

08
In a competitive environment our ancestors eventually became the dominant predatory species through a combination of physical, mental, and social traits that allowed them to become, as physiologist Bernd Heinrich dubbed them, "super-endurance predators." The physical foundation for the emergence of these predators was provided by an interrelated set of attributes that began to develop roughly six million years ago, when our ancestors diverged from other apelike species. Hominids never evolved to outrun or outmuscle either competing predators or the prey that they sought over short distances. Instead, hominids developed an enormous capacity for endurance. They could run-or walk, jog, amble, march, trot, or hike-over long distances, traveling for hours and even days in pursuit of prey. They could make these treks in all sorts of weather and at any time, including the heat of midday, when the competing predator species, such as the great cats and dog packs, hid from the intense African sun. Even hyenas and vultures fled from the sun in the hottest periods of the day, thus giving hominids, who could stand the heat, an important advantage in getting to carcasses.

* carcass: (짐승의) 시체

① Hominids: A Persistent Hunter

② Intensity Comes Before Endurance

③ Hunting in the Heat: Mission Impossible

④ Hunters Need Speed and Power

⑤ Show Respect to Your Prey

09
Competitive sport is often a highly ritualised activity. For example, golfers tend to 'waggle' their clubs a consistent number of times before striking the ball, while tennis players like to bounce the ball a set number of times before serving. These preferred action sequences are called 'pre-performance routines' (PPRs) and involve task-relevant thoughts and actions which athletes engage in systematically prior to

the performance of specific sport skills. Usually, PPRs are evident prior to the execution of closed skills and self-paced actions (i.e. those that are carried out largely at one's own speed and without interference from other people) such as free-throwing in basketball, putting in golf or place-kicking in American football or rugby. Such routines are used extensively by athletes, and recommended by coaches and psychologists, as a form of mental preparation both to improve focusing skills and to enhance competitive performance. In short, the purpose of a PPR is to put oneself in an optimal state immediately prior to execution, and to remain that way during the act.

* waggle: 흔들다
** place-kick: (공을 땅에 놓고) 차다

① Team Play: One for All, All for One
② Competitive Spirits Enable You to Surpass Your Limits
③ Pre-performance Routines: Athletes' Ritual for Better Play
④ Habitual Body Movements Interfere with Successful Performance
⑤ Pre-performance Routines as Superstitious Behaviour Among Athletes

10 다음 글의 주제로 가장 적절한 것은?

The development of the moldboard plow turned Europe's natural endowment of fertile land on its head. People who lived in Northern Europe had long endured difficult farming conditions, but now it was the north, not the south, that enjoyed the best and most productive land. Starting about a thousand years ago, thanks to this new plow-based prosperity, cities of Northern Europe emerged and started to flourish. And they flourished with a different social structure from that of cities around the Mediterranean. The dry-soil scratch plow needed only two animals to pull it, and it worked best with a crisscross plowing in simple, square fields. All this had made farming an individualistic practice: a farmer could live alone with his plow, oxen, and land. But the wet-clay moldboard plow required a team of eight oxen— or, better, horses— and who had that sort of wealth? It was most efficient in long, thin strips often a step or two away from someone else's long, thin strips. As a result, farming became more of a community practice: people had to share the plow and draft animals and resolve disagreements. They gathered together in villages. [4점]

* moldboard plow: 볏 달린 쟁기
** crisscross: 십자형의

① socio-economic changes in Northern Europe caused by the moldboard plow
② difficulties of finding an appropriate farming method for barren land
③ various reasons farming was difficult for Northern Europeans
④ social support required to invent the moldboard plow
⑤ potential problems of using animals to plow a field

11 다음 글에서 필자가 주장하는 바로 가장 적절한 것은?

Like the old advice for married couples, "Don't ever go to bed angry," don't knowingly let students leave the lesson angry or upset. Students' frustrations can stem from difficult content or technique, personal problems, fatigue, and yes, sometimes annoyance with their teacher. Regardless of what might be the cause, don't ignore their emotions. If you see tears starting to well up, stop everything and talk. Avoid overreacting and taking their frustration personally. A certain amount of frustration is a normal part of learning any new skill. When they look discouraged, give them a glass of water, a sympathetic ear, and a tissue. If they have misinterpreted you or don't understand the concept, strip it down to its barest essentials. If your instincts tell you something is bothering a student, don't be afraid to probe a little. Most students will say, "I'm fine," but even when they do, they almost always appreciate your caring. Follow through with a call to the parents if you are concerned.

① 학생과의 상담 내용을 누설하지 말라.
② 학생의 감정을 헤아려 적절하게 대하라.
③ 학생의 강점과 약점을 분명히 알려주라.
④ 학생 스스로 자신의 한계를 극복하게 하라.
⑤ 학생에게 감정을 솔직하게 표현하는 방법을 가르치라.

12 다음 글이 시사하는 바로 가장 적절한 것은?

I believe that the good that people do, small though it may appear, has more to do with the good that manifests broadly in the world than people think, and I believe the same about evil. We are each more responsible for the state of the world than we believe, or would feel comfortable believing. Without careful attention, culture itself tilts toward corruption. Tyranny grows slowly, and asks us to retreat in comparatively tiny steps. But each retreat increases the possibility of the next retreat. Each betrayal of conscience, each act

of silence (despite the resentment we feel when silenced), and each rationalization weakens resistance and increases the probability of the next restrictive move forward. This is particularly the case when those pushing forward delight in the power they have now acquired—and such people are always to be found. Better to stand forward, awake, when the costs are relatively low—and, perhaps, when the potential rewards have not yet vanished.

* tilt: 기울다

① Stay alert and stand up against what is wrong.

② Sometimes retreat is a wise choice.

③ Silence is golden, speech is silver.

④ Expectation is the root of all heartache.

⑤ Success depends more on attitude than aptitude.

13 다음 글의 목적으로 가장 적절한 것은?

My customers at the Smalltown Home Station Hardware store are constantly asking me for advice on how to do some of the larger home repair and improvement jobs. All of the sales associates here do as much as possible to help customers decide to do the work themselves, but we also lose quite a few sales to people who lack the confidence to tackle a do-it-yourself job. I'd like to suggest that Home Station have a day when we can give instruction and demonstrations on doing the most popular do-it-yourself projects. We can have experts take people through jobs like installing a garage door opener, sealing a driveway, installing a faucet, and other common jobs. I'm sure many of our suppliers would be happy to send their own technicians to run the classes, and we can assist them —and sell the hardware and materials.

① 고객이 직접 작업할 때 유의할 사항을 알리려고

② 고객이 신청한 작업 항목과 작업 일정을 확인하려고

③ 판매 실적을 올리기 위해 영업 사원을 늘릴 것을 요청하려고

④ 신상품 사용법을 익히기 위한 직원 교육의 필요성을 강조하려고

⑤ 고객이 직접 작업하는 방법을 알려주는 강좌 개설을 제안하려고

14 Ruth Gardena Birnie에 관한 다음 글의 내용과 일치하지 않는 것은?

On August 15, 1884, Ruth Gardena Birnie was born to Moses and Louise Harrison in Sumter, South Carolina.

Since her parents died while she was very young, Birnie was reared by Martha A. Savage, a teacher. Birnie graduated from Lincoln School, an early African American school in Sumter. Later she taught there for a short period of time. In 1902, when she was eighteen years old, she married Charles Wainwright Birnie, who came to Sumter as its first African American physician. Sixteen years after their marriage, the Birnies gave birth to a daughter, Anna. As Charles W. Birnie's practice grew, he and Martha Savage, Ruth Birnie's foster mother, encouraged Ruth to pursue pharmacy as a profession. She entered Benedict College, then went on to Temple University and received her degree in pharmacy. Upon her return to South Carolina, Birnie became one of the earliest female African American pharmacists in the state.

① 아주 어릴 때 부모를 여의고 Martha A. Savage에 의해 양육되었다.
② 모교인 Lincoln School에서 짧은 기간 동안 가르쳤다.
③ 열여덟 살 때 의사인 Charles Wainwright Birnie와 결혼했다.
④ 남편과 키워준 어머니의 반대를 무릅쓰고 약사가 되려고 했다.
⑤ Temple University에서 약학 학위를 받았다.

[15~19] 다음 빈칸에 들어갈 말로 가장 적절한 것을 고르시오.

15

Some psychologists refer to the knowing feeling as "the feeling of rightness," and it's a strong and pervasive one because we dislike not understanding something that is relevant to us. As psychiatrist Irvin Yalom puts it, "When any situation or set of stimuli defies patterning, we experience dysphoria (a high level of unease), which persists until we fit the situation into a recognizable pattern." We are designed to feel very uncomfortable when something does not make sense to us because discomfort motivates us to figure things out, whether it be a mysterious rustle in the bush, the confusing betrayal of a friend, or the promotion that we didn't get. Not knowing is an "out-of-control" state that we are psychologically motivated to eliminate. Our neuroendocrine system is geared toward this very objective: our sympathetic nervous system secretes stress hormones, such as cortisol and adrenalin, that activate our alertness responses, putting us on edge until we feel that we have _____.

* defy: 거부하다
** rustle: 바스락거리는 소리
*** neuroendocrine system: 신경내분비계

① shared values

② received praise

③ regained control

④ removed inequality

⑤ overcome perfectionism

2023 기출문제

16

Suppose we define ownership as the legal relation between people and the things they own. Because this definition uses the word "own," it defines the concept OWNERSHIP in terms of itself. Instead of explaining what it means to own something, it assumes that we know this already. It tells us how the concept relates to itself, but not how it relates to other concepts or to reality. This definition doesn't go anywhere; it just moves in a circle. The same problem arises if we use synonyms in a definition. Suppose we define ownership as the legal relation between people and things they *possess*. "Own" and "possess" are synonyms, different words that express the same concept. In terms of concepts, therefore, the definition is still circular: The concept OWNERSHIP is still being used to define itself. The same objection would apply if we define *man* as the *human* animal, *large* as the attribute possessed by something that is *big*, or *folly* as a *foolish* act.

In each case, the italicized words are synonyms. To avoid such circularity, it is useful to ask: _____ _____? For example, what is the difference between owning a dress and borrowing it or trying it on in the store? How are humans different from other animals? What makes an action a folly as opposed to a wise action?

① When do you need to define key concepts

② Why then do you suggest such a definition

③ Where can you find the supporting evidence

④ How do you convince people that you're right

⑤ What contrast is the concept intended to draw

17

Change is hard, and we urgently need to get better at creating positive change in the world. Unfortunately, many of the people who make it to leadership positions have a highly developed intellect but are poor on the social side of things. Neuroscience is beginning to explore this phenomenon, too. "The brain network involved in holding

information, planning, working memory and cognitive problem solving tends to be on the lateral, or outer, portions of the brain," Matthew Lieberman explains during an interview at his lab. "Then there are regions more involved in the midline or middle areas, related to self-awareness, social cognition, and empathy. We know that these two networks are inversely correlated: when one is active, the other tends to be deactivated. It does suggest possibly that there is something inversely correlated about social and nonsocial abilities." This makes sense when you understand that the networks you pay attention to are the ones that grow. If you spend a lot of time in cognitive tasks, your ability to have empathy with people reduces simply because _____ _____. [4점]

* lateral: 측면의, 옆의
** inversely: 역으로

① that circuitry doesn't get used much

② the outer brain regions become inactive

③ the brain is built to concentrate on survival

④ the brain's short-term memory function is affected

⑤ some chemicals trigger the growth of new brain cells

18

A key feature of Karl Popper's claim is that scientific laws always go beyond existing experimental data and experience. The inductive method attempted to show that, by building up a body of data, inferences can be made to give laws that are regarded as certain, rather than probable. Popper challenges this on the grounds that all sensation involves interpretation of some sort, and that in any series of experiments there will be variations, and whether or not such variations are taken into account is down to the presuppositions of the person conducting them. Also, of course, the number of experiments done is always finite, whereas the number of experiments not yet done is infinite, so an inductive argument can never achieve the absolute certainty of a piece of deductive logic. At the same time, scientists are likely to favour any alternative theories that can account for both the original, confirming evidence and also the new, conflicting evidence. In other words, progress comes by way of _____ _____. [4점]

① finding the limitations of existing scientific theories and pushing beyond them

② creating sustainable partnerships between scientists and decision-makers

③ publishing research findings in the most reputable academic journals

④ conducting scientific research generally through a proven process

⑤ encouraging innovation through funding from the government

19

Rats can reflect on their own mental processes—and can tell if they are likely to perform well (or not) on a duration-discrimination test. They were asked to decide if a sound that they recently heard was long or short. Short tones lasted from 2 to 3.6 seconds; long ones, from 4.4 to 8 seconds. (Note that 3.6 seconds is more difficult to discern from 4.4 seconds than 2 seconds is to discern from 8 seconds. Rats understand this, apparently.) After hearing the sounds, a rat had two choices: it could abandon the test by sticking its nose into one hole and receiving a small reward, or it could opt to take the test about the difference in duration by sticking its nose into a different hole and receiving a big reward if it made the correct choice (registered by pressing a lever). An incorrect choice resulted in no reward. Rats were more likely to decline the test (and receive the smaller reward) the

more difficult the test was, that is, the more similar in duration the two sounds were. In other words, rats can _____.

[4점]

① cheat other rats to get food

② assess their own cognitive states

③ apply their auditory sense to find objects

④ make certain communication sounds

⑤ act as if they don't mind pain

[20~21] 주어진 글 다음에 이어질 글의 순서로 가장 적절한 것을 고르시오.

20

Mosquitoes can carry and transmit many disease-causing microbes to humans. They also have microbiota. Again, knowledge of this has been exploited to try to thwart mosquitoes' capacity to transmit infections to humans. Many insects carry *Wolbachia* bacteria normally.

(A) The presence of *Wolbachia* infection in the next generation of mosquitoes inhibits viruses such as dengue. Use of this technique in one area of Australia has been extremely effective in interrupting dengue transmission. Tests are also underway in other areas.

(B) In nature, *Aedes aegypti*, the mosquito that transmits dengue, chikungunya, Zika, and other viruses, are not normally infected with *Wolbachia* however, they can survive when infected with *Wolbachia*. It turns out, however, that if infected with *Wolbachia*, they may be unable to transmit certain viruses like dengue and chikungunya and other viruses that cause disease.

(C) Researchers are now studying whether they can use this information to prevent transmission. They are rearing mosquitoes, intentionally infecting male mosquitoes with *Wolbachia*, and releasing them into the wild. Male mosquitoes do not take blood meals and do not transmit infections. The released male mosquitoes mate with local female mosquitoes and *Wolbachia* is passed to the next generation via eggs. [4점]

* microbiota: (특정 장소에 사는) 미생물 군집
** thwart: 방해하다

① (A) − (C) − (B)
② (B) − (A) − (C)
③ (B) − (C) − (A)
④ (C) − (A) − (B)
⑤ (C) − (B) − (A)

21   Stabilizing selection refers to selection against both extremes of a trait's range in values. Individuals with extreme high or low values of a trait are less likely to survive and reproduce, and those with values closer to the average are more likely to survive and reproduce.

(A) Very small ones are more prone to disease and have weaker systems, making their survival more difficult. Newborns who are too large are also likely to be selected against, because a very large child may create complications during childbirth and both mother and child may die. Thus, there is selection against both extremes, small and large.

(B) The weight of a newborn child is the result of a number of environmental factors, such as mother's age and weight, among many others. There is also a genetic component to birth weight. Newborns who are very small (less than 2.5 kg) are less likely to survive than newborns who are heavier.

(C) The effect of stabilizing selection is to maintain the population at the same average value over time. Extreme

values are selected against each generation, but the average value in the population does not change. Human birth weight is a good example of stabilizing selection.

① (A) – (C) – (B)   ② (B) – (A) – (C)
③ (B) – (C) – (A)   ④ (C) – (A) – (B)
⑤ (C) – (B) – (A)

[22~23] 글의 흐름으로 보아, 주어진 문장이 들어가기에 가장 적절한 곳을 고르시오.

22

> And the mechanical looms that displaced Ned and his comrades meant that someone with less skill, without Ned's specialized training, could take his place.

A popular picture of the Industrial Revolution depicts a wave of machines displacing a large number of low-skilled workers from their roles — people who made their living spinning thread and weaving cloth with bare hands and basic tools finding themselves without work. (①) But this is not what happened. (②) It was the high-skilled workers of the time who were under threat. (③) Ned Ludd, the apocryphal leader of the Luddite uprising against automation, was a skilled worker of his age, not an unskilled one. (④) If he actually existed, he would have been a professional of sorts — perhaps even a card-carrying member of the Worshipful Company of Clothworkers, a prestigious club for people of his trade. (⑤) These new machines were "de-skilling," making it easier for less-skilled people to produce high-quality wares that would have required skilled workers in the past.

* loom: 베틀
** apocryphal: (진위가) 의심스러운

23

> Nevertheless, children in their developmental phases (e.g., from the age of 9 or 10 via puberty to solidary growing up) challenge the previous value system.

Morals change over time and across generations. Generational conflicts are therefore precisely due to evolution. (①) What today's generations in many societies regard as opportune was often unacceptable in previous generations. (②) Children are socialized (and thus learn what is good or bad, what is right or wrong), especially through their parents, in the family and at school. (③) By means of explicit rules and prohibitions as well as implicitly through behavior, children are provoked to behave

in a way that is considered desirable. (④) The conflicts at generation transitions lead in the long run to adjustments of the moral conceptions. (⑤) This is to be understood as a clear indication of the social evolution and saves chances of the advancement as well as risks (of the "moral decline").

24 다음 글의 내용을 한 문장으로 요약하고자 한다. 빈칸 (A), (B)에 들어갈 말로 가장 적절한 것은?

Today's technology offers alternatives to the traditional approach in education. Take one feature of the traditional approach, the fact that teaching in a classroom is unavoidably "one size fits all." Teachers cannot tailor their material to the specific needs of every student, so in fact the education provided tends to be "one size fits none." This is particularly frustrating because tailored tuition is known to be very effective: an average student who receives one-to-one tuition will tend to outperform 98 percent of ordinary students in a traditional classroom. In education research, this is known as the "two sigma problem"— "two sigma," because that average student is now almost two standard deviations (in mathematical notation, 2σ) ahead of ordinary students in

achievement, and a "problem" since an intensive tutoring system like this, although it can achieve impressive outcomes, is prohibitively expensive. "Adaptive" or, "personalized" learning systems promise to solve this problem, tailoring what is taught to each student but at a far lower cost than the human alternative.

* standard deviation: 표준 편차

Traditional teaching methods cannot provide students with __(A)__ learning experiences, but technology can help provide these experiences more __(B)__ than the human alternative.

	(A)		(B)
①	customized	……	cost-effectively
②	cooperative	……	cost-effectively
③	competitive	……	expertly
④	collective	……	costly
⑤	individualized	……	costly

[25~26] 다음 글을 읽고, 물음에 답하시오.

Fashion presented a distinctive opportunity because it alone could _____ _____. Most Europeans during the late Middle Ages were

illiterate, and literacy spread only slowly during the Renaissance: for example, historians estimate that more than 90 percent of the English population was illiterate in 1500 and the majority remained so until the nineteenth century. As a consequence, these societies relied on verbal communication and images to convey messages that later societies conveyed through the written word. The church spread the Gospel through icons, paintings, ritual, and spectacle; the state addressed its citizens and the ambassadors of foreign powers with magnificent celebrations, grand palaces, parades, and awe-inspiring monuments—visual arguments for honor and respect. Clothing was an integral part of these image-based polemics; a monarch could *show* other people she was extraordinary and destined to rule; a priest could suggest by his very physical presence the splendor of heaven and the glory of God. New developments in fashion amplified this type of visual persuasion: the tailor's art, which became widespread in the fourteenth century, allowed clothing to communicate not only through luxurious fabrics, vibrant colors, and surface adornments but also through form and shape. Rather than simply draping a body in finery, tailored clothing could transform it into something otherworldly, superhuman.

* polemics: 논증법
** adornment: 장식

25 윗글의 제목으로 가장 적절한 것은?

① Written Words as a Replacement of Images
② Fashion: A Visual Means of Communication
③ What Made the Fashion Industry Prosperous
④ Luxury: Expanding Its Market to More Customers
⑤ Designers Need to Balance Creativity and Business

26 윗글의 빈칸에 들어갈 말로 가장 적절한 것은? [4점]

① facilitate a sustainability agenda based on local production
② transform the body itself into a form of political persuasion
③ foster a strong relationship between consumer and producer
④ generate the largest manufacturing business in human history
⑤ provide a hygienic barrier keeping the body safe from diseases

[27~28] 다음 글을 읽고, 물음에 답하시오.

Immanuel Kant suggested that our experience of the outside world is shaped by our uniquely human cognitive structures. In his view, we perceive external reality through our sensory and mental faculties, which (a) employ specific forms, like time, space and causality, to structure and order the world. We thereby create the world that we experience, a world that is a function of the forms we impart to it. The properties that we associate with the world are features of our cognitive apparatus, not of "things-in-themselves." If pink lenses were implanted over our eyeballs at birth, the world would appear to us with a pink shade, and we would have no way of envisioning reality without this pink overlay. Similarly, we cannot see reality without the (b)influence of how our eyes and brains are constructed to view things.

According to Kant, when we attribute properties like causality, space and time to the world outside our experience we run into conceptual confusion and (c) eliminate contradictions, because these properties are conceptual structures, not structures of things-in-themselves. These contradictions are known as Kant's antinomies of pure reason, and they (d) reveal the limits of our knowledge: we are restricted to things as they appear to us; we cannot know the world as it exists without the form of these appearances. Kant did not (e)deny the existence of objects outside us; rather,

he asserted that we perceive them in a form that is determined by the way the human brain works.

* impart: 주다, 부여하다
** apparatus: 장치
*** antinomy: 모순, 이율배반

27 윗글의 주제로 가장 적절한 것은?

① differences between Kant and preceding philosophers
② Kant's contribution to making philosophy popular
③ strengths and weaknesses of Kantian philosophy
④ Kantian political theory and its effects on politics
⑤ Kant's view of how humanity perceives the world

28 밑줄 친 (a)~(e) 중에서 문맥상 낱말의 쓰임이 적절하지 않은 것은? [4점]

① (a)   ② (b)
③ (c)   ④ (d)
⑤ (e)

2023 기출문제

[29~30] 다음 글을 읽고, 물음에 답하시오.

(A)

Linda was one of my coaching clients. She was a middle-level leader who worked in a large school district that was undergoing a great deal of change. Linda had many ideas and was enthusiastic about them. Her immediate supervisor, Jean, had a high level of visible anxiety about the upcoming changes.

(B)

Linda challenged her own assumption that Jean would never listen and began to take bold action. She approached Jean to schedule a meeting. Linda and I brainstormed what she could say that would be different from their conversations of the past, and would hopefully make a difference, and lead to progress. Within a few short weeks, Linda scheduled and had the meeting with Jean. Jean recognized the change in Linda and was, much to Linda's surprise, open to listening to (a)her ideas.

(C)

They were at a stalemate. Eventually, Linda realized it was (b)she who had to look deeply at her assumptions and how they contributed to her stagnation, and that of the department and the school. Although it took a while for Linda to recognize that it would continue this way until she did something about it, once she realized that change began with (c)

her, she became open to examine what she could do. Linda chose to have a conversation with Jean.

* stalemate: 교착
** stagnation: 정체

(D)

In fact, Jean had a temper that became evident under stress. Linda learned to avoid (d)her. Linda assumed Jean would fly off the handle when Linda wanted to discuss the team's goals and strategies. What did Linda do? Nothing. Linda learned to stay away from Jean. The result? Nothing. In our coaching sessions, Linda recognized that Jean wasn't likely to change alone. Linda wanted to implement some new programs in her department and felt as though (e)she was walking on eggshells around Jean. Linda fell into inaction.

29 주어진 글 (A)에 이어질 내용을 순서에 맞게 배열한 것으로 가장 적절한 것은?

① (B) − (D) − (C) ② (C) − (B) − (D)

③ (C) − (D) − (B) ④ (D) − (B) − (C)

⑤ (D) − (C) − (B)

30 밑줄 친 (a)~(e) 중에서 가리키는 대상이 나머지 넷과 다른 것은?

① (a) ② (b)

③ (c) ④ (d)

⑤ (e)

A discovery is said to be an accident meeting a prepared mind.
발견은 준비된 사람이 맞딱뜨린 우연이다.

2025
사관학교

10개년 영어

2022학년도 기출문제
영어영역(공통)

제2교시 영어영역(공통)

▶정답 및 해설 300p

01 다음 글의 밑줄 친 부분 중, 어법상 틀린 것은?

　Modern archaeological researchers, some of whom are women, ① have unearthed evidence that suggests the historical soundness of Herodotus' account of the Amazons. These scholars have found numerous graves in southern Ukraine dating from the middle of the first millennium BCE ② containing the skeletal remains of women buried with military paraphernalia such as lances, arrows, and armor. Some of the skeletons indicate that the deceased had been struck on the head or stabbed with a sharp blade, providing support for the view ③ which these are the remains of warriors rather than of women who were coincidently buried with weapons. The graves also contain bronze mirrors and gold trim for clothing, as well as jewelry (earrings, necklaces, beads, and arm rings). Perhaps the bodies were buried so that the women would enter the next world with both the weapons they would need as warriors and the ornaments they would desire ④ to enhance their appearance. All in all, the archaeological evidence suggests that Herodotus' account of the Amazons was not, as formerly thought, an illustration of his gullibility, but rather historically ⑤ sound.

　*paraphernalia : (특정 활동에 필요한) 용품
**trim : 장식
***gullibility : (남의 말을) 쉽게 믿음

02 (A), (B), (C)의 각 네모 안에서 어법에 맞는 표현으로 가장 적절한 것은?

　Given their disposition to be attentive to situational cues, high self-monitors (HSMs) are keen to make sure they know the nature of the situations they are about to encounter. The *clarity* of the situational expectations is particularly important to HSMs. This was nicely demonstrated in a study in which students (A) gave / were given the choice of entering or not entering a situation in which they had to behave as extroverts. HSMs were far more likely to enter if the situation was defined clearly, irrespective of their own extroversion level. However, low self-monitors (LSMs)' choices were based on (B) what / whether they were introverts or extroverts; if they were LSM extroverts, in they

2022 기출문제

went. Also, when asked how the situation might be changed to make them more (C) willing / willingly to enter it, HSMs transformed it so as to provide clearer guidelines for conduct. LSMs transformed the situation to more closely match their own dispositions to be introverted or extroverted. [4점]

	(A)	(B)	(C)
①	gave	what	willing
②	gave	whether	willingly
③	were given	whether	willingly
④	were given	what	willingly
⑤	were given	whether	willing

03 다음 글의 밑줄 친 부분 중, 문맥상 낱말의 쓰임이 적절하지 않은 것은?

Sculpture has historically been a significant form of public art, used across cultures and time to produce works that memorialized individuals and events considered ① momentous and worth remembering. As a result, sculptors often chose materials that were as ② permanent as possible, seeking to create art that would last as long as feasible. Popular materials for sculpture have included bronze and stone, especially marble, limestone, and granite. Wood and clay, which were less expensive, have also been popular media for sculpture. Occasionally, precious materials, including gold, silver, jade, and ivory, have been used, although much more ③ rarely because of their cost. Although materials used traditionally reflected those readily accessible to the sculptor, this decision was dictated by ④ availability more than any other reason. This resulted in sculptors in certain regions traditionally working with certain materials. With the advent of less expensive transportation and greater access to global markets, sculptors began using materials once considered ⑤ familiar.

04 (A), (B), (C)의 각 네모 안에서 문맥에 맞는 낱말로 가장 적절한 것은?

According to descriptive realism, states are, as a matter of fact, motivated exclusively by national self-interest. Their behavior is not influenced by moral considerations. On this view, any appeal to ideology and values in world politics is mere rhetoric, (A) concealing / revealing the pursuit of power, which is at the root of every decision taken in the international arena. Some see this as an (B) avoidable / inevitable consequence of human nature. Since humans are naturally self-seeking, the argument goes, it is to be expected that this will be reflected in their

political institutions. For 'structural' realists, by contrast, it is the anarchical nature of the international system-the absence of an 'overarching sovereign' or 'world government'-that explains why states are so preoccupied with their own interests. The absence of a world government makes for an insecure environment which (C) | forbids / forces | states to seek power in order to ensure their own survival. [4점]

	(A)	(B)	(C)
①	concealing	avoidable	forbids
②	concealing	inevitable	forces
③	concealing	inevitable	forbids
④	revealing	inevitable	forbids
⑤	revealing	avoidable	forces

05 다음 글에서 전체 흐름과 관계 없는 문장은?

Subsidies are payments made to businesses or economic sectors with the intention of reducing prices or increasing profitability. ① They are not necessarily used for exports, as farmland is often subsidized with the intention of making food cheaper for domestic consumption, and businesses are often subsidized for the costs of hiring new employees when a government is trying to increase employment levels. ② During the course of economic warfare, one reason subsidies are used is to increase the volume of a specific product, or potentially all products, that the consumers of the targeted nation are purchasing from the businesses of the issuing nation. ③ The other purpose is to make the good produced within one's own nation cheaper to decrease the volume of exports purchased by people domestically. ④ In other words, planned economies are not responsive to market forces, which results in resource inefficiencies and shortages. ⑤ The intended goal of issuing subsidies is to redirect profits and production away from the businesses of the target nation and turn them to benefit one's own businesses. [4점]

06 다음 글의 요지로 가장 적절한 것은?

When art fails to mirror life it fails as art. Mirroring life, however, does not mean copying it. The artist does not merely set down a photographic record of his times. Rather he reflects in his work the tempo, attitudes, aims, hopes, tensions, successes and failures of his era. He transposes these through his work. Because he is a member of society he intuitively expresses its heartbeat. One has but to walk through one of our great museums to realize the feelings and ideas-

the way of life-that were important, consciously and unconsciously, to the people of a particular epoch. The restrained emotional intensity, the medieval mystical mind of the early German and Flemish painters, for example, contrasts strongly with the frivolous, gay, carefree work of the French eighteenth century court painters, such as that of Antoine Watteau.

*transpose : (다른 장소·환경으로) 옮기다
**frivolous : 경박한

① 미술관에서 작품을 보면서 역사를 공부하는 것이 효과적이다.
② 사진과 달리 회화에서는 화가의 상상력이 표현될 수 있다.
③ 명작의 모방을 통해 창작을 위한 영감을 얻을 수 있다.
④ 예술가에 대한 생계 지원은 창작 활동의 기반이 된다.
⑤ 예술가는 자신이 사는 시대를 작품에 반영한다.

07 밑줄 친 epidemic of invisibility가 다음 글에서 의미하는 바로 가장 적절한 것은?

If an alien were to stumble upon an archive of American film and television, this alien would conclude that we are a mostly male, overwhelmingly white, with few people over sixty or with physical disabilities. Female speaking characters are only 29 percent of those in film and 36 percent of those on television. These statistics have not changed meaningfully in more than half a century. Whites are overrepresented, comprising 72 percent of speaking parts (versus 62 percent of the population). In a study of the top one hundred films of 2015, forty-eight did not include a single black character with a speaking part (defined as one word or more). Seventy films did not include an Asian or Asian-American character. Across film and television, only 15 percent of directors are female and 29 percent of writers are female. In film, women are even harder to find in director's chairs; about 4 percent of movies are directed by women. Media scholar Stacy Smith, who leads the massive research effort that produced these findings, calls this an "epidemic of invisibility."

① prevailing ignorance about the causes of infectious diseases
② rapid disappearance of movie-goers during the Internet Age
③ no visible means of economic support for aspiring entertainers
④ widespread failure to reflect diversity in American film and television
⑤ insufficient investments for training young directors in the American film industry

08 밑줄 친 turn them into a big raft to float around on the rivers and lakes가 다음 글에서 의미하는 바로 가장 적절한 것은?

One typical exchange begins with Huizi telling Zhuangzi that a king once gave him a gift of a handful of large gourd seeds: "When I planted them they grew into enormous gourds, big enough to hold twenty gallons! I tried to use them as water containers, but they were too heavy to lift; I tried cutting them to make spoons, but they were too shallow to hold any liquid. It's not that I wasn't impressed by their size, but I decided they weren't really useful for anything, so I smashed them." In China at the time, gourds were used for these two purposes, containers or spoons. Hence Huizi's disappointment. Hearing this story, though, Zhuangzi is incredulous. "You are certainly a fool when it comes to thinking big!" he declares. He tells Huizi some stories about people who took apparently useless or trivial items and used them for unexpected purposes, winning great rewards in the process. "Now you've got these gourds," he concludes. "Why didn't it occur to you that you could turn them into a big raft to float around on the rivers and lakes, instead of lamenting how they're too big to use as spoons! It's as though you've got underbrush growing in your mind!" [4점]

*gourd : 조롱박
**underbrush : (큰 나무 밑에 나는) 덤불

① conform to established conventions

② show respect for other people's possessions

③ take a look at your current spending habits

④ be flexible when considering the uses of objects

⑤ pay attention to the size of the item you are buying

09 다음 글의 주제로 가장 적절한 것은?

Consumers all over the world tend to explore new tastes and constantly pursue opportunities for a good deal, a better price, higher quality and reliable suppliers. It is therefore difficult to retain existing customers if there is no deliberate effort to understand and respond to their needs. Through the use of good communication and reciprocity, the selling process is the best opportunity for producers to engage customers and change them from being mere explorers to loyal and committed members of their initiative. If customers are not satisfied with how you sell your products, they are likely to never do business with you again. Thus, creating a consistent and pleasurable buying experience is an integral part of building trust and

loyalty. Reciprocity, as the process through which customers are somehow rewarded for their loyalty, is another important factor in ensuring that your customers keep returning. Creating loyal consumers requires a strategy which doesn't have to be expensive, it just needs to be smart!

① fierce competition between producers to gain customers' attention

② promoting brand-new products by word of mouth

③ ways to make consumers loyal in the selling process

④ reasons marketers focus on potential customers over existing ones

⑤ difficulties to meet loyal customers' demands for premium services

10 다음 글의 제목으로 가장 적절한 것은?

When negotiating with someone as part of a wider relationship, should you aim at cooperating (being nice) or being selfish (attempting to secure as much as you can for yourself)? Being selfish may give you the highest short-term payoff, but cooperating has the biggest reward in the long run. After organizing computer tournaments where game theorists pitched various negotiation strategies against one another, political scientist Robert Axelrod concluded that you should first cooperate and then imitate the other party's last action. The key is to realize that you and the other party are communicating through your actions. Cooperating (i.e., starting nice) sends the message that you are willing to make some accommodations. If the other party adopts a dominating strategy, then you should reciprocate that aggression. Likewise, if they are nice, then be nice. Continue imitating their last move in each subsequent instance. This creates a cooperative environment where the parties learn to search for an integrative agreement.

① What It Takes to Become a Crisis Negotiator

② Why Being Nice Can Hurt You in Negotiation

③ The Key to Negotiation: First Be Nice, Then Mirror

④ It Pays to Express Anger or Sorrow While Negotiating

⑤ Imitating a Successful Negotiation: Medicine or Poison?

11 다음 글에서 필자가 주장하는 바로 가장 적절한 것은?

When one virtuously reaches the mountaintop, he must not stop there-until 'every' hungry person in the world is fed; 'every' crying person is comforted; 'every' depressed person had cause to smile again; 'every' discouraged person is encouraged; and 'every' lethargic person is motivated. One must not ever stop creating possibilities. "To whom much is given, much is expected." Success carries with it a wonderfully heavy responsibility to use this new power as a lever to shift the world a little closer to God. As an achiever, the time is not to luxuriate, vegetate, or procrastinate, but to dedicate. The achiever has a power base. He must use it. He has influence. He must wield it. He has success. He must share it. To laugh often and much, to win the respect of intelligent people and the affection of children, to earn the appreciation of honest critics and endure the betrayal of false friends, to appreciate beauty, to find the best in others, and to leave the world a bit better because one (the achiever) once existed-this is to have success.

*lethargic : 무기력한
**vegetate : 무기력하게 살다

① 일등을 제외한 모두를 패자로 만드는 경쟁은 줄여야 한다.

② 성공한 사람은 더 나은 세상을 만들기 위해 노력해야 한다.

③ 승자의 성공 요인뿐만 아니라 패자의 패인도 분석해야 한다.

④ 큰 성공을 욕심내기 전에 작은 성공부터 하나씩 쌓아야 한다.

⑤ 경쟁에 참가할 수 있는 기회를 모두에게 공평하게 주어야 한다.

12 다음 글이 시사하는 바로 가장 적절한 것은?

What you hear in the forest but cannot see might be a tiger. It might even be a conspiracy of tigers, each hungrier and more vicious than the other, led by a crocodile. But it might not be, too. If you turn and look, perhaps you'll see that it's just a squirrel. (I know someone who was actually chased by a squirrel.) Something is out there in the woods. You know that with certainty. But often it's only a squirrel. If you refuse to look, however, then it's a dragon, and you're no knight: you're a mouse confronting a lion; a rabbit, paralyzed by the gaze of a wolf. And I am not saying that it's always a squirrel. Often it's something truly terrible. But even what is terrible in actuality often pales in significance compared to what is terrible in imagination. And often what cannot be confronted because of its horror

in imagination can in fact be confronted when reduced to its-still-admittedly-terrible actuality.

① Don't turn away from reality.

② Despair gives courage to a coward.

③ Everything you can imagine is real.

④ Imagine yourself in the other's boots.

⑤ Never chase your prey, just wait with bait.

13 밑줄 친 부분이 가리키는 대상이 나머지 넷과 다른 것은?

Krause describes a memorable encounter with an elder of the Nez Perce tribe named Angus Wilson, who chided ① <u>him</u> one day: "You white people know nothing about music. But I'll teach you something about it if you want." The next morning, Krause found ② <u>himself</u> led to the bank of a stream in northeastern Oregon. He was motioned to sit quietly on the ground there. After a chilly wait, a breeze picked up, and suddenly ③ <u>his</u> surroundings were filled with the sound of a pipe organ chord—a remarkable occurrence, since no instrument was in sight. Wilson brought ④ <u>him</u> over to the water's edge and pointed to a group of reeds, broken at different lengths by wind and ice. "He took out his knife," Krause later recalled, "and cut one at the base, whittled some holes, brought the instrument to his lips and began to play a melody. When ⑤ <u>he</u> stopped, he said, 'This is how we learned our music.'"

*whittle : 깎아서 모양을 만들다

14 다음 글의 목적으로 가장 적절한 것은?

I received a letter from your office, saying that my recent claim for additional compensation had been denied. It appears that the letter is a form letter and does not disclose the reason that I was denied the additional bonus pay for having completed the 14-month language training program with a passing grade. Therefore, I am requesting a review of this claim and a full, specific explanation about the reasons for the denial. If I do not receive a reversal of this decision, I plan to file an appeal within the required time frame to follow up on my rightful claim to this bonus. All appropriate documentation is enclosed (service letter explaining the language bonus, grades, my original letter to you, your form letter to me). I expect to hear from you immediately about this review and to receive the full compensation due me under this recruitment arrangement.

① 언어 연수 프로그램 수료를 보고하려고
② 연수 대상으로 선발되었는지 알아보려고
③ 보너스 수령을 위해 필요한 서류를 확인하려고
④ 추가 보너스 지급 거부에 대한 번복을 요구하려고
⑤ 언어 연수 프로그램 지원 절차에 대해 문의하려고

15 Tilly Edinger에 관한 다음 글의 내용과 일치하지 <u>않는</u> 것은?

Tilly Edinger was born to a wealthy Jewish family in 1897. Her father, Ludwig, was a medical researcher who compared the brain structure of different animals. Edinger studied at the universities of Heidelberg and Munich from 1916 to 1918. After receiving a doctorate in 1921 from the University of Frankfurt, Edinger became a curator at the Senckenberg Museum in 1927. In 1929, she published the founding work of paleoneurology, *Die Fossilen Gehirne* (Fossil Brains), which was based on her discovery that plaster casts of the inside of fossil skulls revealed the shape of brains. She was one of the first to combine geological and biological evidence to show how the brains of animals had evolved over millions of years. After the Nazis took control of Germany, Edinger decided to leave the country. She fled Germany in 1939 and, after staying in London for a year, went to the United States. In her new country, Edinger maintained her reputation as one of the top figures in her field and published a second monumental book, *The Evolution of the Horse Brain*.

*paleoneurology : 고생물 신경학

① 아버지는 다양한 동물의 뇌 구조를 비교한 의학 연구원이었다.
② Frankfurt 대학에서 박사 학위를 받은 후 박물관의 큐레이터가 되었다.
③ 1929년에 Die Fossilen Gehirne를 출간했다.
④ 나치가 독일을 장악한 후 독일을 떠나 바로 미국으로 갔다.
⑤ 미국에서 명성을 유지했고 기념비적인 저서를 출간했다.

[16~19] 다음 빈칸에 들어갈 말로 가장 적절한 것을 고르시오.

16

Specialization of members of a group is a hallmark of advance in social evolution. One of the theorems of ergonomic theory is that for each species in a particular environment there exists an optimum mix of coordinated specialists that performs more efficiently than groups of equal size

2022 기출문제

consisting wholly of generalists. It is also true that under many circumstances mixes of specialists can perform qualitatively different tasks not easily managed by otherwise equivalent groups of generalists, whereas the reverse is not true. Packs of African wild dogs, to cite one case, break into two "castes" during hunts: the adult pack that pursues, and the adults that remain behind at the den with the young. Without this _____, the pack could not hunt down a sufficient number of the large ungulates that constitute its chief prey.

*theorem : 원리, 법칙
**ergonomic : 인체 공학의
***ungulate : 발굽이 있는 동물

① team of rivals

② division of labor

③ pursuit of pleasure

④ balance in nutrition

⑤ distribution of wealth

17 Since the early Chinese philosophers aimed for an action-oriented model of perfection, they focused on training the embodied mind through physical practice, visualization exercises, music, ritual, and meditation. There was little emphasis on abstract theorizing or the learning of general principles. Although memorization played a role-students were expected to know the classics by heart at an early age-the end goal was learning to use this information in real life, flexibly and creatively. Confucius once noted, "Imagine a person who can recite the several hundred Odes by heart but, when delegated a governmental task, is unable to carry it out or, when sent abroad as an envoy, is unable to engage in repartee. No matter how many Odes he might have memorized, what good are they to him?" Simply memorizing the classics does not make one a true gentleman or lady-you need to *incorporate* this knowledge, make it part of your embodied being. This is what early Chinese training focused on. The goal was to produce a kind of flexible *know-how*, exemplified in _____. Education should be analog, holistic, and oriented toward action. [4점]

*Ode : 시경(詩經)에 나오는 시
**repartee : 재치 있는 즉답

① effective engagement with the world

② complete abandonment of selfish actions

③ perfect memorization of all the given information

④ shared commitment to abstract theorizing

⑤ wise imitation of successful people

18

Early behavioral observations already argued against the idea of _____. Researchers demonstrated repeatedly that animals do not associate everything equally and cannot be trained to do all tricks the experimenter expects them to do. Behaviors that relate to the animal's ecological niche can be trained easily because the brain is predisposed or "prepared" to do things that have survival and reproductive advantage. For example, "spontaneous alternation," the tendency in rodents to choose different paths during foraging, is an instance of biological preparedness for the rapid acquisition of species-specific learning. Returning to the same location for food within a limited time window is not an efficient strategy because choosing an alternate route will more likely lead to reward. In contrast, associations that would be detrimental to survival are called "contraprepared." For example, it is virtually impossible to train a rat to rear on its hindlimbs to avoid an unpleasant electric shock to the feet since rearing is an exploratory action and incompatible with the hiding and freezing behaviors deployed in case of danger. [4점]

*ecological niche : 생태(학)적 지위
**rodent : 설치류 동물
***detrimental : 유해한

① the brain as a blank slate
② reward as a double-edged sword
③ emotion as a companion of reason
④ disposition as a predictor of destiny
⑤ animal experiments as a necessary evil

19

We know that focusing conscious awareness on the mechanics of one's performance, while useful in very early stages of skill acquisition, has a disruptive effect on more experienced players or performers. Similarly, regardless of level of expertise, focusing on the environment and effects one wishes to have upon it ("external focus") is more effective than focusing on one's own bodily movements or internal states ("internal focus"). For instance, swimmers told to focus on pushing the water back (external focus) as opposed to pulling their hands backwards (internal focus) swim faster, and this effect has been shown in a large variety of domains. There are various hypotheses about why directing one's attention outward, rather than inward, is more effective in learning and performing a physical skill. When you focus on your own movements, you allow your conscious mind to insert itself where it doesn't belong, disrupting smooth, automatic motor programs

and allowing other distractions-social pressure, personal anxieties, promised material rewards-to invade and degrade your performance. _____ facilitates your ability to get "lost" in the to-and-fro of the play. [4점]

① Expecting reasonable rewards for your efforts
② Focusing on the skill-relevant environment
③ Balancing between work and play
④ Being conscious of others' judgments
⑤ Isolating yourself from your day-to-day environment

[20~21] 주어진 글 다음에 이어질 글의 순서로 가장 적절한 것을 고르시오.

20

While parents are better informed now than they were in the days of Holt and Watson about children's need for affectionate touch, busy work schedules may not give them much opportunity to provide it. Many children are left at daycare or school after breakfast and only return home in time for supper and bed.

(A) Some parents and caretakers may attempt to compensate for the limited tactile attention children receive by providing them with heightened visual stimulation, most notably videos and computer games (which are now directed even at infants).

(B) While this may lead to a heightened visual consciousness appropriate for members of a society of the image, however, it cannot confer the benefits of a personal touch. It would seem that the time has not yet come for us to feel comfortable in our own skins.

(C) This routine may not allow for much more tactile interaction than Watson's ideal of a handshake in the morning and a kiss at bedtime. Nor are children likely to receive their quota of hugs and kisses outside of the home as childcare providers are increasingly fearful that affectionate touch maybe interpreted as an inappropriate, abusive touch.

① (A)-(C)-(B)　　② (B)-(A)-(C)
③ (B)-(C)-(A)　　④ (C)-(A)-(B)
⑤ (C)-(B)-(A)

21

In spite of thousands of research studies, we are still unclear on the most basic question-What is the function of sleep? The most obvious explanation is that sleep is restorative.

(A) In contrast, vulnerable animals that are too large to burrow or hide—for example, horses and cattle—sleep very little. In a study of 39 species, the combined factors of body size and danger accounted for 80% of the variability in sleep time.

(B) Support for this idea comes from the observation that species with higher metabolic rates typically spend more time in sleep. A less obvious explanation is the *adaptive* hypothesis; according to this view, the amount of sleep an animal engages in depends on the availability of food and on safety considerations.

(C) Elephants, for instance, which must graze for many hours to meet their food needs, sleep briefly. Animals with low vulnerability to predators, such as the lion, sleep much of the time, as do animals that find safety by hiding, like bats and burrowing animals.

① (A)-(C)-(B) 　② (B)-(A)-(C)

③ (B)-(C)-(A) 　④ (C)-(A)-(B)

⑤ (C)-(B)-(A)

[22~23] 글의 흐름으로 보아, 주어진 문장이 들어가기에 가장 적절한 곳을 고르시오.

22

Nonetheless, there may be what clinical psychologists call "secondary gain" that derives from the memory.

In many cases, the motivation to adopt (or, at least, to consider) a suggested memory may be complex. Consider, for example, an adult who now recalls some awful childhood event. (①) If the remembered event was painful or shameful, one might think the person gains nothing from this memory; instead, it hurts the person to hold these memories. (②) Perhaps the person gets long-hoped-for attention and respect. (③) Perhaps the person is excused from various responsibilities. (④) Perhaps the person at last gains the powerful feeling reflected in statements like, "Finally, my life makes sense, and I see why all these bad things happened to me," or "At last, I realize that the bad things in my life were not my fault." (⑤) Thus, anyone evaluating the memory and seeking to decide if the memory is accurate or not should weigh these possibilities.

23

Rather, the primary motivators for their behaviors remain spontaneous reactions both to internal, unlearned, genetic programming as well as cues from their environment.

An important issue is that with the unfolding of the bio–ontological shift, primitive humans felt isolated from the natural world. (①) Compared to life forms whose lives are controlled mostly by thoughtless, genetic programming, humans now had the heavy burden of having to think before acting. (②) While genetic programming enacts very specific, inflexible instructions as to how to behave, thinking, by comparison, is very flexible and presents humans with possible ways of choosing and behaving. (③) There is certainly learning among certain nonhuman life as well as primitive, culture transferal; there are also clear indications that some species, particularly nonhuman primates, utilize a degree of thought before acting. (④) Nonetheless, the idea that the actions of nonhuman primates are *thoughtful* and that reflective thinking precedes their behavior is far–fetched. (⑤) For humans, the situation in the world is dramatically different. [4점]

*bio–ontological : 생물 존재론적인
**transferal : 전달, 전승

24 다음 글의 내용을 한 문장으로 요약하고자 한다. 빈칸 (A), (B)에 들어갈 말로 가장 적절한 것은?

Paul Green, Francesca Gino, and Brad Staats studied four years' worth of employee performance data from over 300 full-time workers at one particular company. At this organization, managers did not conduct annual performance reviews. Instead, people engaged in self-evaluation and they reviewed their peers. The researchers examined these data, as well as information about each worker's network within the organization. What did they find? Individuals tended to eliminate colleagues from their network if these co-workers provided negative feedback. If they could not exclude the person, they compensated by bringing others who would be more affirming into their social circle. In short, individuals surrounded themselves with people who told them what they wanted to hear. They paid a price for this behavior. The researchers found that employee performance suffered considerably when workers disassociated themselves from colleagues offering critical feedback.

↓

In the study, workers tended to keep their ___(A)___ colleagues who gave critical feedback and this attitude had ___(B)___ effects on their performance.

	(A)		(B)
①	distance from	……	adverse
②	distance from	……	beneficial
③	confidence in	……	multi-dimensional
④	confidence in	……	unintended
⑤	temper with	……	lasting

[25~26] 다음 글을 읽고, 물음에 답하시오.

Faced with the bewildering variety of moral customs and practices encountered throughout the world, it is tempting to seek refuge in the thought that there really is no morally right or wrong decision. Moral relativism is the idea that the truth of a moral judgment or principle is dependent upon and relative to its acceptance by some person or group of persons. Thus, confronted with a conflict of personal beliefs, we ought simply to follow our own beliefs. Or, perhaps, quite differently, we should adhere to and advocate our own personal beliefs, while learning simply to tolerate the differing beliefs of others. If we are to cultivate tolerance, how widely should our moral latitude extend? For example, would it cover toleration of the violent and brutal suppression of political opponents? Should we stand silently by and tolerate (let alone advise or participate in) the torture of such opponents, simply because it is the practice of another country?

In this instance, according to the concept of moral relativism, no one is in a privileged position of saying what is, in fact, right or wrong-we are only at best able to state with some certainty what we ourselves believe to be right or wrong. In the case of a conflict between accepted moral values (for example, about the rights of women, or of minors, or of ethnic minorities, or the treatment of political opponents) in our society versus another, relativism seems to say that _____. Relativists might further recommend, in keeping with the value of tolerance, that we adopt the moral values and practices of the society in which we find ourselves, as captured in the familiar and well-worn proverb: When in Rome, do as the Romans do.

*latitude : (행동 · 사상 · 활동 등의) 자유[허용 범위]

25 윗글의 제목으로 가장 적절한 것은?

① How Moral Relativists Approach Moral Conflicts

② Moral Relativism Leads to Moral Irresponsibility

③ Moral Individuals in Their Immoral Society

④ Our Ultimate Goal: Universal Morality

⑤ Morality: Is It Innate or Acquired?

26 윗글의 빈칸에 들어갈 말로 가장 적절한 것은? [4점]

① we need to search for a superior moral justification for selfishness

② no criticism of one society by another would be objectively valid

③ moral courage is a higher and rarer virtue than physical courage

④ there is no moral authority like that of self-sacrifice

⑤ we become virtuous by practicing virtue

[27~28] 다음 글을 읽고, 물음에 답하시오.

This might sound like a fevered nightmare, but climate change has triggered the collapse of advanced civilizations dating back nearly 3,000 years. Around 1200 BCE, a perfect storm of calamities-including earthquakes, famines, and a drought that lasted 150 years or more-set in motion the breakdown of the late Bronze Age kingdoms clustered around the eastern Mediterranean in an area that includes much of what is now Greece, Israel, Lebanon, Turkey and Syria. Archaeologists have unearthed persuasive evidence that part of the world experienced vibrant economic (a) growth and cultural and technological advances for more than three centuries. These ancient societies-from the Mycenaeans and Minoans to the Hittites, Assyrians, Cypriots, Canaanites and Egyptians-were intimately (b) interconnected, exchanging the services of physicians, musicians and artisans. Their well-developed trade routes transported goods and natural resources, especially commodities such as tin, essential for making bronze.

But a 2012 study revealed that surface temperatures of the Mediterranean Sea cooled rapidly during the years around 1200 BCE, (c) causing a severe drought that led to food shortages, mass migrations, and internal rebellions by poor and agrarian peasants. Ultimately, the major cities of these once-thriving Bronze Age societies were destroyed by invading armies likely fleeing their own drought-stricken homelands, (d) prompting the loss of culture, languages and technologies. The result was the first Dark Ages when these once-sophisticated and complex societies (e) continued to exist. It took centuries to recover and rebuild.

27 윗글의 주제로 가장 적절한 것은?

① the impact of climate change on the late Bronze Age kingdoms

② the necessity of international efforts to prevent climate change

③ ongoing attempts to reveal a mystery about bronze artifacts

④ ideal climate conditions for building advanced civilizations

⑤ reasons the Bronze Age kingdoms prospered

28 밑줄 친 (a)~(e) 중에서 문맥상 낱말의 쓰임이 적절하지 <u>않은</u> 것은? [4점]

① (a) ② (b)

③ (c) ④ (d)

⑤ (e)

[29~30] 다음 글을 읽고, 물음에 답하시오.

(A)

Danny shouted angrily, "I won't apologize to Miss Hayward. Colin broke the window, not me. I'm not going to say I'm sorry just to please everybody!" Danny's granddad listened patiently to what his grandson had to say. "You both played with the ball, didn't you?" he asked. "Yes, but Colin dodged on purpose when I passed the ball to him. It was his fault that the ball went through Miss Hayward's kitchen window." "Remember, if you don't apologize, you will never be able to play near her house again," Grandpa reminded (a) <u>him</u>.

*dodge : 몸을 피하다

(B)

And so they could both continue their journey. "Why did you show me this picture?" Danny asked. "If you are prepared to be the least, like the goat in the cartoon who lay down, (b) <u>you</u> and Colin can still play together in front of Miss Hayward's house," Grandpa said.

(C)

Danny thought about what his granddad said. Yes, that would be a pity. She had such a great stretch of lawn in front of her house, and she always let them swim in her pool in summer. But (c) <u>he</u> decided, "No, Grandpa! Even if I have nowhere to play and even if I die of heat in summer, I will not go to Miss Hayward and say that I am sorry!" Grandpa went to his desk and browsed through some newspaper clippings. "Come and have a look at this," (d) <u>he</u> said.

(D)

Danny looked at the cartoon that Grandpa held out to (e) <u>him</u>. Two goats were walking in opposite directions on the narrow ledge of a cliff, next to a gaping precipice. In the middle of the path, they came face-to-face with each other. What would happen next? Would they tackle each other until both of them fell down the cliff? No, the one goat went down on his knees and allowed the other to walk over him.

*ledge : (절벽에서 튀어나온) 바위 턱

**precipice : 절벽

29 주어진 글 (A)에 이어질 내용을 순서에 맞게 배열한 것으로 가장 적절한 것은?

① (B)-(D)-(C) ② (C)-(B)-(D)

③ (C)-(D)-(B) ④ (D)-(B)-(C)

⑤ (D)-(C)-(B)

30 밑줄 친 (a)~(e) 중에서 가리키는 대상이 나머지 넷과 <u>다른</u> 것은?

① (a)   ② (b)

③ (c)   ④ (d)

⑤ (e)

A discovery is said to be an accident meeting a prepared mind.
발견은 준비된 사람이 맞딱뜨린 우연이다.

– 알버트 센트 디외르디(Albert Szent–Gyorgyi)

2025
사관학교 10개년 영어

2021 학년도 기출문제
영어영역(공통)

01 Based on the following dialogue, which one is true?

> John : Excuse me. I'm sorry to bother you, but I'm looking for the conference room. Do you know where it is?
>
> Amy : Yes! It's down the hall to your right. Are you here for the annual military leadership seminar?
>
> John : I am! Are you here for that as well? I heard a special guest speaker from the U.S. Navy Command was invited to talk about the future military exercise.
>
> Amy : Well, that speaker is actually me. I'm from the U.S. Navy Command and I'm here to encourage South Korea's participation in our annual Navy exercise to further enhance our alliance.
>
> John : What a nice surprise! It's an honor to meet you in person. I have so many questions.
>
> Amy : Well, I'll do my best to answer them.

① Amy wants to know where the conference room is.

② John is the special guest for the annual military leadership seminar.

③ Amy wants South Korea to participate in the annual Air Force exercise.

④ John wants South Korea to invite the U.S. Navy to the future military exercise.

⑤ Amy is the guest speaker from the U.S. Navy Command.

02 Choose the best answer for the blank.

> Doctor : Based on your X-ray results, your lower back pain is due to muscle strain. It's not a disc problem, so that's good news.
>
> Patient : Does that mean I can go back to work by next week?
>
> Doctor : You could, but you cannot lift any heavy objects or participate in any activity that will strain your lower back muscle. I recommend you take some days off to relax.

Patient : Is there anything else I can do to expedite my recovery? I have to go back to work as soon as possible.

Doctor : I understand you have important things to do, but your body needs to relax. Your back pain is only going to get worse if you don't take care of yourself.

Patient : Okay, _____. Thank you.

① I'll get back to work right away as you recommended

② I'll come back next week for the X-ray results

③ I'll get myself ready for the disc surgery

④ I'll try to get some time off from work

⑤ I'll go do some weight lifting now

03 Which is the best sequence of answers for the blanks? [3점]

Aaron : Good afternoon. Thank you for calling Global Travel Agency. This is Aaron. How may I help you?

Nancy : Yes, hi! I have some questions about the 10-day Southeast Asia package tour.

_____

Aaron : Well, the package includes visiting Thailand, Vietnam, and Malaysia for the first 7 days and you'll be given the option to either stay with the group and go to Cambodia or join a different group to visit Bali.

Nancy : _____

Aaron : Definitely! We can set that up for you. However, you'll have to move to a new hotel. There won't be any additional fee and you can select one on our website.

Nancy : Ah! That sounds great. _____ Thank you.

〈보기〉

a. Would it be possible to stay in Thailand longer instead of selecting Cambodia or Bali?

b. Call me as soon as you choose the package.

c. I'll call you back as soon as I pick the hotel.

d. Do I get to pick the countries that I will visit or are they preset?

① a − b − d   ② a − c − d

③ b − a − d   ④ d − a − b

⑤ d − a − c

04 What is the relationship between the man and the woman?

> Man : Now, for the second question, last time you talked about your passion for women's history. So, is it safe to assume that this is the reason for your involvement in the current project?
>
> Woman : Oh, definitely. And it's not just about representing women's history, but more specifically about women in the scientific field.
>
> Man : Were you ever into science when you were young?
>
> Woman : Yes, I was! I even went to the science camp and completed a NASA internship when I was in college. That's why I am very excited to take on this role.
>
> Man : Well, I can't wait to see you star in the film.
>
> Woman : I also can't wait to read your film review in your next issue.

① news anchor − correspondent

② professor − college student

③ movie director − scriptwriter

④ magazine reporter − actress

⑤ job interviewer − job interviewee

05 Based on the following dialogue, which one is NOT true?

> Mother : Hey honey, is everything okay? You look tired.
>
> Daughter : I don't know, Mom. I just can't seem to focus and I have nasal congestion. I think I am coming down with something.
>
> Mother : Do you want me to take you to the hospital? It might be something serious.
>
> Daughter : Maybe later in the afternoon. I purchased some over-the-counter medication at the pharmacy. I'll let you know if I feel worse.
>
> Mother : Well, try to get some rest and drink lots of water.
>
> Daughter : Okay, I will, Mom.

① The daughter has a stuffy nose.

② The daughter bought some over−the−counter medicine.

③ The mother thinks her daughter might be in a serious condition.

④ The daughter will let her mother know if her condition gets worse.

⑤ The daughter is getting better after she came back from the hospital.

06 Choose the sentence that best describes the situation.

> Michael : Hey Linda. Any plans for the summer break?
>
> Linda : I think I'm just going to stay home and maybe look for a part-time job. I'm really short on cash right now and need to save as much as I can.
>
> Michael : What happened? Is everything okay?
>
> Linda : Well, my dog had a car accident and I had to spend a lot of money on his surgery. He is recovering very well and will come home tomorrow.
>
> Michael : That's good. Well, I'm going to the lake with my friends this weekend. You are more than welcome to join. I'm sure it'll be great for your dog, too.
>
> Linda : That sounds really nice. Just let me know when and where to meet and I'll be there with my dog.

① Linda has found a part-time job at the lake.

② Linda has saved a lot of money for her holiday travel.

③ Michael is inviting Linda to go to the lake with her dog.

④ Michael wants to take care of Linda's dog while she is away.

⑤ Linda is reluctant to go to the lake with Michael and his friends.

07 다음 글에서 필자가 주장하는 바로 가장 적절한 것은?

> In a specialized economy, the food supply of the nation, and to some extent foreign markets, is somewhat contingent upon a dependable, long-term supply of water for irrigation. About 19 percent of crops produced and sold in the United States come from irrigated land. Without irrigation water this production would not occur, and the price of commodities would be much higher. Thus it behooves* the general public as consumers to understand that irrigation water and water conservation are extremely important to their own interests. Consumers must be willing to support public funding for water conservation research and for water supply development. The public must understand more about agricultural water problems and more about the processes for solving them.
>
> *behoove : ~할 필요가 있다

① 소비자에게 안전한 물이 제공될 수 있도록 수질 검사 절차를 개선해야 한다.

② 전 세계는 각 국가의 물 부족 실태를 공유하고 해결책을 함께 모색해야 한다.

③ 대중은 농업용수와 물 보존의 중요성을 이해하고 관련 활동을 지원해야 한다.

④ 일반 대중에게 충분한 식수를 공급하기 위해 농업용수의 사용을 줄여야 한다.

⑤ 물 소비의 불균형 문제 해소를 위한 활동에 전 국민이 적극적으로 참여해야 한다.

08 다음 글이 시사하는 바로 가장 적절한 것은?

My wife, Tami, and I have had our fair share of disagreements and disputes - and will undoubtedly continue to have them. But as a result of confronting these issues and resolving them, our relationship has become stronger and we have matured individually and as a couple. Why? Because underneath the hurt, frustration, irritation, or fear there is always a strong desire to learn and grow and make our relationship better. We dislike conflicts and certainly do not seek them out; but when they find us, we plunge into the storm. And when we reach the ominous stillness in the eye of the storm - the point of realization and recognition, the point of knowing and of clear seeing - we hold one another and together, leading or being led, make it out to safer shores. Conflicts do not necessarily happen for the best, but we are learning to make the best of conflicts that happen.

① A friend in need is a friend indeed.

② After the rain comes the sunshine.

③ Many hands make light work.

④ Strike while the iron is hot.

⑤ Blood is thicker than water.

[09~10] 다음 글의 요지로 가장 적절한 것을 고르시오.

09

Diplomats are almost always kept under close control by their capitals, and this will be truer for the larger developed nations. Diplomats are not free to make up their own foreign policy as they go along but are instead told what to say through *instructions*. The instructions will be carefully reviewed in the capital and sent by encoded means to the nation's embassy or mission abroad. Sometimes there will be an internal conflict in the capital regarding a particular issue, and different departments will take different positions. For example, in the United States, the State Department may not always take the same view as other departments that have an interest in international relations - the Defense Department or the Commerce Department. These internal differences must first be settled in the capital before the diplomat in some foreign city can be issued instructions. And it occasionally happens that internal

disagreements in the capital have left the lonely diplomat having to attend a scheduled meeting without instructions or not knowing what he or she is authorized to say or negotiate.

① 본국 정부 부처 간 의견 불일치는 외교관의 직무 수행을 어렵게 할 수 있다.
② 외교관에게는 긴급 상황 발생 시 신속한 독자적 판단 능력이 요구된다.
③ 외교관의 주요 임무는 주재국에서 본국의 이미지를 제고하는 것이다.
④ 외교관은 주재국의 사정을 본국에 신속 정확하게 알릴 필요가 있다.
⑤ 국가 간의 갈등은 외교로 해결하는 것이 당사국 모두에게 이롭다.

10

Some contact or acquaintance between a pair of people is an essential precondition for the formation of a relationship between them. Evidence from Festinger, Schachter, and Back documents the obvious fact that the less the physical distance between people and the more in the course of their daily activities their required paths cross, the more likely they are to develop social visiting relationships. Presumably this is so because contacts between people depend upon the ecological factors of distance and pathways. Similarly, Powell found that the differential proximity of houses in two Costa Rican villages was associated with the frequency of visiting between families. In a village where the houses are all grouped closely together fifty-three per cent of the visiting was reported to be on a daily basis, whereas in an open-country type of settlement where the houses are spread out over a considerable distance only thirty-four per cent of the visiting was on a daily basis. Gullahorn explicitly investigated rate of interaction as a function of proximity in an office of thirty-seven people in a large corporation. After two and one half months of observation and interviewing, he concluded that distance was the most important factor in determining rate of interaction.

① 집단 구성원 간의 접촉이 많을수록 갈등의 빈도도 높아진다.
② 사람 간의 물리적 거리는 상호작용의 빈도에 영향을 미친다.
③ 사람 간에 만나는 빈도가 높을수록 협동심도 높아진다.
④ 사회 활동의 폭이 넓은 사람일수록 대인관계가 원만하다.
⑤ 친밀도에 영향을 미치는 것은 거리가 아니라 접촉 빈도이다.

[11~12] 다음 글의 주제로 가장 적절한 것을 고르시오.

11

Skepticism, as a method of doubt that demands evidence and reasons for hypotheses, is essential to the process of scientific research, philosophical dialogue, and critical intelligence. It is also vital in ordinary life, where the demands of common sense are always a challenge to us to develop and act upon the most reliable hypotheses and beliefs available. It is the foe of absolute certainty and dogmatic finality. It appreciates the snares and pitfalls of all kinds of human knowledge and the importance of the principles of fallibilism and probabilism in regard to the degrees of certainty of our knowledge. This differs sharply from the skepticisms of old, and it can contribute substantially to the advancement of human knowledge and the moral progress of humankind. It has important implications for our knowledge of the universe and our moral and social life. Skepticism in this sense provides a positive and constructive framework that can assist us in interpreting the cosmos in which we live and in achieving some wisdom in conduct.

① significance of skepticism for the advancement of human knowledge and conduct

② weaknesses of skepticism in the context of artificial knowledge and behavior

③ importance of old skeptical inquiries in studying logical reasoning

④ differences between modified skepticism and scientific reasoning

⑤ ways to distinguish between different forms of skepticism

12

Explorations of the nature of thought, like the rest of psychology, began life in the philosopher's armchair. The study of thought processes, however, took longer than many other areas of psychology to pull loose from philosophy. Because of the elusive*, private, intensely personal nature of thought, on the one hand, and because of its relation to "truth," "knowledge," and "judgment," on the other, philosophers have been reluctant to part with this province of the study, and they have not entirely given it up today. Nevertheless, the study of thinking has moved out of the philosopher's library and into the laboratory - out of the philosopher's head and into the scientist's. Thought was introduced to the laboratory at the beginning of the twentieth century. Before that time, the psychology of thinking was strictly the philosopher's province, and so its history is studded with** names of

the great and near great, especially in the centuries during which empirical philosophy flourished in Great Britain.

*elusive : 파악하기 어려운
**be studded with : ~로 산재해 있다

① various approaches to the nature of thought in philosophy

② harmonious coexistence between philosophy and psychology

③ different views of philosophers and psychologists on thought

④ conversion of the study of thinking from philosophy to psychology

⑤ characteristics of thinking processes revealed by modern psychology

[13~14] 다음 글의 제목으로 가장 적절한 것을 고르시오.

13

So slow and painful is the process of mastering a technique, whether of handicraftsmanship or of art, so imbued* are we with the need of education for the acquirement of knowledge, that we are taken aback by the realization that all around us are creatures carrying on the most elaborate technique, going through the most complicated procedures and apparently possessed of the surest knowledge without the possibility of teaching. The flight of birds, the obstetric** and nursing procedures of all animals, and especially the complicated and systematized labors of bees, ants and other insects, have aroused the wonder, admiration and awe of scientists. The female insect lays its eggs, the male insect fertilizes them, the progeny go through the states of evolution leading to adult life without teaching and without the possibility of previous experience. Since the parent never sees the progeny***, and the progeny assume various shapes and have very varied capacities at these times, there can be no possible teaching of what is remarkably skillful and marvelously adapted conduct.

*imbue : 불어넣다
**obstetric : 출산의
***progeny : 자손

① Evolution: A Process Going on Forever

② Wonder of Knowing Without Being Taught

③ Nature: The True Teacher of Human Beings

④ Superiority of Human Beings over Other Creatures

⑤ Teaching and Learning: All Creatures' Way of Survival

14

A feeling of calm is regulated in part by a pathway of the autonomic nervous system called the *smart vagus*. When you're feeling stressed, your primitive brain wants to kick in - and when the primitive brain is in charge, it tends to make decisions that are bad news for relationships. When you have strong relationships, the smart vagus can modulate the stress response and keep the primitive brain from taking over. You're healthier, can think more clearly, and you're more likely to solve problems through creative thinking instead of exploding in anger or running away. But when you're isolated from other people, your smart vagus can suffer from what neuroscientists call *poor tone*. This means that your primitive brain is more likely to call the shots. In the short term, this leads to relationship problems. Over time, you can expect chronic stress, illness, depression, and big-time irritability.

① The Smart Vagus Brings Distraction to Your Mind

② Having Good Relationships: The Road to Staying Calm

③ The Location of Our Emotion: Still a Mystery to Neuroscientists

④ Understanding Ourselves Through Primitive Human Behaviors

⑤ The Primitive Brain: The Modulator of the Smart Vagus

15 다음 도표의 내용과 일치하지 <u>않는</u> 것은?

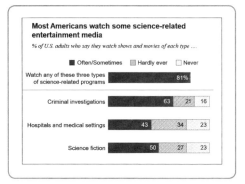

The graph above shows the percentage of U.S. adults who say they watch each type of science—related shows and movies: criminal investigations, hospitals and medical settings, or science fiction. ① About eight-in-ten U.S. adults say they often or sometimes watch any of the three types of shows and movies. ② In all three types of shows and movies, the percentage of adults who say that they often or sometimes watch them is the highest, while the percentage of adults who say they never watch them is the lowest. ③ The percentage of adults who say that they often or sometimes watch shows and movies of criminal investigations is three times larger than that of adults who say they hardly ever do. ④ The percentage of adults who say they often or sometimes watch shows and movies of hospitals and medical settings is more than twice that of adults who say they never do. ⑤ The percentage of adults who say they never watch shows and movies of hospitals and

medical settings is the same as that of adults who say they never watch shows and movies of science fiction.

16 Carl von Clausewitz에 관한 다음 글의 내용과 일치하지 <u>않는</u> 것은?

Carl von Clausewitz was born in Prussia on 1 June 1780 as the fourth and youngest son of a family that made claims to noble status which Carl accepted. Clausewitz entered the Prussian military service at the age of twelve, eventually attaining the rank of major general*. On 14 October 1806, when Napoleon invaded Prussia and defeated the Prussian army, he was captured and held prisoner in France from 1807 to 1808. Returning to Prussia, he assisted in the reform of the Prussian army and state. Opposed to Prussia's enforced alliance with Napoleon I, Clausewitz left the Prussian army and served in the Imperial Russian Army from 1812 to 1813. He wrote a careful, systematic, philosophical examination of war in all its aspects. The result was his principal book, *On War*. Clausewitz died without completing the book, but despite this his ideas have been widely influential in military theory and have had a strong influence on German military thought specifically. He died of cholera on 17 November 1831.

*major general : 소장

① 1780년 6월에 Prussia에서 한 가정의 막내 아들로 태어났다.

② 열두 살에 Prussia 군에 입대하여 결국 소장으로 진급했다.

③ 1807년부터 1808년까지 프랑스에서 포로로 잡혀 있었다.

④ 나폴레옹 1세와 Prussia의 동맹에 반대해 제정 러시아군에서 복무했다.

⑤ 사망 전에 *On War*를 완성하여 군사 이론에 널리 영향을 미쳤다.

17 밑줄 친 부분이 가리키는 대상이 나머지 넷과 <u>다른</u> 것은?

A young officer in the army was training to take parade. He walked along the rows of foot soldiers standing straight and still, all staring ahead as if in a trance*. They were battle worn, they had been fighting and were just back at camp to parade for the young officer before retiring. The young officer was accompanied by an old, seasoned general who was training ① <u>him</u> to be a leader. As they walked along the rows, the officer remembered an important leadership principle and quizzed the general. "Sir," ② <u>he</u> stammered still looking at the men in their emotionless eyes, "how does one learn to become humble while inspecting these men?" "The truth is, I feel superior to every one," ③ <u>he</u> admitted. The general smiled to himself.

"That's easy," ④ he said softly. "Simply look down at their boots." The young officer looked down and saw the rough and ravaged boots of the men. Many were barely holding together and some had blood showing through the toes of men who had driven themselves to the limit. ⑤ He felt a strong and sudden upsurge of emotion and unexpectedly felt compassion and humility. "Thank you," he said.

*trance : 몽환

[18~19] 다음 글의 밑줄 친 부분 중, 어법상 틀린 것을 고르시오.

18 What culture does is take ① what is available in the physical and human environment and interpret it socially and fill it with socially shared meaning and feeling. The world of human beings is a culturally interpreted social world. In this perspective we are somewhat ② like and somewhat unlike the rest of humankind. We are like others, naturally, insofar as all peoples (as far as we know) mate, reproduce, live in some variation of a cave (house), get around (transportation), and the like. We differ from others culturally insofar as different groups of people assign different meanings and values to being a father or mother, a man or a woman, to ③ have children, and to types of housing, modes of transportation, and so on. A child may be viewed as an economic asset or an economic liability. All houses are not constructed ④ equally; there are high-class and low-class houses. Transportation for an Eskimo is not the same as transportation for a typical U.S. suburbanite, and a twenty-year-old, "pre-used" car does not mean the same thing as the latest-model luxury automobile. Culture is all about the distinctive, shared meanings and feelings ⑤ characteristic of a given group at a certain time and place. [3점]

19 Why are our brains located in our heads? Wouldn't they be safer if they were deep in our chest, similar to the location of our hearts? Brains, regardless of ① how small or simple, have evolved at the best possible location to perform their principal function: survival of the individual and the species. With very few exceptions, brains are always located at the front end of an animal's feeding "tube" or mechanism, ② which in humans and many other organisms is the tubular system that extends from the mouth to the anus. Your brain makes it possible for you to find food by sight, sound, and smell and then to organize your behavior so that the front end of your feeding tube can get close enough to taste the food and check it for ③ beneficially or potentially harmful contents before you ingest it. Once the food is in your feeding tube, it is ④ absorbed and becomes available to the cells of your body. Your entire feeding tube and associated organs, also known as the

gastrointestinal system, ⑤ <u>use</u> nearly 70% of the energy you consume just to make the remaining 30% available to the rest of your body. [3점]

	(A)	(B)	(C)
①	capitalize	which	necessary
②	capitalize	what	necessarily
③	capitalize	which	necessarily
④	capitalizes	what	necessary
⑤	capitalizes	which	necessarily

[20~21] (A), (B), (C)의 각 네모 안에서 어법에 맞는 표현으로 가장 적절한 것을 고르시오.

20

Tactical command and control is the process whereby units actually engaged with opposing forces communicate with one another and coordinate their activities. Tactical command and control can improve responsiveness in battle by helping tactical commanders react quickly as the battle unfolds and (A) capitalize / capitalizes on tactical-level opportunities. It can enhance integration by affecting the coordination of deployments* and troop movements on the battlefield. More broadly, tactical command and control can affect the degree to (B) which / what individual units and commands work well together and synchronize their operations. Tactical command and control can improve skill by providing soldiers with the cues (C) necessary / necessarily to perform complicated synchronized fire, maneuver, or other activities.

*deployment : 배치

21

I would like to suggest that when our heads are filled with judgments and analyses that others are bad, greedy, irresponsible, lying, cheating, polluting the environment, valuing profit more than life, or (A) behave / behaving in other ways they shouldn't, very few of them will be interested in our needs. If we want to protect the environment, and we go to a corporate executive with the attitude, "You know, you are really a killer of the planet, you have no right to abuse the land in this way," we have severely impaired our chances of getting our needs (B) to meet / met. It is a rare human being who can maintain focus on our needs when we are expressing them through images of their wrongness. Of course, we may be successful in using such judgments to intimidate people into meeting our needs. If they feel (C) so / such frightened, guilty, or ashamed that they change their behavior, we may come to believe that it is possible to "win" by telling people what's wrong with them.

	(A)		(B)		(C)
①	behave	……	to meet	……	so
②	behave	……	met	……	so
③	behaving	……	met	……	such
④	behaving	……	met	……	so
⑤	behaving	……	to meet	……	such

[22~23] 다음 글의 밑줄 친 부분 중, 문맥상 낱말의 쓰임이 적절하지 <u>않은</u> 것을 고르시오.

22 Political power of any kind creates envy, and one of the best ways to deflect it before it takes root is to seem ① <u>unambitious</u>. When Ivan the Terrible died, Boris Godunov knew he was the only one on the scene who could lead Russia. But if he sought the position ② <u>eagerly</u>, he would stir up envy and suspicion among the boyars*, so he refused the crown, not once but several times. He made people insist that he ③ <u>reject</u> the throne. George Washington used the same strategy to great effect, first in refusing to keep the position of Commander in Chief of the American army, second in ④ <u>resisting</u> the presidency. In both cases he made himself more popular than ever. People cannot envy the power that they themselves have given a person who does not seem to ⑤ <u>desire</u> it.

*boyar : (옛 러시아의) 귀족

23 The key to any successful strategy is to know both one's enemy and oneself, and Gandhi, educated in London, understood the English well. He judged them to be essentially liberal people who saw themselves as ① <u>upholding</u> traditions of political freedom and civilized behavior. This self-image—though riddled with contradictions, as indicated by their sometimes ② <u>brutal</u> behavior in their colonies—was deeply important to the English. The Indians, on the other hand, had been ③ <u>humiliated</u> by many years of subservience* to their English overlords. They were largely unarmed and in no position to engage in a rebellion or guerilla war. If they rebelled ④ <u>violently</u>, as other colonies had done, the English would crush them and claim to be acting out of self-defense; their civilized self-image would suffer no damage. The use of nonviolence, on the other hand—an ideal and philosophy that Gandhi deeply valued and one that had a rich tradition in India—would exploit to perfection the English ⑤ <u>willingness</u> to respond with force unless absolutely necessary. [3점]

*subservience : 종속

[24~25] (A), (B), (C)의 각 네모 안에서 문맥에 맞는 낱말로 가장 적절한 것을 고르시오.

	(A)	(B)	(C)
①	procedures	restricted	specific
②	procedures	expanded	specific
③	procedures	restricted	widespread
④	consequences	expanded	specific
⑤	consequences	restricted	widespread

24

What exactly is metaphysics? What are metaphysical questions and metaphysical answers? Answering these questions requires a distinction between *a* metaphysics and metaphysics. *A* metaphysics is a view of the world that seeks to be accurate, consistent, comprehensive, and supported by sound evidence. Metaphysics, on the other hand, is the learned discipline one practices when one seeks to develop *a* metaphysics, consisting therefore in a set of (A) procedures / consequences . Metaphysics is different from natural science. The sciences are disciplines of learning that, like metaphysics, seek to develop views that are accurate, consistent and supported by sound evidence, but, unlike metaphysics, do not seek to be comprehensive. The sciences have (B) restricted / expanded areas of competence and specialized methods. Astronomy deals only with astral bodies and its method involves observatiaon and mathematical calculations; physics studies only certain properties of the physical universe and does so with very (C) specific / widespread methods; and so on.

25

Police interrogators, corporate personnel interviewers, reporters, and attorneys all know a basic fact about the people they question, which they use to great advantage: Interview subjects fear (A) silence / confrontation ; to avoid it, they will talk, even without thinking. This is why an attorney who questions you may, at the end of your perfectly adequate response, just stare silently at you as if to say, "That can't be all you have to say; you've got to be kidding!" In fact, when most of the people who answer (B) truthfully / untruthfully are faced with such a silence they will wrongly assume the questioner knows something more and will blurt out the truth. It's a neat trick to get more information from you, the witness; if not to (C) cover / uncover a concealed truth, then at least to get you to reveal new areas of information. Now that you know about it, don't get caught. In much of life talking is success

and silence is failure. On the witness stand, having the sense to sustain a silence after your response is success, and talking too much is failure. [3점]

	(A)		(B)		(C)
①	silence	⋯	untruthfully	⋯	cover
②	silence	⋯	untruthfully	⋯	uncover
③	silence	⋯	truthfully	⋯	uncover
④	confrontation	⋯	untruthfully	⋯	cover
⑤	confrontation	⋯	truthfully	⋯	cover

[26~30] 다음 글을 읽고, 빈칸에 들어갈 말로 가장 적절한 것을 고르시오.

26

The mass media bestow prestige and enhance the authority of individuals and groups by _____. Recognition by the press or radio or magazines or newsreels testifies that one has arrived, that one is important enough to have been singled out from the large, anonymous masses, that one's behavior and opinions are significant enough to require public notice. The operation of this status-confirmation function may be witnessed most vividly in the advertising pattern of testimonials to a product by "prominent people." Within wide circles of the population, such testimonials not only enhance the prestige of the product but also reflect prestige on the person who provides the testimonials. They give public notice that the large and powerful world of commerce regards him as possessing sufficiently high status for his opinion to count with many people. In a word, his testimonial is a testimonial to his own status.

① legitimizing their status
② camouflaging their defects
③ recreating their personality
④ revealing hidden facts about their status
⑤ comparing their status with that of the public

27

In its ordinary, normal state, the information-processing system that constitutes consciousness does not focus on any particular range of stimuli. Like a radar dish, attention sweeps back and forth across the stimulus field, noting movements, colors, shapes, objects, sensations, memories, one after the other in no particular order or pattern. This is what happens when we walk down a street, when we lie awake in bed, when we stare out a window-in short, whenever attention is not focused in an orderly sequence. One thought follows another without

rhyme or reason, and usually we cannot link one idea to the other in a sensible chain. As soon as a new thought presents itself, it pushes out the one that was there before. Knowing what is in the mind at any given time does not predict what will be there a few seconds later. This _____ of consciousness, although it produces unpredictable information, is the *probable* state of consciousness. It is probable because that is the state to which consciousness reverts as soon as there are no demands on it. [3점]

① random shift
② strict inflexibility
③ orderly repetition
④ reliable consistency
⑤ constant irreversibility

28

  Many social psychologists are still prone to take the view that the social variables important to their study will inevitably be reflected in their research situation. Even if this were entirely true, it is not true that researchers who hold this view will _____, for they are not primed to look for them. They justify their lack of attention to the other social sciences that study such variables with the declaration that they are studying the *interaction of individuals*, which is the basic stuff of all social sciences. This view has led to literally tons of studies of "leadership" that have no bearing on leadership in real life, to grand psychological models of power relations that omit most of the major variables that make power the central problem in political science, and to a deluge* of experimentation called "small group research" of which about 85 per cent is doomed to gather dust on library shelves, at least as far as anyone is concerned who is genuinely interested in group processes in real life. [3점]

*deluge : 범람

① ask why the social sciences should be integrated into other disciplines
② experience important shifts in their fundamental professional relationships
③ have to balance the gains of a new technology against the risks entailed
④ be highly knowledgeable about how to use experiments for their research
⑤ detect the reflections of sociocultural variables in their miniature experiments

29
　　Pythagoras's most important discovery was ＿＿＿＿＿＿＿＿. This was reinforced by his investigations into music, and in particular into the relationships between notes that sounded pleasant together. The story goes that he first stumbled onto this idea when listening to blacksmiths at work. One had an anvil* half the size of the other, and the sounds they made when hit with a hammer were exactly an octave (eight notes) apart. While this may be true, it was probably by experimenting with a plucked string that Pythagoras determined the ratios of the consonant** intervals (the number of notes between two notes that determines whether they will sound harmonious if struck together). What he discovered was that these intervals were harmonious because the relationship between them was a precise and simple mathematical ratio. This series, which we now know as the harmonic series, confirmed for him that the elegance of the mathematics he had found in abstract geometry also existed in the natural world. [3점]

*anvil : 모루
**consonant : 협화음의

① the beauty of mathematics: theory rules practice

② the theory that the number is the ruler of forms

③ the principle of deductive reasoning in notes of music

④ the artificiality of harmonic relationships in the natural world

⑤ the relationships between numbers: the ratios and proportions

30
　　Examples of the relation between fashion, clothing and "power" include the late 1960s' and early 1970s' youth. These people adapted their fashions and clothing to try to reflect the new roles between different social groups. Thus, attempted changes in power relations between different races and different sexes were expressed or reflected in terms of fashion and dress. Many workers in professions like social work are wary of wearing anything that will distinguish them from their clients and will tend to avoid a show of opulence*. Consequently fashions and clothing that will ＿＿＿＿＿＿＿＿ will be avoided and some sort of attempt made to dress on a level with the client. Doing this, of course, they run the risk of falling into the "sandals and oatmeal—coloured hand—knits" stereotype. In the 1970s and 1980s, various American police forces abandoned their uniforms and adopted civilian clothes in order to appear more

friendly and approachable.

*opulence : 부유함

① show their positive attitudes towards their clients
② mark them out as establishment or authority figures
③ hide their true identity and make them look ordinary
④ jeopardize their roles indicative of power and authority
⑤ reveal them as a person with friendliness and kindness

[31~32] 주어진 글 다음에 이어질 글의 순서로 가장 적절한 것을 고르시오.

31

Darwin justly observed that the struggle between two organisms is as active as they are analogous. Having the same needs and pursuing the same objects, they are in rivalry everywhere.

(A) The dentist does not struggle with the psychiatrist, nor the shoemaker with the hatter. Since they perform different services, they can perform them parallely.

(B) As long as they have more resources than they need, they can live side by side, but if their number increases to such proportions that all appetites can no longer be sufficiently satisfied, war breaks out. It is quite different if the coexisting individuals are of different species or varieties.

(C) As they do not feed in the same manner, and do not lead the same kind of life, they do not disturb each other. Men submit to the same law. In the same city different occupations can coexist without being obliged mutually to destroy one another, for they pursue different objects.

① (A) − (C) − (B) ② (B) − (A) − (C)
③ (B) − (C) − (A) ④ (C) − (A) − (B)
⑤ (C) − (B) − (A)

32

One experiment gave subjects a memory task. Some were asked to remember a two-digit number; some were given a seven-digit number.

(A) The subjects were then led to a lobby where they would await further testing. In front of them in the waiting area were slices of cake and fruit. The real test was what they would choose while they waited, while rehearsing those numbers in their heads.

(B) It requires conscious action to prevent the automatic choice. When our mental bandwidth is used on something else, like rehearsing digits, we have less capacity to prevent ourselves from eating cake.

(C) Those whose minds were not terribly occupied by the two-digit number chose the fruit most of the time. Those whose minds were busy rehearsing the seven-digit number chose the cake 50 percent more often. The cake is the impulsive choice.

① (A) − (C) − (B) ② (B) − (A) − (C)

③ (B) − (C) − (A) ④ (C) − (A) − (B)

⑤ (C) − (B) − (A)

[33~34] 글의 흐름으로 보아, 주어진 문장이 들어가기에 가장 적절한 곳을 고르시오.

33

You will soon find that what you do in such a state of heightened awareness, instead of being stressful, tedious, or irritating, is actually becoming enjoyable.

Here is a spiritual practice that will bring empowerment and creative expansion into your life. Make a list of a number of everyday routine activities that you perform frequently. (①) Include activities that you may consider uninteresting, boring, tedious, irritating, or stressful. (②) The list may include traveling to and from work, buying groceries, doing your laundry, or anything that you find tedious or stressful in your daily work. (③) Then, whenever you are engaged in those activities, let them be a vehicle for alertness. (④) Be absolutely present in what you do and sense the alert, alive stillness within you in the background of the activity. (⑤) To be more precise, what you are enjoying is not really the outward action but the inner dimension of consciousness that flows into the action.

34

The efforts and legacy of those humanists, however, have not always been appreciated in their own right by historians of philosophy and science.

The Renaissance was one of the most innovative periods in Western civilization. New waves of expression in fine arts and literature bloomed in Italy and gradually spread all over Europe. (①) A new approach with a strong philological* emphasis, called "humanism" by historians, was also introduced to scholarship. (②) The intellectual fecundity** of the

Renaissance was ensured by the intense activity of the humanists who were engaged in collecting, editing, translating and publishing the ancient literary heritage, mostly in Greek and Latin, which had hitherto been scarcely read or entirely unknown to the medieval world. (③) The humanists were active not only in deciphering and interpreting these "newly recovered" texts but also in producing original writings inspired by the ideas and themes they found in the ancient sources. (④) Through these activities, Renaissance humanist culture brought about a remarkable moment in Western intellectual history. (⑤) In particular, the impact of humanism on the evolution of natural philosophy still awaits thorough research by specialists.

*philological : 문헌학의
**fecundity : 풍요

[35~36] 다음 글에서 전체 흐름과 관계가 없는 문장을 고르시오.

35 It is man's inherent nature to seek what he believes to be greener pastures in the distance. ① When a man begins to look for a better position and more pay, he usually seeks opportunity in the distance with some other employer. ② Sometimes this may be necessary, but changes in employment, while they may bring advantages, always bring some disadvantages, the most outstanding of which is the fact that one is never as efficient in a new position, a new environment, and among new associates, as he is where he is familiar with the details of his work and has the confidence of his associates. ③ Of course, most people can't afford to leave their current job willingly, but delaying too long can be damaging to yourself and to others. ④ Moreover, the changing of positions deprives an individual of much of the goodwill value built around himself through long association with an employer. ⑤ Therefore, before deciding to change employers, be sure that you have exhausted the possibilities of your present position.

36 Seeing only the good in one's own actions and the bad in those of others is a common human weakness, and validating only the positive or negative aspects of the human experience is not productive. It is very tempting to focus on just the good (or the bad) in the world, *but it is not good science*, and we must not make this mistake in advancing positive psychology. ① Although we do not agree with the principles of the previous pathology models, it would be inaccurate to describe their proponents as being poor scholars, poor scientists, poor practitioners, or bad people. ② Instead, this previous paradigm was advanced by well-meaning,

bright people who were responding to the particular circumstances of their times. ③ Nevertheless, advocates of the previous pathology approach were short-sighted and prejudiced in their portrayals of humankind. ④ Likewise, it is not as if these people were wrong in their depictions of people. ⑤ They developed diagnoses and measurement approaches for schizophrenia, depression, and alcoholism and validated many effective treatments for specific problems such as panic disorder and blood and injury phobia.

37 다음 글의 내용을 한 문장으로 요약하고자 한다. 빈칸 (A), (B)에 들어갈 말로 가장 적절한 것은?

A paradox occurs when you avoid what you fear, because your fear then grows. This is counterintuitive, because when you avoid what you fear for a short time, your fear does decrease. Over a longer period, however, avoidance allows the anxiety to flourish. For example, let's say that you are anxious about going to a dinner party because you fear talking to strangers. For a brief time, avoiding the evening enables your anxiety to lessen. However, if you avoid the next dinner party invitation, and then the next and the next, you have created a problem. Because of your avoidance of those dinner parties, you have

made your anxiety about talking to strangers worse than it was at the start. You have to try to work against avoidance, even though it seems to make you feel better. I call this *challenging the paradox*. Challenging the paradox involves doing away with avoidance and replacing it with exposure. Exposure means facing what makes you feel anxious. By exposing yourself to anxiety-provoking situations, you become habituated to them, and your anxiety will eventually diminish.

A good way to __(A)__ situations that make you feel anxious is to __(B)__ such situations whenever possible without any hesitation.

	(A)		(B)
①	overcome	······	reject
②	overcome	······	experience
③	forget	······	experience
④	avoid	······	ignore
⑤	avoid	······	reject

[38~39] 다음 글을 읽고, 물음에 답하시오.

In considering event possibilities, strive to think creatively; people are attracted to events that are special and unusual. If you have been offering an event for several years, be aware that people can become tired of repeating the same program in the same way. Volunteers become stale, and the audience becomes bored unless you provide something fresh. Developing a distinctive and original event in the charitable marketplace can help (a) attract a following.

Another reason to be creative is competition. In the long run, whatever niche or special advantage you create for your event, there is a tendency for (b) decline, due to others copying your idea. You may enjoy the advantage of uniqueness for a while, but expect this to be (c) temporary. Add innovation to your program or undertaking with different, imaginative events to stay ahead of your competition.

To think creatively, you must first develop an attitude of exploring different ideas. Assume that nothing is fixed and that any fundraising event is open to change. Even though previous events may have been successful, circumstances may have changed or there may be better and different ways to continue the event. You must be open to (d) accepting familiar formats. If necessary, you must be willing to fall out of love with a cherished tradition or program. This openness to ideas involves taking risks. Remember that you are not seeking the unique for the sake of just being different. What matters most in this (e) exploratory process is the willingness to look for worthwhile ideas.

38 윗글의 주제로 가장 적절한 것은?

① the role of experiences in creative thinking

② benefits of participating in a fundraising event

③ the impact of excessive competition on the market

④ ways to make your products attractive to consumers

⑤ the necessity of generating creative ideas for an event

39 밑줄 친 (a)~(e) 중에서 문맥상 낱말의 쓰임이 적절하지 <u>않은</u> 것은?

① (a)　　　　② (b)

③ (c)　　　　④ (d)

⑤ (e)

[40~41] 다음 글을 읽고, 물음에 답하시오.

We often imagine that we generally operate by some kind of plan, that we have goals we are trying to reach. But we're usually ___(A)___ ourselves; what we have are not goals but wishes. Our emotions infect us with hazy desire: we want fame, success, security-something large and abstract. This haziness unbalances our plans from the beginning and sets them on a chaotic course. What have distinguished all history's grand strategists and can distinguish you, too, are specific, detailed, focused goals. Contemplate them day in and day out, and imagine how it will feel to reach them and what reaching them will look like. By a psychological law peculiar to humans, clearly visualizing them this way will turn into a self-fulfilling prophecy.

Having clear objectives was crucial to Napoleon. He visualized his goals in intense detail-at the beginning of a campaign, he could see its last battle clearly in his mind. Examining a map with his aides, he would point to the exact spot where it would end-a ___(B)___ prediction, it might seem, since not only is war in any period subject to chance and to whatever the enemy comes up with to surprise you, but the maps of Napoleon's era were notoriously unreliable. Yet time and again his predictions would prove uncannily correct. He would also visualize the campaign's aftermath: the signing of the treaty, its conditions, how the defeated Russian czar or Austrian emperor would look, and exactly how the achievement of this particular goal would position Napoleon for his next campaign.

40 윗글의 제목으로 가장 적절한 것은?

① The First Step to Success: Have a Wish
② Focus on Your Goals and Envision Them Clearly
③ Not Everything You Dream and Visualize Comes True
④ Don't Let Your Emotions Interfere with Your Objectives
⑤ The Road to Becoming a Grand Strategist: Know Yourself

41 윗글의 빈칸 (A), (B)에 들어갈 말로 가장 적절한 것은? [3점]

	(A)		(B)
①	fooling	……	ridiculous
②	fooling	……	reasonable
③	criticizing	……	ridiculous
④	underestimating	……	reasonable
⑤	underestimating	……	plausible

[42~43] 다음 글을 읽고, 물음에 답하시오.

The primary problem for artists in Leonardo da Vinci's day was the constant pressure to produce more and more work. They had to produce at a relatively high rate in order to keep the commissions coming and remain in the public eye. This influenced the quality of their work. A style had developed in which artists could quickly create effect in their painting that would (a) <u>superficially</u> excite viewers. To create such effects they would depend on bright colors, unusual juxtapositions* and compositions, and dramatic scenes. In the process, they would inevitably gloss over the details in the (b) <u>background</u> and even in the people they portrayed. They did not pay much attention to the flowers or trees or the hands of figures in the foreground. They had to dazzle on the surface. Leonardo recognized this fact early in his career and it (c) <u>distressed</u> him. It went against his grain** in two ways—he hated the feeling of having to hurry with anything, and he loved immersing himself in details for their own sake. He was not interested in creating surface effects. He was animated by a hunger to understand life forms from the inside out and to grasp the force that makes them dynamic, and to somehow express all of this on a flat surface. And so, not fitting in, he went on his own peculiar path, mixing science and art.

To complete his quest, Leonardo had to become what he termed "universal"—for each object he had to be able to render all of its details, and he had to (d) <u>extend</u> this knowledge as far as possible, to as many objects in the world as he could study. Through sheer (e) <u>elimination</u> of such details, the essence of life itself became visible to him, and his understanding of this life force became visible in his artwork.

*juxtaposition : 병렬, 병치

**grain : 기질

42 윗글에 관한 내용으로 적절하지 <u>않은</u> 것은?

① 다빈치 시대의 화가들은 다작에 대한 압박을 끊임없이 느꼈다.

② 다빈치 시대의 화가들은 밝은 색상과 극적인 장면에 의존하곤 했다.

③ 다빈치는 자신의 경력 초기에 당대 화가들의 관행을 인식하고 있었다.

④ 다빈치는 생명체의 역동적인 면 대신 정적인 면을 파악하려고 했다.

⑤ 다빈치는 과학과 예술을 혼합하면서 자신의 독자적인 길을 나아갔다.

43 밑줄 친 (a)~(e) 중에서 문맥상 낱말의 쓰임이 적절하지 <u>않은</u> 것은? [3점]

① (a) ② (b)

③ (c) ④ (d)

⑤ (e)

[44~45] 다음 글을 읽고, 물음에 답하시오.

(A)

Long ago in the great city of Vanasrai the king kept a stable of elephants. His favorite elephant had an unusual best friend-a dog who first came to the stable to eat the rice that fell from the elephant's mouth as she ate her dinner. As time went on, the elephant and the dog developed a close and loving relationship, until it came to pass that the elephant would not eat unless the dog was there to share her meal.

(B)

The adviser carefully examined the elephant. He clearly saw that there was nothing physically wrong with the beast. The elephant's caretaker said, "The elephant had a great friend in a dog, who has vanished recently." With that the adviser went back to the king and said, "Your elephant is heartbroken at the disappearance of a dog she much loved. To find the dog, I recommend putting forth a proclamation declaring that anyone who is found in custody of a dog from the king's elephant stable will be forced to pay a large fine."

(C)

One day an unkind stableman sold the dog to a passing peasant for a few coins. The elephant was miserable. She would not eat, drink, or bathe. When the king was told of the worsening condition of his favorite animal he was very upset. He called in his wisest adviser and told him, "Go to my beloved elephant and find out what is wrong with her."

(D)

So it was done, and as soon as the peasant who had bought the dog heard of the proclamation, he immediately released it, and the dog dashed directly back to the elephant stable. When the exhausted dog returned, the elephant wept tears of joy, and she scooped the dog up with her trunk and cradled it. She would not eat until the dog had been fed; then she ate her food as well and was soon back to her old ways, her canine friend forever at her side.

44 주어진 글 (A)에 이어질 내용을 순서에 맞게 배열한 것으로 가장 적절한 것은?

① (B) − (D) − (C)

② (C) − (B) − (D)

③ (C) − (D) − (B)

④ (D) − (B) − (C)

⑤ (D) − (C) − (B)

45 윗글에 관한 내용으로 적절하지 <u>않은</u> 것은?

① 코끼리는 개와 함께 먹이를 나누지 않으면 먹으려 하지 않았다.

② 코끼리 관리인은 코끼리와 친했던 개가 최근에 사라졌다고 말했다.

③ 고문은 왕에게 개를 데리고 있는 사람에게 큰 상을 주자고 제안했다.

④ 포고문에 대해 듣자마자 농부는 개를 즉시 풀어주었다.

⑤ 개가 돌아왔을 때 코끼리는 기쁨의 눈물을 흘렸다.

A likely impossibility is always preferable to an unconvincing possibility.

불가능해 보이는 것은 불확실한 가능성보다 항상 더 낫다.

– 아리스토텔레스(Aristotle)

2025
사관학교

10개년 영어

2020학년도 기출문제

영어영역(공통)

01 Based on the following dialogue, which one is true?

> Ron : I don't think I can go any further.
>
> Dan : Come on, man! Push it, we have about one more kilometer to the top. Don't quit now!
>
> Ron : That's easy for you to say! You're in great shape, and your bike is carbon fiber! It must weigh 10 kilograms less than my bike!
>
> Dan : If you make it without stopping, I'll buy you dinner after the ride. Anything you want.
>
> Ron : I can't even think about eating. My legs feel like they're going to fall off and my throat is drier than a desert. Seriously I've got to stop and rest. I want to get in better shape, but I'm too tired. This is too hard.
>
> Dan : You have to push yourself. You're not going to lose all that fat by taking rests. You're the one that asked me to help you.
>
> Ron : I see. You're right.

① Ron and Dan managed to reach the top together.

② Ron's bike is lighter than Dan's.

③ Ron says that he can eat anything after the ride.

④ Ron desperately wants to take a break.

⑤ Ron is helping Dan to lose weight.

02 Choose the best answer for the blank.

> Salesman : Well, I think this SUV is exactly what you're looking for.
>
> Bob : It looks nice, but it's much bigger than I expected.
>
> Salesman : In that case, maybe this sedan is more to your interest? It's smaller and the price is reasonable.
>
> Bob : That sounds great. Does it come in navy blue?
>
> Salesman : We have one in navy blue here in the showroom. The sticker price is $75,000. Would you like to take it for a test drive?
>
> Bob : No, I drove the same car at another dealership last week. I think I'm going to just go ahead and buy it.
>
> Salesman : _____

① Great. Let me get the paperwork together and you can get on the road.

② Okay. I can introduce you to another car dealer in your neighborhood.

③ No problem. I can give you enough time for your test drive.

④ Don't worry. Both cars will be within your price range.

⑤ I'm sorry, but we don't have the car in navy blue.

03 Which is the best sequence of answers for the blanks?

Randy : What should we have for dinner?

Martha : Actually, I can't think of anything I really want to eat.

Randy : How about Mexican food? A new Mexican restaurant called El Gordo's has opened nearby.

Martha : _____ Last time I ate spicy food in a Mexican restaurant, my stomach hurt for two days.

Randy : Then what about the Waffle Shack? _____

Martha : So do I, but there's always a really long wait for a table.

Randy : You may be right. What about pizza?

Martha : I can't eat it again. _____

_____

Randy : Mmm.... How about trying El Gordo's? We can choose unspicy food.

Martha : Okay. If you want.

― 〈보기〉 ―

a. I don't think it's a good idea.

b. I really love their dinner menu.

c. I'm so hungry.

d. I've already had it three times this week.

① a ― b ― d   ② a ― c ― d

③ b ― a ― d   ④ d ― b ― c

⑤ d ― c ― b

04 What is the relationship between the man and the woman?

Man : So I think it's exactly what you're in the market for. What do you think?

Woman : Well, honestly, I love it. The neighborhood seems fantastic and it is within my budget.

Man : So, should we make an offer to the owner? I know there are several other people interested in the house.

Woman : Yes, but I have one concern. Does the house next door always look like that? It

looks empty and untidy.

Man : In fact, no one lives there. It needs renovating but the owner doesn't have the mind to do it.

Woman : I don't want to live next to the deserted house. I'd like to see some other places in the area.

① security guard — visitor

② real estate agent — homebuyer

③ tour guide — tourist

④ house owner — tenant

⑤ architect — reporter

05 Based on the following dialogue, which one is NOT true?

Jeff : I was hoping we'd get some nice waves today.

Paul : Yeah, but it doesn't look like they'll be any good. You just missed it. They were fantastic yesterday. We had overhead waves.

Jeff : It seems like I'm always missing the good surf. Last month on the Baja Peninsula was the last time I had a great surfing day.

Paul : I've had those slumps before as well. Sometimes the surf gods smile upon us, and sometimes they don't!

Jeff : What does the forecast look like for tomorrow?

Paul : Rain and no surf, but the day after tomorrow looks like there'll be clear skies and fantastic waves! When are you leaving?

Jeff : Tomorrow night. The surf gods must hate me.

① Paul says that the waves were fantastic yesterday.

② Jeff is having terrible luck with surfing.

③ Jeff had great surf on the Baja Peninsula last month.

④ The forecast says it will rain tomorrow.

⑤ Jeff is going to leave the day after tomorrow after enjoying surfing.

06 Choose the sentence that best describes the situation. [3점]

Tom : Sorry but all of those plastic pipes have to be ripped out and replaced. Then we are going to have to build a new shower in there.

Jane : Oh no! That sounds expensive! How much is something like that going to cost?

Tom : Well, I'd have to write up an estimate, but off the top of my head, I'd say around $2,000. I did a job like this last year.

Jane : Oh boy! That's too expensive. I expected a few hundred maybe. I paid the last person $500. Couldn't you do it for that?

Tom : The reason I'm here is because you paid the last guy $500. He did a terrible job. That's why all your pipes are leaking and your shower has to be replaced.

Jane : Well, I just don't know. I guess I don't really have a choice. How about $700?

Tom : If I did the work for $700, I'd be losing a ton of money. It is going to be at least $1,800.

① Jane is asking Tom where the shower facility is.

② Tom broke Jane's shower, and now she wants him to fix it.

③ Tom and Jane are negotiating the fee for building a new shower.

④ Tom is trying to sell Jane some pipes, but she doesn't want to buy them.

⑤ Jane is willing to pay as much as Tom asks for the repair job.

07 다음 글에서 필자가 주장하는 바로 가장 적절한 것은?

Thought stopping, a term coined by Richard Rawson of UCLA, who works with recovering drug addicts, is a definitive decision not to respond to the pull of a reward: Encounter a stimulus, and shut off the action it provokes. "Think of it like television," says Rawson. "Change the channel." Turning off a thought has to be almost immediate. "You're not helpless about this; you can make a decision, but you have to make the decision quickly," said Rawson. The more seconds you spend thinking about what to do in the face of an urge, the greater the chance that you'll ultimately give in to it. Once you begin to debate "Should I or shouldn't I?" you've lost the battle. Experience a cue, switch off the associated thought. No ambiguity, no maybes. Don't waste time in debate; don't struggle with your response. Just get it out of your working memory. Internalize a response to urges that is absolute, even rigid, leaving no room for doubt.

① 결정을 내리기 전에 심사숙고하라.

② 자신의 생각을 남에게 강요하지 말라.

③ 다른 사람의 의견보다는 자신의 판단을 따르라.

④ 주관적인 판단보다는 전문가의 견해를 들어보라.

⑤ 유혹에 빠지게 하는 생각을 단호하게 중단 하라.

08 다음 글이 시사하는 바로 가장 적절한 것은?

The collective mind of any cultural group, accumulated over time, is typically smarter than any individual human mind. This is why cultural learning is so important, and also why such techniques as crowdsourcing are so effective. Xunzi, a thinker in early China, compares the Confucian Way inherited by his generation to markers used to indicate a ford over an otherwise deep and swift river. People with experience have, through careful trial and error, figured out the best place to cross the river and have left markers to help us find it. We could ignore them and just wing it, but that would be counterproductive and even dangerous. In other words, if a respected member of the local community tells you to boil this root vegetable for two hours, then strain it, and then pound it with a stick blessed by a priest until you've sung this sacred song twenty times, you should probably just shut up and do it, exactly the way you are told.

*ford : (강 따위의) 얕은 곳, 여울
**wing it : 즉흥적으로 하다

① Learn from old wisdom.
② Easy come, easy go.
③ To err is human.
④ Pride comes before a fall.
⑤ Nothing ventured, nothing gained.

[09~10] 다음 글의 요지로 가장 적절한 것을 고르시오.

09

Many decisions that you make will turn out to be wrong in the fullness of time. When you made the decision or commitment, it was probably a good idea, based on the circumstances of the moment. But now the situation may have changed, and it is time to zero-base it again. You can usually tell if you are in a zero-based-thinking situation because of the stress that it causes. Whenever you are involved in something that, knowing what you now know, you wouldn't get into again, you experience ongoing stress, aggravation, irritation, and anger. Sometimes people spend an enormous amount of time trying to make a business or personal relationship succeed. But if you zero-base this relationship, the correct solution is often to get out of the relationship altogether. The only real question is whether or not

you have the courage to admit that you were wrong and take the necessary steps to correct the situation.

① 상황이 바뀌면 원점에서 다시 시작하는 수고를 감내할 필요가 있다.
② 스트레스를 유발하는 상황을 가급적 만들지 않는 것이 좋다.
③ 순간적인 판단이 고심 끝에 내린 판단보다 좋을 수 있다.
④ 합의를 통해 결정한 사항은 쉽게 번복해서는 안 된다.
⑤ 의사결정을 내리는 것을 무한정 미루는 것은 바람직하지 않다.

10

Our natural response to reading or hearing about the darker qualities in human nature is to exclude ourselves. It is always the other person who is narcissistic, irrational, envious, grandiose, or aggressive. We almost always see ourselves as having the best intentions. If we go astray, it is the fault of circumstances or people forcing us to react negatively. Stop once and for all this self-deluding process. We are all cut from the same cloth, and we all share the same tendencies. The sooner you realize this, the greater your power will be in overcoming these potential negative traits within you. You will examine your own motives and look at your own shadow. This will make it that much easier to spot such traits in others. You will also become humbler, realizing you're not superior to others in the way you had imagined. This will not make you feel guilty or weighed down by your self-awareness, but quite the opposite. You will accept yourself as a complete individual, embracing both the good and the bad, dropping your falsified self-image as a saint. You will feel relieved of your hypocrisies and free to be more yourself. People will be drawn to this quality in you.

① 다른 사람의 긍정적인 면을 본받으려는 노력이 필요하다.
② 사람에게는 개별적인 특성뿐만 아니라 보편적인 특성도 있다.
③ 자신의 부정적인 면을 인정하면 그것을 극복하는 데 도움이 된다.
④ 결과뿐만 아니라 의도를 고려하여 행동의 정당성을 판단할 필요가 있다.
⑤ 자신감을 갖고 상대방을 대할수록 자신의 의견에 대한 동의를 얻기 쉽다.

[11~12] 다음 글의 주제로 가장 적절한 것을 고르시오.

11

For all its size and grandeur, the Inca Empire lasted only a century before it was conquered by the Spanish, beginning in 1532. Even before the Spanish Conquistadors arrived in central South America, the Inca had begun to suffer from the European arrival in the New World, for the Europeans brought diseases with them that peoples in the Americas had no immunity to. Shortly after Europeans landed in South America, smallpox, measles, typhoid, influenza, malaria, whooping cough and other diseases killed the indigenous peoples of the Americas. These Old World diseases spread to the Inca Empire by the 1520s. Just before the arrival of the Spanish in the Andes, epidemics killed many Inca leaders, including their Emperor and his successor. Eventually an estimated one-third to one-half of the total population of the Inca Empire died of these viral killers. Those who survived were demoralized, which contributed to the relatively easy Spanish conquest of the Inca.

*conquistador : 정복자

① Spanish conquerors of the New World and their cruelties

② European diseases as a cause of the collapse of the Inca Empire

③ impact of the collision of the Old and New World on Europeans

④ a scientific method to track the rise and fall of the Inca Empire

⑤ Incan natural therapies to treat diseases from the Old World

12

If people know an attack is coming, they can prepare to defend themselves. High school students in a study were forewarned either 2 or 10 minutes in advance that they would hear a speech on "Why Teenagers Should Not Be Allowed to Drive" (not a very popular message, as you might guess). The remaining students heard the same talk, but received no forewarning. The results showed that students who received no forewarning were persuaded the most, followed by those who received 2 minutes' warning, followed by those who received 10 minutes' warning. When people believe that someone is trying to persuade them (and take away their freedom of choice), they experience an unpleasant emotional response called psychological reactance, which motivates them to resist the persuasive attempt. Often people will do exactly the opposite of what they are being persuaded to do. The parents of Romeo and Juliet in Shakespeare's play found this

effect out when their efforts to end the romance only drove the young lovebirds closer together.

① effect of forewarning on persuasion

② characteristics of persuasive speeches

③ importance of an interactive presentation

④ necessity of giving warning signs in advance

⑤ functions of persuasive communication in education

[13~14] 다음 글의 제목으로 가장 적절한 것을 고르시오.

13

To reconstitute democracy in line with our present situation, we need to challenge the frightening, but false, assumption that increased diversity automatically brings increased tension and conflict in society. Indeed, the exact reverse can be true. Conflict in society is not only necessary, it is, within limits, desirable. But if one hundred men all desperately want the same brass ring, they may be forced to fight for it. On the other hand, if each of the hundred has a different objective, it is far more rewarding for them to trade, cooperate, and form symbiotic relationships. Given

appropriate social arrangements, diversity can make for a secure and stable civilization. It is the lack of appropriate political institutions today that unnecessarily sharpens conflict between minorities to the knife-edge of violence. The answer to this problem is not to stifle dissent or to charge minorities with selfishness. The answer lies in imaginative new arrangements for accommodating and legitimating diversity—new institutions that are sensitive to the rapidly shifting needs of changing and multiplying minorities.

① Does Diversity Harm Democracy?

② Are Democracy's Weaknesses Inherent?

③ The Rise of Diversity Is a Threat to Democracy

④ The Majority Rule: A Basic Principle of Democracy

⑤ Democracy Is Contagious: Democratization in Progress

14

Imagine that on your first day working at a record store, your manager says, "Our records are organized alphabetically." Under this direction, you file your first pack of albums with ease. Later, you overhear a coworker saying, "Sorry, it looks like we're sold out

of Michael Jackson right now." Your manager looks under "J" and checks the inventory, which says the store should have a single copy of *Thriller*. You remember that it was part of the shipment of records you just filed. Where else could you have put that record, if not under "J"? Maybe under "M"? The ambiguity that's wrapped up in something as simple as "alphabetize these" is truly amazing. We give and receive instructions all day long. Ambiguous instructions can weaken our structures and their trustworthiness. It's only so long after that first album is misfiled that chaos ensues.

*ensue : (결과로서) 일어나다

① Alphabetical Classification Makes It Easy

② Leave Complexity, Stay with Simplicity

③ A Manager: Coworker or Enemy?

④ Old Albums Are Hard to Collect

⑤ Ambiguity Hides in Simplicity

15 다음 도표의 내용과 일치하지 <u>않는</u> 것은?

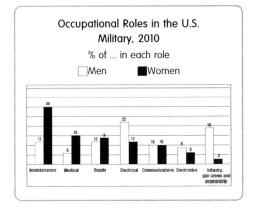

The above graph shows the percentages of men and women in occupational roles in the U.S. military in 2010. ① Active-duty women were much more heavily concentrated in administrative roles than were active-duty men: the percentage of women was more than twice that of men in administrative positions. ② And while only 6% of men in the military held medical roles, 15% of women had these types of jobs. ③ In the electrical field, the percentage of men was larger than that of women: while 22% of men were in electrical positions, only 12% of women served the same roles. ④ Compared to 19% of servicemen in the infantry, gun crews and seamanship, only 3% of servicewomen were in these roles. ⑤ No occupational role showed the same distribution of men and women in the military.

*infantry : 보병
**active-duty : 현역의

16 Herbert Marcuse에 관한 다음 글의 내용과 일치하지 <u>않는</u> 것은?

Born in Berlin in 1898, Herbert Marcuse served with the German army in World War I before completing a PhD in literature in 1922 at the University of Freiburg. After a short spell as a bookseller in Berlin, he studied philosophy under Martin Heidegger. In 1932, he joined the Institute for Social Research, but he never worked in Frankfurt. In 1934 he fled to the US, where he was to remain. While he was in New York with Max Horkheimer, the latter received an offer from Columbia University to relocate the Institute there and Marcuse joined him. In 1958 Marcuse became a professor at Brandeis University, Massachusetts, but in 1965 he was forced to resign because of his outspoken Marxist views. He moved to the University of California, and during the 1960s gained world renown as a social theorist, philosopher, and political activist. He died of a stroke, aged 81.

① 1차 세계대전 중 독일군에서 복무했다.

② Martin Heidegger의 지도하에 철학을 공부했다.

③ 1934년에 미국으로 피신하여 그곳에 머물렀다.

④ California 대학에서 교수가 되어 Brandeis 대학으로 옮겼다.

⑤ 1960년대에 사회이론가, 철학자, 정치활동가로 세계적인 명성을 얻었다.

17 밑줄 친 부분이 가리키는 대상이 나머지 넷과 <u>다른</u> 것은?

Four-year-old Betsy loved to spit. Every time someone said, "Hello, Betsy," she would pucker up and get ready to spray the person with a cloud of saliva. Her parents were embarrassed and couldn't understand how she started such a "bad" habit. ① They were both very respectful people and didn't understand where Betsy learned to do such a "naughty and disgusting" thing. All ② their efforts to get Betsy to stop fell on deaf ears. One day they visited a friend of the family, and when Betsy puckered up to spit, the friend smiled broadly and said, "Betsy, I bet you love to spit. Let's both go in the bathroom and spit into the toilet. I think it's fun to do too." Betsy's parents watched in a mixture of shame and amazement as Betsy took her friend by the hand and the two disappeared into the bathroom. After a few minutes, ③ they returned and Betsy stopped spitting. What Betsy's parents realized is that ④ they had been creating a power struggle by trying to control Betsy's behavior. Now ⑤ they had an option and could tell Betsy, "Spitting is okay as long as you do it in the toilet." It didn't take long for Betsy to give up her "habit."

*pucker up : 입술을 오므리다

[18~19] 다음 글의 밑줄 친 부분 중, 어법상 틀린 것을 고르시오.

18 For women in leadership positions, ① <u>what</u> often works best is a calm, confident expression, warm yet businesslike. Perhaps the best example of this would be current German chancellor Angela Merkel. Her smiles are even less frequent than the average male politician, but when they occur they are especially meaningful. They never seem ② <u>fake</u>. She listens to others with looks of complete absorption, her face remarkably still. She has a way of getting others to do most of the talking while always ③ <u>seeming</u> to be in control of the course of the conversation. She does not need to interrupt to assert herself. When she wants to attack someone, it is with looks of boredom, iciness, or contempt, never with blustering words. When Russian president Vladimir Putin tried to intimidate her by bringing his pet dog into a meeting, ④ <u>know</u> Merkel had once been bitten and had a fear of dogs, she visibly tensed, then quickly composed herself and looked him calmly in the eye. She put ⑤ <u>herself</u> in the one-up position in relation to Putin by not making anything of his ploy. He seemed rather childish and petty in comparison. Her style does not include all of the alpha male body posturing. It is quieter and yet extremely powerful in its own way.

*blustering : 호통치는

19 Rules and incentives are an inevitable and necessary part of our social and political life—the banking crisis would have been far less serious ① <u>had</u> Depression-era regulations not been removed and had existing regulations been enforced. For all the importance of rules and incentives, however, a debate that focuses only on the proper mix of these two mechanisms ② <u>leave</u> out an important ingredient. The kind of work that most practitioners want to do, and ③ <u>that</u> those they serve also want them to do, demands practical wisdom. Rules and incentives may improve the behavior of those who don't care, though they won't make ④ <u>them</u> wiser. But in focusing on the people who don't care—the targets of our rules and incentives—we miss those who do care. We miss those who want to do the right things but ⑤ <u>lack</u> the practical wisdom to do them well. Rules and incentives won't teach these people the moral skill and will they need. Even worse, rules can kill skill and incentives can kill will. [3점]

[20~21] (A), (B), (C)의 가 네모 안에서 어법에 맞는 표현으로 가장 적절한 것을 고르시오.

	(A)	(B)	(C)
①	are	being	which
②	are	was	which
③	are	was	at which
④	is	being	at which
⑤	is	was	which

20

Biodiversity as a whole forms a shield protecting each of the species that together compose it, ourselves included. What will happen if, in addition to the species already extinguished by human activity, say, 10 percent of those remaining (A) are / is taken away? Or 50 percent? Or 90 percent? As more and more species vanish or drop to near extinction, the rate of extinction of the survivors accelerates. In some cases the effect is felt almost immediately. When a century ago the American chestnut, once a dominant tree over much of eastern North America, (B) being / was reduced to near extinction by an Asian fungal blight, seven moth species whose caterpillars depended on its vegetation vanished, and the last of the passenger pigeons plunged to extinction. As extinction mounts, biodiversity reaches a tipping point (C) which / at which the ecosystem collapses. Scientists have only begun to study under what conditions and when this catastrophe is most likely to occur.

[3점]

*blight : 마름병

21

In the 1970s, Stanley Schachter, a Columbia University social psychologist, became convinced that overweight people did not respond (A) appropriate / appropriately to internal signals, such as hunger, satiety, or a need for fuel. He hypothesized that overweight people ate in response to external cues, rather than internal signals. Schachter's cracker study compared the eating behaviors of thin and overweight subjects. He first divided his participants into two groups, offering one all the sandwiches they wanted to eat and (B) ask / asking the other only to fill out a questionnaire about food. Then he gave everyone the same opportunity to sample five different types of crackers. Not surprisingly, the thin people who had already eaten the sandwiches ate fewer crackers than the thin people who had simply completed the questionnaire. But those who were overweight ate about the same number of crackers

whether or not they had eaten the sandwiches first. Schachter theorized that the sight of food was (C) exerted / exerting more pull on the overweight population than any internal messages reporting an absence of hunger.

	(A)	(B)	(C)
①	appropriate	ask	exerted
②	appropriately	asking	exerting
③	appropriately	asking	exerted
④	appropriate	asking	exerting
⑤	appropriately	ask	exerted

[22~23] 다음 글의 밑줄 친 부분 중, 문맥상 낱말의 쓰임이 적절하지 않은 것을 고르시오.

22 Joseph Schumpeter expressed the view that the essence of capitalism is the process of "creative destruction"—the perpetual cycle of destroying the old and less efficient product or service and ① replacing it with new, more efficient ones. Andy Grove took Schumpeter's insight that "only the paranoid survive" and made it in many ways the business model of globalization capitalism. Grove helped to popularize the view that dramatic, industry-transforming ② innovations are taking place today faster and faster. Thanks to these technological breakthroughs, the speed by which your latest invention can be made ③ obsolete is now lightning quick. Therefore, only the paranoid, only those who are constantly looking over their shoulders to see who is creating something new that will destroy them and then staying just one step ahead of them, will survive. Those countries that are most willing to let capitalism quickly destroy inefficient companies, so that money can be freed up and directed to more innovative ones, will ④ perish in the era of globalization. Those which rely on their governments to ⑤ protect them from such creative destruction will fall behind in this era. [3점]

*paranoid : 편집증적인 사람

23 Boston and Cambridge are cities where many people do not stay for too long. Many people here are graduate students and postdoctorals, which means that by definition their positions have an ① expiration date. Boston and Cambridge are melting pots, but also cities where you make new friends at farewell parties. The combination of high resident turnover and friendships produces a situation in which the best apartments in Cambridge never ② reach the market. When someone moves out of a good apartment, there's always a friend looking to move in, and landlords usually are okay with this hand-me-down dynamic because it ③ causes them the burden of finding a new tenant. So the lesson is that, at least in the case of Boston and Cambridge, the real estate market for apartments is ④ secondary to the social network. According to Mark

Granovetter, a sociologist who has studied the economic relevance of social networks throughout much of his life, we can say that in Cambridge the market for student apartments is ⑤ embedded in the network of social interactions.

[24~25] (A), (B), (C)의 각 네모 안에서 문맥에 맞는 낱말로 가장 적절한 것을 고르시오.

24

Behavior is not infinitely flexible, easily moved in any direction. Rather, organisms are born with natural behavior systems and tendencies that (A) constrain / expand how learning occurs and what changes one may expect from a training procedure. These limitations were described elegantly in an analogy by a researcher, who compared learning to sculpting a wooden statue. The sculptor begins with a piece of wood that has little (B) contrast / resemblance to a statue. As the carving proceeds, the piece of wood comes to look more and more like the final product. But the process is not without limitation since the sculptor has to take into account the direction and density of the wood grain and any knots the wood may have. Wood carving is most successful if

it is in (C) conflict / harmony with the preexisting grain and knots of the wood. In a similar fashion, learning is most successful if it takes into account the preexisting behavior structures of the organism.

	(A)	(B)	(C)
①	constrain	contrast	conflict
②	constrain	resemblance	conflict
③	constrain	resemblance	harmony
④	expand	contrast	conflict
⑤	expand	resemblance	harmony

25

Plants are great chemists—and alchemists: they can turn sunbeams into matter! They have evolved to use biological warfare to repel predators—poisoning, paralyzing, or disorienting them—or to reduce their own digestibility to stay alive and protect their seeds, (A) enhancing / reducing the chances that their species will endure. Both these physical and chemical defensive strategies are remarkably effective at keeping predators away, and even sometimes at getting animals to do what they wish. Because their initial predators were insects, plants developed some lectins that would paralyze any unfortunate bug that tried to dine on them. Obviously, there is a

quantum size difference between insects and mammals, but both are (B) resistant / subject to the same effects. Clearly, most of you won't be paralyzed by a plant compound within minutes of eating it, although a single peanut (a lectin) certainly has the potential to kill certain people. But we are not immune to the long-term effects of eating certain plant compounds. Because of the huge number of cells we mammals have, we may not see the (C) beneficial / damaging results of consuming such compounds for years. And even if this is happening to you, you don't know it yet. [3점]

*lectin : 렉틴(주로 식물에서 추출되는 단백질)

(A)	(B)	(C)
① enhancing	⋯ resistant	⋯ beneficial
② enhancing	⋯ subject	⋯ damaging
③ enhancing	⋯ subject	⋯ beneficial
④ reducing	⋯ subject	⋯ damaging
⑤ reducing	⋯ resistant	⋯ beneficial

[26~30] 다음 글을 읽고, 빈칸에 들어갈 말로 가장 적절한 것을 고르시오.

26

Observers have repeatedly noticed that animals in the wild do not live solely by "tooth and claw" but regularly show _____. Once, when an old bull elephant lay dying, human observers noted that his entire family tried everything to help him to his feet again. First, they tried to work their trunks and tusks underneath him. Then they pulled the old fellow up so strenuously that some broke their tusks in the process. Their concern for their old friend was greater than their concern for themselves. Elephants have also been observed coming to the aid of a comrade shot by a hunter, despite their fear of gunshots. The other elephants work in concert to raise their wounded companion to walk again. They do this by pressing on either side of the injured elephant and walking, trying to carry their friend between their gigantic bodies. Elephants have also been seen sticking grass in the mouths of their injured friends in an attempt to feed them, to give them strength.

① self-treatment for injury

② compassion for their fellows

③ family ties for their offspring

④ tricks of deceiving their predators

⑤ collaboration for finding food in the wild

27

A factor which helps people to withstand fear is _____. The front-seat passenger in a car, for example, is usually more anxious than the driver. In the studies of American servicemen this was revealed when aircrew in the European theater of operations were asked in June 1944: "If you were doing it over again, do you think you would choose to sign up for combat flying?" Pilots were always more willing to answer "Yes, I'm pretty sure I would" (51-84 percent) than other enlisted men (39-51 percent), and fighter pilots flying their planes single-handed (84 percent) more so than bomber pilots (51-74 percent). Heavy bomber crews showed increasing reluctance the more missions they had flown, and the reason is not hard to discover. The casualty rates (over 70 percent killed or missing in action after six months and 17.5 percent wounded or injured in action) were dreadful. [3점]

*theater : 작전 구역

① being in control

② to wait and see

③ recalling good events

④ being with a companion

⑤ proper training and practice

28

Some contemporary technologies seem to open new and deeply troubling ethical issues, issues of a kind that humankind has never had to address before. The emerging technology of genetic engineering, for instance, creates the prospect of our designing our own children and turning humanity itself into a kind of artifact. Some authors seem to welcome this prospect, but others believe that we are at a crossroads that requires that we relinquish the opportunity to acquire the knowledge that would enable us to create such a brave new world. Others believe that we can place reasonable limits on how biotechnology and genetic engineering will be employed on human beings that will allow some uses but prohibit others. Genetic engineering of plants and some animal species is already in widespread use, and it may already be impossible to put this particular genie back in the bottle. Hans Jonas believes that technologies such as these that give us the capability _____ should be approached with a sense of "long-range responsibility" and, above all, a sense of humility.

① to make aesthetic use of science

② to alter nature in fundamental ways

③ to produce materials with little variation

④ to detect and locate hidden defects in complex systems

⑤ to defend the organism from external and internal dangers

29

You can almost certainly recall instances when being around a calm person leaves you feeling more at peace, or when your previously sunny mood was spoiled by contact with a grouch. Researchers have demonstrated that this process occurs quickly and doesn't require much, if any, verbal communication. In one study, two volunteers completed a survey that identified their moods. Then they sat quietly, facing each other for a two-minute period, waiting for the researcher to return to the room. At the end of that time, they completed another emotional survey. Time after time, the brief exposure resulted in the less expressive partner's moods coming to resemble the moods of the more expressive one. It's easy to understand how emotions _____. In just a few months, the emotional responses of both dating couples and college roommates become dramatically more similar.

*grouch : 불평이 많은 사람

① can be best managed for optimal functioning

② can operate independently of external stimuli

③ can be even more infectious with prolonged contact

④ are influenced by social and cultural norms

⑤ are related to the whole creative process

30

There is much evidence that the use of language enables us _____, because the stimulation associated with the use of language facilitates a further spurt of brain development. There have been extended attempts to teach chimpanzees the use of language by bringing them up in human family environments. Since they do not have the vocal apparatus for speech, they have been taught using American sign language. It has proved possible to teach chimpanzees up to a few hundred words in their first five years of life, a tiny fraction of what human children achieve. The comparative abilities of human children and chimpanzees are rather similar until the point at which language develops in the children, somewhere between their first and second birthdays, after which our mental development accelerates away from that of chimpanzees. A related point is that we have very few memories of the period before we learn the use of language. It is obvious that our use of language does not merely enable us to communicate, but that it also profoundly affects the way we perceive the outside world. [3점]

① to express our curiosity about nature

② to memorize events much more precisely

③ to share our perceptual experiences

with others

④ to communicate with animals around us

⑤ to put creative thoughts into action

[31~32] 주어진 글 다음에 이어질 글의 순서로 가장 적절한 것을 고르시오.

31

Today, the secret of success of many profitable businesses lies in their ability to process the data using advanced analytical methods. The business of information management encompasses more than just storing the data. It also covers 'data mining' or acquiring information by processing data using a new form of business intelligence.

(A) This ability of knowing 'why' will therefore empower the organization to make the necessary strategic changes. For example, the organization should capitalize on the newfound knowledge by building a stronger, one-to-one relationship with its customers.

(B) However, a report aided by data mining or business intelligence, is not only able to identify the best-selling product in a supermarket but the report is also able to explain the reasons why the product is the best.

(C) Hence, organizations need to invest in data mining techniques (aided by statistical analysis, visualization and neural networks) to uncover hidden patterns, discover new knowledge, and as a consequence gain more insight into the current business situation. For example, a typical report is able to identify the best-selling product in a supermarket.

① (A) – (C) – (B) ② (B) – (A) – (C)
③ (B) – (C) – (A) ④ (C) – (A) – (B)
⑤ (C) – (B) – (A)

32

As the case on the Canada-US Free Trade Agreement shows, it was important for Canada to gain the attention of US political leadership to increase Canadian power in the negotiation. Lack of attention by the stronger party is often a statement that it does not consider the other side particularly powerful or significant.

(A) This action provoked a diplomatic crisis between the two long-time allies and succeeded in getting US attention, which led to high-level American participation in the negotiations. Canada enhanced its power by playing on the historically strong relationship

between the two countries.

(B) Such lack of attention may manifest itself in many ways, but it is almost always demonstrated by entrusting the negotiations to relatively low-level officials who have limited authority and access to their country's political leadership.

(C) Canada faced this problem in this negotiation. The tactics of attention-getting may include stalling and walking out of the negotiations. In the Canada-US Free Trade Agreement talks, Canada walked out when they felt that the United States was not taking the negotiations seriously.

*stall : (교묘하게) 시간을 벌다

① (A) - (C) - (B)   ② (B) - (A) - (C)
③ (B) - (C) - (A)   ④ (C) - (A) - (B)
⑤ (C) - (B) - (A)

[33~34] 글의 흐름으로 보아, 주어진 문장이 들어가기에 가장 적절한 곳을 고르시오.

33

An alternative use, however, treats law generally as a means of enforcing norms or standards of social behavior.

The term 'law' has been used in a wide variety of ways. In the first place, there are scientific laws or what are called descriptive laws. These describe regular or necessary patterns of behavior found in either natural or social life. (①) The most obvious examples are found in the natural sciences; for instance, in the laws of motion and thermodynamics advanced by physicists. (②) But this notion of law has also been employed by social theorists, in an attempt to highlight predictable, even inevitable, patterns of social behavior. (③) This can be seen in Engels's assertion that Marx uncovered the 'laws' of historical and social development, and in the so-called 'laws' of demand and supply which underlie economic theory. (④) Sociologists have thus seen forms of law at work in all organized societies, ranging from informal processes usually found in traditional societies to the formal legal systems typical of modern societies. (⑤) By contrast, political theorists have tended to understand law more specifically, seeing it as a distinctive social institution clearly separate from other social rules or norms and only found in modern societies. [3점]

34

> Another, unexpected, consequence is the ability of bacteria to overcome the mechanisms that give antibiotics their efficacy, rendering them useless.

Initially seen as *miracle drugs*, antibiotics, once they became widely available, were used not only for bacterial infections, but for everything from the common cold to headaches. (①) Indeed antibiotics were a godsend, drastically improving medicine and contributing significantly to the increase in life expectancy achieved during the twentieth century. (②) Like many technological fixes, along with the positive benefits of antibiotics came negative side effects. (③) Antibiotics can kill the many beneficial bacteria in the human body, for instance those that promote digestion, along with invasive bacteria. (④) Antibiotic resistance, first a curiosity seen in the laboratory, became common among populations of bacteria exposed to antibiotics. (⑤) In a matter of years following the introduction of penicillin, penicillin-destroying staphylococci appeared in hospitals where much of the early use of penicillin had taken place.

*staphylococci : 포도상구균

[35~36] 다음 글에서 전체 흐름과 관계 없는 문장을 고르시오.

35   Far from existing inertly, the inhabitants of the pasture—or what the ancient Hellenes called *botane*—appear to be able to perceive and to react to what is happening in their environment at a level of sophistication far surpassing that of humans. ① The sundew plant will grasp at a fly with infallible accuracy, moving in just the right direction toward where the prey is to be found. ② Some parasitical plants can recognize the slightest trace of the odor of their victim, and will overcome all obstacles to crawl in its direction. ③ Plants are in trouble because they are rooted to the ground and therefore unable to pick up and move when they need something or when conditions turn unfavorable. ④ Plants seem to know which ants will steal their nectar, closing when these ants are about, opening only when there is enough dew on their stems to keep the ants from climbing. ⑤ The more sophisticated acacia actually enlists the protective services of certain ants which it rewards with nectar in return for the ants' protection against other insects and herbivorous mammals.

*inertly : 비활동적으로

36 Transport geography is a topical branch of geography that evolved out of economic geography. Like tourism, transportation is, of course, inherently geographic because it connects places and facilitates the movement of goods and people from one place to another. ① Transport geography fundamentally depends on the geographic concepts, such as location or scale. ② For example, location shapes patterns of movement, including whether movement is possible from and/or to a given location and how that movement might occur. ③ Transportation networks exist at local and regional scales and, in the modern world, are increasingly being connected into a global system. ④ With much faster personal and organized transport, afternoon drives, day trips, overnight stays and weekends have added a considerable scope to the tourism industry but also to tourists themselves. ⑤ In addition, there are many geographic factors of places — both physical and human — that either allow or constrain transportation.

37 다음 글의 내용을 한 문장으로 요약하고자 한다. 빈칸 (A)와 (B)에 들어갈 말로 가장 적절한 것은?

Consider a household that dumps sewage into a public lake rather than purchasing a septic system to process and store the waste. This "straight pipe" method of disposal damages the lake's appeal for water sports and as a source of drinking water. Although the social cost of dumping sewage is larger than the cost of a septic system, the household's private cost of dumping is not, because the household bears only a fraction of the overall damage of dumping. If the lake area belonged to the household dumping the sewage, that household would internalize the full social cost of dumping and invest in a septic system. If the lake area belonged to someone else, that person would have an incentive to prohibit and carefully monitor dumping. Biologist Garrett Hardin felt that by assigning property rights to land, water, and air, society could avoid externalities caused by everything from factories to loud music. As evidence of his point, poaching is a far greater problem in countries where property rights are weak than in countries where they are well-defined and strictly enforced.

*septic system : 오수정화 시스템
**poach : (남의 영역을) 침해하다

According to Garrett Hardin, environmental damage to open-access areas, such as lakes, could be (A) if the areas were (B) held.

	(A)		(B)
①	caused	......	exclusively
②	caused	......	commercially
③	disclosed	......	commonly
④	prevented	......	publicly
⑤	prevented	......	privately

[38~39] 다음 글을 읽고, 물음에 답하시오.

We cannot divorce emotions from thinking. The two are completely intertwined. But there is inevitably a (a) <u>dominant</u> factor, some people more clearly governed by emotions than others. What we are looking for is the proper ratio and balance, the one that leads to the most effective action. The ancient Greeks had an appropriate metaphor for this: the rider and the horse.

The horse is our emotional nature continually (b) <u>impelling</u> us to move. This horse has tremendous energy and power, but without a rider it cannot be guided; it is wild, subject to predators, and continually heading into trouble. The rider is our thinking self. Through training and practice, it holds the reins and guides the horse, transforming this powerful animal energy into something (c) <u>productive</u>. The one without the other is useless. Without the rider, no directed movement or purpose. Without the horse, no energy, no power. In most people the horse dominates, and the rider is weak. In some people the rider is too strong, holds the reins too tightly, and is (d) <u>willing</u> to occasionally let the animal go into a gallop. The horse and rider must work together. This means we consider our actions (e) <u>beforehand</u>; we bring as much thinking as possible to a situation before we make a decision. But once we decide what to do, we loosen the reins and enter action with boldness and a spirit of adventure. Instead of being slaves to this energy, we channel it. That is the essence of rationality.

38 윗글의 주제로 가장 적절한 것은?

① necessity of finding the optimal balance of thinking and emotion

② traditional skills of taming and harnessing wild animals

③ effects of emotional suppression on physical health

④ difficulties of getting the right technique to win horse races

⑤ ancient Greek concepts about the importance of philosophy in sports

39 밑줄 친 (a)~(e) 중에서 문맥상 낱말의 쓰임이 적절하지 <u>않은</u> 것은?

① (a)   ② (b)

③ (c)   ④ (d)

⑤ (e)

[40~41] 다음 글을 읽고, 물음에 답하시오.

Yesterday's *Observer* features two pieces about human enhancement in the prospect of the FutureFest festival in London in September. The articles mention Bertolt Meyer, a Swiss man born without a left hand who was recently fitted with a state-of-the-art bionic one (which he controls from his smartphone), and include quotes from well-known authors associated with the topic of human enhancement, such as Nick Bostrom and Andy Miah.

At the moment, prosthetic devices like Meyer's are used to restore normal human functions among those who lack them. Yet as such devices become ever more   (A) , to the point that they eventually outperform "natural" limbs in terms of speed, strength, executive control etc., "will it become the norm to have one of these?" Meyer asks. Also, as the author of the *Observer* editorial worries, "what happens when these technologies and machines get so smart that humans can be written out of the equation altogether?" For instance, what if we could simply turn to our smartphone rather than a human doctor to get a diagnosis for our ailments as well as appropriate treatment recommendations? Such suggestions can   (B) fears of a dystopian future where humans are pressured to become "cyborgs," whether they like it or not, if they are to remain competitive on the job market (including competitive sports) and in other contexts; or where they are increasingly made useless by more effective machines, and real-life human interaction is reduced (machines replacing staff at supermarket checkouts, but also general practitioners, etc.), and becomes less accessible than it is now (think of having to pay a significant premium to see a human doctor).

*prosthetic : 인공 기관의

40 윗글의 제목으로 가장 적절한 것은?

① Where Machines Could Replace Humans and Where They Can't
② Human Enhancement Technologies: Blessing or Curse?
③ Disabled Persons and Their Right to Equal Treatment
④ Artificial Intelligence: Science Fact vs. Science Fiction
⑤ Science Fiction Foretells Future Technologies

41 윗글의 빈칸 (A), (B)에 들어갈 말로 가장 적절한 것은? [3점]

	(A)		(B)
①	expensive	……	calm
②	expensive	……	reflect
③	outdated	……	trigger
④	sophisticated	……	calm
⑤	sophisticated	……	trigger

[42~43] 다음 글을 읽고, 물음에 답하시오.

When Mario came to me for therapy, he explained that he worried about everything. He was newly married and in the midst of purchasing an expensive home that would require investing his life savings, barely leaving money for the necessary renovations. "Did I marry the right person? Am I going crazy? Is my mind working? I seem forgetful. What if the plane I take to Miami crashes? Will my father develop Parkinson's like my grandfather?" The worries were (a) endless, and Mario noticed that the more he worried the more he felt depressed. To ease his tortured mind, he spent time (b) distracting himself by eating.

Over the course of cognitive behavioral therapy with an emphasis on mindfulness and acceptance, Mario began to learn to not panic over his feelings of panic. He became able to bring awareness to his worries as mental processes rather than get (c) stuck in his mind, where he would live in the worst-case scenarios. He practiced asking himself, "Is this worry productive or unproductive?" If a worry was productive, he came up with an action plan. If it was unproductive, he noticed the feelings and thoughts in his body and mind and practiced returning to the present moment. When he noticed urges to reach for sweets and salty foods as he tensed up, he chose to sit with his feelings instead, seeing his feelings as meaningful.

What sat behind his worries? He deeply (d) valued serving as a provider, establishing a secure, loving home, and protecting his father. His feelings (e) denied what mattered to him, though his relationship with his feelings—profound fear and confusion about feeling too much and not understanding his feelings—got in the way of his willingness to accept and learn from his emotions. During our last session, he said, "I feel because things matter to me. I can talk to my wife about our difficulties, take action to solve financial problems, and show my dad how much I care. That tastes sweet in my heart."

42 Mario에 관한 윗글의 내용으로 적절하지 않은 것은?

① 평생 저축한 돈을 투자해야 하는 비싼 집을 구입하는 중이었다.

② 자신의 공황 상태의 감정에 당황하지 않는 법을 배우기 시작했다.

③ 자신의 걱정이 생산적인지 아닌지 스스로에게 질문하는 것을 연습했다.

④ 단것과 짠 음식을 먹고 싶어 하는 충동을 이겨내는 데 결국 실패했다.

⑤ 재정적인 문제를 해결하기 위한 조치를 취할 수 있다고 말했다.

43 밑줄 친 (a)~(e) 중에서 문맥상 낱말의 쓰임이 적절하지 않은 것은? [3점]

① (a)   ② (b)

③ (c)   ④ (d)

⑤ (e)

[44~45] 다음 글을 읽고, 물음에 답하시오.

(A)

Bibs the canary lived with an elderly lady who had a niece who lived next door and checked on her each night to make sure she was all right. A warm and sweet friendship had blossomed between the old woman and the tiny bird. At breakfast each morning, they shared toast and Bibs liked to sip whatever beverage the woman was having. One rainy night, seeing that her aunt's lights were on and assuming everything was fine, the niece retired with her husband for the night rather than going over to the aunt's house.

(B)

The tiny yellow bird had escaped from the aunt's house and flown through the storm to the next house. There it had pecked at the window with such desperate fury that it collapsed in exhaustion and died before their eyes. Now completely alarmed, the niece and her husband raced over to the aunt's house.

(C)

They found the old lady lying unconscious on the floor in a pool of blood. She had slipped and fallen, striking her head on a table corner. Her niece rushed her to the hospital. Because of her little bird's loyalty and determination to get help, even at the sacrifice of his own life, the woman's life was saved.

(D)

As the couple relaxed cozily by a fire, they were startled by an odd tapping at the window. At first they assumed it was a windblown branch, but the tapping grew louder and continued persistently, followed by a strange cry. Finally, the niece went to the window, pulled back the curtains and found Bibs, who had been furiously beating on the window and chirping.

44 주어진 글 (A)에 이어질 내용을 순서에 맞게 배열한 것으로 가장 적절한 것은?

① (B) − (D) − (C)   ② (C) − (B) − (D)

③ (C) − (D) − (B)   ④ (D) − (B) − (C)

⑤ (D) − (C) − (B)

45 윗글에 관한 내용으로 적절하지 않은 것은?

① 노부인의 조카딸은 노부인의 옆집에 살았다.

② 노부인과 Bibs는 토스트를 나눠 먹었다.

③ Bibs는 폭풍우를 뚫고 옆집으로 날아갔다.

④ 노부인은 의식을 잃고 바닥에 쓰러져 있었다.

⑤ 조카딸 집의 창문에 나뭇가지가 부딪쳐 소리가 났다.

2025
사관학교

10개년 영어

2019학년도 기출문제

영어영역(공통)

01 Based on the following dialogue, which one is true?

> Ms. Smith : OK, class, it's time to look at the solar system again!
>
> Sunny : Oh, Ms. Smith, do we have to? We just did that last week, and it's so boring, all planets and moons and stuff.
>
> Ms. Smith : Well, Sunny, then perhaps you can answer some questions. If you get them all right, we can study whatever you want. Does it sound good?
>
> Sunny : Yes, that's great! Ms. Smith, you're the best teacher! Ask away.
>
> Ms. Smith : First question: how many moons does Mars have?
>
> Sunny : That's easy! There's one.
>
> Ms. Smith : Sorry, Sunny, you're wrong on the first try. There are two.
>
> Sunny : Aw, how could I know that? I've never been there!

① Ms. Smith doesn't think students have to learn about the solar system again.

② Sunny is very interested in the planets and moons.

③ Sunny doesn't understand why she has to answer Ms. Smith's questions.

④ Sunny gives the right answer to Ms. Smith's first question.

⑤ Ms. Smith tells Sunny that Mars has two moons.

02 Which is the best sequence of answers for the blanks?

> Julie : I'm starving. There are lots of places down by the river that sell good chicken.
>
> Rachel : That sounds great. It's pretty far from here, though, right? _____
>
> Julie : Well, there's the subway. I've got my transit pass. Do you have yours?
>
> Rachel : No, and besides, my feet already hurt from all the running around we've done. We'd have to walk all the way to the subway station.
>
> Julie : _____ That would be easier, if not cheaper.

Rachel : Oh, no. I don't have that much money.

Julie : Then, I think we should just hop a bus. _____

───〈보기〉───

a. We could grab a taxi.

b. I'm not sure how to get there.

c. There's one right there.

d. It's not that far.

① a – b – d   ② b – a – c

③ b – d – a   ④ c – a – b

⑤ c – b – d

03 Where is the dialogue most likely taking place?

Dan : Look at that, over there! Have you ever seen anything like it?

Paul : Well, on TV of course, but the plant looks kind of scary when I see it with my own eyes. It looks like it has teeth.

Dan : Yes, it does. But they're not teeth. They're just special leaves. That's one of the most unique plants here.

Paul : Well, then, let's get a closer look.

Dan : Fine, but you know what? Now that I think of it, if the smell is too much, I'm leaving. I had a big breakfast

and I don't want to lose it.

Paul : Grow up! It's nature, man! Some flowers smell bad.

Dan : Have it your way, then, but I'm holding my nose.

① at a haunted house

② at a botanical garden

③ at a recycling center

④ at a cosmetics store

⑤ at an aquarium

04 Based on the following dialogue, which one is NOT true?

Nick : I really liked that movie we saw last night. It was fantastic!

John : Really? It didn't meet my expectation. Sequels are never as good as the originals.

Nick : No, I disagree. I think the second *Avengers* movie was just as good as the first.

John : Okay, I'll grant you that, but what about the *Iron Man* movies? *Iron Man 2* wasn't good.

Nick : You may be right, but the other *Iron Man* sequel, the third one, was excellent!

John : Okay, that's true. You've got a point about that.

Nick : And ... *Ant-Man 2*! Ha! It was also just as good as, and maybe even better than, the

2019 기출문제

first one, right?

John : Okay, you're right. I should think more before making generalizations.

① The two people saw a movie together last night.

② Nick doesn't agree with John's idea that sequels are worse than the originals.

③ John admits that the second *Avengers* movie was as good as the first.

④ The two people agree that *Iron Man 2* was excellent.

⑤ John accepts Nick's idea that *Ant-Man 2* was a good movie, like the first one.

05 Choose the best answer for the blank.

Doctor : What seems to be the trouble?

Patient : Well, I have this pain in my stomach, down here on the right side.

Doctor : Lie down here. *[Pause]* Does it hurt when I push on it, like this?

Patient : Ow! Yes! It's very painful. Please don't do that again.

Doctor : Well, let's take your temperature. Hmm. Yes, it's pretty high, as I expected.

Patient : As you expected? Do you already know what the trouble is, Doctor?

Doctor : I'm pretty sure what it is. I think you need surgery, but to be certain, there's one more step before we schedule it. _____

① We should do another test.

② I want to apply for health insurance.

③ I need to go have lunch with my staff.

④ Can I get something for my stomachache?

⑤ Don't worry, your temperature is not high.

06 Choose the sentence that best describes the situation. [3점]

Lisa : John and I are going to open a restaurant!

Suzy : That's pretty brave. I've heard that 50% of all restaurants fail within the first year.

Lisa : You've got to have faith. We've been cooking for a long time, and we think we'll be able to create a great place.

Suzy : What kind of cuisine are you thinking about offering?

Lisa : We've got it narrowed down to Mexican or Vietnamese.

Suzy : Wow, those are quite different styles. What made you consider those two particularly?

Lisa : Mexican is super popular, but there's a lot of competition.

Vietnamese is rather unusual, so that's good, but on the other hand, people aren't familiar with it.

Suzy : Well, you'll have to make up your minds before you go to the bank for a loan.

① Suzy is going to open a new restaurant and is trying to find a good cook.

② Lisa and John will open a restaurant, but haven't made a final decision on the cuisine.

③ Lisa and Suzy are trying to decide what kind of food to eat tonight in the restaurant.

④ Suzy will go to the bank with Lisa so that Lisa can get a loan for her restaurant.

⑤ Suzy is confident that Lisa's new restaurant will succeed, but Lisa is not sure.

07 다음 글에서 필자가 주장하는 바로 가장 적절한 것은?

Not all decisions are made from perfect data. Even though it is important to use all data at hand to render the best possible solution, sometimes you are still missing information and the solution doesn't seem clear. In cases like this, your intuition needs to be your guide. This means having faith in yourself and listening to what you believe is truth, regardless of what direction the data may point. When you are going through the decision-making process and you are sifting through the net to weed out the garbage and gather only the good information, remember to ask yourself how you feel about the information you have gathered. This is extremely important. The best decisions are the ones that combine good data that points to an obvious choice and that gut feeling that says, "You did the right thing."

① 반론을 제기할 때 타당한 근거를 제시하라.

② 연구 주제와 무관한 정보를 과감하게 버리라.

③ 자료를 선정하고 결정을 내릴 때 직관을 동원하라.

④ 객관적인 자료를 바탕으로 합리적인 결정을 내리라.

⑤ 자료 수집 과정에서 정보의 양보다 질을 중요시하라.

2019 기출문제

08 다음 글이 시사하는 바로 가장 적절한 것은?

There are difficulties that we cannot deal with right away, or perhaps ever. As well as remembering to have the patience to bear what cannot be changed, there are other ways of adjusting to seemingly impossible situations. Many spiritual teachers regard afflictions, trials, sufferings, and deprivations as "blessings in disguise" through which our inner spiritual powers are stimulated, purified, and ennobled. Confucius stated that "the gem cannot be polished without friction, nor man perfected without trials," while Helen Keller wrote, "I thank God for my handicaps, for, through them, I have found myself, my work, and my God." If we use them correctly, the failures, tests, and difficulties in our lives can become the means of purifying our spirits and strengthening our characters. A quote from 'Abdu'l-Baha illustrates this particularly well: "We should try to make every stumbling block a stepping stone to progress."

① The more educated, the more civilized.

② Adversity can lead to achievement.

③ Do as you would be done by.

④ Cooperation works miracles.

⑤ Look before you leap.

[09~10] 다음 글의 요지로 가장 적절한 것을 고르시오.

09

When websites ask you to check a box saying "Don't ask me again," a lot of people are happy to check that box. If public officials, or doctors, ask you to fill out numerous forms with the same questions, registering choices of multiple kinds, you may get immensely frustrated and wish that at least some of those choices had been made for you. People would be better off if public and private institutions cut existing form-filling requirements dramatically. And if a cab driver insists on asking you to choose which route you want to take in an unfamiliar city, you might wish he hadn't asked, and just selected the route that he deems best. When you are having lunch or dinner with a friend, it's often most considerate to suggest a place, rather than asking the friend to choose.

① 사람들은 선택의 부담이 줄어드는 것을 더 좋아한다.

② 사람들은 자신이 직접 선택한 것에 더 애착심을 갖는다.

③ 고객 선호도 조사를 통해 서비스의 질을 개선할 수 있다.

④ 인터넷상에서는 개인 정보 보호 의식이 여전히 미흡하다.

⑤ 사람들은 선택의 기회가 많을수록 자신의 의사를 잘 표현한다.

10

There are those who think that the skill is everything and they evaluate a work of art entirely on the amount of skill involved. Such people are more interested in realism in painting because of the skill associated with painting a subject realistically. They also are usually more interested in crafted items and are awed by the skill involved in making the item. Certainly we should give credit for many elements that go into making a piece of art, but there is a distinction between those elements and the aesthetic element. We can give credit for effort, for technique, for skill, for material, for scale, and the time it took to make the work. The value of art should not be measured by such qualities. No matter how hard one tries to make a work of art, it still may fail aesthetically. One could make a work out of gold, but it could also fail aesthetically. There is nothing worse in bad art than big, bad art. What a shame to work for years on one piece of art that is not successful in the end. If the skill is not developed well enough to get the aesthetic elements of the art across, then the value of the work lessens.

① 기술적 요소에 미학적 요소를 더해야 예술 작품의 가치가 높아진다.

② 위대한 예술 작품은 기존의 틀에서 벗어난 새로운 양식을 추구한다.

③ 비평가에게는 예술 작품의 진가를 알아보는 심미안이 필요하다.

④ 많은 시간과 자원을 투입해야 예술 작품의 수준이 높아진다.

⑤ 예술 작품을 평가하는 기준이 사람에 따라 다를 수 있다.

[11~12] 다음 글의 주제로 가장 적절한 것을 고르시오.

11

Knowledge transfer has received a tremendous amount of publicity recently with advances in groupware and networking tools, designed to enable the flow of knowledge among groups and individuals. The goal of such tools is ultimately shared memory and understanding. In fact, this is difficult to achieve because knowledge is "sticky," alive, and rich. It is "sticky" because it is very tightly bound to the context which gives it meaning; without context it is just information. Knowledge can be thought of as being alive in that it must be constantly attended to as it is ever-changing and growing. It also dies, goes out of date, becomes irrelevant and must be discarded, but who is its rightful steward? Lastly, it is rich in its multi-

2019 기출문제

dimensionality, containing a tremendous amount of content, context, and experience. All three of these factors make it very difficult to distribute knowledge.

① protection of traditional cultural knowledge

② close relationship between knowledge and context

③ importance of experience as a source of knowledge

④ characteristics of knowledge that make its transfer difficult

⑤ easier knowledge distribution with information technology

12

A number of unique security problems are associated with carrying air cargo. Air cargo often contains more expensive items than those shipped by other freight-carrying methods; hence, the potential for loss is greater. It is also more difficult to identify where losses occur. In other methods of shipment, items are simply picked up, moved, and delivered to loading docks. Air cargo movement is much more complex: cargo is first moved from freight terminals to flight terminals, then loaded onto freight aircraft before shipping, with

opportunities for theft all along the way. When freight is placed on a passenger airplane, risk is increased because it must go to a passenger terminal and is exposed to additional handlers. At many airports, carts travel to and from flights along unlit routes, creating still more opportunities for theft. Moreover, 90 percent of air cargo is shipped at night, the time period when most crime occurs.

① factors that make air cargo more vulnerable to theft

② problems of airline passenger security screening

③ benefits and drawbacks of air freight transport

④ a brief history of air freight delivery service

⑤ different methods of transporting cargo

[13~14] 다음 글의 제목으로 가장 적절한 것을 고르시오.

13

What is truly arresting about human beings is well captured in the story of the Tower of Babel, in which humanity, speaking a single language, came so close to reaching heaven that God himself felt threatened. A common language connects the members of a community into an information-sharing network with formidable collective powers. Anyone can benefit from the strokes of genius, lucky accidents, and trial-and-error wisdom accumulated by anyone else, present or past. And people can work in teams, their efforts coordinated by negotiated agreements. As a result, *homo sapiens* is a species, like blue-green algae and earthworms, that has made far-reaching changes on the planet. Archaeologists have discovered the bones of ten thousand wild horses at the bottom of a cliff in France, the remains of herds stampeded over the clifftop by groups of paleolithic hunters seventeen thousand years ago. These fossils of ancient cooperation and shared ingenuity may shed light on why saber-tooth tigers, mastodons, giant wooly rhinoceroses, and dozens of other large mammals went extinct around the time that modern humans arrived in their habitats. Our ancestors, apparently, killed them off.

*stampede : (동물 등을) 우르르 몰다

① Breaking the Language Barrier: A Hard Task
② Language: A Basis of Cooperative Human Power
③ Changes in Languages from Ancient to Modern Times
④ Communicating with Animals, Understanding Animal Language
⑤ How Language Began: Gesture and Speech in Human Evolution

14

Education, either formal or informal, plays a major role in the passing on and sharing of culture. Educational levels of a culture can be assessed using literacy rates and enrollment in secondary or higher education, information available from secondary data sources. International firms need to know about the qualitative aspects of education, namely, varying emphases on particular skills, and the overall level of the education provided. The Republic of Korea and Japan, for example, emphasize the sciences, especially engineering, to a greater degree than do Western countries. Educational levels will have an impact on various business functions. Training programs for a production facility will have to take the educational backgrounds of trainees into account. For example, a high level of illiteracy will suggest the use of visual aids rather than printed manuals. Local recruiting for sales jobs will be affected by the availability of suitably trained personnel. In some cases, international firms routinely send locally recruited personnel to headquarters for training.

① Education as a Means of Social Mobility

② Educational Background and Economic Status

③ Trends in Education and Occupational Structure

④ Education: One Vital Consideration for Foreign Businesses

⑤ Educated Labor Force: A Driving Force for Economic Growth

15 다음 도표의 내용과 일치하지 <u>않는</u> 것은?

The graph above shows the global shares of arms purchases of seven countries over two time periods, 2007−2011 and 2012−2016. ① In the 2012−2016 period, India accounted for the largest share of global arms imports, followed by Saudi Arabia, the United Arab Emirates (UAE), China, Algeria, Turkey and Australia. ② Compared with the 2007−2011 period, the global shares of arms imports of India, Saudi Arabia, the UAE, and Turkey increased in the 2012−2016 period. ③ In contrast, the global shares of arms imports of China, Algeria, and Australia fell in the 2012−2016 period, compared with the previous period. ④ Specifically, China's share of global arms imports fell the most, from 5.5 percent to 4.5 percent, between the two periods. ⑤ The gap in global

shares of arms purchases between 2007–2011 and 2012–2016 was the largest in Saudi Arabia, and the smallest in Turkey.

16 Bertolt Brecht에 관한 다음 글의 내용과 일치하지 <u>않는</u> 것은?

> Bertolt Brecht was a major influence on 20th century drama. He explored a new style of drama, using unusual staging and different styles of acting in order to achieve his aim of making audiences think about the moral and political implications of his plays. Brecht was born in Augsburg, Germany, and studied medicine and philosophy at the universities of Munich and Berlin. After serving in World War I, he achieved success with his play *Drums in the Night*. Throughout the 1920s and early 1930s he wrote many more plays. In 1933 Brecht and his wife were forced to flee from Germany after Hitler came to power. Brecht eventually reached America, but there he was investigated for having Communist beliefs. He left America and returned to East Berlin in 1947, where he founded The Berliner Ensemble, a theater company that became world famous.

① 독특한 연출 및 다른 연기 방식을 이용하여 새로운 양식의 연극을 탐구했다.

② 뮌헨 대학교와 베를린 대학교에서 의학과 철학을 공부했다.

③ 1차 세계대전 이전에 연극 *Drums in the Night*로 성공을 거두었다.

④ 히틀러가 집권한 후 아내와 함께 독일을 떠나야 했다.

⑤ 1947년에 동베를린으로 돌아와 그곳에서 극단을 세웠다.

17 밑줄 친 <u>he</u>가 가리키는 대상이 나머지 넷과 다른 것은?

At the height of the Civil War, President Lincoln and his Secretary of War visited the battle side house of General George McClellan on some urgent business. Since ① <u>he</u> was not at home, they waited in his parlor. When the General finally returned home, he saw that he had visitors but did not acknowledge them. Instead, he went straight to his room. Assuming that ② <u>he</u> would come out soon, they waited for him. An hour later, when he had still not appeared, they sent the maid to inquire. A minute later, she returned and said, "I am sorry, Mr. President, but the General has asked me to tell you that ③ <u>he</u> is very tired and has gone to bed." The Secretary of War was shocked and said, "Mr. President, this is unacceptable. You must immediately dismiss him from the post of General!"

Lincoln thought about it for a minute and then ④ he said, "No, I will not dismiss him. He is a good general. He wins battles. I would hold his horse and wash the dirt from his boots if ⑤ he could shorten this bloodshed even by one hour."

[18~19] 다음 글의 밑줄 친 부분 중, 어법상 틀린 것을 고르시오.

18 Given the dominance in Western cultures of naturalistic views of the body, the concept of the body in culture is ① potentially a difficult one to grasp. The bodies of accident victims, transplant patients and others ② undergoing cosmetic surgery are literally and physically reconstructed every day by surgeons. Such commonplace practices make ③ it relatively easy to think of the body as a machine. Like machines, bodies have components that can, up to a point, be taken apart and reassembled. The workings of the body can in similar fashion to other machine-like objects ④ be examined and malfunctions diagnosed and remedied. Mary Shelley's monster, literally constructed by Dr. Frankenstein, is the classical working out of the body-as-machine idea. So familiar are these ways of thinking about the body ⑤ which to some of us the ideas of the social construction of the body and of the body in culture may seem to be nonsense.

19 Adolescence is a period of rebellion and of striving for independence; consequently, there will be many areas ① where children will disagree with you or not see things exactly the way you do. Remember, *what* they say ② is not as important as *how* they say it. If they communicate their disagreements with family policies and the way they are treated, certainly listen to them and when ③ possible try to respond positively. The child who says to his parent rationally, "I think I should be able to spend more time on the phone. Fifteen minutes a day is not enough. I've been doing all my homework and my grades are good," should ④ respond to in a very different manner from the child who begins by shouting and complaining angrily about his lack of phone time. It should be acceptable for a teenager to tell his mother that he does not like eating liver on Monday nights. However, it would be totally unacceptable for him to come into the kitchen on Monday evening and ⑤ start threatening that he will not eat this "garbage" and that his mother had better learn to cook something "decent."

[3점]

[20~21] (A), (B), (C)의 각 네모 안에서 어법에 맞는 표현으로 가장 적절한 것을 고르시오.

20

If you want something to happen in your life, you need to focus on it. Without focusing, and believing in what you want to achieve, you cannot accomplish the task at hand. This law of focus reminds you not to give up, no matter how (A) exhausted / exhausting the task may seem. By continuing to believe in it and focusing on it, you clearly stand a better chance of achieving the desired results. Through the law of energy and attraction, you will attract into your life (B) that / what you give energy to and focus on. A magnifying glass used to focus the sun's energy can start a fire. You can manifest what you want through your focused energy of thought and belief. You will continue to be faced with challenges, struggles and mishaps as other laws, such as the law of ups and downs, (C) are / is working in the background. You give power and life to whatever you focus on. You bring magic into what you want as you increase its vibration through your focus. [3점]

	(A)	(B)	(C)
①	exhausted	that	are
②	exhausted	what	is
③	exhausting	what	are
④	exhausting	what	is
⑤	exhausting	that	are

21

Although hunter-gatherers had previously led semi-settled rather than entirely nomadic lives, moving between a number of temporary or seasonal shelters, the ability to store cereal grains began to encourage people to stay in one place. An experiment carried out in the 1960s shows why. An archaeologist used a flint-bladed sickle to see how (A) efficient / efficiently a prehistoric family could have harvested wild grains, which still grow in some parts of Turkey. In one hour he gathered more than two pounds of grain, which suggested that a family (B) worked / that worked eight-hour days for three weeks would have been able to gather enough to provide each family member with a pound of grain a day for a year. But this would have meant staying near the stands of wild cereals to ensure the family did not miss the most suitable time (C) harvested / to harvest them. And having gathered a large quantity of grain, they would have been reluctant to leave it unguarded.

*sickle : 낫

	(A)	(B)	(C)
①	efficient	worked	harvested
②	efficient	that worked	to harvest
③	efficiently	worked	harvested
④	efficiently	that worked	to harvest
⑤	efficiently	that worked	harvested

[22~23] 다음 글의 밑줄 친 부분 중, 문맥상 낱말의 쓰임이 적절하지 않은 것을 고르시오.

22 The embedding of reporters, as ground-breaking as it may have been, proved to be a ① controversial policy. Some critics charged that embedded reporters might endanger the troops or the mission. Others were concerned that journalists would become "too close" to those they covered, and naturally identify more directly with those whom they lived with and were protected by, thereby ② gaining their objectivity. This phenomenon was likened to Stockholm Syndrome, where hostages come to empathize with their captors. Nevertheless, advocates of embedding argue it has several advantages. It provides an "up close and personal" view and ③ allows journalists to experience war as the troops do, so that they can portray the efforts of those doing the fighting. It provides ④ direct access to the battlefield and the war's events in ways not otherwise possible. The live footage and "real time" reporting provide a ⑤ realistic "first cut of history" and document the war as it happens.

*embed : (종군 기자 등을) 파견하다

23 Stand at the edge of your favorite beach and look out. You are seeing one of the most unusual sights our universe has to offer: large amounts of liquid water. This perception of the oceans of the Earth as a ① unique phenomenon is fairly new. Those who read science fiction will have vivid memories of the "canals of Mars" and the "swamps of Venus." Less than a quarter century ago the best scientific guess as to the nature of our planetary neighbors presupposed the ② presence of large amounts of water. On Mars, the white polar caps indicated that the temperature might be too cold for the water to be liquid, so that it was thought to be ③ locked in ice sheets. On Venus, the cloud cover prevented us from seeing the surface, but it didn't prevent us from ④ imagining the planet as an overgrown version of the Amazon rainforest. In both cases, our view of neighboring planets was shaped by the expectation that water, so plentiful on the Earth, must be ⑤ scarce everywhere else in the solar system. [3점]

[24~25] (A), (B), (C)의 각 네모 안에서 문맥에 맞는 낱말로 가장 적절한 것을 고르시오.

24

According to Nassim Taleb, author of the brilliant book *Black Swan*, we try to make sense of all the data around us because there are costs attached to information storage. So the more orderly we can make that information, the easier and less costly it is to store in our minds. This means that we prefer our data to be more ordered and less random. We have a drive to (A) increase / reduce the number of dimensions that we handle, so we place complex data into a much simpler order as a way to achieve this. Taleb considers that this is not only the purpose of narrative but also causality. We will try to attribute causality to events so that we can explain and understand, rather than leaving us to deal with the complexity and randomness of the world. And the purpose of (B) denying / imposing a narrative is that it can generate a sense of chronology, so both move in a single direction. The narrative means that we tend then to recall those facts that fit the story, that meet the requirements of the causality the narrative has perpetuated. We then don't recall the true sequence of events but a reconstructed one that makes the causality appear much more

(C) complicated / straightforward than it was. [3점]

*perpetuate : 영속화하다

	(A)	(B)	(C)
①	increase	denying	complicated
②	increase	imposing	complicated
③	reduce	denying	straightforward
④	reduce	imposing	complicated
⑤	reduce	imposing	straightforward

25

Alongside the wounded, ill, and injured service members and veterans exists a group of individuals who help care for them, whom we term *military caregivers*. Military caregivers are heroes in their own right, but their efforts are often (A) honored / unrecognized. They serve in the shadow of war, as their caregiving responsibilities persist for months and years after conflicts end. The men and women of the military who have made sacrifices for their country often receive honors, awards, and benefits in recognition of their service — accolades and opportunities that they (B) hardly / rightly deserve. However, their caregivers help the disabled walk and eat, tend to wound care, or take them to their medical appointments, and rarely receive honors and awards. These caregivers are an

incidental population, one that has received policy attention only as a consequence of the focus on the ones for whom they provide care. Yet their value is (C) enormous / insignificant . Military caregivers provide benefit not only to their loved one, but also to society. The care they render helps reduce health care costs to the government and society. [3점]

*accolade : 표창

	(A)	(B)	(C)
①	honored	hardly	enormous
②	honored	hardly	insignificant
③	unrecognized	rightly	enormous
④	unrecognized	rightly	insignificant
⑤	unrecognized	hardly	enormous

[26~30] 다음 글을 읽고, 빈칸에 들어갈 말로 가장 적절한 것을 고르시오.

26

Several historians declare that the foreign correspondent — the reporter covering events outside the country — is _____. This description applies to traditional mass media correspondents in particular. Since 1980, American networks have closed most of their overseas bureaus and have decreased their international news coverage. Neither the terrorism of September 11, 2001, nor the war in Iraq has reversed these trends. In a review of the year 2007, for example, the *Tyndall Report*, which monitors network television news, found that while the war in Iraq was the story of the year by a wide margin, the networks' foreign bureaus had their lightest workload since 2001. Economic pressures, global interdependence, and technological innovations — and a perception of public disinterest — have changed the way foreign news is reported and consumed.

① an endangered species

② an amateur ambassador

③ a fountain of exotic ideas

④ a particularly hated figure

⑤ the storyteller of a secret war

27

If you live in a country like the United States, it is easy to say that population is the major problem for preserving the environment. But if you think about it a little more deeply, you could rapidly come to understand that consumption and the kinds of technology that we use are also very important in setting the stage for the world of the future. For example, people in rural Brazil or rural Indonesia, like most of their counterparts in developing countries, live at about one-fortieth of the consumption level of people in the United States. If you consider that we've added 135 million people to the population of the United States since the end of World War II, then you realize that the impact of the extra people in the United States on the world — in terms of levels of consumption, levels of pollution, uses of inappropriate technologies that may themselves be destructive — is about equal to the impact on the world of all the entire population of developing countries — 4.2 billion people. It is not justifiable to say that population is the only factor. It's _____ that is truly significant. [3점]

① our way of dealing with the world

② our viewpoint on the welfare problem

③ humanitarian aid to developing countries

④ how to put an end to poverty and violence

⑤ how to measure the degree of economic equality

28

Personality characteristics are important not only for how we define ourselves, but also for _____. Social psychologists have shown that when we form impressions of others we try to extract information about their personality attributes from how they look and act: whether they are friendly, trustworthy, emotional, dominant, and so on. Impression formation is all about making what are known as 'dispositional inferences' about other people's personalities. Similarly, the stereotypes that we hold about particular social groups are saturated with personality characteristics. Whether accurate or inaccurate, these stereotypes represent personality portraits of group members, such as whether they are happy-go-lucky, aggressive, socially awkward, greedy, and so on. Once again, personality characteristics matter to us as social perceivers because they are such centrally important aspects of people.

① how we form our character

② sorting out false information

③ how we perceive other people

④ making inferences about causality

⑤ finding a career fit for our personality

② work within the confines of a frame

③ want their work to incite controversy

④ get thousands of step—by—step solutions

⑤ depend on patrons for financial support

29

Due to the efforts of Renaissance artists to elevate their profession as a liberal art, the Western world has popularized the idea of a lone individual creating his or her own art to express something very personal. In the nineteenth and twentieth centuries it became more common for artists to determine individually the appearance and content of their own work, and, in their search for new forms of self-expression, to make art that was often very controversial. This remains true today. But for many centuries before this, very few artists worked alone. Even Renaissance artists who promoted the idea of creative genius operated workshops staffed by artist assistants who carried out most of the labor involved in turning their master's design into a work of art. Even today, some famous artists, such as Jeff Koons, _____ .

① employ other artists to realize their ideas

30

Of all the thinkers of antiquity, Aristotle was perhaps the most comprehensive, his works ranging over the landscape of knowledge, such as physics, politics, and ethics. But the very scale of Aristotle's achievement left a problematic legacy. There are authors like Aristotle who are too clever for our own good. Having said so much, they appear to have had the last word. Their genius inhibits the sense of irreverence vital to creative work in their successors. Aristotle may, paradoxically, prevent those who most respect him from behaving like him. He rose to greatness only by doubting much of the knowledge that had been built up before him, not by refusing to read Plato or Heraclitus, but by mounting significant critiques of some of their weaknesses based on an appreciation of their strengths. To act in a truly Aristotelian spirit may mean allowing for some _____ . [3점]

① opportunities to work together across disciplines

② credits to humanities such as politics, ethics, and literature

③ significant ties based on the values shared by philosophers

④ generalizations to be made about the features of individual cases

⑤ intelligent departures from even the most accomplished authorities

[31~32] 주어진 글 다음에 이어질 글의 순서로 가장 적절한 것을 고르시오.

31

To parents and the general public, class size seems to be the "litmus test" of the quality of a school. Schools with small class sizes are perceived as being better than schools with large class sizes. Surveys show that parents care more about class size than anything else except school safety.

(A) Furthermore, discipline is much more difficult: for example, students may be able to doze in class without the teacher knowing it, and surely the teacher cannot correct every student who shows evidence of daydreaming.

(B) After all, if a teacher has only fifteen or so students in a class, it is far more possible for that teacher to provide individual attention to each student.

None will be left behind, and none will have to move forward on their own.

(C) On the other hand, teachers of class sizes of thirty or so students simply cannot teach to each individual student. These teachers have huge numbers of papers to grade, grades to calculate, makeup work for students who are absent, parents to contact, and e-mails to answer.

① (A) − (C) − (B)   ② (B) − (A) − (C)
③ (B) − (C) − (A)   ④ (C) − (A) − (B)
⑤ (C) − (B) − (A)

32

Eating is still fun for the one-year-old, but it is no longer the main interest in the child's life. Children's need for food is determined mostly by their activity level and by the rate at which they are growing in height and weight.

(A) If this happens everybody loses. The parents lose because they never get over their frustration at the way their children eat. The children lose because they really do become picky, difficult eaters or else chronic overeaters.

(B) That concern often leads parents to try to force children to eat more. When parents force and children

resist, a chronic battle is set up which may become more important to all concerned than the question of food which started it all in the first place.

(C) Because this rate slows down greatly in the second year of life, many children are actually eating less at 15–18 months than they were at 8–10 months. Not unexpectedly this concerns a great many parents who feel it is obvious that the bigger and older children are, the more they should eat.

① (A) − (C) − (B)   ② (B) − (A) − (C)
③ (B) − (C) − (A)   ④ (C) − (A) − (B)
⑤ (C) − (B) − (A)

[33~34] 글의 흐름으로 보아, 주어진 문장이 들어가기에 가장 적절한 곳을 고르시오.

33

That prompted the military to take the chemical-repelling technology that it had developed to protect soldiers against biological weapons and apply it to T-shirts and underwear.

Who knew that the largest number of casualties from Operation Desert Storm in the 1991 Gulf War would be from bacterial infections? Soldiers in combat don't always have the luxury of being able to change into fresh underwear, if they even *have* a clean pair to change into. (①) Underwear worn day after day in those hot desert conditions turned out to be a significant cause of bacterial infections and discomfort. (②) The underwear is manufactured by using microwave energy to bond tiny "nanoparticles" to the fibers in the underwear fabric. (③) Then chemicals that repel oil, water, bacteria, and other substances are bonded to the nanoparticles. (④) The result was underwear that is very, very difficult to get dirty, because virtually nothing will stick to it. (⑤) And because bacteria never gets established, undergarments made with the stuff can be worn for weeks without washing and without risk to the wearer's health. [3점]

34

However, private property rights are not sacred, even in societies with strong views on this subject.

Landscape-level restoration will almost always involve public property (especially where water is concerned) and a mixture of organizational and personal private property. (①) Consequently, a formidable

barrier to a landscape approach is the inevitable conflicts between environmental protection and property rights. (②) The individual property owner with a small wetland is likely to be angry when told that filling, draining or altering the wetland in major ways is illegal. (③) This property, the owner sometimes says, is private "and I will do as I wish with my property." (④) Each person lives not only on private property, but in a larger ecological landscape shared with others. (⑤) So, a key question is: to what extent should individual, organizational or national behavior and attitudes be modified for the betterment of others of the human species and for other species as well?

[35~36] 다음 글에서 전체 흐름과 관계 없는 문장을 고르시오.

35 Gifted children, with their extreme emotional sensitivity and idealism, often notice great gaps between how things are and how they ought to be — in their family, their school, their community, and the larger world. ① Because of their keen minds and their sharp thinking and reasoning abilities, they find themselves sharply aware of mediocrity, greed, poverty, corruption, violence, abuse, pollution, hypocrisy, and other flaws in society. ② They become discouraged and disillusioned that no one else cares or that these problems can never be fixed. ③ They may feel relieved and act swiftly to conform to the social or behavioral norms of their age group. ④ As a result of this "What's the point?" attitude, many intellectually gifted youngsters choose to underachieve in school, and some drop out of high school, college, or even society altogether. ⑤ They may search for a life or career where they don't have to deal with social hypocrisy or other aspects of society that make them uncomfortable.

36 Scientific evidence is mounting that some animals use tools, live by moral codes, use complex communication systems, and have culture. ① These findings fit squarely within Charles Darwin's theory of evolution, which predicts that differences between humans and other animals are in degree, not kind. ② Yet there is an ongoing debate about the nature and sufficiency of the evidence for culture among animals. ③ Some scholars aren't convinced that ecological and genetic explanations for animal behavior have been ruled out in all cases, while others define culture in ways that exclude nonhuman animals. ④ In order to understand the legal status of nonhuman animals it is necessary to understand what is fundamental about how legal systems work. ⑤ The unresolved debate makes this an active, exciting field of study, with new discoveries and important advances appearing regularly.

37 다음 글의 내용을 한 문장으로 요약하고자 한다. 빈칸 (A)와 (B)에 들어갈 말로 가장 적절한 것은?

Consider a new manager who wants to test her employees' planning skills. She may ask her employees to develop a written plan for a particular project. The manager could use very concrete and specific language to describe the assignment: "I want you to develop a five-page plan for this proposed project. First, make sure you include an overview of the project in the introduction. Second, I want a section that highlights your analysis of why we have embarked on this project. Third, I want a solutions section in the report. Finally, I want a description of the criteria and benchmarks for assessing the success of your proposed solution." This request uses very concrete and specific language, but does it meet this manager's needs? By outlining the length and format for the project proposal, the manager clearly specifies what she wants, and in doing so, she reduces her chances to assess her employees' planning abilities. She could have made her request more ambiguous: "Please develop a proposal for this project. I don't want to tell you too much more, because I don't want to limit your creativity." Although this language is more abstract, it may give the manager better insight into how each employee thinks and plans.

When assessing employees' planning skills, a manager can provide them with an opportunity to show their ___(A)___ by adjusting the level of ___(B)___ in the instructions for an assignment.

	(A)	(B)
①	creativity	agreement
②	creativity	abstraction
③	experience	frequency
④	experience	abstraction
⑤	enthusiasm	frequency

[38~39] 다음 글을 읽고, 물음에 답하시오.

You never know when a so-called *bad idea* will contain the seeds of greatness within it. We've seen it countless times in our work. A *bad*, even absurd, idea is offered up, and within minutes it has transformed into a brilliant example of innovative thinking. We make use of some effective idea generation methods that invite participants to come up with the worst, most ridiculous, even distasteful ideas imaginable — and then to turn around or transform those ideas into great ones.

Consider the extreme "what if we all jumped out of the window" example. From this bad idea, you might develop an innovative emergency personal parachute product for individuals working in tall city buildings. Or conceive an improved process for evacuation from high floors during a fire. A new "team hang-gliding" extreme sports event. A breakthrough advertising concept where a group of people are able to fly after consuming a new beverage. An infinite number of other possibilities could be born from the bad idea that everyone in the room should jump out of a window. That is, unless the idea is shot down prematurely before the great idea within it has a chance to blossom. So, _____ until an idea has had a fair chance to show all it's got.

38 윗글의 제목으로 가장 적절한 것은?

① Creative Ads Will Inspire You

② Bad Ideas Can Lead to Big Ideas

③ Why Doesn't Group Brainstorming Work?

④ Good Intentions Can Have Bad Outcomes

⑤ Are People More Creative Alone or Together?

39 윗글의 빈칸에 들어갈 말로 가장 적절한 것은?

① detect errors

② follow tradition

③ suspend judgment

④ punish wrongdoing

⑤ reduce daydreaming

[40~41] 다음 글을 읽고, 물음에 답하시오.

As an example of the ability of language to direct our attention, think about the term 'politically correct,' or PC, language. Its proponents argue that we can rid our minds of discriminatory thoughts by removing from our language any words or phrases that could offend people by the way they reference differences and handicaps. Los Angeles County in California asked suppliers to stop using the terms *master* and *slave* on computer equipment, even though these are commonly used terms that refer to primary and secondary hard disk drives, because of cultural sensitivity. Other substitutions, such as *police officer* for *policeman*, are intended to highlight that such positions are held by both men and women.

Using PC language and being PC have come to be viewed negatively, __(A)__, and even ridiculed and satirized because they overcompensate for others' sensitivities. One reason that PC language is fairly easy to ridicule is that

its political agenda is not always connected to large social and cultural institutions. (B) , it is one thing to say that we need to rid the workplace of sexist language in an effort to create equal relationships between men and women, but unless this directive is connected to a broader agenda of fostering gender pay equity and equal opportunity for promotions and advancement, merely ridding the workplace of sexist language may not generate the hoped-for effect.

40 윗글의 주제로 가장 적절한 것은?

① grounds for supporting political correctness

② effects of social progress on language changes

③ pros and cons of using politically correct language

④ differences between male and female language use

⑤ necessity of getting a clear idea with a clear expression

41 윗글의 빈칸 (A), (B)에 들어갈 말로 가장 적절한 것은?

	(A)	(B)
①	however	For example
②	however	In contrast
③	that is	For example
④	thus	In contrast
⑤	thus	Furthermore

[42~43] 다음 글을 읽고, 물음에 답하시오.

A boy was born in England to parents from Ghana. Because he was born in England, the boy was automatically a British citizen. As a youngster, he returned to Ghana to live with his father, leaving behind his mother, two sisters, and a brother. Some years later he returned, intending to live with his mother and siblings. At this point, the story gets (a) complicated. Immigration authorities suspected that the boy was an impostor and thought he was either an unrelated child or a nephew of the boy's mother. On the basis of their suspicions, the boy's application for residency was (b) denied. The boy's family fought to establish his identity so that he could live in the country of his birth. The first round of medical tests used blood types as well as genetic markers normally employed to match organ donors and recipients. The results (c) confirmed that the boy was closely related to the woman he claimed was his mother, but the tests could not tell whether she was his mother or an aunt.

The family turned to Alec Jeffreys, a scientist at the University of Leicester, for help. They asked if DNA fingerprinting,

a technique developed in Jeffreys's research laboratory, could establish the boy's identity. However, the mother's sisters and the boy's father were not available for testing. Despite these problems, Jeffreys agreed to take on the case. He took blood samples from the boy, the children he believed were his brother and sisters, and the woman who claimed to be his mother. The pattern of bands, known as a DNA fingerprint, was analyzed to determine the boy's identity. The results showed that the boy had the same father as his brother and his sisters because they all (d) shared DNA fragments associated with the father. The most important question was whether the boy and his "mother" were related.

Jeffreys found that 25 fragments of the woman's DNA matched those of the boy, indicating that she was in fact the boy's mother. Faced with this evidence, immigration authorities had to (e) maintain their position. They allowed the boy to live in England with his family.

*impostor : 남의 이름을 사칭하는 사람

42 윗글에 관한 내용으로 적절하지 <u>않은</u> 것은?

① 소년은 영국에서 태어나 자동적으로 영국 시민이 되었다.

② 소년은 어렸을 때 아버지와 살려고 Ghana 로 갔다.

③ 소년의 가족은 소년이 영국에서 살 수 있도록 그의 신원을 증명하려고 애썼다.

④ 소년의 가족은 Alec Jeffreys에게 DNA 지문 검사를 요청했다.

⑤ Alec Jeffreys는 소년의 아버지의 혈액 샘플을 받았다.

43 밑줄 친 (a)~(e) 중에서 문맥상 낱말의 쓰임이 적절하지 <u>않은</u> 것은? [3점]

① (a) ② (b)

③ (c) ④ (d)

⑤ (e)

[44~45] 다음 글을 읽고, 물음에 답하시오.

(A)

It was summer and Mary was 14. Her whole family spent weekend after weekend at the river, waterskiing and swimming and just having a great time. But Mary couldn't ski like her big brothers and sisters. She was too embarrassed to try. (a) She was horrified at the idea of looking ridiculous, and looking like a novice next to her skilled and experienced siblings. One day she told her mother all about this.

(B)

On that day, Mary learned to ski. Her mother was patient and careful. It wasn't nearly as difficult as Mary had thought it would be, and with no audience (b) she

had no discomfort about being hunched over her skis. As the afternoon wore on, she stood up straighter and straighter on the skis. The next weekend river trip would see Mary happily skiing along with her brothers and sisters, (c) her embarrassment erased by her mother's kind act.

(C)

Mary explained that when beginning skiers got up out of the water for the first time, they started off crouched over their skis with their bottoms stuck out, looking absolutely absurd. And there were so many people on the river on any sunny weekend. Some of them were boys, and they would all see Mary as (d) she adopted that humiliating pose. Mary told her mom that she was not willing to risk this shame.

(D)

One Thursday soon after this talk, Mary's mother left work after lunch and came home. Mary didn't understand why her mom was home, but Mary's mom just told her to help hook the boat trailer to the car. Her mother was offering something, and Mary had to accept (e) her offer. Before she knew what had happened, Mary and her mom were in the boat, heading up the river in the warm sunshine on quiet water. It was a Thursday, so no one else was about. No one was there to see Mary look ridiculous.

44 주어진 글 (A)에 이어질 내용을 순서에 맞게 배열한 것으로 가장 적절한 것은?

① (B) − (D) − (C) ② (C) − (B) − (D)

③ (C) − (D) − (B) ④ (D) − (B) − (C)

⑤ (D) − (C) − (B)

45 밑줄 친 (a)~(e) 중에서 가리키는 대상이 나머지 넷과 다른 것은?

① (a) ② (b)

③ (c) ④ (d)

⑤ (e)

2025
사관학교
10개년 영어

01 Based on the following dialogue, which one is NOT true?

> Jimmy : Let's go camping this weekend.
>
> Joanne : Not again. We just went last weekend and the rain soaked us.
>
> Jimmy : Yes, the tent leaks a bit, but the forecast says there won't be a cloud in the sky this weekend.
>
> Joanne : Can't we just go to see a play, or something else cultural?
>
> Jimmy : Fair enough. Since we did what I wanted last weekend, you get to make the plan this time. So what do you want to do?
>
> Joanne : I heard about an amazing ballet performance at the cultural center downtown. You'll love it.
>
> Jimmy : Sorry, but please don't make me go to a ballet! Ballet is the worst. How about anything else?

① Joanne is not interested in camping this weekend.

② It rained last weekend.

③ Their tent is not completely waterproof.

④ The weather is expected to be good this weekend.

⑤ Jimmy is a fan of the ballet.

02 Which is the best sequence of sentences for the blanks?

> Janet : I must say I really like this apartment, but I do have some concerns. First of all, I have a young son and don't want him to walk too far to school.
>
> Dave : I totally understand. There's a good school very near here. _____
>
> Janet : How about the utilities? We don't have a lot of money to spend, actually.
>
> Dave : This building is quite modern and energy-efficient. _____
>
> Janet : Oh, that's a relief. And what about the neighbors? We prefer to live in a quiet place.
>
> Dave : There are currently only a young family with no kids and some older couples living in the building. _____
>
> Janet : Great! I think this may be the place.

〈보기〉

a. There's nothing available.
b. It shouldn't be noisy at all.
c. It's just a block away.
d. They're very affordable.

① a – b – d   ② b – c – d
③ c – d – b   ④ c – b – a
⑤ d – c – a

03 Where is the dialogue most likely taking place?

Aaron : Good morning. I was wondering if you have anything available for today. I'm in town for the day, flying out tonight, and was hoping to visit some of the sites.

Krista : Well, it is short notice, but I do have several options to offer you. Did you have any preferences?

Aaron : Actually, I was kind of hoping that you would have something compact that gets good mileage.

Krista : That shouldn't be a problem. I have the perfect one. And would you like the extra insurance? I would recommend it.

Aaron : I sure would. Better safe than sorry.

Krista : Great. I just need to see your license, and then I can prepare the contract. Just make sure the tank is full when you return it.

Aaron : No problem. I'll drop it off sometime this evening.

① at a gas station
② at a car repair shop
③ at a car rental agency
④ at a travel agency
⑤ at an insurance company

04 Based on the following dialogue, which one is true?

Bill : Honey, on this day, our first wedding anniversary, I wanted to get you something special. I think you'll love it. Please, open it up.

Diane : Oh my lord, a puppy! We can't keep a dog. It just costs too much to raise one, and it's a huge responsibility.

Bill : It really doesn't cost that much, and now with me working at home these days it'll be quite easy for me to take care of him. You won't have to do a thing.

Diane : Are you sure? Do you promise that you'll take full responsibility for him?

Bill : Absolutely. Plus, look at him! He's adorable, and he seems to have bonded with you already. He's snuggling right up to you.

Diane : To be honest, he is awfully cute. You may have a point. Let's give it a try.

① Bill forgot their anniversary last year.

② Diane got Bill a pet for their anniversary.

③ Diane thinks raising a dog will be a piece of cake.

④ Bill doesn't work at home these days.

⑤ Bill and Diane are going to keep the dog.

05 Choose the most appropriate sentence for the blank.

Taxi Driver : Hi there. Where are you headed?

Passenger : Across town to the Smythe Building. And please hurry.

Taxi Driver : Don't worry, there shouldn't be much traffic at this time.

[5 minutes later]

Passenger : Sorry to bother you, but why are you going through the city instead of using the expressway? I have to be at a meeting in just 40 minutes.

Taxi Driver : There's major construction clogging up the expressway, and I know all the short cuts. I'll get you there in time.

Passenger : Okay, I hope you know what you are doing.

[25 minutes later]

Taxi Driver : Here we are sir, at your destination with time to spare.

Passenger : Apologies for my skepticism. _____

① Here's the fare and a well-earned tip.

② I'm not going to make it on time.

③ I should've taken the subway.

④ Let's take the expressway, then.

⑤ I'm going to complain to your supervisor.

06 Choose the sentence that best describes the situation. [3점]

> Father : I can't believe my oldest is finally leaving the nest and moving out on his own. It's going to be so hard.
>
> Tim : Don't worry, dad. You and mom will do fine without me. I'm only two hours away, so we can visit each other anytime.
>
> Father : I'm not worried about us, son. I'm worried about you being able to take care of yourself like doing your laundry, cleaning your apartment, and paying your bills.
>
> Tim : Actually, I was kind of hoping that I could bring my laundry here for you guys to do, that mom would come visit to clean my place, and that you would pay my bills.
>
> Father : You must be joking. You're on your own young man. This is independence.
>
> Tim : Of course I'm kidding. I'm more than capable of doing my own housework. Plus, my new job pays me more than enough. You don't have to worry about a thing.

① Tim moved back home so that he could take care of his parents.

② Tim's parents decided to visit Tim regularly to take care of him.

③ Tim's father is happy to have Tim back home after a long absence.

④ Tim is moving away and thinks he is prepared for his independence.

⑤ Tim is going away to university but will still need his parents' support.

07 밑줄 친 부분이 가리키는 대상이 나머지 넷과 다른 것은?

Dr. J. F. Cowan once told the story of a small college that was having financial difficulties, even though their academic standards had been exceptionally high. One day a very wealthy man came on the campus, found ① a white-haired man in overalls painting the wall, and asked where he could find the president. The painter pointed out a house on the campus and said ② he was sure the president could be seen there at noon. At the designated time the visitor knocked at the president's door and was admitted by the same man ③ he had talked to on the grounds, though now he was attired differently. The visitor accepted an invitation to have lunch with ④ the painter-president, asking a number

of questions about the needs of the college, and told him he would be sending a little donation. Two days later a letter arrived enclosing a check for $50,000. The humility of a man who was fitted for ⑤ his position as a college president, but who was not too proud to put on the clothes of a workman and do the job that needed doing so badly, had opened the wealthy man's purse strings.

[08~09] 다음 글에서 전체 흐름과 관계 <u>없는</u> 문장을 고르시오.

08 When the first Olympic victor was recorded in 776 B.C., Rome was a mere farm community surrounded by warring tribes. ① By 500 B.C., as the athletic program at Olympia settled into a fixed, predictable pattern, the Romans were rising up against the rule of the Etruscans, their hostile neighbors to the north. ② Within two centuries Roman military might, administrative officials, language, and culture dominated all of Italy. ③ Then began their imperial conquest of Sicily, Carthage, and Greece. ④ Furthermore, Greek sports and games were too individualistic, too geared to the participants rather than to spectator appeal. ⑤ By the end of the first century B.C., the Roman empire covered the entire rim of the Mediterranean, extending to the northern reaches of Britain, to the Danube in Europe, and east to the Caspian Sea.

09 The fact that most organizations, large and small, are now filled with data is no bad thing. ① In fact, it is a huge opportunity for businesses to acquire insight and understanding in ways never before considered possible. ② However, what is a problem is that most organizations don't step back to consider how the data should be explored and understood. ③ Understanding data relating to human behavior is a long-standing skill of marketers and social scientists. ④ Analysis processes designed to uncover new insights are confused and mixed with those used to measure performance. ⑤ There is a lack of attention to which methods of analysis actually make a difference to the business — there is still too much focus on measurement as a function of ease for accessing the number rather than relevance to business outcomes. [3점]

[10~11] 다음 글의 밑줄 친 부분 중, 어법상 <u>틀린</u> 것을 고르시오.

10 For years, psychology turned its attention to the study of negative emotions or negative affect, including depression, sadness, anger, stress and anxiety. Not surprisingly, psychologists found them ① <u>interesting</u> because they may often lead to, or signal the presence of, psychological disorders. However, positive emotions are no less fascinating, if only because of many common-sense misconceptions that ② <u>exist</u> about positive affect. We tend to think, for example, that positive affect

typically, by its very nature, distorts or disrupts orderly, effective thinking, that positive emotions are somehow "simple" or ③ <u>what</u>, because these emotions are short-lived, they cannot have a long-term impact. Research has shown the above not to be the case, but it took it a while ④ <u>to get</u> there. It is only relatively recently that psychologists realized that positive emotions can be seen as valuable in their own right and ⑤ <u>started</u> studying them.

11 In Ancient Rome, messages sent over short distances, for which a quick reply was expected, were written with a stylus on wax tablets ① <u>mounted</u> in wooden frames that folded together like a book. To modern eyes these tablets, with their flat writing surfaces surrounded by a wooden frame, look strikingly ② <u>similar</u> to tablet computers. The recipient's response could be scratched onto the same tablet, and the messenger who had ③ <u>delivered</u> it would then take it straight back to the sender. The tablets could be erased and reused by smoothing the colored wax with the flat end of a stylus. Within the city, this was a handy way to send a quick question to someone and ④ <u>get</u> a reply within an hour or two. Letters sent over longer distances ⑤ <u>written</u> on papyrus, which was more expensive but lighter and therefore more suitable for transport. A single sheet of papyrus typically measured about six inches wide by ten inches tall, which was enough for a short letter.

*stylus : 철필

[12~13] (A), (B), (C)의 각 네모 안에서 어법에 맞는 표현으로 가장 적절한 것을 고르시오.

12

The personal computer can be thought of as a commodity, as an everyday object. It can end its days as a piece of junk, a "bygone object," (A) are / to be disposed of somehow, either by literally throwing it away, or by resale, or by passing it on to someone else, or by keeping it somewhere out of sight. Christine Finn (2001) has written a brilliant book on computers-as-junk, (B) which / in which she looks at the ways they are disposed of, all the activities that take place at the supposed end of a PC's days, whether that means having its reusable bits removed, or being snapped up by a vintage computer collector. People from my generation don't like to think about computers as junk, because to us they're still such new things. I find (C) it / them much harder to throw one out than, say, a tumble drier, and I can see much more (symbolic) value in a 20-year-old computer than I can in a 20-year-old car.

	(A)	(B)	(C)
①	are	which	them
②	are	in which	them
③	to be	in which	it
④	to be	in which	them
⑤	to be	which	it

13

Fairy stories are filled with frogs turning into princes, or pumpkins turning into coaches drawn by white horses (A) transformed / are transformed from white mice. Such fantasies are profoundly unrealistic. They couldn't happen, not for biological reasons but mathematical ones. Such transitions would be virtually impossible, which means that for practical purposes we can rule them out. But for a caterpillar (B) to turn / turns into a butterfly is not a problem: It happens all the time, the rules having been built up over the ages by natural selection. And although no butterfly has ever been seen to turn into a caterpillar, (C) it / which should not surprise us in the same way as, say, a frog turning into a prince. Frogs don't contain genes for making princes. But they do contain genes for making tadpoles.

*tadpole : 올챙이

	(A)	(B)	(C)
①	transformed	······ to turn ······	it
②	transformed	······ to turn ······	which
③	are transformed	······ turns ······	it
④	are transformed	······ turns ······	which
⑤	are transformed	······ to turn ······	it

[14~17] 다음 글을 읽고, 빈칸에 들어갈 말로 가장 적절한 것을 고르시오.

14

By examining the various functions of religion, we can see that religion is a(n) _____ force in a society. In a general sense religions support the status quo by keeping people in line through supernatural sanctions, relieving social conflict, and providing explanations for unfortunate events. Moreover, some of the major world religions, through both philosophical convictions and political interpretations, have tended to inhibit social change. To illustrate, orthodox Hindu beliefs, based on the notion that one's present condition in life is determined by deeds in past lives, have had the effect of making people so fatalistic that they accept their present situations as unchangeable. Such a worldview is not likely to bring about major revolutions or even minor initiatives for change. Likewise, some Muslim leaders have taken a strong stand against the introduction of new values and behaviors, particularly from the Western world.

① conservative   ② democratic

③ impartial   ④ intellectual

⑤ stimulating

15

Imagine that you are standing in a large, square field. On one side of the field a noisy road crew is doing some repairs with a jackhammer. On an adjacent side of the field a street vendor with a food cart is playing a loud, repetitive jingle. With your eyes closed, you could wander around in the field and work out your distance from either the road crew or the food cart by gauging the loudness of the sounds. Knowing both distances would allow you to triangulate your position on the field with an accuracy limited only by your ability to discriminate loudness. What is even more interesting about this example is that you could work out your position in the field even from locations that you had never visited before, provided you had a basic understanding of the principle — two sources of sound in two different locations _____. [3점]

① keep you alert for longer periods

② provide unambiguous cues to position

③ hinder your positional awareness

④ lead to higher distraction levels

⑤ diminish auditory functions

16

Like speech, most forms of nonverbal communication are symbolic behaviors: A particular body motion or distance does not inherently convey a certain message but does so only because of conventions, or common understandings. Because much nonverbal communication is arbitrary and conventional, there is great potential for misunderstanding when people do not share the same meanings for nonverbal messages — that is, when people have learned different conventions. Probably the potential for misunderstanding is even greater with nonverbal messages than with spoken language. When two people from different cultures converse, both generally know that they do not understand the other's language, so at least each person is aware of his or her own ignorance. However, both are more likely to think they understand nonverbal messages, so they _____. [3점]

① have to focus on verbal messages more carefully

② might give or take offense when none is intended

③ might end communication by clarifying the other's intention

④ will make their feelings clear to each other verbally

⑤ will be better at communicating with each other

2018 기출문제

165

17

When people are stressed they react differently. It is difficult for them to eat and sleep. They become irritable and short-tempered. They may say things in the heat of the moment they would not otherwise say. As couples tend to react differently under stress, one partner may be affected far more than the other and so the relationship is damaged. The answer is to identify the source of stress and see what can be done about it. First, you must accept that you are under stress and that this is causing problems in the relationship. Then sit down together and talk about the issues. That alone is often enough to relieve some of the stress. Whatever the cause of the stress, it is not likely to be resolved easily or quickly, but just recognizing it and having some sort of plan to tackle it is reassuring. Much more important, by sitting down with your partner and talking about it you can work together to resolve it. There is a lot of truth in the saying "_____."

① Too many cooks spoil the broth

② A bad workman blames his tools

③ Absence makes the heart grow fonder

④ A problem shared is a problem halved

⑤ Better a live coward than a dead hero

18 다음 글이 시사하는 바로 가장 적절한 것은?

Quite often, people will come up to me after a seminar and say that they have decided upon their financial goal. When I ask them what it is, they tell me that they have decided to become a millionaire or even a billionaire in the next year or two. In almost every case, these people turn out to have no money or very little. They are often in their thirties or forties and have a lifetime of financial mismanagement behind them. Nonetheless, they think that they can neutralize all their past experiences and somehow leap into wealth and affluence with little preparation, few resources, and no clear idea of how to get there. They believe that all they need to do is to think happy thoughts and they will magically attract everything they need to overcome decades of frustration and failure. When people say to me that they want to be a millionaire as soon as possible, I suggest that they first become a "thousandaire." After they have managed to save a thousand dollars and get out of debt, they can then become a "ten thousandaire," and so on.

① Positive thinking can lead one out of debt.

② Each person must walk before he or she can run.

③ If you work really hard, you will get rich in a short period of time.

④ You must develop multiple courses of action before leaving your job.

⑤ One's quality of life depends on how he or she neutralizes past experiences.

19 다음 글에서 필자가 주장하는 바로 가장 적절한 것은?

Some of the biggest fears of pre-service teachers include what they are required to teach and whether or not they know enough of the subject matter to teach the class. Your jurisdiction's department of education will have mandated a curriculum for you to follow. Treat the curriculum as the stepping stones of information you are required to teach and your students are to learn. While you are required to follow the curriculum's learning outcomes, curriculum documents don't say how to teach them or how to assess them. Along with the curriculum, there are often approved textbooks that align with the jurisdiction's vision of student learning. Some of the best teachers do not solely rely on the curriculum and textbooks, but will expand on some areas based on student interest. Remember, although you should use the curriculum and textbooks as your guide to lesson planning and instruction, they shouldn't be everything.

*jurisdiction : 관할구역

① 예비교사를 위한 교육실습 기회가 확대되어야 한다.

② 교사는 교과과정과 교과서에 전적으로 의존해서는 안 된다.

③ 교육청은 교사들에게 교과과정과 평가방법을 제시해야 한다.

④ 교과과정을 수립할 때 교사들의 의견을 충분히 수렴해야 한다.

⑤ 교과서를 집필할 때 학생들의 관심 분야를 적극 반영해야 한다.

[20~21] 다음 글의 빈칸 (A), (B)에 들어갈 말로 가장 적절한 것을 고르시오.

20

Both internationally and domestically, tourism is seen as an effective means of transferring wealth and investment from richer, developed countries or regions to less developed, poorer areas. This ___(A)___ of wealth occurs, in theory, as a result of both tourist expenditures in destination areas and also of investment by the richer, tourist-generating countries in tourism facilities. In the latter case,

developed countries are, in principle, supporting the economic growth and development of less developed countries by investing in tourism. However, it has long been recognized that the net retention of tourist expenditures varies considerably from one destination to another, while overseas investment in tourism facilities more often than not may lead to   (B) . This can be seen in profits often largely being diverted away from the less developed countries, potentially leaving them subject to the investor nations and corporations. [3점]

	(A)	(B)
①	concentration	exploitation and dependency
②	redistribution	exploitation and dependency
③	imbalance	prosperity and security
④	redistribution	prosperity and security
⑤	imbalance	collaboration and development

21

A kind of personal knowledge that we have stored in our memory is the knowledge of our likes and dislikes. This is a highly personal kind of knowledge, dependent on individual taste. If we ask you,   (A) , what your favorite kind of soup is, you might tell us that it's Borscht or Chicken Noodle or Egg Drop. You know because you have eaten many kinds of soup before, and you remember which one you liked the best. Based on that memory, you probably ask for it over and over again at home or in restaurants.   (B) , you can easily tell us who your best friend is, who your favorite singer is, and which soccer team you like best, as well as what your favorite color or book or television program is. All of these things you remember because you have had extensive direct experience with them in the past, and you can easily compare and contrast the various experiences to determine which one gave you the most pleasure.

	(A)	(B)
①	for example	Similarly
②	for example	Therefore
③	on the contrary	Similarly
④	on the contrary	Otherwise
⑤	in other words	Therefore

[22~23] 다음 글의 밑줄 친 부분 중, 문맥상 낱말의 쓰임이 적절하지 <u>않은</u> 것을 고르시오.

22 Domesticated animals were frequently utilized as weapons and equipment in ancient wars. The Greeks often used elephants as war equipment. Intended primarily to ① <u>terrify</u> the enemy, elephants were elaborately decorated with ornaments, such as headpieces and clanging bells. They were occasionally given fermented wine to drink, ② <u>encouraging</u> fierce behavior. However, the use of elephants on the front lines was probably more a ③ <u>display</u> of strength than of their practical use as a war animal. Elephants are not ④ <u>effective</u> in fighting human wars; if bombarded by arrows, an elephant will simply turn around and retreat, often inflicting more damage on his own army than on the enemy. Further, a female elephant will refuse to fight if separated from her young, and she would immediately ⑤ <u>assume</u> all military duties and rush to the rescue if her offspring cried out when wounded or trampled upon.

23 Firms exist in capitalistic societies to make a profit. If the firm's product were viewed as a one-time-only purchase by consumers (e.g., novelty items such as the pet rock), if the level of performance were not subject to regulation, and if only ① <u>limited</u> cross-communication channels were open to consumers, then customer satisfaction would be an unimportant goal for the purely profit-oriented firm. Few producers, however, ② <u>encounter</u> these conditions. Most find that repeat purchasing is essential to a continued stream of ③ <u>profitability</u>. Even for products with long purchase intervals (e.g., major appliances, automobiles), satisfaction is important because of word of mouth and the activities of numerous watchdog organizations, such as Consumers Union, that ④ <u>track</u> reports of satisfaction over time. Now becoming more available, empirical data on the influence of satisfaction, quality, and other such measures are ⑤ <u>contradicting</u> the long-held assumption that customer satisfaction is one key to profitability. [3점]

[24~25] 다음 글의 제목으로 가장 적절한 것을 고르시오.

24 Psycholinguistic researchers have found that a person will understand a positive statement in approximately two-thirds the time it takes to understand a negative one. Even if your only objective in life is to motivate others to do what you want them to do, constructive criticism will carry you much further than a negative attack. If someone has done something half right and half wrong, emphasize

how great the end product would be if he consistently employed the techniques that worked well. If someone's clothing is attractive and stylish, but his hair looks like it was cut by a blind barber, compliment him on the tastefulness of his attire; and if you have a legitimate need to change his appearance, suggest that he would look even better if he conformed his hairstyle to his clothing style. Offer solutions, not just criticism; and give others the chance to take the hint. If they don't, you can always turn up the criticism until they do.

① Keep Your Criticism Positive

② Why Criticism Is So Hard to Take

③ Accept Negative Criticism for Growth

④ How to Recognize Empty Compliments

⑤ The Value of Offering Negative Feedback

25

People unconsciously signal that they are lying through inconsistencies in their nonverbal behavior. If you have ever caught someone in a lie, you might have noticed that statements made later in the conversation contradicted statements made at the beginning, or perhaps his or her gestures seemed to contradict the words being spoken. The person may have acted calm and aloof, but at the same time kept tapping his or her foot, playing with a button or piece of jewelry, and speaking with a higher pitch. Examinations of people's perceptions of courtroom testimony reveal that stereotypically deceptive behaviors don't necessarily trigger suspicion, but inconsistent nonverbal behaviors are frequently interpreted as deceptive regardless of the specific actions that are performed. Research has also shown that familiarity with a person's typical nonverbal behaviors makes it easier to detect deception. In particular, people are better able to tell whether a partner is telling the truth or lying when they have previous experience with that person's truthful behavior.

*aloof : 초연한, 무관심한

① Patterns of Behavior That Reveal Deception

② Psychological Factors That Lead to Deception

③ Common Characteristics of Nonverbal Messages

④ Developing a Strong Relationship Free of Deception

⑤ Inaccurate Assessments of People's Truth or Deception

[26~27] 글의 흐름으로 보아, 주어진 문장이 들어가기에 가장 적절한 곳을 고르시오.

26

However, the same sport can have different meanings to different groups of people.

As with education, sport has a common core of shared meaning and a periphery of additional meanings that are very much context-dependent. (①) In other words, although most of us have a common understanding of what sport is, it can still mean different things to different people. (②) In general terms we recognize that football is sport, but that ballroom dancing is not; motor racing is sport, but driving to work is not; sailing a boat on an ocean is sport, but sailing on a tanker delivering oil is not. (③) It is not necessary to define what we mean by sport whenever the word is used. (④) As an example of these differing meanings let us consider the sport of tennis. (⑤) To a professional tennis player tennis is a job; to a club player, however competitive, tennis is essentially a recreation; to a spectator at Wimbledon, tennis may be a temporary diversion or an all consuming vicarious passion.

*vicarious : 대리의

27

In a stable, fully occupied habitat, there may not be enough nest sites or food available in a given year for new breeders to strike out on their own.

Flamingos, penguins, ostriches, giraffes, dolphins, crocodiles, and many other species leave their young in the care of other adults for a while. This gives parents the freedom to track down the most nutritious foods for their growing family. (①) Just who are these surrogate parents that care for the young? (②) The sitters may be parents taking random turns, or they may be nonbreeding individuals that are related to the parents. (③) Though it may look like altruism, the sitters are merely promoting their own genes tied up in the young nieces, nephews, or siblings that they are caring for. (④) If their aim is to further their genes, you may ask, why not just have their own brood? (⑤) Rather than be forced into a marginal nesting site, they might hold off for a year, learning tricks in the meantime that will make them better parents. [3점]

*surrogate : 대리의

[28~29] 다음 글의 요지로 가장 적절한 것을 고르시오.

28

In everyday life, people are repeatedly exposed to different aspects of consumption. Advertising, traveling on a train, grocery shopping, watching television, listening to music, surfing the Internet, clothes shopping, and reading a book are all examples of things that people consume. Almost all behaviors that humans engage in are directly or indirectly linked to consumption. Even traditional holidays such as Christmas are these days mainly about consumption. What was originally a religious holiday has mainly been overtaken by aspects of consumption with the most typical example of this being Santa Claus delivering presents. Basically there is no way of escaping the fact that consumption is a part of humans' everyday lives. Hence, without studying how consumption affects individuals and groups, one can never truly say that we understand humans.

① 다양한 제품 개발로 소비 활동이 촉진될 수 있다.

② 개인의 선호에 따라 서로 다른 소비 양상이 나타난다.

③ 소비자는 자극적인 광고에 영향을 많이 받는 경향이 있다.

④ 인간을 이해하기 위해서는 소비에 대한 연구가 반드시 필요하다.

⑤ 크리스마스와 같은 종교적인 휴일에는 더 많은 소비가 발생한다.

29

Complications arise when an artist attempts to illustrate a story from outside his or her realm of cultural experience. If the artist has little or no background in a particular area and is unwilling or unable to do thorough research, he or she is in danger of misrepresenting the story through illustrations, especially if an attempt is made to imitate "native" styles. It is very difficult for an outsider to extract details effectively without an understanding of the overall context from which they come. That is not to say it can't be done. Ed Young, for example, is known for his attention to authentic detail in the artwork he creates for traditional stories from other cultures. In Kimiko Kajikawa's *Tsunami!*, for example, Young accurately depicts the clothing, hairstyles, and architecture characteristic of mid-nineteenth-century Japan.

① 예술작품에 관해서는 문화 간의 우열을 가리는 것이 무의미하다.

② 삽화는 독자가 이야기의 세부내용을 이해하는데 많은 도움을 준다.

③ 타문화를 제대로 이해하려면 그 문화를 모방하려는 노력이 필요하다.

④ 배경지식이 부족하면 타문화권 이야기의 삽화를 정확하게 그리기 어렵다.

⑤ 타문화를 무분별하게 받아들이면 자국 문화에 부정적인 결과가 초래된다.

[30~31] 다음 글의 주제로 가장 적절한 것을 고르시오.

30

Sports marketing is not new. The first known athletic event that required paid admission was a baseball game in Long Island, New York, in 1858, where spectators were charged 50 cents. Sports organizers soon realized the financial potential of sporting events and professional athletes. Golfer Gene Sarazen signed an endorsement deal with Wilson Sporting Goods in 1923. The original agreement was for $6,000 a year plus an equal amount for travel expenses. In 1949 Babe Didrikson Zaharias signed the first significant female endorsement with Wilson Sporting Goods for $100,000 a year. Coca-Cola partnered with the Summer Olympics in 1928 and remains a sponsor to this day. The first pay-per-view athletic event was

a boxing match, the "Thrilla in Manila," with Muhammad Ali taking on Joe Frazier in the Philippines in 1975. It was broadcast to 276 closed-circuit locations. Capitalizing on the popularity of sports, ESPN made its debut in 1979, offering advertisers a new way to reach their target markets. Today many high schools and colleges offer sports marketing programs.

① the emergence and expansion of sports marketing

② effective budgeting for sports marketing activities

③ social changes affecting sports marketing

④ misconceptions about sports marketing

⑤ the dark side of sports sponsorship

31

At the start of the century, interest in advertising was growing and it was not only manufacturers who could see its potential. Politicians also became interested when they realized that "how to sell products" could be applied to sell their own ideas. This was particularly evident during World War I when propaganda campaigns were used as tools to encourage people to continue fighting. For example,

the British and Americans spread rumors about the appalling behavior of the Germans, such as making soap out of enemy soldiers. This was done so that people would feel that they could not possibly let such a horrible nation win the war and hence think that it was worth continuing to fight. Many so-called "atrocity stories" were used, and while some did contain an element of truth, many were invented solely for the benefit of the British and American governments. Nevertheless, they appeared to be effective in selling political agendas to the people.

*atrocity : 잔학 (행위)

① different methods of advertising in different cultures

② political and social conflicts caused by propaganda

③ increasing influence of propaganda on advertising

④ differences between advertising and propaganda

⑤ the application of advertising to political matters

32 Romain Rolland에 관한 다음 글의 내용과 일치하지 <u>않는</u> 것은?

Romain Rolland was a French dramatist, novelist, and art historian who was awarded the Nobel Prize for Literature in 1915 as a tribute to the lofty idealism of his literary production. He was born at Clamecy, Nièvre in 1866. An excellent student, he entered the École Normale Supérieure, where he studied philosophy before gravitating toward the arts and music. After graduation in 1889, he spent several years in Italy studying the Italian masterpieces of the Renaissance. Upon his return to France, Rolland earned a doctorate in the study of early European opera in 1895. That same year, he earned a master's degree for a thesis on Italian oil paintings of the 16th century. He then taught at the university level until 1912, when he resigned his position to turn his full attention to writing. His greatest literary contributions came in the form of plays. He firmly believed that theater should be physically and intellectually welcoming to the masses. He favored plays that reminded audiences of France's revolutionary history.

① 프랑스인으로서 1915년에 노벨문학상을 수상했다.

② École Normale Supérieure에서 철학을 공부했다.

③ 16세기 이탈리아 유화에 관한 논문으로 박사학위를 받았다.

④ 저술 활동에 전념하기 위해 가르치는 일을 그만두었다.

⑤ 관객들에게 프랑스의 혁명 역사를 상기시키는 희곡을 선호했다.

33 다음 도표의 내용과 일치하지 <u>않는</u> 것은?

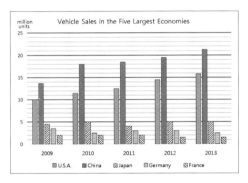

The above graph shows the number of vehicles sold in each of the five largest economies between the years of 2009 and 2013. ① Each year during the 5-year period China showed the largest vehicle sales, consistently followed by the U.S.A. ② The number of vehicles sold in China continued to increase from year to year with close to 14 million units sold in 2009 and over 21 million units sold in 2013. ③ The gap in the numbers of vehicles sold in China and the U.S.A. was more than 3 million units in 2009 and over 5 million units in 2013. ④ While the third most vehicles were sold in Japan each year, the number of vehicles sold there in 2013 was a third of what was sold in China in the same year. ⑤ Each year the fourth most vehicles were sold in Germany, with the number of vehicles sold in the country failing to reach 4 million units in any of the 5 years, and France had the smallest vehicle sales each year.

[34~35] 주어진 글 다음에 이어질 글의 순서로 가장 적절한 것을 고르시오.

34

You see your friend running towards you. As he approaches he gets larger and larger. However, you know your friend is coming closer, not actually growing.

(A) Likewise, as a car passes you and moves off into the distance, it appears to get smaller. However, it is known that perception of size does not vary as much as would be expected from the change in size of the retinal image.

(B) This is because you have knowledge in your memory about the size of people and know that people do not rapidly change size. In fact, the retinal

2018 기출문제

image is expanding, and the rate of expansion is an indication of how fast something, in this case your friend, is approaching.

(C) These are the examples of *perceptual constancy*. Basically we experience a car moving away, or a person coming nearer. We do not concern ourselves with the changing size; we interpret the information as giving movement in the depth plane.

*retinal : 망막의

① (A) − (C) − (B)

② (B) − (A) − (C)

③ (B) − (C) − (A)

④ (C) − (A) − (B)

⑤ (C) − (B) − (A)

35

One of the most valuable outcomes from coaching people is that you also develop yourself in the process of coaching. It is the genuine passion and intention to grow others that spurs us on to transform ourselves.

(A) This cycle of learning returns over and over again throughout the entire coaching relationship. As we coach more people, we inculcate knowledge,

skills, and competencies in coaching that will help us in many aspects of our professional and personal lives.

(B) During the coaching session, we gain hands-on experience and practice coaching skills and techniques. After coaching, we reflect on what happened during the dialogue and what went well, what didn't, and how we can do better next time.

(C) To develop others, we have to first develop ourselves. And to continuously change others, we can't help but continuously transform ourselves. Before we coach, we learn, we prepare, and we reflect on how we can be an effective coach. [3점]

*inculcate : 되풀이하여 가르치다

① (A) − (C) − (B)

② (B) − (A) − (C)

③ (B) − (C) − (A)

④ (C) − (A) − (B)

⑤ (C) − (B) − (A)

36 (A), (B), (C)의 각 네모 안에서 문맥에 맞는 표현으로 가장 적절한 것은? [3점]

In the past, economy and thrift were the order of the day. Nothing was thrown away no matter how

little value it seemed to have. Every purchased product was important and every dollar was worth saving. Today, products are less (A) durable / fragile and are meant to be disposed of. Cigarette lighters, contact lenses, and even watches and cameras have become throwaways. Similarly, clothing and accessories are perishables in the sense that once they are out of style their usefulness (B) expires / prevails. In regard to the new shopping trend this means that consumers, young and old, are becoming more used to living in a world where things are disposed of quickly and readily, and new things are bought to replace them. As the pace of life increases steadily there is more demand for more throwaway products. Our emotional (C) attachment / aversion to personal products is becoming less over time and that means that there is ever more demand for more products.

	(A)	(B)	(C)
①	durable	expires	attachment
②	durable	prevails	attachment
③	durable	expires	aversion
④	fragile	expires	attachment
⑤	fragile	prevails	aversion

37 다음 글의 내용을 한 문장으로 요약하고자 한다. 빈칸 (A)와 (B)에 들어갈 말로 가장 적절한 것은?

In a psychological study, researchers gave questionnaires to two groups of students and asked them to respond by email. All the questions had to do with some mundane task, such as opening a bank account. But the two groups were given different instructions for answering the questions. The students in the first group were to write about what the activity implied about some intangible information such as personal traits — what kind of person has a bank account, for example. The second group wrote simply about the specific steps in the process — speaking to a bank teller, filling out forms, making an initial deposit, and so forth. There proved to be a significant difference between the response times of the two groups. The students in the first group tended to delay — in fact, some never completed the task at all. By contrast, the students in the second group, who were focused on the how, when, and where of the task, completed the task sooner than the first group.

*mundane : 일상적인

In the study, the first group of students, who were given a task requiring thinking in more ___(A)___ terms, turned out to ___(B)___ their answers to a greater extent than the other group of students.

	(A)		(B)
①	abstract	……	postpone
②	abstract	……	emphasize
③	quantitative	……	postpone
④	practical	……	exaggerate
⑤	practical	……	emphasize

[38~39] 다음 글을 읽고, 물음에 답하시오.

Ecological approaches to human health consider human beings as part of a broader ecosystem. Disease ecologists focus on interactions between humans and the environments in which they live, helping to describe and explain patterns of health and disease across space. Humans interact with their environment in many ways that make them more or less susceptible to ill-health. Staying out too long in cold weather can lead to hypothermia, a condition of dangerously low body temperature, or too much exposure to the sun may promote the development of skin cancer, for instance. ___(A)___, not all connections are this direct. One of the main ways in which disease ecology has been useful in explaining disease patterns is by considering how characteristics of the environment influence where disease-causing organisms, or the vectors that carry them, can live. ___(B)___, many diseases are restricted to tropical climates where year-round warm temperatures allow vectors such as mosquitoes to thrive. Warm temperatures can also speed up the reproduction rates of micro-organisms such as viruses and bacteria, as well as the invertebrates that transmit them, leading to more rapid transmission of disease among humans. Analyzing relationships between people and infectious agents of disease was one of the first focuses of disease ecologists and remains a fundamental part of disease ecology today.

*vector : (병균의) 매개 곤충
**invertebrate : 무척추 동물

38 윗글의 제목으로 가장 적절한 것은?

① Effective Hygiene Practices to Combat Diseases
② The Origin of Disease Ecology as a Scientific Field
③ The Evolution of Typical Disease-Causing Organisms
④ Effects of Environmental Change on the Spread of Diseases
⑤ Disease Ecologists' Concerns: Environment and Human Diseases

39 윗글의 빈칸 (A), (B)에 들어갈 말로 가장 적절한 것은?

	(A)	(B)
①	However	······ As a result
②	However	······ For example
③	Furthermore	······ As a result
④	In other words	······ Similarly
⑤	In other words	······ For example

[40~41] 다음 글을 읽고, 물음에 답하시오.

Machu Picchu is surrounded by the Urubamba River located 2,000 feet below the citadel. This river was considered sacred to the Inca partly because nature was sacred to them but also because of the advantages it brought. It curves around the mountain in which Machu Picchu is located and some of the agricultural terraces extend all the way down to the river. The river cannot be navigated at the location of Machu Picchu, but further down it is possible to use boats to navigate to the Amazon River and all the way to the Atlantic Ocean and move people and goods. This may have been purposeful to avoid having people navigate directly to Machu Picchu but still offer a relatively close route of   (A)   .

Proximity to the rainforest was certainly another advantage of the geography of Machu Picchu. The rainforest was the only source of rare products that were prized by the Incas such as colorful bird feathers, butterflies, coca leaves, exotic fruits and vegetables and healing herbs among other products. The Inca would exchange these products with tribes from the rainforest for things that they did not have such as potatoes, guinea pigs, precious stones, quinoa, and gold and use them for religious ceremonies. When building Machu Picchu, the Inca must have considered the benefits from being so close to the rainforest as a(n)   (B)   source.

*citadel : 요새

40 윗글이 시사하는 바로 가장 적절한 것은?

① With no written language, the Inca left no record of how Machu Picchu was built.

② In building Machu Picchu, the Inca took into account their surrounding geography.

③ Conservation efforts are necessary for the future of Machu Picchu's tourism industry.

④ Machu Picchu is set in a rainforest providing a stable habitat for some endangered species.

⑤ The lack of direct route from the Atlantic Ocean delayed the development of Incan civilization.

2018 기출문제

41 윗글의 빈칸 (A), (B)에 들어갈 말로 가장 적절한 것은?

	(A)	(B)
①	invasion	…… trading
②	invasion	…… energy
③	tourism	…… labor
④	transportation	…… trading
⑤	transportation	…… labor

[42~43] 다음 글을 읽고, 물음에 답하시오.

During World War II, the composer Dmitry Shostakovich and several of his colleagues were called into a meeting with the Russian ruler Joseph Stalin, who had commissioned them to write a new national anthem. Shostakovich heard meetings with Stalin were (A) fascinating / terrifying ; one misstep could lead you into a very dark alley. He would stare you down until you felt your throat tighten. And, as meetings with Stalin often did, this one took a bad turn: The ruler began to criticize one of the composers for his poor arrangement of his anthem. Scared silly, the man admitted he had used an arranger who had done a bad job. Here he was digging several graves: Clearly the poor arranger could be called to task. The composer was responsible for the (B) hire / dismissal , and he, too, could pay for the mistake. And what of the other composers, including Shostakovich?

Stalin could be relentless once he smelled fear.

Shostakovich had heard enough: It was foolish, he said, to blame the arranger, who was mostly following orders. He then subtly redirected the conversation to a different subject — whether a composer should do his own orchestrations. What did Stalin think on the matter? Always eager to prove his expertise, he swallowed the bait. The dangerous moment passed.

Shostakovich maintained his presence of mind in several ways. First, instead of letting Stalin intimidate him, he forced himself to see the man as he was: short, fat, ugly, unimaginative. So the dictator's famous piercing gaze was just a trick, a sign of his own (C) creativity / insecurity . Second, Shostakovich faced up to Stalin, talking to him normally and straightforwardly. By his actions and tone of voice, the composer showed that he was not intimidated.

42 (A), (B), (C)의 각 네모 안에서 문맥에 맞는 표현으로 가장 적절한 것은? [3점]

	(A)	(B)	(C)
①	fascinating	…… hire	…… creativity
②	fascinating	…… dismissal	…… insecurity
③	terrifying	…… hire	…… insecurity
④	terrifying	…… dismissal	…… insecurity
⑤	terrifying	…… hire	…… creativity

43 윗글의 내용으로 적절하지 <u>않은</u> 것은?

① Shostakovich와 그의 동료들은 Stalin으로 부터 국가를 작곡하라는 의뢰를 받았다.

② Stalin은 국가를 잘 편곡하지 못한 작곡자 중 한 명을 비난했다.

③ Shostakovich는 지시를 따른 편곡자를 나무라는 것은 어리석은 일이라고 말했다.

④ Stalin은 자신이 전문적 지식을 지녔음을 입증하는 것을 원하지 않았다.

⑤ Shostakovich는 Stalin을 두려워하지 않는다는 것을 보여줬다.

[44~45] 다음 글을 읽고, 물음에 답하시오.

(A)

When Don was 25, he went backpacking around South East Asia. For three of those weeks, he traveled around Indonesia, including a stop in a lovely town called Bukittinggi. At his guesthouse, he met a nice fellow from Sweden, Stephen, who recommended that (a) <u>he</u> explore a nearby lake atop a long inactive volcano.

(B)

In starting (b) <u>his</u> trek around the lake, Don knew that the last bus down the mountain left at 5:00p.m., so he had to be sure to be back at the bus stop by then. As it was 1:00p.m., he figured he had loads of time to make it all the way around the lake and back in time to catch the last bus down the mountain. It was an amazing hike. However, at about 4:00p.m. he realized that (c) <u>he</u> was nowhere near half-way around the lake.

(C)

He decided to race back the way he came. As he neared the bus stop, he saw the last bus driving away without (d) <u>him</u>. Breathless, he had no choice but to start walking down the mountain and hope that some kind person would pick him up. He walked for hours before any vehicles even came by. Fortunately, eventually, a wonderful Indonesian gentleman stopped to help. He was very sympathetic to the situation and offered Don a ride all the way back to his guesthouse. Don was more grateful than words could express.

(D)

Following (e) <u>his</u> advice, Don found a bus that would take him up there. It turned out to be not so close, but rather a four-hour ride up steep, windy, and rather dangerous roads. It was worth it, though, because the view was unbelievable at the top. There was an absolutely majestic lake at the top of the mountain where the mouth of the volcano once was. It was surrounded by a lovely walking path, which according to Stephen, would take about two hours to walk around.

44 주어진 글 (A)에 이어질 내용을 순서에 맞게 배열한 것으로 가장 적절한 것은?

① (B) − (D) − (C)

② (C) − (B) − (D)

③ (C) − (D) − (B)

④ (D) − (B) − (C)

⑤ (D) − (C) − (B)

45 밑줄 친 (a)~(e) 중에서 가리키는 대상이 나머지 넷과 <u>다른</u> 것은?

① (a)　　　　　② (b)

③ (c)　　　　　④ (d)

⑤ (e)

2025

사관학교

10개년 영어

2017학년도 기출문제

영어영역(공통)

제2교시 영어영역(공통)

▶ 정답 및 해설 391p

01 Based on the following dialogue, which one is NOT true? [2점]

> Rachel : Hello, Dave. Welcome to the gym. Are you ready to start exercising?
> Dave : Good morning, Rachel. Actually, before we start, do you have any nutritional advice that might help me get in shape?
> Rachel : Okay. Did you drink plenty of fluids this morning?
> Dave : I sure did. You told me how important hydration is during your last lesson.
> Rachel : Great! Next up, are you eating a balanced diet? It should include grains, like bread or rice, healthy fats and oils, and plenty of fruits and vegetables.
> Dave : Oh, I love rice! Wow, I didn't realize that some fats are good for our bodies!
> Rachel : Of course! Healthy fats can be found in fish and are essential to a balanced diet. Also, rice is a great source of energy, but it contains many calories. Try replacing a little bit of rice with some fish in the future.

① Rachel is a gym instructor.
② Dave is well-hydrated.
③ A balanced diet should contain several types of food.
④ Some fats are important to a healthy diet.
⑤ Dave should eat more rice.

02 Which is the best sequence of answers for the blanks? [2점]

> Ben : Hello, ma'am. You look lost. Could I help you?
> Susan : Oh, yes. Thank you so much! This is my first time in New York City and I don't have a clue where I'm going.
> Ben : It's my pleasure. Well, luckily for you, there's a great tourist site just around that corner. Have you visited the Empire State Building yet? _____
> Susan : Not yet, but I certainly plan to! Where else should I visit?
> Ben : If you love sports, then head up 5th Avenue toward the Yankees store on 36th Street. _____

Susan : Great! I also love reading. Could you recommend somewhere, please?

Ben : Actually, the New York Public Library is just past there, on 42nd Street. _____

Susan : Oh, I should hurry. Thank you so much for all of your advice!

──〈보기〉──

a. People buy baseball souvenirs there.

b. Just be aware that it closes at 6 p.m.

c. It was one of the first major skyscrapers.

d. It's a well-known hair salon.

① a − b − d   ② b − c − d

③ c − a − b   ④ c − b − a

⑤ d − c −a

03 Where is the dialogue most likely taking place? [2점]

Laura : Wow, it's beautiful out here! Oh, those look really fresh; I'd love to get some for myself! Where did you find them?

Steven : Well, that depends. Are you talking about the strawberries or the appels?

Laura : How about both? Strawberries are definitely

my favorite fruit, but I also enjoy baking apple pie. My grandmother's recipe is famous in my hometown.

Steven : Okay! Do you promise to share some pie with me if I help you pick some?

Laura : Sure thing. Where did you get them and how much were they, anyway?

Steven : Well, the strawberries cost $1 per kilogram and the plot is over there by the stream; the apples cost $2 per kilogram and they can be found in the southern field. Let's go!

① in a florist's

② in an orchard

③ in a greenhouse

④ in a grocery store

⑤ in a fruit processing plant

04 Based on the following dialogue, which one is true? [2점]

[Telephone rings.]

Sam : Good morning. You've reached the customer service department of Big Electronics. This is Sam speaking. How may I help you?

Joe : Hi, I'm Joe Lee. I recently bought one of your cellphones and the screen is faulty.

Sam : I'm sorry, Sir. Can you tell me the date and location of the purchase, please?

Joe : Of course. I bought it two weeks ago, on the 3rd of July. The location was one of your LA stores, the large one on San Pedro Street.

Sam : Okay, Sir. Your phone is still within its warranty. You can choose to send your device to the manufacturer and receive a replacement. Or, one of our technicians can repair it for you if you'd prefer to visit a branch.

Joe : Well, I'd like it fixed quickly. I guess I can drop by the San Pedro store at 10 a.m.

Sam : I see, Sir. I'll call ahead and inform them that you'll be arriving in about an hour.

① Joe works at an electronics store.

② The phone won't turn on.

③ The phone's warranty has expired.

④ Joe prefers his phone to be replaced.

⑤ Joe wants to visit the store in the morning.

05 Choose the best answer for the blank. [3점]

Emma : Hi, Tom. You're in advertising, right? I'd be grateful if you could offer me some expert marketing advice.

Tom : Sure, Emma. I'd love to help! What kind of business is it?

Emma : It's a take-out chicken place. I know my recipe is delicious, but there's just so much competition these days. Plus, TV advertising is very costly.

Tom : Okay. Have you considered online marketing? It's a lot cheaper.

Emma : Really? But I can't use computers very well. I don't even have a blog!

Tom : It's okay. It's a simple strategy that's very effective. You can create a business page on social media sites and offer discounts to subscribers. It's proven way for businesses to become well-known quickly.

Emma : Wow! I really appreciate your advice. _____

① It sounds like a great idea! Could you help me set it up, please?

② However, I'm really worried about the high cost.

③ Okay. I'll give it a shot. My blog is linked to my business page.

④ I think I'd perfer to advertise on television, however. The prices are cheaper.

⑤ But I'm worried if this strategy is really effective. You made it sound too risky.

06 Choose the sentence that best describes the situation. [2점]

> Julia : Hi, Diana. Thanks for responding to my ad.
>
> Diana : Oh, no problem. I just hope that I'm making a good first impression!
>
> Julia : You certainly are. However, I just need to know a few things if we're to live together. First of all, can you cook and do you own any pets?
>
> Diana : Yes, I can. I try to live healthily. And I do have a cat, but she's quiet, well-trained and very affectionate.
>
> Julia : That sounds fine. I don't have any pets, but I prefer cats over dogs. Next, are you an organized person? I must admit that cleanliness is really important to me.
>
> Diana : Me too. I absolutely hate mess!

① Julia wants Diana's advice about raising a pet.

② Julia is searching for a roommate.

③ Julia and Diana are talking about their hobbies.

④ Diana is trying to make a new friend.

⑤ Diana is being interviewed for a job.

07 밑줄 친 부분이 가리키는 대상이 나머지 넷과 다른 것은? [2점]

J. R. Kline liked to tell stories of other mathematicians. This one about Norbert Wiener was a favorite: One summer, the Klines and the Wieners had adjacent cottages on a lake in New Hampshire. Wiener was in the habit of swimming from ① his dock to a small island in the middle of the lake. On these swims, Kline would keep Wiener company by paddling a rowboat alongside, and they would carry on a conversation while Wiener was steadfastly progressing towards ② his goal. Wiener always tried to keep control of the conversation, even as ③ he was puffing and gasping towards the small land mass. On one such day, near the end of the swim, ④ he bleated out, "Kline, who are the five greatest living mathematicians?" Quietly, Kline replied, "That is an interesting question. Let's see." ⑤ He quickly ticked off four names (none of them "Wiener"). "Yes, yes, go on," spluttered Wiener. With delicate humor, Kline avoided mentioning the name of the fifth one.

[08~09] 다음 글에서 전체 흐름과 관계 <u>없는</u> 문장을 고르시오.

08 Scientific research clearly shows that a sustained high level of cortisol, triggered by chronic stress, has negative effects on long-term health. ① Among these effects is an increase in appetite and cravings for certain foods. ② Because one of the roles of cortisol is to encourage the body to refuel itself after responding to a stressor, an elevated cortisol level keeps your appetite high. ③ In addition, the type of fat that accumulates as a result of this stress-induced appetite will typically locate itself in the abdominal region to be ready for the next stress response. ④ Exercise increases cortisol levels, but this short-term increase is good for immune function, memory, and weight loss. ⑤ The major problem with abdominal fat is that his type of fat is also highly associated with the development of heart disease, diabetes, and cancer. [2점]

*cortisol : 부신피질에서 생성되는 스테로이드 호르몬

09 One study evaluated the efficacy of daily multivitamin to prevent cognitive decline among 5,947 elderly males. ① After 12 years of follow-up, there were no differences between the multivitamin and placebo groups in overall cognitive performance or verbal memory. ② The researchers concluded that the use of a multivitamin supplement in a well-nourished elderly population did not prevent cognitive decline. ③ This conclusion was further supported by a review of some other studies that evaluated supplementation with multivitamins, B vitamins, vitamins E, C and omega-3 fatty acids, in persons with mild cognitive impairment or mild to moderate dementia. ④ While all vitamins are required for optimal health and brain function, there are a few that stand out above the rest as being essential for a healthy brain. ⑤ None of the supplements improved cognitive function, indicating that multivitamin intake has no effect on the treatment of dementia. [2점]

*dementia : 치매

10 다음 글이 시사하는 바로 가장 적절한 것은?
[2점]

In an experiment, two groups of mice were conditioned to feel fear in a certain location, and later the researchers put them back in that location to see if the mice showed fear. Interestingly, the mice whose eating schedule was shifted to the normal sleeping time felt fear less often in the fearful situation than their normal-schedule peers, suggesting the odd eating and sleeping schedule affected the animals' memory of scary situations. "The misaligned mice showed severe deficits in their recall of the training that they received," Colwell

said. His research team previously found that jet lag has similar effects on memory in both human and mouse studies. The researches also measured the strengthening of neural connections — a measure of learning in the brain. Not surprisingly, they found that the mice that ate during normal sleeping periods learned less quickly than the mice that ate at normal mealtimes.

① 양질의 음식 섭취는 학습 능력을 강화시켜 준다.

② 음식 섭취를 늘리는 것은 학습 능력 향상에 도움이 되지 않는다.

③ 정상적인 수면 시간에 음식을 먹는 것은 인지 능력을 약화시킬 수 있다.

④ 시차증을 쉽게 극복하려면 정상적인 수면 시간에 잠을 자야 한다.

⑤ 규칙적인 식사 습관이 규칙적인 수면 습관으로 이어질 수 있다.

[11~12] 다음 글의 밑줄 친 부분 중, 어법상 틀린 것을 고르시오.

11 Before jeans were pants, *jean* was a cotton cloth used for making sturdy work clothes. The textile was produced in Genoa, Italy, ① which French weavers called *Genes*, the origin of our word "jeans." The origin of blue jeans, though, ② is really the story of Levi Strauss, an American immigrant tailor. When he arrived in San Francisco during the gold rush in the 1850s, he sold canvas for tents and covered wagons. A clever observe, he realized that miners went through trousers ③ quickly, so Strauss stitched some of his canvas into pants. Though heavy and stiff, the pants held up so well ④ that Strauss was in demand as a tailor. In the 1860s, he replaced canvas with denim. And Strauss discovered that dying neutral-colored denim pants dark blue to minimize soil stains greatly ⑤ increasing their popularity. [2점]

12 New experiences trigger change only if they cause us ① to question our beliefs. Remember, whenever we believe something, we no longer question it in any way. The moment we begin to honestly question our beliefs, we no longer feel absolutely certain about ② them. We are beginning to shake the reference legs of our cognitive tables, and as a result start to lose our feeling of absolute certainty. Have you ever doubted your ability to do something? How did you do it? You probably asked ③ yourself some poor questions like "What if it doesn't work out?" But questions can obviously be tremendously empowering if we use them to examine the validity of beliefs we may have just blindly accepted. In fact, many of our beliefs ④ supported by information we've received from others that we failed to question at the time. If we scrutinize them, we may find that ⑤ what we've unconsciously believed for years may be based on a false set of presuppositions. [3점]

[13~14] (A), (B), (C)의 각 네모 안에서 어법에 맞는 표현으로 가장 적절한 것을 고르시오.

	(A)	(B)	(C)
①	how	do	Understanding
②	how	are	Understanding
③	how	do	Understand
④	what	do	Understanding
⑤	what	are	Understand

13

Communication in its broadest sense occurs both verbally (via language) and nonverbally. Despite the importance of nonverbal behaviors, however, we often take them for granted. Although we receive no formal training in (A) how / what to send or receive nonverbal messages and signals, by adulthood we have become so skilled at it that we do so unconsciously and automatically. Nonverbal behaviors are just as much a language as any other. Just as verbal languages differ from culture to culture, so (B) do / are nonverbal languages. Because we are aware of the differences between verbal languages, we do not hesitate to use dictionaries and other resources to help us understand different languages. But when it comes to nonverbal language, we often mistakenly assume that our systems of communicating nonverbally are all the same. (C) Understanding / Understand cultural differences in nonverbal behavior is a step in the process of truly appreciating cultural differences in communication. [2점]

14

In the developed world the widespread use of water-based toilets form the mid-nineteenth century meant that extensive, connected systems of sewage pipes (A) sending / sent the outflow into sewage processing plants were built in cities. These systems helped solve the cholera outbreaks that devastated so many urban populations in the growing industrial-commercial cities of the early nineteenth century, (B) where / which the untreated human waste was just dumped into the local rivers, contaminating the ground water and local water supplies. Although it took time to establish the link between out breaks of disease and the faecal-contaminated water supplies, most cities in the developed world created extensive water supply systems from reservoirs and (C) build / built separate sewer systems to take the flow from the increasing numbers of toilets in buildings, which led to the development of

sewage treatment systems to filter out the harmful material. [3점]

*faecal : 배설물의

	(A)	(B)	(C)
①	sending	where	built
②	sending	where	build
③	sent	which	built
④	sent	which	build
⑤	sent	where	built

[15~18] 다음 글을 읽고, 빈칸에 들어갈 말로 가장 적절한 것을 고르시오.

15

The producers of manufactured foods have an advantage over farmers because they buy the farm output and have flexibility over what ingredients to use and where to source them. For example, the manufactured food requires a sweetener, but not necessarily sugar derived from the sugarcane plant. It requires oil, yet not necessarily oil from corn. It requires a starch, but that could be derived from a potato or wheat or a number of other grains. The production of potato chips provides a good example of this _____ effect : Producers can fry the chips in whatever oil is cheapest at the moment of production. This illustrates why farmers are often at a disadvangaged position within the agrofood system. [2점]

① integration　② substitution
③ conservation　④ simplification
⑤ overconsumption

16

Theodore Berger has achieved successes with _____ by using implanted chips to replace damaged parts of the hippocampus in rats. Berger and his team at the University of Southern California have succeeded in recording and transforming into computer code memories that have been stored for an extended period of time in the hippocampus of these animals. They had the rats perform a memory task. Then, they downloaded and transformed the memory of that task into digital code. Afterwards, they removed the section of the rats' hippocampus that carried these memories and replaced that bit of the brain with a special computer chip, onto which they reloaded the artificially stored memories. They found that the rats' memories could be fully restored using this technique. [2점]

*hippocampus : (뇌의) 해마상(狀) 융기

① long−term memory regeneration
② memory capacity increase
③ the selective distortion of memory
④ the deletion of traumatic memories
⑤ memory transfer speed enhancement

17

There are at least two reasons why a subjective sense of "foreignness" may implicitly suggest the possibility of spreading disease. First, historically, contact with exotic peoples increased exposure to exotic germs, which tend to be especially contagious when introduced to the local population. Secondly, outsiders are often ignorant of local behavioral norms that serve as barriers to germ transmission (e.g., norms pertaining to hygiene, food-preparation); as a consequence, they may be more likely to violate these norms, thereby increasing the danger of germ transmission within the local population. Thus, in addition to other risks suggested by outgroup status, people perceived to be subjectively foreign are likely to be implicitly judged _____ . [2점]

① to isolate a local population

② to pose the threat of infection

③ to transmit novel technologies

④ to harm a local economy

⑤ to meet local hygiene standards

18

When Josephine Baker moved to Paris, in 1925, as part of an all-black revue, her exoticism made her an overnight sensation. But Baker sensed that the French's interest in her would quickly pass to someone else. To seduce them for good, she learned French and began to sing in it. She started dressing and acting as a stylish French lady, as if to say that she preferred the French way of life to the American. Countries are like people: they feel threatened by other customs. It is often quite seductive to a people to see an outsider adopting their ways. Benjamin Disraeli was born and lived all his life in England, but he was Jewish by birth, and had exotic features; the provincial English considered him an outsider. Yet he was more English in his manners and tastes than many an Englishman, and this was part of his charm, which he proved by becoming the leader of the Conservative Party. Should you be an outsider, turn it to your advantage in such a way as to show the group _____ . [3점]

*revue : 익살극 **exoticism : 이국정서

① how deeply you prefer their tastes and customs to your own

② that you don't complain about how misunderstood you are

③ that you have distinct tastes, opinions, and experiences

④ how hard you try to do noble and charitable deeds

⑤ that you are willing to disclose your own identity

19 다음 글에서 필자가 주장하는 바로 가장 적절한 것은? [2점]

Every member of the family is an individual, as well as a part of the whole family. As a parent, you have to balance your role as a caregiver with your needs as an individual. If you sacrifice all of your time and energy to your family without finding a way to socialize with adults, to feel intellectually stimulated, or to maintain a healthy body and mind, the whole family will suffer. Remember: You're modeling adulthood for your children — don't create a martyr model of parenthood. Being an empty, self-sacrificing shell of a person is hardly the role model you want them to see. Of course, it's tough, if not impossible, to satisfy all of these needs to the fullest every single day. Parenting usually involves some level of self-sacrifice, but you need to strive for a healthy balance that works for you and your family.

*martyr : 순교자

① 부모와 자녀는 서로의 만족을 위해 함께 애써야 한다.
② 부모는 어른의 기준으로 자녀를 평가하지 말아야 한다.
③ 부모는 자녀 양육과 자신의 삶 사이에서 균형을 잡아야 한다.
④ 부모는 주위에서 자녀에게 좋은 역할 모델을 찾아 주어야 한다.
⑤ 부모는 자녀에게 권리에는 책임이 따른다는 것을 가르쳐야 한다.

[20~21] 다음 글의 빈칸 (A), (B)에 들어갈 말로 갖아 적절한 것을 고르시오.

20

The very systematicity that allows us to comprehend one aspect of a concept in terms of another (e.g., comprehending an aspect of arguing in terms of battle) will necessarily   (A)   other aspects of the concept. In allowing us to focus on one aspect of a concept (e.g., the battling aspects of arguing), a metaphorical concept can keep us from focusing on other aspects of the concept that are inconsistent with that metaphor. For example, in the midst of a heated argument, when we are intent on attacking our opponent's position and defending our own, we may lose sight of the cooperative aspects of arguing. Someone who is arguing with you can be viewed as giving you his or her time, a valuable commodity, in an effort to achieve mutual understanding. But when we are   (B)   the battle aspects, we often lose sight of the cooperative aspects. [2점]

	(A)	(B)
①	hide	indifferent to
②	reveal	engaged in
③	hide	preoccupied with
④	reveal	preoccupied with
⑤	affect	indifferent to

	(A)	(B)
①	On the other hand	therefore
②	On the other hand	for instance
③	In the same way	nevertheless
④	As a result	nevertheless
⑤	As a result	for instance

21

Your body image doesn't develop overnight. Rather, it is something that develops slowly over time, and many things influence it. For example, years of playing sports and being involved in athletic activities can help build a positive body image by giving a person confidence in his or her body and its strengths and abilities.   (A) , hearing one thoughtless or unkind comment about your body can have a long-lasting negative impact on your body image. Furthermore, body image continues to evolve and change throughout your whole life. Most people adjust their body images as they physically, mentally, and emotionally age and mature. You can have a negative body image at one time in your life and a positive body image at another time. Building a positive body image,   (B) , is a never-ending process. [2점]

[22~23] 다음 글의 밑줄 친 부분 중, 문맥상 낱말의 쓰임이 적절하지 <u>않은</u> 것을 고르시오.

22

In November 2007, a team of researchers from the National Institute of Mental Health and McGill University announced that they had ① <u>uncovered</u> the specific deficits of the ADHD brain. The disorder turns out to be largely a developmental problem; often, the brains of children with ADHD develop at a significantly ② <u>slower</u> pace than normal. This lag was most obvious in the prefrontal cortex, which meant that these children literally lacked the mental muscles needed to resist tempting stimuli. The good news, however, is that the brain almost always ③ <u>recovers</u> from its slow start. By the end of adolescence, the frontal lobes in these children reached normal size. It's not a coincidence that their behavioral problems began to ④ <u>emerge</u> at about the same time. The children who had had the developmental lag were finally able to ⑤ <u>counter</u> their urges and compulsions. They could look at the tempting marshmallow and decide that it was better to wait. [2점]

*prefrontal cortex : (뇌의) 전전두엽 피질
**frontal lobes : 전두엽

23 It has been said that the clothes make the man, and nowhere is this truer than in the military. A soldier's uniform ① <u>represents</u> everything from loyalty to title and rank. And as for camouflage, it can mean the difference between life and death —a point brought up by U.S. lawmakers as they prepared to pass a $106 billion emergency war-spending bill that will ② <u>fund</u>, among other things, some 70,000 new uniforms for troops in Afghanistan. Evidently, the country's muddy, mountainous terrain doesn't ③ <u>match</u> the "universal camouflage pattern" designed for dusty desert cities like Baghdad. The emergence of aerial and trench warfare during World War I gave rise to the strategy — and art — of camouflaged battle dress, resulting in a fruitful ④ <u>collaboration</u> among soldiers, artists and naturalists like Abbott Thayer, whose 1909 book *Concealing Coloration in the Animal Kingdom* became required reading for the U.S. Army's newly launched unit of camouflage designers. Now that troops had to avoid bombs and bullets from all directions, the traditional glorious uniform worn in an earlier era of warfare began to seem ⑤ <u>up-to-date</u>, if not downright dangerous. [3점]

*camouflage : 위장 **trench : 참호

[24~25] 다음 글의 제목으로 가장 적절한 것을 고르시오.

24 When it comes to happiness, comparisons are rarely, if ever, helpful. Happiness is a subjective phenomenon; it is experienced differently by everyone and it means different things to different people. As the saying goes, one man's meat is another man's poison — our needs and desires vary, so what makes one person happy might not have the same impact on the next person. Although most of us realize the disparity between our individual requirements, it is easy to fall into the trap of looking over the fence, seeing what the neighbors have and thinking that we need that too. Simply put, this is unhelpful and almost certainly a direct path to unhappiness. Research strongly indicates that those who are happiest appreciate what they have and focus less on what they don't have. Long-term happiness studies clearly purport that, rather than judging themselves in relation to others, happy people simply clarify what's important to them and then focus on achieving and fulfilling their priorities. [2점]

*purport : 주장하다

① Avoid the Trap of Self-satisfaction
② Subjectivity Comes from Objectivity
③ Happiness Is Tailored to Each Person
④ Assess Yourself Through the Eyes of Others
⑤ The More You Achieve, the Happier You Will Be

25

Many people understand that eating too much salt, a major source of sodium, is a significant cause of cardiovascular diseases including a stroke or heart attack. However, fewer people know that too much sodium intake may also be harmful to bones. The amount of calcium that your body loses via urination increases with the amount of salt you eat. Triggered by low blood calcium levels, cells called osteoclasts break down bone to release calcium into the blood, potentially causing bone mass reduction. So, a diet high in sodium could have an additional unwanted effect — the bone-thinning disease known as osteoporosis. A 2009 study on elderly women, for example, showed that the loss of hip bone density over two years was related to the 24-hour urinary sodium excretion at the start of the study, and that the connection with bone loss was as strong as that for calcium intake. Other studies have shown that reducing sodium intake helps maintain calcium balance, suggesting that eating less salt could slow the calcium loss from your bones that occurs with aging. [2점]

*urination : 배뇨(작용) **excretion : 배출

① Significant Impact of Aging on Bone Thinning

② Relationship Between Losing Weight and Bone Weakness

③ Overlooked Causes of Abnormal Urinary Sodium Excretion

④ Bone Weakening: Another Threat of Excessive Sodium Intake

⑤ Calcium Balance: A Newly Discovered Shortcut to a Healthy Heart

[26~27] 글의 흐름으로 보아, 주어진 문장이 들어가기에 가장 적절한 곳을 고르시오.

26

That let him loosen the reins of command; with actors like Max von Sydow, he could just suggest what he had in mind and watch as the great actor brought his ideas to life.

[2점]

Early in his career, the great Swedish film director Ingmar Bergman was often overwhelmed with frustration. (①) He had visions of the films he wanted to make, but the work of being a director was so demanding and the pressure so immense that he would scold his cast and crew, shouting orders and attacking them for not giving him what he wanted. (②) Some would stew with resentment at his dictatorial ways; others became obedient automatons. (③) With almost every new film, Bergman would have to start again with a new cast and crew, which only made things worse. (④) But eventually he put together a team of the finest camera operators, editors, art directors,

and actors in Sweden, people who shared his high standards and whom he trusted. (⑤) Greater control could now come from letting go.

27

> Yet nations tend to restrict the import of certain goods for a variety of reasons. [2점]

There are a growing number of companies, large and small, that are doing business with firms in other countries. Some companies sell to firms in foreign countries; others buy goods around the world to import into their countries. (①) Whether they buy or sell products across national borders, these businesses are all contributing to the volume of international trade that is fueling the global economy. (②) Theoretically, international trade is every bit as logical and worthwhile as interstate trade between, say, California and Washington. (③) For example, in the early 2000s, the United States restricted the import of Mexican fresh tomatoes because they were undercutting the price levels of domestic fresh tomatoes. (④) Despite such restrictions, international trade has increased almost steadily since World War II. (⑤) Many of the industrialized nations have signed trade agreements intended to eliminate problems in international business and to help less-developed nations participate in world trade.

[28~29] 다음 글의 요지로 가장 적절한 것을 고르시오.

28

> Listening and reading critically — that is, reacting with systematic evaluation to what you have heard and read — requires a set of skills and attitudes. These skills and attitudes are built around a series of related critical questions. While we will learn them one by one, our goal is to be able to use them together to identify the best decision available. We could have expressed them as a list of things you should do, but a system of questions is more consistent with the spirit of curiosity, wonder, and intellectual adventure essential to critical thinking. Thinking carefully is always an unfinished project, a story looking for an ending that will never arrive. Critical questions provide a stimulus and direction for critical thinking; they move us forward toward a continual, ongoing search for better opinions, decisions, or judgements. [2점]

① 비판적인 질문은 비판적인 사고를 하는 데 필요하다.

② 어려서부터 비판적인 사고력을 길러 주는 것이 중요하다.

③ 상대방의 비판을 무조건 수용하는 것은 바람직하지 않다.

④ 작가가 독자의 비판적인 질문을 예상하며 글을 쓸 필요는 없다.

⑤ 호기심을 자극하는 질문은 학생의 수업 참
여도를 높이는 데 효과적이다.

29

Spatial cognition is a fundamental design requirement for every mobile species with a fixed territory home base. And there is little doubt that it plays a central role in human thinking and reasoning. Indeed, the evidence for that centrality is all around us, in our language where spatial metaphors are used for many other domains and in the special role of place in memory. The idea that space is a fundamental intuition built into our nature goes back at least to Kant, and the idea that our perception of space is governed by cognitive universals informs much current cognitive science. But in some ways human spatial cognition is puzzling. First, it is unspectacular — we are not as a species, compared to bees or pigeons, bats or whales, particularly good at finding our way around. Second, human spatial cognition is obviously variable — hunters, sailors and taxi-drivers are in a different league from the ordinary city-dweller. This suggests that many aspects of effective spatial thinking depend on cultural factors, which in turn suggests limits to cognitive universals in this area. [3점]

① 언어와 공간의 개념은 인간의 삶에서 상호
작용한다.
② 인간의 공간적 사고에는 인지적 보편성의
한계가 있다.
③ 인간의 공간적 사고는 시대와 문화를 초월
하여 보편적이다.
④ 인간의 공간 인지 능력은 동물과 비교해서
뒤지지 않는다.
⑤ 인지과학은 공간 인지의 개념에 바탕을 두
어야 한다.

[30~31] 다음 글의 주제로 가장 적절한 것을 고르
시오.

30

inexperienced writers often make the mistake of thinking that they have a firmer grasp on their ideas than on their words. they frequently utter the complaint, "I know what I want to say; I just can't find the words for it." This claim is almost always untrue, not because beginning writers are deliberate liars but because they confuse their intuitive sense that they have something to say with the false sense that they already know precisely what that something is. When a writer is stuck for words, the problem is rarely a problem only of words. Inexperienced writers may think they need larger vocabularies when what they really

need are clearer ideas and intentions. Being stuck for words indicates that the thought one wants to convey is still vague, unformed, cloudy, and confused. Once you finally discover your concrete meaning, you will discover the proper words for expressing it at the same time. [2점]

① reasons why some writers are not truthful in their writings
② ways of training students how to develop ideas systematically
③ importance of a large vocabulary in making a piece of writing effective
④ beginning writer' mistake of confusing unclear ideas with a lack of words
⑤ difficulty of getting a clear idea without having enough words to express it

31

　The seemingly simple question of "what defines a sport?" has been the subject of argument and conversation for years, among professional and armchair athletes alike. There seems to be no doubt that vigorous and highly competitive activities such as baseball, football, and soccer are truly "sports," but when the subject of other activities such as darts, chess, and shuffleboard is brought up we find ourselves at the heart of

a controversy. If say, billiards, is not a sport, then what exactly is it? Those who would dispute that it is a sport first and foremost requires some form of physical exertion. More to the point, if a player does not break a sweat, what he or she plays is not a sport. Beyond that, more important criteria would be the need for decent hand-eye coordination and the ever-present possibility of sustaining injury. Billiards only fits one of those specifications (hand-eye coordination), so according to the doubters, it is not a real sport. [2점]

① leisure activities embedded in sports
② popularity of highly competitive activities
③ dispute over the defining criteria for sports
④ influence of sports on humans' mental health
⑤ characteristics that define billiards as a sprot

32 Andy Warhol에 관한 다음 글의 내용과 일치하지 <u>않는</u> 것은? [2점]

　In 1967, Andy Warhol was asked to lecture at various colleges. He hated to talk, particularly about his own art; "The less something has

to say," he felt, "the more perfect it is." But the money was good, so Warhol always found it hard to say no. His solution was simple: he asked an actor, Allen Midgette, to impersonate him. Midgette was dark-haired, tan, part Cherokee Indian. He did not resemble Warhol in the least. But Warhol and friends covered his face with powder, sprayed his brown hair silver, gave him dark glasses, and dressed him in Warhol's clothes. Since Midgette knew nothing about art, his answers to students' questions tended to be as short and enigmatic as Warhol's own. The impersonation worked. Warhol may have been an icon, but no one really knew him, and since he often wore dark glasses, even his face was unfamiliar any detail.

*enigmatic : 수수께끼 같은

① 자신의 예술에 대해 이야기하는 것을 싫어했다.

② 돈 때문에 강연 요청을 거절하기 힘들었다.

③ 자신을 전혀 닮지 않은 배우를 자신처럼 분장시켰다.

④ 예술에 조예가 깊은 사람을 골라 대신 강연하게 했다.

⑤ 짙은 색의 안경을 자주 썼기에 얼굴이 상세하게 알려지지 않았다.

33 다음 도표의 내용과 일치하지 <u>않는</u> 것은?

[2점]

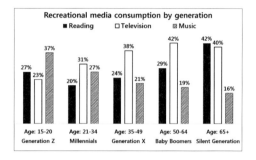

The graph above shows the generational participation percentages for three popular recreational media activities. ① Of the three leisure pursuits, music is the most popular spare-time activity among Generation Z, while reading is the most popular among the silent generation. ② The percentage of millennials who spend their spare time reading is visibly smaller than that of their counterparts from other generations. ③ Television is the most popular spare-time activity for all generations, except for Generation Z, less than a quarter of whom chose television as their favorite recreational activity. ④ Among Generation X, baby boomers, and the silent generation, music is less popular than reading. ⑤ The two generations that read more than the youngest are baby boomers and the silent generation.

[34~35] 주어진 글 다음에 이어질 글의 순서로 가장 적절한 것을 고르시오.

34

Twentieth-century medicine has been marked by the emergence of medical specialties and the focus on an organ systems approach to treat disease.

(A) Changes in one tissue or organ can lead to physiological effects in other subsystems. Integration also means therapy can have broad-ranging effects. Treatment of disease in one tissue may have complicating effects in another tissue, for instance.

(B) This local systems approach is now giving way to an integrative methodology to medical management. A sick patient does not represent a biochemistry problem or an anatomy problem or a genetics problem or an immunology problem.

(C) Instead, each person is the product of multiple molecular, cellular, genetic, environmental, and social influences that interact in complex ways to determine health and disease. The human body is a highly integrated set of subsystems. [2점]

① (A) − (C) − (B)
② (B) − (A) − (C)
③ (B) − (C) − (A)
④ (C) − (A) − (B)
⑤ (C) − (B) − (A)

35

There are certain rules that, to break them, would give us such intense pain that we don't even consider the possibility. We will rarely, if ever, break them. I call these rules threshold rules.

(A) Conversely, we have some rules that we don't want to break. I call these personal standards. If we do break them, we don't feel good about it, but depending upon the reasons, we're willing to break them in the short term. The difference between these two rules is often phrased with the words must and should.

(B) We have certain things that we *must* do, certain things that we must not do, certain things that we *must never* do, and certain things that we *must always* do. the "must" and the "must never" rules are threshold rules; the "should" and "should never" rules are personal standard rules. All of them give a structure to our lives.

(C) For example, if I asked you, "what's something you would never do?," you'd give me a threshold rule. You'd tell me a rule that you would never violate. Why? Because you link too much pain to it. [3점]

① (A) − (C) − (B)
② (B) − (A) − (C)
③ (B) − (C) − (A)
④ (C) − (A) − (B)
⑤ (C) − (B) − (A)

36 (A), (B), (C)의 각 네모 안에서 문맥에 맞는 표현으로 가장 적절한 것은? [2점]

Even in today's modern society, many people still perform rituals on a daily basis; they knock on wood to ward off bad luck or throw salt over their shoulders to (A) accept / repel evil spirits. Every culture has its own superstitions, and now anthropologists and psychologists think they know why. It is because our brains are always working to find the causes of the significant events that we perceive. When something strange happens that we can't explain, our minds are (B) uncomfortable / satisfied with the uncertainty. However, we fill this cognitive gap with whatever explanations are available to us, and superstitions provide a simple way to explain mysterious events. They believe that spirits that live in wood have to be appeased, or that throwing salt blinds the devil. Superstitions may seem silly to nonbelievers not sharing them. To believers those rituals on the other hand are providing a sense of control over situations otherwise which would be (C) secure / unsettling.

	(A)	(B)	(C)
①	accept	uncomfortable	secure
②	accept	satisfied	unsettling
③	repel	uncomfortable	unsettling
④	repel	satisfied	secure
⑤	repel	uncomfortable	secure

37 다음 글의 내용을 한 문장으로 요약하고자 한다. 빈칸 (A)와 (B)에 들어갈 말로 가장 적절한 것은? [3점]

Here is an interesting experiment which was conducted on a group of elementary students in the U.S. over thirty years ago. The teacher who partook in the experiment told her students: "According to a recent study, children with blue eyes have a higher learning aptitude than children with brown eyes." After telling her students this bit of uncertified information, she had the children write the color of their eyes on a card and hang them around their necks. The children were monitored for a week and the results were as follows. Learning motivation for children with brown eyes dropped, and the blue-eyed children became drastically better in class. Then, the teacher told the students, "There have been reports that the experimental results were wrong. In fact, brown-eyed children do better in class than blue-eyed

children." What were the results? This time the children with brown eyes excelled in class and learning ambition for the children with blue eyes dropped.

↓

According to the experiment above, (A) projected by teachers can determine students' (B) .

	(A)	(B)
①	self-images	academic achievement
②	self-images	career choice
③	traditional values	psychological wellbeing
④	traditional values	academic achievement
⑤	prejudices	career choice

[38~39] 다음 글을 읽고, 물음에 답하시오.

For many children, their first experiences with print occur in the home. Children from families that make literacy development a focal point of home activities via shared reading are at an advantage. (A) , there is little research on the precise mechanisms by which early literacy experiences influence children's subsequent language and print skills. A variety of factors, including cultural beliefs, socioeconomic status, parenting styles and parental beliefs may affect children's reading development. Moreover, establishing directional causality among these factors is difficult.

It is also difficult to disentangle the effects of children's genetic make-up from the effects on them of their biological parents. Although parents' motivations, enthusiasm, and willingness to read are behavioral influences on their children, their effects may be minimal relative to a child's own wants and needs. Parents who read a lot to their children may primarily be responding to the fact that their children are interested in reading. Such influence is, at least in part, genetically determined. (B) , parents who read little to their children may be responding to their children's lack of interest or to the fact that, genetically, both parents and children find reading-related activities boring or difficult. children's genetic endowments strongly influence how their parents interact with them. Given the confounds of parents' behaviors with the family genetic make-up, experiments on parent-child shared reading are perhaps the clearest evidence thus far that home environment can affect reading-related skills.

*confound : 혼동 요인

38 윗글의 제목으로 가장 적절한 것은? [2점]

① Children Are Inherently Good Readers

② What Influences Children's Literacy Development?

③ Relationship Between Literacy Skills and Cultural Beliefs

④ Social Intelligence: Determined by Home Environment

⑤ What Makes Your children Unwilling to Read?

39 윗글의 빈칸 (A), (B)에 들어갈 말로 가장 적절한 것은? [2점]

	(A)	(B)
①	Therefore	Otherwise
②	However	Similarly
③	As a result	Moreover
④	However	Otherwise
⑤	As a result	Similarly

[40~41] 다음 글을 읽고, 물음에 답하시오.

As Jim Collins pointed out in *Good to Great*, __(A)__ and a failure to see the situation as it is can be not only unhelpful - it can be fatal. He called this the Stockdale paradox, after James Stockdale, a U.S. military officer. Stockdale was held captive for eight years during the Vietnam War. he was tortured numerous times and had little reason to believe he would live to see his wife again. Although Stockdale understood his predicament, he also never lost hope that he might endure it and not only survive his ordeal but use it as a defining experience in his life. And here is the paradox:

While Stockdael had remarkable faith in the unknowable, he noted that it was always the most optimistic of his prisonmates who failed to make it out of there alive. "They were the ones who said, 'We're going to be out by Christmas.' And Christmas would come, and Christmas would go. Then they'd say, 'We're going to be out by Easter.' And Easter would come, and Easter would go. And then Thanksgiving, and then it would be Christmas again. And they died of a broken heart." What the optimists failed to do was confront the reality of their situation. They __(B)__ the ostrich approach, sticking their heads in the sand and hoping for the difficulties to go away. That self-delusion might have made it easier on them in the short term, but when they were eventually forced to face reality, it had become too much and they couldn't handle it.

And, of course, such unfounded optimism often precluded taking action to deal with the situation as best one could, which is precisely what Stockdale did.

*predicament : 곤경

40 윗글의 빈칸 (A), (B)에 들어갈 말로 가장 적절한 것은? [3점]

	(A)	(B)
①	irrational negativity	criticized
②	irrational negativity	preferred
③	unrealistic optimism	rejected
④	unrealistic optimism	preferred
⑤	unconditional devotion	rejected

41 윗글의 James Stockdale에 관한 내용과 일치하지 <u>않는</u> 것은? [2점]

① 그의 이름을 따서 Stockdale paradox라는 표현이 생겨났다.

② 베트남 전쟁 중에 8년 동안 포로로 잡혀 지냈다.

③ 자신이 처한 곤경을 견뎌낼 수 있다는 희망을 잃지 않았다.

④ 가장 낙관적인 수용소 동료들이 살아 나오지 못하는 것에 주목했다.

⑤ 수용소 동료들에게 곧 풀려날 것이라는 희망을 불어 넣어주었다.

[42~43] 다음 글을 읽고, 물음에 답하시오.

The trend which has impacted the application of the laws of armed conflict is the increasing civilianisation of modern conflict. this trend is taking place through a number of processes, including the escalating prominence of internal armed conflicts in which the majority of war fighters are civilians, and the (A) shift / removal of the conduct of hostilities into civilian population centres. In addition, modern militaries increasingly outsource support and even core functions to contractors — some of whom, like private military or security firms, are engaged in armed tactical roles.

In the three-and-a-half centuries since the Treaty of Westphalia, the nation state has been the defining actor in international relations, and has held the monopoly on power and military force. The emergence of transnational armed groups, the increasing number of non-international armed conflicts and the (B) reduction / expansion of the battlespace to encompass entire territories have all meant that civilians are involved in conflicts more than ever.

Militaries are also under pressure to downsize and reduce budgets. As part of this trend, civilian contractors and employees are increasingly used to augment defence forces as an easy and flexible way to maintain military strength according to constantly changing needs. Further, as weapons and equipment become more technologically advanced, civilians are (C) excluded / recruited to provide essential maintenance and support functions, sometimes from the 'factory to the foxhole'. Civilians are an easy and less expensive way maintaining access to the latest technical expertise; they can be hired when needed and discharged when the need is no longer urgent.

*hostilities : 교전

42 윗글의 주제로 가장 적절한 것은? [2점]

① conflict resolution without military intervention

② civilian involvement in a variety of military affairs

③ maintenance of military power for national security

④ competition between private sectors and public sectors

⑤ how military technological advancement benefits civilians

43 (A), (B), (C)의 각 네모 안에서 문맥에 맞는 표현으로 가장 적절한 것은? [3점]

	(A)	(B)	(C)
①	shift	expansion	recruited
②	shift	reduction	excluded
③	shift	reduction	recruited
④	removal	expansion	excluded
⑤	removal	reduction	excluded

[44~45] 다음 글을 읽고, 물음에 답하시오.

(A)

One summer when he was in high school, Colin attended church camp and made some new friends who proved to be a bad influence. They talked (a) him into sneaking out of camp with them to buy beer, and then they hid it one of the toilet tanks to keep it cold. They thought no one would ever find out. But they were wrong.

(B)

He stood silent as she lectured (b) him about trust and responsibility, knowing there was no good defense for his actions. Then it was his father's turn to tell Colin how disappointed he was in his son. In the middle of the family crisis, Father Weeden — the priest at St. Margaret's — called to tell Colin's parents the whole story — about how their son had stood up like a man and taken responsibility for (c) his actions. The family was proud that Colin had done the right thing.

(C)

Because of his honesty, two other boys also admitted their guilt. All of their parents were notified, and the boys were sent home in disgrace. Riding on the train, Colin thought about what (d) he had done and regretted his involvement. How embarrassing for him and his parents! To get kicked out of church camp was worse than anything he could imagine. After walking slowly home from the train, Colin was met at the door by his scowling mother.

*scowl : 얼굴을 찌푸리다

(D)

The camp director called all the boys together to confront them with the fact that the beer had been discovered. The priest didn't yell or scream. (e) He firmly asked the guilty parties to stand up and act like men and to accept the responsibility for their misdeed. Colin Powell, because of his mother's firm hand throughout his childhood years, was the one who came clean first. "Father, I did it," Colin confessed.

44 주어진 글 (A)에 이어질 내용을 순서에 맞게 배열한 것으로 가장 적절한 것은? [2점]

① (B) − (D) − (C)

② (C) − (B) − (D)

③ (C) − (D) − (B)

④ (D) − (B) − (C)

⑤ (D) − (C) − (B)

45 밑줄 친 (a)~(e) 중에서 가리키는 대상이 나머지 넷과 다른 것은? [2점]

① (a)　　　② (b)

③ (c)　　　④ (d)

⑤ (e)

There is nothing like a dream to create the future.
미래를 창조하기 위해서 꿈만 한 것은 없다.

– 빅토르 위고(Victor Hugo)

2025
사관학교
10개년 영어

2016학년도 기출문제
영어영역(공통)

제2교시 영어영역(공통)

▶정답 및 해설 413p

01 Based on the following dialogue, which one is NOT true? [2점]

> Mr. Sanders : You'll never guess who I met when I picked up our daughter from her violin lesson today!
>
> Mrs. Sanders : Don't keep me in suspense. Who?
>
> Mr. Sanders : Our girl's first boyfriend. I can't believe she's already dating.
>
> Mrs. Sanders : Oh my goodness! Well, she is all grown up, isn't she? What did you think of him?
>
> Mr. Sanders : I'm a father! At first glance, of course I wasn't impressed. No one is good enough for our precious daughter.
>
> Mrs. Sanders : Come on! Objectively, tell me, what was he like?
>
> Mr. Sanders : Honestly, in talking with him for a minute, he seemed like a pretty decent guy. But I still want to know everything about him.

① The Sanders' daughter is learning violin.

② The Sanders' daughter is dating.

③ Mrs. Sanders says she doesn't like the guy.

④ Mrs. Sanders hasn't met the guy.

⑤ Mr. Sanders was originally skeptical about the guy.

02 Which is the best sequence of answers for the blanks? [2점]

> Librarian : Hi there. What can I do for you?
>
> Tom : To be honest, this is my first time in a library and I need to find a book called "Bob's Big Barbecue," but I don't know who wrote it.
>
> Librarian : No problem. First of all, we'll just type the _____ of the book here in the computer, and it will give us a series of numbers. The first digit will tell us what _____ to look on, so it shows us we must take the stairs over there.
>
> Tom : What about the next

numbers?

Librarian : Those indicate what
_____ to look on, so
check the numbers on
each bookcase until you
find the correct range of
numbers.

Tom : Thanks so much for your
help.

─────〈보기〉─────

a. title   b. author
c. floor   d. shelf

① a — c — d   ② a — d — c
③ b — d — c   ④ d — a — c
⑤ d — c — a

03 Where is the dialogue most likely taking
place? [2점]

Mr. Gupta : I'm glad you brought
Mia in for treatment.
The good news is that
she will be okay, but
the bad news is that
her injury will require
surgery.

Susan : I was afraid of that. Since
the accident, she has been
limping badly, and that
back paw just won't heal
completely.

Mr. Gupta : Yes, unfortunately, she
has a broken bone in
her back leg that will

require an operation.

Susan : But after that, she'll be fine?

Mr. Gupta : Then she'll still have
a few weeks of home
recovery, during which
she will have to wear a
big plastic cone around
her head to make sure
she doesn't lick at
her wound. But then
she should be 100%
recovered.

Susan : Great! What a relief!

① Veterinary Clinic

② Dentist's Office

③ Pharmacy

④ Medical Supply Center

⑤ Hospital Information Desk

04 Based on the following dialogue, which
one is true? [2점]

Steve : Wow, what a beautiful place!
I could stay here forever. So
where do you want to set up
the tent?

Dean : Are you sure you want to
sleep out here? There was a
reasonable hotel just down
the road.

Steve : Come on. What about over
there near the water? The
ground looks nice and flat.

Dean : I don't know. It's right in the
sun without any shade.

2016 기출문제

Steve : So, what about back there a bit, under those trees?

Dean : That's even worse, surrounded by bugs and closer to any wild animals stalking around in the dark.

Steve : You're such a baby! Fine. I give up. But you're paying for the room.

Dean : No problem. As long as we don't sleep outdoors.

① Dean wants to set up the tent near the water.

② Dean isn't fond of sleeping outdoors.

③ Steve and Dean are going to sleep in the tent.

④ Steve is afraid of wild animals.

⑤ Steve will pay for the accommodation.

05 Choose the best answer for the blank. [3점]

Bank Manager : We've reviewed your small business loan a'pplication, but we are not entirely convinced of the potential of your plan.

Loan Applicant : What are you talking about? It's fool-proof. Everyone loves ice cream, and there is not another ice cream store around for hundreds of miles.

Bank Manager : The general desirability of your product is not really the problem.

Loan Applicant : I don't understand. Is it my lack of experience? Because I promise you, I have learned everything there is to know about ice cream.

Bank Manager : No, the real issue is location. You've chosen to open your business in a small village in Alaska where it is winter almost year-round. We just don't think an ice-cream shop is a viable business in such a place. _____

① It sounds like a great idea and we wish you luck.

② Please fill out these forms to begin your loan application.

③ We look forward to a long and healthy business relationship.

④ We're pleased to tell you that you've been approved for the loan.

⑤ We're sorry, but we will not be able to process your loan application.

06 Choose the sentence that best describes the situation. [2점]

> Sam : This is Sam's Office Supplies, how can I help you?
>
> Donna : I'm calling because over a month ago I ordered 10 boxes of A4 printer paper, and at the time I was told delivery would only take one week.
>
> Sam : Absolutely, our orders are guaranteed to be delivered in one week or less, depending on your location. What seems to be the problem?
>
> Donna : The problem is, not only was the shipment two weeks late, but only half was delivered, and I'm still waiting for the rest.
>
> Sam : I'm terribly sorry. Our records show that all 10 boxes were delivered, but I will get to the bottom of the problem and get those remaining 5 boxes shipped out immediately.
>
> Donna : Thank you, and please make sure it doesn't happen again.

① Donna was completely satisfied with Sam's delivery service.

② Donna regrets that Sam has ignored her complaints for weeks.

③ The order was properly filled so there is nothing Sam can do.

④ Sam will try to solve the problem and make his customer happy.

⑤ Donna is planning to cancel her order with Sam's Office Supplies.

07 밑줄 친 부분이 가리키는 대상이 나머지 넷과 다른 것은? [2점]

> Misty May-Treanor and Kerri Walsh are great athletes, and they are great people. In the semifinals of the beach volleyball event at the 2008 Olympics in Beijing, ① they defeated a very good Brazilian team. Afterward, they shook hands with the members of the Brazilian team and said "thank you." ② They then shook hands with many, many volunteers who do such things as retrieve balls and rake the sand. In awe, journalist Mike Celizic wrote, "They literally chased down some of the volunteers from behind as they were leaving the court, not wanting ③ them to get away without knowing how much their efforts were appreciated." ④ They also waved to the fans and promised to come back after the mandatory drug testing. They did come back, posing

for photographs and signing autographs for many, many fans. And yes, the fans really appreciated shaking hands with ⑤ <u>them</u>.

[08~09] 다음 글에서 전체 흐름과 관계 없는 문장을 고르시오.

08 MSG is essentially a concentrated form of sodium, which is extracted from seaweed, beets, and grains. ① The Glutamate Association insists that MSG is perfectly safe. ② They argue that MSG is no different from the glutamate that is liberated by our bodies when we eat food protein, and that MSG added to food represents only a small fraction of the glutamate contained naturally in most foods. ③ For many of the same reasons, a number of chefs dislike MSG, believing that it deadens the taste of foods and is too often used to compensate for inferior products. ④ For example, most recipes call for half a teaspoon of MSG per pound of meat. ⑤ With these proportions, the MSG in a serving of chicken would constitute less than 10 percent of the glutamate already found in the chicken.

* glutamate 글루타민산염

09 Traditional advertisements are typically defined as persuasive, nonpersonal communications delivered to consumers via the mass media on behalf of identifiable sponsors, and humor is often a key tool employed. ① Because most consumers are exposed to a large number of advertisements on a daily basis, humorous advertisements may be the most frequent way that many come into contact with intentional humor. ② Advertisers use humor as a message tactic, with the intent of enhancing an advertisement's potential for achieving various strategic objectives. ③ Humor was used rather infrequently during the early years of modern advertising; researchers, however, have confirmed that its use in contemporary advertising is prevalent, especially in the broadcast media. ④ It is widely accepted in the advertising industry that humor is quite ineffective and even counterproductive. ⑤ Although this is generally true for most industrialized, First World countries, humor is found somewhat more frequently in the advertising of Western countries and cultures than in Eastern ones.

10 다음 글의 요지로 가장 적절한 것은? [3점]

Most people have two potentially opposing needs: one is to be available to others for social contact; the other is to have privacy. Some people need more privacy, others more social contact. If we think about the environment, whether at the level of public spaces or domestic spaces, we can see

features which reflect these two needs. In western society the door is a ubiquitous architectural feature, and curtains are almost obligatory parts of our domestic props. The possibility of closing or opening doors and curtains is a device for signalling availability. Goffman has drawn attention to the prevalence of back (private) regions and front (public) regions both in domestic settings and in public settings. Back regions, which in houses include bedrooms, bathrooms and sometimes kitchens, are regions in which only intimates may penetrate without invitation. Front regions are open to the public.

① 현대사회는 사생활보다 사회생활을 중시한다.

② 사생활에 대한 인식과 중요성은 문화마다 다르다.

③ 사생활과 사회생활의 구분이 점차 희미해지고 있다.

④ 가정이 사회생활의 장이 되는 것은 바람직하지 않다.

⑤ 생활공간에는 사생활과 사회생활에 대한 필요가 반영된다.

[11~12] 다음 글의 밑줄 친 부분 중, 어법상 틀린 것을 고르시오.

11 The triumph of antibiotics over disease-causing bacteria is one of modern medicine's greatest success ① <u>stories</u>. Since these drugs first became widely used in the World War II era, they have saved countless lives and ② <u>blunted</u> serious complications of many feared diseases and infections. After more than 50 years of widespread use, however, many antibiotics don't have the same effect that they once ③ <u>were</u>. Over time, some bacteria have developed ways to outwit the effects of antibiotics. Widespread use of antibiotics is thought to have spurred evolutionary changes in bacteria ④ <u>that</u> allow them to survive these powerful drugs. While antibiotic resistance benefits the microbes, it presents humans with two big problems: it makes it more ⑤ <u>difficult</u> to purge infections from the body; and it heightens the risk of acquiring infections in a hospital.

12 In a survey, when the response options are presented visually, it seems reasonable to assume that respondents typically start at the top of the list and ① <u>work</u> their way through the remaining options in order. Primacy effects would, therefore, seem to be the rule: Respondents will tend to prefer options at the beginning of the list over ② <u>those</u> at the end. However, the picture becomes somewhat murkier when the interviewer reads the response options to the respondent. Survey interviewers tend to read questions ③ <u>quickly</u> so that respondents will not generally have time to evaluate the first option before they must turn to the next. It is quite likely

that respondents will begin by considering the final option, since that option is the one that will remain in working memory when the interviewer stops ④ to read. Consequently, we should expect recency effects — the tendency to choose options at the end of the list — when the question ⑤ is presented aloud to the respondent. [3점]

[13~14] (A), (B), (C)의 각 네모 안에서 어법에 맞는 표현으로 가장 적절한 것을 고르시오.

13

"Hat-trick" was originally an English cricket term used to describe the tremendous feat of a bowler's taking three wickets on successive balls. The reward for this accomplishment at many cricket clubs (A) was / were a new hat. Other clubs honored their heroes by "passing the hat" among fans and giving the scorer the proceeds. The term spread to other sports (B) which / in which scoring is relatively infrequent — "hat-trick" is also used to describe the feat of scoring three goals in soccer. According to Belinda Lerner of the National Hockey League, the expression surfaced in hockey during the early 1900s: "There is some confusion about its actual meaning in hockey. Today, a 'true' hat-trick occurs when one player scores three successive goals without another goal (C) scoring / being scored by other players in the contest."

*take a wicket : (크리켓 경기에서 투수가) 타자를 아웃시키다

	(A)	(B)	(C)
①	was	in which	being scored
②	was	which	scoring
③	was	in which	scoring
④	were	which	being scored
⑤	were	in which	scoring

14

Most of us choose the kinds of lives we lead. Although we may not be aware of it, each day we make choices that determine (A) what / whether we will be happy or unhappy, healthy or ill, creative or barren. We make the majority of these choices on an unconscious level, (B) guide / guided primarily by a sense of what has happened to us in the past and what might happen to us in the future. This apparently automatic process of decision making tends to hide the fact that we are making choices constantly. Over time, we lose the sense of making a choice at each new moment of life; as a result, we come to believe that a vague external force — destiny, fate, or luck — (C) influences / influencing

how we live, what we accomplish, and sometimes, how we die.

	(A)	(B)	(C)
①	what	guide	influencing
②	what	guided	influences
③	whether	guided	influencing
④	whether	guide	influences
⑤	whether	guided	influences

[15~18] 다음 글을 읽고, 빈칸에 들어갈 말로 가장 적절한 것을 고르시오.

15

The melting pot view of society has some appeal, because it suggests that everyone can succeed if only they try hard enough. However, at some point we should realize that this type of equity usually means eliminating differences and variety. The melting pot ideal generally requires that an individual sacrifice his or her uniqueness to fit into an existing system. The only way to become successful, at least in a socially acceptable fashion (as opposed to becoming a famous gangster), requires developing ways to fit in while giving up on one's cultural background. We use the idea of the melting pot as a way to blend different ingredients, but we should recognize that the result of this melting pot is a homogeneous

product wherein distinctive features are diluted. In short, the melting pot metaphor reflects a desire for _____.

① diversity   ② challenge

③ sameness   ④ originality

⑤ independence

16

Time adds an important and necessary dimension to our understanding of the world and our place in it — it seems almost impossible to conceive of what our world of experience might be like in the absence of time; after all, events happen in time. This has resulted in physicists treating time, along with space, as a theoretical and an empirical primitive. The view that time constitutes, at some level, part of the physical fabric of the cosmos, and as such is physically real, accords with what I will term the common-place view of time. Most people believe in this view of time, a 'true' time, a time that actually exists in a physical sense; on this account, time _____, as reflected in the physical laws which govern the environment we inhabit. While time may itself be "imperceptible," it is nonetheless real, manifesting tangible consequences. Without

time's "passage" there could be no succession and thus no experience of duration.

① passes with its own driving force

② cannot be perceived physically

③ is not dealt with in the field of physics

④ is objectively embedded in the external world

⑤ is an imaginary construct of human experience

whelms us; ＿＿＿＿＿＿＿＿ makes them seem realizable. There is nothing more therapeutic than action.

*antidote : 해독제, 교정수단

① getting help from others

② taking that small first step

③ looking back into the past

④ sharing our desires with someone

⑤ sacrificing ourselves for a good cause

17

The problem that many of us face is that we have great dreams and ambitions. Caught up in the emotions of our dreams and the vastness of our desires, we find it very difficult to focus on the small, tedious steps usually necessary to attain them. We tend to think in terms of giant leaps toward our goals. But in the social world as in nature, anything of size and stability grows slowly. The piecemeal strategy is the perfect antidote to our natural impatience: it focuses us on something small and immediate, a first bite, then how and where a second bite can get us closer to our ultimate objective. It forces us to think in terms of a process, a sequence of connected steps and actions, no matter how small, which has immeasurable psychological benefits as well. Too often the magnitude of our desires over-

18

Anxiety, believe it or not, ＿＿＿＿＿＿＿. For you are born and raised with desires, preferences, and goals, and if you had no anxiety whatever, and were totally unconcerned about achieving your desires, you would tolerate all kinds of obnoxious things and would do nothing to ward them off or escape from them. Anxiety, basically, is a set of uncomfortable feelings and action tendencies that make you aware that unpleasant happenings — meaning things that go against your desires — are happening or are likely to happen and warn you that you'd better do something about them. Thus, if you are in danger of being attacked, and you desire to remain unhurt, you have a choice of several possible actions, such as running away, fighting off your attacker, calling the police, and so on. But you would probably

do none of these things unless you were concerned, watchful, anxious, tense, cautious, vigilant, or panicked. You would perceive the danger of the attack, perhaps, but do nothing about it.

*obnoxious : 불쾌한

① instills a sense of responsibility in you

② helps keep you alive and comfortable

③ makes you tolerate all kinds of insults

④ prevents you from pursuing your desires

⑤ inhibits clear thinking in stressful situations

19 다음 글에서 필자가 주장하는 바로 가장 적절한 것은?

Right from the start, the main focus in AI research has always been with the issue of problem solving. Seen from this point of view, intelligence corresponds to the ability to solve complex problems, from the accurate autonomous movement of a robot arm to the understanding of a natural language sentence. The classical setting is that of a search in a space of solutions for the problem, where an intelligent agent looks for the best choices. One of the most common criticisms made of Artificial Intelligence methods of problem solving is their limited ability to deal with situations not predicted in the specification. The search space is normally strictly defined, however flexible, complex and adaptable the system seems to be. When facing a problem with no satisfactory solution in its search space, an AI system simply returns, at best, the least unsuccessful result that exists in that search space even when the solution is achievable via the simplest operation of changing perspective, relaxing a constraint or adding a new symbol. In other words, such systems are hardly capable of performing what we normally call creative behavior, a fundamental aspect of intelligence.

① 인공지능의 탐색 공간은 무한히 확장될 수 있다.

② 인공지능을 활용한 범죄에 대한 대책이 시급하다.

③ 도덕성 논란은 인공지능 기술 발전의 장애 요인이다.

④ 인공지능 기술 개발 및 연구에 대한 투자가 부족하다.

⑤ 인공지능은 창의성 결여라는 한계를 극복하지 못하고 있다.

[20~21] 다음 글의 빈칸 (A), (B)에 들어갈 말로 가장 적절한 것을 고르시오.

20

What we call "mind" and what we call "body" are not two things, but

rather aspects of one ___(A)___ process, so that all our meaning, thought, and language emerge from the aesthetic dimensions of this embodied activity. Chief among those aesthetic dimensions are qualities, images, patterns of sensorimotor processes, and emotions. For at least the past three decades, scholars and researchers in many disciplines have piled up arguments and evidence for the embodiment of mind and meaning. However, the implications of their research have not entered public consciousness, and so the denial of mind/body dualism is still a highly provocative claim that most people find objectionable and even threatening. Coming to grips with your embodiment is one of the most profound philosophical tasks you will ever face. Acknowledging that every aspect of the human mind is ___(B)___ specific forms of bodily engagement with an environment requires a far-reaching rethinking of who and what we are, in a way that is largely at odds with many of our inherited Western philosophical and religious traditions.

*sensorimotor : 감각운동성의

	(A)	(B)
①	dividing	grounded in
②	organic	grounded in
③	organic	separated from
④	dividing	separated from
⑤	imaginary	unrelated to

21

In the early history of warfare, military leaders were faced with the following predicament: The success of any war effort depended on the ability to know as much about the other side — its intentions, its strengths and weaknesses — as possible. But the enemy would never willingly disclose this information. ___(A)___, the enemy often came from an alien culture, with its peculiar ways of thinking and behaving. A general could not really know what was going on in the mind of the opposing general. From the outside the enemy represented something of an impenetrable mystery. And yet, lacking some understanding of the other side, a general would be operating in the dark. The only solution was to scrutinize the enemy for outward signs of what was going on within. ___(B)___, a strategist might count the cooking fires in the enemy camp and the changes in that number over time; that would show the army's size.

*predicament : 곤경
*scrutinize : 면밀히 조사하다

	(A)	(B)
①	Instead	Otherwise
②	Instead	However
③	In addition	However
④	In addition	For example
⑤	On the contrary	For example

(C) blurry / jerky to produce realistic movement.

	(A)	(B)	(C)
①	considerably	resting	blurry
②	considerably	moving	jerky
③	slightly	resting	blurry
④	slightly	resting	jerky
⑤	slightly	moving	blurry

[22~23] (A), (B), (C)의 각 네모 안에서 문맥에 맞는 표현으로 가장 적절한 것을 고르시오.

22

Stop-motion photography is used to fool the eye into seeing motion. A still photograph is made of an object, such as a clay model of a dinosaur. The object is moved (A) considerably / slightly and another photograph is taken. This delicate process is repeated thousands of times. When the photographs, or frames, are shown at the speed of a motion picture camera, 24 frames per second, the clay model appears to be (B) resting / moving . A major problem with stop-motion filming is that there are no "blurs." If you film a man running down the street, there will be a slight blur on each frame. Although not noticed by the audience, the blur helps make the running motion smooth and realistic. In stop-motion films, a running creature seems to have jerky movements. This problem has been solved with computer animation, which can be used to make frames

23

Modern technology has provided us with countless time-saving devices. Cell phones with headsets (A) allow / forbid people to talk to friends or colleagues and battle rush hour at the same time. In a matter of seconds a computer can perform calculations that would take months if done by hand. Nonetheless, most of us complain about not having enough time. Surveys suggest that a majority of people subjectively feel that they have less and less time for themselves. Time has become a truly (B) common / precious commodity; one national survey found that 51% of the adult respondents would rather have more time than more money. Part of the problem is that in our modern society, work follows people home. Thus, people find themselves bound to their jobs around the clock by the same nomadic tools — cell phones, tablets, wireless e-mail —

2016 기출문제

221

that were heralded first as instruments of (C) constraint / liberation. To deal with this time crunch, more and more people are cutting back on their sleep as they attempt to juggle work, family, and household responsibilities.

	(A)	(B)	(C)
①	allow	precious	liberation
②	allow	precious	constraint
③	allow	common	liberation
④	forbid	common	constraint
⑤	forbid	precious	constraint

[24~25] 다음 글의 제목으로 가장 적절한 것을 고르시오.

24

According to explanatory critical theories of capitalism, crises occur when the inherent contradictions of capitalism lead to imbalances, i.e. the loss of the balances (e.g. between what is produced and what is consumed) which are necessary for the existing system to continue to function. Crises are not only inevitable but also necessary, for when imbalances develop, people have to impose some order on a situation of collapse and chaos. We can say that crises have a rationalizing function, the function of restoring rationality where it has been undermined. In Harvey's words, crises are "the irrational rationalisers of an always unstable capitalism." Crises have an objective or systemic aspect, but they also have a necessary and indeed crucial subjective aspect, which is agentive and strategic. In a crisis, people have to make decisions about how to act in response and to develop strategies for pursuing particular courses of action or policies which will hopefully restore balance and rationality.

① Destructive Nature of Crises

② Necessity of Crises in Capitalism

③ Avoiding Crises in a Capitalist System

④ Competition : Driving Force of Capitalism

⑤ Capitalism : Way Out of Crises and Chaos

25

"Children's playing is not sport and should be considered their most serious action," Montaigne, a sixteenth-century essayist, wrote. If we wish to understand our child, we need to understand his play. Freud, a founder of modern psychology, regarded play as the means through which a child expresses himself. He also noted how much and how well children express their thoughts and feelings

through play. From a child's play we can gain understanding of how he sees and interprets the world — what he would like it to be, what his concerns and problems are. A child does not play spontaneously only to while away the time, although the adults observing him may think he does. Even when he engages in play partly to fill empty moments, what he chooses to play at is motivated by inner processes, desires, problems, anxieties.

① Harm Caused by Children's Violent Play

② Play: Expression of Children's Inner Self

③ Importance of Restricting Children's Play

④ How to Raise Physically Healthy Children

⑤ Children's Play: Means of Making Friends

[26~27] 글의 흐름으로 보아, 주어진 문장이 들어가기에 가장 적절한 곳을 고르시오.

26

And this will not ever go away — not now, not in the twenty-second century, not in a thousand years: *All leaders die.*

In looking at the charismatic leader model, we think the world is heading in exactly the opposite direction. Just look at the twenty-first century. Nearly the entire world has moved toward democracy. (①) The very essence of democracy is to avoid overdependence on any single leader and put the primary focus on the process. (②) Even Churchill — perhaps the single greatest leader of the last century — was secondary to the nation and its processes, kicked out of office at the end of World War II. (③) Hitler, Stalin, Mussolini — these were charismatic leaders who did not understand that they were fundamentally *less* important than the institutions they served. (④) And even if you don't buy the analogy between the shift to democracy and the evolution of corporations, the great charismatic leader model has one fundamental flaw. (⑤) To transcend this unchanging reality of human mortality, the focus must be first and foremost on building the characteristics of the organization, instead of being a great charismatic leader.

27

If there is disagreement or confusion at this stage, it is unlikely that the ensuing encounter will be fruitful.

In many interpersonal transactions, one encounter is influenced by decisions made and commitments undertaken in

the previous meeting. (①) Again, it is important to establish that all parties are in agreement as to the main points arising from prior interactions and the implications of these for the present discussion. (②) This problem is formally overcome in many business settings, where minutes of meetings are taken. (③) The minutes from a previous meeting are reviewed, and agreed at the outset, before the main agenda items for the current meeting are discussed. (④) This procedure ensures that all participants are in agreement about what has gone before, and have therefore a common frame of reference for the forthcoming meeting. (⑤) In addition, agenda items are usually circulated prior to the meeting, and this in itself is a form of cognitive set, allowing individuals to prepare themselves for the main areas to be discussed.

[28~29] 다음 글이 시사하는 바로 가장 적절한 것을 고르시오.

28

When historians look at this period, they're going to conclude that we're in a different type of revolution: a revolution in war, like the invention of the atomic bomb. But it may be even bigger than that, because our unmanned systems don't just affect the "how" of war-fighting, but they affect the "who" of fighting at its most fundamental level. That is, every previous revolution in war, be it the machine gun or atomic bomb, was about a system that either shot faster, went further, or had a bigger boom. That's certainly the case with robotics, but they also change the experience of the warrior and even the very identity of the warrior. Another way of putting this is that mankind's 5,000-year-old monopoly on the fighting of war is breaking down in our very lifetime. It is likely that the effects of this may ripple outwards over time, substantially changing the very direction of human development, our society, our laws and our ethics, etc.

① Robotics is bringing about a revolution in warfare whose effects reach far into society.

② Unmanned systems are the only way to save human soldiers from the battlefield.

③ Robotics, which is developing rapidly, will eventually bring an end to warfare.

④ There will be little change in the way wars are fought.

⑤ Governments must make robotics investment a priority.

29

"What matters is not what people say or intend but the results of their actions." This is what Machiavelli called the "effective truth" — the real truth, in other words, what happens in fact, not in words or theories. You can apply the same barometer to your attempts at communication. If a man says or writes something that he considers revolutionary and that he hopes will change the world and improve mankind, but in the end hardly anyone is affected in any real way, then it is not revolutionary or progressive at all. Communication that does not advance its cause or produce a desired result is just self-indulgent talk, reflecting no more than people's love of their own voice. The effective truth of what they have written or said is that nothing has been changed. The ability to reach people and alter their opinions is a serious affair.

① It is important to remain consistent in applying your principles.

② The search for truth through actions has proven to be difficult.

③ People interpret others' words according to their own preconceptions.

④ Good speakers focus not only on their message but on their presentation.

⑤ Communication is effective only when it has the power to influence others.

[30~31] 다음 글의 주제로 가장 적절한 것을 고르시오.

30

Religion can exert strong influences over commerce. In medieval Europe, for example, the Christian Church was strongly opposed to money-lending at interest, and because Jews were not bound by these religious rules they took on the role of money-lenders. Until quite recently, banking institutions have not developed among Muslims because the Prophet prohibited acceptance of interest from borrowers. On the other side of the coin, literally, are the vast sums of money exchanged by religious pilgrims to holy sites. Pilgrimage plays a significant role in the economy of religious centres such as Mecca in Saudi Arabia, Lourdes in France, and Banaras in India. Religion can also strongly influence what type of employment a person has, particularly in Hindu society where caste prescribes certain duties and occupations by birthright rather than suitability.

*pilgrim : (성지) 순례자

① how economic boom supports religion

② geographical features of religious centres

③ significant impact of religion on economy

④ pilgrimage as the heart of religious activity

⑤ why different religions exist in different regions

31

Perhaps the most important dimension of the way that we think about ourselves is that of evaluation, that is our level of self-esteem. The degree to which we globally approve of ourselves has an impact on how we behave, particularly with other people. To a certain degree our evaluations of ourselves are dependent on comparisons with other people. For example, in judging specific abilities our judgements can really only be relative: the question of how good a tennis player/musician/cook one is can only be meaningful with reference to a scale derived from other people's performances. There is ample evidence that we look for opportunities to compare ourselves with relevant others. By *relevant* we mean others who are likely to be sufficiently close to us in terms of some overall scale for the comparison to be meaningful. For example, the local tennis club provides a more meaningful set of comparisons about our tennis skills than international championships would.

① damaging effects of over-focusing on competition

② role of relevant comparison in self-evaluation

③ importance of having high self-esteem

④ development of a competitive spirit

⑤ sports as a measure of self-worth

32 러시아 문학에 관한 다음 글의 내용과 일치하지 <u>않는</u> 것은?

During the century that it has existed in adequate English translation, the Russian canon of novels and plays has acquired a reputation and a certain "tone." It is serious (that is, tragic or absurd, but rarely lighthearted and never trivial), somewhat preacherly, often politically oppositionist, and frequently cast in a mystifying genre with abrupt or bizarre beginnings and ends. The novels especially are too long, too full of metaphysical ideas, too manifestly eager that readers not just read the story for fun or pleasure but learn a moral lesson. These books are deep into good and evil even while they parody those pretensions. If there is comedy, there is a twist near the end that turns your blood to ice. Russian literary characters don't seek the usual money, career, success in society for its own sake, trophy wife or husband, house in the suburbs, but instead crave some other unattainable thing.

*canon : 진짜 작품(목록)

① 소설과 희곡은 명성을 얻었다.

② 소설과 희곡은 다소 설교적인 색채를 띤다.

③ 소설은 도덕적 교훈을 배제하고 즐거움을 추구한다.

④ 희곡의 끝부분에서는 뜻밖의 전개가 일어난다.

⑤ 문학작품의 등장인물은 얻기 어려운 것을 갈망한다.

33 다음 도표의 내용과 일치하지 <u>않는</u> 것은?

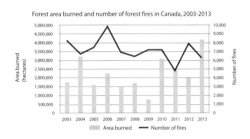

Forest area burned and number of forest fires in Canada, 2003-2013

The graph above shows forest area burned and the number of forest fires in Canada between 2003 and 2013. ① The number of hectares burned in this period is shown to have three significant spikes of over 3 million in 2004 and in 2010, and more than 4 million in 2013. ② There was also a substantial drop in forest area burned in 2009 with much less than 1 million hectares. ③ In this period, the number of hectares burned was largest in 2013, which was over three times greater than in the previous year. ④ There were some significant fluctuations in the number of forest fires, such as in 2006 when there was a high of nearly 10,000 and a low of less than 5,000 in 2011. ⑤ Overall, there is no consistent correlation between forest area burned and the number of forest fires per year.

[34~35] 주어진 글 다음에 이어질 글의 순서로 가장 적절한 것을 고르시오.

34

Pesticides are an important component in pest management strategies for food production and public health. Despite their importance, these chemicals are often blamed for environmental pollution.

(A) In fact, few other chemicals commonly used by our society are more closely scrutinized. Moreover, insects can develop resistance with frequent applications of pesticides.

(B) Therefore, in order to use pesticides safely and effectively, not only must we know which pesticides to use in specific conditions, but we must also understand all biological, physiological, and environmental consequences.

(C) All of these issues have changed pest control from a simple task in the old days into the complex, publicly-sensitive operation of today. People who develop and supervise modern pest control methods must be highly trained in many areas of pesticide usage.

2016 기출문제

① (A) − (C) − (B)   ② (B) − (A) − (C)

③ (B) − (C) − (A)   ④ (C) − (A) − (B)

⑤ (C) − (B) − (A)

35

I was never a dog person. I'd even say I hated them. That was, until one day I found a pathetic ball of fur cowering under my car. It was a scared little dog. It looked as if she hadn't eaten or bathed in weeks.

(A) I had to go on a business trip the next day, but she was too weak to be left alone, so I asked a friend to watch her. When I got back I ran to pick her up, but apparently she had "escaped." I scoured the neighborhood through the night but came up empty.

(B) I made up posters with her description and my phone number, and put them up around the area. But nothing for over a week. Until finally, the phone rang. She was returned to me and we haven't been apart since. Needless to say, my feelings on dogs have drastically changed.

(C) She was so scared that I couldn't get her to come out, so I crawled under there and snatched her. And that's when it happened. She snuggled up to me. From that moment the bond was made; she was mine, my responsibili−ty, my best friend.

① (A) − (C) − (B)   ② (B) − (A) − (C)

③ (B) − (C) − (A)   ④ (C) − (A) − (B)

⑤ (C) − (B) − (A)

36 다음 글의 밑줄 친 부분 중, 문맥상 낱말의 쓰임이 적절하지 않은 것은?

Physiological comfort is the sensation experienced in conditions relatively ① free of physiological stress. This comfort exists in certain ranges of temperature, incoming radiation, humidity, and wind speed deemed by a sophisticated instrument to be ② pleasant. The sophisticated instrument used to measure comfort is the human body. As long as the internal temperature of the body remains within a desirable range, the perception is one of comfort. Discomfort occurs when environmental conditions ③ exceed the range that supports this internal condition. As environmental temperatures rise, or as increased activity or fever raise internal temperatures, evaporative cooling (perspiration) on the surface of the skin increases to remove additional body heat. Increased air speed or decreased humidity can ④ reduce the stress that rising temperatures produce by increasing the benefit of evaporative cooling. Conversely, as ambient temperatures drop, provisions must be made to ⑤ accelerate the escape of body heat or to allow more solar radiation to be captured.

*ambient : 주위의, 환경의

37 다음 글의 내용을 한 문장으로 요약하고자 한다. 빈칸 (A)와 (B)에 들어갈 말로 가장 적절한 것은?

Many teenagers want to be like everyone in the school lunchroom. "We are not as unique as we would like to think," said Erica van de Waal, who conducted a study on monkey behavior. "We can find many of the roots of our behaviors in animals." Her study team gave 109 vervet monkeys, living in groups in the wild, food tinted pink or blue. One color for each group was tainted with aloe to give it a bad flavor, but only for the first few meals. Even after the flavor returned to normal the monkeys would not eat the color that they thought was bad. Then some blue-eating monkeys went to the pink-eating tribes and some pink-eating monkeys went to the blue-eating tribes. That is when the researchers saw peer pressure in action. The blue-food eaters that moved to an area full of pink-food eaters switched even though they had avoided pink food before. Pink eaters also changed when they moved to a blue-food area. They ate what everyone else ate.

The vervet monkeys' act of ____(A)____ is thought to be a result of ____(B)____ in a new group.

	(A)	(B)
①	switching food	social conformity
②	switching food	food abundance
③	refusing to eat	power struggle
④	refusing to eat	food abundance
⑤	avoiding contact	social conformity

[38~39] 다음 글을 읽고, 물음에 답하시오.

Suppose you are having an argument with a friend and you "accidentally" knock off a shelf an irreplaceable statue belonging to that friend. The statue shatters beyond repair. You apologize, saying that you did not mean to do it. But is this really an accident? In Freud's view, many apparent accidents are in fact intentional actions stemming from unconscious impulses. Freud might argue that you were expressing an unconscious desire to hurt your friend when you broke his or her prized possession. Clients who claim to accidentally forget their regular therapy appointment might be displaying what Freud called *resistance*. Consciously, the clients believe they simply did not remember the appointment. Unconsciously, there has been a deliberate effort to _____ a therapist who may be close to uncovering threatening unconscious material. Similarly, reckless drivers might be setting themselves up for an accident to satisfy an unconscious desire for self-inflicted harm. To Freudian psychologists, many unfortun-ate events

are accidents in the sense that people do not consciously intend them, but not in the sense that they are unintended.

38 위 글의 제목으로 가장 적절한 것은?

① How to Avoid Accidents

② Resistance to Undesirable Urges

③ Good Intention Matters More than Result

④ Unconscious Intention Hidden in Accidents

⑤ Unconscious Desire for Safety and Comfort

39 위 글의 빈칸에 들어갈 말로 가장 적절한 것은?

① hinder   ② support

③ consult   ④ impress

⑤ motivate

[40~41] 다음 글을 읽고, 물음에 답하시오.

In later life, Arthur Rimbaud was an anarchist, businessman, arms dealer, financier, and explorer. But as a teenager, all (a) he wanted to be was a poet. In May 1871, the sixteen-year-old Rimbaud wrote two letters, one to Georges Izambard, (b) his former teacher, and one to Paul Demeny, a publisher he was keen to impress. Rimbaud waited around for Izambard every day, palely hanging around outside the school gates, eager to show the young professor his most recent verse. He also presented Demeny with copies of his work, accompanied by notes in which (c) he spoke about his poems and dropped heavy hints that he wanted to see them in print. In the letter to Demeny, Rimbaud outlined his vision for a new kind of poetry. "A Poet makes himself a visionary," Rimbaud lectured (d) him, "through a long, boundless, and systematized disorganization of all the senses." Only that, Rimbaud argued, could create a language that "will include everything: perfumes, sounds, colors, thought grappling with thought." (e) His poetic program involved upsetting conventional orders of perception, deranging habitual ways of seeing, hearing, smelling, touching, and tasting, and rearranging them in novel combinations. Fresh, vivid, and sometimes shocking images resulted when sense impression jostled sense impression, when thought grappled with thought.

*jostle : 부딪치다

40 위 글의 밑줄 친 (a)~(e) 중에서, 가리키는 대상이 나머지 넷과 다른 것은?

① (a)   ② (b)   ③ (c)

④ (d)   ⑤ (e)

41 위 글의 "Arthur Rimbaud"에 관한 내용과 일치하지 않는 것은? [3점]

① He worked in fields unrelated to

literature as an adult.

② He wanted to be a poet as a teenager.

③ He acquired his own unique vision for poetry from his teacher.

④ He hoped his poems would be published.

⑤ His poetic images were based on a conflict of senses or thoughts.

[42~43] 다음 글을 읽고, 물음에 답하시오.

Humans deliberately make and remake their social networks all the time. The primary example of this is *homophily*, the conscious or unconscious tendency to associate with people who resemble us (the word literally means "love of being alike"). Whether it's stamp collectors, coffee drinkers, or bungee jumpers, the truth is that we seek out those people who share our interests, histories, and dreams. As the saying goes, "_____"

But we also choose the *structure* of our networks in three important ways. First, we decide how many people we are connected to. Do you want one partner for a game of checkers or many partners for a game of hide-and-seek? Do you want to stay in touch with your crazy uncle? Second, we influence how densely interconnected our friends and family are. Should you seat the groom's college roommate next to your bridesmaid at the wedding? Should you throw a party so all your friends can meet each other? Should you introduce your business partners? And third, we control how central we are to the social network. Are you the life of the party, mingling with everyone at the center of the room, or do you stay on the sidelines?

Diversity in these choices yields an astonishing variety of structures for the whole network in which we come to be embedded. And it is diversity in these choices that places each of us in a unique location in our own social network. Of course, sometimes these structural features are not a matter of choice; we may live in places that are more or less conducive to friendship, or we may be born into large or small families. But even when these social-network structures are thrust upon us, they still rule our lives.

*conducive : 도움이 되는

42 위 글의 주제로 가장 적절한 것은?

① how we shape our social networks

② how online social networks affect our life

③ tips for restoring damaged social networks

④ dangers of diversifying your social networks

⑤ necessity of social networks in finding a job

43 위 글의 빈칸에 들어갈 말로 가장 적절한 것은?

① Familiarity breeds contempt.

② Birds of a feather flock together.

③ Too many cooks spoil the broth.

④ Don't judge a book by its cover.

⑤ A rolling stone gathers no moss.

[44~45] 다음 글을 읽고, 물음에 답하시오.

(A)

When we were children, my brothers and I would get several presents from our parents for Christmas. Usually, our mother and father would give each of us one very expensive gift, as well as a few less costly items. This, however, was not the only gift-giving that happened in my house at Christmas time.

(B)

Since the papers were folded up, no one could tell whose name they were selecting. Also, no one would tell anyone else whose name they had chosen. In this way, our family members secretly bought something for one other person in the family. We really looked forward to Christmas Day, wondering from whom we would receive a gift.

(C)

We also had a unique tradition of our family. Every year, sometime in November, each person's name would be written on a small piece of paper, and the pieces of paper would be folded up and then placed into a hat. Next, one by one, we

would each choose a piece of paper. The person whose name was on the paper was the family member that the person who chose it would buy a gift for.

(D)

Then one year something unexpected happened. On Christmas Day, when the time came to give out the "secret presents," my parents, my older brother, and I were all shocked to learn that each of us had purchased a gift for my younger brother, Joe. It was then that we realized that Joe had been the one to prepare the pieces of paper, and that _____ !

44 주어진 글 (A)에 이어질 내용을 순서에 맞게 배열한 것으로 가장 적절한 것은?

① (B) − (D) − (C)　　② (C) − (B) − (D)

③ (C) − (D) − (B)　　④ (D) − (B) − (C)

⑤ (D) − (C) − (B)

45 위 글 (D)의 빈칸에 들어갈 말로 가장 적절한 것은?

① he'd saved enough money to buy a present

② he'd written his own name on every one of them

③ he'd been proud of this unique tradition of our family

④ he'd properly finished what he had been expected to do

⑤ he'd wanted to give a gift to every member of our family

2025
사관학교
10개년 영어

2015학년도 기출문제
영어영역(공통)

제**2**교시 영어영역(공통)

▶정답 및 해설 431p

01 Where is the following dialogue most likely taking place? [2점]

> Captain Sim : And what can I do for you, young lady?
> Sonya : I'm not sure. I've been trying to figure out what I want to do with my life, and a friend recommended that I come here.
> Captain Sim : Wise decision. We have great career options to offer a bright young person such as yourself. What branch of service are you considering?
> Sonya : I have no idea really. I'd sure appreciate some advice.
> Captain Sim : Well, let me ask you to close your eyes and imagine yourself proudly wearing a uniform and serving your nation. Do you see yourself sailing the high seas, soaring into the vast skies, or traversing exotic foreign lands?
> Sonya : Well ... I think flying

> sounds great.
> Captain Sim : Then, let me show you our Air Force brochures.

① at a military recruitment center

② in a soldiers' dining hall

③ in a cadet dormitory

④ in an air control tower

⑤ at a war memorial

02 Based on the following dialogue, which is NOT true? [2점]

> Mr. Perez : I need to talk to you for a minute.
> Mrs. Perez : Sure, honey. What's up?
> Mr. Perez : I was offered a promotion today. It's a great opportunity and I'm excited, but it means being transferred to Sweden for a few years.
> Mrs. Perez : Wow! But ... I don't know. I'd have to resign from work. Plus, how can I get a new job there? I don't know the

234

language.

Mr. Perez : You don't have to worry about that, because the promotion comes with such a big pay raise that you wouldn't have to work.

Mrs. Perez : Can we really leave our home and friends for so long? We really have to think about this.

① Mr. Perez will get a promotion if he accepts the transfer.

② Mrs. Perez is currently unemployed.

③ Mrs. Perez cannot speak Swedish.

④ Mr. Perez will make more money if he takes the job.

⑤ Mrs. Perez is hesitant to go to Sweden.

03 Which is the best sequence of sentences for the blanks? [2점]

Mrs. Won : Thanks so much for coming, finally! I've been calling for three days!

Frank : _____
But due to the heat wave, it seems everyone in town needs their air conditioners serviced. I've been working twelve hours a day all week.

Mrs. Won : I totally understand. However, my family and I have been baking in here.

Frank : Well, then let's get this fixed and cool you guys off as fast as possible.

_____

Mrs. Won : When I turn it on, it just blows warm air.

Frank : _____
It probably just needs its Freon gas refilled. If nothing is leaking, I can take care of that in no time.

Mrs. Won : Great. But please hurry. I think I may be melting.

〈보기〉

a. What seems to be the problem?

b. There's nothing I can do about that.

c. That should be a simple fix.

d. I do apologize.

① b − d − c ② c − a − b

③ c − b − d ④ d − a − c

⑤ d − b − a

04 What is the relationship between the woman and the man? [2점]

> Woman : I'm calling because I'm in trouble and in need of your services.
>
> Man : How can I help?
>
> Woman : I got arrested because my boss reported me for stealing from his company. Now the police tell me I'll have to go to court.
>
> Man : Tell me the whole story, and don't leave anything out.
>
> Woman : I didn't do it exactly. It was a big misunderstanding. I just borrowed the money. I was going to pay it back.
>
> Man : Now don't worry. I can take care of this. But if I am going to properly represent you in a court of law, we should meet and talk about this.

① client ...... attorney

② judge ...... accused

③ criminal ...... victim

④ police officer ...... suspect

⑤ employer ...... employee

05 Choose the best sentence for the blank. [3점]

> Sam's Teacher : Thanks for coming in to school today. As I told you on the phone, I'm a little worried about Sam.
>
> Sam's Dad : I was surprised to hear from you. Did he do something wrong?
>
> Sam's Teacher : No, not at all. It's just that he seems distracted lately, unable to concen-trate. At the beginning of the term, he was one of my best students. But recently he's been late with homework, his scores are dropping, and he seems distant from his classmates. Has something been going on at home?
>
> Sam's Dad : That's so strange. I always though he was good in school. I have no idea what the issue might be. In fact, family life has been great.
>
> Sam's Teacher : _____

① If he does something like that again, he could be suspended.

② I hope he can continue his current level of school performance.

③ Sam has consistently improved as the semester has progressed.

④ Due to his disinterest in the class from the start, I've given up on him.

⑤ Please talk with him, because if he doesn't improve, he could fail the class.

06 Choose the sentence that best describes the situation. [2점]

> Bobby : I'm, bored, Grandpa. Can I play games on your smart-phone?
>
> Grandpa : Those games are such a waste of time and energy. Why don't you go outside and play? It's a beautiful day.
>
> Bobby : But there's nothing to do out there. When are Mom and Dad coming back from their trip?
>
> Grandpa : There's a whole world to explore out there. When I was young, I played outside from sunrise to sunset. I always found ways to have fun without smart-phones or video games. We have one more week together, so we best find some ways to entertain ourselves.
>
> Bobby : Would you come out and play with me?
>
> Grandpa : I'd love to. Let's go.

① Grandpa is looking after Bobby.

② Bobby's parents are working late.

③ Bobby is playing a smart-phone game.

④ Bobby and Grandpa are on a trip together.

⑤ Grandpa doesn't want to play outside with Bobby.

07 밑줄 친 부분이 가리키는 대상이 나머지 넷과 다른 것은? [2점]

> Memories can be easily fabricated so people become convinced of the reality of something that never happened. A famous example occurred to no less a personage than the Swiss psychologist Jean Piaget. Throughout ① his life, Piaget frequently spoke of a vivid memory of an incident from his early childhood. One day, while his nanny walked ② him in a pram down the street, a man leaped out from the bushes in an attempt to kidnap Piaget. The man struggled with the nanny, who successfully

fought him off, but not before ③ he inflicted scratches on her face. Piaget's memory of the frightening event was exquisitely detailed. ④ He recalled the faces of the people at the scene, the uniform of the policeman, the scratches on his nanny's face, and the exact location of the assault. And yet, as Piaget and ⑤ his family subsequently learned, the episode had never taken place. Years later, the nanny wrote to Piaget's parents and confessed to making up the whole story, including the scratches.

*pram : 유모차

[08~09] 다음 글에서 전체 흐름과 관계<u>없는</u> 문장을 고르시오.

08 Muhammad Ali refused to fight in the usual way. Ali's style ran counter to the boxing wisdom of the time in almost every way, but this unconventional style was exactly what made him a legendary boxer. ① As children and young adults, we are taught to conform to certain codes of behavior and ways of doing things, learning that being different comes with a social price. ② But there is a greater price to pay for blindly conforming: we lose the power that comes from our individuality, from a way of doing things that is authentically our own. ③ Following social conventions forms the basic ground-work for building a safe and stable society. ④ The way to be truly unconventional is to imitate no one, to fight and operate according to your own rhythms. ⑤ If your peculiarity is authentic enough, it will bring you attention and respect — the kind the crowd always has for the unconventional and extraordinary. [2점]

09 Developmental psychologists studying the impact of texting worry especially about young people because their interpersonal skills have not yet fully formed. ① Unlike kids, most adults were already stable social entities when they first got their hands on a text-capable mobile device. ② Besides, their ability to have a face-to-face conversation dramatically declines after extensive reliance on text messages. ③ However, this may not be the case with kids, according to Sherry Turkle, an interpersonal development researcher at MIT. ④ She believes kids are unlikely to develop face-to-face conversation skills if they overly rely on texting to communicate. ⑤ This may also prevent them from learning skills to think, reason, and self-reflect, as these skills are hard to acquire without sufficient experience in verbal communication. [2점]

10 다음 글의 요지로 가장 적질한 것은?

Katrina was the first hurricane to hit the United States to the accompaniment of continuous (24/7) television coverage. In social science terms, television constructed the frame of meaning with which audiences and decision-makers came to understand Katrina. For some along the coast, personal experience with Katrina might have helped. If you were on Dauphin Island, Biloxi Bay, St. Louis, or in a bar on Bourbon Street, the storm was slightly different. However, for most of us, the reality of the storm came through television networks. Even for "victims" who lost electrical power, if it came back, the coffee pot and the television were the first appliances back on so that their own experiences would be understood and confirmed in the context of the information provided by the media.

* 24/7 : 24 hours a day/7 days a week

① 재난에 대처하는 방법은 각 개인이 처한 상황에 따라 다르다.

② 텔레비전 보도가 자연재해의 경험에 대한 이해의 틀을 제공한다.

③ 부정적인 사건·사고에 치중하는 보도 관행은 바람직하지 못하다.

④ 자연재해 정보를 전문으로 다루는 텔레비전 네트워크가 필요하다.

⑤ 대중매체는 재난 복구와 이재민 구호 활동에서 핵심적인 역할을 한다.

[11~12] 다음 글의 밑줄 친 부분 중, 어법상 틀린 것을 고르시오.

11 Your communication with others ① involves some kind of risk, since communication means presenting to others a statement of your self, your role, the situation, and the others that they may reject. The communication climate is an important part of your guessing how much risk is involved for you in a given situation. You behave on the basis of how safe you think you are. If you do not feel secure, you will ② likely use defensive strategies. Perhaps you have been in a classroom situation in which the teacher keeps ③ insisting that students participate by discussing issues openly, and then the teacher shoots down their comments or ridicules them when they do. It does not take you long ④ to figure out that publicly being cut down by sarcasm is not comfortable. You learn quickly that the climate is not safe. Your communication takes on defensive strategies ⑤ are designed to protect yourself. [2점]

12 The quest of science has seen many triumphs and agonies. They usually went hand in hand and ① evidenced equally well the role of faith for science. The first major triumph was Copernicus' outline of the planetary order. He was far from proving definitely the heliocentric proposition. But he supplemented ② what he lacked in physical proofs with his faith in nature. From his belief ③ that nature was the handiwork of the Creator, he readily concluded that nature was simple. His system of the planets gave no better prediction of the motion of planets than did ④ Ptolemy's; the most attractive proof of Copernicus lay in the geometrical simplicity of the new ordering of the planets. It was a bold view, and he clung to it though people shook their heads in disbelief. But Galileo, whom people consider the father of the experimental method, ⑤ to praise Copernicus precisely for what he did: for staying with his belief. [3점]

doors, hood, and so on, is drawing attention as a potential breakthrough in dealing with this problem. Some researchers have already started experimenting with a prototype electric vehicle with an energy-storing trunk floor, whose extra energy storage could (B) reduce / be reduced the battery's weight by 15 percent. Ultimately, if this new technology reached the efficiency of the current lithium-ion battery, cars of this sort could store enough electricity to power (C) them / themselves for 80 miles in non-battery parts such as the roof or the doors. [3점]

	(A)	(B)	(C)
①	increase	reduce	them
②	increase	be reduced	themselves
③	increasing	reduce	them
④	increasing	reduce	themselves
⑤	increasing	be reduced	them

[13~14] (A), (B), (C)의 각 네모 안에서 어법에 맞는 표현으로 가장 적절한 것을 고르시오.

13 One of the biggest obstacles to (A) increase / increasing a hybrid car's range is the weight of the battery. More powerful batteries can power a car for a longer distance, but they also weigh more. A newly emerged concept of hybrid car, which can hold electricity in its

14 The following represents a classic study in perception. Twenty-three middle-level managers were asked to read a comprehensive case (A) describing / described the operational activities in a steel company. Six of the 23 executives worked in the area of sales, five in

production, four in accounting, and eight in miscellaneous functions. After reading the case, each of these executives was then asked to identify the problem that a new company president should deal with first. Eighty-three percent of the sales executives rated sales most important, but only 29 percent of the others (B) were / did . Similarly, the production executives gave priority to the production area, and the accounting people focused on accounting problems. These findings led to the conclusion (C) that / which these participants interpreted the case's priorities in terms of the activities and goals of the functional areas to which the executives were attached. [2점]

	(A)	(B)	(C)
①	describing	were	that
②	describing	did	that
③	describing	did	which
④	described	did	which
⑤	described	were	that

15 다음 글의 밑줄 친 부분 중, 문맥상 낱말의 쓰임이 적절하지 <u>않은</u> 것은? [2점]

Not much learning takes place unless you concentrate carefully on what you are learning. Concentration is basically thinking. Concentration can ① enhance your ability to do both mental and physical tasks. This is why many failures in school are due more to poor concentration than to ② low intelligence. Researchers note that one enemy of concentration is indecision: Indecision about when to study and which subject to study first is not only a great time-waster, but also a sure way to ③ eliminate a negative attitude toward studying. Personal problems also interfere with concentration. You will not make good use of your intelligence if you are ④ preoccupied with personal problems. After you have taken some ⑤ constructive action on your problem, you will then be in a better position to learn or perform well.

[16~18] 다음 글을 읽고, 빈칸에 들어갈 말로 가장 적절한 것을 고르시오.

16

The psychological effects of activities are not linear, but depend on their systematic relation to everything else we do. For instance, even though food is a source of pleasure, we cannot achieve happiness by eating around the clock. Meals raise our level of happiness, but only when we spend around five percent of our waking time eating; if we spent one hundred percent of the day eating, food would quickly cease to be rewarding. The same is true of most of the other good things in life: relaxation and television watching in small doses tend to improve the quality of daily life, but the effects are not _____; a point of diminishing returns is quickly reached. [3점]

① additive
② reductive
③ temporary
④ immediate
⑤ avoidable

17

Over the course of the past century, *National Geographic* magazine has come to be one of the primary means by which people in the United States receive information and images of the world outside their own borders. While *National Geographic* covers a range of topics—including the geographic and cultural wonders of the United States, wildlife and nature stories, and accounts of exploration of space, the oceans, and the polar ice caps—a good portion of its text and photographs is devoted to curious and exotic images of the peoples and cultures of the third world. *National Geographic* is located in a long tradition of travelogue as it sends its staff on expeditions to bring back stories and photos of faraway people and places. While its photographs and stories can be marveled at by readers in the privacy of their own homes, it draws people into contact with _____. [2점]

① their own traditions
② local economic issues
③ environmental movements
④ the realities of labor conditions
⑤ different cultures from their own

18

Suppose five competing firms all manage to lower the production cost and selling price of a standard product that they all produce. One does it by cutting its workers' pay. One does it by working them longer hours. One does it by getting some of its materials at lower prices from a poorer country. One does it by replacing some of its workers with robots. One does it by inventing an improvement to some of its machinery that allows it to cut work hours with no harm to anyone—no loss of output, profit, jobs, or pay. Ask which change was the most desirable, and scarcely will anybody name either of the first two. There may be votes for each of the other three, though perhaps on conditions. Were the foreign supplies produced by cruelly exploited labor, or with pollutant wastes? Could the workers displaced by robots depend on finding other jobs? Has the inventor of the improved machinery patented it, so that other firms and workers can't share its benefits? The respondents thus take _____ into account when considering the question. [3점]

① upcoming elections

② familiar social values

③ maximum productivity

④ national competitiveness

⑤ new technological advances

19 다음 글의 목적으로 가장 적절한 것은? [2점]

Dear Ms. Hart,

Upon completion of the screening of over one-hundred applicants, we are pleased to inform you that we were extremely impressed with your resume, interview, and test results. Therefore, you have been chosen for one of the five job positions currently being filled here at the ACME Consulting Firm. Should you choose to accept, you would immediately enter a six month, unpaid, internship program. Upon successful completion, you would then become a regular employee at full salary, including all standard benefits. There may also be the opportunity to transfer to one of our many branches around the country, or stay at our main office here in town. Congratulations, Ms. Hart! Please inform us of your decision no later than the end of the month.

Sincerely,
Cheryl Smith
Human Resources,
ACME Consulting Firm

① to encourage Ms. Hart to apply at the ACME Consulting Firm

② to congratulate Ms. Hart on the completion of her internship

③ to offer Ms. Hart a position at the ACME Consulting Firm

④ to inform Ms. Hart of her upcoming contract renewal

⑤ to notify Ms. Hart of her job application rejection

[20~21] 다음 글의 빈칸 (A), (B)에 들어갈 말로 가장 적절한 것을 고르시오.

20

Genes are pure information— information that can be encoded, recoded, and decoded, without any change of meaning. Pure information can be copied, and the accuracy of the copying can be __(A)__. In fact, DNA characters are copied with an exactness that rivals anything modern engineers can do. They are copied down through the generations, with just enough occasional errors to introduce variety. Among this variety, those coded combinations that become more numerous in the world will obviously and automatically be the ones that, when decoded and obeyed inside bodies, make those bodies take active steps to preserve and propagate those same DNA messages. We—and that means all living things—are survival machines programmed to __(B)__ the database that did the programming. Darwinism is now seen to be the survival of the survivors at the level of pure code. [2점]

*propagate : 유전시키다

	(A)	(B)
①	immense	remove
②	immense	reproduce
③	moderate	remove
④	insignificant	improve
⑤	insignificant	reproduce

21

A transition to an alternate energy cannot be motivated by a scarcity of fossil fuels. For decades, energy producers have continually identified new fossil fuel reserves and developed technologies to economically recover oil and gas from deposits previously deemed too difficult to access. __(A)__, Japan recently announced that they were able to extract methane from undersea hydrate deposits, which appear to contain more than twice as much carbon as in all of Earth's

fossil fuel combined. This means that humanity has burned just a small portion of our fossil fuels to date. Even though we have used such a small fraction of our fossil fuels, the planet has already experienced serious warming problems. If we continue to rely heavily on fossil fuels for our energy supply, climate-change related damage will become very severe long before there is any real pressure on our fossil fuel supply. _____(B)_____, movement for an alternate energy must be driven by a concerted effort to keep the climate livable and healthy. [2점]

	(A)	(B)
①	For example	Therefore
②	On the other hand	Nevertheless
③	For example	On the contrary
④	On the other hand	Therefore
⑤	In the same way	Nevertheless

[22~23] (A), (B), (C)의 각 네모 안에서 문맥에 맞는 표현으로 가장 적절한 것을 고르시오.

22

The autotrophic nature of plants makes them very dependent upon light and there are only a few plant species that cannot photosynthesize. Therefore, it is crucial that plants can sense light and respond to it. Plants need to locate light sources and grow towards them. Then they need to ensure that their leaves are orientated in the correct way to (A) maximize / minimize light exposure to the photosynthetic organs. But there is further information than this that plants gain from sensing light. Plants live in a changing environment, with day and night changes, seasonal changes, weather changes, and habitat changes. This means that plants need to be able to see their surroundings and then need to be very (B) flexible / rigid in their behavior to respond to these changes. Even photosynthesis has to be modified continually to cope with changing illumination. The sun should be brightest at midday, but few days are without clouds that can temporarily block out the sun. This leads to huge (C) constancy / variation in light intensity with which a plant needs to be able to deal. [3점]

*autotrophic : 자가[자급] 영양의

	(A)	(B)	(C)
①	maximize	flexible	variation
②	maximize	flexible	constancy
③	minimize	rigid	constancy
④	minimize	flexible	variation
⑤	minimize	rigid	variation

23

Once you begun to use rewards to control people, you cannot easily go back. When behaviors become (A) irrelevant / instrumental to monetary rewards — in other words, when people behave to get rewards — those behaviors will last only so long as the rewards are forthcoming. In some cases that may be fine, but in most cases the activities we reward are ones that we would like to have (B) persist / cease long after the rewards have stopped. For example, if you offered rewards to your children for studying — a dollar for each "A" on their report cards — you would want the children to remain enthusiastic about studying after your reward system was (C) initiated / terminated . But it is pretty likely that if they study for the rewards, they will stop studying when there are no longer rewards.

[2점]

	(A)	(B)	(C)
①	irrelevant	persist	terminated
②	irrelevant	cease	terminated
③	instrumental	cease	initiated
④	instrumental	persist	initiated
⑤	instrumental	persist	terminated

[24~25] 다음 글의 제목으로 가장 적절한 것을 고르시오.

24

We are accustomed to brushing our teeth every day. We know it to be a healthful ritual that preserves our teeth and gums and widens our smile. Its benefits are personal as well as social. But archaeologists working among the remains of eighteenth-century Annapolis — where a new class of people were eager for work — have suggested a new view of how and why we came to all this brushing and flossing and fussing. Mark Leone and his team of urban archaeologists found numerous toothbrushes under the streets of Annapolis. Eighteenth-century toothbrushes suggest a new emphasis on personal hygiene and the notion of the self-maintained individual. It's important: to have workers arrive on time and do a job, they have to develop discipline. So an industrial society emphasizes toothbrushes and a lot of other things like combs and clocks to help people make themselves orderly. Toothbrushes, it turns out, were instrumental in easing us into the Industrial Revolution. [2점]

① Annapolis: A Grand Archaeologist Attraction

② Appearance of "Toothbrush" in the English Language

③ Impact of the Toothbrush on the Dental Care Industry

④ Role of the Toothbrush in Developing an Industrial Workforce

⑤ Economic Changes Brought About by the Industrial Revolution

25

Researchers have noted a correlation between diet drink consumption and poor health for years. But many people simply believe that this undesirable correlation is due to the fact that people who are already unhealthy or heavy tend to drink diet soda in the first place. However, Susan Swithers of Purdue University claims that this superficial behavioral explanation does not address the health problems caused by unfounded faith in diet drinks. She points out that when the body responds normally to sugar, it releases the hormones needed to prepare itself for the increased intake of both calories and sugar. "What happens when you have diet soda is you sense the sweet taste — but calories and sugar don't show up," Swithers said. Accordingly, she warns that if this unnatural situation happens over time, people's brains and bodies may be trained not to release the protective hormones any longer, even when you actually intake real sugar. [2점]

① Preventing and Curing Soda Addiction

② Prevalence of Sugar Substitutes in Diet Drinks

③ Recent Consumer Preferences in the Soda Market

④ Disruptive Effect of Diet Drinks on Protective Hormones

⑤ How the Brain Copes with Excessive Sugar Consumption

[26~27] 글의 흐름으로 보아, 주어진 문장이 들어가기에 가장 적절한 곳을 고르시오.

26

Even so, modern weather forecasting is one of the great achievements of modern meteorology and all of science.

Modern weather forecasting today fuses advanced computer modeling with collective human insight. Together, they save lives and protect property through increasingly accurate predictions, as in the "Storm of the Century" in March 1993 and Superstorm Sandy in October 2012. (①) Ensemble forecasting allows meteorologists to get many "second opinions" on which to base even better forecasts. (②) Limits exist on how

good forecasts can become, however.
(③) Imperfect data, imperfect knowledge of how the atmosphere works,
limits on computing power, and even
chaos theory cause inaccurate forecasts.
(④) Our ability to forecast weather
skillfully has improved at the rate of about
one more day into the future every decade.
(⑤) It will continue to improve during
your lifetime, through new techniques
such as ensemble forecasting. [2점]

*ensemble forecasting : 종합적 분석에 기반한 기상예보

27

> Rather, we are witnessing the rise of
> an increasingly homogenized popular
> culture underwritten by a Western
> "culture industry."

Does globalization make people around the
world more alike or more different? This is
the question most frequently raised in the
subject of cultural globalization. (①) One
group of people argue that the former may
be unfortunately true. (②) They suggest
that we are not moving towards a cultural
rainbow that reflects the diversity of the
world's existing cultures. (③) As evidence
for their interpretation, these people
point to Amazonian Indians wearing Nike
training shoes, inhabitants of the Southern
Sahara purchasing Yankees baseball

caps, and Palestinian youths proudly
displaying their Chicago Bulls sweatshirts
in downtown Ramallah. (④) Referring to
the spread of Anglo–American values and
consumer goods as the "Americanization
of the world," the proponents of this
cultural homogeni–zation theory argue
that Western norms and lifestyles are
overwhelming more vulnerable cultures.
(⑤) Although there have been serious
attempts by some countries to resist these
forces of "cultural imperialism," the spread
of American popular culture seems to be
unstoppable. [3점]

28 Samuel Adams에 관한 다음 글의 내용과 일
치하지 <u>않는</u> 것은? [2점]

> As a young man, Samuel Adams
> (1722-1803) of colonial-era Boston
> developed a dream: the American
> colonies, he believed, should one
> day win complete independence
> from England and establish a
> government based on the writings of
> the English philosopher John Locke.
> According to Locke, a government
> should reflect the will of its citizens;
> a government that did not do so had
> lost its right to exist. Adams had
> inherited a brewery from his father,
> but he did not care about business.
> While the brewery went into

bankruptcy, he spent his time writing articles on the ideas of Locke and the need for independence. He was an excellent writer, good enough to get his articles published. But few took his ideas seriously at that time: he seemed to be somewhat out of touch with the world. Adams began to sink into a depression, because his self-appointed mission seemed hopeless.

① 영국의 철학자 John Locke로부터 영향을 받았다.

② 아버지로부터 물려받은 사업을 돌보지 않았다.

③ Locke의 사상과 독립의 필요성에 관한 글을 썼다.

④ 자신의 글을 출판할 정도로 훌륭한 작가였다.

⑤ 그의 사상은 그 당시 많은 사람들의 공감을 얻었다.

29 다음 글이 함축하는 바로 가장 적절한 것은?

[3점]

A recent study conducted by Mueller and Oppenheimer points to new evidence that people have better learning outcomes when they have taken handwritten notes, rather than typed ones. The researchers observed that the laptop note takers in their study generally produced long, word-for-word notes, while the handwriting note takers created relatively brief notes. Close attention was paid to the fact that the more copious, in-detail notes led to inferior retrieval of facts and concept comprehension, as revealed by the test scores. Those who were taking notes on the laptops did not have to choose what to type, as keyboarding is fast enough for word-for-word transcription. On the contrary, the longhand note takers had to process information more carefully to choose what to write down because their handwriting was not as fast. This initial selectivity is regarded as the reason for better long-term grasp of the lecture materials.

① Keyboard note-taking yields better factual content memorization.

② There is no evidence of the superiority of handwriting note-taking.

③ Handwriting note-taking is recommended for better academic performance.

④ Paper-and-pencil note-taking generally leads to more complete, detailed notes.

⑤ Word-for-word notes taken with laptops generally guarantee higher test scores.

[30~31] 다음 글의 주제로 가장 적절한 것을 고르시오.

30

Social networks seem to be particularly important as they increase access of employees to individuals with varying areas and levels of expertise. Consequently, facilitating the development of network ties, particularly weak ties, will have a positive impact on creativity. It is also clear that within the workplace, both informational and emotional support from colleagues is related to higher levels of creativity. Therefore, organizations (or leaders) interested in generating creativity should encourage strong relationships among employees. Finally, the presence of creative colleagues may be necessary for leaders to realize the impact of their own efforts to enhance creativity. Individuals display the highest level of creativity in response to supervisor feedback when they are in the presence of creative coworkers. Clearly, fostering individual creativity requires a consideration not just of the individual, but of his or her social context. [2점]

① harmful effects of strong network ties on creativity

② need for social networks to support the underprivileged

③ importance of respecting individuality within the workplace

④ danger of placing too much emphasis on creative outcomes

⑤ value of supportive social networks for enhancing creativity

31

For a period of more than a thousand years, Rome was hub of Western civilization. Eventually, however, the very life of the Empire was threatened by economic unrest and a series of rapid changes in government. Matters reached such a state that no person of importance dared to walk the streets of the capital without armed bodyguards, who were known as satellites. When the Empire fell, classical Latin ceased to be the language of commerce and science. But educated men brought back the ancient tongue ten centuries later and used it for most formal speech. Among the revived terms was *satellite*, which medieval rulers applied to their personal body-guards. When Johannes Kepler heard about the strange bodies revolving about Jupiter, he thought of guards and countries encircling the king. So, in 1611 Kepler named them *satellite*; soon the term was

applied to all heavenly bodies that revolve about primary masses. [2점]

① discovery of Jupiter's satellites
② rise and fall of the Roman Empire
③ revival of classical Latin for formal speech
④ Roman citizens' need for armed bodyguards
⑤ evolution of the meaning of the word satellite

32 다음 글이 시사하는 바로 가장 적절한 것은?
[2점]

The brilliance of warfare is that no amount of eloquence or talk can explain away a failure on the battlefield. A general has led his troops to defeat, lives have been wasted, and that is how history will judge him. You must strive to apply this ruthless standard in your daily life, judging people by the results of their actions, the deeds that can be seen and measured, and the steps they have taken to achieve their goals. What people say about themselves does not matter; people will say anything. Look at what they have done; deeds do not lie. You must also apply this logic to yourself. Stop bragging and set out to prove your worth by the fruits of your hard work. People will judge you by what you do, not what you say.

① Look before you leap.
② Do as you would be done by.
③ Actions speak louder than words.
④ The pen is mightier than the sword.
⑤ One swallow does not make a summer.

33 다음 도표의 내용과 일치하지 않는 것은?
[2점]

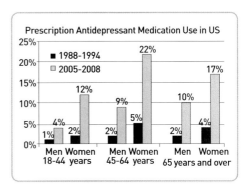

The above graph shows the percentage of Americans who answered yes to the question "Did you take prescription antidepressant medication in the past month?" by gender and age over two time periods, 1988–1994 and 2005–2008. ① There were general increases in the prescription antidepressant medication use across both genders and age groups between those two time frames. ② For men in the two older age categories, there were

significant increases from 2% to 9% and 2% to 10%, respectively, yet men aged 18−44 showed a rather moderate increase from 1% to 4%. ③ In contrast, all three female groups showed more drastic increases of 10% in the 18−44 group, 17% in the 45−64 group, and 13% in the oldest group. ④ Men showed the greatest increase in the oldest group, while for women it was in the 45−64 year age range. ⑤ In the period 2005−2008, for those 45−64 years old, over twice as many males took prescription antidepressant medication as females.

[34~35] 주어진 글 다음에 이어질 글의 순서로 가장 적절한 것을 고르시오.

34
> To be beautiful a thing must possess certain characteristics which awaken a feeling of appreciation in the normal person. It is true that the artistic judgment is not possessed equally by all, or at least it is not equally developed in all.

(A) The man without a musical education does not possess such knowledge, but he appreciates the harmony of tones when he hears it. The colorist knows how to produce pleasing effects with colors. He has acquired this knowledge which others do not possess, although they are able to appreciate his work.

(B) There are, however, certain combinations of sounds which are universally called harmonies and others which are called discords. There are certain combinations of colors which are regarded as pleasing and others which are displeasing.

(C) There are likewise certain geometrical forms or space arrangements which are beautiful, and others which are displeasing. The musician knows what tones will harmonize and which ones will not. [2점]

① (A) − (C) − (B)
② (B) − (A) − (C)
③ (B) − (C) − (A)
④ (C) − (A) − (B)
⑤ (C) − (B) − (A)

35
> One day as John was riding to work on his bike, his cell-phone began to ring. As he reached for his phone to pull it from his pocket with his right hand, he hit the brake with his left hand. He lost control and went flying over the front of his bike.

(A) While John didn't feel much pain, his ego was hurt. He quickly pulled himself up and looked around to make sure no one had seen his embarrassing tumble. Lucky for John, there were no witnesses. He brushed the dirt off his

face and got back on his way.

(B) After arriving at work, John became aware that he had severely scratched up his face and had a large cut across is cheek. He rushed to the hospital, where he was bandaged and received a few stitches. While not seriously injured, he still faced the shame of explaining the accident to his family.

(C) In that split second, his instinct was to protect his phone from damage at the cost of his own physical well-being. He held his arm up to keep his phone from hitting the pavement, instead using his face to break his fall. [2점]

① (A) − (C) − (B)
② (B) − (A) − (C)
③ (B) − (C) − (A)
④ (C) − (A) − (B)
⑤ (C) − (B) − (A)

blind you to the treacherous actions of those apparently on your side. Even the subtlest gradations of these emotions can color the way you look at events. The only remedy is to be aware that the pull of emotion is inevitable, to notice it when it is happening, and to compensate for it. When you have success, be extra wary. When you are angry, take no action. When you are fearful, know you are going to exaggerate the dangers you face. The more you can limit or compensate for your emotional responses, the closer you will come to seeing things as they are.

*treacherous : 배신하는

① 자신의 감정을 솔직하게 표현하라.
② 현실을 바로 보려면 감정에 휘둘리지 말라.
③ 원만한 문제 해결을 위해 이성에 호소하라.
④ 업무에 개인적인 감정을 개입시키지 말라.
⑤ 대화 시 상대방의 감정을 상하지 않게 하라.

36 다음 글에서 필자가 주장하는 바로 가장 적절한 것은? [2점]

Fear will make you overestimate a problem and act too passively. Anger and impatience will draw you into rash actions that will cut off your options. Overconfidence, particularly as a result of success, will make you go too far. Love and affection will

37 다음 글의 내용을 한 문장으로 요약하고자 한다. 빈칸 (A)와 (B)에 들어갈 말로 가장 적절한 것은? [3점]

Dr. Zeray Alemseged made a remarkable contribution to the field of anthropology. Inspired by his experience of working in Ethiopia's National Museum, Alemseged went to the University of Paris for a

Ph.D. program. After he returned to Ethiopia, he set his sight on an isolated region as an optimal place to look for new fossils. Other scientists had avoided this area, due to a centuries-old tribal conflict that made it too dangerous to work in, but he did not give up convincing both sides to allow him to work there. Alemseged and his team finally discovered the fossilized skeleton of a 3.3 million-year-old baby girl. It included the shoulder blades almost intact, which had never been found fossilized as they are paper-thin. Based on the shape of these blades, Alemseged and his colleagues published a study suggesting that Australopithecus afarensis was still a capable climber 3.3 million years ago, which means our ancestors gave up tree-climbing considerably later than many researchers had previously suggested.

*Australopithecus afarensis : 에티오피아 Afar 지역에서 화석이 발견된 오스트랄로피테쿠스

Thanks to his ____(A)____, Dr. Zeray Alemeseged has contributed to a remarkable advancement in anthropology by finding evidence that human ancestors ____(B)____ their tree-climbing ability significantly later than other researchers had claimed.

	(A)	(B)
①	perseverance	abandoned
②	generosity	abandoned
③	perseverance	acquired
④	generosity	improved
⑤	creativity	acquired

[38~39] 다음 글을 읽고, 물음에 답하시오.

One of the most moving piano recitals I ever heard was by the late Rudolf Serkin, who delivered a luminous performance of the Beethoven *Waldstein Sonata* and the Schubert *Wanderer Fantasy*. During one of the virtuoso runs that make up the Schubert work, Serkin's fingers became audibly tangled. Despite the apparent mistake, Serkin wouldn't have this bother him, and went on playing. When he rose from the bench at the conclusion of the piece, he openly acknowledged his error by good-naturedly shaking his fist at the piano. In what could have been an embarrassing situation, Serkin was able to evoke laughter from the audience with his witty action. Needless to say, the audience were moved by the lovely performance as a whole. It was a more revealing, more beautiful version of this piece than many other "perfect" ones I have heard played by other musicians before or since. The lesson is obvious: Deliver a good performance overall, and you will be forgiven an error or two,

even an obvious one. All the more, do not allow your mistakes to interrupt your performance. Just as Serkin's audience did not attend his recital for the purpose of catching him in a blunder, so it is highly unlikely that your audience will have gathered for the express purpose of seeing you make a mistake. And if you do err while performing, embrace the mistake and _____.

38 윗글의 빈칸에 들어갈 말로 가장 적절한 것은? [2점]

① take a brief time out

② get on with the show

③ shake your fist in anger

④ restart from the beginning

⑤ choose another piece to play

39 윗글의 Rudolf Serkin에 관한 내용과 일치하지 않는 것은? [2점]

① 연주회에서 Beethoven과 Schubert의 곡을 연주했다.

② 연주를 하다가 명백한 실수를 했다.

③ 연주를 중단하고 일어나서 청중에게 사과했다.

④ 재치 있는 행동으로 청중의 웃음을 자아냈다.

⑤ 아름다운 연주로 청중을 감동시켰다.

[40~41] 다음 글을 읽고, 물음에 답하시오.

I'm always looking for communicators who create exciting ways to engage an audience. I've rarely seen anyone use more props than a young Italian entrepreneur and television host, Marco Montemagno.

Montemagno frequently speaks on the topic of Internet culture, showing Italians why the Internet should be embraced and not feared. He presents to groups as large as three thousand people in places such as Rome, Milan, and Venice. Since the majority of people in his audience are beginners in using the Web, (a) he uses language that everyone can understand (well, assuming you know Italian). His slides are very simple and visual; he often employs just photographs, animation, and video. But what truly differentiates Montemagno from the majority of presenters is (b) his unbelievable number of props and demonstrations.

In parts of his presentation, Montemagno will ask for his audience to join him onstage. For example, (c) he asks a volunteer to fold a T-shirt on the stage. Like most people, the volunteer will take about twenty seconds to fold the shirt in a conventional way. When (d) he's done, the audience watch a popular YouTube video of someone demonstrating how to fold a shirt in five seconds. Montemagno then duplicates it as the audience cheer. (e) His point is that the Internet can instruct on a deep, intellectual level, but it can also make

the most mundane tasks easier.

*prop : 소품

40 윗글의 밑줄 친 (a)~(e) 중에서, 가리키는 대상이 나머지 넷과 다른 것은? [2점]

① (a) ② (b)

③ (c) ④ (d)

⑤ (e)

41 윗글의 Marco Montemagno에 관한 내용과 일치하지 않는 것은? [2점]

① He engages in business and also hosts a TV program.

② He encourages his audience not to fear the Internet.

③ He makes presentations to very large groups in English.

④ He utilizes props and other visual materials in his presentations.

⑤ He incorporates the audience into his presentations.

[42~43] 다음 글을 읽고, 물음에 답하시오.

(A)

Haydn was delighted with London in most of its aspects, but there was one kind of pupil that he perfectly willing to leave behind when he returned to his beloved Vienna. One day a nobleman visited him and, expressing his fondness for music, said he would like Haydn to give him a few lessons in composition at one pound per lesson.

(B)

Then Haydn suggested that the pupil rewrite the music to his own taste; but this he declined to do, though he persisted in his question about Haydn's composition choices. At last, Haydn lost all patience with this noble critic, and said, "I see that it is you who are so good as to give lessons to me. I do not want your lessons, for I feel that I do not deserve the honor of having such a master as yourself. I must say farewell," and showed the nobleman the door.

(C)

Haydn could offer no objection to this. They then set to work to examine the music. Several places were found which, when asked why he did this and that, Haydn could only say he wrote it so to obtain a good effect. But the nobleman was not satisfied with such a reason and declared that unless the composer gave him a better reason for his innovations, they were good for nothing.

(D)

Haydn agreed and asked when they should begin, "At once, if you have no objection," said he, drawing from his pocket one of Haydn's quartets. "For the first lesson, let us examine this quartet and you tell me the reasons for some modulations and certain progressions that are contrary to all rules of composition."

*quartet : 4중주곡
**modulation : 조음(조 바꾸기)

42 주어진 글 (A)에 이어질 내용을 순서에 맞게 배열한 것으로 가장 적절한 것은? [3점]

① (B) − (D) − (C)

② (C) − (B) − (D)

③ (C) − (D) − (B)

④ (D) − (B) − (C)

⑤ (D) − (C) − (B)

43 윗글의 제목으로 가장 적절한 것은? [2점]

① Money Buys Patience

② Pleasure of Examining Music

③ A Most Beautiful London Memory

④ Not a Good Pupil, But a Harsh Critic

⑤ Inspiration from a Challenging Question

[44~45] 다음 글을 읽고, 물음에 답하시오.

Despite the many eco-friendly movements to prevent global warming, Arctic ice melting at previously unseen rates. The melting has led to coastal ice in parts of Canada and Alaska becoming quite   (A) . That ice easily breaks away in large chunks (a process known as calving) and melts in the open ocean.

There is also less sea ice in the Arctic Ocean because ice has floated into the Atlantic Ocean. A record low for Arctic sea ice was recorded on August 15, 2005, but the Arctic saw another milestone in the summer of 2007. In August, the Northwest Passage had almost no floating ice. It was the first time the Passage had been completely open to shipping since people started keeping records in 1972.

Arctic sea ice that was previously considered   (B)   is now rapidly disappearing. The disappearance of this ice must be noted seriously because it plays an important role in keeping temperatures down around the world. Whereas sea ice reflects eighty percent of sunlight back into the atmosphere, ocean water absorbs ninety percent. As melting ice exposes more ocean to direct sunlight, scientists expert water temperatures to rise even more, causing the melting ice to disappear at an ever-increasing rate.

44 윗글의 제목으로 가장 적절한 것은? [2점]

① Developing a Plan to Battle Arctic Ice Melt

② Scientific Ways to Monitor Global Warming

③ Differing Effects of Sunlight on Land and Ocean

④ Vicious Circle of Global Warming and Arctic Ice Melt

⑤ Changes in Ocean Navigation Owing to Global Warming

45 윗글의 빈칸 (A)와 (B)에 들어갈 말로 가장 적절한 것은? [2점]

	(A)	(B)
①	brittle	permanent
②	brittle	vulnerable
③	solid	defenseless
④	solid	permanent
⑤	soft	vulnerable

Chance is always powerful.

Let your hook be always cast;

in the pool where you least expect it, there will be a fish.

우연은 항상 강력하다.

항상 낚시바늘을 던져두라.

전혀 기대하지 않은 곳에 물고기가 있을 것이다.

— 오비디우스(Ovid)

A weak man has doubts before a decision,

a strong man has them afterwards.

약한 사람은 결정을 내리기 전에 의심하고,

강한 사람은 결정을 내린 후 의심한다.

– 카를 크라우스(Karl Kraus)

MeMo

MeMo

MeMo

MeMo

SPECIAL INFORMATION
· 2025 ·
SERVICE COMPANY

육사 | 해사 | 공사 | 국군간호사관

사관학교 기출문제

영 어

2024~2015
10
개년
연차별 동형
기출문제

정답 및 해설

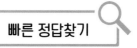

빠른 정답찾기

2024 학년도

01 ②	02 ②	03 ⑤	04 ①	05 ②	06 ①	07 ④	08 ④	09 ②	10 ⑤
11 ②	12 ①	13 ⑤	14 ④	15 ①	16 ①	17 ②	18 ③	19 ②	20 ③
21 ⑤	22 ③	23 ⑤	24 ①	25 ④	26 ③	27 ③	28 ⑤	29 ③	30 ④

2023 학년도

01 ④	02 ④	03 ⑤	04 ③	05 ④	06 ④	07 ②	08 ①	09 ③	10 ①
11 ②	12 ①	13 ⑤	14 ④	15 ③	16 ⑤	17 ①	18 ①	19 ②	20 ③
21 ⑤	22 ⑤	23 ④	24 ①	25 ②	26 ②	27 ⑤	28 ③	29 ⑤	30 ④

2022 학년도

01 ③	02 ⑤	03 ⑤	04 ②	05 ④	06 ⑤	07 ④	08 ④	09 ③	10 ③
11 ②	12 ①	13 ⑤	14 ④	15 ④	16 ②	17 ①	18 ①	19 ②	20 ④
21 ③	22 ②	23 ⑤	24 ①	25 ①	26 ②	27 ①	28 ⑤	29 ③	30 ④

2021 학년도

01 ⑤	02 ④	03 ⑤	04 ④	05 ⑤	06 ③	07 ③	08 ②	09 ①	10 ②
11 ①	12 ④	13 ②	14 ②	15 ④	16 ⑤	17 ④	18 ③	19 ③	20 ①
21 ④	22 ③	23 ⑤	24 ①	25 ②	26 ①	27 ①	28 ⑤	29 ⑤	30 ②
31 ③	32 ①	33 ⑤	34 ⑤	35 ③	36 ①	37 ②	38 ⑤	39 ④	40 ②
41 ①	42 ④	43 ⑤	44 ②	45 ③					

2020 학년도

01 ④	02 ①	03 ①	04 ②	05 ⑤	06 ③	07 ⑤	08 ①	09 ①	10 ③
11 ②	12 ①	13 ①	14 ⑤	15 ⑤	16 ④	17 ③	18 ④	19 ②	20 ③
21 ②	22 ④	23 ③	24 ③	25 ②	26 ②	27 ①	28 ②	29 ③	30 ②
31 ⑤	32 ③	33 ④	34 ④	35 ③	36 ④	37 ⑤	38 ①	39 ④	40 ②
41 ⑤	42 ④	43 ⑤	44 ④	45 ⑤					

빠른 정답찾기

2019 학년도

01 ⑤	02 ②	03 ②	04 ④	05 ①	06 ②	07 ③	08 ②	09 ①	10 ①
11 ④	12 ①	13 ②	14 ④	15 ⑤	16 ③	17 ④	18 ⑤	19 ④	20 ③
21 ④	22 ②	23 ⑤	24 ⑤	25 ③	26 ①	27 ①	28 ③	29 ①	30 ⑤
31 ③	32 ⑤	33 ②	34 ④	35 ③	36 ④	37 ②	38 ②	39 ③	40 ③
41 ①	42 ⑤	43 ⑤	44 ③	45 ⑤					

2018 학년도

01 ⑤	02 ③	03 ③	04 ⑤	05 ①	06 ④	07 ③	08 ④	09 ③	10 ③
11 ⑤	12 ③	13 ①	14 ①	15 ②	16 ②	17 ④	18 ②	19 ②	20 ②
21 ①	22 ⑤	23 ⑤	24 ①	25 ①	26 ④	27 ⑤	28 ④	29 ④	30 ①
31 ⑤	32 ③	33 ④	34 ②	35 ⑤	36 ①	37 ①	38 ⑤	39 ②	40 ②
41 ④	42 ③	43 ④	44 ④	45 ⑤					

2017 학년도

01 ⑤	02 ③	03 ②	04 ⑤	05 ①	06 ②	07 ⑤	08 ④	09 ④	10 ③
11 ⑤	12 ④	13 ①	14 ①	15 ②	16 ①	17 ②	18 ①	19 ③	20 ③
21 ①	22 ④	23 ⑤	24 ③	25 ④	26 ⑤	27 ③	28 ①	29 ②	30 ④
31 ③	32 ④	33 ③	34 ③	35 ④	36 ③	37 ①	38 ②	39 ②	40 ④
41 ⑤	42 ②	43 ①	44 ⑤	45 ⑤					

2016 학년도

01 ③	02 ①	03 ①	04 ②	05 ⑤	06 ④	07 ③	08 ③	09 ④	10 ⑤
11 ③	12 ④	13 ①	14 ⑤	15 ③	16 ④	17 ②	18 ②	19 ⑤	20 ②
21 ④	22 ⑤	23 ①	24 ②	25 ②	26 ⑤	27 ②	28 ①	29 ⑤	30 ③
31 ②	32 ③	33 ③	34 ①	35 ④	36 ⑤	37 ①	38 ④	39 ①	40 ④
41 ③	42 ①	43 ②	44 ②	45 ②					

2015 학년도

01 ①	02 ②	03 ④	04 ①	05 ⑤	06 ①	07 ③	08 ③	09 ②	10 ②
11 ⑤	12 ⑤	13 ④	14 ②	15 ③	16 ①	17 ⑤	18 ②	19 ③	20 ②
21 ①	22 ①	23 ⑤	24 ④	25 ④	26 ④	27 ③	28 ⑤	29 ③	30 ⑤
31 ⑤	32 ③	33 ⑤	34 ③	35 ④	36 ②	37 ①	38 ②	39 ③	40 ④
41 ③	42 ⑤	43 ④	44 ④	45 ①					

2024학년도 기출문제 정답 및 해설

2024학년도

[영어]

정답 및 해설

▌[영어] 2024학년도 | 정답

01	②	02	②	03	⑤	04	①	05	②
06	①	07	④	08	④	09	②	10	⑤
11	②	12	①	13	⑤	14	④	15	①
16	①	17	②	18	③	19	②	20	③
21	⑤	22	③	23	⑤	24	①	25	④
26	③	27	③	28	③	29	③	30	④

[영어] 2024학년도 | 해설

01 어법상 틀린 것 고르기 ②

[정답해설]

which → in which(=where)

which는 관계대명사로 선행사 markets를 수식하기 위한 형용사절을 이끈다. 그런데 뒤에 완전한 문장이 왔으므로, '전치사+관계대명사'의 형태인 in which로 고쳐 쓰거나 장소를 나타내는 관계부사 where로 고쳐 써야 옳다.

[오답해설]

① it은 앞의 단수 보통명사 money를 가리키는 지시대명사로 옳게 사

용되었다.

③ to earn은 앞의 명사 income을 수식하는 to부정사의 형용사적 용법으로 옳게 사용되었다.

④ that은 앞의 It is와 함께 It is ~ that의 강조구문으로 옳게 사용되었다.

⑤ 주격 관계대명사 that 다음의 동사는 선행사 purpose와의 수의 일치에 따라 3인칭 단수 현재의 형태인 transcends를 사용한 것은 적절하다.

[핵심어휘]

▫ component (구성) 요소, 부품

▫ isolation 고립, 분리, 격리

▫ coherently 밀착하여, 시종 일관하여

▫ configuration (각 요소의) 상대적 배치, 배열

▫ facilitate 가능하게 하다, 용이하게 하다

▫ distribution 분배, 배분, 유통

▫ transcend 초월하다, 능가하다

[본문해석]

경제 체제의 필수적인 구성요소들과 그것들이 어떻게 작동하는지는 분리하여 보았을 때가 아니라, 오히려 더 큰 사회적 그리고 문화적 환경과 연결되어 있을 때 가장 잘 이해가 된다. 돈은 어떤 경제의 필수적인 구성요소이지만, 그것으로 살 수 있는 어떤 것이 기업에 의해 생산되지 않는 한 그것은 그 자체로 아무런 도움이 되지 않는다. 기업도 핵심적인 역할을 하지만, 그들의 상품을 살 의지와 능력이 있는 가계들이 없고, 상품을 사고 팔 수 있는 시장이 없다면, 그들은 이익을 낼 수 없다. 시장에서 소비할 돈을 벌 수입원이 없는 가계는 미국의 경제 체제에서 소비자가 될 수 없다. 그것들이 경제적인 생산, 분배, 그리고 소비를 가능하게 하는 것은 오직 돈, 시장, 기업, 그리고 가계가 특정한 배치로 일관되게 합쳐질 때이다. 그것들은 하나의 체제를 구성하고 그 체제는 구성요소 그 자체의 특정 목적을 능가하는 더 넓은 목적에 도움을 준다.

02 어법상 맞는 것 고르기 ②

[정답해설]

(A) placing / (B) those / (C) discovered

(A) compare A with B 구문에서 A와 B는 동일 형태가 와야 한다. 해당

문장에서 B에 동명사인 moving이 쓰였으므로 A에도 동명사의 형태인 placing을 쓰는 것이 적절하다.

(B) 투명한 병에 담긴 초콜릿과 불투명한 병에 담긴 초콜릿을 비교하는 것이므로, chocolates를 대신하는 지시대명사 those를 쓰는 것이 적절하다.

(C) 연구원들이 실험을 통해 음식이 과잉 공급된 가정에서 두 배의 비율로 소비된 사실을 발견하였다. 즉, 행위의 주체인 사람이 주어이므로 능동태 동사인 discovered를 쓰는 것이 적절하다.

[핵심어휘]

- experimenter 실험자
- strategically 전략상, 전략적으로
- transparent 투명한, 명료한
- opaque 불투명한, 흐릿한
- principle 원리, 원칙
- apply to ~에 적용되다
- stock 채우다, 갖추다
- moderate 보통의, 중간의
- quantity 양, 다량
- ready-to-eat 즉석의, 바로 먹을 수 있는
- overstocked 공급 과잉의, 필요 이상의

[본문해석]

단지 음식이나 음료를 눈에 보이지 않게 두거나 그것을 몇 피트 떨어진 곳에 두는 것이 소비에 큰 영향을 미칠 수 있음을 연구에서 보여준다. 일련의 연구에서, 실험자들은 전략적으로 사무실 주변에 초콜릿 병을 놓아두고 얼마나 많이 소비되었는지 신중하게 숫자를 세었다. 한 조건에서, 그들은 사람들의 책상 위에 병을 놓는 것과 그것들을 단지 6피트 떨어진 곳에 놓는 것을 비교했다. 다른 조건에서, 그들은 초콜릿을 투명한 병 또는 불투명한 병 중 하나에 담았다. 사람들의 책상 위에 초콜릿을 놓아 둔 것은 직원 일인당 매일 평균 6개의 초콜릿을 더 소비하는 결과를 낳았고, 투명한 병에 있는 초콜릿은 불투명한 병에 있는 것보다 46% 더 빨리 소비됐다. 비슷한 원리가 집 주위의 음식에도 적용된다. 다른 연구에서, 연구원들은 사람들의 가정에 많은 양 또는 적당한 양 중 하나의 즉석 식사를 제공했고, 음식이 과잉 공급된 가정에서 두 배의 비율로 소비된 것을 발견했다.

03 　　　문맥상 부적절한 낱말 고르기　　　⑤

[정답해설]

slower → faster

제시문에 따르면 지구와 달리 화성과 금성에서 활성산소가 축적되지 않은 결정적인 이유는 활성산소의 생성 속도에 있다고 하였다. 즉, 새로운 암석과 광물이 노출되어 산화되는 속도보다 산소가 더 빠르게 생성되어야만 공기 중에 산소가 축적될 수 있으므로, ⑤의 slower는

faster로 고쳐 써야 옳다.

[핵심어휘]

- ultraviolet radiation 자외선 방사[복사]
- cost 잃게 하다, 희생시키다
- sterile 불모의, 메마른
- crust 지각, 껍질
- oxidize 산화시키다, 녹슬게 하다
- carbon dioxide 이산화탄소
- a trace of 약간의, 소량의
- free oxygen 활성 산소
- critical 대단히 중요한, 결정적인
- weathering 풍화(작용)
- volcanic activity 화산 활동

[본문해석]

수십 억 년에 걸쳐, 자외선 방사의 영향으로 인한 물의 손실로 화성과 금성이 바다를 잃은 것으로 생각된다. 오늘날, 두 행성 모두 건조하고 메마르며, 지각은 산화되고 대기는 이산화탄소로 가득 차 있다. 두 행성 모두 서서히 산화되었고, 대기에 소량의 활성 산소조차 결코 축적되지 않았다. 왜 이런 일이 화성과 금성에서는 일어나고, 지구에서는 일어나지 않았을까? 결정적인 차이는 산소의 생성 속도에 있었을 수도 있다. 풍화와 화산 활동에 의해 새로운 암석, 광물, 그리고 가스가 노출되는 속도보다 산소가 더 빠르지 않게 천천히 생성된다면, 이 모든 산소는 공기 중에 축적되는 대신 지각에 의해 소모될 것이다. 지각은 천천히 산화시킬 것이지만, 산소는 결코 공기 중에 축적되지 않을 것이다. 새로운 암석과 광물이 노출되는 속도보다 산소가 더 느리게 (→ 더 빠르게) 생성되어야만 그것이 공기 중에 축적되기 시작할 수 있다.

04 　　　문맥에 맞는 낱말 고르기　　　①

[정답해설]

(A) evident / (B) relevant / (C) included

(A) 작가들이 명확한 언급 없이 독자로 하여금 이야기를 추론하고, 결론 내리고, 예측하도록 충분한 단서를 제공하는 글쓰기 장르는 미스터리 소설이 가장 확실하므로, (A)에 들어갈 말은 'evident(분명한, 명백한)'가 적절하다.

(B) 미스터리 소설의 독자들은 스스로 단서를 찾아 본문의 퍼즐을 짜 맞추기를 원하지만, 작가가 그 이야기와 관련된 정보를 바로 밝힌다면 독자들은 그 소설을 읽는 것을 상당히 지루해할 것이다. 그러므로 (B)에 들어갈 말은 'relevant(관련 있는)'가 적절하다.

(C) 미스터리 소설에서 독자가 추론과 결론을 내리는 동안, 작가는 독자를 그 방향으로 이끌 수 있는 단서들을 이미 제공해 왔으므로, (C)에 들어갈 말은 'included(포함하다)'가 적절하다.

[핵심어휘]

- there are times when ~할 때가 있다.
- explicitly 명쾌하게, 명료하게, 분명하게
- state 말하다, 언급하다, 진술하다
- genre 장르
- evident 분명한, 명백한
- inference 추론, 추리, 추정
- prediction 예측, 예견
- forthcoming 기꺼이 말하는[밝히는]
- relevant 관련 있는, 의의가 있는
- irrelevant 무관한, 상관없는
- take A out of B B에서 A를 제거하다
- savvy 잘 아는, 박식한
- piece ~ together ~을 조립하다[짜 맞추다]
- figure out 이해하다, 생각해 내다
- identify 알아보다, 확인하다
- unfold 펼치다, 전개하다

[본문해석]

작가들은 우리가 특정한 메시지를 결정하고 그것을 명확하게 언급함이 없이 우리를 올바른 방향으로 인도하기 위한 충분한 단서를 제공하기를 바랄 때가 있다. 아마도 이것이 가장 (A) 분명한 글쓰기 장르는 미스터리 소설이다. 작가는 독자로 하여금 추론 후에 추론, 결론 후에 결론, 그리고 예측 후에 예측을 하도록 하는 단서들의 그물망을 만든다. 만일 작가가 가장 (B) 관련 있는 정보를 바로 밝힌다면 미스터리 이야기를 읽는 것이 얼마나 지루할지 상상해보라. 그것은 모든 재미를 없앨 것이다. 박식한 독자로서, 우리는 단서를 찾아 마음속으로 본문의 퍼즐을 짜 맞추기를 원한다. 등장인물이 식별할 수 없거나 상황이 전개되기 전에 결과를 아는 것에 대한 해결책을 생각해 내는 것보다 독자에게 더 만족스러운 것은 없다. 기억하라, 독서는 계속되는 대화이다. 그것은 독자가 추론과 결론을 내리는 동안, 작가가 독자를 그 방향으로 이끌 수 있는 단서를 (C) 포함해 왔다는 것을 의미한다.

05 글의 요지 파악하기 ②

[정답해설]

제시문에 따르면 습관의 지속성을 유지하기 위해서는 어떤 외부 요인이나 그날의 성향과 기분에 따라 좌우되지 않고, 마치 근육처럼 처음부터 습관을 강하게 길러 깨지지 않도록 할 것을 주문하고 있다. 그러므로 습관을 꾸준히 유지하려면 훈련을 통해 처음부터 강화해야 한다는 ②의 설명이 제시문의 요지로 가장 적절하다.

[핵심어휘]

- prove to be ~임이 판명[입증]되다, ~임이 드러나다
- fragile 깨지기 쉬운, 허약한

- predictably 예측[예견]할 수 있게
- regret 후회하다, 유감스럽게 생각하다
- continuity 지속성, 연속성
- muscle 근육, 힘
- external factor 외부 요인
- disposition 기질, 성향
- vulnerable 취약한, 연약한
- interruption 중단, 가로막음
- by all means 기어코, 반드시
- per se 그 자체로
- a bunch of 다수의

[본문해석]

습관은 우리의 삶에서 변화가 예측 가능하거나 예측 불가능하게 나타날 때 종종 꽤 깨지기 쉬운 것으로 드러난다. 누군가가 결혼 전 '시간이 있을 때' 자신의 '좋은 취미'에 대해 불평하거나 후회하는 것을 몇 번이나 들어본 적이 있는가? 나는 그 소리를 수십 번 들었고 사람들은 항상 지속성이 부족한 것에 대한 구실을 찾으려고 한다. 그게 우리가 하는 행동이다. 우리는 변명을 찾아낸다. 하지만 우리가 어떻게 기능하고 습관이 어떻게 기능하는지를 생각하고 이해하려고 노력하는 데 시간을 좀 쓴다면, 마치 근육이 그런 것처럼 습관을 강화하는 훈련이 필요하다는 것을 알 수 있고, 습관들이 어떤 외부 요인이나 혹은 유지해야 할 성향과 기분에 더 의존하면 할수록, 습관이 중단에 더 취약하다는 것을 알 수 있다. 처음부터 여러분의 습관을 강하게 길러라. 조깅을 시작하고 싶다면, 날씨가 좋을 때, 바람이 불거나 비가 올 때, 행복할 때, 그리고 반드시 슬플 때 하라. 그것은 수행해야 할 다수의 조건들을 충족시키는 것을 넘어 그 자체로 즐거움의 영역과 연결하는 것이다.

06 글의 요지 파악하기 ①

[정답해설]

제시문의 마지막 문장에서 사려 깊은 사람들은 행복을 얻는 가장 좋은 방법이 우리의 욕망을 지배하는 것이라고 주장해 왔지만, 보통 사람들은 이 충고를 무시해왔다고 서술하고 있다. 그러므로 많은 사람들은 욕망을 통제하는 것이 우리를 행복하게 할 수 있다는 생각을 쉽게 묵살한다는 ①의 설명이 제시문의 요지로 가장 적절하다.

[오답해설]

② 일반적인 믿음과 달리, 우리의 욕망을 지배하는 것은 거의 불가능하다.
③ 행복은 사랑하는 사람들의 도움 없이는 거의 이루어지지 않는다.
④ 우리의 욕망이 자라는 것은 바로 우리 환경 안에서 이다.
⑤ 아무것도 원하지 않으면, 아무것도 얻지 못한다.

[핵심어휘]

- unanimously 이의 없이, 만장일치로
- convince 납득시키다, 설득하다
- enhance 강화하다, 증진시키다
- suppress 진압하다, 억압하다
- eradicate 근절하다, 없애다
- master 참다, 억누르다
- dismiss 묵살하다, 일축하다
- contrary to ~에 반해서
- breed 기르다, 양육하다

[본문해석]

사람들은 보통 행복을 얻는 가장 좋은 방법은 그들의 환경 즉, 집, 옷, 차, 직업, 교유관계를 바꾸는 것이라고 생각한다. 그러나 욕망에 관해 면밀하게 생각한 사람들은 지속적인 행복을 얻는 가장 좋은 방법은 아마도 정말 유일한 방법이지만, 우리 주변의 세상 또는 그 안에서 우리의 위치를 바꾸는 것이 아니라 우리 스스로를 변화시키는 것이라는 결론을 만장일치로 도출했다. 특히, 우리가 이미 소유한 것을 원한다고 스스로를 설득할 수 있다면, 우리 환경에 아무런 변화 없이 우리의 행복을 극적으로 증진시킬 수 있다. 만족은 우리 내부에서 발견한 욕망을 충족시키기 위해 일하는 것이 아니라 우리의 욕망을 선택적으로 억압하거나 없앰으로써 얻는 게 최선이라는 사실은 일반인들에게 떠오르지 않는다. 시대와 문화를 통해, 사려 깊은 사람들은 행복을 얻는 가장 좋은 방법이 우리의 욕망을 억누르는 것이라고 주장해 왔지만, 시대와 문화를 통해, 보통 사람들은 이 충고를 무시해왔다.

---

07 밑줄 친 문장의 의미 파악하기 ④

[정답해설]

제시문에서 '긴 녹색 탁자 앞에 서다'는 말의 요점은 긴 녹색 탁자에 둘러앉아 있는 장교들에게 좋은 주장을 펼칠 수 없다면, 여러분의 행동을 재고하라고 서술되어 있다. 그러므로 'stand before the long green table(긴 녹색 탁자 앞에 서다)'는 말은 ④의 "권위 있는 인사들에게 당신의 행동을 설득력 있게 정당화하다"이다.

[오답해설]

① 지속적으로 변화하는 현장 조건에 맞게 전략을 수정하다
② 더 많은 지식이 있는 사람들에게 업무에 대한 도움을 요청하다.
③ 동료의 승인 없이 용기 있게 계획을 실행하다
⑤ 그들의 캠페인 전략이 현실적이지 않다고 동료들을 설득하다

[핵심어휘]

- serve the military 군복무를 하다
- conference table 회의 탁자
- boardroom 중역 회의실, 이사회실

[핵심어휘]

- felt 펠트(모직이나 털을 압축해서 만든 천)
- formal proceeding 공식적인 절차
- adjudicate 판결하다, 심판하다
- make a good case 좋은 사례를 들다, 좋은 주장을 펼치다
- reconsider 재고하다, 다시 생각하다
- take a step 조치를 취하다
- courageously 용감하게, 대담하게
- approval 승인, 인정
- peer 또래, 동료
- convincingly 설득력 있게, 납득이 가도록
- authority figure 권위 있는 인사, 실세

[본문해석]

군 복무를 할 때, 나는 이 말에 굳게 의지하여 내 행동을 인도했다. 어려운 결정을 내릴 때마다, 나는 "긴 녹색 탁자 앞에 설 수 있습니까?"라고 스스로에게 물었다. 제2차 세계대전 이후, 군 회의실에서 사용되는 회의 탁자는 녹색 천으로 덮인 길고 폭이 좁은 가구로 만들어졌다. 여러 명의 장교들이 어떤 문제를 판단해야 하는 공식적인 절차가 진행될 때마다, 장교들은 탁자 주변에 모이곤 했다. 그 말의 요점은 간단하다. 긴 녹색 탁자에 둘러앉아 있는 장교들에게 좋은 주장을 펼칠 수 없다면, 여러분의 행동을 재고해야만 한다. 중요한 결정을 내리려고 할 때마다, 나는 "긴 녹색 탁자 앞에 서서 내가 정말 올바른 행동을 했다고 만족할 수 있을까?"라고 스스로에게 물었다. 이것은 지도자가 스스로에게 물어야 하는 가장 근본적인 질문 중 하나이다. 그리고 그 옛 격언은 내가 어떤 조치를 취해야 하는지 기억하도록 도와주었다.

---

08 전체 흐름과 관계 없는 문장 고르기 ④

[정답해설]

제시문은 피카소의 대표작인 '게르니카'가 그려진 의도와 그 이름이 붙여진 유래 등에 대해 서술하고 있다. 그런데 말년에 피카소가 새로운 양식과 기법으로 실험을 하면서 계속해서 관심에 변화를 주었다는 ④의 설명은 피카소의 말년 화풍의 변화에 대해 설명하고 있으므로, 제시문의 전체 흐름과 어울리지 않는다.

[핵심어휘]

- mastery 숙련, 숙달, 통달
- name after ~의 이름을 따다
- dump 버리다, 덤핑하다
- range (범위가) 이르다, 다양하다
- puzzlement 어리둥절함, 혼란
- confusion 혼란, 혼동
- direction 지시, 지휘, 지도
- presumably 아마, 짐작건대

[본문해석]

피카소의 강렬한 그림 '게르니카'를 처음 보는 사람을 생각해 보자. 누구나 이 그림에서 기술적 숙련도와 매우 감성적인 내용을 볼 수 있다. ① 그러나 우리가 '게르니카'를 처음 보는 사람에게 이 그림은 그가 18세였을 때 피카소를 차버린 소녀의 이름을 따서 붙여졌다고 말했다. ② 이 그림에 대한 관람객의 감정은 어리둥절하고 혼란스러울 수도 있다. 즉, 작품의 규모와 내용을 고려할 때, 그것은 약간의 과잉반응처럼 보일 것이다. ③ 그런 다음 우리는 관람객에게 이 그림이 1937년 4월 프랑코 지휘 하의 스페인 민족주의자들의 요청에 따라 독일과 이탈리아의 연합 파시스트 군대에 의해 심하게 폭격을 당한 작은 바스크 마을을 기념하기 위해 그려졌다고 말한다. ④ 심지어 말년에도, 피카소는 새로운 양식과 기법으로 실험을 하면서, 계속해서 관심에 변화를 주었다. ⑤ 아마도, 관람객의 감정은 바뀔 것이고 피카소는 그 그림을 관람하는 사람들이 의도했던 감정을 더 많이 반영할 것이다.

09	**글의 제목 유추하기**	②

[정답해설]

진화 인류학적 관점에서 신체 구성과 얼굴 형태가 더 부드럽고 온화하게 변한 것은 폭력으로부터 벗어난 진화의 일부였으며, 성공한 집단들은 폭력적이고 파괴적인 사람들을 제거하고 남은 더 온화한 사람들의 성공을 보장했다고 설명하고 있다. 그러므로 제시문의 제목으로 ②의 "더 온화한 사람들: 진화 전쟁의 승리자들"이 적절하다.

[오답해설]

① 원시 인류의 온화함: 인류학적 신화
③ 화석 증거에 의해 드러난 폭력적인 인간의 본성
④ 성공적인 전쟁 캠페인 개최: 멋진 예술
⑤ 인간의 갈등을 끝내는데 방해가 되는 것은 무엇인가?

[핵심어휘]

- aversion 싫음, 혐오
- recognition 알아봄, 인식
- evolutionary anthropology 진화 인류학
- body composition 신체 구성
- blunt 무딘, 뭉툭한
- claw 손[발]톱
- brow-ridge 눈 위의 뼈가 돌출한 부분
- violence 폭력, 폭행
- sophisticated 지적인, 학식 있는
- shelter 주거지, 은신처
- bound up with ~와 밀접한 관련이 있는
- weed out 잡초를 뽑다, 제거하다
- disruptive 분열시키는, 파괴적인
- intertwine 엮이다, 뒤얽히다

- ensure 보장하다, 보증하다
- fossil 화석
- obstacle 장애, 방해

[본문해석]

아마도 전쟁은 근본적으로 나쁜 것이며, 이는 서서히 우리에게 하나의 종(種)으로 분명해지고 있다. 아마도 전쟁에 대한 혐오, 심지어 그것이 나쁘다는 인식조차 인간 조건에 깊이 내재한다. 진화 인류학에서 이러한 생각을 지지하는 이들이 있다. 지능이 높은 유인원에서 호모 사피엔스에 이르기까지 신체 구성과 얼굴 형태의 변화 즉, 더 부드러운 피부, 더 무른 치아와 발톱, 더 낮은 눈썹 위 뼈는 폭력으로부터 벗어난 진화의 일부였을지도 모른다. 사냥하고, 채집하고, 집을 짓고, 아이들을 기르는 지적인 방식으로 협력하는 것이 점점 더 잘 되어감에 따라, 개인들의 성공은 그 집단의 성공과 밀접하게 연관되었다. 성공한 집단들은 폭력적이고 파괴적인 사람들을 제거한 집단들이었다. 사회적 진화와 생물학적 진화는 그렇게 뒤얽혔고, 남은 더 온화한 사람들의 성공을 보장했다.

10	**글의 제목 유추하기**	⑤

[정답해설]

제시문에 신용카드의 출현은 현금을 필요로 하지 않는 편이성 때문에 소비의 지혜에 대한 신중한 평가보다 충동적인 소비 본능의 고양이라는 결과를 낳았다고 서술되어 있다. 그러므로 제시문의 제목으로는 ⑤의 '즉각적인 소비문화를 조성하는 신용카드'가 적절하다.

[오답해설]

① 신용카드: 사회적 불안정의 씨앗
② 미국 파산의 외부 기원
③ 건전한 신용: 재정적 행복으로 가는 길
④ 개인주의를 신장시키는 신용카드의 폭발적 증가

[핵심어휘]

- anti-thrift 반절약, 소비
- take on debt 부채를 떠안다, 빚을 책임지다
- emerge 출현하다, 나타나다
- distribute 분배[배포]하다, 유통시키다
- usher 도입하다, 안내하다
- hard cash 현금
- gratification (욕구의) 충족, 만족감
- regulate 규제하다, 조절하다
- behavioral 행동의, 행동에 관한
- elevation 승진, 승격, 고양
- impulsive 충동적인, 감정에 끌린
- evaluation 평가, 감정

□ instability 불안정, 변덕

□ imported 수입된, 외부에서 들어온

□ bankruptcy 파산, 파탄

□ explosion 폭발, 폭파

□ boost 신장시키다, 북돋우다

□ foster 조성하다, 발전시키다

[본문해석]

개인적인 채무를 지려는 광범위한 의향이 없었다면 소비문화의 출현은 불가능했을 것이고, 신용카드의 개발이 없었다면 그러한 의지는 출현하지 않았을 것이다. 1958년과 1970년 사이에 1억 장의 신용카드가 미국 전역에 배포되었는데, 이것은 구매 패턴뿐만 아니라 미국인들이 그들 자신과 그들의 욕망을 경험하기 시작한 방식에 있어서 중대한 변화로 드러났다. 신용카드는 구매를 뒷받침하는데 현금이 필요하지 않은 새로운 시대에 사용의 편의성을 도입했고, 결과적으로 소비자들 사이의 즉각적인 만족감 때문에 폭넓은 욕망과 기대로 이어졌다. 이러한 편리함은 역사적으로 그것을 방해함으로써 즉각적인 만족감을 규제했던 사회적, 자연적, 경제적 환경과 대조적으로 나타났다. 지난 한 세기 동안, 우리 문화는 흔히 우리가 원하는 것을 바로 얻는데 행동적 장애가 거의 없도록 바뀌었고, 소비의 지혜에 대한 신중한 평가보다 충동적인 소비 본능의 고양이라는 결과를 낳았다.

11   글의 주제 파악하기   ②

[정답해설]

제시문에 따르면 글로벌 기업들은 보통 외국 공급업체들과 독립된 거래를 하고 있다고 생각했지만, 소비자들은 공급망과 하청 업체들의 근로 조건 및 환경 영향에 대한 책임도 글로벌 기업에게 물었고, 결국 인터넷 시대에 글로벌 기업들은 한 번도 들어보지 못한 관련 회사들의 비윤리적인 행동으로 인해 브랜드 평판이 손상되는 위험에 직면하게 되었다고 설명하고 있다. 그러므로 ②의 '글로벌 기업에 닥친 확대된 윤리적 책임'이 제시문의 주제로 가장 적절하다.

[오답해설]

① 해외 공장에서의 작업 환경 관리의 어려움

③ 구매 결정에 미치는 브랜드 평판의 영향 감소

④ 글로벌 제조업에 대한 자원 부족 위험 증가

⑤ 글로벌 기업이 사용하는 위험 관리 전략

[핵심어휘]

□ vulnerability 취약성, 상처[비난]받기 쉬움

□ arms-length 공정한, 독립한, 대등한

□ transaction 거래, 매매

□ head office 본사

□ outsourcing 아웃소싱, 외주처리

□ athletic shoes 운동화

□ confectionary 제과의, 과자 제조의

□ ship lines 선박 회사

□ harbor 마음속에 품다

□ tarnish 손상하다, 흐려지다, 퇴색하다

□ allegation (증거 없는) 주장, 혐의

□ unethical 비윤리적인, 비도덕적인

□ top executives 고위 간부, 최고 경영자

□ reputational 평판의, 명성이 있는

□ resource shortage 자원 부족

[본문해석]

2000년대 초에 기업들은 세계화로 인해 발생하는 새로운 위험에 직면해 있다는 사실을 깨닫기 시작했다. 유력 글로벌 브랜드는 이익뿐만 아니라 취약성의 근원이 될 수 있는 것으로 드러났다. 그러한 브랜드를 소유하고 있는 기업들은 보통 외국 공급업체들과 독립된 거래를 하고 있다고 생각했지만, 소비자들은 본사로부터 수마일 떨어진 곳에 있는 공급망, 관련 업체를 통틀어 노동 및 환경 조건에 대한 책임을 그들에게 물었다. 운동화 생산을 인도네시아에 있는 공장에 외주처리하거나 스위스에 있는 무역회사를 통해 가나에서 재배된 코코아를 구입하는 것도 신발 및 제과업체들의 근로 조건 및 환경 영향에 대한 책임을 덜어주지는 못했다. 심지어 선박 회사 및 플라스틱 제조업체와 같이 소비자와 직접적으로 거래하지 않은 회사들도 기업 고객들이 비슷한 기대를 품고 있다는 사실을 알았다. 인터넷 시대에, 기업의 브랜드는 최고 경영자들이 결코 들어보지 못한 회사들에서 비윤리적인 행동을 했다는 주장들로 인해 쉽게 퇴색될 수 있었고, 그러한 평판의 손상은 되돌리기 어려웠다.

12   글의 목적 파악하기   ①

[정답해설]

버니 미니 제품을 생산하는 ABC 토이 컴퍼니가 피부 발진을 일으킬 수 있다는 안전상의 문제로 제품을 전량 회수하고, 고객에게 환불받는 방법에 대해 안내하고 있다. 그러므로 제시문의 목적은 제품의 회수 및 환불 조치에 관해 알리기 위해서이다.

[오답해설]

② 새로운 상품의 예약 구매 방법을 안내하려고 → 신상품의 예약 판매가 아니라 기존 상품의 회수와 환불에 대한 공지임

③ 인기 장난감의 빠른 품절에 대해 사과하려고 → 품절에 대한 사과가 아니라 회수와 환불에 대한 사과임

④ 변경된 환불 및 제품 보증 정책을 공지하려고 → 환불 및 제품 보증 정책이 변경된 것은 아님

⑤ 판매 실적에 따른 고객 감사 행사를 홍보하려고 → 고객 감사 행사에 대한 홍보가 아니라 회수와 환불에 대한 사과 공고임

[핵심어휘]

- appreciate 감사하다, 고마워하다
- loyalty 충실, 충성
- attention 주의, 관심
- skin rash 피부 발진
- precautionary 예방 조치, 선제적 조치
- refund 환불
- disappointment 실망, 낙심
- assure 확신하다, 보장하다

[본문해석]

아이들에게 재미와 즐거움을 주는 믿을 만한 기업으로 ABC 토이 컴퍼니를 선택해 주셔서 감사합니다. 우리 브랜드에 대한 지속적인 지지와 충성에 감사드립니다. 하지만 주의를 받은 안전 문제에 대해 알려드리게 되어 유감입니다. 우리는 최근에 버니 미니 인형이 사용된 페인트로 인해 피부 발진을 일으킬 수 있다는 사실을 알았습니다. 고객의 안전과 건강이 최우선이기에, 우리는 이 문제를 매우 심각하게 받아들이고 있습니다. 선제적 조치로, 우리는 버니 미니 제품을 시장에서 전량 회수하고 있습니다. 만약 이 장난감을 구매하셨다면, 그 제품을 매장 중 한 곳으로 가져가 환불받기를 요청 드립니다. 우리 장난감을 사랑하는 아이들에게 특히 실망을 줄 수 있다는 것을 이해합니다. 우리는 이 상황을 신속하게 해결하기 위해 모든 필요한 조치를 취하고 있음을 확신합니다.

[핵심어휘]

- breed 품종
- furry 털로 덮인, 털 같은
- intuition 직관, 직감
- intact 그대로의, 완전한, 온전한
- tune 음을 맞추다, 조율하다
- veneer 겉치장, 허식

[본문해석]

많은 사람들이 자신의 개를 아기로 대하는 실수를 저지른다. 개에게 이것 이상의 더 많은 부분이 있다는 것을 인정하는 한 그것은 문제가 되지 않는다. 먼저 동물을 존중해야 하고, 그 다음에 개를 존중해야 하며, 그 다음에 품종을 존중하고, 마지막으로 개별 반려동물을 존중해야 한다. 만일 이렇게 할 수 있다면, 일대일 긴밀한 의사소통은 그 다음 단계이다. 당신의 개가 그저 작고 털 많은 사람이 아니라, 그 이상이라는 것을 인정해라. 그 개는 동물로서 인간과 달리 모든 직관과 본능을 그대로 가지고 있다. 그 개는 당신보다 훨씬 더 예민한 후각과 청각을 가지고 있고, 따라서 당신보다 자연 세계에 대해 훨씬 더 잘 알고 있다. 이것은 당신의 개가 대부분의 시간을 당신과 다른 세계에 존재하므로, 비범한 능력을 존중하고, 할 수 있는 한 당신 자신의 본능과 직관의 많은 부분을 다시 조율해야 한다는 것을 의미한다. 우리는 아직도 이러한 능력을 가지고 있다. 그것들은 단지 우리의 문명화된 겉치장 밑에 묻혀 있을 뿐이다.

13	필자의 주장 이해하기	⑤

[정답해설]

제시문에 따르면 반려견은 동물로서 인간과 달리 모든 직관과 본능을 그대로 가지고 있으므로, 그들의 비범한 능력을 존중하고 이에 맞춘다면 반려견과 진정한 소통을 할 수 있다고 설명하고 있다. 그러므로 제시문에서 필자가 주장하는 바는 ⑤의 '반려견과의 진정한 소통을 위해 그들의 본능과 직감을 존중해야 한다.'이다.

[오답해설]

① 반려견을 입양하기 전에 가족 구성원의 동의를 구해야 한다. → 반려견의 입양에 대한 내용은 제시문에 나타나 있지 않음

② 반려견의 건강한 삶을 위해 함께 활동하는 시간을 늘려야 한다. → 반려견에 대한 존중과 진정한 소통에 대해 다루고 있음

③ 반려견의 개별적 특성을 고려하여 행동 교정 훈련을 해야 한다. → 반려견의 비범한 능력을 존중하라고 설명하고 있으나, 반려견의 행동 교정 훈련에 대한 설명은 나타나 있지 않음

④ 반려견이 자연과 교감할 수 있도록 다양한 기회를 제공해야 한다. → 반려견과 자연과의 교감이 아니라 반려견과 사람과의 교감임

14	내용과 불일치 문장 고르기	④

[정답해설]

제시문에 따르면 플로렌스 핀치는 1945년 미군에 의해 석방된 후 미국으로 이주해 미국 시민이 되었고, 2016년에 뉴욕 이타카에서 101세의 나이로 사망했다. 그러므로 1945년에 미군에 의해 풀려난 후 필리핀에 남아 여생을 마쳤다는 ④의 설명은 제시문의 내용과 일치하지 않는다.

[오답해설]

① 필리핀에서 태어나 마닐라에 주둔한 U.S. Army에서 근무했다. → 1915년 필리핀에서 필리핀인 어머니와 미국인 아버지의 딸로 태어났으며, 마닐라에 있는 미 육군에서 근무함

② Philippine Liquid Fuel Distributing Union에서 직업을 구했다. → 마닐라가 1942년에 일본에 함락된 후, 일본이 통제하는 필리핀 액체 연료 배급 단체에서 직업을 구함

③ 연료를 저항군에게 빼돌리고 미군 포로에게 음식을 몰래 제공했다. → 필리핀 지하조직과 긴밀히 협력하면서, 저항군에게 연료 공급을 전용했고 굶주린 미국인 전쟁 포로들에게 몰래 음식을 구해다 줌

⑤ 필리핀에서의 공적을 인정받아 Medal of Freedom을 받았다. → 1947년에 미국인 포로들을 구하고 필리핀에서 다른 저항 행동들을 수행한 것

으로 자유 훈장을 받음

[핵심어휘]

□ prior to ~에 앞서, ~이전에

□ fall to ~에게 무너지다[함락되다]

□ disguise 변장하다, 위장하다

□ liquid 액체

□ distributing 분배의, 배급의

□ Philippine Underground 필리핀 지하조직

□ divert 전용하다, 전환시키다, 우회시키다

□ starve 굶주리다, 굶어 죽다

□ interrogate 심문하다, 추궁하다

□ liberate 해방하다, 자유롭게 하다

□ pass away 죽다, 사망하다, 없어지다

□ funeral 장례식

[본문해석]

플로렌스 핀치는 1915년 필리핀에서, 필리핀인 어머니와 미국인 아버지의 딸로 태어났다. 일본의 침략 이전에, 핀치는 마닐라에 있는 미 육군에서 근무했다. 마닐라가 1942년에 일본에 함락된 후, 핀치는 미국과의 관계를 위장했고 일본이 통제하는 필리핀 액체 연료 배급 단체에서 직업을 구했다. 필리핀 지하조직과 긴밀히 협력하면서, 그녀는 저항군에게 연료 공급을 전용했고 굶주린 미국인 전쟁 포로들에게 몰래 음식을 구해다 주었다. 1944년에 그녀는 일본 군대에 의해 체포되었고 심문을 받았지만 어떤 정보도 밝히기를 거부했다. 1945년 미군에 의해 석방된 후, 그녀는 미국으로 이주해 시민이 되었고 미국 해안경비대에 입대했다. 1947년에 그녀는 미국인 포로들을 구하고 필리핀에서 다른 저항 행동들을 수행한 것으로 자유 훈장을 받았다. 그녀는 2016년에 뉴욕 이타카에서 101세의 나이로 사망했고, 최고의 명예 군 장례식을 수여했다.

15   빈칸 추론하기   ①

[정답해설]

아기가 걸음마를 배울 때 넘어지는 것은 일어서려고 노력하는 과정의 일부로서 너무나 자연스러운 행동인 것처럼, 우리가 성공하는 법을 배우려고 할 때 실패도 성공하려고 노력하는 과정의 일부로서 너무나 자연스러운 행동인 것이다. 그러므로 제시문의 빈칸에 들어갈 말은 ①의 'natural(자연스러운)'이 가장 적절하다.

[오답해설]

② 사교적인

③ 지능적인

④ 지략이 풍부한

⑤ 신뢰할 수 있는

[핵심어휘]

□ positiveness 명백함, 긍정적 태도

□ in itself 실질상, 본질적으로

□ integrate 통합하다, 통일하다

□ persistence 고집, 끈기, 인내

□ manage to 간신히 ~하다, 그럭저럭 ~하다

□ to a great extent 대부분은, 상당 부분은

□ in a way 어느 정도는, 어떤 면에서는

□ sociable 사교적인, 붙임성 있는

□ resourceful 지략이 풍부한, 수완이 좋은

□ trustworthy 신뢰할 수 있는, 믿을 수 있는

[본문해석]

긍정성, 더 정확하게는 항상 균형을 잘 유지하는 것은 본질적으로 결코 현장을 떠나지 않는 기본 목표이다. 아기 때 바닥에 수십 번 넘어진 후 다시 일어서려고 노력하지 않는 것과 같은 그런 가능성이 결코 존재한다고 생각하지 않을 것이다. 넘어지는 것은 일어서려고 노력하는 과정의 일부로서 너무나 자연스럽게 통합되어 있어서 아무도 "불쌍한 아기, 서려고 너무 많이 실패했어!"라고 생각하지 않을 것이다. 우리는 인내심과 이미 올바른 사고방식을 가지고 태어나는데 – 절대 포기하지 않고, 항상 탐험하고, 항상 그것을 할 수 있다고 믿지만 – 어떻게든 도중에 그것들을 '그럭저럭' 잃어버린다. 그래서 성공하는 법을 배우려고 할 때 실제 우리가 하고 있는 것은 대부분 태어날 때 우리에게 주어진 일련의 기술들을 다시 배우거나 기억하는 행위이다. 더 생산적이고자 하는 우리의 목표는 어떻게 보면 더 자연스러워지려는 우리의 목표가 된다.

16   빈칸 추론하기   ①

[정답해설]

우리가 사랑하는 감정을 말로 표현하기가 매우 어려우며 "그냥 느낌이 그렇기" 때문이라고 빙빙 돌려 말하거나 이치에 맞지 않는 말을 하는 것은 우리의 감정을 조절하는 뇌의 부분에 어떤 능력이 없기 때문이다. 그러므로 제시문의 빈칸에 들어갈 말은 ①의 '언어 능력이 없다'이다.

[오답해설]

② 우리의 운동 능력을 방해하다

③ 기억과 별개로 작동하다

④ 어떠한 도덕적 판단도 하지 않다

⑤ 의사 결정이 차단되어 있다

[핵심어휘]

□ disconnection 단절, 분리

□ put into words 말로 표현하다, 말로 형용하다

- talk around 빙빙 돌려서 말하다, 에둘러 말하다
- rationalize 합리화하다, 이론적으로 설명하다
- obviously 확실히, 분명히
- personality 성격, 개성
- competence 능력, 능숙함
- make rational sense 이치에 맞다
- capacity 용량, 능력, 지위
- obstruct 막다, 방해하다
- motor function 운동 기능
- independently 독립하여, 자주적으로, 별개로

[본문해석]

우리의 감정을 조절하는 뇌의 부분은 언어 능력이 없다. 우리의 감정을 말로 표현하는 것을 매우 어렵게 만드는 것은 바로 이러한 단절이다. 예를 들어, 우리는 왜 우리가 결혼했던 사람과 결혼했는지 설명하는 데 어려움이 있다. 우리는 그들을 사랑하는 진짜 이유를 말로 표현하기 위해 애쓰며, 그것을 빙빙 돌려 말하거나 혹은 합리화한다. "그녀는 재미있고, 똑똑합니다."라고 시작한다. 그러나 세상에는 재미있고 똑똑한 사람들이 많이 있지만, 우리는 그들을 사랑하지 않으며 결혼하고 싶어하지 않는다. 분명 사랑에 빠지는 것은 단지 성격과 능력 이상의 것이 있다. 이성적으로, 우리의 설명이 진짜 이유가 아니라는 것을 알고 있다. 그것이 사랑하는 사람들이 우리가 느끼도록 하는 방법이지만, 그러한 감정들은 말로 표현하기는 정말 어렵다. 그래서 추궁할 때, 우리는 그것을 빙빙 돌려 말하기 시작한다. 심지어 이치에 맞지 않는 말을 할 수도 있다. 예를 들어, "그녀가 나를 완전하게 합니다"라고 말할 수도 있다. 그 말이 무슨 의미이고 어떻게 그렇게 말하는 사람을 찾아 결혼할 수 있을까? 왜냐하면 그것은 "그냥 느낌이 그렇기" 때문에 우리가 오직 사랑을 찾았을 때만 아는 사랑의 문제이다.

17   빈칸 추론하기   ②

[정답해설]

제시문에서 공격자보다 방어자가 더 많으면 방어자들이 남아서 싸우는 것이 타당하고, 공격자가 더 많으면 재빨리 달아나는 것이 더 현명한 전략임이 사자들의 실험을 통해 입증되었다. 이는 사자들에게 어느 무리가 더 많은 지 그 개체수를 파악하는 능력이 있기 때문이므로, 빈칸에는 ②의 '무리 지은 개체수를 비교하다'가 빈칸에 들어갈 말로 가장 적절하다.

[오답해설]

① 무리들과 효율적으로 소통하다
③ 움직이는 물체의 방향을 확인하다
④ 위장하여 주위 환경에 어울리다
⑤ 다른 종(種)의 울음소리를 흉내 내다

[핵심어휘]

- obvious 분명한, 확실한
- territory 영역, 구역, 지역
- retreat 후퇴하다, 물러나다
- make sense 타당하다, 이치가 맞다
- make a bolt for it 재빨리 달아나다, 쏜살같이 달아나다
- colleague 동료
- roar 으르렁거리다, 포효하다
- exceed 낫다, 능가하다, 초과하다
- intruder 침입자, 불청객
- versus 대(對), ~에 비해
- efficiently 효율적으로, 능률적으로
- collection 무리, 더미
- identify 찾다, 확인하다
- blend into ~와 뒤섞이다
- disguise 변장[가장]하다, 위장하다
- mimic 모방하다, 흉내 내다

[본문해석]

무리지은 개체수를 비교할 수 있는 한 가지 분명한 생존 이점은 한 무리의 동물들이 공격으로부터 그들의 영역을 방어할 것인지 아니면 후퇴할 것인지를 알 수 있도록 도와준다는 것이다. 만약 공격자보다 방어자가 더 많다면 방어자들이 남아서 싸우는 것이 타당할 수 있고, 만약 공격자가 더 많다면 가장 현명한 전략은 재빨리 달아나는 것일 수도 있다. 이러한 의견은 Karen McComb와 그녀의 동료들에 의해 몇 년 전에 시험되었다. 그들은 탄자니아의 세렝게티 국립공원에서 작은 무리의 암컷 사자들에게 포효하는 사자들의 테이프 녹음을 재생시켰다. 포효하는 다른 사자의 수가 그 무리의 사자 수를 초과할 때는 암컷들이 물러났지만, 암컷들이 더 많을 때는 땅에 서서 침입자들을 공격할 준비를 했다. 그들은 두 가지 다른 감각을 통해 숫자를 비교할 수 있는 것 같았다. 즉, 그들이 들은 포효하는 사자의 수 대 그들이 관찰한 암사자의 수로, 꽤 추상적인 숫자 감각을 필요로 하는 일처럼 보인다.

18   빈칸 추론하기   ③

[정답해설]

제시문에 우리는 기능을 상실한 사람들이 존엄성을 위협하지 않도록 지원할 힘이 있고, 여전히 헌신적인 만남과 친밀함을 유지하고 있다고 서술하고 있다. 그러므로 ③의 '우리가 그들과 맺고 있는 방식을 바꾸지는 못한다'가 빈칸에 들어갈 말로 가장 적절하다.

[오답해설]

① 그들에게 굴욕을 참으라고 강요하다
② 남의 도움을 필요로 하지 않다

④ 우울증에 대한 그들의 회복력을 약화시키다

⑤ 그들이 인생에서 가치 있게 여기는 것을 극적으로 변화시키다

[핵심어휘]

- faculty (신체 또는 정신의) 기능, 능력
- dignity 존엄성, 자존감
- paralysed 마비된
- tremor 떨림, 전율
- dizziness 어지럼증, 현기증
- in and of itself 그것 자체로
- autonomy 자주성, 자율성
- powerlessness 무력함, 무력감
- humiliation 굴욕, 수치, 수모
- committed 헌신적인, 열성적인
- entanglement 복잡한 관계, 얽힘
- uphold 지탱하다, 유지하다
- intimacy 친밀, 친분
- diminish 줄이다, 약화시키다
- resilience 회복력, 쾌활성
- depression 우울증, 우울함

[본문해석]

우리 삶의 한 부분이었던 사람들이 점차 이전의 기능을 잃어가는 일이 일어날 수 있다. 이 과정의 여러 면이 고통을 수반하지만 존엄성을 위협하지는 않는다. 장님이나 귀머거리가 되거나, 마비되거나, 떨림을 겪거나, 더 이상 집을 떠날 수 없을 정도로 심한 고통, 불안 또는 어지러움을 감당해야 하는 이 모든 일은 끔찍하고 때로는 참을 수 없지만, 이미 그 자체로 존엄성을 위협하는 것은 아니다. 이 모든 것은 자율성의 상실과 더불어 다양한 의존성의 경험을 수반하며, 때로는 이러한 의존성이 무력감으로 경험되기도 한다. 그러나 우리는 이를 겪는 사람들이 그들의 무력감이 굴욕이 되고 그들의 존엄성을 위협하지 않도록 지원할 힘이 있다. 우리는 여전히 그들과 헌신적인 만남을 하고 있고, 지적이고 감정적인 얽힘은 우리 관계의 친밀함을 유지한다. 그들의 기능 상실이 <u>우리가 그들과 맺고 있는 방식을 바꾸지는 못한다</u>.

19 　　빈칸 추론하기 　　②

[정답해설]

포식자가 단 한 끼의 단기적인 이익보다 생존이라는 장기적인 이익을 선호하도록 진화한 것처럼, 야생 버섯을 먹을지 말지 결정할 때도 목숨 값은 지불하기에 너무 큰 대가이므로 절대적인 확신이 없다면 응당 먹지 않는 게 낫다는 뜻이다. 그러므로 ②의 '맛있는 보상품 생각에 자신을 희생시키지 마라'가 빈칸에 들어갈 말로 가장 적절하다.

[오답해설]

① 절망적인 시기를 위해 지금 할 수 있는 한 많은 음식을 비축하라

③ 생존의 이름으로 과감히 도전하라

④ 누군가에겐 독이지만 다른 누군가에겐 즐거움이라는 것을 잊지 마라

⑤ 사냥하는 포식자를 조심하라.

[핵심어휘]

- predator 포식자, 육식 동물
- spot 찾다, 발견하다
- of the essence 중요한, 절대적으로 필요한
- twist 전환, 반전
- venomous 독이 있는
- coral snake 산호 뱀
- non-venomous 독이 없는
- tradeoff 거래, 교환
- favor 편들다, 선호하다
- conservative 보수적인
- mimic 모방하다, 흉내 내다
- evolutionary arms race 진화적 군비[무기] 경쟁
- fall prey to ~의 먹이가 되다, ~의 희생물이 되다
- desperate 절망적인, 자포자기의

[본문해석]

당신을 포식자, 아마도 매라고 상상해보라. 높은 곳에서, 당신은 맛있는 뱀으로 보이는 것을 발견한다. 만약 단 몇 초 동안이라도 망설이면, 식사는 사라질지도 모른다. 시간은 절대적으로 필요하고, 당신은 빨리 행동해야 한다. 그러나 중대한 반전이 있다. 만일 독이 있는 산호 뱀을 독이 없는 왕 뱀으로 착각한다면, 그것은 당신의 목숨을 빼앗을 것이다. 식사와 목숨의 거래에서, 그 선택은 명백하다. 포식자에게 자연 선택은 보수적인 선택 즉, 단 한 끼의 단기적인 이익보다 생존이라는 장기적인 이익을 선호하도록 의사 결정 과정을 형성했다. 따라서 왕 뱀이 진화론적 무기 경쟁의 라운드에서 이기기 위해 산호 뱀의 색깔을 완벽하게 모방할 필요는 없다. 똑같은 논리가 야생 버섯을 먹을지 말지를 결정할 때 적용된다. 만일 절대적인 확신이 없다면, <u>맛있는 보상품 생각에 자신을 희생시키지 마라</u>. 목숨 값은 지불하기에 너무 큰 대가일 것이다.

20 　　글의 배열순서 정하기 　　③

[정답해설]

주어진 문장에서 HDTV와 온라인 동영상 공유 플랫폼의 참여 방식이 어떻게 변화했는지 비교해 볼 것을 제안하고 있다. 그런데 (C)에서 'on the other hand(반면에)'로 시작하며 동영상 공유 플랫폼의 참여 방식에 대해 서술하고 있으므로, HDTV의 참여 방식에 대해 서술한 (B) 다음에 와야 함을 알 수 있다. 그리고 마지막으로 (A)에서 동영상 공유

플랫폼의 참여 방식에 대해 추가적으로 설명하고 있으므로, 주어진 글 다음에 (B)-(C)-(A) 순으로 배열되어야 글의 흐름이 가장 적절하다.

[핵심어휘]

□ engagement 참여, 관계
□ respective 각자의, 각각의
□ keystroke 키 누름
□ enthusiast 열정적인 팬, 열렬한 지지자
□ stitch 꿰매다, 봉합하다
□ immersive 몰입형의, 실감형의
□ radically 급진적으로, 근본적으로
□ alter 바꾸다, 변경하다
□ for starter 우선, 먼저
□ mass phenomenon 대중 현상
□ rate 평가하다, 여기다

[본문해석]

이 두 아이디어 즉, HDTV와 온라인 동영상 공유 플랫폼이 각 미디어 플랫폼의 기본적인 참여 규칙을 변경한 방식을 비교해 보라.

(B) 아날로그 텔레비전에서 HDTV로의 이동은 정도의 변화이지, 종류의 변화가 아니다. 즉, 픽셀들이 더 많을수록 소리는 더 실감나고 색상은 더욱 선명하다. 그러나 소비자들은 구식의 아날로그 TV를 보는 것과 똑같이 HDTV를 본다. 그들은 채널을 선택하고, 가만히 앉아서 본다.

(C) 반면, 이 온라인 동영상 공유 플랫폼은 미디어의 기본적인 규칙들을 근본적으로 변화시켰다. 우선, 이 플랫폼은 웹상에서 동영상을 시청하는 것을 대중 현상으로 만들었다. 그러나 이 온라인 동영상 공유 플랫폼 덕택에 앉아서 TV와 같은 쇼를 보는 것에 국한되지 않고, 자신의 동영상 클립을 업로드하거나, 다른 동영상 클립을 추천 또는 평가하며, 그것들에 관한 대화도 나눌 수 있었다.

(A) 몇 번의 쉬운 키 누르기만으로, 다른 사람의 사이트에서 동영상 클립을 실행시킬 수 있고, 자기 사이트에 복사할 수도 있다. 그 기술은 일반적인 열광자들이 자신만의 개인 방송 네트워크를 효과적으로 프로그램하고, 지구 전역의 동영상 클립을 수집하도록 했다.

21 글의 배열순서 정하기 ⑤

[정답해설]
주어진 문장에서 현재 인간의 법적, 정치적, 문화적 관행에 따라 동물은 사물로 간주되고 있음을 밝히고 있고, (C)에서 이에 이의를 제기한 동물권(animal rights)에 대해 소개하고 있다. 그리고 (B)에서 윤리적 측

면 외에 정치적 측면으로의 동물권 확장에 대해 서술하고 있고, 마지막으로 (A)에서 윤리적 고려에서 정치적 참여 움직임으로 인한 동물 문제에 대한 새로운 고찰을 서술하고 있다. 그러므로 주어진 글 다음에 (C)-(B)-(A) 순으로 배열되어야 글의 흐름상 가장 적절하다.

[핵심어휘]

□ perspective 관점, 시각
□ ethical 윤리적인, 도덕적인
□ consideration 고려, 숙고
□ drawing on ~에 근거하여, ~에 기초하여
□ inclusion 함유, 포용, 포괄
□ interspecies 종(種)간의, 이종간의
□ sentient 지각(력)이 있는, 감각이 있는
□ relevant 관련 있는, 적절한

[본문해석]

인간이 아닌 동물들은 자신만의 삶의 관점을 가진 개체로서, 인간 및 인간이 아닌 다른 동물들과 관계를 형성한다. 현재 인간의 법적, 정치적 체계에서, 그리고 많은 문화적 관행에서 그들은 사물로 간주되고 이용된다.

(C) 동물권 이론가들은 1970년대부터 인간이 아닌 동물들이 도덕과 관련된 측면에서 인간과 비슷하고 따라서 우리의 도덕적 공동체의 일부로 간주되어야 하는 지각 있는 존재라고 주장하며 이에 이의를 제기해 왔다.

(B) 이러한 견해와 민주적 포용에 초점을 맞춘 사회 정의 운동이 제공하는 통찰력에 근거하여, 정치 철학의 최근 연구는 인간이 아닌 동물을 정치 집단으로, 그리고 이들 중 일부를 공유된 종간 공동체의 구성원으로 볼 것을 제안한다.

(A) 윤리적 고려에서 정치적 참여로의 이러한 움직임은 인간이 아닌 동물에 대한 문제들을 그들이 어떻게 취급되어야만 하는지부터 그들이 살아가고 싶은 방식에 대해 어떻게 더 많은 통찰력을 얻을 수 있는지, 그들이 서로 간에 그리고 인간과 어떤 형태의 관계를 원하는지, 그리고 우리 모두가 살고 있는 지구를 어떻게 공유할 수 있고 공유해야 하는지로 이동시킨다.

22 주어진 문장의 위치 찾기 ③

[정답해설]
제시문에서 초보자들은 표면 특징 유사성에 근거하여 물리학 문제들을 분류하였고, 전문가들은 심층 특징 유사성에 근거하여 물리학 문제들을 분류하였다. 주어진 문장이 'on the other hand(반면에)'를 사용

하여 전문가들의 분류 방법에 대해 서술하고 있으므로, 초보자들의 분류 방법에 대한 설명이 끝나고 전문가들의 분류 방법에 대한 설명이 시작되는 ③에 들어가는 것이 가장 적절하다.

[핵심어휘]
- similarity 유사성, 닮음
- expertise 전문성, 전문 지식
- influential 영향력 있는, 유력한
- novices 선무당, 초심자
- configuration 배열, 배치, 조합
- schemata 선험적 도식
- solution-oriented 해결 지향의, 해결 중심의

[본문해석]

> 반면에 전문가들은 각 문제의 해결을 좌우하는 주요 물리학 원리와 관련된 심층 특징 유사성에 근거하여 그들의 문제를 분류했다.

유사성이 문제 해결에서 중요한 역할을 수행하는 가장 좋은 사례 중 하나는 물리학에서 유사성과 전문성의 역할과 관계된 것이다. 영향력 있는 논문에서, 연구자들은 물리학 박사과정 학생들(전문가들)과 학부생들(초보자들)에게 24개의 물리학 문제를 그룹으로 분류한 후 그렇게 그룹으로 나눈 이유를 설명하라고 요청했다. (①) 초보자들은 일반적으로 표면 특징 유사성을 기준으로 문제를 분류했다. (②) 즉, 그들은 문제에서 언급된 문자 그대로의 물리학 용어와 문제에서 설명된 물리적 조합에 따라 문제를 분류했다. (③) 이것은 전문가들이 기존의 도식에 접근하였고 해결 중심의 분류를 만들기 위해 물리학에 관한 지식을 사용했음을 시사한다. (④) 문제들이 이 범주에 따라 분류되었기 때문에, 어떤 문제를 해결하는 방법을 결정할 때 이 범주에 접근할 가능성이 높다는 것도 시사한다. (⑤) 즉, 전문가들은 문제들 간의 유사성에 의존하여 문제를 빠르고 효율적으로 해결할 수 있도록 도울 가능성이 높다.

23	주어진 문장의 위치 찾기	⑤

[정답해설]
⑤의 앞 문장에서 그들의 기대가 방해받을(are disrupted) 때 감정을 경험한다고 하였고, ⑤의 다음 문장에서 그러한 개인은(Such a person)은 다른 사람들과 상호작용하도록 동기부여가 되어야만 한다고 서술되어 있다. 즉, 주어진 문장에서 '그 방해(the disruption)'는 ⑤의 앞 문장에서 언급하고 있고, '한 개인(a person)'은 ⑤의 다음 문장에서 언급하고 있으므로, 주어진 문장은 ⑤에 들어가는 것이 가장 적절하다.

[핵심어휘]
- disruption 분열, 방해, 지장
- intense 강렬한, 치열한
- assumption 추정, 가정
- stem from ~에서 유래하다, ~에서 비롯되다
- cognitive-motor 인지 운동적
- encode 암호로 바꾸다, 표현하다
- retain 유지하다, 지탱하다
- nonverbal 말을 사용하지 않는, 비언어적인
- affect-related 정서와 관련된
- visceral 뱃속으로부터의, 내장의
- assimilate 동화시키다, 완전히 이해하다
- put into words 말로 표현하다, 말로 형용하다
- anticipation 예상, 기대
- disrupt 방해하다, 지장을 주다
- disconfirm 확인하지 않다, 거절하다

[본문해석]

> 그 방해가 매우 심하다면, 그것은 자아와 세계에 대한 한 개인의 기본적인 가정에 도전할 지도 모른다.

사람들이 자신의 감정적인 경험을 다른 사람들에게 드러내는 다른 동기들을 설명하는 것을 넘어, 연구자들은 왜 사람들이 이렇게 하는지에 대해 더 깊은 설명을 제시했다. (①) 한 가지 설명은 인지 운동적 표현 관점에서 비롯된다. (②) 이 관점에 따르면, 한 사람의 경험의 중요한 부분들은 정신적인 이미지, 신체적인 움직임, 그리고 (배가 뒤틀리거나 심장이 뛰는 것과 같은) 정서와 관련된 뱃속으로부터의 변화의 형태로 암호화되거나 비언어적인 수준으로 유지된다. (③) 이러한 비언어적인 형태들은 그것들이 동화되고 말로 표현될 수 있을 때까지, 특히 그 경험들이 정서적으로 더 강렬할 때, 관심의 대상으로 남아 있다. (④) 또 다른 생각은 사람들이 세상이 어떻게 작동되어야 하는지에 대한 그들의 기대가 방해받을 때, 감정을 경험한다는 것이다. (⑤) 그러한 개인은 자신에 대한 믿음을 확인하거나 확인하지 못하게 돕고 세상에 대한 가정을 재구성하는 수단으로서 다른 사람들과 상호작용하도록 동기부여가 되어야만 한다.

24	한 문장으로 요약하기	①

[정답해설]
(A) 제시문의 첫 문장에서 비행기를 날게 하는 것은 물리학에 반하는 끊임없는 도전이라고 하였으므로, 빈칸에 들어갈 말은 'challenges(도전하다)'이다.
(B) 제시문의 마지막 문장에서 한 개인이 그들의 직무를 망각하거나 혹은 부적절하게 수행하는 것조차 재앙적인 결과를 초래할 수 있

다고 하였으므로, 빈칸에 들어갈 말은 'flawless(완벽한)'이다.

[오답해설]
② 도전하다 …… 용감한
③ 재정립하다 …… 독특한
④ 재정립하다 …… 보수적인
⑤ 지원하다 …… 보수적인

[핵심어휘]
▫ fail-safe 안전장치가 되어 있는, 실패를 방지하는
▫ default 불이행, 과실, 잘못
▫ crash 추락하다, 부딪치다
▫ ingenuity 독창성, 훌륭한 솜씨
▫ unforgiving 용서가 안 되는, 관대하지 못한
▫ disastrous 처참한, 재앙[재난]의
▫ bet-the-company 회사를 걸다
▫ fraction 부분, 일부
▫ aviation 비행, 항공
▫ optimum 최상의, 최적의
▫ unstable 불안정한, 흔들리는
▫ improperly 부적절하게, 부당하게
▫ catastrophic 대참사의, 처참한, 비극적인
▫ high-stake 고위험의, 위험 부담이 큰
▫ flawless 무결점의, 완벽한
▫ redefine 재정립하다, 재정의하다
▫ conservative 보수적인, 바뀌지 않는
▫ responsive 즉각 반응하는, 관심이 보이는

[본문해석]
비행기를 날게 하는 것은 물리학에 반하는 끊임없는 도전이다. 3만 피트에서 시속 600마일로 이동하는 비행기는 저절로 일어나는 것이 아니다. 그것은 실패가 방비된 행위가 아니며, 과실이 의미하는 것은 추락이다. 추락을 막는 것은 훌륭한 솜씨와 의사 결정에 달려 있다. 그것은 조금도 용서가 안 되는 특수한 환경이다. 자동차의 동력 상실이 일반적으로 도로가에서 몇 시간이라는 결과를 낳는 반면, 공중에서의 동력 상실은 대개 처참하다. 사업에서조차 회사를 담보한 결정은 드물며, 그런 결정에 직면했을 때 극히 일부의 직원들만이 그 결정에 참여한다. 하지만 항공은 단지 비행기를 계속 날게 하기 위해서 최적의 수준에서 일하는 모든 사람에게 의존한다. 그것은 심지어 한 개인이 그들의 직무를 망각하거나 혹은 부적절하게 수행하는 것조차 재앙적인 결과를 초래할 수 있는 불안정한 시스템이다.

↓

비행은 물리학 법칙에 (A) 도전하기 때문에, 안전을 보장하기 위해 각 구성원의 (B) 완벽한 수행이 요구되는 위험 부담이 큰 환경을 내포한다.

[25~26]

[핵심어휘]
▫ plain wrong 명백한 잘못
▫ stubbornly 완고[완강]하게, 고집스럽게
▫ come up with ~을 생산하다, 제시하다, 찾아내다
▫ prerequisite 선행 조건, 전제 조건
▫ keep track of ~을 기록하다, ~을 추적하다
▫ engage with ~에 관여[참여]하다
▫ proactive 사전 행동의, 주도적인, 선도적인
▫ on the spot 즉각, 즉석에서
▫ stumble onto ~를 우연히 만나다[관여하다]
▫ annoyance 짜증, 골칫거리
▫ friction 마찰, 충돌, 갈등
▫ multiply 증식하다, 번식하다
▫ appreciate 감상하다, 알아보다
▫ trigger 방아쇠, 계기, 도화선
▫ behave oneself 예의 바르게 행동하다
▫ mindful 염두에 두는, 신경 쓰는
▫ reliant 의존하는, 의지하는

[본문해석]
우리는 잘 작동하지 않는 제품들, 느린 서비스들, 그리고 명백하게 잘못된 설정들에 매일 둘러싸여 있다. 주차장에서 노트북과 연결하는 것을 완강히 거부하는 프로젝터에서 한두 번만 클릭하면 되는 것을 열 번의 클릭을 요구하는 웹사이트는 지불을 매우 어렵게 만든다. 무언가가 고장 났다는 것을 인지하는 것은 그것을 고칠 수 있는 창의적인 해결책을 찾아내기 위한 필수적 전제 조건이다. "버그 리스트"를 만드는 것은 창의성을 적용할 더 많은 기회들을 보도록 도와줄 수 있다. 주머니 속 종이를 이용하든 스마트폰에 아이디어를 기록하든, 개선의 기회들을 계속 추적하는 것은 더 주도적인 방식으로 주변 세계에 관여하도록 도울 수 있다. 실행 리스트는 씨름할 새로운 프로젝트를 찾을 때 유용한 아이디어의 원천이 될 수 있다. 혹은 즉석에서 버그 리스트를 만들 수 있다. 괴롭히는 것들을 적어라, 그러면 그것들을 더 신경 쓰기 시작할 것이다. 부정적인 것들에 집중하는 것처럼 보이지만, 요점은 일을 더 잘 처리하기 위한 더 많은 기회들을 인지하는 것이다. 그리고 버그 리스트의 많은 항목들은 고칠 수 없지만, 그것을 정기적으로 추가한다면, 영향을 줄 수 있는 문제들과 해결하는 데 도움을 줄 수 있는 문제들을 우연히 만날 것이다. 거의 모든 골칫거리, 모든 갈등은 창의적 기회를 숨기고 있다. 단지 불평하기 보다는 "내가 어떻게 이 상황을 개선할 수 있을까?"하고 스스로에게 물어보라.

25　글의 제목 파악하기　④

[정답해설]
제시문에서 버그 리스트를 만드는 것은 창의성을 적용할 더 많은 기회들을 보도록 도와줄 수 있으며, 더 주도적인 방식으로 주변 세계에 관여하도록 도울 수 있다고 하였다. 또한 실행 리스트는 씨름할 새로운 프로젝트를 찾을 때 유용한 아이디어의 원천이 될 수 있다고 하였다. 그러므로 ④의 '버그 리스트: 창의적인 해결책을 위한 방아쇠'가 제시문의 제목으로 가장 적절하다.

[오답해설]
① 벌레를 무시하는 것이 벌레를 번식하게 하는가? → 잘못된 것을 그냥 방치하면 잘못이 더 커진다.
② 혁신적인 디자인: 실천보다 말이 쉽다 → 혁신은 말하기는 쉬워도 실행하기는 어렵다.
③ 깨진 것은 잊어버리고, 아름다운 것을 감상하라 → 부정적인 것은 버리고 긍정적인 것을 바라보라.
⑤ 자기 비판: 강력한 개선 도구 → 스스로 반성하는 것은 자기를 발전시키는 강력한 도구가 된다.

26　빈칸 추론하기　③

[정답해설]
제시문에서 일상생활에서 일어나는 버그들을 기록하면 그것들을 더 유념하고 신경 쓰게 되며, 그 문제들을 해결하는 데 도움을 줄 수 있는 문제들을 언젠가는 만나게 된다고 설명하고 있다. 그러므로 ③의 'being more mindful of them(그것들을 더 신경 쓰기)'이 빈칸에 들어갈 말로 가장 적절하다.

[오답해설]
① 일상을 당연하게 여기기
② 공공장소에서 예의 바르게 행동하기
④ 기술에 덜 의존하기
⑤ 자신의 약점을 인정하기

[27~28]

[핵심어휘]
- morality 도덕, 도덕성
- arbitrary 임의적인, 제멋대로인
- value framework 가치 체계
- orientation 방향, 지향
- time immemorial 태고, 아득한 옛날
- consistent 한결같은, 일관된
- norm 표준, 규범
- organize 체계를 세우다, 준비[조직]하다
- solidarity 연대, 결속
- distribution 분배, 배분
- denominator 분모
- underlying 근본적인, 밑에 있는
- unpredictable 예측[예견]할 수 없는
- uncertainty 불확실성, 반신반의
- disregard 무시, 묵살
- moral code 도덕률, 도덕 법규
- violation 위반, 위배

[본문해석]
도덕성은 변화 가능하고 문화에 의존적이며 사회적으로 바람직한 행동을 표현한다. 그러나 도덕성이 변화 가능하더라도, 특히 변화 과정 자체가 비교적 (a) 오랜 시간(몇 주가 아닌 몇 년 이상)이 걸리기 때문에 결코 임의적이지 않다. 이것은 또한 사회적 가치 체계 즉, 도덕성이 중요한 지향 기능을 제공하기 때문이다. 먼 옛날부터 사람들은 도덕적 문제에 대해 생각하고 그것들을 다루어 왔다. 이것은 사람들이 사회 공동체에서 자신을 세울 때 (b) 일관된 가치, 규범, 그리고 도덕적 개념이 항상 주요한 역할을 한다는 것을 분명히 한다. 궁극적으로, 이것은 또한 상품과 자원의 분배뿐만 아니라 정의, 연대, 그리고 돌봄이란 질문의 대답이 된다.
여기서 도덕성은 특정 사회의 (c) 공통된 최저 분모로 작용한다. 그 (d) 이점은 도덕성의 근간이 되는 가치들이 사회적으로 수용된 기본 이해를 전달하고 구체적인 의사결정 상황에서 방향을 제공한다는 사실에 기초한다. 이는 도덕성이 사회 집단을 기능적이고 효율적으로 만든다. 즉, 공동체에 수용되기 위해서 개인은 이 공동체에 반하는 행동을 하지 않도록 노력할 것이다. 역으로 이것은 개인과 사회집단의 행동이 궁극적으로 (e) 예측할 수 없다는(→ 예측 가능하다는) 것을 의미한다. 결과적으로 행동에 대한 불확실성이 감소하고 신뢰가 구축된다.

27　글의 주제 파악하기　③

[정답해설]
제시문에서 도덕성은 인간 사회에서 상품과 자원의 분배뿐만 아니라 정의, 연대, 돌봄의 역할을 하며, 도덕성이 사회 집단을 기능적이고 효율적으로 만든다고 설명하고 있다. 그러므로 '인간 사회에서 도덕성의 기본 역할'이 제시문의 주제로 가장 적절하다.

[오답해설]
① 극한 상황에서 보이는 도덕성의 무시 → 극한 상황에 처했을 때 사람들이 도덕성을 무시하는 사례는 제시문에 나타나 있지 않음
② 도덕성의 기본 요소인 정의와 연대 → 정의와 연대는 도덕성의 역할을 포괄하는 개념이 아니라 하위 개념임

④ 문화 교류를 통한 도덕성의 발전 → 도덕성과 관련된 문화 교류의 사례는 제시문에 나타나 있지 않음

⑤ 사회 전반에 걸친 도덕 법규 위반에 대한 처벌 → 도덕 법규 위반에 대한 처벌 내용은 제시문에 나타나 있지 않음

28 문맥상 부적절한 낱말 고르기 ⑤

[정답해설]

unpredictable → predictable

도덕성의 근간이 되는 가치들이 사회적으로 반영된 공동체에 수용되기 위해서 개인은 그 공동체에 반하는 행동을 하지 않도록 노력하기 때문에 개인의 행동에 대한 불확실성이 감소되고 신뢰가 구축된다. 이것은 역으로 개인과 사회집단의 행동이 궁극적으로 예측 가능하다는 것을 의미하므로 (e)의 'unpredictable(예측할 수 없는)'은 'predictable(예측 가능한)'로 고쳐 써야 옳다.

[29~30]

[핵심어휘]

▢ at the base of ~의 기슭에
▢ huge 거대한, 엄청난
▢ clay 점토, 찰흙
▢ statue 조각상
▢ broom 빗자루
▢ glinting 반짝이는
▢ head monk 주지 스님
▢ precious 귀중한, 값진
▢ nod 끄덕이다, 절[인사]하다
▢ underneath ~의 밑에, 속으로
▢ exterior 외부, 외피, 겉모습
▢ peek 훔쳐보다, 엿보다
▢ sure enough 과연, 아니나 다를까
▢ chip (조금씩) 깎다[쪼다]
▢ chisel 끌
▢ reveal 드러내다, 밝히다

[본문해석]

(A)

오래 전 히말라야 산 기슭에 한 가난한 마을이 있었다. 그 마을의 중심에는 거대한 점토 불상이 있었다. 누가 그것을 만들었는지 아무도 몰랐다. 어느 날, 한 젊은 승려가 빗자루로 불상의 눈을 쓸고 있을 때, 점토에 작은 틈이 있는 것을 발견했다. 해가 떠오르자, 그는 내부 깊은 곳에서 무언가 반짝이는 것을 볼 수 있었

다. (a) 그는 주지 스님에게 달려가, 불상이 부서졌고 빛나는 무언가가 그 안에 있다고 말했다.

(C)

주지 스님은 "그 불상은 수 세대 동안 여기에 있었지. 그것에는 많은 틈이 있단다. 그냥 내버려두렴. 나는 아주 바쁘단다."라고 말했다. 그 젊은 승려는 다시 돌아가 쓸었다. 그러나 (c) 그는 그 틈을 엿보는 것을 참을 수 없었다. 아니나 다를까, 그 안에는 빛나는 무언가가 있었다. 그는 아버지를 불렀고, 아버지는 아들이 발견한 것에 호기심이 있었다. 아버지는 반짝이는 것을 보고 놀랐다. (d) 그는 수년 동안 그 불상을 지나쳤지만 반짝이는 것을 결코 보지 못했다.

(D)

아버지는 달려가 (e) 그의 아들이 발견한 것을 마을 사람들에게 말했다. 곧, 마을의 모든 사람들이 그 불상 주위에 모였다. 주지 스님은 끌로 틈 주변을 조심스럽게 깎아 냈다. 반짝임이 강해졌다. 점토 외피 밑에 드러나길 기다리는 금상이 있다는 사실은 아무도 부인할 수 없었다. 마을 사람들은 밤늦게까지 논쟁을 벌였다. 그들이 점토 불상을 부수고 다시는 돈 걱정을 할 필요가 없거나 아니면 늘 있던 대로 놔둬야 할까?

(B)

주지 스님은 최종 발언을 해야 할 것으로 생각되었다. 그는 틈을 발견한 소년에게 돌아서서 어떻게 생각하는지 물었다. 그에게 쏠린 마을 사람들의 시선에, (b) 그 소년은 말했다. "저는 이 불상을 만든 스님들은 무엇을 해야 할지 알고 있었을 것이라고 생각합니다. 아무도 평범한 점토 불상을 훔치거나 파괴하고 싶어하지는 않을 것입니다. 그러나 값비싼 금으로 만들어진 불상은 모든 사람의 욕망의 대상이 될 것입니다." 스님은 고개를 끄덕였고, "그 불상을 부수지 맙시다. 아마도 우리 모두는 평범한 겉모습 속에 금이 있다는 사실을 깨달았을 것입니다."라고 말했다.

29 글의 배열순서 정하기 ③

[정답해설]

(A)에서는 점토 불상의 갈라진 틈에서 반짝이는 무언가를 발견한 젊은 승려가 주지 스님에게 이 사실을 알리고 있고, (C)에서 이 사실을 전해들은 주지 스님은 무관심하게 받아들인다. 그러자 젊은 승려는 자신의 아버지에게 알린다. (D)에서 아버지는 그의 아들이 발견한 것을 마을 사람들에게 알리고, 마을 사람들은 그 점토 불상을 부숴야 할지 그대

로 나눠야 할지 논쟁을 벌인다. 마지막으로 (B)에서 주지 스님은 평범한 겉모습 속에 금이 있다는 교훈을 일깨우고 그 불상을 부수지 말자고 마을 사람들을 설득한다. 그러므로 글 (A) 다음에 (C)―(D)―(B) 순으로 배열하는 것이 글의 내용 흐름상 적절하다.

30   지칭 대상과 다른 것 고르기   ④

[정답해설]

(a), (b), (c), (e)는 모두 점토 불상에서 작은 틈을 발견한 젊은 승려를 가리키지만, (d)는 젊은 승려의 아버지를 가리킨다.

2023학년도 기출문제 정답 및 해설

✎ 제2교시 **영어영역(공통)**

01 ④	02 ④	03 ⑤	04 ③	05 ④	06 ④
07 ②	08 ①	09 ③	10 ①	11 ②	12 ①
13 ⑤	14 ④	15 ③	16 ⑤	17 ①	18 ①
19 ②	20 ③	21 ⑤	22 ⑤	23 ④	24 ①
25 ②	26 ②	27 ⑤	28 ③	29 ⑤	30 ④

01 ④ 'which'가 관계대명사라면 종속절은 주어나 목적어가 없는 불완전한 문장이 와야 한다. 그러나 해당 문장의 종속절은 완전한 문장이므로, 앞의 'the Moluccas'를 선행사로 하는 장소를 나타내는 관계부사 'where'나 전치사+관계대명사인 'in which'를 사용해야 옳다.

어휘

- crew : 선원, 승무원, 뱃사람
- mislead : 오인하다, 호도하다
- straits : 해협
- prevailing : 우세한, 탁월한
- trade winds : 무역풍
- be rumored to be : 소문에 들리다
- spice : 양념, 향신료
- pilot chart : 항해도, 항공도

해석

마젤란과 그의 선원들은 날씨에 운이 좋았다. 약 12,000마일의 먼 바다를 항해하던 3개월 하고도 20일의 기간 내내, 단 한 번의 폭풍우도 없었다. 이 한 번의 경험을 오인하여, 그들은 그곳을 태평양이라고 명명했다. 마젤란이 바람의 달인이 아니었다면, 그는 결코 태평양을 횡단할 수 없었을 것이다. 해협을 출발한 그는 자신이 원하는 스파이스 아일랜드에 도달하기 위해 북서쪽으로 곧장 가지 않고, 남아메리카의 서쪽 해안을 따라 북쪽으로 먼저 항해하였다. 그의 목적은 포르투갈인들이 장악하고 있다고 소문난 몰루카 섬이 아니라, 스페인 사람들에게 여전히 개방되어 있는 다른 향신료 섬들로 그를 운반해 줄 북동부 우세 무역풍을 잡으려는 것임에 틀림없었다. 그 당시 그의 동기가 무엇이든 간에, 그가 선택한 코스는 여전히 그 계절에 케이프 혼에서 호놀룰루까지 항해하는데 미국 정부의

항해도로 추천된 코스이다.

02 ④ (A) 'choosing'이 무생물로써 문장 전체의 주어이고 내용상 수동태가 되어야 한다. 조동사 'can'이 있으므로, 수동태 형태인 'be seen(be + 과거분사)'을 조동사 'can' 다음에 써야 한다.

(B) 내용상 앞에서 사용한 동사 'sacrifice(희생하다)'를 대용하기 위해 대동사 'do'를 사용해야 한다. 'much as~' 이하에서 'those'가 주어에 해당하므로 3인칭 복수 현재 시제의 형태인 'do'를 그대로 사용하면 된다.

(C) 등위 접속사 'and'에 의해 연결된 'A and B'의 구문으로, A와 B는 동일 형태가 되어야 한다. 앞의 A는 조동사 'should' 다음의 'look'이므로 B에 해당하는 'investigate'의 형태는 동사원형인 'investigate'가 되어야 한다.

어휘

- analogous to : ~와 비슷한[유사한]
- run for : ~에 입후보하다, 출마하다
- knowingly : 다 알고도, 고의로, 일부러
- anonymity : 익명성
- opt in : ~에 참여하기로 하다
- varying degrees : 다양한 수준[정도]
- election : 선거, 선출, 당선
- tacit : 무언의, 암묵적인
- feed : 피드(웹 콘텐츠를 배포하는 데 사용되는 기술)
- legal : 합법적인, 법률과 관련된
- feed : 공급하다, 제공하다
- safeguard : 보호하다, 옹호하다
- craft : 정교하게[세밀하게] 만들다
- investigate : 조사하다, 연구하다, 살피다

해석

우리는 사회에 참여하기 위해, 예를 들어 은행 계좌와 의료 기록에 접속하기 위해 인터넷을 사용할 필요성이 증가하고 있다는 이유만으로 권리를 포기해서는 안 된다. 우리는 이러한 서비스에 대한 사생활 보호를 요구해야 한다. 그러나 소셜 미디어와 같은 것에 참여하기로 결정한 것은 공직에 출마하기로 결정한 사람과 비슷하다고 볼 수 있다. 활동을 하기로 결심했을 때 인스타그램, 트위터 또는 페이스북의 게시글 올리기에

참여한 사람들 만큼이나 익명성과 일부 사생활을 알면서도 희생한다. 우리 모두는 소셜 미디어 피드에 출마 중이며, 그것은 플랫폼이 우리의 정보를 분석하고 그들의 비즈니스 모델을 지원하기 위해 광고를 제공할 거라는 암묵적인 수용(그리고 작은 인쇄물에서는 합법적 수용)을 수반한다. 우리의 권리를 옹호하고 우리의 동료 사이버 시민들을 위해로부터 보호하기 위해 가능한 모든 것을 해야 하지만, 아마도 우리는 개인과 기업이 우리의 정보를 수집하고 거래할 수 있도록 새로운 규칙을 만드는 것을 넘어 데이터 수집 과학 자체를 더 면밀히 조사해야 할 것이다.

03 ⑤ 제시문은 생산과 관련된 혁신을 꾀할 때 소프트웨어적인 문화보다 하드웨어적인 기술 변화에 치중하는 것에 대한 문제점을 지적하고 있다. 즉, 기술적인 수정을 선호하는 것은 제품 전반에 미치는 실질적인 영향을 소홀히 하고, 소프트웨어적인 변화의 중요성을 간과하며, 선택과 행동에 대한 책임을 회피하려는 경향을 증가시킨다. 그러므로 ⑤의 'reduce(감소시키다)'는 'increase(증가시키다)'로 바꿔 써야 옳다.

어휘

- sustainability : 지속[유지] 가능성
- prevalence : 만연, 팽배
- improvement : 향상, 개선, 호전
- ameliorate : 개선하다, 개량하다
- favour : 선호하다, 편들다
- behavioural : 행동의, 행동적인
- inevitable : 불가피한, 필연적인
- textile : 직물, 옷감, 섬유
- neglect : 방치하다, 소홀히 하다
- substantial : 중요한, 본질적인, 실질적인
- significant : 중요한, 의미가 있는
- sideline : 열외시키다, 제외시키다
- contribution : 기여, 공헌
- subtle : 미묘한, 교묘한, 예민한
- insidious : 서서히 퍼지는, 암암리에 퍼지는
- reduce : 줄이다, 감축하다
- accountability : 해명, 책임

해석

생산과 관련된 지속가능성 혁신의 한 가지 특징은 '소프트웨어' 문화 변화보다 '하드웨어' 기술 기반 개선이 만연하다는 것이다. 많은 제조업체에게 혁신적이라는 것은 특히 기존 기술의 부정적인 영향을 개선하려고 할 때, 어떤 문제에 기술을 '추가'하는 것을 의미한다. 더 소프트웨어적이고, 행동적이며, 문화적인 것들보다 기술적인 수정을 선호하는 것은 아마도 18

세기 산업혁명 이후 기술을 개선함으로써 원료를 더 빠르고 저렴하게 가공해 온 섬유와 같은 산업에서 불가피할 것이다. 그러나 그 결과는 행동이 제품의 전반적인 환경 영향을 결정하는 데 미치는 매우 실질적인 영향을 소홀히 하는 경향이 있다. 그것은 또한 지속가능성 개선을 하는 데 있어 소프트웨어적인 변화의 중요한 역할을 간과하고 디자이너와 소비자와 같은 비기술자의 기여를 제외시킨다. 모든 문제를 '수정'하기 위해 기술에 의존하는 것은 또한 선택과 행동에 대한 책임을 회피하려는 경향을 감소시키는(→ 증가시키는) 더 교묘하고 암암리에 퍼지는 영향을 미칠 수 있다.

04 ③ (A) 제1차 세계 대전 이후 새로운 용도로 재활용되어야 할 군수용 물품들이 창고에 많이 쌓여 있다는 의미이므로, 빈칸 (A)에는 'abundance(많음, 풍부함)'가 들어갈 말로 적절하다.

(B) 전쟁 중에 절약과 재사용의 문화가 불필요한 것을 버리고 새로운 물건에 기꺼이 돈을 쓰는 소비 문화로 바뀌어야 한다는 의미이므로, 빈칸 (B)에는 'willingness(기꺼이 하기)'가 들어갈 말로 적절하다.

(C) 전쟁기간 동안에는 낭비하지 말라는 포스터를 제작한 반면에 전쟁 이후에는 소비를 장려하기 위해 현명하지 못한 절약에 주의하라는 표지판을 제공했다는 내용이므로, 빈칸 (C)에는 'encourage(장려하다)'가 들어갈 말로 적절하다.

어휘

- manufacturer : 제조업자, 생산자
- abundance : 풍부, 많은, 다량
- pile : 쌓다, 포개다
- warehouse : 창고
- absorbent : 잘 빨아들이는, 흡수력 있는
- celluloid : 셀룰로이드
- military bandage : 군사용 붕대
- disposable : 사용 후 버리는, 일회용의
- sanitary napkin : 생리대
- figure out : 생각해 내다, 이해하다
- ethic : 윤리, 도덕
- darn : 깁다, 꿰매다
- odd : 외짝의, 한 짝만 있는, 짝이 안 맞는
- sew : 바느질하다, 깁다
- rag : 해진 천[누더기]
- rug : 깔개, 무릎덮개
- embrace : 포용하다, 받아들이다
- hesitation : 주저, 망설임
- stuff : 것, 물건

- declare : 단언하다, 선언하다
- beware of : ～에 주의하다
- restrain : 제한하다, 억제하다
- repetitive : 반복적인, 되풀이하는

해석

제조업체의 경우, 사용 후 버려지는 제품은 고객에게 계속해서 더 많이 돌려달라고 강요하며 끝없는 이익 가능성을 창출한다. 그것은 제1차 세계 대전 이후 창고에 높이 쌓여 있는 (A) 많은 군수용 물품들에 대한 새로운 용도를 찾아야할 필요성이 컸던 때인 지난 몇 년 간 처음 발견된 가능성이다. 예를 들어, 군용 붕대와 방독면 필터에 사용되었던 셀룰로이드로 만들어진 흡수성 물질을 후에 일회용 코텍스 생리대라는 새로운 용도로 사용되었다. 제조업자들은 또한 절약과 재사용, 즉 양말을 깁고, 짝이 안 맞는 끈을 보관하고, 찻잎을 사용하여 카펫을 청소하고, 누더기 천을 꿰매 깔개를 만드는 전시 윤리를 어떻게 "버리기 습관"과 새로운 "물건"에 (B) 기꺼이 돈을 쓰는 것을 포용하는 문화로 변화시킬지 생각해 내야 했다. 전쟁 기간 동안 미국 정부는 "낭비하지 않으면 부족함이 없다"고 선언한 포스터를 제작했다. 1917년 말에, 정부는 지속적인 소비를 (C) 장려하기 위해 전국의 상점들 창문에 전시할 "검소와 현명하지 못한 절약에 주의하라"라는 표지판을 제공했다.

05 ④ 주어진 제시문은 그리스 신화와 중세의 연금술 그리고 무슬림 화학자와 유대교 학자에 이르기까지 인공 생명체를 창조하는 것에 대해 언급하고 있다. 그러므로 종교적인 관점에서 이슬람교와 유대교의 유사점에 대해 설명한 ④의 내용은 윗글의 전체적인 흐름과 관계가 없다.

어휘

- humanity : 인류, 인간성
- millennia : 천년, 새로운 천년이 시작되는 시기
- reference : 말하기, 언급
- craftsman : 공예가, 수공업자
- artisan : 장인, 기능인
- sculptor : 조각가
- alchemical : 연금술의
- synthetic : 합성한, 인조 물질의
- similarity : 유사성, 닮음
- perspective : 관점, 시각
- inanimate : 무생물의, 생기 없는, 죽은 것 같은
- clay : 점토, 찰흙
- folklore : 민속 신앙, 신화

해석

스마트 기계는 수천 년 동안 인류의 환상이었다. ①기계적이

고 인공적인 존재에 대한 초기 언급은 그리스 신화에 등장하는데, 황금 로봇을 만든 대장장이, 목수, 공예가, 기능인 그리고 조각가들의 신인 헤파이스토스에서 시작한다. ②중세에는 인공적인 형태의 생명을 창조하는 신비한 연금술의 수단이 계속되었다. ③무슬림 화학자 자비르 이븐 하이얀이 언급한 목표는 탁원으로, 실험실에서 인간의 생명을 포함한 그 이상의 인조 생명체를 창조하는 것을 말한다. ④한때 유대인들과 무슬림교인들은 함께 살았고, 함께 일하고, 함께 공부했으며, 오늘날에도 이슬람교와 유대교를 종교적인 관점에서 관찰할 때 비슷한 점이 많다. ⑤프라하의 마하랄로 유대교 학자들에게 널리 알려진 랍비 유다 로우는 이제는 민속 신앙이 되어버린 골렘 즉, 진부 무생물(대개 찰흙이나 진흙)로 만들어진 존재에 대한 이야기를 했다.

06 ④ 위의 제시문은 어떤 문제에 대한 한 가지 접근법은 어느 한 쪽으로 시각이 편향될 수 있으므로, 서로 다른 접근 방식을 반복적으로 추구함으로써 새롭고 유용한 생각을 얻을 수 있다고 설명하고 있다. 그러므로 "문제에 다각적으로 접근하면 새롭고 유용한 생각에 이를 수 있다."는 ④의 설명이 윗글의 요지로 가장 적절하다.

어휘

- have in common with : ～와 공통점을 지니다
- variation : 변이, 변화, 다양성
- generate : 발생시키다, 만들어 내다
- exemplify : 예를 들다, 귀감이 되다
- restructure : 재구성하다, 재구축하다
- biased : 편향된, 선입견이 있는
- perspective : 관점, 시각
- essence : 본질, 정수
- once in a while : 때로는, 가끔

해석

미칼코는 창의적 사고가 자연 선택에 의한 진화와 많은 공통점이 있다고 말한다. 진화의 기본은 다양성인데, 왜냐하면 다양성이 없으면 선택할 수 있는 것이 없기 때문이다. 마찬가지로 창의적인 사람들은 처리할 문제를 선택하기에 앞서 어떤 문제에 대한 매우 다양한 아이디어를 만들어내는 데 능숙하다. 이러한 사고방식의 귀감이 되는 레오나르도 다빈치는 그의 문제들을 다른 각도에서 보기 위해 반복적으로 재구성하는 것으로 유명하다. 그는 첫 번째 접근법이 평소 자신의 시각에 너무 치우쳐 있다고 생각했다. 각각의 새로운 관점에서 그는 그 문제에 대한 이해를 깊게 하고 그것의 본질을 보기 시작할 것이다. 그는 이 방법을 사퍼 비데어 즉, '보는 방법을 아는 것'이라고 불렀다. 언뜻 보기에 이러한 사고방식은 대부분의 아이디어가 결코 직접적으로 사용되지 않기 때문에 낭비적인 것

처럼 보일 수 있다. 요점인 즉, 서로 다른 접근 방식을 반복적으로 추구함으로써, 일반적인 사고방식에서 점차 새로운 사고방식으로 이동한다는 것이다. 때때로 이 과정은 모든 노력을 가치 있게 만드는 진정 새롭고 유용한 아이디어로 귀결될 것이다.

07 ② Victor Shklovsky가 제시한 문학 예술을 만드는 기준인 '비익숙화'는 생소하고 낯선 단어와 구문을 사용함으로써 예술을 처음 보았던 것처럼 만드는 것이다. 그러므로 밑줄 친 make 'a stone a stone again'('돌을 다시 돌'로 만드는)이 의미하는 바는 ②의 'make ordinary things unordinary(평범한 것을 비범하게 만들다)'가 가장 적절하다.

어휘

- criterion : 표준, 기준
- strangeness : 이상함, 진기함
- valid : 유효한, 타당한
- novelty : 새로움, 참신함, 신기함
- article : 글, 기사
- assert : 단언하다, 주장하다
- defamiliarization : 낯설음, 비익숙화
- economize : 절약하다, 아끼다
- cliches : 상투적인 문구
- prolong : 미루다, 연기하다
- deautomatize : 비자동화하다
- perception : 지각, 인지, 깨달음
- deviate from : ~에서 일탈하다, 벗어나다
- rhymeless : 리듬이 없는, 운율이 없는
- unordinary : 보통이 아닌, 비범한
- precisely : 꼭, 바로, 정확하게

오답풀이

① replace symbols with ordinary words(기호를 평범한 말로 바꾸다)
③ turn a word into an image(단어를 이미지로 바꾸다)
④ define a thing more precisely(사물을 보다 정확하게 정의하다)
⑤ make readers read between the lines(독자들에게 행간을 읽게 하다)

해석

이상함의 기준이 유효하다면 새로움의 기준에 속할 것이다. 장치 예술에 관한 유명한 글에서, Victor Shklovsky는 비익숙화가 문학 예술을 만드는 기준이라고 단언한다. 일상생활에서 우리는 사물을 실제로 인지하지 않은 채 당연하게 여기는 경향이 있고, 일상어로 그것에 대해 이야기할 때, 청자가 즉시

이해하는 상투적인 문구와 같은 잘 알려진 단어와 말을 사용하여 표현을 아끼는 경향이 있다. 생소하고 낯선 단어와 구문을 사용함으로써, 예술은 '돌을 다시 돌'로 만드는 즉, 마치 그것을 처음 보았던 것처럼 만들기 위해 인식의 과정을 연장하고 비자동화하려고 한다. 비익숙화는 독자의 주의를 그가 간과하기 쉬운 현실의 측면에 집중시킨다. Shklovsky는 의사소통 과정의 다른 수준을 구별하지 않고 글, 정신적 모델 그리고 행동에서 비익숙화의 사례를 제시한다. 비익숙화는 일상적인 것에서 벗어난 어떤 것이든 될 수 있다. 예를 들어, 운율이 흔한 시기에는 운율이 없는 시가 이상하며, 그 반대도 마찬가지이다. 메시지의 수준에서, 비익숙화는 그 행동이 독자들이 다르게 생각하도록 어떻게든 강요할 것이라는 것을 의미할 것이다.

08 ① 제시문에 인류의 조상은 결코 경쟁적인 포식자나 먹잇감보다 빨리 달리거나 힘이 세지 않았지만, 한낮의 더위도 견딜 수 있는 엄청난 지구력 덕분에 먹잇감을 사냥을 할 수 있었다고 서술되어 있다. 그러므로 ①의 'Hominids: A Persistent Hunter(인류의 조상: 끈질긴 사냥꾼)'가 윗글의 제목으로 가장 적절하다.

어휘

- dominant : 우세한, 우성의, 지배적인
- predatory : 포식성의, 포식 동물 같은
- trait : 특성, 특징
- physiologist : 생리학자
- dub : 별명을 붙이다, 더빙하다
- super-endurance : 초내구성
- emergence : 출현, 나타남
- interrelated : 상호 관련된, 밀접한 관계인
- attribute : 속성, 특성
- diverge from : ~에서 나뉘다
- apelike : 유인원 같은
- hominid : 인류, 인류의 조상
- outrun : 보다 빨리 달리다, 넘어서다
- outmuscle : 힘으로 압도하다[이기다]
- seek over : ~을 찾아내다[구해내다], 색출하다
- enormous : 거대한, 엄청난
- amble : 느긋하게 걷다, 느릿느릿 걷다
- trot : 빨리 걷다, 속보로 가다
- trek : 트레킹, 오지 여행
- midday : 정오, 한낮
- pack : (사냥개, 늑대 따위의) 한 떼[무리]
- intense : 강한, 극심한, 강력한
- vulture : 독수리, 콘도르

- flee from : ~에서 달아나다, 도망치다
- carcass : 사체, 죽은 동물
- persistent : 끈질긴, 집요한
- intensity : 강렬함, 강인함

오답풀이

② Intensity Comes Before Endurance(지구력보다 우선인 강인함)
③ Hunting in the Heat: Mission Impossible(더위 속 사냥: 미션 임파서블)
④ Hunters Need Speed and Power(속도와 힘을 필요로 하는 사냥꾼)
⑤ Show Respect to Your Prey(먹이에 경의를 표하라)

해석

경쟁적인 환경에서 우리 조상은 생리학자 Bernd Heinrich가 그들을 "초내구적 포식자"라고 불렀던 것처럼 신체적, 정신적, 사회적 특징들의 결합을 통해 결국 지배적인 포식동물이 되었다. 이러한 포식자들의 출현을 위한 신체적 토대는 우리 조상들이 다른 유인원 같은 종들에서 나뉘었을 때인 약 600만년 전에 발달하기 시작한 상호 연관된 특성들에 의해 제공되었다. 인류의 조상은 결코 경쟁하는 포식자나 짧은 거리에서 찾아낸 먹잇감 보다 빨리 달리거나 힘으로 압도하도록 진화하지 않았다. 대신에 인류의 조상은 지구력을 위한 엄청난 능력을 발달시켰다. 그들은 먼 거리를 달리거나 혹은 걸어가거나, 조깅하거나, 느리게 걷거나, 행진하거나, 빨리 걷거나, 하이킹을 할 수 있으며, 먹잇감을 쫓기 위해 몇 시간 동안 심지어 며칠 동안 이동할 수 있다. 그들은 거대한 고양이와 개 무리들과 같은 경쟁적인 포식동물들이 강렬한 아프리카의 태양으로부터 숨을 때, 한낮의 더위는 물론, 모든 종류의 날씨에서 언제든지 이러한 트레킹을 할 수 있었다. 하이에나와 독수리조차 가장 뜨거운 낮에 태양으로부터 도망쳤고, 따라서 더위를 견딜 수 있는 인류의 조상들에게 사체에 접근하는데 중요한 이점을 제공했다.

09 ③ 윗글에서는 농구에서 자유투, 골프에서 퍼팅 혹은 미식축구나 럭비에서 플레이스킥을 실행하기에 앞서 나타나는 '실행 전 루틴(PPRs)'에 대해 설명하고 있다. 이러한 루틴은 집중력과 경쟁적 성과를 향상시키기 위한 정신적 준비의 한 형태로 운동선수들이 널리 이용하고 있으며 코치와 심리학자들도 추천하고 있다고 서술되어 있다. 그러므로 ③의 'Pre-performance Routines: Athletes' Ritual for Better Play(실행 전 루틴: 더 나은 경기를 위한 선수들의 의식)'가 윗글의 제목으로 가장 적절하다.

어휘

- ritualised : 의례적인, 의식화된
- waggle : 흔들다, 움직이다
- preferred : 우선의, 선호하는
- task-relevant : 업무[직무]와 관련된
- evident : 분명히 나타난, 눈에 띄는
- execution : 실행, 수행
- closed skill : 폐쇄 기술(환경이 변하지 않는 안정된 상태에서 수행하는 운동 기술)
- interference : 간섭, 방해
- place-kick : (공을 땅에 놓고) 차다
- extensively : 널리, 광범위하게
- enhance : 높이다, 강화하다, 향상시키다
- optimal : 최적의, 적기의
- competitive spirit : 경쟁심
- ritual : 의례, 의식
- superstitious : 미신의, 미신적인

오답풀이

① Team Play: One for All, All for One(팀 플레이: 모두를 위한 하나, 하나를 위한 모두)
② Competitive Spirits Enable You to Surpass Your Limits(경쟁심을 통해 한계를 뛰어넘을 수 있다)
④ Habitual Body Movements Interfere with Successful Performance(습관적인 몸 동작이 성공적인 수행을 방해한다)
⑤ Pre-performance Routines as Superstitious Behaviour Among Athletes(운동선수들 사이의 미신적 행동, 실행 전 루틴)

해석

경쟁적인 스포츠는 종종 매우 의식화된 활동이다. 예를 들어 테니스 선수들은 서브하기 전에 정해진 횟수만큼 공을 튀기는 것을 좋아하는 반면, 골퍼들은 공을 치기 전에 일정한 횟수만큼 클럽을 '흔들기'하는 성향이 있다. 이러한 선호되는 일련의 행동은 '실행 전 루틴'(PPRs)이라고 하며 특정 스포츠 기술의 실행에 앞서 선수들이 체계적으로 참여하는 직무 관련 사고와 행동을 포함한다. 보통 PPRs는 농구에서 자유투, 골프에서 퍼팅 혹은 미식축구나 럭비에서 플레이스킥과 같은 폐쇄 기술과 자기 페이스대로 하는 행동(즉, 주로 자신의 속도로 다른 사람의 간섭 없이 실행되는 것)을 실행하기 전에 분명히 나타난다. 이러한 루틴은 집중력을 요하는 기술을 개선하거나 경쟁적 성과를 향상시키기 위해 정신적인 준비의 한 형태로 운동선수들에 의해 광범위하게 이용되며 코치와 심리학자들에 의해 추천된다. 요컨대, PPR의 목적은 실행 직전에 자신을 최적의 상태로 두는 것이며, 실행 중에 그 상태

를 유지하는 것이다.

10 ① 제시문에 따르면 북유럽 사람들은 볏 달린 쟁기를 개발하기 전까지 농사 조건이 좋지 않았지만, 길고 좁은 땅에서 많은 동물들을 필요로 하는 볏 달린 쟁기의 특성으로 인해 농사가 지역 공동체의 일이 되었고, 따라서 북유럽에 도시들이 생겨나고 번영하기 시작했다고 서술되어 있다. 그러므로 ①의 'socio-economic changes in Northern Europe caused by the moldboard plow(볏 달린 쟁기로 인한 북유럽의 사회 경제적 변화)'가 윗글의 주제로 가장 적절하다.

어휘

- moldboard plow : 볏 달린 쟁기
- endowment : 기부(금)
- fertile : 비옥한, 기름진
- plow-based : 쟁기 기반의
- prosperity : 번영, 번성, 번창
- flourish : 번창하다, 번영하다
- dry-soil : 건식
- crisscross : 열십자의, 십자형의
- plowing : 밭 갈기, 경작
- individualistic : 개인주의의, 개인주의적인
- wet-clay : 습식
- efficient : 능률적인, 효율적인
- strip : 길고 좁은 땅
- draft : 뽑다, 선발하다
- appropriate : 적당한, 타당한
- barren land : 불모지

오답풀이

② difficulties of finding an appropriate farming method for barren land(불모지에 적합한 농사 방법을 찾기 어려움)
③ various reasons farming was difficult for Northern Europeans(북유럽 사람들에게 농사가 어려웠던 다양한 이유)
④ social support required to invent the moldboard plow(볏 달린 쟁기를 발명하는 데 필요한 사회적 지원)
⑤ potential problems of using animals to plow a field(밭을 갈기 위해 동물을 이용하는 잠재적인 문제점)

해석

볏 달린 쟁기의 개발은 유럽의 비옥한 토지에 대한 자연의 기부를 뒤집었다. 북유럽에 살던 사람들은 오랫동안 어려운 농사 조건을 견뎌왔지만, 지금은 가장 좋은 생산적인 땅이 남쪽이 아닌 북쪽이 되었다. 약 천 년 전에 시작된 이 새로운 쟁기로 인한 번영 덕분에, 북유럽의 도시들이 생겨나고 번영하기

시작했다. 그리고 그 도시들은 지중해 주변의 도시들과는 다른 사회 구조로 번창했다. 건식 스크래치 쟁기는 그것을 끌기 위해 두 마리 동물만 필요했고, 단순히 네모난 밭의 십자형 밭 갈기에 가장 적합했다. 이 모든 것이 농사를 개인주의적인 일로 만들었다. 농부는 쟁기, 소, 땅이 있으면 혼자 살 수 있었다. 하지만 습식의 볏 달린 쟁기는 여덟 마리가 한 팀인 황소, 아니 더 낫게는 말이 필요했으니 누가 그렇게 부자였겠는가? 그것은 종종 다른 사람의 길고 좁은 땅에서 한두 걸음 떨어져 있는 길고 좁은 땅에서 가장 효율적이었다. 결과적으로 농사는 더욱 지역 공동체의 일이 되었다. 즉, 사람들은 쟁기를 공유하고 동물을 선발하고 의견 차이를 해결해야 했다. 그들은 마을에서 함께 모였다.

11 ② 제시문은 학생들이 화가 나고 마음 상하고 좌절하는 등 그 원인이 무엇이든 간에 학생들의 감정을 무시하지 말고 끝까지 보살피라고 서술되어 있다. 그러므로 "학생의 감정을 헤아려 적절하게 대하라."는 ②의 설명이 필자의 주장으로 가장 적절하다.

어휘

- knowingly : 다 알고도, 고의로
- upset : 속상하게 하다, 마음 상하게 하다
- frustration : 불만, 좌절감
- stem from : ~에 기인[유래]하다, ~에서 비롯되다
- fatigue : 피로, 피곤
- annoyance : 짜증, 골칫거리
- well up : 고이다, 샘솟다
- overreact : 과잉[과민] 반응을 보이다
- sympathetic : 동정적인, 공감하는
- misinterpret : 잘못 이해하다, 오해하다
- probe : 캐묻다, 조사하다
- appreciate : 감사하다, 고마워하다
- follow through with : ~을 이행[완수]하다

해석

"절대 화가 나서 잠자리에 들지 말라"는 부부들의 오랜 조언처럼, 학생들을 일부러 화나게 하거나 마음 상하게 해서 수업을 그만두게 하지 마라. 학생들의 좌절은 어려운 내용이나 기술, 개인적인 문제, 피로, 그리고 때로는 선생님에 대한 짜증에서 비롯될 수 있다. 그 원인이 무엇이든 간에, 그들의 감정을 무시하지 마라. 만약 눈물이 고이기 시작하는 것을 본다면, 모든 것을 멈추고 이야기하라. 과민반응과 그들의 좌절감을 개인적으로 받아들이는 것을 피하라. 어느 정도의 좌절감은 새로운 기술을 배우는 데 정상적인 부분이다. 그들이 낙담해 보일 때, 그들에게 물 한 잔, 공감하는 귀, 그리고 휴지를 건네라. 만약 그들이 당신을 오해했거나 개념을 이해하지 못했다

면, 가장 원초적인 것까지 벗겨내라. 만약 본능적으로 무언가가 학생을 괴롭히고 있다고 느끼면, 알아보는 것을 조금도 두려워하지 마라. 대부분의 학생들은 "전 괜찮아요"라고 말하겠지만, 그렇게 말할 때조차도 그들은 거의 항상 당신의 보살핌에 고마워한다. 만약 걱정이 된다면 부모님께 전화를 걸어 끝까지 챙겨라.

12 ① 제시문은 세심한 주의를 기울이지 않으면 문화는 곧 타락하므로 폭정에 맞서 침묵하지 말고 깨어나 앞장서라고 설명하고 있다. 그러므로 윗글이 시사하는 바는 ①의 'Stay alert and stand up against what is wrong.(정신을 바짝 차리고 옳지 못한 일에 맞서라.)'이다.

어휘

• manifest : 나타내다, 드러내 보이다
• tilt : 기울다, 젖히다
• corruption : 부패, 타락, 오염
• tyranny : 폭정, 학정
• comparatively : 비교적, 어지간히, 꽤
• tiny : 아주 작은, 조그마한
• retreat : 후퇴하다, 물러나다
• betrayal : 배신, 배반
• rationalization : 합리화, 정당화
• resentment : 분함, 분개, 울분
• restrictive : 제한하는, 구속하는
• delight : 기쁨, 즐거움
• vanish : 사라지다, 없어지다
• alert : 방심하지 않는, 경계하는, 주의 깊은
• attitude : 자세, 태도
• aptitude : 적성, 소질

오답풀이

② Sometimes retreat is a wise choice.(때로는 후퇴하는 것이 현명한 선택이다.)
③ Silence is golden, speech is silver.(침묵은 금이고, 연설은 은이다.)
④ Expectation is the root of all heartache.(기대감은 모든 심적 고통의 근원이다.)
⑤ Success depends more on attitude than aptitude.(성공은 적성보다도 태도에 달려 있다.)

해석

비록 작아 보일지라도, 나는 사람들이 행하는 선이 그들이 생각하는 것보다 세상에 널리 나타나는 선과 더 관련이 있다고 믿으며, 악에 대해서도 똑같다고 믿는다. 우리 모두 우리가 생각하는 것보다 세계 정세에 더 많은 책임이 있으며, 또한 그

렇게 믿는 것이 편할 것이다. 세심한 주의를 기울이지 않으면, 문화는 바로 타락으로 기운다. 폭정은 느리게 성장하고, 우리에게 아주 조금씩 후퇴하라고 요구한다. 그러나 각각의 후퇴는 다음 후퇴의 가능성을 높인다. 양심의 배신 하나하나가, 침묵의 행동 하나하나가(침묵할 때 느끼는 울분에도 불구하고), 그리고 합리화 하나하나가 저항을 약화시키고 다음의 제한적인 전진 가능성을 높인다. 이것은 그들이 지금 획득한 권력에 대한 기쁨을 만끽하는 경우 특히 그러하며 그리고 그러한 사람들은 항상 발견된다. 비용이 상대적으로 저렴할 때, 그리고 아마도 잠재적인 보상이 아직 사라지지 않았을 때, 깬 채로 앞장 서는 것이 더 낫다.

13 ⑤ 본문에서 "가장 인기 있는 DIY 프로젝트를 수행하는 설명과 시범을 Home Station에서 할 수 있는 날을 제안하고 싶다"고 서술되어 있다. 그러므로 ⑤의 '고객이 직접 작업하는 방법을 알려주는 강좌 개설을 제안하려고'가 윗글의 목적으로 가장 적절하다.

어휘

• sales associate : 영업 사원, 판매 사원
• tackle : 부딪치다, 대처하다
• expert : 전문가, 숙련가
• take A through B : A가 B를 익히도록 하다
• install : 설치하다, 설비하다
• seal : 밀봉하다, 봉쇄하다
• driveway : 차도, 진입로
• faucet : 수도 꼭지

해석

Smalltown Home Station Hardware 상점에서 내 고객들은 더 큰 집수리 및 개선 작업을 어떻게 해야 하는지에 대한 조언을 끊임없이 요청하고 있다. 여기 있는 모든 판매 사원들은 고객이 직접 작업을 결정하도록 돕기 위해 가능한 한 많은 노력을 하지만, 또한 DIY(손수 만드는 상품)를 다룰 자신이 없는 사람들에게 꽤 많은 판매량을 놓치고 있다. 가장 인기 있는 DIY 프로젝트를 수행하는 설명과 시범을 Home Station에서 할 수 있는 날을 제안하고 싶다. 우리는 전문가들로 하여금 사람들이 차고 문 개폐기 설치, 진입로 봉쇄, 수도꼭지 설치, 그리고 다른 평범한 작업들을 익히도록 할 수 있다. 많은 공급업체가 자체 기술자를 파견하여 수업을 운영하고 하드웨어 및 자재 판매를 지원할 수 있다.

14 ④ 윗글에 따르면 남편인 Charles W. Birnie와 양어머니인 Martha Savage는 Ruth가 약학을 직업으로 삼도록 장려했다. 그러므로 "남편과 키워준 어머니의 반대를 무릅쓰고 약

사가 되려고 했다."는 ④의 설명은 윗글의 내용과 일치하지 않는다.

어휘

- rear : 기르다, 양육하다
- physician : 의사, 내과 의사
- foster mother : 양어머니
- pharmacy : 약국, 약학
- degree : 학위

해석

1884년 8월 15일, Ruth Gardena Birnie는 South Carolina의 Sumter에서 Moses와 Louise Harrison 사이에서 태어났다. 그녀의 부모님이 그녀가 매우 어릴 때 돌아가셨기 때문에, Birnie는 Martha A. Savage 선생님에 의해 양육되었다. Birnie는 Sumter에 있는 초기 아프리카계 미국인 학교인 Lincoln School을 졸업했다. 후에 그녀는 그곳에서 짧은 기간 동안 가르쳤다. 1902년, 그녀가 18살이 되었을 때, 그녀는 최초의 아프리카계 미국인 의사로서 Sumter에 온 Charles Wainwright Birnie와 결혼했다. 결혼 16년 후, Birnie 부부는 딸 Anna를 낳았다. Charles W. Birnie의 일이 커지자, 그와 Ruth Birnie의 양어머니인 Martha Savage는 Ruth가 약학을 직업으로 삼도록 장려했다. 그녀는 Benedict College에 입학한 후, Temple University에 진학하여 약학 학위를 받았다. South Carolina로 돌아온 Birnie는 그 주에서 가장 최초의 아프리카계 미국인 여성 약사가 되었다.

15 ③ 어떤 일련의 상황이 정형화를 거부하거나 이치에 맞지 않아 통제 불능 상태가 될 때, 우리의 신체는 교감신경계에서 코르티솔과 아드레날린과 같은 스트레스 호르몬을 분비하여 심리적으로 마음이 통제될 때까지 경계 반응을 활성화시키고 신경을 곤두서게 한다. 그러므로 빈칸에 들어갈 말은 ③의 'regained control(통제권을 되찾았다)'이다.

어휘

- pervasive : 만연하는, 스며드는, 퍼지는
- be relevant to : ~와 관련이 있다, ~와 연관되다
- psychiatrist : 정신과의사
- stimuli : 고무, 격려, 자극(stimulus의 복수 형태)
- defy : 반항하다, 거부하다
- patterning : 정형화
- dysphoria : 불쾌감
- recognizable : 인식할 수 있는, 알 수 있는
- make sense : 앞뒤가 맞다, 이치에 맞다
- rustle : 바스락거리다, 사각거리다
- betrayal : 배신, 배반

- out-of-control : 통제불능의
- eliminate : 없애다, 제거하다
- neuroendocrine system : 신경내분비계
- be geared toward : ~에 맞춰지다, ~에 적합되다
- sympathetic nervous system : 교감신경계
- secrete : 분비하다
- cortisol : 코티솔
- adrenalin : 아드레날린
- activate : 작동시키다, 활성화시키다
- alertness : 경계심, 경각심
- put ~ on edge : 신경을 곤두서게 하다, 과민하게 만들다
- regain : 되찾다, 되돌아오다
- perfectionism : 완벽주의, 완전주의

오답풀이

① shared values(가치를 공유했다)
② received praise(칭찬을 받았다)
④ removed inequality(불평등을 제거했다)
⑤ overcome perfectionism(완벽주의를 극복했다)

해석

몇몇 심리학자들은 안다는 느낌을 "옳다는 느낌"이라고 말하는데, 우리와 관련된 것을 알지 못하는 것을 싫어하기 때문에 그것은 강하고 만연된 느낌이다. 정신과 의사 Irvin Yalom이 말했듯이, "어떤 상황이나 일련의 자극이 정형화를 거부할 때, 우리는 그 상황을 인식할 수 있는 패턴에 맞출 때까지 지속되는 불쾌감(높은 수준의 불안)을 경험한다." 우리는 불편함이 덤불 속의 수상한 바스락 소리인지, 친구의 혼란스러운 배신인지, 혹은 우리가 하지 못한 승진이든지 간에, 무언가를 이해하도록 동기를 부여하기 때문에 어떤 것이 이치에 맞지 않을 때 매우 불편하게 느끼도록 설계되었다. 무지는 우리가 심리적으로 제거하려고 동기가 부여된 "통제 불능" 상태이다. 신경내분비계는 바로 이 목표에 맞춰져 있다. 즉, 교감신경계는 경계 반응을 활성화시키는 코르티솔과 아드레날린과 같은 스트레스 호르몬을 분비하여, 통제권을 되찾았다고 느낄 때까지 신경을 곤두서게 한다.

16 ⑤ 개념 속에 있는 단어의 반복이나 동의어의 사용으로 인한 순환적 정의를 피하는 방법으로, 빈칸 다음에 대조의 예시들을 열거하고 있다. 그러므로 ⑤의 'What contrast is the concept intended to draw(그 개념이 그리려고 하는 것은 어떤 대조인가?)'가 윗글의 빈칸에 들어갈 말로 가장 적절하다.

어휘

- ownership : 소유(권)

• definition : 정의, 뜻풀이

• in terms of : ~면에서, ~에 관하여

• synonym : 동의어, 유의어

• circular : 원형의, 순환적인

• attribute : 속성, 특성

• folly : 어리석음, 어리석은 행동[생각]

• circularity : 환형, 순환, 환상성

• supporting evidence : 증거물, 입증 자료

오답풀이

① When do you need to define key concepts(언제 주요 개념을 정의할 필요가 있는가?)

② Why then do you suggest such a definition(왜 그 때 그러한 정의를 제안하는가?)

③ Where can you find the supporting evidence(증거물을 어디서 찾을 수 있는가?)

④ How do you convince people that you're right(네가 옳다는 것을 사람들에게 어떻게 납득시킬 수 있는가?)

해석

소유권을 사람과 그들이 소유한 물건 사이의 법적 관계로 정의해 보자. 이 정의는 "소유"라는 단어를 사용하기 때문에 소유권이라는 개념을 그 자체로 정의한다. 무언가를 소유한다는 것이 무슨 의미인지 설명하는 대신, 그것은 우리가 이미 이것을 알고 있다고 가정한다. 그것은 그 개념이 그 자체와 어떻게 관련되는지 알려주지만, 다른 개념이나 현실과 어떻게 관련되는지는 알려주지 않는다. 이 정의는 어디도 가지 않고 단지 원을 그리며 움직인다. 만약 정의에 동의어를 사용한다면 똑같은 문제가 발생한다. 소유권을 사람과 그들이 소유한 물건 사이의 법적 관계로 정의해 보자. "own"과 "possess"는 같은 개념을 표현하는 다른 단어인 동의어이다. 따라서 개념 면에서 그 정의는 여전히 순환적이다. 즉, 소유권이라는 개념은 여전히 스스로를 정의하는 데 사용되고 있다. 만약 '사람'을 '인간 동물'로, '크다'는 것을 '큰' 무언가가 가진 속성으로, 또는 '어리석음'을 '어리석은' 행동으로 정의한다면, 그 반대도 똑같이 적용될 것이다. 각각의 경우에 이탤릭체로 된 단어들은 동의어이다. 이러한 순환을 피하려면 다음과 같이 묻는 것이 효과적이다. 그 개념이 그리려고 하는 것은 어떤 대조인가? 예를 들어, 드레스를 소유하는 것과 빌리는 것 또는 가게에서 입어보는 것의 차이점은 무엇인가? 인간은 다른 동물들과 어떻게 다른가? 현명한 행동과 반대되는 어리석은 행동은 무엇인가?

17 ① 사회적 능력과 비사회적 능력을 관장하는 뇌의 부위는 서로 다르며, 두 신경망은 역 상관관계에 있다. 즉, 한 쪽이 활성화되면 다른 쪽이 비활성화되는데, 인지 작업을 관장하는 뇌의 부위가 활성화되면 다른 쪽이 많이 사용되지 않

아 비활성화 된다. 그러므로 ①의 'that circuitry doesn't get used much(그 회로는 많이 사용되지 않는다)'가 윗글의 빈칸에 들어갈 말로 가장 적절하다.

어휘

• urgently : 급히, 시급히

• neuroscience : 신경 과학

• cognitive : 인식의, 인지의

• lateral : 옆의, 측면의

• portion : 부분, 일부

• region : 부위, 영역

• self-awarness : 자아 인식

• empathy : 감정이입, 공감

• inversely : 역으로, 거꾸로

• correlated : 상관된, 연관성이 있는

• deactivate : 정지시키다, 비활성화시키다

• circuitry : 전기 회로

• trigger : 촉발하다, 유발하다

오답풀이

② the outer brain regions become inactive(뇌의 바깥쪽 부위가 비활동적이게 된다)

③ the brain is built to concentrate on survival(뇌는 생존에 집중하도록 만들어졌다)

④ the brain's short-term memory function is affected(뇌의 단기 기억 기능이 영향을 받는다)

⑤ some chemicals trigger the growth of new brain cells(어떤 화학 물질이 새로운 뇌세포의 성장을 촉발시킨다)

해석

변화는 어렵고, 우리는 세계에 긍정적인 변화를 만드는 데 시급히 더 나아져야 한다. 불행하게도, 리더 자리에 오르는 많은 사람들은 매우 발달된 지성을 가지고 있지만, 사회적 측면에서는 부족하다. 신경 과학도 이 현상을 탐구하기 시작했다. "정보 보유, 계획, 작업 기억, 인지 문제 해결과 관련된 뇌 신경망은 뇌의 측면 또는 바깥 부분에 있습니다"라고 Matthew Lieberman은 그의 연구실에서 인터뷰를 하는 동안 설명했다. "자아 인식, 사회적 인식, 공감과 관련되어 중간선이나 중간 영역에 더 많이 포함된 부위가 있습니다. 우리는 이 두 신경망이 역 상관관계에 있다는 것을 알고 있습니다. 즉, 한 쪽이 활성화되면 다른 쪽이 비활성화됩니다. 그것은 사회적 능력과 비사회적 능력에 관해 역 상관관계에 있는 무언가가 있을 수 있다는 가능성을 암시합니다." 이것은 여러분이 주목하는 신경망이 성장하는 신경망이라고 이해할 때 타당하다. 만약 인지 작업에 많은 시간을 보낸다면, 그 회로가 많이 사용되지 않는다는 이유만으로 사람들과 공감하는 능력이 감소한다.

18 ① 기존의 실험 데이터와 경험을 아무리 많이 축적하더라도 아직 실행되지 않은 실험의 수가 무한하므로, 기존의 과학 이론은 필연적으로 한계가 있고 이를 넘어선 새로운 과학 이론이 출현한다. 이것이 진보이다. 그러므로 ①의 'finding the limitations of existing scientific theories and pushing beyond them(기존 과학 이론의 한계를 찾고 이를 넘어서는)'이 윗글의 빈칸에 들어갈 말로 가장 적절하다.

<어휘>

• experimental : 실험의, 실험적인
• inductive method : 귀납법
• inference : 추론, 추리
• probable : 있을[사실일] 것 같은, 가능성 있는
• sensation : 느낌, 기분, 감각
• interpretation : 해석, 이해, 설명
• take into account : ~을 고려하다, 참작하다
• be down to : ~의 책임이다, ~에 달려 있다
• presupposition : 전제, 추정
• finite : 한정된, 유한한
• certainty : 확실성, 확실한 것
• deductive : 추론적인, 연역적인
• favour : 좋아하다, 선호하다
• alternative : 선택적인, 양자택일의
• confirming evidence : 확실한 증거, 확증
• conflicting evidence : 상충 증거, 상반되는 증거
• sustainable : 지속 가능한, 유지 가능한
• reputable : 평판이 좋은, 덕망이 있는
• proven : 입증된, 증명된

<오답풀이>

② creating sustainable partnerships between scientists and decision-makers(과학자와 의사결정자 간의 지속적인 파트너십을 창출하는)
③ publishing research findings in the most reputable academic journals(가장 평판이 좋은 학술지에 연구 결과를 발표하는)
④ conducting scientific research generally through a proven process(일반적으로 입증된 과정을 통해 과학적 연구를 수행하는)
⑤ encouraging innovation through funding from the government(정부로부터 조달된 자금을 통해 혁신을 장려하는)

<해석>

Karl Popper 주장의 핵심적 특징은 과학 법칙이 항상 기존의 실험 데이터와 경험을 넘어선다는 것이다. 귀납법은 데이터 본체를 구축함으로써 추론이 가능하기보다는 확실한 법칙

으로 간주될 수 있다는 것을 보여주려고 했다. Popper는 모든 감각은 어떤 종류의 해석을 수반하며, 어떤 일련의 실험에서도 변수가 있을 것이며, 그러한 변수가 고려되는지의 여부는 그것을 수행하는 사람의 전제에 달려 있다는 근거로 이에 이의를 제기한다. 또한, 물론 실행된 실험의 수는 항상 유한한 반면, 아직 실행되지 않은 실험의 수는 무한하기 때문에 귀납적 논쟁은 결코 연역적 논리의 한 가지 절대적인 확실성도 얻을 수 없다. 동시에 과학자들은 원래의 확인된 증거와 새롭고 상반되는 증거 모두를 설명할 수 있는 어떤 양자택일의 이론도 좋아할 것 같다. 바꾸어 말하면, 진보는 기존 과학 이론의 한계를 찾고 이를 넘어서는 방식으로 온다.

19 ② 지속시간 식별 시험에서 쥐들은 어려운 시험을 통과하여 큰 보상을 받기 보다는 작은 보상을 받더라도 시험을 포기하는 쪽을 선택한다는 사실이 밝혀졌다. 즉, 쥐들은 시험이 어려운지 쉬운지를 인지한다는 것이다. 그러므로 ②의 'assess their own cognitive states(자신의 인지 상태를 평가한다)'가 빈칸에 들어갈 말로 적절하다.

<어휘>

• duration 지속, (지속되는) 기간
• discrimination : 차별, 식별
• discern : 알아차리다, 식별하다
• apparently : 명백히, 분명히
• abandon : 버리다, 포기하다
• stick : 박다, 찌르다
• register : 등록하다, 기입하다
• decline : 줄어들다, 감소하다, 거절[사양]하다
• assess : 재다, 평가하다
• cognitive : 인식의, 인지의
• cheat : 속이다, 기만하다
• auditory sense : 청각
• pain : 아픔, 고통

<오답풀이>

① cheat other rats to get food(먹이를 얻기 위해 다른 쥐들을 속인다)
③ apply their auditory sense to find objects(청각으로 사물을 찾는다)
④ make certain communication sounds(특정한 의사소통의 소리를 낸다)
⑤ act as if they don't mind pain(고통을 마다하지 않는 것처럼 행동한다)

<해석>

쥐들은 자신의 정신 작용을 반영할 수 있으며, 지속시간 식

별 시험을 잘 수행할 수 있는지(또는 그렇지 않을지) 알 수 있다. 쥐들이 최근에 들은 소리가 긴지 짧은지를 결정하는 요구를 받았다. 짧은 음은 2초에서 3.6초, 긴 음은 4초에서 8초까지 지속되었다. (2초와 8초를 구별하는 것보다 3.6초와 4.4초를 구별하는 것이 더 어렵다는 점에 주목하라. 쥐들은 분명 이것을 알아차린다.) 소리를 들은 쥐들은 두 가지 선택권이 있었는데, 한 구멍에 코를 찔러서 시험을 포기하고 작은 보상을 받을 수도 있고, 다른 구멍에 코를 찔러 올바른 선택을 하면 큰 보상을 받음으로써 지속시간 차이에 대한 시험을 치를 수도 있다(레버를 눌러 기록한다). 잘못된 선택은 아무런 보상도 없었다. 쥐들은 시험이 어려울수록, 즉 두 소리의 지속시간이 더 비슷할수록 그 시험을 거절할 가능성이 더 높았다(그리고 더 적은 보상을 받는다). 바꾸어 말하면, 쥐들은 <u>자신의 인지 상태를 평가할 수 있다.</u>

20 ③ 윗글은 볼바키아 바이러스에 감염된 모기가 질병을 일으키는 다른 바이러스를 전염시킬 수 없다는 특성을 이용하여 전염병 감염을 억제하는 연구에 대한 설명이다. 주어진 글 다음에 볼바키아에 감염된 모기가 질병을 일으키는 다른 바이러스를 전염시킬 수 없다는 사실을 밝힌 글 (B)가 와야 한다. 다음으로 방사시킨 모기가 짝짓기를 통해 볼바키아 바이러스를 다음 세대에 전달시킨다는 글 (C)가 와야 한다. 마지막으로 볼바키아에 감염된 다음 세대의 모기가 전염을 억제한다는 내용인 글 (A)가 와야 한다.

어휘

- mosquito : 모기
- transmit : 옮기다, 전염시키다
- disease-causing : 질병을 일으키는[유발하는]
- microbe : 세균, 미생물
- microbiota : (특정 장소에 사는) 미생물 군집
- exploit : 이용하다, 착취하다
- thwart : 좌절시키다, 방해하다, 억제하다
- infection : 감염, 전염병
- dengue : 뎅기열
- chikungunya : 치쿤구니아 바이러스 병
- Zika : 지카 바이러스
- intentionally : 고의로, 일부러, 의도적으로
- release : 놓아 주다, 방사[방류]하다
- mate with : ∼와 교미하다, 짝짓기하다
- via : 경유하여, 통하여
- presence : 있음, 존재
- inhibit : 억제하다, 못하게 하다
- interrupt : 방해하다, 중단시키다, 차단하다
- underway : 진행중인, 여행중인

해석

> 모기는 질병을 일으키는 많은 미생물을 사람에게 옮기거나 전염시킬 수 있다. 모기는 또한 미생물 군집도 가지고 있다. 다시금 이 지식은 모기가 인간에게 전염병을 옮기는 능력을 억제하기 위해 이용되었다. 많은 곤충들이 보통 볼바키아 박테리아를 옮긴다.

(B) 자연에서 뎅기열, 치쿤구니아, 지카 등의 바이러스를 옮기는 에데스아집티 모기는 보통 볼바키아에 감염되지 않지만, 볼바키아에 감염되더라도 살 수 있다. 그러나 볼바키아에 감염되면 뎅기열이나 치쿤구니아와 같은 특정 바이러스와 질병을 일으키는 다른 바이러스를 전염시킬 수 없는 것으로 밝혀졌다.

(C) 연구원들은 현재 전염을 막기 위해 이 정보를 사용할 수 있는지 연구하고 있다. 그들은 모기를 기르고, 의도적으로 수컷 모기를 볼바키아에 감염시켜 야생에 방사하고 있다. 수컷 모기는 피를 먹지 않고 전염병을 옮기지 않는다. 방사된 수컷 모기는 현지 암컷 모기와 짝짓기를 하고 볼바키아는 알을 통해 다음 세대로 전해진다.

(A) 다음 세대의 모기에 볼바키아 감염이 있으면 뎅기열과 같은 바이러스가 억제된다. 호주의 한 지역에서 이 기술을 사용한 것은 뎅기열의 전염을 차단하는 데 매우 효과적이었다. 다른 분야에서도 시험이 진행 중이다.

21 ⑤ 윗글은 양극단보다는 평균값을 지닌 모집단이 생존과 번식 가능성이 높다는 안정화 도태에 대해 설명하고 있다. 출생 시 몸무게를 안정화 도태의 사례로 들겠다고 전제한 글 (C)가 주어진 글 다음에 와야 하고, 그 사례를 구체적으로 설명한 글 (B)가 그 다음에 온다. 마지막으로 아주 작은 신생아와 아주 큰 신생아의 도태를 비교하여 설명한 글 (A)가 와야 한다.

어휘

- stabilizing selection : 안정화 도태
- extreme : 극단, 극도
- trait : 특성, 특징
- range : 범위, 다양성
- reproduce : 복사[복제]하다, 번식하다
- population : 인구[동물들], 모집단
- genetic : 유전의, 유전적인
- component : 요소, 성분, 인자
- be prone to : ∼하기 쉽다, ∼에 치우치다
- complication : 합병증
- select against : 도태시키다, 가려내다

해석

> 안정화 도태란 특성 값의 범위 양극단에 반(反)하는 선
> 택을 말한다. 특성이 극단적으로 높거나 낮은 값을 가
> 진 사람들은 생존하고 번식할 가능성이 낮고, 평균에
> 가까운 값을 가진 사람들은 생존하고 번식할 가능성이
> 더 높다.

(C) 안정화 도태의 효과는 시간이 지남에 따라 모집단을 동일
한 평균값으로 유지하는 것이다. 극값이 각 세대에 반해
선택되지만, 모집단의 평균값은 변경되지 않는다. 인간의
출생 시 몸무게는 안정화 도태의 좋은 예이다.

(B) 신생아의 몸무게는 다른 많은 요인들 중 산모의 나이와 몸
무게와 같은 몇 가지 환경적 요인의 결과이다. 출생 시 몸
무게는 유전적 요인도 있다. 아주 작은 신생아(2.5kg 미만)
는 더 무거운 신생아보다 생존 가능성이 낮다.

(A) 아주 작은 신생아는 질병에 더 걸리기 쉽고 신체 조직이
약해서 생존이 더 어렵다. 아주 큰 아이는 출산 중에 합병
증이 발병할 수 있고 산모와 아이 모두 죽을 수 있기 때문
에 너무 큰 신생아 또한 도태될 가능성이 높다. 그러므로
작고 큰 양극단 모두에 반대되는 선택이 있다.

22
⑤ 산업혁명 당시 직조 기계는 일반적인 생각과 달리 비숙련
공을 대체한 것이 아니라 숙련공들을 대체하였다. 그것은
전문적 훈련을 못 받은 덜 숙련된 사람들도 새로운 직조
기계를 이용하여 Ned와 그의 동료들과 같은 숙련공들을
필요로 했던 고품질의 제품을 더 쉽게 생산할 수 있게 되
었기 때문이다. 그러므로 주어진 문장은 ⑤에 들어가는 것
이 가장 적절하다.

어휘

- loom : 직기, 직조기, 베틀
- displace : 대신하다, 쫓아내다
- comrade : 동료, 동무
- depict : 그리다, 묘사하다
- spin thread : 실을 잣다
- bare hands : 맨손
- apocryphal : 출처가 불분명한, 사실이 아닐 듯한, 가상의, 허구의
- uprising : 봉기, 반란, 폭동
- card–carrying member : 정식 회원
- clothworker : 직물 직공, 의류 노동자
- prestigious : 명망 있는, 일류의
- de–skilling : 단순화, 비숙련화

해석

> 그리고 Ned와 그의 동료들을 대체한 직조 기계는 Ned
> 의 전문적인 훈련 없이 덜 숙련된 사람이 그의 자리를
> 대신할 수 있다는 것을 의미했다.

산업혁명에 관한 인기작은 그들의 역할에서 많은 수의 저숙
련 노동자들, 즉 맨손으로 실을 잣고 천을 짜며 생계를 유지하
는 사람들과 할 일 없이 나뒹구는 기본 도구들을 대체하는 기
계들의 물결을 묘사한다. (①) 그러나 이것은 일어난 일이 아
니다. (②) 위협을 받고 있던 사람들은 바로 당시의 고숙련
노동자들이었다. (③) 자동화에 반대하는 Luddite 봉기의 가
상의 지도자 Ned Ludd는 비숙련 노동자가 아니라 그 시대의
숙련된 노동자였다. (④) 만약 그가 실제로 존재했다면, 그는
아마도 그런 부류의 전문가들 즉, 상인들의 명망 있는 클럽인
고명한 의류 직공 협회의 정식 회원이었을 것이다. (⑤) 이러
한 새로운 기계들은 "비숙련화" 되어, 덜 숙련된 사람들이 과
거에 숙련된 노동자를 필요로 했던 고품질의 제품을 더 쉽게
생산할 수 있게 되었다.

23
④ 글의 시작에서 도덕은 시대와 세대에 걸쳐 변한다고 전제
하였다. 그리고 명시된 규칙과 금지 및 암묵적인 행동에 자
극받는 아이들이 이전의 가치 체계에 도전하는 것은 결국
도덕적 개념이 세대에 따라 달라지기 때문이다. 그러므로
주어진 문장은 ④에 들어가는 것이 가장 적절하다.

어휘

- developmental phase : 발달 단계
- puberty : 사춘기, 성숙기
- solidary : 공동의, 연대의, 합동의
- generational conflict : 세대 갈등
- explicit : 명시된, 명백한
- prohibition : 금지
- implicitly : 암암리에, 암묵적으로
- provoke : 불러일으키다, 유발하다, 자극하다
- generation transition : 세대 교체[전이]
- adjustment : 수정, 적응, 조정
- indication : 지시, 표시, 암시
- moral decline : 도덕적 쇠퇴[타락]

해석

> 그럼에도 불구하고, 발달 단계에 있는 아동들(예: 사춘
> 기를 거치는 9세 또는 10세부터 연대 성장기까지)은 이
> 전의 가치 체계에 도전한다.

295

도덕은 시대와 세대에 걸쳐 변화한다. 그러므로 세대 갈등은 바로 진화에 기인한다. (①) 많은 사회에서 오늘날의 세대가 기회라고 여기는 것을 이전 세대에서는 종종 받아들일 수 없었다. (②) 아이들은 특히 부모를 통해, 가정과 학교에서 사회화 된다(따라서 선과 악을 배우고, 옳고 그름을 배운다). (③) 명시된 규칙과 금지를 통해서뿐만 아니라 암묵적으로 행동을 통해서, 아이들은 바람직하다고 생각되는 방식으로 행동하도록 자극받는다. (④) 세대 교체의 갈등은 결국 도덕적 개념의 조정으로 이어진다. (⑤) 이것은 사회 진화의 명확한 표시로 이해되어야 하며, ("도덕적 쇠퇴"의) 위험뿐만 아니라 진보의 기회를 절약한다.

통적인 교실에서 일반 학생들의 98%를 능가할 것이다. 교육 연구에서, 이것은 "두 시그마 문제"로 알려져 있는데, "두 시그마"는 평균적인 학생이 현재 성취도에서 일반 학생보다 거의 두 가지 표준 편차(수학 표기, 2σ)에 앞서 있고, 이와 같은 집중 교육 시스템이 인상적인 결과를 얻을 수 있지만, 엄청나게 비싸기 때문에 "문제"이다. "보정된" 또는 "개인 맞춤형" 학습 시스템이 이 문제를 해결할 것으로 보이며, 인간의 대안보다 훨씬 더 저렴한 비용으로 개별 학생들에게 가르치는 것을 맞춤화한다.

> 전통적인 교수법은 학생들에게 (A) 맞춤형 학습 경험을 제공할 수 없지만, 기술은 이러한 경험을 인간의 대안보다 더 (B) 비용 효율적으로 제공하는 데 도움을 줄 수 있다.

24

① (A) 제시문에 전통적인 교수법은 모든 학생들의 특정한 요구에 선생님들이 자료를 맞출 수 없기 때문에 불만족스럽다고 서술되어 있다. 그러므로 빈칸 (A)에 들어갈 말은 'customized(맞춤형의)'이다.

(B) 제시문에서 집중 교육 시스템이 매우 효과적인 것으로 검증되었지만 엄청나게 비싸기 때문에 개인 맞춤형 학습 시스템과 같은 기술이 보다 저렴한 비용으로 이를 해결할 수 있다고 하였다. 그러므로 빈칸 (B)에 들어갈 말은 'cost-effectively(비용 효율적으로)'이다.

어휘

- alternative : 대체, 대안
- unavoidably : 마지못해, 불가피하게
- tailor : 맞추다, 조정하다
- one size fits all : 범용의, 널리[두루] 적용되는
- frustrate : 좌절시키다, 불만스럽게 만들다
- tuition : 수업, 교습
- outperform : 능가하다, 뛰어나다
- sigma : 시그마
- standard deviation : 표준 편차
- mathematical notation : 수학적 표기[표시]
- intensive tutoring : 집중 교육[과외]
- prohibitively : 엄청나게, 터무니 없이
- adaptive : 조정의, 적응할 수 있는

해석

오늘날의 기술은 교육에서 전통적인 접근 방식에 대한 대안을 제공한다. 전통적인 접근 방식의 한 가지 특징을 살펴보면, 교실에서 가르치는 것은 불가피하게 "모든 사람에게 맞는 한 가지 크기"라는 사실이다. 선생님들이 모든 학생들의 특정한 요구에 그들의 자료를 맞출 수는 없기 때문에, 사실 제공되는 교육은 "한 가지 크기로는 아무도 맞지 않는" 경향이 있다. 맞춤형 수업이 매우 효과적인 것으로 알려져 있기 때문에 이것은 특히 불만족스럽다. 즉, 일대일 교습을 받는 평균의 학생들은 전

[25~26]

어휘

- distinctive : 독특한, 차별화된
- persuasion : 설득, 신념
- illiterate : 글을 모르는, 문맹의
- literacy : 글을 읽고 쓸 줄 아는 능력
- verbal : 언어의, 말로 된
- Gospel : 복음, 신조
- ritual : 의식, 의례
- ambassador : 대사
- magnificent : 장엄한, 웅장한
- awe-inspiring : 경외심을 불러일으키는, 장엄한
- integral : 필수적인, 완전한
- polemics : 논쟁, 논증법
- monarch : 군주, 제왕
- splendor : 훌륭함, 화려함, 영예, 영광
- amplify : 확대[확장]하다, 증폭시키다
- fabrics : 섬유, 직물, 옷감
- vibrant : 활기찬, 강렬한
- adornment : 장식, 치장
- drape : 걸치다, 드리우다, 씌우다
- finery : 화려한 옷, 아름다운 장식품
- tailored : 맞춤의, 잘 맞도록 만든
- facilitate : 가능하게[용이하게] 하다, 촉진하다
- sustainability : 지속 가능성
- agenda : 의제, 안건

- foster : 기르다, 양육하다
- hygienic : 위생적인, 청결한
- barrier : 장벽, 보호막

해석

패션은 그것만으로도 신체 자체를 정치적 설득의 형태로 변화시킬 수 있기 때문에 차별화된 기회를 제공했다. 중세 후기의 대부분의 유럽인들은 문맹이었고, 글을 읽고 쓰는 능력은 르네상스 시대 동안 천천히 퍼져나갔다. 예를 들어 역사학자들은 1500년에 영국 인구의 90% 이상이 문맹이었으며, 대다수는 19세기까지 여전히 그러했다고 추정한다. 결과적으로 이들 사회는 후대 사회가 문자 언어를 통해 전달했던 메시지를 전달하기 위해 언어적 의사소통과 이미지에 의존했다. 교회는 성화, 그림, 의식 그리고 행사를 통해 복음을 전파했다. 반면에 국가는 명예와 존경을 위한 장엄한 축하, 웅장한 궁전, 열병식, 경외감을 불러일으키는 기념물로 시민들과 외세의 대사들에게 연설했다. 의복은 이러한 이미지 기반 논쟁의 필수적인 부분이었다. 군주는 다른 사람들에게 자신이 특별하고 통치할 운명이라는 것을 보여줄 수 있었다. 성직자는 그의 육체적인 존재로 천국의 영예와 신의 영광을 암시할 수 있었다. 패션의 새로운 발전은 이러한 유형의 시각적 설득을 증폭시켰다. 즉, 14세기에 널리 퍼진 재단사의 기교는 고급스러운 옷감, 선명한 색, 표면 장식뿐만 아니라 형태와 모양을 통해서도 옷으로 의사소통 할 수 있게 하였다. 단순히 몸을 화려한 옷으로 치장하기보다, 맞춤 의상은 육체를 다른 세상의 어떤 초인으로 바꿀 수 있었다.

25 ② 제시문에 따르면 패션의 새로운 발전은 군주가 자신의 특별함과 통치의 정당성을 부여하기 위해 그리고 성직자가 천국과 신의 영광을 암시하기 위해 시각적 설득을 증폭시켰고, 14세기에 널리 퍼진 재단사의 기교는 고급스러운 옷감, 선명한 색, 표면 장식뿐만 아니라 형태와 모양을 통해서도 옷으로 의사소통 할 수 있게 하였다라고 서술되어 있다. 그러므로 ②의 'Fashion: A Visual Means of Communication(패션: 시각적인 의사소통 수단)'이 윗글의 제목으로 가장 적절하다.

오답풀이

① Written Words as a Replacement of Images(이미지를 대체하는 문어(文語))
③ What Made the Fashion Industry Prosperous(패션 산업을 번영시킨 것)
④ Luxury: Expanding Its Market to More Customers(고급화: 더 많은 고객을 위한 시장 확대)
⑤ Designers Need to Balance Creativity and Business(디자이너는 창의성과 일의 균형을 맞춰야 한다)

26 ② 제시문에 따르면 중세 후기의 대부분의 유럽인들은 문맹이었기 때문에, 군주와 성직자들은 패션을 시각적인 의사소통 수단으로 활용하여 그들의 메시지를 전달하였다. 즉, 의복을 통해 군주는 자신의 특별함과 통치의 정당성을 보여주었고, 성직자는 천국의 영예와 신의 영광을 보여주었다. 그러므로 ②의 'transform the body itself into a form of political persuasion(신체 자체를 정치적 설득의 형태로 변형시키다)'가 빈칸에 들어갈 말로 가장 적절하다.

오답풀이

① facilitate a sustainability agenda based on local production(지역 생산에 기반한 지속 가능한 의제를 촉진하다)
③ foster a strong relationship between consumer and producer(소비자와 생산자 사이의 강력한 관계를 형성하다)
④ generate the largest manufacturing business in human history(인류 역사상 최대의 제조업을 창출하다)
⑤ provide a hygienic barrier keeping the body safe from diseases(질병으로부터 몸을 지키는 위생 보호막을 제공하다)

[27~28]

어휘

- cognitive : 인식의, 인지의
- perceive : 깨닫다, 감지[인지]하다
- sensory : 감각의, 지각의
- faculty : 능력, 기능
- causality : 인과[상호] 관계
- impart : 주다, 부여하다, 덧붙이다
- properties : 성질, 특성
- apparatus : 기구, 기관, 조직체
- envision : 마음속에 그리다[상상하다]
- overlay : 덧씌움
- eliminate : 없애다, 제거하다
- contradiction : 모순, 반박
- antinomy : 이율배반, 자가당착
- pure reason : 순수 이성
- appearance : 모습, 출현, 나타남
- preceding : 앞선, 이전의

해석

임마누엘 칸트는 외부 세계에 대한 우리의 경험은 독특한 인간 인지 구조에 의해 형성된다고 제안했다. 그의 관점에서, 우

리는 감각과 정신적인 능력을 통해 외부 현실을 인식하는데, 그것은 세계를 구조화하고 질서화하기 위해 시간, 공간, 인과관계와 같은 특정한 형태를 이용한다. 따라서 우리는 우리가 경험하는 세계 즉, 우리가 그것에 부여하는 기능적 형태의 세계를 창조한다. 우리가 세상과 연관짓는 속성들은 "그 안에 내재된 것"이 아니라 우리 인지 기관의 특징들이다. 만약 태어날 때 분홍색 렌즈가 안구에 이식되었다면, 세상은 분홍색 그림자로 보일 것이고, 우리는 이 분홍색 덮개 없는 현실을 상상할 수 없을 것이다. 마찬가지로 우리는 우리의 눈과 뇌가 사물을 보기 위해 어떻게 구성되어 있는지에 대한 영향 없이는 현실을 볼 수 없다.

칸트에 따르면, 인과관계, 공간, 시간과 같은 속성을 우리 경험 밖의 세계에 귀속시킬 때, 우리는 개념적 혼란에 부딪히고 모순을 제거하는데(→ 추가하는데). 이러한 특성들은 그 안에 내재된 구조가 아니라 개념적 구조이기 때문이다. 이러한 모순은 순수한 이성에 대한 칸트의 이율배반으로 알려져 있으며, 그것들은 우리 지식의 한계를 드러낸다. 우리는 우리에게 보이는 대로 사물에 제한되어 있다. 하지만 우리는 이러한 모습의 형태 없이 존재하는 그대로의 세계를 알 수 없다. 칸트는 우리 밖의 사물의 존재를 부정하지 않았다. 오히려 그는 우리가 인간의 뇌가 작동하는 방식에 의해 결정되는 형태로 그것들을 지각한다고 주장했다.

27 ⑤ 칸트는 글의 서두에서 외부 세계에 대한 우리의 경험은 독특한 인간 인지 구조에 의해 형성된다고 하였고, 글의 말미에서 인간의 뇌가 작동하는 방식에 의해 결정되는 형태로 그것들을 지각한다고 주장하였다. 그러므로 ⑤의 'Kant's view of how humanity perceives the world(인류가 세상을 어떻게 인식하는지에 관한 칸트의 견해)'가 윗글의 주제로 가장 적절하다.

오답풀이

① differences between Kant and preceding philosophers(칸트와 이전 철학자들 사이의 차이점)
② Kant's contribution to making philosophy popular(철학을 대중화시킨 칸트의 공헌)
③ strengths and weaknesses of Kantian philosophy(칸트 철학의 장점과 단점)
④ Kantian political theory and its effects on politics(칸트의 정치 이론과 정치에 미친 영향)

28 ③ 칸트에 따르면 우리는 감각과 정신적인 능력을 인식하기 위해 시간, 공간, 인과관계와 같은 속성을 이용하는데, 그 속성들이 우리의 경험 밖에 있게 되면 혼란에 부딪히고 모순이 생긴다는 것이다. 그러므로 (c)의

'eliminate(제거하다)'는 'add(추가하다)' 등으로 바꿔 써야 한다.

[29~30]

어휘

- school district : 학군
- enthusiastic : 열렬한, 열광적인
- immediate supervisor : 직속 상사, 직속 상관
- evident : 분명한, 눈에 띄는, 알기 쉬운
- fly off the handle : 버럭 화를 내다, 발끈하다
- implement : 시행하다, 이행하다
- department : 부서, 부처, 학과
- walk on eggshells around : ~의 눈치를 살피다
- inaction : 무활동, 활동하지 않음
- stalemate : 교착 상태, 파국, 난국
- assumption : 가정, 추측, 추정
- stagnation : 침체, 정체, 부진
- brainstorm : 구상하다, 쥐어짜내다, 머리를 모으다

해석

(A) Linda는 내 코칭 고객 중 한 명이었다. 그녀는 커다란 변화를 겪고 있는 큰 학군에서 일하던 중간 지도자였다. Linda는 많은 아이디어를 가지고 있었고 그것에 열정적이었다. 그녀의 직속상관인 Jean은 다가오는 변화에 대해 높은 수준의 가시적인 불안감을 가지고 있었다.

(D) 사실 Jean은 스트레스를 받으면 금방 눈에 띄는 성격이었다. Linda는 (d)그녀를 피해야 한다고 생각했다. Linda가 팀의 목표와 전략에 관해 논의하고 싶었을 때 Jean이 발끈할 거라고 생각했다. Linda는 어떻게 했을까? 아무 것도 하지 않았다. Linda는 Jean을 멀리해야 한다고 생각했다. 결과는? 아무 일도 없었다. 코칭 기간 동안, Linda는 Jean이 혼자서는 변하기 쉽지 않다는 사실을 깨달았다. Linda는 자신의 학과에서 몇 가지 새로운 프로그램을 시행하고 싶었고 마치 (e)그녀는 Jean 주변의 계란 껍데기 위를 걷는 것처럼 느꼈다. Linda는 활동을 중단하게 되었다.

(C) 그들은 교착 상태에 빠져 있었다. 결국, Linda는 그녀의 추측이 어떻게 그녀의 침체를 가져왔고 이어서 학과와 학교의 침체를 가져왔는지 깊이 살펴봐야 하는 사람은 바로 (b)자신이라는 사실을 깨달았다. 비록 Linda가 뭔가 조치를 취하기 전까지는 이런 식으로 계속될 거라는 사실을 깨닫는 데 시간이 걸렸지만, 일단 (c)그녀에게 시작된 변화를 깨닫고 나면, 그녀는 자신이 무엇을 할 수 있는지 검토하기 위해 마음을 열었다. Linda는 Jean과 대화하기로 결정했다.

(B) Linda는 Jean이 절대 말을 듣지 않을 것이라는 자신의 추측에 도전하여 과감한 행동을 취하기 시작했다. 그녀는 회의 일정을 잡기 위해 Jean에게 다가갔다. Linda와 나는 과거의 대화와는 다른 말을 쥐어짜냈고, 바라건대 차이를 만들어 발전시킬 것이다. 몇 주의 짧은 기간 내에 Linda는 일정을 잡아 Jean과 미팅을 했다. Jean은 Linda의 변화를 알아챘고, Linda가 놀랍게 (a)그녀의 생각을 경청할 마음이 있었다.

29 ⑤ 주어진 글 (A) 다음에 Linda와 Jean의 불편한 관계에 대해 설명한 글 (D)가 와야 한다. 그리고 이를 개선하기 위해 Linda가 Jean과 대화하기로 결심한 글 (C)가 와야 한다. 마지막으로 글 (C) 다음에 Jean과의 관계 개선을 위한 Linda의 과감한 행동과 그로인한 Jean의 변화를 서술한 글 (B)가 와야 하다.

30 ④ (a)의 'her', (b)의 'she', (c)의 'her', (e)이 'she'는 모두 Linda를 가리키나, (d)의 'her'는 Linda의 직속상관인 Jean을 가리킨다.

2022학년도 기출문제 정답 및 해설

✏️ 제2교시 **영어영역(공통)**

01 ③	02 ⑤	03 ⑤	04 ②	05 ④	06 ⑤
07 ④	08 ④	09 ③	10 ③	11 ②	12 ①
13 ⑤	14 ④	15 ④	16 ②	17 ①	18 ①
19 ②	20 ④	21 ③	22 ②	23 ⑤	24 ①
25 ①	26 ②	27 ①	28 ⑤	29 ③	30 ④

01 ③ 선행절 뒤에 관계대명사 which가 쓰일 경우, 후행절은 'which'가 주격이나 목적격을 대신하기 때문에 불완전문장이어야 한다. 그러나, 지문의 ③ which 뒤에 이어지는 문장은 선행절의 'the view'와 동격의 의미를 가지는 완전한 문장이다. 그러므로 이 같은 경우 'which'가 아니라 'that'을 써야 올바르다.

　어휘

• soundness : 건실함

• sound : 건실하다

• the first millennium BCE : 기원전 제1천년기

• deceased : 사망한

• provide support : 지지하다, 힘을 보태다

• ornament : 장식

　해석

일부 여성이 포함된 현대 고고학 연구자들은 아마존에 대한 헤로도투스의 언급의 역사적인 건실함을 시사하는 증거를 발굴했다. 이 학자들은 우크라이나 남부에서 창, 화살, 갑옷 같은 군사 도구와 함께 묻힌 여성들의 유골이 있는 기원전 제1천년기 중반에 세워진 수많은 무덤들을 발견했다. 유골 중 일부는 사망자가 머리를 맞거나 날카로운 칼날에 찔렸다는 것을 나타내며, 이들이 무기들과 우연히 매장된 여성이라기보다는 전사들의 유골이라는 관점을 뒷받침한다. 무덤 속에는 옷을 위한 청동거울과 금장식에 더하여 귀금속(귀걸이, 목걸이, 구슬, 팔찌)도 있다. 시체는 아마도 여성들이 다음 세상으로 갈 때 전사로서 필요한 무기와 외모를 꾸미기 위하여 갖고 싶은 장식들과 묻혔을 것이다. 이 고고학적 증거는 대체적으로 아마존에 대한 헤로도투스의 언급이, 이전의 평가대로, 그가 남의 말을 쉽게 믿는다는 일종의 예시가 아니었으며, 오히려 역사적으로 건실하다는 것을 시사한다.

02 ⑤ (A) 지문에서 언급된 연구에서 'students'가 피실험자의 입장이기 때문에 선택을 주는 입장이 아니라 주어지는 입장이므로 'give'의 수동형인 'were given'을 사용하는 것이 적절하다.

   (B) 후행절의 문장이 완전문장이므로 관계대명사 'what'을 쓸 수 없고, 대신 '~인지 아닌지'의 뜻인 'whether'를 사용하는 것이 적절하다.

   (C) 'make + 목적어 + 형용사'의 어순에서 부사인 'willingly' 대신 형용사 'willing'을 사용하는 것이 적절하다.

　어휘

• high self-monitor : (심리학) 자기주시 경향이 높은 사람

• extrovert : 외향적인 사람

• introvert : 내성적인 사람

• irrespective of : 상관(관계)없이

　해석

상황적 신호에 주의를 기울이는 성향으로 볼 때, 자기주시 경향이 높은 사람들(HSMs)은 직면하게 될 상황의 본질을 확실히 알고 싶어 한다. 상황에 따른 기대의 명확성은 HSMs에게 특히 중요하다. 이것은 학생들에게 외향적인 사람처럼 행동해야만 하는 상황에 들어가거나 그렇지 않은 선택이 주어진 연구에서 잘 입증되었다. HSMs은 상황이 명확하게 정의되면, 그들의 외향적 수준과는 상관없이 상황에 진입할 가능성이 훨씬 더 높았다. 그러나 자기주시 경향이 낮은 사람들(LSMs)의 선택은 그들이 내성적인 사람인지 외향적인 사람인지에 달렸고, 그들이 외향적인 LSM이라면, 그들은 진입했다. 또한 HSMs은 더 적극적으로 진입하게 하기 위해 상황이 어떻게 바뀔 수 있나는 질문에 보다 명확한 행동지침을 제공하기 위해 이를 변형시켰다. LSMs은 내성적이거나 외향적인 성향을 자신의 성향과 더 가깝게 일치시키기 위해 상황을 전환시켰다.

03 ⑤ 제시된 지문에서는, 조각가들이 조각의 재료를 선택하는 데에 있어서 가용성이라는 것이 가장 중요하다고 말하고 있다. 그러므로, 전통적으로는 대중적인 조각 재료를 사용했지만, 마지막 문장에서는 '보다 저렴한 교통수단과 세

계 시장에 대한 접근성 확대'로 생소하다고 여겨졌던 재료들의 가용성이 높아져 조각가들이 사용하기 시작했다고 해야 글의 흐름이 자연스럽다. 따라서 쓰임이 적절하지 않은 ⑤의 'familiar(친숙한)'를 'unfamiliar(생소한)'으로 바꿔 써야 한다.

어휘

• significant : 의미심장한, 중요한
• memorialize : 추모하다, 기념하다
• momentous : 중대한, 중요한
• permanent : 영구적인
• feasible : 실현 가능한
• jade : 옥
• rarely : 드물게
• readily : 손쉽게
• dictate : 지시하다
• availability : 유용성, 효용; (입수) 가능성

해석

조각은 역사적으로 대중 예술의 중요한 형태였으며, 문화와 시간을 넘나들며 중요하고 기억할 가치가 있다고 여겨지는 개인과 사건들을 추모하는 작품을 제작하는 데 사용되었다. 그 결과 조각가들은 가능한 한 영구적인 재료를 선택해 실현 가능한 한 오래 지속되는 예술을 추구했다. 대중적인 조각 재료로는 청동과 돌, 특히 대리석, 석회석, 화강암 등이 있다. 값이 싼 나무와 점토도 조각의 대중적인 매체였다. 종종 금, 은, 옥, 상아 등 귀한 재료들이 사용되기도 하지만, 그 비용 때문에 훨씬 더 드물게 사용되어 왔다. 사용된 재료들은 전통적으로 조각가가 쉽게 접근할 수 있는 재료들을 반영했지만, 이러한 결정은 다른 어떤 이유보다 가용성에 의해 좌우되었다. 이는 전통적으로 특정 지역의 조각가들이 특정 재료로 작업하는 결과를 낳았다. 보다 저렴한 교통수단과 세계 시장에 대한 접근성 확대로 조각가들은 한때는 ~~친숙하다고(→생소하다고)~~ 여겨졌던 재료들을 사용하기 시작했다.

04 ② (A) 국가는 오로지 국가 이기주의에 의해 동기가 부여된다고 하였으므로, 이념과 가치에 대한 어떤 호소 역시 권력 추구를 밝히는 것이 아니라 감추는 것이라고 해야 문장이 자연스럽다. 따라서 'concealing(감추는)'이 문맥상 적절하다.
    (B) 이어지는 문장에서 인간은 본래 자기중심적이기 때문이라고 하였으므로, 문맥상 'inevitable(필연적인)'이 적절하다.
    (C) 세계정부의 부재라는 무정부적 특성이 국가 이기주의에 대해 뒷받침하고 있으므로, 문맥상 'forces(강요하다)'가 적절하다.

어휘

• descriptive : 서술하는, 서술적, 기술적인
• exclusively : 오로지
• mere : ~에 불과한, 단순한
• rhetoric : 수사법, 미사여구
• reveal : 밝히다
• avoidable : 피할 수 있는
• forbid : 금지하다
• ensure : 보장하다

해석

서술적 사실주의에 따르면, 국가는 사실상 오로지 국가 이기주의에 의해 동기가 부여된다. 그들의 행동은 도덕적 고려에 의해 영향을 받지 않는다. 이런 시각에서, 세계 정치에서 이념과 가치에 대한 어떤 호소도 국제무대에서 취해지는 모든 결정의 근저인 권력 추구를 (A) 감추는 수사법에 불과하다. 어떤 사람들은 이것을 인간 본성의 (B) 필연적인 결과로 본다. 인간은 본래 자기중심적이기 때문에, 이것이 그들의 정치제도에 반영될 것으로 예상된다는 주장이다. 반면에, '구조적' 현실주의자들에게는, 각 국가들이 왜 자신들의 이익에만 몰두하는지 설명해주는 것이 국제 시스템의 무정부적 특성 – '절대군주'나 '세계정부'의 부재 – 이다. 세계정부의 부재는 국가들로 하여금 자신들의 생존을 보장하기 위해 권력을 추구하도록 (C) 강요하는 불안정한 환경을 만든다.

05 ④ 윗글은 보조금에 대한 개념과, 정부가 기업에 보조금을 지급하는 이유와 목적에 대하여 설명하고 있으며, 그에 따른 긍정적인 효과를 예상되게 하므로, 계획 경제에 대한 부정적인 관점을 제시하는 ④의 설명은 전체 흐름과 관계가 없는 문장이다.

어휘

• subsidies : subsidy(보조금)의 복수형
• intention : 의도, 목적
• profitability : 수익성, 이윤율
• export : 수출하다, 수출, 수출품
• domestic consumption : 국내 소비(내수)
• subsidize : 보조금을 주다
• economic warfare : 경제 전쟁
• issue : 발부하다, 지급하다

해석

보조금은 가격을 낮추거나 수익성을 높이기 위해 기업이나 경제 부문에 지급되는 지급액이다. ① 내수를 위해 식량을 싸게 할 목적으로 농지를 보조받는 경우가 많고, 정부가 고용 수준을 높이려 할 때 신규 채용 비용을 기업이 보조금을 받는 경

우가 많기 때문에 꼭 수출에 쓰이지는 않는다. ② 경제 전쟁 과정에서 보조금이 사용되는 이유 중 하나는 대상 국가의 소비자들이 해당 국가의 기업으로부터 구매하는 특정 제품, 또는 잠재적으로 모든 제품의 양을 늘리기 위해서이다. ③ 자국 내에서 생산되는 상품을 저렴하게 만들어 국민이 국내에서 구매하는 해외 수출품의 물량을 줄이는 것이 또 다른 목적이다. ④ 다시 말해, 계획 경제는 시장의 힘에 대응하지 못해 자원 비효율성과 부족을 초래한다. ⑤ 보조금 지급의 목적은 목표 국가의 사업에서 수익과 생산을 다른 방향으로 전환하고 자신의 사업에 이익을 주는 것이다.

06 ⑤ 윗글에 따르면 예술가는 삶을 단순하게 복사하는 것이 아니라, 사회의 일원으로서 사회가 살아 숨 쉬는 것을 작품에 반영한다. 그러므로 윗글의 요지는 ⑤의 "예술가는 자신이 사는 시대를 작품에 반영한다."이다.

어휘

• mirror : 반영하다
• photographic : 사진(술)의
• transpose : 바꾸다, 옮기다
• intuitively : 직감적으로, 직관에 의하여
• consciously : 의식적으로
• unconsciously : 무의식적으로
• epoch : 시대
• frivolous : 경박한
• gay : 명랑한
• carefree : 태평한

해석

예술이 삶을 반영하지 못하면 그것은 예술로서 실패한다. 그러나 삶을 반영한다는 것은 삶을 복사한다는 의미가 아니다. 예술가는 단순하게 자신의 시대가 담긴 사진 기록을 남기는 것이 아니다. 오히려 그 시대의 템포, 태도, 목표, 희망, 긴장, 성공과 실패를 작품에 반영한다. 예술가는 자신의 작품을 통해 이것들을 옮긴다. 예술가가 사회의 일원이기 때문에 직감적으로 사회가 살아 숨 쉬는 것을 표현한다. 우리의 위대한 박물관 중 하나를 거닐어야만 특정 시대의 사람들에게 의식적으로 무의식적으로 중요했던 감정과 아이디어—삶의 방식—를 깨달을 수 있다. 예를 들어 초기 독일과 플랑드르 화가들의 중세 신비주의 정신인 절제된 감정적 강렬함은 앙투안 와토와 같은 18세기 궁정 화가들의 경박하고 명랑하며 태평한 작품과 강하게 대조된다.

07 ④ 윗글에서는 미국 영화와 텔레비전이 백인 남성 중심적으로 이루어졌다는 근거를 제시함으로써, 이에 대한 사회비판적인 입장을 보이고 있다. 그러므로, "보이지 않는 전염병"이

의미하는 바는 ④의 'widespread failure to reflect diversity in American film and television(미국 영화와 텔레비전의 다양성을 반영하는 광범위한 실패)'이 가장 적절하다.

어휘

• stumble upon : 우연히 만나다
• overwhelmingly : 압도적으로
• overrepresented : 대표가 지나치게 많은
• epidemic : 전염병

오답풀이

① 전염병의 원인에 대한 일반적인 무지
② 인터넷 시대에 영화 관람객의 급속한 소멸
③ 연예인 지망생에 대한 가시적인 경제적 지원 수단의 부재
⑤ 미국 영화 산업에서 젊은 감독들을 양성하기 위한 불충분한 투자

해석

만약 한 외계인이 우연히 미국 영화와 텔레비전의 기록 보관소를 발견하게 된다면, 이 외계인은 우리가 대개 남성이며 백인이 압도적으로 많고, 60세 이상의 사람이나 신체적 장애를 가진 사람은 거의 없다고 결론내릴 것이다. 말을 하는 여성 인물은 영화에 나오는 인물의 29%와 텔레비전에 나오는 인물의 36%에 불과하다. 이러한 통계는 반세기가 넘도록 의미 있게 바뀌지 않았다. 백인은 대사의 72%를 차지할 정도로 지나치게 많았다(62%의 인구와 대비). 2015년 상위 100편의 영화를 대상으로 한 연구에서 48편은 대사(한 단어 이상을 기준)를 가진 흑인 캐릭터를 포함하지 않았다. 70편의 영화에는 아시아인이나 아시아계 미국인 캐릭터가 포함되어 있지 않았다. 영화와 텔레비전을 통틀어 감독들의 15%만이 여성이고 29%의 작가들이 여성이다. 영화계에서 여성은 감독의자에서 찾기가 더 어렵고, 영화의 약 4%가 여성에 의해 연출된다. 이러한 연구 결과를 도출한 대규모 연구 작업을 주도하고 있는 미디어 학자인 스테이시 스미스는 이것을 "보이지 않는 전염병"이라고 부른다.

08 ④ 윗글에서는 큰 조롱박들을 얻은 혜자가 물통이나 숟가락으로 쓸 수 없다며 버린 것에 대하여, 장자가 어째서 큰 뗏목으로 만들 생각은 하지 못했느냐며 꾸짖는 이야기를 보여준다. 그러므로, '물건의 용도를 생각할 때는 유연해져라'라는 ④의 설명이 가장 적절하다.

어휘

• Huizi : 혜자(惠子)
• Zhuangzi : 장자(庄子)
• enormous : 거대한, 막대한
• hence : 이런 이유로

① 전설에 따르라

② 타인의 물건을 소중히 하라

③ 소비 습관을 살펴라

⑤ 구매하는 물건의 크기에 주의하라

해석

혜자가 왕이 자신에게 한 줌의 큰 조롱박 씨앗을 선물로 주었다고 장자에게 말하는 것으로 일상적인 대화가 시작한다. "내가 그 씨앗들을 심으니 20갤런을 담을 수 있을 만큼이나 거대한 박으로 자라나더군! 물통으로 쓰려고 했는데 너무 무거워서 들어올릴 수가 없었고, 숟가락을 만들기 위해 자르려고 했는데 너무 얕아서 액체를 담을 수가 없었다네. 크기에 감명을 받기 했지만, 아무짝에도 쓸모가 없는 것 같아 부숴버렸지." 당시 중국에서는 조롱박을 용기나 숟가락 두 가지 용도로 사용했다. 그래서 혜자는 실망이 컸다. 하지만 이 이야기를 듣고 장자는 믿을 수 없었다. "크다는 것을 생각하는 한 자네는 얼간이나 다름없네!"라며 그가 분명히 말했다. 그는 혜자에게 쓸모없거나 하찮은 물건을 가져다가 예상치 못한 용도로 사용하여, 그 과정에서 큰 보상을 얻게 된 사람들에 대한 이야기들을 들려준다. "지금 자네에게는 이런 조롱박들이 생겼는데,"라며 그는 결론을 내린다. "그것들을 숟가락으로 사용하기에는 너무 크다고 탄식하는 대신, 강과 호수에 띄울 수 있는 큰 뗏목으로 만들 생각은 왜 하지 못하는 겐가! 마치 자네 마음속에 덤불이 자라고 있는 것 같군!"

09 ③ 윗글에서는 판매 과정이 충성스러운 고객을 만드는 데에 최상의 기회라며, 그에 대한 방법에 대해 말하고 있다. 그러므로, ③의 'ways to make consumers loyal in the selling process(판매 과정에서 소비자의 충성도를 높이기 위한 방법)'이 윗글의 주제로 가장 적절하다.

• constantly : 끊임없이, 부단히

• existing : 기존의

• deliberate : 의도적인

• reciprocity : 상호주의

① 고객의 관심을 끌기 위한 생산자 간의 치열한 경쟁

② 입소문에 의한 신제품 홍보

④ 마케터가 기존 고객보다 잠재 고객에게 초점을 맞추는 이유

⑤ 프리미엄 서비스에 대한 충성 고객의 요구를 충족하기 위한 어려움

해석

전 세계 소비자들은 새로운 취향을 탐구하고 좋은 거래, 더 나

은 가격, 더 높은 품질 및 신뢰할 수 있는 공급업체를 끊임없이 추구한다. 따라서 고객의 니즈를 이해하고 대응하려는 의도적인 노력이 없다면 기존 고객을 유지하기가 어렵다. 좋은 의사소통과 상호주의를 통해, 판매 과정은 생산자들이 고객을 참여시켜 단순한 탐험가에서 자신들의 계획의 충성스럽고 헌신적인 구성원으로 변화시킬 수 있는 최상의 기회이다. 고객이 제품 판매 방식에 만족하지 않으면 다시는 거래하지 않을 가능성이 높다. 따라서 일관되고 즐거운 구매 경험을 만드는 것은 신뢰와 충성도를 쌓는 데 필수적인 부분이다. 상호주의는 고객의 충성도에 대한 보상을 받는 과정으로서 고객이 계속 돌아오도록 보장하는 또 다른 중요한 요소이다. 충성스러운 소비자를 만들기 위해서는 비용이 많이 들지 않아도 되는 전략이 필요하고, 현명하기만 하면 된다!

10 ③ 윗글에서는 정치학자 로버트 액슬로드를 따라서, 협상을 할 경우에는 먼저 협력을 한 뒤에 상대방의 행동을 흉내 내라고 말한다. 따라서 ③의 'The Key to Negotiation: First Be Nice, Then Mirror(협상의 핵심 : 먼저 친절하게 대하고, 흉내 내라)'이 윗글의 제목으로 가장 적절하다.

• attempt : 시도하다

• i.e. : 예를 들어, 즉

• accommodation : 합의

• dominating : 지배적인

• subsequent : 그 후의, 후속

• instance : 사례, 경우

• integrative : 통합하는, 완전하게 하는

① 위기 협상가가 되기 위해 필요한 것

② 친절하게 대하는 것이 협상에서 피해를 줄 수 있는 이유

④ 협상 중에 분노나 슬픔을 표현하는 것은 득이 된다

⑤ 성공적인 협상의 모방 : 악인가 독인가?

해석

더 넓은 관계의 일부로서 누군가와 협상할 때, 당신은 친절하게 협력하는 것을 목표로 해야 하는가 아니면 자신의 이익을 위해 최대한 많은 것을 확보하려는 이기적인 것을 목표로 해야 하는가? 이기적인 것이 단기적으로 가장 높은 보상을 줄 수도 있지만, 협력하는 것이 장기적으로 가장 큰 보상을 준다. 정치학자 로버트 액슬로드는 게임 이론가들이 서로 다양한 협상 전략을 펼치는 컴퓨터 토너먼트를 기획하고 나서, 당신이 먼저 협력한 다음에 상대방의 마지막 행동을 흉내 내야 한다고 결론을 내렸다. 핵심은 당신과 상대방이 당신의 행동을 통해 소통하고 있다는 것을 깨닫는 것이다. 협력하는 것(즉, 친절하게 시작하는 것)은 몇 가지 협상을 할 의사가 있다는 메시

지를 보낸다. 상대방이 지배적인 전략을 채택한다면, 당신은 그 공격에 대응해야 한다. 마찬가지로, 그들이 친절하다면, 친절하게 대하라. 이어지는 각 상황에서 마지막 행동을 계속 따라하라. 이를 통해 당사자들 간의 완전한 합의를 찾는 것을 배우는 협력 환경이 조성된다.

11 ② 윗글에서는 성공한 사람이 성공에 그치지 말고 더 나은 세상을 만들기 위한 책임을 강조하였으므로, 필자는 성공한 사람이 더 나은 세상을 만들기 위해 노력해야 한다고 주장하고 있다.

> **어휘**
> • virtuously : 덕이 높아서, 도덕적으로
> • luxuriate : 사치를 부리다
> • vegetate : 무위도식하다
> • procrastinate : 미루다
> • wield : 휘두르다
> • betrayal : 배신

> **해석**
> 어느 한 사람이 덕적으로 경지에 이르면, 그는 세상의 굶주린 '모든' 사람이 음식을 먹고, '모든' 우는 사람이 위로받고, '모든' 우울한 사람이 다시 웃을 이유가 생기고, '모든' 낙담한 사람이 격려 받고, '모든' 무기력한 사람이 동기부여를 받을 때까지 거기에 그쳐서는 안 된다. 가능성을 만드는 것을 절대 멈춰서는 안 된다. "누구에게나 많은 것이 주어질 것이며, 많은 것이 기대될지어다." 성공은 이 새로운 힘을 지렛대로 사용하여 세상을 신에게 조금 더 가까이 옮겨야 하는 놀랍도록 무거운 책임을 수반한다. 성취자로서, 시간은 사치를 부리거나, 무위도식하거나, 해야 할 일을 미루는 것이 아니라, 헌신하는 것이다. 성취자는 권력 기반을 가지고 있다. 그것을 활용해야 한다. 그는 영향력이 있다. 그것을 휘둘러야 한다. 그는 성공했다. 그것을 공유해야 한다. 자주 웃는 것, 지적인 사람들의 존경을 받는 것, 아이들의 애정을 얻는 것, 정직한 비평가들의 인정을 받는 것, 거짓 친구의 배신을 견뎌내는 것, 아름다움에 감사하는 것, 남에게서 최고를 찾는 것, 그리고 성취자가 존재했기 때문에 더 나은 세상이 되는 것-이것이 성공이다.

12 ① 윗글은 상상 속의 공포라는 것이 실제로 현실에서 마주했을 때는 그다지 끔찍한 것이 아니라고 설명하고 있다. 그러므로 윗글이 시사하는 바는 "현실을 외면하지 말라."는 ①의 설명이다.

> **오답풀이**
> ② 절망은 겁쟁이에게 용기를 준다
> ③ 당신이 상상할 수 있는 모든 것이 현실이다
> ④ 다른 사람의 입장을 상상해보라

⑤ 먹이를 쫓지 말고 미끼를 물고 기다려라

> **해석**
> 숲에서 들리지만 보이지 않는 것이 호랑이일 수도 있다. 그것은 다른 호랑이들보다 제각각 더 굶주리고 포악하며, 악어가 이끄는 호랑이들의 음모일지도 모른다. 하지만 아닐 수도 있다. 돌아서서 보면 다람쥐라는 걸 알 수 있을 거다. (실제로 다람쥐에게 쫓기는 사람을 알고 있다.) 숲속에 뭔가가 있다. 당신은 그걸 확실히 알고 있다. 하지만 그것은 대개 다람쥐일 뿐이다. 그러나 만약 당신이 보려 하지 않는다면, 그것은 용서되지만 당신은 기사가 아니다. 당신은 사자와 맞서는 쥐이고, 늑대의 시선에 마비된 토끼이다. 그리고 나는 그게 언제나 다람쥐라고 말하지 않는다. 가끔은 정말 끔찍한 일이기도 하다. 하지만 실제로 끔찍한 것조차도 상상 속의 끔찍한 것에 비하면 종종 의미가 없어진다. 그리고 상상 속의 공포로 인해 맞설 수 없던 것은 종종 끔찍한 현실로 전락할 때 실제로 맞설 수 있다.

13 ⑤ 윗글에서 ①, ②, ③, ④는 모두 크라우즈를 가리키고, ⑤는 네즈퍼스족의 장로 앵거스 윌슨을 가리킨다.

> **어휘**
> • memorable : 기억에 남는
> • encounter : 만남
> • remarkable : 놀라운
> • occurrence : 발생
> • water's edge : 물가

> **해석**
> 크라우즈는 어느 날 ① 그를 꾸짖었던 네즈퍼스족의 장로 앵거스 윌슨과의 추억의 만남을 묘사했다. "너희 백인들은 음악에 대해 아무것도 모른다. 하지만 원한다면 내가 어느 정도 가르쳐줄 수 있다." 다음날 아침, 크라우즈는 ② 자신이 오리건 주 북동부의 하천 둑으로 인도된 것을 알아차렸다. 그는 그곳에 조용히 앉으라는 몸짓을 받았다. 쌀쌀한 속에 기다린 끝에 산들바람이 일더니 갑자기 ③ 그의 주위가 파이프 오르간 화음소리로 가득 찼다. 악기가 보이지 않아 놀라운 광경이었다. 윌슨은 ④ 그를 물가로 데려와 바람과 얼음 때문에 길이가 다르게 부러진 갈대 무리를 가리켰다. 크라우즈는 이후 "그가 칼을 빼들었다"며 "그리고 거기서 하나를 잘라 구멍을 내고, 그 악기를 입술에 가져가 멜로디를 연주했어. ⑤ 그가 연주를 멈추고 말했지. '우리는 음악을 이렇게 배운다.'"라고 회상했다.

14 ④ 윗글에서는 해당 회사에 추가 보너스 지급 거부에 대한 구체적인 설명과 번복을 요구하고 있다. 그러므로 ④가 윗글의 목적으로 가장 적절하다.

• compensation : 보상금

• form letter : (똑같은 내용의) 양식 편지

• disclose : 밝히다

• file : (소송 등을) 제기하다

• appropriate : 적절한

해석

귀사로부터 최근 추가 보상 청구가 거절되었다는 편지를 받았습니다. 이 편지는 똑같은 내용이 복사된 편지이며, 제가 14개월 어학연수를 합격 학점으로 마친 것에 대한 추가 보너스 지급이 거부된 이유를 밝히지 않은 것으로 보입니다. 따라서 이 청구에 대한 검토와 거절 사유에 대한 완전하고 구체적인 설명을 요청합니다. 만약 제가 이 결정을 번복하지 못한다면, 저는 이 보너스에 대한 정당한 주장에 따라 필요한 기간 내에 항소를 제기할 계획입니다. 관련된 모든 서류(어학 보너스에 대한 서비스 설명서, 성적, 귀사에 보냈던 원본 편지, 귀사로부터 받은 양식 편지)가 동봉되어있습니다. 즉시 귀사로부터 이 검토에 대한 소식을 듣고, 이번 채용 약정에 따라 저에게 필요한 모든 보상을 받을 수 있기를 바랍니다.

15 ④ 윗글에서는 틸리 에딩거가 독일을 떠나 1년 동안 런던에 머무른 후 미국으로 갔다고 하였으므로, 독일을 떠나 바로 미국으로 갔다는 ④의 설명은 적절하지 않다.

어휘

• doctorate : 박사학위

• plaster cast : 석고 모형(깁스)

• maintain : 유지하다

해석

틸리 에딩거는 1897년 부유한 유대인 가정에서 태어났다. 그녀의 아버지 루드비히는 서로 다른 동물들의 뇌 구조를 비교하는 의학 연구원이었다. 에딩거는 1916년부터 1918년까지 하이델베르크와 뮌헨 대학에서 공부했다. 1921년에 프랑크푸르트 대학에서 박사학위를 받은 에딩거는 1927년에 센켄베르크 박물관의 큐레이터가 되었다. 1929년에 그녀는 화석 두개골 내부의 석고 주형으로 뇌 모양이 드러난다는 사실을 발견한 고생물 신경학, '화석의 뇌'를 발표했다. 그녀는 동물들의 뇌가 수백만 년 동안 어떻게 진화했는지 보여주는 지질학적, 생물학적인 증거를 결합시킨 최초의 사람 중 한 명이었다. 나치가 독일을 점령한 후, 에딩거는 나라를 떠나기로 결정했다. 1939년, 그녀는 독일을 떠나 1년 동안 런던에 머무른 후 미국으로 갔다. 그녀의 새로운 나라에서, 에딩거는 그녀의 분야에서 정상급 인물 중의 하나로 명성을 유지했고, 두 번째 기념비적인 책, '말의 뇌의 진화'를 출판했다.

16 ② 윗글에서는 사회 진화의 특징으로 그룹 구성원들의 전문화를 강조하고 있다. 즉, 그룹 안에서의 구성원들 간의 역할 분리를 말한다. 그러므로, 빈칸에 들어갈 말로는 ②의 'division of labor(분업)'이 가장 적절하다.

어휘

• hallmark : 특징

• optimum : 최적의

• circumstance : 상황

• caste : 계층

오답풀이

① 라이벌 팀

③ 쾌락의 추구

④ 영양의 균형

⑤ 부의 분배

해석

그룹 구성원들의 전문화는 사회 진화의 특징이다. 인체공학적 이론 중 하나는 특정 환경에 있는 각 종에 대해 일반학자로 구성된 동일한 크기의 그룹보다 더 효율적으로 수행하는 최적의 조정된 전문가 집단이 존재한다는 것이다. 또한 많은 상황에서 전문가 집단은 일반학자들의 동등한 집단이 쉽게 관리하지 못하는 질적으로 다른 업무를 수행할 수 있는 반면, 그 반대의 경우는 그렇지 않다 아프리카 들개 무리는 사냥을 할 때 두 개의 '계층'으로 나뉘어 사냥을 한다. 바로 추적을 하는 성체와 새끼들과 동굴에 남는 성체이다. 이러한 분업이 없었다면, 그 무리는 주요 먹잇감을 구성하는 발굽을 가진 커다란 동물들을 충분히 사냥할 수 없었을 것이다.

17 ① 윗글에서는 초기 중국 철학자들의 아날로그적이고 행동 지향적인 교육 방식에 빗대어 교육이 어떻게 되어야 하는가를 주장하고 있다. 그러므로, 빈칸에 들어갈 말로는 'effective engagement with the world(자연과의 효과적인 조화)'의 ①이 가장 적절하다.

오답풀이

② 이기적인 행동의 완전한 포기

③ 주어진 모든 정보에 대한 완벽한 암기

④ 추상적 이론화에 대한 공동의 약속

⑤ 성공한 사람들에 대한 현명한 모방

해석

초기 중국 철학자들은 행동 지향적인 완벽의 모델을 지향했기 때문에 육체적 연습, 시각화 운동, 음악, 의식, 명상을 통해 체화된 정신을 단련하는 데 초점을 맞췄다. 추상적 이론화나 일반 원칙의 학습에 대한 강조는 거의 없었다. 학생들은 어린 나이에 고전을 암기했을 것으로 예상되었으며 암기가 제 역할을

하더라도, 최종 목표는 이 정보를 생활에 유연하고 창의적으로 사용하는 법을 배우는 것이었다. 공자는 "수백 시를 암송할 수 있는 사람이 정부 업무를 위임받았을 때 그것을 수행할 수 없거나, 사절로 해외에 파견되었을 때 재치 있는 즉답에서 주의를 사로잡을 수 없다고 상상해보라. 얼마나 많은 시를 외웠다 한들, 그게 무슨 도움이 되겠는가?"라고 말했다. 단순히 고전을 외운다고 해서 진정한 신사나 숙녀가 되는 것은 아니다. 그 지식을 통합하여 당신의 일부가 되게 만들어야 한다. 이것이 초기 중국 교육의 초점이다. 그 목표는 자연과의 효과적인 조화에 대한 모범을 보이는 일종의 유연한 노하우를 만들어내는 것이었다. 교육은 아날로그적이고, 총체적이며, 행동 지향적이어야 한다.

18 ① 윗글에서는 뇌가 생존과 생식에 유리한 일을 하기 위한 성향이 있거나 준비가 되어 있다고 하였으므로, 빈칸에 들어갈 말로는 ①의 'the brain as a blank slate(뇌는 백지상태)'가 가장 적절하다.

어휘

- predispose : ∼하는 성향을 갖게 하다
- spontaneous : 자발적인
- tendency : 경향
- forage : 먹이를 찾다
- acquisition : 습득

해석

초기 행동적 관찰 연구에서는 이미 뇌는 백지상태라는 생각에 반대했다. 연구자들은 동물들이 모든 것을 동등하게 연관시키지 않으며 실험자가 기대하는 모든 재주를 부리도록 훈련받을 수 없다는 것을 반복해서 증명했다. 뇌가 생존과 생식에 유리한 일을 하기 위한 성향이 있거나 '준비'가 되어 있기 때문에 동물의 생태학적 지위와 관련된 행동들은 쉽게 훈련될 수 있다. 예를 들어, 설치류에서 먹이를 구하는 동안 다른 경로를 선택하는 경향인 '자발적 교대'는 생물종별 학습의 신속한 습득에 대한 생물학적 준비의 한 예이다. 제한된 시간 내에 같은 장소에서 식량을 찾는 것은 효율적인 전략이 아니다. 왜냐하면 대체 경로를 선택하는 것이 보상으로 이어질 가능성이 더 높기 때문이다. 반면에, 생존에 해가 될 수 있는 연계는 '대비된 것'이라고 불린다. 예를 들어, 발에 불쾌한 감전 사고를 피하기 위해 뒷다리로 쥐를 훈련시키는 것은 탐색적인 행동이며 위험에 처했을 때 전개되는 은닉 및 동결 행동과 양립할 수 없기 때문에 사실상 불가능하다.

19 ② 윗글에서는 기술을 습득할 때에 자신의 신체 운동이나 내적 상태보다 자신이 원하는 환경과 효과에 집중하는 것이 더 효과적이라고 강조하고 있다. 그러나 빈칸이 포함된 문장에서는 그렇지 못한 경우를 설명하고 있으므로, 빈칸에 들어갈 말로는 ②의 'Focusing on the skill-relevant environment(기술 관련 환경에 초점을 맞추는 것)'이 가장 적절하다.

오답풀이

① 노력에 대한 합당한 보상을 기대하는 것
③ 일과 놀이에서 균형을 잡는 것
④ 타인의 판단을 의식하는 것
⑤ 일상적인 환경에서 스스로를 격려하는 것

해석

자신의 수행 역학에 의식적인 인식을 집중하는 것은 기술 습득의 초기 단계에서 유용하지만, 더 경험이 많은 선수나 연주자에게는 지장을 준다는 것을 우리는 알고 있다. 마찬가지로 전문지식의 수준과 상관없이 자신이 원하는 환경과 효과에 집중하는 것('외부 초점')이 자신의 신체 운동이나 내적 상태에 집중하는 것('내부 초점')보다 더 효과적이다. 예를 들어, 손을 뒤로 당기는(내부 초점) 대신 물을 뒤로 밀어내는(외부 초점) 것에 집중하라고 말한 수영선수들이 더 빠르게 수영하고, 이러한 효과는 매우 다양한 분야에서 나타나고 있다. 자신의 주의를 내면이 아닌 밖으로 향하게 하는 것이 신체적 기술을 배우고 수행하는 데에 어째서 더 효과적인지에 대한 다양한 가설이 있다. 자신의 움직임에 집중할 때, 자신의 의식이 그것이 속하지 않는 곳에 스스로를 삽입하도록 허용함으로써 부드럽고 자동적인 모터 프로그램을 방해하고 다른 방해물(사회적 압력, 개인적인 걱정, 약속된 물질적 보상)이 성과를 침해하고 저하시키도록 한다. 기술 관련 환경에 초점을 맞추면 플레이의 시작과 끝에서 기량을 '잃어버릴' 수 있다.

20 ④ 윗글은 바쁜 부모로 인해 애정 어린 손길을 받지 못하는 아이들과 그 부모에 대하여 설명한 글이다. 주어진 글이 바쁜 부모가 처한 일상을 설명하고 있으므로, 그다음에는 그 일상으로 인해 나타날 수 있는 상황을 제시하는 (C)가 와야 하고, 다음으로 그 상황에 대한 부모와 보호자들의 대비책에 해당하는 (A)가 와야 한다. 그리고 (A)의 효과에 대한 긍정적이지 못한 시선에 해당하는 (B)가 마지막에 위치한다.

어휘

- inform : 알리다
- affectionate : 다정한, 애정 어린
- tactile : 촉각의
- notably : 특히
- infant : 유아
- heighten : 고조시키다
- appropriate : 적절한

- confer : 수여하다, 부여하다
- childcare : 보육
- abusive : 학대하는; 모욕적인

해석

부모들이 홀트와 왓슨 시절보다 아이들에게 애정 어린 손길이 필요하다는 것을 더 잘 알고 있지만, 바쁜 업무 스케줄은 아이들에게 그 기회를 많이 주지 못할 수도 있다. 많은 아이들이 아침 식사 후 어린이집이나 학교에 남겨져 저녁 식사나 취침 시간에만 귀가한다.

(C) 이 루틴은 왓슨이 아침에 악수하고 잠자리에 들 때 키스를 하는 것보다 훨씬 더 촉각적인 상호작용을 못하게 할 수도 있다. 보육제공자들이 애정 어린 손길이 부적절하고 학대적인 손길로 해석될까 봐 점점 더 두려워하고 있기 때문에 아이들은 집 밖에서 포옹과 키스 할당량을 받을 것 같지도 않다.

(A) 일부 부모와 보호자들은 아이들이 받는 촉각적 관심, 특히 지금은 유아들까지도 대상으로 하는 비디오와 컴퓨터 게임을 통해 아이들에게 높은 시각적 자극을 줌으로써 보상하려 할지도 모른다.

(B) 이것이 한 사회의 구성원들에게 적절한 시각적 의식의 고양으로 이어질 수 있지만, 개인적인 손길의 이점을 줄 수는 없다. 아직 우리 자신의 피부로 편안함을 느낄 때가 오지는 않은 것 같다.

21 ③ 윗글은 동물의 종이 처해진 상황에 따라 수면 시간이 다르다는 것을 설명하고 있다. 주어진 글이 수면의 기능에 대하여 설명하고 있으므로, 그것을 뒷받침해주고 있는 (B)가 와야 한다. 다음으로는 그 예시에 해당하는 (C)가 와야 하며, 그와 대비되는 설명에 해당하는 (A)가 그 뒤에 와야 한다.

어휘

- vulnerable : 취약한
- variability : 가변성, 변동성
- metabolic : 신진대사의

해석

수천 가지의 연구에도 불구하고, 우리는 여전히 가장 기본적인 질문에 대해 불명확하다. 수면의 기능은 무엇일까? 가장 확실한 설명은 수면이 원기를 회복시킨다는 것이다.

(B) 신진대사율이 더 높은 종들이 일반적으로 더 많은 시간을 잠자는 데 보낸다는 관찰에서 이 설명을 지지한다. 덜 명

확한 설명은 적응 가설인데, 이 관점에 따르면, 동물이 잠을 자는 양은 음식의 입수 가능성과 안전 고려사항에 따라 달라진다.

(C) 예를 들어, 먹이 욕구를 충족시키기 위해 몇 시간 동안 풀을 뜯어야 하는 코끼리들은 잠을 조금 잔다. 사자와 같이 포식자에 대한 취약성이 낮은 동물들도 박쥐나 굴을 파고 사는 동물처럼 숨어서 안전을 찾는 동물들처럼 많은 시간을 잔다.

(A) 반대로 크기가 너무 커서 굴을 파거나 숨기에 취약한 동물들(예를 들어, 말이나 소)은 매우 적게 잔다. 39종을 대상으로 한 연구에서는 체격과 위험이 결합된 요소가 수면시간 변동의 80%를 차지했다.

22 ② 윗글에서는 기억에서 비롯되는 2차적 이득에 대하여 설명하고 있다. 주어진 글은 고통스럽거나 수치스러운 기억으로부터는 아무것도 얻지 못한다고 생각할 수 있다는 것에 반대하는 주장의 시작을 의미하고 있으므로, ②에 들어가는 것이 가장 적절하다.

해석

그럼에도 불구하고, 임상 심리학자들이 말하는 기억에서 비롯되는 '2차적 이득'이 있을 수 있다.

많은 경우에, 제안된 기억을 채택하려는 동기(혹은 적어도 고려하려는 동기)는 복잡할지도 모른다. 예를 들어, 지금 어떤 끔찍한 어린 시절의 일을 떠올리는 어른을 생각해보아라. (①) 만약 기억된 사건이 고통스럽거나 수치스러웠다면, 그는 이 기억으로부터 아무것도 얻지 못한다고 생각할 수 있다. 대신, 이 기억을 간직하는 것은 그 사람에게 상처를 준다. (②) 그는 아마도 관심과 존중을 오랫동안 바랄 거다. (③) 그는 아마도 여러 가지 책임에서 벗어난 것 같다. (④) 어쩌면 "드디어 내 인생이 이해되고, 왜 이런 나쁜 일들이 나에게 일어났는지 알겠다."라거나, "마침내 내가 겪은 나쁜 일들이 내 잘못이 아니었음을 깨달았다."와 같은 문장에 비친 강력한 감정을 비로소 얻을지도 모른다. (⑤) 그러므로, 기억을 평가하고 기억이 정확한지 아닌지를 결정하려는 사람은 이러한 가능성을 따져봐야 한다.

23 ⑤ 윗글에서는 원시인류가 생각을 가지고 있었다는 징후들이 있더라도 원시인류의 생각이 행동보다 앞선다는 주장은 설득력이 없다고 말하므로 ⑤에는 이에 해당하는 이유나 근거가 와야 한다. 그러므로 주어진 글은 ⑤에 들어가는 것이 가장 적절하다.

정답 및 해설

어휘

- unfold : 펴다, 펼쳐지다
- burden : 짐, 짐을 지우다
- enact : (법을) 제정하다
- inflexible : 융통성 없는
- transferal : 이동, 전이
- indication : 지시, 암시
- utilize : 활용하다

해석

> 오히려, 그들의 행동의 주요 동기는 그들 환경의 단서뿐만 아니라 내부의, 학습되지 않은, 유전자 프로그래밍에 대한 자발적인 반응으로 남아 있다.

중요한 이슈는 생물생태학적 변화가 전개되면서 원시인류가 자연계로부터 고립된 느낌을 받았다는 점이다. (①) 생명이 대부분 무분별한 유전자 프로그래밍에 의해 통제되는 생명체들에 비해, 이제 인간은 행동하기 전에 생각해야 하는 무거운 짐을 지고 있었다. (②) 유전자 프로그래밍은 행동하는 방법에 대해 매우 구체적이고 융통성 없는 지시를 내리는 반면, 생각은 그에 비해 매우 유연하며 인간에게 가능한 선택 및 행동 방식을 제시한다. (③) 원시적이고 문화적인 전달뿐만 아니라 특정 비인간 생물들 사이에서도 분명히 학습이 있고, 또한 몇몇 종들, 특히 비인간 영장류들이 행동하기 전에 어느 정도의 생각을 활용한다는 분명한 징후들이 있다. (④) 그럼에도 불구하고, 비인간 영장류들의 행동이 사려 깊고 그들의 행동보다 반사적인 사고가 앞선다는 주장은 설득력이 없다. (⑤) 인간에게 있어 세상의 상황은 극적으로 다르다.

24 ① (A) 비판적인 피드백을 하는 동료들과는 거리를 둔다고 하였으므로, 빈칸 (A)에는 'distance from(거리를 두다)'이 들어갈 말로 가장 적절하다.
(B) 비판적인 피드백을 하는 동료들과 거리를 두었던 태도가 성과에 상당한 타격을 입었다고 하였으므로 빈칸 (B)에는 'adverse(불리한)'이 들어갈 말로 가장 적절하다.

어휘

- exclude : 제외하다
- compensate : 보상하다
- affirm : 단언하다

오답풀이

	(A)		(B)
②	~와의 거리	……	이로운
③	~에 대한 자신감	……	다차원적인

④ ~에 대한 자신감 …… 의도하지 않은
⑤ ~로 인한 성질(성미) …… 지속적인

해석

폴 그린, 프란체스카 지노 및 브래드 스태츠는 한 특정 회사의 300명 이상의 정규직 근로자의 4년치 직원 성과 데이터를 연구했다. 이 조직에서는 관리자들이 연간 성과 검토를 실시하지 않았다. 대신, 사람들은 자기 평가에 참여했고 동료들을 평가했다. 연구원들은 이러한 데이터뿐만 아니라 조직 내 각 직원의 네트워크에 대한 정보도 조사했다. 그들은 무엇을 발견했을까? 개개인은 동료들이 부정적인 피드백을 제공하면 그들의 네트워크에서 동료들을 제거하는 경향이 있었다. 만약 그 사람을 배제할 수 없다면, 그들은 더 긍정할 수 있는 다른 사람들을 그들의 관계로 들임으로써 보상했다. 한마디로, 개개인은 각자 듣고 싶은 것을 말해주는 사람들로 자신을 둘러쌌다. 그들은 이 행동에 대한 대가를 치렀다. 연구진은 직원들이 비판적 피드백을 제공하는 동료들과 관계를 끊었을 때, 직원 성과에 상당한 타격을 입었다는 사실을 발견했다.

↓

> 연구에 따르면, 근로자들은 비판적인 피드백을 하는 동료들과 (A) 거리를 두는 경향이 있었으며 이러한 태도는 그들의 성과에 (B) 불리한 영향을 끼쳤다.

[25~26]

어휘

- bewildering : 어리둥절하게 하는
- relativism : 상대주의
- dependent : 의존하는
- adhere to something : ~을 고수하다
- tolerate : 참다
- privilege : 특권을 주다, 특권
- ethnic minority : 소수 민족
- justification : 정당성, 정당한 이유
- objectively : 객관적으로
- virtuous : 도덕적인, 고결한

해석

세계 곳곳에서 마주치는 황당한 도덕적 관습과 관행의 다양성에 직면하여, 도덕적으로 옳고 그른 결정이 정말로 없다는 생각에서 벗어나고 싶은 것은 일리가 있다. 도덕적 상대주의는 도덕적 판단이나 원칙의 진실이 어떤 사람이나 집단의 수용에 의존하고 상대적이라는 견해이다. 그러므로 개인적인 믿음의 충돌에 직면할 때, 우리는 단순히 우리 자신의 신념을 따라

야 한다. 아니면, 상당히 다르게, 우리는 단순히 다른 사람들의 다른 신념을 용인하는 법을 배우면서, 우리 자신의 개인적인 신념을 고수하고 옹호해야 할 것이다. 만약 우리가 관용을 기르려면, 우리의 도덕적 관용도는 얼마나 넓게 확장되어야 하는가? 예를 들어, 정치적 반대자들에 대한 폭력적이고 잔혹한 탄압에 대한 관용을 포함할 것인가? 단순히 타국의 관행이라는 이유만으로 그런 반대자들에 대한 고문을 (충고나 관여는 고사하고) 묵묵히 방관하고 참아야 하는가?

이 경우에, 도덕적 상대주의의 개념에 따르면, 사실 옳고 그름을 말할 수 있는 특권적 위치에 있는 사람은 아무도 없다. 우리는 기껏해야 우리 자신이 옳고 그르다고 믿는 것을 어느 정도 확실하게 말할 수 있을 뿐이다. 우리 사회에서 받아들여지는 도덕적 가치(예를 들어, 여성, 미성년자, 소수 민족의 권리 또는 정적에 대한 대우)와 그렇지 못한 것이 충돌하는 경우, 상대주의는 한 사회에 대한 다른 사회의 어떤 비판도 객관적으로 타당하지 않을 거라고 말하는 것 같다. 상대주의자들은 관용의 가치에 따라 '로마에서는 로마법을 따르라'는 친숙하고 진부한 격언에서 볼 수 있듯이, 우리 스스로 발견하는 사회의 도덕적 가치와 관행을 채택할 것을 더 나아가 권고할지도 모른다.

25 ① 윗글에서는 우리가 우리 사회에서 받아들여지는 도덕적 가치와 다른 국가에서 받아들여지는 도덕적 가치가 충돌했을 때 상대주의자들이 접근하는 방식에 대하여 설명하고 있다. 그러므로 ①의 'How Moral Relativists Approach Moral Conflicts(상대주의자들이 도덕적 갈등에 접근하는 방식)'이 윗글의 제목으로 가장 적절하다.

오답풀이
② 도덕적 상대주의가 도덕적 무책임으로 이어지다
③ 비도덕 사회의 도덕적 개인
④ 우리의 궁극적인 목표 : 보편적 도덕
⑤ 도덕 : 선천적인가 후천적인가?

26 ② 윗글에서는 상대주의자들은 우리 사회에서 적용되는 도덕적 가치로 다른 국가의 도덕적 가치를 평가해서는 안 된다는 입장이라고 설명하고 있다. 그러므로 빈칸에는 'no criticism of one society by another would be objectively valid(한 사회에 대한 다른 사회의 어떤 비판도 객관적으로 타당하지 않을 거라고)'가 들어갈 말로 가장 적절하다.

오답풀이
① 우리는 이기심에 대한 우월한 도덕적 정당성을 찾아야 한다고
③ 도덕적 용기는 육체적 용기보다 높고 드문 미덕이라고
④ 자기중심적인 도덕적 권위는 없다고
⑤ 우리는 덕을 행함으로써 도덕적인 사람이 된다고

[27~28]

어휘
• famine : 기근
• breakdown : 붕괴, 고장, 실패
• cluster : 무리를 이루다
• persuasive : 설득력 있는
• intimately : 친밀하게; 직접적으로
• artisan : 장인
• commodity : 상품
• thriving : 번영하는, 번화한
• flee : 달아나다, 도망치다
• sophisticated : 세련된, 교양 있는

해석
이것은 열병하는 악몽처럼 들릴지 모르지만, 기후 변화는 거의 3,000년 전으로 거슬러 올라가는 선진 문명의 붕괴를 촉발시켰다. 기원전 1200년경, 후기 청동기 왕국들의 붕괴가 시작된 완전한 (지진, 기근, 가뭄을 포함하여 150년 이상 지속된) 재난의 폭풍이 현재의 그리스, 이스라엘, 레바논, 터키, 시리아를 포함하는 지역인 동부 지중해 주변에 몰려들었다. 고고학자들은 그 세계의 일부가 3세기 이상 활발한 경제 성장과 문화적, 기술적 발전을 경험했다는 설득력 있는 증거를 발견했다. 미케네인과 미노아인으로부터 히타이트인, 아시리아인, 키프로스인, 가나안인, 이집트인까지, 이들 고대 사회는 의사, 음악가, 장인의 서비스를 주고받으며 밀접하게 연결되어 있었다. 그들의 잘 발달된 무역로는 상품과 천연 자원, 특히 주석과 같은 청동을 만드는 데 필수적인 상품들을 수송했다.

그러나 2012년 연구에 따르면 기원전 1200년경 지중해의 지표면 온도가 급격히 냉각되면서 극심한 가뭄이 발생하여 이로 인해 식량 부족, 대규모 이주, 가난하고 농경한 농민들의 내부 반란이 일어났다고 한다. 결국, 한때 번영했던 청동기 시대의 주요 도시들은 가뭄에 찌든 고국을 떠나 침략한 군대에 의해 파괴되었고, 이는 문화, 언어, 기술의 상실을 초래했다. 그 결과 한때 세련되고 복잡했던 사회가 계속 존재했던(→ 사라진) 최초의 암흑시대였다. 그걸 복구하고 재건하는 데에 수 세기가 걸렸다.

27 ① 윗글에서는 첫 문단의 'climate change has triggered the collapse of advanced civilizations dating back nearly 3,000 years.'를 통해 알 수 있듯이 기원전 1200년경의 후기 청동기 왕국이 기후변화로 인해 어떻게 붕괴되었는지를 설명하고 있다. 그러므로 ①의 'the impact of climate change on the late Bronze Age kingdoms(기후변화가 청동기 후기 왕국에 미친 영향)'이 윗글의 주제로 가장 적절하다.

오답풀이

② 기후변화를 막기 위한 국제적 노력의 필요성

③ 청동 유물에 대한 신비를 밝히기 위해 계속되는 시도

④ 선진 문명을 건설하기 위한 이상적인 기후 조건

⑤ 청동기 왕국이 번영한 이유

28 ⑤ 윗글에서는 기후변화로 인한 후기 청동기 왕국의 붕괴를
설명하고 있으므로, 기후변화의 결과로 청동기 왕국이 계
속 존재했던 암흑시대가 나타난 것이 아니라 청동기 왕
국이 사라진 암흑시대가 나타났을 것이다. 그러므로 ⑤
의 'continued(계속했던)'은 'discontinued(끝이 난)' 또는
'stopped(멈춘)' 등으로 고쳐 써야 옳다.

오답풀이

① (a) 성장

② (b) 서로 연결하다

③ (c) 야기하다, 초래하다

④ (d) 유도하다

[29~30]

어휘

• please : 비위를 맞추다, 기쁘게 하다

• stretch : 뻗은

• lawn : 잔디밭

• gaping : 입을 크게 벌린, 크게 갈라진

• face-to-face : 얼굴을 맞대고

해석

> 대니는 "헤이워드 씨에게 사과하지 않을 거예요. 콜린
> 이 창문을 깼지, 내가 아니라구요. 사람들의 비위를 맞
> 추려고 사과하지 않을 거예요!"라고 화를 내며 소리쳤
> 다. 대니의 할아버지는 손자가 하는 말을 잠자코 들었
> 다. "너희 둘 다 공을 가지고 놀았어, 그렇지?"라며 그
> 가 물었다. "네, 하지만 제가 공을 패스했을 때 콜린은
> 일부러 피했어요. 공이 헤이워드 씨의 부엌 창문을 통
> 해 들어간 것은 걔 잘못이에요." "만약 사과를 하지 않
> 는다면 다시는 그녀의 집 근처에서 놀지 못할 줄 알아
> 라." 할아버지가 (a) 그에게 일러두었다.

(C) 대니는 할아버지가 한 말을 떠올렸다. 그래, 아쉬운 일이
야. 그녀의 집 앞엔 아주 넓게 펼쳐진 잔디밭이 있고, 여름
마다 수영장에서 수영하게 해주었어. 하지만 (c) 그는 "싫
어요, 할아버지! 아무리 내가 놀 데가 없고 여름에 더위로

죽더라도 헤이워드 씨에게 가서 미안하다고 말하지 않을
거예요!"라고 말했다. 할아버지는 책상으로 가서 신문 스
크랩을 훑어보았다. "와서 이걸 좀 보려무나."라고 (d) 그
가 말했다.

(D) 대니는 할아버지가 (e) 그에게 내민 만화를 보았다. 두 염
소가 갈라진 벼랑 옆에 있는 절벽의 좁은 가장자리에서 서
로 반대 방향으로 걷고 있었다. 길 한가운데서 그들은 얼
굴을 마주 보았다. 다음엔 무슨 일이 벌어졌을까? 둘 다
절벽에서 떨어질 때까지 서로 덤벼들었을까? 아니다. 염
소 한 마리가 무릎을 꿇고 다른 한 마리가 자기 위로 걷도
록 했다.

(B) 그래서 둘은 여행을 계속할 수 있었다. "왜 이 그림을 보
여주시는 거예요?"라며 대니가 물었다. 할아버지는 "만화
에서 누워있는 염소처럼 자세를 낮출 준비가 되어 있다면,
(b) 너와 콜린은 헤이워드 씨의 집 앞에서 계속 함께 놀 수
있을 거야."라고 말했다.

29 ③ 윗글에서는 대니와 콜린이 공놀이를 하다 헤이워드 씨의
창문을 부순 뒤에, 대니가 사과하려고 하지 않자 할아버지
가 타이르는 것을 보여주고 있다. 그러므로 (A) 다음에는
할아버지의 말에 반발하는 대니의 말이 이어지는 (C)가 와
야 하며, 그다음에는 그런 대니에게 할아버지가 신문의 만
화를 보여주는 (D)가 와야 한다. 그리고 할아버지가 대니에
게 조언을 해주는 내용의 (B)가 마지막에 위치한다.

30 ④ (C)의 (d)는 대니에게 신문의 만화를 보여주려는 할아버지를
가리키며, 나머지 (a), (b), (c), (e)는 모두 대니를 가리킨다.

2021학년도 기출문제 정답 및 해설

제2교시 영어영역(공통)

01 ⑤	02 ④	03 ⑤	04 ④	05 ⑤	06 ③
07 ③	08 ②	09 ①	10 ②	11 ①	12 ④
13 ②	14 ②	15 ④	16 ⑤	17 ④	18 ③
19 ③	20 ①	21 ④	22 ③	23 ⑤	24 ①
25 ②	26 ①	27 ①	28 ⑤	29 ⑤	30 ②
31 ③	32 ①	33 ⑤	34 ⑤	35 ③	36 ③
37 ②	38 ⑤	39 ④	40 ②	41 ①	42 ④
43 ⑤	44 ②	45 ③			

01 ⑤ 제시문은 John과 Amy가 연례 군사지도자 세미나에 참가하면서 대화한 내용이다. 대화 도중 John이 미 해군사령부의 특별 초청연설자가 세미나에 왔다는 말을 들었다고 하자 Amy가 그 연설자가 사실 자신이며 매년 실시하는 훈련에 한국이 참여하도록 격려하러 왔다고 대답하였으므로 대화의 내용으로 알 수 있는 사실은 ⑤의 "Amy is the guest speaker from the U.S. Navy Command.(Amy는 미 해군사령부의 초청 연사로 있다.)"가 적절하다.

오답풀이

① Amy는 회의실이 어디에 있는지 알고 싶어 한다.
② John은 연례 군사지도자 세미나의 특별 초대 손님이다.
③ Amy는 한국이 연례 공군 훈련에 참여하기를 원한다.
④ John은 한국이 미 해군을 향후 군사 훈련에 초대하기를 원한다.

어휘

- bother : 신경 쓰다, 괴롭히다, 성가신 일
- conference : 회의, 회담, 협의
- guest speaker : 초청 연사
- invite : 초대하다, 요청하다
- enhance : (좋은 점, 가치, 지위를) 높이다

해석

John : 실례합니다. 방해해서 죄송하지만 회의실을 찾고 있는데요. 어딘지 아시나요?
Amy : 네! 복도 오른쪽에 있어요. 연례 군사지도자 세미나에

오셨나요?
John : 맞아요! 당신도 그것 때문에 여기 온 건가요? 미 해군사령부의 특별 초청연사가 향후 군사훈련에 대해 이야기하기 위해 초대받았다고 들었어요.
Amy : 그게, 그 연설자는 사실 저예요. 저는 미 해군사령부에서 왔고, 우리의 동맹을 더욱 강화하기 위해 매년 실시하는 해군 훈련에 한국이 참가하도록 격려하기 위해 이곳에 왔어요.
John : 정말 놀랍군요! 직접 만나게 되어 영광입니다. 전 정말 많은 질문거리를 가지고 있어요.
Amy : 그럼, 최선을 다해 답변 드릴게요.

02 ④ 의사가 가능한 한 빨리 회복되길 바라는 환자에게 몸을 돌보지 않으면 허리 통증이 더 심해질 것이니 휴식을 취해야 한다고 충고하고 있으므로 환자의 답변으로는 ④의 "I'll try to get some time off from work(일을 좀 쉬도록 노력해야겠어요.)"가 적절하다.

오답풀이

① 당신이 추천한 대로 바로 일하러 갈게요.
② 다음 주에 엑스레이 결과를 위해 다시 올게요.
③ 디스크 수술 준비할게요.
⑤ 저는 이제 역도 좀 하러 갈게요.

어휘

- based on : ~에 근거하여
- lower back pain : 허리 통증
- due to : ~ 때문에
- go back to : (중단했던 것을) 다시 시작하다
- participate in : ~에 참가하다
- strain : 긴장, 부담, 압력, (근육의) 염좌
- expedite : 더 신속히 처리하다
- recovery : 회복
- as soon as possible : 되도록 빨리
- worse : 더 나쁜, 더 심한

해석

Doctor : 엑스레이 결과를 토대로 볼 때, 환자분의 허리 아래 통증은 근육의 긴장 때문입니다. 디스크 문제가 아니니 다행이네요.
Patient : 그럼 다음 주까지 복직할 수 있다는 뜻인가요?

Doctor : 할 수는 있지만, 무거운 물건을 들거나 허리 아래 근육을 긴장시키는 어떤 활동에도 참여할 수는 없습니다. 저는 환자분이 휴식을 취하기 위해 며칠 쉬는 것을 추천하네요.

Patient : 빠른 회복을 위해 더 할 수 있는 일이 없을까요? 저는 가능한 한 빨리 일하러 돌아가야 해요.

Doctor : 저는 환자분이 중요한 일이 있다는 것을 알지만, 환자분의 몸은 휴식을 취해야 합니다. 몸을 돌보지 않으면 허리 통증이 더 심해질 뿐이에요.

Patient : 그래요, 일을 좀 쉬도록 노력하겠어요. 고마워요.

03 ⑤ • **첫 번째 빈칸** : Nancy는 여행사에 전화하여 동남아시아 여행에 대한 궁금증을 물어보고 있으므로 빈칸에는 d의 "Do I get to pick the countries that I will visit or are they preset?(제가 방문할 국가를 선택해야 하나요, 아니면 여기서 미리 정해 놓은 것인가요?)가 들어갈 말로 적절하다.

• **두 번째 빈칸** : 패키지여행 동안 캄보디아나 발리를 가기 위한 다른 그룹에 가입하는 선택권이 주어진다는 Aron의 말에 Nancy가 해당 정보와 관련된 질문을 하고 있으므로 빈칸에는 여행 경로와 관련된 질문인 a의 "Would it be possible to stay in Thailand longer instead of selecting Cambodia or Bali?(캄보디아나 발리를 선택하는 대신 태국에 더 오래 머무르는 것이 가능할까요?)"가 들어갈 말로 적절하다.

• **세 번째 빈칸** : 태국에 더 오래 머무르도록 여행사에서 준비해 줄 수 있지만 그렇게 하려면 새로운 호텔로 옮겨야 한다는 Aron의 답변에 Nancy가 긍정의 반응을 보이고 있으므로 빈칸에는 c의 "I'll call you back as soon as I pick the hotel.(호텔을 고르는 대로 다시 전화할게요.)"가 들어갈 말로 적절하다.

• sequence : 순서, 장면
• package : 포장물
• stay with : 남의 집에서 머물다, 일에 열중하다, 일 따위를 계속하다
• definitely : 확실히, 분명히
• additional fee : 추가요금
• instead of : ~대신에
• preset : 미리 조정하다, 미리 결정하다

Aron : 안녕하세요. Global Travel Agency에 전화해줘서 감사합니다. Aron입니다. 무엇을 도와드릴까요?

Nancy : 안녕하세요! 저는 동남아시아 패키지여행 10일에 대해 몇 가지 궁금한 점이 있어요. 제가 방문할 국가를 선택해야 하는가요, 아니면 여기에서 미리 정해 놓은 것인가요?

Aron : 음, 이 패키지에는 처음 7일 동안 태국, 베트남, 말레이시아를 방문하는 것이 포함되어 있어요. 그리고 여러분은 이 그룹에 머물면서 캄보디아로 가거나 발리를 방문하기 위해 다른 그룹에 가입할 수 있는 선택권이 주어질 겁니다.

Nancy : 캄보디아나 발리를 선택하는 대신 태국에 더 오래 머무르는 것이 가능할까요?

Aron : 당연하죠! 우리가 준비해 줄 수 있어요. 하지만, 새로운 호텔로 옮겨야 할 겁니다. 추가 요금은 없으며, 저희 웹사이트에서 고르십시오.

Nancy : 아! 그거 좋은 생각이네요. 호텔을 고르는 대로 다시 전화할게요. 고마워요.

04 ④ 남자가 여자에게 이런저런 질문을 던지고 여자가 이에 답변을 하고 있으며 자신이 과학 분야의 여성 배역을 맡게 돼서 기쁘다고 한 것으로 봤을 때 여자는 'actress(여배우)'임을 알 수 있다. 또한 마지막에 여자가 남자의 영화 리뷰를 빨리 읽고 싶다고 하는 부분에서 남자는 'magazine reporter(매거진 기자)'라는 사실도 알 수 있다.

① 뉴스 앵커 – 특파원
② 교수 – 대학생
③ 영화감독 – 각본가
⑤ 구직면접관 – 구직면접자

• passion : 열정, 격정
• assume that : ~라 가정하여, ~라 하면
• involvement : 관련, 관여, 개입, 열중
• definitely : 절대로, 확실히, 분명히
• representing : ~의 대표로서
• specifically : 분명히, 특별히, 명확하게
• correspondent : 기자, 특파원, 통신원

Man : 자, 두 번째 질문으로, 지난번에는 여성 역사에 대한 열정에 대해 이야기했죠. 그렇다면, 이것이 현재 프로젝트에 참여하게 된 이유라고 봐도 무방할까요?

Woman : 오, 물론이죠. 그리고 그것은 단지 여성의 역사를 대변하는 것이 아니라, 과학 분야의 여성에 관한 것이에요.

Man : 당신은 어렸을 때 과학에 빠져본 적 있나요?

Woman : 네, 그랬어요! 나는 심지어 과학 캠프에 가서 대학을 다닐 때 NASA 인턴 과정을 마쳤죠. 그래서 나는 이 역할을 맡게 되어 매우 흥분돼요.

Man : 그렇군요. 난 당신이 그 영화에 출연하는 걸 보고 싶어요.

Woman : 저도 다음 호에서 당신의 영화 리뷰를 빨리 읽고 싶어요.

05 ⑤ 엄마가 딸에게 병원에 데려다 줄지 물어봤을 때 딸은 약국에서 처방전 없이 살 수 있는 약을 샀고 기분이 안 좋을 때 다시 알려주겠다고 한 것으로 봐서 아직 병원에 가지 않았다는 사실을 알 수 있다. 그러므로 "The daughter is getting better after she came back from the hospital.(딸은 병원에서 돌아온 후 점점 나아지고 있다.)"이라는 ⑤의 설명은 윗글의 내용과 일치하지 않는다.

오답풀이
① 딸은 집중이 안 되고 코막힘이 있다고 말했다.
② 딸은 처방전 없이 살 수 있는 약을 샀다.
③ 엄마는 딸이 심각한 상태일 수도 있다고 생각한다.
④ 딸은 상태가 나빠지면 엄마에게 알려줄 것이다.

어휘
• seem to be : (현재) ~한 모양이다
• nasal congestion : 코막힘
• serious : 심각한, 진지한
• maybe later : 다음 기회로
• purchase : 구입, 구매, 매입
• over-the-counter : 약이 처방전 없이 살 수 있는
• pharmacy : 약국
• stuffy : 답답한, 딱딱한

해석
Mother : 얘야. 별일 없니? 너 피곤해 보이는구나.
Daughter : 몰라, 엄마. 집중이 안 되고 코막힘이 있어. 내가 무슨 일이 있는 것 같아.
Mother : 병원에 데려다 줄까? 뭔가 심각한 것일 수도 있어.
Daughter : 아마 오후 늦게 갈 거 같아. 나는 약국에서 처방전 없이 살 수 있는 약을 샀어. 기분이 안 좋으면 알려줄게.
Mother : 그럼, 좀 쉬도록 하고 물을 많이 마셔.
Daughter : 알았어, 그럴게, 엄마.

06 ③ Linda의 강아지는 교통사고를 당해서 수술 후 내일 집에 올 것이며 Michael이 친구들과 호수로 놀러가는 데 Linda와 강아지도 초대하자 Linda가 승낙하고 있다 그러므로 "Michael is inviting Linda to go to the lake with her dog.(Michael은 Linda를 그녀의 개와 함께 호수에 가도록 초대하고 있다.)라는 ③의 설명이 윗글의 대화 내용과 일치하다.

오답풀이
① Linda는 호수에서 아르바이트를 찾았다.
② Linda는 휴가 여행을 위해 많은 돈을 모았다.
④ Michael은 Linda가 없는 동안 Linda의 강아지를 돌보고 싶어 한다.
⑤ 린다는 마이클과 그의 친구들과 함께 호수에 가는 것을 꺼린다.

어휘
• look for : 찾다, 구하다
• short on : ~이 부족하여
• as much as : ~만큼, ~정도
• accident : 사고, 우연
• spend : (돈을) 쓰다, (시간을) 보내다
• lake : 호수
• reluctant : 꺼리다, 주저하다

해석
Michael : 안녕 Linda. 여름방학 계획은 있어?
Linda : 난 그냥 집에 있으면서 아르바이트를 찾을 것 같아. 나는 지금 현금이 너무 부족해서 최대한 저축해야 해.
Michael : 무슨 일이야? 모두 괜찮은 거야?
Linda : 그게. 우리 강아지가 교통사고를 당해서 나는 강아지의 수술에 많은 돈을 써야 했어. 그는 매우 잘 회복되고 있고 내일 집에 올 거야.
Michael : 잘됐네. 음. 나는 이번 주말에 친구들과 함께 호수에 갈 거야. 너도 같이 왔으면 좋겠어. 너의 강아지에게도 좋을 거야.
Linda : 정말 좋은 생각이야. 언제 어디서 만날지 알려주면 강아지와 함께 갈게.

07 ③ 미국에서 생산되고 판매되는 작물의 약 19%가 관개용지에서 나온다는 근거를 들어 일반 대중이 농업용수와 물 보존이 그들 스스로의 이익에 매우 중요하다는 것을 이해해야 한다는 중심내용을 주장하고 있다. 그러므로 ③의 "대중은 농업용수와 물 보존의 중요성을 이해하고 관련 활동을 지원해야 한다."가 필자가 주장하는 바로 가장 적절하다.

어휘
• specialized : 전문적인, 전문화된
• food supply : 식량공급
• extent : 정도, 크기
• somewhat : 어느 정도, 약간, 다소
• contingent : 대표단, 분견대, 파견대
• dependable : 믿을 수 있는
• irrigation : 관개, 물을 끌어들임
• crop : 농작물, 수확량
• occur : 일어나다, 발생하다, 존재하다
• commodities : 상품, 물자
• consumer : 소비자
• conservation : 보호, 보존, 관리
• be willing to : 흔쾌히 ~하다
• research : 연구, 조사
• agricultural water : 농업용수

• solve : 해결하다

해석

전문화된 경제에서 국가의 식량 공급은 관개를 위한 신뢰할 수 있고 장기적인 물의 공급에 어느 정도 좌우된다. 미국에서 생산되고 판매되는 작물의 약 19%는 관개용지에서 나온다. 관개수가 없다면 이 생산은 일어나지 않을 것이고, 원자재 가격은 훨씬 더 높을 것이다. 따라서 일반 대중은 관개수와 물 보존이 그들 자신의 이익에 극히 중요하다는 것을 이해해야 한다. 소비자들은 물 보존 연구와 물 공급 개발을 위한 공공 기금을 기꺼이 지원해야 한다. 국민들은 농업용수 문제에 대해 더 많이 이해하고, 농업용수 문제를 해결하기 위한 과정에 대해 더 많이 이해해야 한다.

08 ② 제시문에 따르면 우리가 서로 갈등하는 상황에 처했을 때 갈등에서 벗어나고 문제를 해결하러 끊임없는 노력을 하고 있으며, 이를 통해 갈등이 일어나는 상황을 최대한 현명하게 활용하는 법을 배운다고 말한다. 그러므로 제시문이 시사하는 바는 ②의 "After the rain comes the sunshine.(비가 온 후 햇빛이 쬐인다.)"이 가장 적절하다.

오답풀이

① 어려울 때 친구가 진정한 친구다.
③ 많은 손이 가벼운 일을 만든다.
④ 쇠가 뜨거울 때 두드려라.
⑤ 피는 물보다 진하다.

어휘

• disagreement : 의견 충돌, 다툼, 불일치
• dispute : 분쟁, 분규, 논란, 논쟁
• undoubtedly : 의심의 여지없이, 확실히
• confront : (문제나 상황에) 맞서다
• resolve : 해결하다, 다짐하다
• mature : 어른스러운, 분별 있는, 숙성된
• individually : 개별적으로
• underneath : ～의 밑에, 속으로
• frustration : 불만, 좌절감
• irritation : 짜증, 격앙, 자극, 흥분, 염증
• conflict : 갈등, 물리적 충돌
• certainly : 틀림없이, 분명히
• plunge : 거꾸러지다, 급락하다
• ominous : 불길한
• stillness : 고요, 정적
• realization : 깨달음, 자각, 인식, 실현
• shore : 기슭, 해안, 호숫가

해석

내 아내 Tami와 나는 의견 불일치와 분쟁의 공정한 몫을 가지고 있었고 의심할 여지없이 계속 그럴 것이다. 그러나 이러한 문제에 직면하고 해결한 결과, 우리의 관계는 더욱 돈독해졌고, 개별적이고 부부로서 성숙해지게 되었다. 왜일까? 왜냐하면 상처, 좌절, 짜증, 또는 두려움 밑에는 언제나 배우고 성장하고 우리의 관계를 더 좋게 만들고자 하는 강한 욕망이 있기 때문이다. 우리는 갈등을 싫어하고 갈등을 찾아내지 않는다. 그러나 갈등이 우리를 발견하면 우리는 폭풍에 빠진다. 그리고 우리가 폭풍의 눈에서 불길한 고요에 도달했을 때, 즉 깨달음과 인식의 지점, 아는 것과 분명한 보기의 지점에 도달했을 때, 우리는 서로를 붙들고, 이끌든 이끌리든, 함께 안전한 해안으로 나아간다. 갈등이 반드시 최선의 선택을 위해 일어나는 것은 아니지만, 우리는 갈등이 일어나는 것을 최대한 활용하는 법을 배우고 있다.

09 ① 제시문에 따르면 때때로 외교 정책의 특정 사안으로 인해 수도 내부에서 갈등이 빚어지고 부처마다 입장이 달라질 수도 있는데 이러한 내부적인 의견 불일치로 인해 외국의 외교관은 본국의 지시 없이 예정된 회의에 참석해야 하거나 협상할 권한이 자신에게 있는지 알지 못하는 어려움을 겪는다고 서술하고 있다. 그러므로 ①의 "본국 정부 부처 간 의견 불일치는 외교관의 직무 수행을 어렵게 할 수 있다."가 제시문의 요지로 가장 적절하다.

어휘

• diplomat : 외교관
• foreign policy : 외교 정책
• instruction : 설명, 지시
• encoded : 암호화된
• embassy : 대사관
• internal : 내부의, 체내의
• regarding : ～에 관하여
• interest in : ～에 대한 관심
• Defense Department : 국방부
• Commerce Department : 상무부
• settle in : 적응하다
• occasionally : 가끔
• authorized : 인정받은, 공인된, 올바른
• negotiate : 협상하다, 성사시키다, 타결하다

해석

외교관들은 거의 항상 그들의 수도에 의해 철저한 통제를 받고 있고, 이것은 더 큰 선진국들일수록 더욱 그럴 것이다. 외교관들은 외교 정책을 계속 진행함에 따라 자유롭게 자신의

외교 정책을 결정할 수 없는 대신 지시를 통해 무엇을 말해야 할지를 듣게 된다. 이 지침서는 수도에서 면밀히 검토되고 암호화된 방법으로 한국의 대사관이나 해외 공관에 보내질 것이다. 때로는 특정 사안과 관련해 수도 내부 갈등이 빚어지고, 부처마다 입장이 달라진다. 예를 들어, 미국에서 국무부는 국제 관계에 관심이 있는 다른 부서– 국방부나 상무부–과 항상 같은 견해를 가지지는 않을 수 있다. 일부 외국 도시의 외교관이 지시를 내리기 전에 이러한 내부적 차이는 먼저 수도에서 해결되어야 한다. 그리고 가끔 수도의 내부적인 의견 불일치로 인해 이 외로운 외교관은 지시 없이 예정된 회의에 참석해야 하거나, 무슨 말을 하거나 협상할 권한이 있는지 알지 못하는 경우가 있다.

10 ② 제시문에 따르면 사람들 사이의 접촉은 거리와 경로의 생태적 요인에 의존하며 코스타리카의 두 마을에 있는 집들과 대기업에 근무하는 사무실의 상호 작용 비율을 예시로 들어 거리가 상호작용의 비율을 결정하는 가장 중요한 요소라는 사실을 설명하고 있다. 그러므로 ②의 "사람 간의 물리적 거리는 상호작용의 빈도에 영향을 미친다."가 제시문의 요지로 가장 적절하다.

어휘
- acquaintance : 아는 사람, 친분
- essential : 필수적인
- precondition : 전제 조건
- formation : 형성 과정
- relationship : 관계
- evidence : 증거, 흔적
- document : 서류, 문서
- obvious : 분명한, 확실한, 너무 뻔한
- presumably : 아마, 짐작건대
- factor : 요인, 양
- depend upon : ～에게 의존하다
- pathway : 좁은 길, 오솔길, 진로, 경로
- proximity : (거리, 시간상으로) 가까움
- frequency : 빈도, 반발, 잦음, 진동수
- spread out : 몸을 뻗다, 넓은 공간을 쓰다
- explicitly : 명쾌하게
- interaction : 상호작용

해석
한 쌍의 사람들 사이에 어떤 접촉이나 친분이 있는 것은 그들 사이의 관계를 형성하기 위한 필수적인 전제조건이다. Festinger, Schachter, 그리고 Back의 기록은 사람 사이의 물리적 거리가 적고 일상 활동 과정에서 필요한 경로가 교차할수록 사회적 방문 관계를 발전시킬 가능성이 높다는 명백한

사실을 문서화한다. 아마도 이것은 사람들 사이의 접촉이 거리와 경로의 생태학적 요인에 의존하기 때문일 것이다. 마찬가지로, Powell은 코스타리카의 두 마을에 있는 집들의 서로 다른 근접성은 가족 간의 방문 빈도와 관련이 있다는 것을 발견했다. 집들이 빽빽이 모여 있는 마을에서는 방문자의 5할3푼이 일상생활인 반면, 상당히 먼 곳에 집이 펼쳐지는 개간지 형태의 정착촌에서는 방문자의 3할4푼만이 일상생활인 것으로 보고되었다. Gullahorn은 대기업의 377명이 근무하는 사무실에서 근접성의 함수로서 상호 작용의 비율을 명시적으로 조사했다. 2개월 반의 관찰과 인터뷰 후에, 그는 거리가 상호작용의 비율을 결정하는 가장 중요한 요소라고 결론지었다.

11 ① 제시문의 마지막에서 회의주의는 우리가 살고 있는 우주를 해석하고 행동에서 지혜를 얻는 데 도움이 될 수 있는 긍정적이고 건설적인 틀을 제공한다고 서술되어 있으므로 ①의 'significance of skepticism for the advancement of human knowledge and conduct(인간의 지식과 행동의 발전을 위해 회의론이 가지는 의의)'가 제시문의 주제로 가장 적절하다.

오답풀이
② 인위적인 지식 · 행동 맥락에서 회의론의 약점
③ 논리적인 추론을 연구하는 데 있어서 오래된 회의적 질문의 중요성
④ 수정된 회의론과 과학적 추론의 차이점
⑤ 다른 형태의 회의론을 구별하는 것

어휘
- skepticism : 회의론, 무신론
- doubt : 의심, 의혹, 의문
- evidence : 증거, 흔적
- hypothesis : 가설, 추정
- ordinary life : 평범한 삶
- reliable : 믿을 만한
- certainty : 확실성
- dogmatic : 독단적인
- appreciate : 진가를 알아보다
- snare : 사냥용 덫, (위험한) 유혹
- pitfall : (눈에 안 띄는) 위험
- principle : 원칙, 신조
- fallibilism : 오류가능주의
- probabilism : 개연성
- in regard to : ～에 대한
- constructive : 건설적인
- framework : (건물 등의) 뼈대, (판단, 결정 등을 위한)틀, 체제, 체계

정답 및 해설

• achieve : 달성하다, 성취하다, 해내다

• wisdom : 지혜, 슬기, 현명함, 타당성

• conduct : (특정한 활동을) 하다, 지휘하다, (어떤 장소로) 안내하다

해석

회의론은 가설에 대한 증거와 이유를 요구하는 의심의 방법으로 과학 연구, 철학적 대화 및 비판적 기능의 과정에 필수적이다. 또한 그것은 상식의 요구가 항상 우리에게 가장 신뢰할 수 있는 가설과 신념에 따라 발전하고 행동해야 하는 도전적인 평범한 삶에서도 필수적이다. 그것은 절대적으로 확실성과 독단적인 최종성의 적이다. 그것은 모든 종류의 인간 지식의 함정에 감사하며, 우리 지식의 확실성과 관련하여 오류주의와 확률주의의 원칙의 중요성을 인식한다. 이것은 오래된 회의론과는 확연히 다르며, 인류 지식의 진보와 인류의 도덕적 진전에 실질적으로 기여할 수 있다. 그것은 우주에 대한 우리의 지식과 도덕적이고 사회적인 삶에 중요한 의미를 가지고 있다. 이런 의미에서 회의론은 우리가 살고 있는 우주를 해석하고 행동에서 지혜를 얻는 데 도움이 될 수 있는 긍정적이고 건설적인 틀을 제공한다.

12 ④ 제시문에서는 사상의 본질에 대한 탐구 역시 다른 심리학과 마찬가지로 철학에서부터 시작되었고 철학으로부터 벗어나기 위해 다른 심리학의 분야보다 더 오랜 시간이 걸렸다고 설명하고 있다. 그러므로 ④의 'conversion of the study of thinking from philosophy to psychology(사상 연구의 철학에서 심리학으로의 전환)'이 제시문의 주제로 가장 적절하다.

오답풀이

① 철학의 사상의 본질에 대한 다양한 접근법

② 철학과 심리학의 조화로운 공존

③ 사상에 대한 철학자와 심리학자의 다른 견해들

⑤ 현대 심리학에 의해 드러난 사고 과정의 특성

어휘

• exploration : 탐사, 탐험, 탐구

• intensely : 강렬하게, 격하게, 열심히

• on the one hand : 한편으로는

• entirely : 전적으로 완전히, 전부

• strickly : 깐깐하게

• empirical : 경험에 의거한, 실증적인

• flourish : 번창하다, 잘 자라다, 잘 지내다

해석

사상의 본질에 대한 탐구도 다른 심리학과 마찬가지로 철학자의 안락의자에서 삶을 시작했다. 그러나 사고 과정에 대한 연구는 철학에서 벗어나기 위해 심리학의 다른 많은 분야보다 더 오랜 시간이 걸렸다. 한편으로 사상이란 이해하기 어렵고, 사사롭고, 강렬하게 개인적인 성격 때문에, 또 한편으로는 '진리', '지식', '판단'과의 관계 때문에, 철학자들은 이 연구의 영역과 결별하기를 꺼려왔으며, 오늘날 완전히 포기한 것은 아니다. 그럼에도 불구하고 사고의 연구는 철학자의 도서관을 벗어나 실험실로 ─ 철학자의 머리에서 과학자의 머릿속으로 ─ 이동했다. 사상은 20세기 초에 실험실에 소개되었다. 그 이전까지 사고의 심리학은 엄밀히 말하면 철학자의 영역이었고, 따라서 그 역사에는 특히 경험철학이 영국에서 번성했던 수세기 동안 위대하고 가까운 위대한 사람들의 이름이 연구되어 있다.

13 ② 제시문의 전반부에서 우리 주의의 생명체들이 어떠한 가르침 없이도 자신들의 생존 기술을 이어가는 것에 과학자들이 놀라움과 감탄 및 경외심을 불러일으켰다고 서술하고 있다. 그러므로 ②의 "Wonder of Knowing Without Being Taught(가르치지 않고 아는 것의 불가사의)"가 제시문의 제목으로 가장 적절하다.

오답풀이

① 진화 : 영원토록 진행되는 과정

③ 자연 : 인간의 진정한 스승

④ 다른 생물들에 대한 인간의 우월성

⑤ 교육 및 학습 : 모든 생명체의 생존 방법

어휘

• painful : (몸이) 아픈, (마음이) 괴로운

• handicraftsmanship : 수세공인의 지위

• acquirement : 취득, 획득, 습득

• aback : 돛이 역풍을 받고

• realization : 깨달음, 자각, 인식

• elaborate : 정교한

• apparently : 듣자하니

• possessed : 흘린

• admiration : 감탄, 존경

• awe : 경외감, 외경심

• fertilize : 수정시키다

• progeny : 자손

• marvelously : 놀라울 만큼, 불가사의하게

해석

수공예든 예술이든 이렇게 느리고 고통스러운 것은 기술을 터득하는 과정이다. 그래서 지식 습득을 위한 교육의 필요성에 젖어 있다. 그래서 우리는 우리 주위가 가장 복잡한 절차를 거치며 가장 정교한 기술을 이어가는 생명체라는 깨달음에 당황한다. 가르칠 가능성 없이 가장 확실한 지식을 부모에게 빼앗

겼다. 새들의 비행, 모든 동물의 출산과 산후조리 절차, 특히 벌, 개미와 다른 곤충들의 복잡하고 체계화된 노동력은 과학자들의 놀라움과 감탄, 경외심을 불러일으켰다. 암컷 곤충은 알을 낳고, 수컷 곤충은 수정하며, 자손은 가르치지 않고 이전의 경험도 없이 어른들의 삶으로 이어지는 진화의 상태를 거친다. 부모는 자손을 보지 못하며, 자아는 다양한 모양을 하고 있으며, 이 시기에 매우 다양한 능력을 가지고 있기 때문에, 놀랄 만큼 능숙하고 경이롭게 적응된 행동에 대한 가르침이 있을 수 없다.

14 ② 제시문에 따르면 평온한 느낌은 부분적으로 스마트 미주신경이라는 자율신경계의 경로로 조절되며 우리가 강한 관계를 가질 때 스마트 미주신경이 스트레스 반응을 조절하여 건강하고 명확하게 생각할 수 있도록 돕는다고 서술하였다. 그러므로 ②의 "Having Good Relationships: The Road to Staying Calm(좋은 관계: 침착하게 지내는 길)"이 제시문의 제목으로 가장 적절하다.

오답풀이

① 마음을 산만하게 하는 스마트 미주신경
③ 우리 감정의 위치 : 신경과학자들에게는 여전히 미스터리
④ 원시적인 인간의 행동을 통해 우리 자신을 이해하는 것
⑤ 원시 뇌 : 스마트 미주신경의 변조기

어휘

• calm : 평온한, 침착한, 차분한
• regulated : 통제된, 규제된, 조정된
• autonomic : 자율적인, 자발적인
• nervous : 신경의
• primitive : 원시적인
• modulate : 조절하다
• exploding : 증가하는
• isolated : 외딴
• neuroscientist : 신경 과학자
• chronic : 만성적인
• depression : 우울증
• irritability : 화를 잘 냄, 성급함

해석

평온한 느낌은 부분적으로 스마트 미주신경이라 불리는 자율신경계의 경로에 의해 조절된다. 여러분이 스트레스를 받을 때, 여러분의 원초적인 뇌는 도움을 주기를 원하고 원초적인 뇌가 책임자일 때 그것은 관계에 나쁜 소식이 되는 결정을 내리는 경향이 있다. 당신이 강한 관계를 가지고 있을 때, 스마트 미주신경들은 스트레스 반응을 조절할 수 있고 원시적인 뇌가 그 자리를 차지하지 못하게 할 수 있다. 당신은 더 건강하고, 더 명확하게 생각할 수 있으며, 분노에 폭발하거나 도망

가는 대신 창의적인 사고를 통해 문제를 해결할 가능성이 더 높다. 하지만 여러분이 다른 사람들과 격리되어 있을 때, 여러분의 스마트 미주신경들은 신경과학자들이 말하는 나쁜 어조에 시달릴 수 있다. 이것은 당신의 원시적인 뇌가 더 주사들을 부를 가능성이 높다는 것을 의미한다. 단기적으로는 이것이 관계 문제로 이어진다. 시간이 지나면서 만성적인 스트레스, 질병, 우울증, 그리고 큰 시간의 짜증을 기대할 수 있다.

15 ④ 위의 그래프를 보면 병원 및 의료 환경의 쇼와 영화를 절대 보지 않는 성인의 비율은 23이고 그 두 배는 46인데 같은 종류의 영화를 자주 보거나 가끔 본다고 한 성인의 비율은 43이라서 두 배에 미치지 못하므로 "병원이나 의료 환경의 쇼와 영화를 자주 보거나 가끔 본다고 말하는 성인의 비율은 절대 안 본다고 하는 성인의 2배가 넘는다."는 ④의 설명이 도표의 내용과 일치하지 않는다.

어휘

• above : ~보다 위에, ~보다 많은, ~을 넘는
• criminal : 범죄의
• investigation : 조사

해석

위의 그래프는 범죄 수사, 병원과 의료 환경, 또는 공상과학 소설과 같은 과학 관련 쇼와 영화를 각각 본다고 말하는 미국 성인의 비율을 보여준다. ① 약 8명의 미국 성인들은 3가지 유형의 쇼와 영화 중 어떤 것도 자주 혹은 가끔 본다고 말한다. ② 세 가지 유형의 쇼와 영화에서 모두 자주 혹은 가끔 본다고 말하는 성인의 비율이 가장 높은 반면, 절대 본 적이 없다고 말하는 성인의 비율은 가장 낮다. ③ 범죄수사의 쇼와 영화를 자주, 혹은 가끔 본다고 말하는 성인의 비율은 거의 하지 않는다고 말하는 성인의 3배에 달한다. ④ 병원이나 의료 환경의 쇼와 영화를 자주 보거나 가끔 본다고 말하는 성인의 비율은 절대 안 본다고 하는 성인의 2배가 넘는다. ⑤ 병원이나 의료 환경의 쇼와 영화를 절대 보지 않는다고 말하는 성인의 비율은 공상과학의 쇼와 영화를 절대 보지 않는다고 말하는 성인의 비율과 같다.

16 ⑤ 제시문에 따르면 Clausewitz는 자신의 주요 저서인 《On War》를 완성하지 못하고 죽었다. 그러므로 "사망 전에 On War를 완성하여 군사 이론에 널리 영향을 미쳤다."는 ⑤의 설명은 제시문의 내용과 일치하지 않는다.

어휘

• claim : 주장하다, 요구하다
• status : 법적 신분, 사회적 지위
• accept : 받아들이다
• military service : 병역, 군 복무

317

- attain : 이루다, 이르다
- defeat : 패배시키다, 무산시키다
- reform : 개혁하다, 교화되다
- opposed to : ~에 반대하여
- enforce : 집행하다, 가용하다
- alliance : 동맹, 연합
- principal : 주요한, 주된
- specifically : 분명히, 명확하게

해석

Carl von Clausewitz는 1780년 6월 1일 프로이센에서 카를이 받아들인 귀족 지위를 주장하는 집안의 넷째이자 막내아들로 태어났다. Clausewitz는 열두 살에 프로이센군에 입대하여 결국 소장의 계급을 획득했다. 1806년 10월 14일 나폴레옹이 프로이센을 침공하여 프로이센군을 격파하자, 1807년부터 1808년까지 프랑스에 잡혀 포로가 되었다. 프로이센으로 돌아온 그는 프로이센 군대와 국가의 개혁을 도왔다. 프로이센과 나폴레옹 1세와의 강제적인 동맹에 반대하여, Clausewitz는 프로이센 군대를 떠나 1812년부터 1813년까지 러시아 제국의 군대에서 복무했다. 그는 전쟁의 모든 면에 있어서 신중하고 체계적이며 철학적인 조사를 기록으로 남겼다. 그 결과 그의 주요 저서인 《On War》를 완성하지 못하고 죽었지만, 그럼에도 불구하고 그의 사상은 군사 이론에 널리 영향을 미쳐 독일군 사상에 구체적으로 큰 영향을 끼쳤다. 그는 1831년 11월 17일에 콜레라로 죽었다.

17 ④ ①, ②, ③, ⑤의 'he'는 모두 젊은 장교를 가리키나 ④의 'he'는 늙은 장군을 가리킨다.

어휘

- worn : 해진, 닳은, 몹시 지쳐 보이는
- row : (사람과 사물들이 옆으로 늘어서 있는) 열, (극장 등의 좌석) 줄
- stammer : 말을 더듬다
- emotionless : 감정이 없는
- inspect : 점검하다, 사찰하다
- admit : 인정하다
- ravage : 황폐하게 만들다, 유린하다
- upsurge : 급증
- emotion : 감정, 정서
- compassion : 연민, 동정심

해석

군대의 젊은 장교 한 명이 퍼레이드를 하기 위해 훈련을 하고 있었다. 그는 마치 몽환에 빠진 것처럼 앞을 응시하며 똑바로 서 있는 보병들의 줄을 따라 걸었다. 그들은 전투로 지쳐 있었고, 지금까지 싸워왔으며, 전역하기 전에 막 캠프에 돌아와 젊

은 장교를 위해 퍼레이드를 하고 있었다. 젊은 장교는 그를 지도자로 훈련시키고 있는 늙고 노련한 장군과 동행했다. 그들이 줄을 따라 걸을 때, 장교는 중요한 지도력 원칙을 기억하고 장군에게 질문했다. "선생님." 그는 감정이 없는 눈으로 사내들을 바라보고 여전히 더듬거리며 "이 사람들을 살피면서 어떻게 겸손해지는 법을 배웁니까?"라고 물었다. 그는 "사실은 내가 모든 사람보다 우월하다고 느낍니다."고 인정했다. 장군은 혼자 미소를 지었다. "그건 쉬운 일이지." 그가 부드럽게 말했다. "그들의 부츠를 간단히 내려다보게." 젊은 장교가 아래를 내려다보니 사내들의 거칠고 황폐한 부츠가 보였다. 많은 사람들이 간신히 버티고 있었고 극한까지 자신을 몰아붙인 어떤 이들은 발가락 사이로 피가 보였다. 그는 강렬하고 갑작스런 감정의 격앙을 느꼈고 뜻밖에도 연민과 겸손함을 느꼈다. "감사합니다." 그가 말했다.

18 ③ 동사원형 'have'의 앞의 'to'는 전치사이고 같은 전치사 to + being과 전치사 to + types가 병렬 구조를 이루므로 ③의 'have'는 명사의 형태인 'having'으로 바꿔야 한다.

오답풀이

① 선행사가 포함된 목적격 관계대명사 'What'을 사용한 것은 적절하다.
② 주어인 'we'와의 시제 일치를 위해 's'를 생략한 'like'가 와야 한다.
④ 동사인 'constructed'를 꾸며주는 부사로 'equally'가 온 것은 적절하다.
⑤ 주격관계대명사 + be동사가 생략 가능한 구문이다.

어휘

- available : 이용할 수 있는, 시간이 있는
- interpret : 설명하다, 이해하다
- perspective : 관점, 시각
- humankind : 인류, 인간
- reproduce : 복사하다, 재현하다
- variation : 변화, 변형
- transportation : 수송
- insofar : ~하는 한에 있어서는
- liability : 법적 책임
- suburbanite : 교외 거주자
- distinctive : 독특한
- certain : 확실한, 틀림없는

해석

문화가 하는 일은 물리적 환경과 인간 환경에서 이용 가능한 것을 취하여 사회적으로 해석하고 이를 사회적으로 공유된 의미와 느낌으로 채우는 것이다. 인간의 세계는 문화적으로 해석되는 사회 세계이다. 이러한 관점에서 우리는 어느 정도 닮았

고, 다른 인류와는 다소 다르다. 우리는 자연적으로 다른 사람들과 같다. 모든 사람들(우리가 아는)이 짝짓기를 하고, 번식하고, 동굴의 변형된 모습(집)에서 살고, 돌아다니며(이동), 그와 비슷한 것이다. 우리는 서로 다른 집단의 사람들이 아버지나 어머니, 남자나 여자, 그리고 아이를 갖는 것, 그리고 주택의 종류, 교통수단 등에 다른 의미와 가치를 부여하고 있는 한 문화적으로 다른 사람들과 다르다. 어린이를 경제적 자산이나 경제적 부채로 볼 수 있다. 모든 집들이 똑같이 지어지는 것은 아니다; 높은 층과 낮은 층의 집들이 있다. 에스키모의 교통수단은 전형적인 미국 교외 거주자의 교통수단과 같지 않으며, 20년 된 "예비된" 자동차는 최신형 고급 자동차와 같은 것을 의미하지 않는다. 문화는 모두 특정한 시간과 장소에서 주어진 집단의 특징인 독특하고 공유된 의미와 감정에 관한 것이다.

19 ③ 구조만 살펴봐서 풀 수 있는 것이 아닌 해석이 필요한 병렬구조 문제이며, 'potentially'가 아닌 'harmful'과 병렬구조가 이루어져야 하므로 ③의 'beneficially'가 'beneficial'로 바뀌어야 한다.

오답풀이

① 주어 + 동사가 생략된 구문으로 'how'만 홀로 들어오는 것이 가능하다.
② 'organism' 뒤의 동사 'is'와 관련된 주격관계대명사의 자리이고 주어인 'brains'가 사물이므로 'which'가 오는 것이 적절하다.
④ 수동태가 사용된 동사+ed 구문이다.
⑤ 동사 'Your~organs'와 수일치를 해주면서 동사로 'use'가 가능하다.

어휘

- chest : 가슴, 흉부
- similar : 비슷한, 유사한
- regardless : 개의치 않고
- evolve : 발달하다
- principal : 주요한, 주된
- exception : 예외
- feeding : 먹이 주기
- organism : 생물체, 유기체
- tubular : 관으로 된
- anus : 항문
- harmful : 해로운
- ingest : 삼키다
- gastrointestinal : 위장의
- consume : 소모하다

해석

왜 우리의 뇌는 우리의 머릿속에 위치하는가? 그들이 우리 가슴 깊숙한 곳에, 우리 마음의 위치와 비슷하다면 더 안전하지 않을까? 뇌는 얼마나 작거나 단순한지 상관없이, 주요한 기능을 수행할 수 있는 최적의 위치에서 진화했다. 즉, 개인과 종의 생존이다. 극히 소수의 예외를 제외하고는, 뇌는 항상 동물의 먹이인 "튜브"나 메커니즘의 앞 끝에 위치하는데, 인간을 비롯한 많은 유기체에서 입에서부터 항문까지 확장되는 관상 계통이다. 당신의 뇌는 당신이 음식을 시각, 소리, 냄새로 찾을 수 있게 해주고 그리고 나서 당신의 행동을 정리해서 당신의 먹이 튜브의 앞쪽 끝이 음식을 맛 볼 수 있을 만큼 충분히 가까워지도록 하고 그것을 섭취하기 전에 그것의 유익하거나 잠재적으로 해로운 내용물들을 확인할 수 있게 해준다. 일단 그 음식이 당신의 먹이 튜브에 들어가면, 그것은 흡수되어 당신의 몸의 세포에 이용될 수 있게 된다. 위장계라고도 알려진 당신의 전체 급유관과 관련 기관들은 남은 30%를 신체의 나머지 사람들에게 공급하기 위해 소비하는 에너지의 거의 70%를 사용한다.

20 ① (A) 'by helping' 이하 문장의 주어는 'tactical commanders'이고 복수인 주어 뒤에 오는 동사는 s가 생략되므로 'capitalize'를 사용하는 것이 적절하다.
(B) 'the degree'는 사물을 나타내는 목적어이므로 뒤에 오는 목적격 관계대명사는 'which'를 사용하는 것이 적절하다.
(C) 'cues'는 '신호'를 나타내는 명사이므로 명사를 수식하는 형용사인 'necessary'를 사용하는 것이 적절하다.

어휘

- tactical : 전략적인, 전술적인
- whereby : (그것에 의하여) ~하는
- engaged : (~을 하느라) 바쁜, ~하고 있는
- opposing forces : 적군, 대항군
- coordinate : 조직화하다, 조정하다
- improve : 개선되다, 나아지다, 향상시키다
- responsiveness : 민감성
- unfold : 펴다, 펼쳐지다
- enhance : 높이다, 향상시키다
- integration : 통합
- affect : 영향을 미치다, 충격을 주다
- synchronize : 동시에 발생하다
- maneuver : 책략, 술책, 공작

해석

전술지휘통제란 실제로 적대세력과 교전하는 부대들이 서로 소통하고 활동을 조정하는 과정이다. 전술지휘통제(Tactical

Command and Control)는 전투가 전개될 때 전술지휘관들이 신속하게 대응하도록 도와 전술지휘관급 기회를 활용함으로써 전투 대응력을 향상시킬 수 있다. 전장의 배치 조정과 병력 이동에 영향을 주어 통합을 강화할 수 있다. 보다 광범위하게, 전술적 명령과 통제는 개별 단위와 명령이 잘 작동하고 운영을 동기화하는 정도에 영향을 미칠 수 있다. 전술적 지휘와 통제는 병사에게 복잡한 동기화된 사격, 기동 또는 기타 활동을 수행하는 데 필요한 신호를 제공함으로써 기술을 향상시킬 수 있다.

21 ④ (A) 주어가 존재하지 않은 채 동사+목적어만 가지고 있는 구조이므로 동명사인 'behaving'을 사용하는 것이 적절하다.

(B) 'have severely impaired'는 과거완료 형태이므로 과거의 모든 시간까지 포함한 과거형 'met'를 사용하는 것이 적절하다.

(C) 'frightened'는 '겁먹은'이란 뜻을 가진 형용사이므로 형용사를 수식하는 부사인 'so'를 사용하는 것이 적절하다.

어휘

- be filled with : ~로 가득 차다
- judgement : 판단, 비판, 판결, 심판
- irresponsible : 무책임한
- profit : 이익, 수익, 이윤
- corporate : 기업의, 법인의, 공동의
- executive : 경영 간부
- abuse : 오남용
- impair : 손상시키다
- severely : 심하게, 엄하게, 혹독하게
- frightened : 겁먹은, 무서워하는
- ashamed : 부끄러운

해석

나는 우리의 머릿속에 다른 사람들이 나쁘고, 탐욕스럽고, 무책임하고, 거짓말을 하고, 부정행위를 하고, 환경을 오염시키고, 삶보다 이윤을 더 중시하거나, 혹은 그들이 해서는 안 되는 다른 방식으로 행동한다는 판단과 분석으로 가득 차 있을 때, 그들 중 극소수가 우리의 필요성에 관심을 가질 것이라고 제안하고 싶다. 만약 우리가 환경을 보호하기를 원한다면, 그리고 기업 임원을 찾아가 "당신은 정말 지구의 살인자야, 이런 식으로 땅을 남용할 권리는 없어"라는 태도를 취한다면, 우리는 우리의 요구를 충족시킬 수 있는 기회를 심각하게 손상시켰다. 우리가 그들의 그릇된 모습을 통해 표현하고 있을 때 우리의 욕구에 초점을 맞출 수 있는 것은 드문 인간이다. 물론, 우리는 그러한 판단을 사용하여 사람들을 위협하여 우리의 요구를 충족시키는 데 성공할 수도 있다. 만약 그들이 그럴

게 겁을 먹거나, 죄책감을 느끼거나, 부끄러워서 행동을 바꾼다면, 우리는 사람들에게 무엇이 문제인지 말해줌으로써 "승리"가 가능하다고 믿게 될지도 모른다.

22 ③ 제시문에 따르면 Boris Godunov는 러시아에서 유일하게 왕위를 받을 사람이 자신임을 알고 있었으나 귀족들의 의심과 부러움을 사지 않기 위해 왕관을 여러 번 거절했다고 하였다. 그러므로 무욕적으로 보인 모습 덕분에 다른 사람들이 그가 왕위를 '거부하도록' 강요했다는 내용이 아니라 '받아들이도록' 강요한 것이다. 따라서 ③의 'reject(거부하다)'는 'accept(받아들이다)'로 바꿔야 한다.

어휘

- envy : 부러움, 선망
- deflect : 방향을 바꾸다
- eagerly : 열망하여, 열심히, 간절히
- unambitious : 야망이 없는
- suspicion : 혐의, 느낌, 의심
- refuse : 거절하다
- presidency : 대통령직
- desire : 욕구, 갈망, 바람

해석

어떤 종류의 정치력이든 부러움을 자아내고, 그것이 뿌리내리기 전에 그것을 비껴갈 수 있는 가장 좋은 방법 중 하나는 무욕적으로 보이는 것이다. 끔찍한 Ivan이 죽었을 때, Boris Godunov는 러시아를 이끌 수 있는 유일한 사람이라는 것을 알았다. 그러나 열심히 그 자리를 노리면 보야르들의 부러움과 의심을 불러일으킬 것이기에 그는 왕관을 한 번이 아니라 몇 번 거절했다. 그는 사람들이 그에게 왕좌를 거부하도록(→받아들이도록) 만들었다. George Washington은 같은 전략을 사용하여 큰 효과를 보았다. 첫째는 미군 최고사령관의 직위 유지를 거부한 것이고, 둘째는 대통령직에 저항한 것이다. 두 경우 모두 그를 그 어느 때보다 자신을 유명하게 만들었다. 욕심이 없는 것 같은 사람에게 자기 자신이 부여한 힘을 부러워할 수는 없다.

23 ⑤ 제시문에 따르면 간디는 비폭력적 운동을 함으로써 영국이 식민지에서 일어나는 격렬한 저항에 자신들을 지키기 위한 무력을 동원해야 한다는 정신적 압박을 받게 되는 상황을 이용하였다고 서술하였다. 그러므로 ⑤의 'willingness(기꺼이 하는 마음)'은 'pressure(정신적 압박)'로 바꿔야 한다.

어휘

- essentially : 근본적으로
- liberal : 자유민주적인
- uphold : 유지시키다, 확인하다, 인정하다

- riddle : 수수께끼
- indicate : 나타내다
- colony : 식민지, 집단
- contradiction : 모순
- unarm : ～로부터 무기를 빼앗다, ～의 무장을 해제하다
- violently : 격렬하게, 맹렬히
- overlord : 지배자, 권력자
- rebellion : 반란, 모반
- nonviolence : 비폭력 시위
- absolutely : 전적으로, 틀림없이, 전혀

해석

어떤 성공적인 전략의 열쇠는 자신의 적과 자신을 모두 아는 것이고 런던에서 교육을 받은 간디는 영국인을 잘 이해했다. 그는 그들이 본질적으로 정치적 자유와 문명화된 행동의 전통은 유지하는 것으로 간주하는 자유주의자들이라고 판단했다. 때로는 식민지에서 잔혹한 행동을 보였다는 점에서 알 수 있듯이 모순으로 가득 차 있기는 하지만 이러한 자아상은 영국인들에게 매우 중요한 것이었다. 반면에 인도인들은 수년간 그들의 영국 지배층에 대한 복종에 굴욕감을 느껴왔다. 그들은 대체로 비무장 상태였고 반란이나 게릴라전을 벌일 처지가 아니었다. 만약 그들이 다른 식민지가 그랬던 것처럼 격렬하게 반란을 일으킨다면, 영국인들은 그들을 분쇄하고 자기 방어에서 행동하고 있다고 주장할 것이다; 그들의 문명화된 자아 형상은 피해를 입지 않을 것이다. 반면에, 비폭력 시위의 사용은 간디가 깊이 소중히 여기는 이상과 철학 그리고 인도에서 풍부한 전통을 가진 철학으로, 절대적으로 필요하지 않은 한 무력으로 대응하려는 영국의 의지(→ 정신적 압박)를 완벽하게 이용한 것이다.

24 ① (A) 형이상학은 형이상을 발전시키기 위해 실천하는 학문으로 일련의 절차로 구성되었다고 하였으므로, 'procedures(절차)'가 문맥상 적절하다.
(B) 형이상학과 달리 과학은 역량과 특화된 방법의 영역을 제한하였다고 하였으므로 'restricted(제한했다)'가 문맥상 적절하다.
(C) 물리학은 매우 구체적인 방법으로 물리적 우주의 어떤 특성만을 연구한다고 하였으므로 'specific(구체적인)'이 문맥상 적절하다.

어휘

- metaphysics : 형이상학
- distinction : 차이, 뛰어남, 탁월함
- accurate : 정확한, 정밀한
- consistent : 한결같은, 일관된, 변함없는
- comprehensive : 포괄적인, 종합적인

- evidence : 증기, 흔적
- discipline : 규율, 훈육, 절제력
- astronomy : 천문학
- astral body : 천체
- observation : 관찰, 관측, 감시, 주시
- physics : 물리학
- certain : 확실한
- properties : 성질, 특징

해석

형이상학이란 정확히 무엇인가? 형이상학적 질문과 형이상학적 해답은 무엇인가? 이러한 질문에 답하려면 형이상학과 형이상의 구분이 필요하다. 형이상은 정확하고, 일관되고, 포괄적이며, 건전한 증거에 의해 뒷받침되기를 추구하는 세계관을 말한다. 반면에 형이상학은 형이상을 발전시키려고 할 때 실천하는 학문으로서, 일련의 절차로 구성된다. 형이상학은 자연과학과 다르다. 과학은 형이상학처럼 관점을 발전시키려고 하는 학문이다. 그것은 정확하고, 일관되며, 건실한 증거에 의해 뒷받침되지만, 형이상학과는 달리 포괄적이 되려고 하지 않는다. 과학은 역량과 특화된 방법의 영역을 제한했다. 천문학은 오직 천체만을 다루고 그 방법은 관찰과 수학적 계산을 포함하며 물리학은 매우 구체적인 방법으로 물리적 우주의 어떤 특성만을 연구한다.

25 ② (A) 문맥상 인터뷰의 피실험자들은 실험자들의 침묵을 두려워하므로 'silence(침묵)'가 적절하다.
(B) 허위로 대답하는 사람들이 침묵에 직면했을 때, 질문자는 그들이 무언가 더 알고 있다고 잘못 생각하게 된다는 것이므로 문맥상 'untruthfully(허위로)'가 적절하다.
(C) 만약 은폐된 진실을 알아내지 못한다면, 적어도 당신이 새로운 정보 영역을 밝히도록 만들어야 한다는 것이므로 문맥상 'uncover(알아내다)'가 적절하다.

어휘

- interrogators : 질문자, 심문자
- corporate : 기업의, 공동의
- advantage : 이점, 장점
- attorney : 변호사, 대리인
- adequate : 충분한
- assume : 추정하다, 맡다
- blurt : 불쑥 내뱉다
- witness : 목격자, 증인
- concealed : 감추다, 숨기다

해석

경찰 심문관, 기업 인사 면접관, 기자, 변호사 모두 그들이 질문하는 사람들에 대한 기본적인 사실을 알고 있다. 인터뷰 피

실험자들은 침묵을 두려워한다. 그것을 피하기 위해 그들은 심지어 생각 없이 말할 것이다. 그렇기 때문에 질문을 던질 수 있는 변호사가 완벽하게 적절한 답변의 마지막에 "그것만 말할 수는 없어. 농담이야!"라고 말하려는 것처럼 조용히 당신을 응시하는 것이다. 사실, 거짓으로 대답하는 대부분의 사람들이 그런 침묵에 직면했을 때, 그들은 질문자가 무언가를 더 알고 있다고 잘못 생각하고 진실을 말할 것이다. 목격자인 당신으로부터 더 많은 정보를 얻는 것은 깔끔한 속임수다. 은폐된 진실을 밝혀내지 못한다면, 적어도 당신이 새로운 정보 영역을 밝히도록 만드는 것이다. 이제 알았으니 들키지 마라. 인생의 많은 부분에서 말하는 것은 성공이고 침묵은 실패다. 증인석에 서면, 당신의 답변이 끝난 후에도 침묵을 유지할 수 있는 감각을 갖는 것은 성공이고, 너무 많은 말을 하는 것은 실패다.

26
① 제시문에서 대중 매체가 개인과 집단의 위신을 높이고 권위를 높이는 방법으로는 한 사람이나 집단의 증언을 통해 그 신분을 증명하는 것이라고 서술하고 있다. 그러므로 빈칸에는 ①의 'legitimizing their status(그들의 지위를 정당화)'가 들어갈 말로 가장 적절하다.

[오답풀이]
② 결함을 위장하는 것
③ 그들의 개성을 재현하다
④ 신분상 숨겨진 사실 공개
⑤ 그들의 위상과 대중들의 위상 비교

[어휘]
• bestow : (존경의 뜻으로) 수여하다
• prestige : 위신, 명망
• authority : 지휘권, 권한
• legitimize : 정당화하다, 합법화하다
• newsreels : 뉴스 영화
• testify : 증언하다, 증명하다
• anonymous : 익명인
• vividly : 생생하게, 선명하게, 발랄하게
• prominent : 중요한, 유명한
• testimonial : 추천서, 추천사

[해석]
대중 매체는 그들의 지위를 정당화함으로써 개인과 집단의 위신을 높이고 권위를 높인다. 언론이나 라디오나 잡지나 영화 뉴스에 의한 인식은 한 사람이 도착했다는 것을 증명하고, 한 사람이 거대하고, 익명의 대중들 중에서 뽑혔을 정도로 중요하며, 한 사람의 행동과 의견은 공고를 요할 만큼 충분히 유의하다는 것을 증명한다. 이 상태 확인 기능의 작동은 "유명인"에 의한 상품에 대한 추천서의 광고 패턴에서 가장 생생하게

목격할 수 있다. 인구의 광범위한 영역에서, 그러한 추천서는 제품의 위신을 높일 뿐만 아니라 추천서를 제공하는 사람에게도 위신을 반영한다. 그들은 크고 강력한 상업세계는 그의 의견이 많은 사람들에게 반영될 수 있을 만큼 충분히 높은 지위를 소유하고 있다고 간주하고 있다는 것을 대중에게 알려준다. 한 마디로 그의 증언은 자신의 신분을 증명하는 것이다.

27
① 제시문에 따르면 주어진 시간 안에 마음속에 무엇이 있는지 아는 것은 몇 초 후에 무엇이 있을지 예측하지 못한다고 하였다. 그러므로 빈칸에는 ①의 'random shift(무작위적인 변화)'가 들어갈 말로 가장 적절하다.

[오답풀이]
② 엄격한 경직성
③ 질서정연한 반복
④ 신뢰할 수 있는 일관성
⑤ 일정한 불가역성

[어휘]
• ordinary : 보통의, 일상적인
• constitute : ~을 구성하다, 설립하다
• consciousness : 의식, 자각
• range : 다양성
• stimulus : 자극
• unpredictable : 예측할 수 없는
• revert : 되돌아가다, 복귀하다
• demand : 요구

[해석]
평범하고 정상적인 상태에서 의식을 구성하는 정보처리 시스템은 어떤 특정한 범위의 자극에 초점을 맞추지 않는다. 레이더 접시처럼 주의력은 특별한 순서나 패턴 없이 차례로 움직임, 색깔, 모양, 물체, 감각, 기억을 주목하면서 자극장을 왔다 갔다 한다. 이것은 우리가 거리를 걸을 때, 침대에 누워 있을 때, 우리가 창문 밖을 짧게 응시할 때, 순서에 따라 주의가 집중되지 않을 때마다 일어나는 일이다. 하나의 생각은 운율이나 이성 없이 다른 생각을 따르고, 보통 우리는 감각적인 사슬에서 다른 생각과 연결시킬 수 없다. 새로운 생각이 나타나자마자, 그것은 전에 있던 것을 밀어낸다. 어떤 주어진 시간에 마음속에 무엇이 있는지 아는 것은 몇 초 후에 무엇이 있을지 예측하지 못한다. 이러한 의식의 무작위적인 변화는 예측할 수 없는 정보를 생산하지만, 의식은 개연성 있는 상태다. 그것에 대한 요구가 없자마자 의식이 되돌아가는 상태이므로 개연성이 있다.

28
⑤ 제시문에 따르면 많은 사회심리학자들이 사회적 변수가 자신들의 연구 상황에 반영될 수 없다는 견해를 취

하며 이 변수가 사실이라 하더라도 이를 찾을 준비가 되어있지 않다고 하였다. 그러므로 빈칸에는 ⑤의 'detect the reflections of sociocultural variables in their miniature experiments(작은 실험에서 사회문화적 변수의 반사를 감지함)'이 들어갈 말로 가장 적절하다.

[오답풀이]
① 사회과학이 다른 분야로 통합되어야 하는 이유를 묻는다.
② 그들의 근본적인 직업관계에서 중요한 변화를 경험한다.
③ 신기술의 이익과 수반되는 위험의 균형을 맞춰야 한다.
④ 실험의 연구 활용에 관한 지식이 풍부하다.

[어휘]
• prone : 하기 쉬운
• variable : 변동이 심한
• inevitably : 예상대로, 아니나 다를까
• even if : ~에도 불구하고
• researcher : 연구원, 조사자
• justify : 정당화시키다, 옹호하다
• sociocultural : 사회문화적인
• declaration : 선언, 공표, 맹세, 신고서
• stuff : 물건, 물질, 재료
• literally : 문자 그대로, 그야말로, 정말로
• relation : 관계
• omit : 빠뜨리다, 누락시키다, 생략하다
• variable : 변동이 심한, 가변적인
• experimentation : 실험
• genuinely : 진정으로, 성실하게, 순수하게
• disciplines : 학문

[해석]
많은 사회심리학자들은 여전히 연구에 중요한 사회적 변수가 연구 상황에 반영될 수밖에 없다는 견해를 취하는 경향이 있다. 비록 이것이 전적으로 사실이었다 하더라도, 이러한 견해를 가진 연구자들이 그들의 작은 실험에서 사회문화적 변수의 반사를 탐지할 것이라는 것은 사실이 아니다. 왜냐하면 그들은 그것들을 찾을 준비가 되어 있지 않기 때문이다. 그들은 모든 사회과학의 기본인 개인의 상호작용을 연구하고 있다는 약속으로 그러한 변수를 연구하는 다른 사회과학에 대한 관심이 부족함을 정당화한다. 이러한 견해는 말 그대로 실생활에서 리더십과 무관한 '리더십'에 대한 수많은 연구, 권력을 정치학의 중심 문제로 만드는 주요 변수 대부분을 생략한 권력 관계의 대 심리학적 모델, 그리고 그 중 약 85%에 달하는 '소그룹 연구'라는 실험이 쇄도하는 결과를 가져왔다. 적어도 실생활에서 그룹 과정에 관심이 있는 사람이라면 도서관 책꽂이에 먼지를 모으게 될 것이다.

---

29 ⑤ 제시문에 따르면 피타고라스가 발견한 것은 간격들이 정확하고 단순한 수학적 비율이었기 때문에 조화롭다고 설명하고 있다. 그러므로 빈칸에는 ⑤의 'the relationships between numbers: the ratios and proportions(숫자 간의 관계: 비와 비율)'이 들어갈 말로 가장 적절하다.

[오답풀이]
① 수학의 아름다움 : 이론규칙 실천
② 수가 형식의 지배자라는 이론
③ 음악주조의 연역적 추리의 원리
④ 자연계에서의 조화 관계의 인위성

[어휘]
• reinforce : 강화하다, 보강하다, 증강하다
• stumble : 발을 헛디디다, 비틀거리다
• blacksmith : 대장장이
• octave : 옥타브
• interval : 간격
• abstract : 추상적인, 관념적인
• geometry : 기하학

[해석]
피타고라스의 가장 중요한 발견은 숫자 사이의 관계였던 비와 비율이었다. 이것은 음악에 대한 그의 조사, 특히 함께 유쾌하게 들리는 음들 사이의 관계에 의해 강화되었다. 그가 일터의 대장장이들의 말을 들을 때 이런 생각을 처음 접했다는 후문이 있다. 한 개는 다른 한 개보다 절반 크기인 앤빌을 가지고 있었고, 그들이 망치로 때렸을 때 내는 소리는 정확히 옥타브(8음)가 떨어져 있었다. 이것이 사실일지 모르지만, 피타고라스가 자음 간격의 비(함께 치면 조화롭게 들릴지 여부를 결정하는 두 음 사이의 음의 수)를 결정한 것은 아마도 뽑은 끈으로 실험을 함으로써 그랬을 것이다. 그가 발견한 것은 이들 간격은 서로 간의 관계가 정밀하고 단순한 수학적 비였기 때문에 조화롭다는 것이다. 지금 우리가 조화 시리즈로 알고 있는 이 시리즈는 그가 추상 기하학에서 발견한 수학의 우아함이 자연계에도 존재한다는 것을 그에게 확인시켜 주었다.

---

30 ② 제시문에 의하면 사회사업과 같은 직업에 종사하는 많은 근로자들은 자신들과 고객을 구별할 수 있는 옷을 입는 것을 경계하고 과시하는 것을 피하는 경향이 있으며 고객들과 동등한 수준의 옷을 입으려고 할 것이라고 하였다. 그러므로 빈칸에는 ②의 'mark them out as establishment or authority figures(기득권 또는 권위자의 표시)'가 들어갈 말로 가장 적절하다.

[오답풀이]
① 고객에 대한 긍정적 태도

③ 그들의 진짜 정체를 숨기고 평범하게 보이게 하다.

④ 권력과 권위를 나타내는 그들의 역할을 위태롭게 하다.

⑤ 친근함과 친절함이 있는 사람으로서 그들을 드러내다.

어휘

- adapt : 맞추다, 적용하다, 개작하다
- tend to : ~하는 경향이 있다
- reflect : 비추다, 반사하다
- consequently : 그 결과, 따라서
- attempt to : 시도하다
- civilian : 민간인

해석

패션, 의복, 그리고 "힘"의 관계의 예로는 1960년대 후반과 1970년대 초반의 젊은층을 들 수 있다. 이 사람들은 다른 사회 집단들 사이의 새로운 역할을 반영하기 위해 그들의 패션과 옷을 개조했다. 따라서 인종과 성별이 다른 권력관계의 변화를 패션과 의복의 관점에서 표현하거나 반영했다. 사회사업과 같은 직업에 종사하는 많은 근로자들은 자신들과 고객을 구별할 수 있는 옷을 입는 것을 경계하고 있으며, 과시하는 것을 피하는 경향이 있다. 결과적으로 그들을 <u>기득권 또는 권위 있는 인물로 표시하는 패션과 의복은 피할 것</u>이고 고객들과 동등한 수준의 옷을 입으려고 할 것이다. 물론 이렇게 함으로써, 그들은 "샌들과 오트밀 색깔의 손뜨개" 고정관념에 빠질 위험이 있다. 1970년대와 1980년대에, 다양한 미국 경찰대는 더 친근하고 접근하기 쉬운 것처럼 보이기 위해 그들의 유니폼을 버리고 민간 복장을 채택했다.

31 ③ 주어진 글 다음에는 개체수가 모두를 만족할 수 없을 만큼 늘어난 생물체들은 한정된 자원을 놓고 전쟁을 벌인다는 글 (B)가 와야 하고 글 (B) 다음에는 서로 다른 종류가 공존할 경우 다른 방식의 삶을 살기 때문에 서로 방해받지 않는다고 설명한 (C)가 와야 한다. 마지막으로는 의사와 구두닦이를 예로 들면서 서로 다른 종이 공존하는 경우를 설명하는 (A)가 와야 한다. 그러므로 주어진 글 다음에 (B) − (C) − (A)의 순서로 이어져야 한다.

어휘

- justly : 정확하게, 바르게, 공정하게, 당연하게도
- struggle : 투쟁하다, 싸우다, 몸부림치다
- organism : 생물체, 유기체
- analogous : 유사한
- side by side : 나란히, 함께
- appetite : 식욕, 욕구
- coexist : 동시에 있다, 공존하다
- disturb : 방해하다, 건드리다, 불안하게 만들다
- occupation : 직업, 심심풀이, 점령 기간

- coexist : 공존하다, 동시에 있다
- obliged : 고마운
- mutually : 서로, 상호간에, 공통으로
- psychiatrist : 정신과 의사

해석

다윈은 두 생물체 사이의 투쟁이 유사성만큼이나 활발하다는 것을 정확하게 관찰했다. 같은 욕구를 갖고 같은 대상을 추구하는 그들은 곳곳에서 라이벌 관계에 있다.

(B) 필요한 것보다 많은 자원을 갖고 있는 한 나란히 살 수 있지만, 그 수가 모든 식욕을 채울 수 없을 정도로 늘어나면 전쟁이 일어난다. 공존하는 각각이 다른 종이나 품종이라면 사뭇 다르다.

(C) 같은 방식으로 먹이를 찾지 않고, 같은 종류의 생활을 하지 않기 때문에 서로 방해하지 않는다. 사람은 같은 법에 복종한다. 같은 도시에서 서로 다른 직업들은 서로 다른 대상을 추구하기 때문에 서로를 파괴할 필요가 없이 공존할 수 있다.

(A) 치과의사는 정신과 의사나 모자 쓰는 구두장이와 몸싸움을 하지 않는다. 서로 다른 서비스를 수행하기 때문에 병행할 수 있다.

32 ① 주어진 글 다음에는 이어지는 실험 과정으로 케이크와 과일 중 피실험자들이 무엇을 선택할 것인지에 대한 내용인 글 (A)가 와야 한다. 글 (A) 다음에는 실험결과로 두 자리 숫자를 기억했던 사람들은 과일을, 일곱 자리 숫자를 기억했던 사람들은 케이크를 선택했다는 내용인 글 (B)가 와야 한다. 마지막으로는 실험이 알려주는 결론으로 무의식적 선택을 막기 위해서는 의식적인 행동이 필요하다는 내용인 글 (B)가 와야 한다. 그러므로 주어진 글 다음에 (A) − (C) − (B)의 순서로 이어져야 한다.

어휘

- digit : (0에서 9까지의) 숫자
- await : 기다리다
- prevent : 막다, 예방하다
- impulsive : 충동적인
- conscious : 의식적인, 자각하는
- bandwidth : 대역폭

해석

한 실험에서 피실험자들에게 기억 과제를 주었다. 어떤 이들은 두 자리 숫자를 기억하도록 요청받았고, 어떤 이들은 일곱 자리 숫자를 기억했다.

(A) 그 후 실험 대상자들은 로비로 안내되어 추가 시험을 기다리고 있었다. 대기 장소의 그들 앞에는 케이크와 과일 조각들이 놓여 있었다. 실제 시험은 그들이 머릿속에서 그 숫자들을 외우면서 기다리는 동안 무엇을 선택할 것인가 하는 것이었다.

(C) 두 자리 숫자에 의해 마음이 몹시 바쁘지 않은 사람들은 대부분 과일을 선택했다. 일곱 자리 숫자를 외우느라 정신이 없던 사람들은 케이크를 50% 더 자주 선택했다. 케이크는 충동적인 선택이다.

(B) 무의식적 선택을 막기 위해서는 의식적인 행동이 필요하다. 우리의 정신적 대역폭이 리허설 같은 다른 것에 사용될 때, 우리는 우리 자신이 케이크를 먹는 것을 막을 능력이 줄어든다.

33 ⑤ 제시문에서는 우리의 삶에 힘을 주고 창의적인 성장을 가져올 정신적 훈련으로 자주 수행하는 일상적인 활동 목록을 작성할 때 지루하고 스트레스 받는 일들도 포함하면 그렇게 우리가 즐기는 것은 행동으로 흘러드는 의식의 내적인 차원이라고 설명하고 있으므로, 정신적 훈련을 통해 얻게 되는 효과를 설명한 ⑤에 위치하는 것이 가장 적절하다.

어휘
• awareness : 의식
• empowerment : 권한
• tedious : 지루한, 싫증나는
• irritating : 화나는, 신경질 나는, 자극하는
• groceries : 식료품류
• engaged : (~하느라) 바쁜, ~하고 있는
• alertness : 빈틈없음, 조심성 없음
• outward : 표면상의, 겉보기의, 외형의
• dimension : 크기, 치수, 규모, 관점

해석
여러분은 곧 여러분이 스트레스를 받거나, 지루하거나, 짜증나는 대신에, 그러한 높은 인식 상태에서 하는 일이 실제로 즐거워지고 있다는 것을 알게 될 것이다.

여기 여러분의 삶에 힘을 주고 창의적인 성장을 가져올 정신적 훈련이 있다. 자주 수행하는 일상적인 활동 목록을 만들어라. (①) 재미없고, 지루하고, 싫증나고, 짜증나거나, 스트레스를 받는다고 생각할 수 있는 활동을 포함하라. (②) 이 목록에는 출퇴근 여정, 식료품 구입, 세탁 또는 일상 업무에서 지루하거나 스트레스를 받는 모든 것이 포함될 수 있다. (③) 그리고 나서, 여러분이 그러한 활동에 참여할 때마다, 그것들을 경계하는 수단이 되게 하라. (④) 여러분이 하는 일에 전적으로 참여하여 활동 배경에서 여러분 안에 있는 경고, 살아있는 고요를 감지하라. (⑤) 좀 더 정확히 말하면, 당신이 즐기고 있는 것은 정말로 겉으로 보이는 행동이 아니라 행동으로 흘러 들어가는 의식의 내적인 차원이다.

34 ⑤ 제시문은 르네상스 시기 중세 유럽의 인문주의가 끼친 영향에 대한 글이다. 르네상스 시기 인문주의자들의 노력과 유산으로 서양 지성사는 놀라운 순간이 찾아왔지만, 이것이 철학과 과학사학자들에 의해 항상 인정받았던 것은 아니며, 자연철학에 대한 휴머니즘의 영향에 대한 경우에는 여전히 전문가들의 연구가 필요하다는 내용이 되어야 하므로 ⑤에 위치하는 것이 가장 적절하다.

어휘
• spread : 펼치다
• scholarship : 학문
• intense : 극심한, 강렬한, 치열한, 진지한
• heritage : 유산
• deciphering : 판독하다

해석
그러나 이러한 인문주의자들의 노력과 유산은 철학과 과학사학자들에 의해 항상 그들 자신의 권리로 인정받았던 것은 아니다.

르네상스는 서구 문명에 있어서 가장 혁신적인 시기 중 하나이다. 이탈리아에서 미술과 문학의 새로운 표현의 물결이 피어나고 점차 유럽 전역으로 퍼져나갔다. (①) 역사학자들의 '인문주의'라고 불리는 언어학적으로 강조된 새로운 접근법도 학문에 도입되었다. (②) 르네상스의 지적 풍요는 고대 문학 유산을 수집, 편집, 번역, 출판하는 데 종사하는 인문주의자들의 강렬한 활동에 의해 보장되었는데, 주로 중세에는 거의 읽히지 않았거나 전혀 알려지지 않았던 그리스어와 라틴어로 이루어졌다. (③) 인문주의자들은 이러한 '새롭게 복구된' 원문을 해독하고 해석하는 데만 적극적일 뿐 아니라 고대 자료에서 발견한 사상과 주제에서 영감을 받은 원작을 제작하는 데에도 적극적이었다. (④) 이러한 활동을 통해 르네상스 휴머니스트 문화는 서양 지성사에 놀라운 순간을 가져왔다. (⑤) 특히 자연철학의 진화에 대한 휴머니즘의 영향은 여전히 전문가들의 철저한 연구를 기다리고 있다.

35 ③ 제시문은 고용의 변화가 이익을 가져올 수도 있지만 새로운 직책과 환경, 동료들 사이에 효율적이지 않기 때문에 직장을 바꾸려면 현재 직책의 가능성을 모두 소진해야 한다고 설명하고 있다. 그러므로 직장을 떠나는 것을 미루지 말라는 내용의 ③은 전체적인 글의 흐름과 어울리지 않는다.

어휘

• inherent : 내재하는
• greener : 무경험자
• pasture : 초원, 목초지
• confidence : 신뢰, 자신감, 확신
• deprive : 빼앗다, 허용치 않다, 박탈하다
• goodwill : 친선, 호의

해석

멀리 있는 목초지가 더 푸르다고 믿는 것을 추구하는 것은 인간의 본성이다. ① 누군가 더 좋은 직책과 더 많은 보수를 찾기 시작할 때, 그는 보통 다른 고용주와 함께 먼 곳에서 기회를 찾는다. ② 때로는 이것이 필요할 수도 있지만, 고용의 변화는 그들이 이익을 가져오면서도 항상 약간의 불이익을 가져다 주는데, 그중에서도 가장 두드러진 것은, 새로운 직책, 새로운 환경, 그리고 새로운 동료들 사이에서 결고 효율적이지 않다는 사실인데, 그는 자신의 작품의 세부사항에 익숙하고 동료들의 자신감을 가지고 있기 때문이다. ③ 물론 대부분의 사람들이 현 직장을 기꺼이 떠날 수는 없지만 너무 오래 미루는 것은 자신과 타인에게 피해를 줄 수 있다. ④ 게다가, 지위의 변화는 고용주와의 오랜 관계를 통해 개인이 주변에 쌓아올린 호의적 가치를 많이 박탈한다. ⑤ 따라서 고용주를 바꾸기로 결정하기 전에, 현재의 직책의 가능성을 모두 소진했는지 확인하라.

36 ③ 제시문은 이전의 병리학을 지지했던 사람들을 가난하고 나쁜 사람들로만 묘사하는 건 부정확하며 이 사람들이 다양한 진단과 측정 접근법을 개발하고 특정 문제에 대한 효과적인 치료법을 검증한 사실도 알아야 한다고 설명하고 있다. 그러나 ③은 이전의 병리학적 접근법을 옹호하는 자들이 인간에 대한 근시안적인 편견을 가졌다는 부정적인 서술을 하고 있으므로 전체적인 글의 흐름과 어울리지 않는다.

어휘

• validate : 입증하다, 승인하다
• tempting : 솔깃한
• inaccurate : 부정확한, 오류가 있는
• proponent : 지지자
• practitioner : 전문직 종사자
• depiction : 묘사, 서술
• measurement : 측정, 측량
• schizophrenia : 조현병
• depression : 우울증
• alcoholism : 알코올 중독
• injury : 부상, 상처

해석

자신의 행동에서 좋은 점만 보고 다른 사람의 행동에서 나쁜 점만 보는 것은 일반적인 인간의 약점이며, 인간 경험의 긍정적이거나 부정적인 면만 검증하는 것은 생산적이지 않다. 세상의 좋은 것(또는 나쁜 것)에만 집중하는 것은 매우 유혹적이지만, 그것은 좋은 과학이 아니며, 긍정적인 심리를 진전시키는 데 이런 실수를 범해서는 안 된다. ① 비록 우리가 이전의 병리학 모델의 원칙에는 동의하지 않지만, 그들의 지지자들을 가난한 학자, 가난한 과학자, 가난한 실천가, 혹은 나쁜 사람들로 묘사하는 것은 부정확할 것이다. ② 대신 이 이전의 패러다임은 자기 시대의 특정한 상황에 대응하고 있는 선의의, 밝은 사람들에 의해 진전되었다. ③ 그럼에도 불구하고 이전의 병리학적 접근법을 옹호하는 사람들은 인간에 대한 묘사에 있어서 근시안적이고 편견을 가지고 있었다. ④ 마찬가지로, 이 사람들이 사람들을 묘사하는 데 있어서 잘못된 것 같지는 않다. ⑤ 그들은 정신분열증, 우울증, 알코올 중독에 대한 진단과 측정 접근법을 개발했고 공황장애와 혈액 및 부상 공포증 같은 특정 문제에 대한 많은 효과적인 치료법을 검증했다.

37 ② 제시문에서는 우리가 짧은 시간 동안 두려워하는 것을 피할 때 두려움은 줄어들지만 더 긴 기간 동안 불안을 키워주므로 불안을 유발하는 상황에 자신을 노출시킴으로써 불안을 줄여야 한다고 하고 있다. 그러므로 (A)에는 'overcome(극복하다)', (B)에는 'experience(경험)'이 들어가야 적절하다.

오답풀이

	(A)		(B)
①	극복하다	…	거부하다
③	잊다	…	경험하다
④	피하다	…	무시하다
⑤	피하다	…	거부하다

어휘

• paradox : 역설
• counterintuitive : 직관에 어긋나는
• anxiety : 불안, 염려, 걱정거리
• exposure : 노출, 폭로
• diminish : 줄어들다, 약해지다, 폄하하다

해석

역설은 두려운 것을 피할 때 일어난다. 왜냐하면 두려움은 그 후에 커지기 때문이다. 이것은 직관에 반하는 것인데, 왜냐하면 여러분이 짧은 시간 동안 여러분이 두려워하는 것을 피할 때, 여러분의 두려움은 줄어들기 때문이다. 그러나 더 긴 기간 동안, 회피는 불안이 번성하게 한다. 예를 들어, 낯선 사람과 대화하는 것을 두려워하기 때문에 저녁 파티에 가는 것이 걱

정된다고 하자. 짧은 시간 동안, 저녁 시간을 피하는 것은 걱정을 덜게 해 준다. 그러나 다음 회식 파티 초대를 피하고, 그 다음, 그 다음, 그 다음은 문제를 일으킨다. 당신이 그런 저녁 파티를 피했기 때문에, 당신은 처음보다 낯선 사람들과 대화하는 것에 대한 걱정을 더 심하게 했다. 비록 그것이 기분을 좋게 하는 것처럼 보이지만 회피에 맞서려고 노력해야 한다. 나는 이것을 역설이라고 부른다. 역설에 도전하는 것은 회피하는 것을 없애고 그것을 노출로 대체하는 것을 포함한다. 노출은 당신을 불안하게 만드는 것을 마주하는 것을 의미한다. 불안감을 주는 상황에 자신을 노출시킴으로써, 당신은 그것에 익숙해지게 되고, 당신의 불안감은 결국 줄어들 것이다.

↓

불안감을 느끼게 하는 상황을 (A) 극복할 수 있는 좋은 방법은 이런 상황을 언제든 주저 없이 (B) 경험하는 것이다.

[38~39]

어휘

- bored : 지루해하는
- niche : 아주 편한 자리, 틈새시장
- tendency : 성향, 기질, 경향, 동향, 추세
- ahead of : (공간, 시간상으로) ~앞에, 보다 빨리
- fundraising : 모금
- cherish : 소중히 여기다, 아끼다
- exploratory : 탐사의, 탐구의
- worthwhile : 가치 있는

해석

사건 가능성을 고려할 때, 창의적으로 생각하도록 노력하라. 사람들은 특별하고 특이한 사건에 끌린다. 만약 당신이 몇 년 동안 행사를 제공했다면, 사람들은 같은 방식으로 같은 프로그램을 반복하는 것에 싫증을 낼 수 있다는 것을 알아두어라. 자원봉사자들은 퀴퀴해지고, 관객들은 신선한 것을 제공하지 않으면 지루해진다. 자선 시장에서 독특하고 독창적인 이벤트를 개발하는 것은 다음을 (a) 유치하는 데 도움이 될 수 있다. 창의적인 생각이 필요한 또 다른 이유는 경쟁이다. 장기적으로 볼 때, 당신이 당신의 행사를 위해 어떤 틈새나 특별한 이점을 만들든 간에, 다른 사람들이 당신의 아이디어를 모방하기 때문에, (b) 감소하는 경향이 있다. 당신은 잠시 동안 독특함의 이점을 누릴 수 있지만, 이것이 (c) 일시적일 것으로 예상한다. 프로그램에 혁신을 추가하거나 다양한 상상력을 갖춘 이벤트를 통해 경쟁에서 앞서 나가라.
창의적으로 생각하려면 먼저 다른 생각을 탐구하는 태도를 길러야 한다. 고정된 것이 없고 어떤 모금 행사도 바뀔 수 있다

고 가정해보자. 이전 이벤트가 성공적이었더라도 상황이 바뀌었거나 이벤트를 지속할 수 있는 더 좋고 다른 방법이 있을 수 있다. 친숙한 형식을 (d) 받아들일(→ 거부할) 수 있어야 한다. 필요하다면 소중한 전통이나 프로그램에 기꺼이 빠져들어야 한다. 이러한 아이디어에 대한 개방성은 위험을 감수하는 것을 포함한다. 단지 다르다는 것을 위해서 독특한 것을 추구하는 것이 아니라는 것을 기억하라. 이 (e) 탐구 과정에서 가장 중요한 것은 가치 있는 아이디어를 찾으려는 의지다.

38 ⑤ 제시문에서 사람들은 특별하고 특이한 일에 끌리며 다른 아이디어를 모방할 경우 일시적인 이점만을 누릴 수 있으므로 행사를 기획할 때는 창조적인 아이디어가 필요하다고 하였다. 그러므로 ⑤의 "the necessity of generating creative ideas for an event(행사를 위한 창의적인 아이디어 창출의 필요성)"이 윗글의 주제로 가장 적절하다.

오답풀이
① 창의적 사고에서 경험의 역할
② 모금행사 참여 혜택
③ 과당경쟁이 시장에 미치는 영향
④ 제품을 소비자에게 매력적으로 만드는 방법

39 ④ 창의적인 생각을 창출하려면 이미 다른 사람들에게 친숙한 형식을 '받아들인다'가 아니고 '거부한다'고 해야 문맥상 적절하다. 그러므로 'accepting'을 'refusing'으로 고쳐 써야 옳다.

오답풀이
① (a) 유치하다
② (b) 감소하다
③ (c) 일시적인
⑤ (e) 탐구의

[40~41]

어휘

- emotion : 감정, 정서
- infect : 감염시키다, 오염시키다
- hazy : 흐릿한
- desire : 욕구, 갈망, 바람
- abstract : 추상적인
- contemplate : 고려하다, 생각하다
- prophecy : 예언
- aide : 보좌관
- prediction : 예측, 예견
- uncannily : 이상하게

• aftermath : (전쟁, 사고 등의) 여파
• achievement : 업적, 성취, 달성

해석

우리는 보통 우리가 도달하려고 하는 목표가 있다는 어떤 종류의 계획에 의해 작동한다고 상상하곤 한다. 하지만 우리는 보통 스스로를 (A) 속이고 있다. 우리가 가진 것은 목표가 아니라 소망이다. 우리의 감정은 우리를 흐릿한 욕망에 감염시킨다. 우리는 명성, 성공, 보안, 크고 추상적인 것을 원한다. 이 위험성은 처음부터 우리의 계획을 통일시키고 그들을 혼란스러운 길로 가게 한다. 모든 역사의 위대한 전략가들과 여러분을 구별할 수 있는 것은 구체적이고 상세하며 집중적인 목표들이다. 매일매일 그들을 생각하고, 그들에게 도달하는 것이 어떤 기분일지, 그리고 그들에게 도달하는 것이 어떤 모습일지 상상해 보라. 인간 특유의 심리학적 법칙에 의해, 이런 식으로 명확하게 시각화하면 자기희생적 예언으로 변하게 될 것이다.

명확한 목표를 갖는 것은 나폴레옹에게 결정적이었다. 그는 자신의 목표를 강렬한 세부사항으로 시각화했다. 군사 작전이 시작될 때, 그는 그의 마음속에서 그것의 마지막 전투를 분명히 볼 수 있었다. 측근들과 함께 지도를 살펴보면서, 그는 그것이 (B) 어처구니없는 예측을 끝낼 정확한 지점을 가리킬 것이다. 왜냐하면 어떤 시기에서든 전쟁이 당신을 놀라게 할 수 있을 뿐만 아니라, 나폴레옹 시대의 지도는 믿을 수 없을 정도로 불안정했기 때문이다. 그러나 그의 예측은 몇 번이고 엉뚱하게 옳다는 것이 증명될 것이다. 그는 또한 조약의 서명, 조약의 조건, 패배한 러시아 황제나 오스트리아 황제가 어떻게 행동을 보일지, 그리고 이 특별한 목표의 달성이 나폴레옹을 다음 군사 작전으로 어떻게 배치할 것인지 이 군사 작전의 여파를 시각화할 것이다.

40 ② 제시문은 우리가 도달하고자 하는 목표는 소망이며 그 소망을 이루기 위해선 나폴레옹의 예를 들어 자신의 목표를 세부적으로 구성해야 한다고 서술하고 있다. 그러므로 ②의 "Focus on Your Goals and Envision Them Clearly(목표에 집중하여 명확하게 구상하라)"가 윗글의 제목으로 가장 적절하다.

오답풀이

① 성공을 위한 첫걸음 : 소망을 가져라
③ 꿈과 시각화가 모두 실현되는 것은 아니다
④ 감정이 목표에 지장을 초래하지 않도록 하라
⑤ 위대한 전략가가 되는 길 : 자신을 알아라

41 ① (A) 문맥상 보통 우리가 도달하고자 하는 것을 위해 가지는 것이 목표라고 알고 있지만 우리가 가진 것은 소망

이기 때문에 우리 스스로를 속이고 있다는 의미이므로 'fooling(속이는)'이 들어갈 말로 적절하다.

(B) 나폴레옹이 측근들과 지도를 살펴볼 때 당시의 지도는 매우 불안정했으므로 자신의 목표를 통해 터무니없는 결과가 나올 예측을 미리 이끌었다는 의미이다. 그러므로 빈칸 (B)에는 'ridiculous(터무니없는)'가 들어갈 말로 적절하다.

오답풀이

	(A)		(B)
②	속이는	…	합리적인
③	비판하는	…	터무니없는
④	과소평가하는	…	합리적인
⑤	과소평가하는	…	그럴듯한

[42~43]

어휘

• constant : 끊임없는, 거듭되는
• relatively : 비교적
• commission : 수수료
• superficially : 표면적으로
• composition : 구성 요소, 작품
• portrayed : (그림, 글로) 그리다, (정확하지 못하게) 나타내다, (특정 역할을) 연기하다
• foreground : 전경, 중요한 위치
• dazzle : 눈이 부시게 하다
• distressed : 괴로워하는
• render : 만들다, 제시하다
• elimination : 제거, 삭제, 배제
• visible : 눈에 보이는, 알아볼 수 있는

해석

레오나르도 다빈치 시대의 예술가들에게 가장 큰 문제는 점점 더 많은 작품을 생산해야 한다는 끊임없는 압박이었다. 그들은 수수료가 계속 나오고 대중의 관심을 끌기 위해 비교적 높은 비율로 생산해야 했다. 이것은 그들의 작품의 질에 영향을 미쳤다. 예술가들이 그들의 그림에서 (a) 피상적으로 시청자들을 흥분시킬 수 있는 효과를 빠르게 만들어낼 수 있는 스타일이 발전했다. 그러한 효과를 만들어내기 위해 그들은 밝은 색, 특이한 병렬과 구성, 그리고 극적인 장면에 의존했다. 그 과정에서 그들은 필연적으로 (b) 배경과 심지어 그들이 그려낸 인물들의 세세한 부분까지 얼버무렸다. 그들은 꽃이나 나무나 전경에 있는 인물들의 손에는 별로 신경을 쓰지 않았다. 그들은 표면에서 눈부시게 빛나야 했다. 레오나르도는 이 사실을 경력 초기에 인지했고 그것이 그를 (c) 괴롭혔다. 그것은 두 가

지 면에서 그의 기질에 어긋났다-그는 무슨 일이든 서둘러야 한다는 느낌을 싫어했고, 그 스스로를 위해 세부적인 것에 몰두하는 것을 좋아했다. 그는 표면적인 효과를 만들어내는 것에 관심이 없었다. 그는 내면에서 생명체를 이해하고, 생명체를 역동적으로 만드는 힘을 파악하여, 어떻게 해서든지 이 모든 것을 평평한 표면에 표현하고자 하는 갈망에 의해 활기를 띠었다. 그래서 그는 과학과 예술을 섞어가며 자신만의 독특한 길을 나아갔다.

그의 탐구를 완성하기 위해 레오나르도는 자신이 "범용"이라고 부르는 사람이 되어야 했다. 그는 각 목적의 모든 세부사항을 전달할 수 있어야 했고, 그는 이 지식을 가능한 한, 세계의 많은 사물까지 (d) 확장해야 했다. 그런 디테일을 순전히 (e) 제거함으로써(→ 회복시킴으로써) 삶의 본질 자체가 그에게 보여지게 되었고, 이 생명력에 대한 그의 이해는 그의 작품에서 엿볼 수 있게 되었다.

42 ④ 제시문에서 다빈치는 표면적으로만 화려한 당대 작품의 느낌을 싫어했고 세부적인 면에 몰두하는 것을 좋아했으며 생명체를 역동적으로 만드는 힘을 파악하여 과학과 예술을 섞어가며 자신만의 독특한 길을 나아갔다고 서술했으므로 "다빈치는 생명체의 역동적인 면 대신 정적인 면을 파악하려고 했다."는 ④의 설명은 윗글의 내용과 일치하지 않는다.

43 ⑤ 다빈치가 생명체를 역동적으로 표현한 독자적인 길을 가기 위해 작품의 모든 세부사항에 관한 디테일을 회복시켰다는 의미이므로 ⑤의 'elimination(제거)'는 'revival(회복)'으로 바꿔야 한다.

[44~45]

어휘

• stable : 마구간
• peasant : 소작농
• miserable : 비참한
• worsen : 악화되다
• caretaker : 관리인, 경비원
• forth : ~에서 멀리, 밖으로, ~쪽으로
• custody : 양육권, 보호권
• proclamation : 성명서, 선언서
• release : 석방하다, 풀어주다
• exhausted : 기진맥진한, 탈진한
• scoop : 들어올리다
• canine : 개의

해석

(A) 오래 전에 Vanasrai라는 큰 도시에서 왕이 마구간의 코끼리를 기르고 있었다. 그가 가장 좋아하는 코끼리에게는 특이하고 절친한 친구가 있었는데, 그녀가 저녁을 먹으면서 코끼리 입에서 떨어진 밥을 먹기 위해 마구간에 처음 온 개였다. 시간이 흐를수록 코끼리와 개는 친밀하고 사랑스런 관계를 맺게 되었는데, 그 관계가 계속될 때까지 코끼리는 밥을 나눠먹기 위해 그곳에 개가 없으면 먹지 않았다.

(C) 어느 날 불친절한 마부가 지나가는 농민에게 그 개를 동전 몇 개에 팔았다. 코끼리는 상심했다. 그녀는 먹지도 마시지도 목욕도 하지 않으려 했다. 왕은 자신이 가장 좋아하는 동물의 상태가 나빠진다는 말을 들었을 때 매우 화가 났다. 그는 가장 현명한 고문을 불러서 "내가 사랑하는 코끼리에게 가서 무엇이 문제인지 알아봐라"고 말했다.

(B) 고문은 코끼리를 주의 깊게 살폈다. 그는 그 짐승에게 육체적으로 아무런 문제가 없다는 것을 분명히 보았다. 코끼리의 관리인은 "코끼리는 대단한 개 친구가 있었는데, 그는 최근에 사라졌다"고 말했다. 그 말과 함께 고문은 왕에게 돌아가 "대왕의 코끼리는 그녀가 많이 사랑했던 개가 없어지는 것을 보고 가슴이 아픕니다. 개를 찾으려면 대왕께서 코끼리 마구간에서 개를 감금한 채 발견되는 사람은 거액의 벌금을 내야 한다는 포고문을 내기를 권합니다."라고 말했다.

(D) 그래서 그렇게 하자, 개를 산 농민은 포고 소식을 듣자마자 즉시 풀어주었고, 개는 코끼리 마구간으로 곧장 달려왔다. 지친 개가 돌아왔을 때 코끼리는 기쁨의 눈물을 흘렸고, 코끼리는 개를 자신의 코로 감싸 안았다. 그녀는 개가 먹이를 줄 때까지 먹지 않았다. 그러고 나서 그녀는 그녀의 음식도 먹었다. 그리고 곧 그녀의 옛 방식으로 돌아왔고, 그녀의 개와 같은 친구는 영원히 그녀 곁에 있었다.

44 ② (A) 왕이 기르는 코끼리와 개가 친구가 됨
(C) 개가 딴 곳으로 팔려가자 코끼리는 슬퍼했고 왕은 이를 알아봄
(B) 왕의 고문은 개를 데려간 사람에게 벌금을 내도록 하자고 함
(D) 그렇게 하자 개는 돌아왔고 코끼리는 다시 기뻐함

45 ③ 글 (C)를 보면 왕의 고문은 누군가 개를 데리고 갔다는 사실을 알게 되었고 왕에게 그 개를 데려간 사람에게 벌금을 내도록 하라는 조언을 하였다. 그러므로 "고문은 왕에게 개를 데리고 있는 사람에게 큰 상을 주자고 제안했다."는 ③의 설명은 윗글의 내용과 다르다.

2020학년도 기출문제 정답 및 해설

---

01 ④	02 ①	03 ①	04 ②	05 ⑤	06 ③
07 ⑤	08 ①	09 ①	10 ③	11 ②	12 ①
13 ①	14 ⑤	15 ⑤	16 ④	17 ②	18 ④
19 ②	20 ③	21 ②	22 ④	23 ③	24 ③
25 ②	26 ④	27 ①	28 ④	29 ③	30 ②
31 ⑤	32 ③	33 ④	34 ④	35 ③	36 ④
37 ⑤	38 ①	39 ④	40 ②	41 ⑤	42 ④
43 ⑤	44 ④	45 ⑤			

01 ④ 제시문은 Ron이 Dan의 도움을 받아 몸을 건강하게 유지하기 위해 산악자전거에 도전한 내용이다. 대화내용 중 Ron은 다리가 떨어져 나간 것 같고, 목이 사막보다 건조하다며 너무 지쳐서 쉬고 싶다고 말한다. 그러므로 "Ron desperately wants to take a break, (Ron은 몹시도 휴식을 원했다.)"는 ④의 설명은 적절하다.

오답풀이

① Ron과 Dan은 함께 가까스로 정상에 도달했다.
② Ron의 자전거는 Dan의 자전거보다 가볍다.
③ Ron은 자전거를 탄 후에 아무거나 먹을 수 있다고 말했다.
⑤ Ron은 Dan이 살을 빼는 것을 돕고 있는 중이다.

어휘

• in good shape : (몸의) 상태가 좋은
• carbon fiber : 탄소섬유
• make it : 성공하다, 해내다
• fall off : 떨어지다
• seriously : 심각하게, 심하게, 몹시
• push oneself : 스스로 채찍질하다
• manage to : 가까스로 ~하다, 그럭저럭 ~하다
• desperately : 필사적으로, 몹시

해석

Ron : 나는 더 이상은 못 갈 것 같아.
Dan : 어서, 힘내! 정상까지 1킬로미터 정도 남았어. 지금 그만두면 안 돼!

Ron : 말은 쉽지! 너는 몸이 건장하고, 네 자전거는 탄소섬유야! 무게가 내 자전거보다 10킬로그램은 덜 나간다구!
Dan : 그만두지 않고 성공한다면, 자전거를 다 탄 후 저녁 사 줄 게. 원하는 건 뭐든지.
Ron : 먹을 생각조차 나지 않아. 다리가 떨어져 나간 것 같고 목이 사막보다 건조해. 정말이지 그만두고 쉬고 싶어. 몸이 더 좋아지길 원하지만, 너무 지쳤어. 너무 힘들어.
Dan : 스스로를 채찍질해야 해. 휴식을 취하게 되면 살을 다 뺄 수가 없어. 도와달라고 부탁한 건 바로 너야.
Ron : 알겠어. 네 말이 옳아.

02 ① Bob이 자동차 대리점에서 판매사원과 함께 차를 고른 후 바로 구매하기로 결정하였으므로, 빈칸에는 ①의 "Great. Let me get the paperwork together and you can get on the road. (좋습니다. 함께 서류 작업을 마무리 하시고 출발 하시면 됩니다.)"가 들어갈 내용으로 가장 적절하다.

오답풀이

② 좋습니다. 근처의 다른 자동차 판매원을 소개해 드리죠.
③ 그럼요. 시험 운전할 시간은 충분합니다.
④ 걱정하지 마세요. 두 차 모두 원하시는 가격대에 있습니다.
⑤ 죄송하지만, 군청색 차량은 없습니다.

어휘

• in that case : 그런 경우에는, 그렇다면
• sedan : 세단형 자동차
• reasonable : 합리적인, 적당한
• sticker price : (가격표의) 표시 가격
• dealership : 대리점
• paperwork : 서류 작업, 문서 업무
• get on the road : 출발하다, 시작하다
• price range : 가격폭, 가격대

해석

Salesman : 음. 제 생각에 이 SUV가 찾고 계신 것과 꼭 같습니다.
Bob : 보기에는 좋은데, 생각보다 훨씬 크네요.
Salesman : 그렇다면 이 세단이 더 나을까요? 더 작고 가격도 적당합니다.
Bob : 그게 좋아 보이네요. 군청색으로도 나오나요?

Salesman : 여기 전시실에 군청색이 하나 있습니다. 가격표에 붙은 가격은 7만 5천 달러입니다. 시험운전 해보시겠어요?

Bob : 아뇨, 지난주에 다른 대리점에서 같은 차를 운전했어요. 그냥 가서 사야 할 것 같아요.

Salesman : 좋습니다. 함께 서류 작업을 마무리 하시고 출발 하시면 됩니다.

03 ① • **첫 번째 빈칸** : 저녁으로 멕시코 음식은 어떠냐는 Randy 의 말에 Martha가 지난번에 멕시코 식당에서 매운 음식 을 먹고 이틀 동안 배가 아팠다고 부정적으로 말하고 있 으므로, 빈칸에는 a의 "I don't think it's a good idea. (좋 은 생각이 아닌 것 같아.)"가 들어갈 말로 적절하다.

• **두 번째 빈칸** : 저녁으로 와플 가게는 어떠냐는 Randy 의 말에 Martha가 자기도 그렇다고 동의하고 있으므로, 빈칸에는 그 가게에 대한 긍정적인 내용인 b의 "I really love their dinner menu. (나는 그 가게의 저녁 메뉴가 정 말 맘에 들어.)"가 들어갈 말로 가장 적절하다.

• **세 번째 빈칸** : 피자를 권하는 Randy의 말에 Martha가 그걸 또 먹을 순 없다고 했으므로, 빈칸에는 d의 "I've already had it three times this week. (이번 주에 벌써 세 번이나 먹었어.)"가 들어갈 말로 가장 적절하다.

어휘

• spicy : 맛이 강한, 매운 ↔ unspicy : 맵지 않은

• stomach : 위, 복부

해석

Randy : 저녁으로 무얼 먹을까?

Martha : 사실, 난 정말로 먹고 싶은 게 생각나지 않아.

Randy : 멕시코 음식은 어때? 근처에 El Gordo라는 멕시코 식당이 새로 문을 열었어.

Martha : 좋은 생각이 아닌 것 같아. 지난번에 멕시코 식당에 서 매운 음식을 먹고, 이틀 동안 배가 아팠어.

Randy : 그렇다면 와플 가게는 어때? 나는 그 가게의 저녁 메 뉴가 정말 맘에 들어.

Martha : 나도 그렇지만, 그곳은 자리를 잡으려면 항상 오랫동 안 기다려야 해.

Randy : 네 말이 맞을지도 몰라. 피자는 어때?

Martha : 그걸 또 먹을 순 없어. 이번 주에 벌써 세 번이나 먹 었어.

Randy : 음…. El Gordo 식당의 음식을 먹어보는 건 어때? 우 리는 맵지 않은 음식을 고를 수 있어.

Martha : 좋아, 네가 원한다면.

04 ② 집이 마음에 들고 이웃도 아주 좋고 예산도 범위 내에 있 다는 여자의 말에, 남자가 주인에게 제안을 해보겠다고 말

하고 있으므로, 남자는 주택 매매를 알선하는 'real estate agent(부동산 중개업자)'이고 여자는 살 집을 구하고자 하 는 'homebuyer(주택 구입자)'임을 알 수 있다.

오답풀이

① 경비원 – 방문객

③ 관광 안내원 – 관광객

④ 집 주인 – 세입자

⑤ 건축가 – 기자

어휘

• budget : 예산, (지출 예상) 비용

• make an offer : 제안하다

• concern : 근심, 걱정, 우려

• empty : 빈, 비어 있는

• untidy : 어수선한, 너저분한

• renovate : 집을 수리하다, 개조[보수]하다

• deserted : 버려진, 사람이 살지 않는, 황폐한

• security guard : 경비원, 보안 요원

• real estate agent : 부동산 중개인

• tenant : 세입자, 임차인

• architect : 건축가

해석

Man : 제 생각에 시장에서 구하시는 것과 똑같습니다. 어떻게 생각하세요?

Woman : 솔직히, 맘에 듭니다. 이웃도 멋지고 예산도 범위 내 에 있습니다.

Man : 그럼, 주인에게 제안을 넣을까요? 그 집에 관심이 있는 사람들이 몇 분 더 있는 걸로 알고 있습니다.

Woman : 네, 하지만 한 가지 걱정이 있어요. 옆집은 항상 그 런가요? 텅 비고 어수선해 보여요.

Man : 사실 그곳에는 아무도 살지 않습니다. 보수가 필요하지 만 집 주인이 그럴 마음이 없나 봐요.

Woman : 저는 버려진 집 옆에 살고 싶지는 않습니다. 그 지역 의 다른 곳들을 좀 더 볼게요.

05 ⑤ 일기예보에 따르면 내일은 비가 오고 파도도 없지만, 내일 모레는 하늘도 맑고 파도도 좋다고 하였다. 그러나 불행히 도 Paul과 Jeff는 내일 밤 떠날 예정이어서 제대로 서핑을 즐기지 못할 것으로 여겨진다. 그러므로 "Jeff is going to leave the day after tomorrow after enjoying surfing. (Jeff는 서핑을 즐긴 후 내일 모레 떠날 것이다.)"라는 ⑤의 설명은 윗글의 내용과 일치하지 않는다.

오답풀이

① Paul은 어제 파도가 굉장히 좋았다고 말한다.

② Jeff는 서핑을 하는 데 지독히 운이 없다.

③ Jeff는 지난 달 Baja 반도에서 큰 파도를 탔다.

④ 일기예보에 따르면 내일 비가 올 것이다.

어휘

• peninsula : 반도

• forecast : 예측, 예보

• hate : 증오하다, 미워하다

• terrible luck : 악운, 지독히 운이 없음

해석

Jeff : 오늘도 멋진 파도가 왔으면 좋겠네.

Paul : 응, 하지만 파도가 늘 좋지는 않아. 방금 놓쳤어. 어제는 굉장히 좋았는데, 파도가 머리 위로 왔어.

Jeff : 난 항상 좋은 파도를 놓치는 것 같아. 지난 달 Baja 반도에서 마지막으로 멋진 서핑을 했어.

Paul : 나도 전에 그런 슬럼프를 겪어본 적이 있어. 가끔은 서핑 신들이 미소를 짓고, 가끔은 그렇지 않아!

Jeff : 내일의 일기예보는 어때?

Paul : 비가 오고 파도는 없어. 하지만 내일 모레는 맑은 하늘과 멋진 파도가 있을 것 같아! 우리는 언제 떠나?

Jeff : 내일 밤. 서핑 신들이 날 싫어함에 틀림없어.

06 ③ Tom은 파이프를 교체하고 샤워기를 새로 설치하는 비용으로 2,000달러를 요구했으나, Jane은 지난번 작업자에게는 500달러를 지불했다고 하면서 700달러에 하자고 제안한다. 이에 Tom은 700달러는 적자라며 1,800달러는 돼야 한다고 말하고 있다. 그러므로 "Tom and Jane are negotiating the fee for building a new shower. (Tom과 Jane은 새 샤워기를 설치하는 데 드는 비용을 협상하고 있다.)"는 ③의 설명이 윗글의 대화 내용과 일치한다.

오답풀이

① Jane은 Tom에게 샤워 시설이 어디 있는지 묻고 있다.

② Tom이 Jane의 샤워기를 부셔서, 그녀는 지금 그가 샤워기를 고쳐주기를 원한다.

④ Tom은 Jane에게 파이프를 좀 팔려고 했지만, 그녀는 그것을 사고 싶지 않았다.

⑤ Jane은 Tom이 수리 작업에 드는 비용을 청구하는 만큼 기꺼이 지불할 것이다.

어휘

• rip : 찢다, 떼어[뜯어] 내다

• expensive : 비싼, 돈이 많이 드는

• estimate : 견적서 cf) write up an estimate 견적서를 작성하다

• off the top of one's head : 별 생각 없이, 즉석에서, 깊이 생

각하거나 정확한 지식 없이

• leak : 새다, 누설[유출]하다

• a ton of money : 많은 돈, 큰 돈

• facility : 시설, 설비

• negotiate : 협상하다, 교섭하다

• fee : 수수료, 요금

해석

Tom : 죄송하지만 저 플라스틱 파이프들 모두 터져서 교체해야 합니다. 그리고 그 안에 샤워기도 새로 설치해야 합니다.

Jane : 오, 안 돼! 그건 돈이 많이 드는데! 그 일은 비용이 얼마나 들까요?

Tom : 음, 견적서를 작성해야 하지만, 대충 2,000달러 정도 들 겁니다. 작년에도 이런 일을 했거든요.

Jane : 오 이런! 너무 비싸요. 저는 몇 백 달러 정도로 생각했거든요. 지난번 분에게는 500달러를 지불했어요. 그 비용으로 할 수 없나요?

Tom : 제가 여기 오게 된 것도 지난번 분에게 500달러를 지불했기 때문이에요. 그는 일을 엉망으로 해놨어요. 그래서 파이프가 모두 새고 샤워기도 교체해야만 해요.

Jane : 음, 저는 잘 모르겠어요. 저는 정말 여유가 없어요. 700달러는 어때요?

Tom : 700달러에 일을 하게 되면, 적자가 많이 납니다. 적어도 1,800달러는 돼야 합니다.

07 ⑤ Richard Rawson이 만든 용어인 '사고 중단'이란 보상의 유혹에 반응하지 않는 최종 결정으로, 텔레비전의 채널을 바꾸는 것처럼 즉각적으로 이루어져야 한다고 서술하고 있다. 그러므로 ⑤의 "유혹에 빠지게 하는 생각을 단호하게 중단하라."가 필자가 주장하는 바로 가장 적절하다.

어휘

• coin : 주조하다, 만들다

• drug addict : 마약 중독

• definitive : 분명한, 명백한 cf) definitive decision 최종 결정

• the pull of a reward : 보상의 유혹

• encounter : 만나다, 접하다

• stimulus : 자극, 고무, 격려

• shut off : 멈추다, 그만두다, 차단하다

• provoke : 일으키다, 유발하다

• immediate : 즉각적인, 당면한

• in the face of : ～에도 불구하고, ～에 직면하여

• urge : 욕구, 충동

• ultimately : 궁극적으로, 결국

• give in : 굴복하다, 항복하다

• debate : 토론, 논쟁

- cue : 신호, 단서
- associated : 관련된, 연관된
- ambiguity : 모호성, 애매모호함
- struggle with : ~와 싸우다[투쟁하다]
- get out of : ~을 버리다, 지우다
- internalize : (사상 · 태도 등을) 내면화하다
- absolute : 완전한, 완벽한, 절대적인
- rigid : 엄격한, 융통성 없는
- room for doubt : 의심의 여지

해석

마약 중독자를 회복시키는 일을 하는 UCLA의 Richard Rawson이 만든 용어인 '사고 중단'은 보상의 유혹에 반응하지 않는 최종 결정이다. 즉, 자극에 접하고 그것을 유발하는 행동을 차단한다. Rawson은 "그것을 텔레비전과 같다고 생각하세요."라고 말한다. "채널을 바꾸세요." 생각을 끄는 것은 거의 즉각적이어야 한다. "당신은 이 일에 무기력하지 않아요. 즉, 결정을 내릴 수 있지만 빨리 결정해야 합니다."라고 Rawson은 말했다. 충동에 직면하여 무엇을 할지 생각하며 보내는 시간이 많을수록, 결국에는 그것에 굴복할 가능성이 더욱 커진다. 일단 "내가 해야 하나 아니면 하지 말아야 하나?"라는 논쟁을 시작하면, 당신은 전투에서 진 것이다. 단서를 경험하고, 관련된 생각을 꺼라. 모호하지도 않고, 어쩌면 아닐지도 모른다. 토론하는 데 시간을 낭비하지 마라. 당신의 반응에 저항하지 마라. 그냥 네 작업 기억에서 그것을 지워라. 의심의 여지를 남기지 말고, 절대적이고 심지어 융통성 없는 충동에 대한 반응을 내면화하라.

08 ① 제시문에 따르면 오랜 시간 동안 축적된 문화적 학습은 일반적으로 개인의 정신보다 더 똑똑하며 효과적이라고, 유교사상과 종교행사의 두 사례를 예로 들어 이를 설명하고 있다. 그러므로 제시문이 시사하는 바는 ①의 "Learn from old wisdom. (옛 지혜로부터 배워라)"이 가장 적절하다.

오답풀이

② 쉽게 얻는 것은 쉽게 잃는다.
③ 실수하는 것은 인간이다.
④ 자만하다 낭패 보기 쉽다.
⑤ 모험 없인 얻는 것도 없다.

어휘

- collective : 집단의, 단체의, 공동의
- accumulate : 모으다, 축적하다
- crowdsourcing : 크라우드 소싱
- Xunzi : 순자(기원전 3세기 중국의 사상가)
- Confucian : 유교의
- inherited : 상속한, 승계한, 물려받은

- marker : 표시[표지](물)
- ford : (강 따위의) 얕은 곳, 여울
- swift : 신속한, 재빠른
- trial and error : 시행착오
- figure out : 생각해내다, 이해하다
- wing it : 즉흥적으로 하다
- counterproductive : 역효과를 낳는
- strain : (체 같은 것을 받쳐) 물기를 빼다[거르다]
- pound : 치다, 두드리다
- priest : 사제, 신부, 성직자
- sacred : 신성한, 종교적인 cf) sacred song 성가

해석

시간이 흘러 축적된 모든 문화 집단의 집단 정신은 일반적으로 개인의 정신보다 더 똑똑하다. 이것이 바로 문화 학습이 그렇게 중요한 이유이며, 크라우드 소싱과 같은 기술이 또한 그렇게 효과적인 이유이기도 하다. 중국 초기의 사상가인 순자는 자신의 세대가 물려받은 유교 방식을 그와 다르게 깊고 빠른 강 위의 얕은 곳을 나타내는 데 사용된 표시물과 비교한다. 유경험자들은 세심한 시행착오를 거쳐 강을 건너기에 가장 좋은 위치를 파악하고, 그것을 찾는 데 도움이 될 표시를 남겨왔다. 우리는 그것들을 무시하고 그냥 즉흥적으로 갈 수 있지만, 그것은 역효과를 내고 심지어 위험할 것이다. 바꾸어 말하면, 지역 공동체에서 존경을 받는 분이 이 뿌리 채소를 2시간 동안 끓이고, 그것을 채에 받쳐 물기를 뺀 다음, 이 성가를 20번이나 부를 때까지 신부님이 축복한 막대기로 그것을 두드리라고 말한다면, 당신은 아마도 그저 입을 다물고 들은 대로 정확히 그것을 수행해야 한다.

09 ① 제시문에 따르면 결정을 내릴 당시의 상황에선 옳다고 생각했던 것도 상황이 바뀌면 틀린 것으로 판명될 수도 있으므로, 원점에서 다시 시작해야 한다고 서술하고 있다. 그러므로 ①의 "상황이 바뀌면 원점에서 다시 시작하는 수고를 감내할 필요가 있다."가 제시문의 요지로 가장 적절하다.

어휘

- turn out : …인 것으로 드러나다, 판명되다
- in the fullness of time : 때가 무르익었을 때, 마침내 때가 되었을 때
- commitment : 약속, 책무
- zero-base : 출발점부터 재결정[재검토]하다, 원점에서 다시 시작하다
- be involved in : ~에 개입되다, 관계되다
- aggravation : 악화, 격화, 화남, 약오름
- irritation : 짜증, 격앙, 화
- enormous : 거대한, 엄청난

• get out of : 회피하다, 벗어나다
• take steps : 조치를 취하다

해석

당신이 내리는 많은 결정들은 때가 되면 틀린 것으로 판명될 것이다. 당신이 결정이나 약속을 했을 때, 그것은 아마도 그 상황에선 옳은 생각이었다. 하지만 이제 상황은 바뀌었을지 모르며, 원점에서 다시 시작할 때이다. 당신은 보통 그것이 유발하는 스트레스 때문에 원점에서 다시 생각하는 상황에 놓여 있는지 알 수 있다. 지금까지 알고 있는 것을 알면서 다시 개입하지 못하는 무언가와 연관될 때마다. 당신은 계속되는 스트레스, 악화, 짜증, 분노를 겪는다. 때로는 사람들은 사업이나 개인적인 관계를 성공시키기 위해 엄청난 시간을 보낸다. 그러나 이런 관계를 원점에서 다시 시작한다면, 올바른 해결책은 종종 그 관계를 완전히 벗어나는 것이다. 유일한 진짜 질문은 당신이 틀렸다는 것을 인정하고 상황을 바로잡기 위해 필요한 조치를 취할 용기가 있느냐 하는 것이다.

10 ③ 제시문에 따르면 인간의 본성 중 어두운 면에 대해서는 자신을 배제하는 것이 자연스러운 현상이지만, 이러한 자기 기만적인 과정을 멈추고 모두가 똑같은 부류라는 사실을 빨리 깨달을수록 내면에 잠재하고 있는 부정적인 특성들을 극복하는 데 더 큰 힘을 발휘할 수 있다고 하였다. 그러므로 ③의 "자신의 부정적인 면을 인정하면 그것을 극복하는 데 도움이 된다."가 제시문의 요지로 가장 적절하다.

어휘

• exclude : 제외하다, 배제하다
• narcissistic : 자애적인, 자기도취의
• irrational : 비이성적인, 비논리적인
• envious : 시기[질투]하는, 샘내는
• grandiose : 거창한, 뽐내는, 거만한
• aggressive : 공격적인, 적극적인
• intention : 의도, 의향, 목적 cf) best intention 선의, 호의
• go astray : 길을 잃다, 길을 잘못 들다
• self-deluding : 자기 기만의
• once and for all : 마지막으로 한 번만 더, 최종적으로[완전히]
• cut from the same cloth : 똑같은 부류이다
• trait : 특징, 특성
• spot : 발견하다, 찾다, 알아채다
• humble : 겸손한, 미천한
• guilty : 죄책감이 드는, 유죄의
• weigh down by : …로 내리누르다
• self-awareness : 자기 인식, 자각
• opposite : 다른 편[쪽]의, 반대편의
• embrace : 포옹하다, 껴안다

• falsified : 거짓된, 조작된, 꾸민
• saint : 성인, 성자
• relieve : 없애주다, 완화하다
• hypocrisy : 위선

해석

인간의 본성 중 더 어두운 면에 대해 읽고 듣는 것에 대한 자연스러운 반응은 자신을 배제하는 것이다. 자기도취의 비이성적이며 샘 많고 거만하며, 혹은 공격적인 사람은 언제나 상대방이다. 우리는 거의 항상 자신이 선의를 가지고 있다고 여긴다. 우리가 길을 잘못 들면, 그것은 부정적으로 반응하도록 하는 상황이나 사람들의 잘못이다. 마지막으로 한 번 더 이러한 자기 기만적 과정을 멈춰라. 우리 모두 똑같은 부류이며, 똑같은 성향을 공유한다. 이러한 사실을 빨리 깨달을수록, 당신의 내면에 잠재하고 있는 부정적인 특성들을 극복하는 데 더 큰 힘을 발휘할 것이다. 당신은 자신의 동기를 조사하고 자신의 그림자를 바라볼 것이다. 이로 인해 다른 사람의 그런 특징들을 발견하는 것이 훨씬 쉬워질 것이다. 또한 자신이 상상했던 것만큼 다른 사람들보다 우월하지 않다는 것을 깨닫고 겸손해질 것이다. 이것은 죄책감을 느끼게 하거나 또는 자기 인식에 짓눌리지 않을 것이며, 오히려 그 반대이다. 당신은 자신을 완전한 개인으로 받아들이고, 선과 악을 모두 포용하며, 성자로써 거짓된 자아상을 버릴 것이다. 위선에서 해방되고 더욱 자유를 느낄 것이다. 사람들은 당신의 이런 특성에 끌릴 것이다.

11 ② 제시문의 마지막 부분에서 잉카제국은 전체 인구의 약 3분의 1에서 절반이 유럽인들의 바이러스성 질병 때문에 사망했고, 이로 인해 스페인은 비교적 쉽게 잉카를 정복할 수 있었다고 서술되어 있다. 그러므로 ②의 'European diseases as a cause of the collapse of the Inca Empire(잉카제국의 붕괴 원인인 유럽의 질병)'가 제시문의 주제로 가장 적절하다.

오답풀이

① 스페인 신세계 정복자들과 그들의 잔혹함
③ 구세계와 신세계의 충돌이 유럽인들에게 미치는 영향
④ 잉카제국의 흥망성쇠를 추적하는 과학적인 방법
⑤ 구세계의 질병을 치료하기 위한 잉카의 자연 요법

어휘

• grandeur : 장엄함, 위엄
• conquer : 정복하다, 이기다
• conquistador : 정복자
• immunity : 면역력, 면제
• smallpox : 천연두
• measles : 홍역
• typhoid : 장티푸스

- influenza : 인플루엔자, 유행성 감기
- malaria : 말라리아
- whooping cough : 백일해
- indigenous : 원산의, 토착의
- epidemics : 전염병
- successor : 후계자, 계승자
- estimated : 어림의, 추측의
- population : 인구, 주민
- viral : 바이러스성의, 바이러스에 의한
- demoralize : 사기를 꺾다, 의기소침하게 만들다
- contribute to : ~에 기여하다
- relatively : 상대적으로, 비교적
- cruelty : 잔인함, 학대
- collapse : 붕괴되다, 무너지다
- collision : 충돌, 부딪침
- therapy : 치료, 요법

해석

그 규모와 웅장함에도 불구하고, 잉카제국은 1532년부터 스페인에 의해 정복되기 전까지 불과 1세기 동안 지속되었다. 스페인 정복자들이 남아메리카 중부에 도착하기 전부터, 유럽인들이 아메리카 사람들에게 면역력이 없는 질병을 가지고 왔기 때문에 잉카는 유럽인들의 신세계 도착으로 고통받기 시작했다. 유럽인들이 남아메리카에 상륙한 직후 천연두, 홍역, 장티푸스, 인플루엔자, 말라리아, 백일해 및 기타 질병으로 아메리카 원주민들이 사망했다. 이러한 구세계 질병은 1520년대까지 잉카제국에 퍼졌다. 안데스 산맥에 스페인이 도착하기 직전, 전염병으로 황제와 그의 후계자를 포함한 많은 잉카 지도자들이 사망했다. 결국 잉카제국 전체 인구의 약 3분의 1에서 절반이 이러한 바이러스성 암살자 때문에 사망했다. 살아남은 사람들은 사기가 떨어졌고, 이는 비교적 쉽게 스페인이 잉카를 정복하는데 기여했다.

12 ① 제시문에서는 사전 경고를 받은 학생들과 받지 않은 학생들 중 어느 집단이 더 설득이 되었는지 실험을 통해 밝혀내고 있다. 그러므로 ①의 'effect of forewarning on persuasion(설득에 대한 사전 경고의 효과)'이 제시문의 주제로 가장 적절하다.

오답풀이

② 설득력 있는 말의 특징
③ 대화형 프레젠테이션의 중요성
④ 사전 경고 표시의 필요성
⑤ 교육에서 설득적인 의사소통 기능

어휘

- forewarn : 미리 주의를 주다, 사전에 경고하다

- in advance : 사전에, 미리
- persuade : 설득하다 a. persuasive 설득력 있는 n. persuasion 설득력
- take away : 제거하다, 빼앗다
- psychological : 심리의, 심리적인
- reactance : 유도저항
- lovebird : 원앙, 잉꼬, 열애 중인 남녀
- interactive : 상호작용을 하는, 대화형의

해석

만일 사람들이 공격이 있을 거라는 사실을 안다면, 그들은 스스로를 방어할 준비를 할 수 있다. 한 연구에서 고등학생들은 "왜 십대들이 운전을 못하도록 해야 하는가"에 대한 연설을 듣게 될 것이라고 2분 또는 10분 전에 미리 경고를 받았다(짐작하는 것처럼, 별로 관심 있는 메시지는 아님). 나머지 학생들은 같은 말을 들었지만, 미리 경고를 받지는 않았다. 그 결과 사전 경고를 받지 않은 학생들이 가장 많이 설득되었고, 그 다음으로 2분 전에 경고를 받은 학생들이, 그 다음으로 10분 전에 경고를 받은 학생들이 설득되었다. 사람들은 누군가가 그들을 설득하려고 한다고 믿을 때(그리고 선택의 자유를 빼앗으려고 할 때), 그들은 심리적 저항이라고 불리는 불쾌한 감정적 반응을 경험하는데, 이것이 설득력 있는 시도에 그들이 저항하도록 하는 원인이 된다. 사람들은 종종 그들이 설득당하는 것과 정확히 반대되는 행동을 할 것이다. 셰익스피어의 연극에서 로미오와 줄리엣의 부모가 로맨스를 끝내려는 그들의 노력이 그 젊은 연인을 더 가깝게 만들었을 때 이러한 효과가 나타났다.

13 ① 글의 서두에서 다양성의 증가가 저절로 사회의 긴장과 갈등을 증가시킨다는 무섭지만 잘못된 가정에 맞설 필요가 있으며, 사실은 그와 정반대라고 서술하고 있다. 그러므로 ①의 "Does Diversity Harm Democracy? (다양성은 민주주의에 해로운가?)"가 제시문의 제목으로 가장 적절하다.

오답풀이

② 민주주의의 약점은 내재하는가?
③ 다양성의 증가는 민주주의에 대한 위협이다.
④ 다수결의 원칙 : 민주주의의 기본 원리
⑤ 민주주의는 전염되기 쉽다 : 진보의 민주화

어휘

- reconstitute : 재구성[편성]하다, 원상태로 만들다[복원하다]
- in line with : ~에 맞춰, ~와 함께
- frightening : 무서운, 겁나는
- assumption : 가정, 추측
- diversity : 다양성, 포괄성
- tension : 긴장, 불안, 갈등

• conflict : 갈등, 충돌
• within limits : 어느 정도까지는, 어느 한도 내에서는
• desirable : 바람직한, 가치 있는
• desperately : 필사적으로, 기를 쓰고
• brass : 놋쇠, 황동 cf) brass ring 큰 돈벌이[성공]의 기회
• rewarding : 보람 있는, 돈을 많이 버는, 수익이 많이 나는
• symbiotic : 공생의, 공생하는
• appropriate : 적절한, 타당한
• arrangement : 준비, 방안, 합의, 협의, 배열
• secure : 안전한, 확실한
• stable : 안정된, 안정적인
• unnecessarily : 불필요하게, 쓸데없이
• minorities : 소수자
• knife−edge : 칼날
• violence : 폭행, 폭력
• stifle : 억누르다, 억압하다
• dissent : 반대하다, 의견을 달리하다
• selfishness : 이기심, 이기적임
• imaginative : 창의적인, 상상력이 풍부한
• accommodate : 공간을 제공하다, 수용하다
• legitimate : 합법적인, 적법한, 정당한
• multiplying : 중복하는, 복합적인
• inherent : 고유의, 본래의, 내재하는
• contagious : 전염되는, 옮기 쉬운

해석

현재의 상황에 맞춰 민주주의를 재구성하려면, 다양성의 증가가 저절로 사회의 긴장과 갈등을 증가시킨다는 무섭지만 잘못된 가정에 맞설 필요가 있다. 사실은 그와 정반대이다. 사회에서 갈등은 필요할 뿐만 아니라, 어느 정도까지는 바람직하다. 하지만 100명의 사람들 모두가 필사적으로 동일한 성공 기회를 원한다면, 그들은 그것을 위해 싸울 수밖에 없을지도 모른다. 반면, 100명 모두가 각기 다른 목표를 가지고 있다면, 그들이 거래하고, 협력하고, 공생 관계를 형성하는 것이 훨씬 더 수익이 많이 난다. 적절한 사회적 합의를 고려한다면, 다양성은 안전하고 안정적인 문명을 만들 수 있다. 쓸데없이 소수자들 사이의 갈등을 폭력의 칼날로 예리하게 만드는 것은 오늘날 적절한 정치 제도의 부재 때문이다. 이 문제에 대한 해답은 반대 의견을 억누르거나 소수자들의 이기심을 비난하는 것이 아니다. 그 답은 다양성을 수용하고 정당화하기 위한 창의적인 새로운 방안, 즉 다양하고 복합적인 소수자들의 급변하는 요구에 민감하게 반응하는 새로운 제도에 있다.

14 ⑤ 제시문에 따르면 '이것을 알파벳 순서로 배열하라'처럼 단순한 어떤 것으로 포장된 모호함은 정말 놀라우며, 모호한

지시는 우리의 체계와 신뢰를 약화시킬 수 있다고 서술되어 있다. 그러므로 ⑤의 "Ambiguity Hides in Simplicity(모호함은 단순함 속에 숨어 있다.)"가 제시문의 제목으로 가장 적절하다.

오답풀이

① 알파벳 순서는 분류를 쉽게 만든다.
② 복잡함을 버리고, 단순함을 유지하라.
③ 관리자: 동료인가 적인가?
④ 오래된 앨범은 수집하기 어렵다.

어휘

• alphabetically : 알파벳순으로
• direction : 방향, 쪽
• overhear : 우연히 듣다, 엿듣다
• inventory : 물품 목록, 재고
• shipment : 수송, 수송품, 화물
• ambiguity : 애매모호함 a. ambiguous 모호한, 막연한
• wrap : 싸다, 포장하다
• alphabetize : 알파벳순으로 배열하다
• instruction : 지시, 명령
• trustworthiness : 신뢰성, 신용
• misfile : 잘못 철하다[정리하다]
• chaos : 혼돈, 혼란
• ensue : 뒤따르다, 일어나다
• classification : 분류, 범주

해석

레코드 가게에서 일하는 첫날에, 관리자가 "우리 레코드들은 알파벳순으로 정리되어 있어요."라고 말한다고 상상해보자. 이 순서대로 여러분은 첫 번째 앨범들을 쉽게 정리한다. 후에 함께 일하는 동료가 "죄송합니다. 지금 막 마이클 잭슨 앨범이 다 팔린 것 같아요."라고 말하는 것을 우연히 듣게 된다. 관리자는 'J' 밑을 보고 물품 목록을 확인하는데, 그 물품 목록에는 가게에 '스릴러' 앨범 한 장이 있어야 한다고 되어있다. 당신은 그것이 방금 정리한 레코드 물품 중 일부라는 걸 기억한다. 'J' 밑이 아니라면, 그 레코드를 어디에 둘 수 있었겠는가? 'M' 밑에? '이것을 알파벳 순서로 배열하라'처럼 단순한 어떤 것으로 포장된 모호함은 정말 놀랍다. 우리는 하루 종일 지시를 주고받는다. 모호한 지시는 우리의 체계와 신뢰를 약화시킬 수 있다. 첫 번째 앨범이 잘못 정리된 지 너무 오래되어서 혼란이 일어난다.

15 ⑤ 위의 그래프를 보면 통신 분야에 종사하는 남녀 군인의 비율이 각각 10%로 동일하므로, "군대에서 남녀가 동일한 분포를 보이는 직업적 역할은 없었다."는 ⑤의 설명은 도표의 내용과 일치하지 않는다.

- occupational : 직업의, 직업과 관련된
- active-duty : 현역의
- concentrate : 집중하다, 전념하다
- administrative : 관리상의, 행정상의
- serviceman : 군인
- infantry : 보병
- gun crew : 포수
- seamanship : 배를 부리는 기술, 선박 조종술
- distribution : 배분, 유통, 분포

해석

위의 그래프는 2010년 미국의 직업적 역할에 따른 남성과 여성의 비율을 보여준다. ① 현역 여성들은 현역 남성들보다 행정적 역할에 훨씬 더 집중되어 있었다. 즉, 여성의 비율은 행정직 남성의 두 배가 넘었다. ② 그리고 군대의 남성 중 6%만이 의학적 역할을 수행한 반면, 여성의 15%가 이러한 유형의 직업을 가지고 있었다. ③ 전기 분야에서 남성의 비율은 여성보다 컸다. 즉, 남성의 22%가 전기 종사직에 있는 반면, 여성의 12%만이 동일한 역할을 수행했다. ④ 보병, 포수 및 선박 항해사에 종사하는 19%의 남성 군인에 비해, 여성 군인의 3%만이 이러한 역할을 수행했다. ⑤ <u>군대에서 남녀가 동일한 분포를 보이는 직업적 역할은 없었다.</u>

16 ④ 제시문에 따르면 Marcuse는 1958년에 매사추세츠 주 Brandeis 대학의 교수가 되었지만, 1965년 노골적인 마르크스주의 사관 때문에 사임해야 했고 그 후 California 대학으로 옮겼다. 그러므로 "California 대학에서 교수가 되어 Brandeis 대학으로 옮겼다."는 ④의 설명은 제시문의 내용과 일치하지 않는다.

어휘

- completing : 가능한 최대의, 완벽한
- spell : 한동안, 잠깐 cf) a short spell 짧은 기간
- institute : 기관, 협회
- flee to : …로 달아나다, 피신하다
- the latter : 후자
- relocate : 이전하다, 이동하다
- resign : 사임하다, 퇴임하다
- outspoken : 노골적으로[거침없이] 말하는
- Marxist : 마르크스주의의
- renown : 유명, 명성, 평판
- die of a stroke : 뇌졸중으로 죽다

해석

1898년 베를린에서 태어난 Herbert Marcuse는 1922년 Freiburg 대학에서 문학 박사 학위를 받기 전인 제1차 세계대전 당시 독일군에서 복무했다. 베를린에서 잠시 동안 도서판매원으로 일한 그는 Martin Heidegger 밑에서 철학을 공부했다. 1932년 그는 사회 연구 기관에 입사했지만, 결코 프랑크푸르트에서 근무한 적이 없다. 1934년에 그는 미국으로 피신했고, 그곳에서 머물러야 했다. 그가 Max Horkheimer와 함께 뉴욕에 있는 동안, Max Horkheimer는 콜롬비아 대학교로부터 연구소를 그곳으로 이전하라는 제안을 받았고 Marcuse는 그와 합류했다. 1958년 Marcuse는 매사추세츠 주 Brandeis 대학의 교수가 되었지만, 1965년 노골적인 마르크스주의 사관 때문에 사임해야 했다. 그는 California 대학으로 옮겼으며, 1960년대에는 사회이론가, 철학자 및 정치활동가로서 세계적인 명성을 얻었다. 그는 81세의 나이에 뇌졸중으로 사망했다.

17 ③ ①, ④, ⑤의 'they'와 ②의 'their'는 모두 Betsy의 부모님을 가리키나, ③의 'they'는 Betsy와 그녀의 친구를 가리킨다.

어휘

- spit : 침을 뱉다
- pucker up : 입술을 오므리다
- spray : 뿌리다, 퍼붓다
- saliva : 침, 타액 cf) a cloud of saliva 타액
- embarrass : 당황스럽게 만들다, 어쩔 줄을 몰라 하다
- naughty : 버릇없는, 말을 안 듣는
- disgusting : 역겨운, 혐오스러운
- fall on deaf ears : 다른 사람 귀에 들어가지 않다, 무시되다, 허사다
- broadly : 대략, 활짝
- bet : 틀림없다, 분명하다
- in a mixture of : 뒤섞인
- shame : 수줍음, 부끄러움, 창피
- amazement : 놀라움, 경악
- disappear : 사라지다, 보이지 않게 되다
- struggle : 투쟁, 고투

해석

네 살 난 Betsy는 침을 뱉는 것을 좋아했다. 매번 누군가가 "안녕, Betsy"라고 말할 때, 그녀는 입술을 오므리고 그 사람에게 한 움큼 침을 뿌릴 준비를 했다. 그녀의 부모는 당황했고, 그녀가 어떻게 그런 '나쁜' 습관을 시작했는지 이해할 수 없었다. 그들은 둘 다 매우 존경받는 사람들이었고, Betsy가 어디서 그런 '버릇없고 혐오스러운' 것을 배웠는지 이해하지 못했다. Betsy를 멈추게 하려는 그들의 모든 노력은 허사였다. 어느 날 그들은 가족의 친구를 방문했고, Betsy가 침을 뱉으려고 입술을 오므렸을 때, 친구는 활짝 웃으며 "Betsy, 틀림없

이 침 뱉는 거 좋아할 거야. 둘이 욕실로 가서 화장실에 침을 뱉어보자. 내 생각에 그것도 재미있을 거야." Betsy가 친구의 손을 잡고 둘이 욕실로 사라졌을 때, Betsy의 부모는 부끄러움과 놀라움에 뒤섞여 지켜보았다. 몇 분 후, 그들은 돌아왔고 Betsy는 침 뱉는 것을 멈추었다. Betsy의 부모가 깨달은 것은 Betsy의 행동을 통제하려고 애쓰면서 그들이 힘 겨루기를 하고 있었다는 것이다. 이제 그들은 선택권이 있었고, Betsy에게 "화장실에서 하는 한 침 뱉는 건 괜찮아."라고 말할 수 있었다. Betsy가 자기 습관을 포기하는 데는 그리 오래 걸리지 않았다.

18 ④ 해당 문장은 원래 'as(while) he knew Merkel had once been bitten ~'으로써, 부대상황을 나타내는 분사구문으로 바꾸면 접속사 'as(while)'와 주어 'he'를 생략하고, 동사 'knew'는 현재분사인 'knowing'으로 바꿔야 한다.

오답풀이

① 선행사가 포함된 주격 관계대명사로써 'what'을 사용한 것은 적절하며, 문장의 주어로써 'the thing that'의 의미를 지닌다.

② 동사 'seem' 다음에 'to be'가 생략된 형용사 'take'를 사용한 것은 적절하다.

③ 접속사 'while' 다음에 주어+be동사인 'she is'가 생략되고, 현재분사 'seeming'을 사용한 것은 적절하다.

⑤ 'put oneself in the one-up position'는 '유리한 입장에 있다'는 의미로, 앞의 주어 'She'에 맞추어 재귀대명사 'herself'를 사용한 것은 적절하다.

어휘

• confident : 자신감 있는, 확신하는
• businesslike : 효율적인, 업무에 충실한, 사무적인
• chancellor : 수상, 총장
• fake : 가짜의, 거짓된, 가식의
• absorption : 흡수, 몰두, 몰입
• have a way of ~ing : 흔히 ~하게 되어 가다
• remarkably : 두드러지게, 현저하게, 몹시, 매우
• interrupt : 방해하다, 끼어들다
• assert : 단언하다, 주장하다
• boredom : 지루함, 따분함
• iciness : 쌀쌀함, 냉담함
• blustering : 세차게 몰아치는, 호통치는
• intimidate : 겁을 주다, 위협하다
• bite : 물다, 깨물다
• visibly : 눈에 띄게, 분명히
• tense : 긴장한, 신경이 날카로운
• compose : (감정·표정 등을) 가다듬다, 가라앉히다, 진정시키다

• one-up : 한 걸음 앞선, 유리한 cf) put oneself in the one-up position : 유리한 입장에 있다
• ploy : 책략, 계략
• petty : 사소한, 하찮은, 옹졸한
• childish : 어린애 같은, 유치한
• in comparison : ~와 비교하여
• alpha male : 우두머리 수컷
• posturing : 가식적인[꾸민] 태도
• in one's own way : 자기 나름대로

해석

리더십을 발휘하는 위치에 있는 여성들에게 가장 효과적인 것은 침착하고 자신감 넘치는 표정이며, 따뜻하지만 사무적인 것이다. 아마도 이것의 가장 좋은 사례는 현재의 독일 수상인 Angela Merkel일 것이다. 그녀의 미소는 평균적인 남성 정치인보다 빈도가 훨씬 덜 하지만, 미소를 지을 때는 특별한 의미가 있다. 그녀의 미소는 결코 가식처럼 보이지 않는다. 그녀는 완전히 몰입된 표정으로 다른 사람의 말을 경청한다. 그녀는 다른 사람들이 대화를 주도하게 하며, 항상 대화의 과정을 통제하는 것처럼 보인다. 그녀는 자기 주장을 위해 끼어들 필요가 없다. 그녀가 누군가를 비난하고 싶을 때, 지루하고 냉담하며 혹은 경멸의 표정을 짓지, 결코 호통치는 말을 하지 않는다. 블라디미르 푸틴 러시아 대통령이 메르켈이 한 때 물려서 개에 대한 두려움을 가지고 있다는 것을 알고 애완견을 회의에 데려와 그녀를 겁주려고 했을 때, 그녀는 눈에 띄게 긴장했지만, 재빨리 마음을 가라앉히고 조용히 그의 눈을 쳐다보았다. 그녀는 푸틴의 계략에 아무런 대응도 하지 않음으로써 푸틴과의 관계에서 유리한 입장에 놓았다. 이에 비하면 그는 다소 유치하고 옹졸해 보였다. 그녀의 스타일에는 우두머리 남성의 가식이 전혀 없다. 자기 나름대로 더 조용하면서도 아주 강력하다.

19 ② 관계대명사 'that'의 수식을 받는 'a debate'가 문장 전체의 주어이고, 'leave out'이 본동사에 해당하므로 3인칭 단수 현재 시제에 맞추어 'leaves out'이 되어야 한다.

오답풀이

① 주절의 시제가 'would have + p.p'이므로 가정법 과거완료 구문이다. 종속절은 원래 'if Depression-era regulations had not been removed ~'인데, 접속사 'if'가 생략되고 주어와 동사가 도치되어 'had Depression-era regulations not been removed ~'로 된 것이다.

③ 앞의 선행사 'The kind of work'을 수식하기 위해 관계대명사 'that'이 A and B의 형태로 연결된 것으로 적절하다.

④ 앞의 'those who don't care'를 대신하는 지시대명사 'them'을 사용한 것은 적절하다.

⑤ 주어 'We'의 동사가 등위접속사 'but'에 의해 A but B의
형태로 연결된 것이므로, 앞의 동사 'miss'에 맞추어 동사
'lack'을 사용한 것은 적절하다.

어휘

- inevitable : 불가피한, 필연적인
- depression-era : 대공황 시대
- regulation : 규제, 통제
- enforce : 집행[시행]하다, 강요하다
- debate : 토론, 논쟁
- mechanism : 매커니즘, 방법, 구조
- leave out : ~을 빼다[배제시키다]
- ingredient : 재료, 성분, 구성 요소
- practitioner : 전문직 종사자, 실무자
- moral : 도덕의, 도덕적인

해석

규칙과 인센티브는 우리 사회 및 정치 생활에서 불가피하고
꼭 필요한 부분이다. 만약 대공황 시대의 규제가 제거되지 않
고 현재의 규제가 시행되었다면 은행 위기는 훨씬 덜 심각했
을 것이다. 그러나 규칙과 인센티브의 중요성에도 불구하고,
이 두 메커니즘의 적절한 혼합에만 초점을 맞춘 논쟁은 한 가
지 중요한 요소를 배제시킨다. 대부분의 실무자들이 하고 싶
어 하고 그들이 서비스하는 사람들 또한 하고 싶어 하는 종류
의 일들은 실용적인 지혜를 요구한다. 규칙과 인센티브는 비
록 관심 없는 사람들을 더 현명하게 만들지는 못하더라도, 그
들의 행동을 개선할 수도 있다. 그러나 우리의 규칙과 인센티
브의 대상인 관심 없는 사람들에게 초점을 맞추다 보면 관심
있는 사람들을 놓치게 된다. 우리는 옳은 일을 하고 싶지만 그
것을 잘 할 수 있는 실용적인 지혜가 부족한 사람들을 놓친다.
규칙과 인센티브는 이 사람들에게 그들이 필요로 하는 도덕적
기술과 의지를 가르쳐주지 않을 것이다. 더 나쁜 것은 규칙은
기술을 죽일 수 있고 인센티브는 의지를 죽일 수 있다.

20 ③ (A) if 이하의 조건의 부사절에서 'the species'를 가리키는
지시대명사 'those'가 주어이므로, be동사의 복수형인
'are'를 사용하는 것이 적절하다.
(B) When 이하의 부사절에서 주어가 'the American
chestnut'이므로, 부사절의 본동사에 해당하는 'was'를
사용하는 것이 적절하다.
(C) 'the ecosystem collapses at a tipping point'에서 'a
tipping point'가 앞으로 나가 선행사의 역할을 하므로,
'전치사+관계대명사'의 형태인 'at which'를 사용하는
것이 적절하다. 참고로 'at which'는 관계부사 'where'로
바꾸어 쓸 수 있다.

어휘

- biodiversity : 생물의 다양성
- shield : 방패, 보호막
- extinguish : 소멸하다, 멸종하다 n. extinction 소멸, 멸종
- take away : 없애다, 제거하다
- vanish : 사라지다, 없어지다
- survivor : 생존자, 살아남은 사람
- accelerate : 가속화하다, 속도를 높이다
- chestnut : 밤나무
- dominant : 우세한, 지배적인 cf) dominant tree 우세목
- fungal 균류[곰팡이]에 의한
- blight : 마름병
- moth : 나방
- caterpillar : 애벌레
- vegetation : 초목, 식물
- pigeon : 비둘기
- plunge to : …로 돌입하다
- mount : 증가하다, 올라가다
- tipping point : 티핑 포인트, 분기점
- ecosystem : 생태계
- collapse : 붕괴하다, 무너지다
- catastrophe : 재앙, 재난

해석

생물의 다양성은 우리 인간을 포함해서 전체적으로 그것을 함
께 구성하는 개별 종(種)들의 보호막을 형성한다. 인간의 활동
으로 이미 멸종된 종 외에, 가령 남은 종의 10%, 아니면 50%,
아니면 90%가 사라진다면 어떻게 될까? 점점 더 많은 종들이
사라지거나 거의 멸종될 무렵, 살아남은 종들의 멸종 속도는
점점 빨라진다. 어떤 경우에는 그 효과가 거의 즉시 나타난다.
1세기 전 한때 북아메리카 동부의 많은 지역에서 우세목이었
던 미국 밤나무가 곰팡이에 의한 마름병으로 거의 멸종되었을
때, 애벌레가 그 식물에 의존하는 일곱 종의 나방이 사라졌고,
그리고 마지막 탑승객인 비둘기들이 멸종하기 시작했다. 멸종
이 증가함에 따라 생물의 다양성은 생태계가 붕괴되는 분기점
에 도달한다. 과학자들은 단지 어떤 조건 하에서 그리고 언제
이 재앙이 일어날 가능성이 가장 높은지에 대해서만 연구하기
시작했다.

21 ② (A) 앞의 동사 'respond'를 수식하기 위해 부사의 형태인
'appropriately'를 사용하는 것이 적절하다. 형용사인
'appropriate'를 사용하기 위해서는 뒤에 명사가 오거나
보어로써 사용되어야 한다.
(B) 부대상황을 나타내는 분사구문이 A and B의 형태로 연
결된 것으로, 앞의 'offering'에 맞추어 'asking'을 사용하

는 것이 적절하다.

(C) 주어인 'the sight of food'가 무생물로 능동의 역할을 수행하므로, 현재분사 'exerting'을 사용하는 것이 적절하다.

어휘

- convince : 납득시키다, 확신시키다
- appropriate : 적절한, 타당한
- internal : 내부의 ↔ external 외부의
- satiety : 만족감, 포만감
- fuel : 연료, 식량, 음식물
- hypothesize : 가설을 세우다[제기하다]
- eating behavior : 섭식 행동
- subject : 연구[실험] 대상, 피험자
- divide A into B : A를 B로 나누다
- participant : 참가자, 참여자
- questionnaire : 질문지, 설문지
- theorize : 이론을 제시하다[세우다]
- exert : 가하다, 행사하다, 노력하다
- population : 인구, 주민

해석

1970년대에 콜롬비아 대학의 사회 심리학자인 Stanley Schachter는 비만인 사람들이 배고픔, 포만감, 혹은 음식물의 필요와 같은 내부 신호에 적절하게 반응하지 못한다고 확신하게 되었다. 그는 비만인 사람들이 내부 신호보다는 오히려 외부 신호에 반응하여 먹는다는 가설을 제기했다. Schachter의 크래커 연구는 마른 피험자들과 비만인 피험자들의 섭식 행동을 비교했다. 그는 먼저 참가자들을 두 그룹으로 나누었는데, 한 그룹에게는 그들이 먹고 싶은 샌드위치를 모두 제공하고 다른 그룹에게는 음식에 대한 설문지를 작성하도록 요청했다. 그러고 나서 그는 모두에게 다섯 종류의 각기 다른 크래커를 맛볼 수 있는 동등한 기회를 주었다. 당연히 샌드위치를 이미 먹은 마른 사람들은 간단한 설문지를 작성한 마른 사람들보다 크래커를 덜 먹었다. 하지만 비만인 사람들은 샌드위치를 먼저 먹었든 안 먹었든 거의 같은 수의 크래커를 먹었다. Schachter는 음식을 보는 것이 배고픔이 없다는 사실을 알리는 내부적인 메시지보다 비만 인구를 견인했다는 이론을 제시했다.

22 ④ 제시문에 따르면 자본주의의 본질이 '창조적 파괴'에 있으며 오래되고 덜 효율적인 제품이나 서비스를 파괴하고 새롭고 더 효율적인 것으로 대체하는 과정이라고 하였다. 그러므로 자본주의가 비효율적인 기업들을 빠르게 망하도록 그냥 내버려두는 나라들은 자본이 풀리고 더 혁신적인 기업으로 나아가게 되어 세계화 시대에 '사라지는' 것이 아니

라 '생존하거나 번영할' 것이다. 따라서 ④의 'perish(사라지다)'는 'survive(살아남다)' 또는 'prosper(번영하다)' 등으로 바꿔 써야 한다.

어휘

- capitalism : 자본주의
- perpetual : 끊임없이 계속되는, 영구적인
- efficient : 효율적인, 능률적인
- paranoid : 편집증 환자, 피해망상 환자
- popularize : 대중화하다, 보급하다
- innovation : 혁신, 쇄신
- take place : 발생하다, 일어나다
- breakthrough : 돌파구
- obsolete : 한물간, 구식의
- constantly : 끊임없이, 지속적으로
- be freed up : 해방되다, 해소되다
- perish : 죽다, 소멸하다, 사라지다
- fall behind : 뒤떨어지다, 낙오하다

해석

Joseph Schumpeter는 자본주의의 본질이 '창조적 파괴'의 과정이라는 견해를 표명했다. 즉, 오래되고 덜 효율적인 제품이나 서비스를 파괴하고 새롭고 더 효율적인 것으로 대체하는 영구적인 사이클이다. Andy Grove는 Schumpeter의 통찰을 "편집증 환자만이 살아남는다."고 인정하고 여러 면에서 세계화 자본주의의 비즈니스 모델로 만들었다. Grove는 극적이고 산업적으로 변화하는 혁신이 오늘날 점점 더 빨리 일어나고 있다는 견해를 대중화하는 데 도움을 주었다. 이러한 기술적 돌파구 덕분에, 최신 발명품이 구식이 될 수 있는 속도는 이제 번개처럼 빠르다. 따라서 누가 그것들을 파괴하고 그것들에 한 걸음 앞선 새로운 것을 창조하고 있는지를 보기 위해 끊임없이 어깨 너머로 바라보고 있는 사람들, 즉 편집증 환자만이 살아남을 것이다. 자본주의가 비효율적인 기업들을 빠르게 망하도록 그냥 내버려두는 나라들은 자본이 풀리고 더 혁신적인 기업으로 나아가게 되어 세계화 시대에 <u>사라질(→ 살아남을)</u> 것이다. 이러한 창조적 파괴로부터 기업들을 보호하기 위해 정부에 의존하는 나라들은 이 시대에 뒤처질 것이다.

23 ③ 제시문에 따르면 보스턴과 케임브리지 아파트들은 오래 머물지 못하는 거주자의 특성상 시장에서 거래되는 것이 아니라 친구에서 친구로 대물림되기 때문에 집주인들은 새로운 세입자를 구해야 하는 부담을 덜어주는 이러한 대물림 행태를 좋아한다. 그러므로 ③의 'causes(초래하다)'는 'relieves(덜어주다)' 등으로 바꿔 써야 한다.

어휘

- postdoctoral : 박사 학위 취득자 후의 연구원, 박사 학위 취

득자

- definition : 정의 cf) by definition 정의상, 당연히
- expiration : 만료, 만기
- melting pot : (여러 인종과 문화가 뒤섞인 곳) 용광로, 도가니
- combination : 조합, 결합
- resident : 거주자, 주민
- turnover : 전환, 회전, 이동
- landlord : 주인, 지주, 임대주
- hand-me-down : 물려주는, 기성의, 만들어 놓은
- burden : 짐, 부담
- tenant : 세입자, 임차인
- real estate : 부동산
- secondary : 부수적인, 부차적인, 2차적인 cf) be secondary to ~에 버금가다.
- relevance : 연관성, 관련성, 적합성, 타당성
- embed : 박다, 끼워 넣다, 내재되다

해석

보스턴과 케임브리지는 많은 사람들이 그리 오래 머물지 않는 도시들이다. 이곳 사람들의 대다수가 대학원생과 박사 학위 취득자들로, 당연히 그들의 지위에 만료일이 있다는 것을 의미한다. 보스턴과 케임브리지는 여러 인종과 문화가 뒤섞인 곳이지만, 또한 작별 파티에서 새로운 친구를 사귀는 도시이기도 하다. 높은 거주자 이전률과 우정의 공존은 케임브리지에서 가장 좋은 아파트가 결코 시장에서 거래되지 못하는 상황을 만든다. 누군가가 좋은 아파트에서 이사 갈 때 항상 이사를 고려하는 친구가 생기고, 집주인들은 새로운 세입자를 구해야 하는 부담을 주기(→ 덜기) 때문에 보통 이러한 대물림 행태를 좋아한다. 그래서 교훈인 즉, 적어도 보스턴과 케임브리지의 경우, 아파트를 위한 부동산 시장은 소셜 네트워크에서 부차적이라는 것이다. 생애의 대부분을 소셜 네트워크의 경제적 연관성에 관해 연구한 사회학자 Mark Granovetter에 따르면, 케임브리지에서 학생용 아파트 시장은 소셜 네트워크에 내재되어 있다고 말할 수 있다.

24 ③ (A) 다음 문장에서 이러한 한계들은 학습을 나무를 조각하는 것에 비교하여 묘사되었다고 하였으므로, '한계'에 해당하는 'constrain(제한하다)'이 문맥상 적절하다.

(B) 처음에는 조각상과 거의 (B) 닮지 않은 나무 조각으로 시작하지만, 조각이 진행되면서 점차 최종 생산품처럼 보이게 된다는 의미이므로, 'resemblance(닮음)'가 문맥상 적절하다.

(C) 다음 문장에서 학습은 생물의 기존 행동 구조를 고려한다면 가장 성공적이라고 하였으므로, 나무를 조각하는 것은 기존의 결이나 나무 옹이와 조화를 이룰 때 가장

성공적이라고 할 수 있다. 그러므로 'harmony(조화)'가 문맥상 적절하다.

어휘

- infinitely : 무한히, 한없이, 대단히, 엄청
- flexible : 신축성[융통성] 있는, 유연한
- tendency : 성향, 경향, 성질
- constrain : 제한[제약]하다, 억제하다
- expand : 넓히다, 확장하다
- limitation : 국한, 제한, 한정
- elegantly : 우아하게, 고상하게
- analogy : 비유, 유추 cf) in an analogy 비유하여
- sculpt : 조각하다, 형상[형태]를 만들다
- resemblance : 닮음, 유사, 비슷함
- take into account : ~을 고려하다
- density : 밀도, 농도
- wood grain : 나뭇결
- knot : (나무 줄기의) 마디, 옹이
- conflict : 충돌, 갈등
- preexisting : 기존의
- in a similar fashion : 비슷한 방식으로

해석

행동은 무한히 유연하지 않고, 어떤 방향으로든 쉽게 움직인다. 오히려, 생물은 어떻게 학습하며 훈련 과정에서 기대되는 어떤 변화를 (A) 제한하는 자연스러운 행동 체계와 성향을 가지고 태어난다. 이러한 한계들은 학습을 나무조각상을 만드는 것에 비교한 연구자에 의해 우아하게 비유적으로 묘사되었다. 조각가는 조각상과 거의 (B) 닮지 않은 나무 조각으로 시작한다. 조각이 진행되면서, 나무 조각이 점점 더 최종 생산품처럼 보이게 된다. 그러나 조각가는 나뭇결의 방향과 밀도 그리고 나무가 지닌 옹이를 고려해야만 하기 때문에 그 과정은 제한이 없지 않다. 나무를 조각하는 것은 기존의 결이나 나무 옹이와 (C) 조화를 이룬다면 가장 성공적이다. 마찬가지로, 학습은 생물의 기존 행동 구조를 고려한다면 가장 성공적이다.

25 ② (A) 문맥상 식물이 그들의 종(種)이 지속될 수 있는 기회를 높이는 것이므로 'enhancing(향상시키다)'이 적절하다.

(B) 분명 곤충과 포유류 사이에는 크기에 차이가 있지만 둘 다 똑같이 영향을 받는 것이므로, 문맥상 'be subject to(~을 받다, 당하다)'가 적절하다.

(C) 우리가 특정 식물 성분들을 먹는 것에 장기적으로는 면역이 되어 있지 않지만, 우리 포유류들이 가지고 있는 엄청난 수의 세포들 때문에, 수년 동안 그러한 화합물을 소비하면서 나쁜 결과를 얻지 못할 수도 있다는 의미이다. 그러므로 문맥상 'damaging(해로운)'이 적절하다.

- alchemist : 연금술사
- sunbeam : 태양광선, 햇빛
- evolve : 발달하다, 진화하다
- biological warfare : 생물전, 세균전
- repel : 격퇴하다[물리치다], 접근하지 못하게 하다
- paralyze : 마비시키다
- disorient : 방향감각을 잃게 하다
- digestibility : 소화성[율], 소화능력
- enhance : 높이다, 향상시키다
- reduce : 줄이다, 축소하다
- remarkably : 두드러지게, 매우, 몹시
- lectin : 렉틴(주로 식물에서 추출되는 단백질)
- dine on : ~으로 식사를 하다, ~를 먹다
- quantum : 양자(量子)
- be subject to : ~을 받다, 당하다
- resistant : ~에 잘 견디는, 저항[반대]하는
- immune : 면역성이 있는, 면제되는
- compound : 화합물, 혼합물
- huge : 거대한, 엄청난

해석

식물은 훌륭한 화학자이자 연금술사이다. 즉, 그들은 햇빛을 물질로 바꿀 수 있다! 식물은 중독시키기, 마비시키기, 방향감각을 잃게 하기 등으로 포식자들이 접근하지 못하도록 생물학전을 이용하거나 그들의 종이 지속될 수 있는 기회를 (A) 향상시켜 생존과 종자 보전을 위한 자신의 소화능력을 감소시키도록 진화해왔다. 이러한 물리적이고 화학적인 방어 전략 모두 포식자들을 멀리하고, 때로는 식물들이 원하는 대로 동물들이 행동하도록 하는 데 몹시 효과적이다. 식물의 초기 포식자는 곤충이었기 때문에, 식물은 그들을 먹으려 하는 불운한 벌레들을 마비시킬 수 있는 렉틴을 개발했다. 분명히 곤충과 포유류 사이에는 양자 크기에 차이가 있지만, 둘 다 똑같은 영향을 (B) 받는다. 분명 여러분 대부분은 그것을 먹은 지 몇 분 내에 식물 화합물에 의해 마비되지는 않을 것이다. 물론 땅콩 한 알이 특정 사람들을 죽일 수 있는 가능성이 분명 있다. 그러나 우리는 특정 식물 성분들을 먹는 것은 장기적인 효과에 면역이 되어 있지 않다. 우리 포유류들이 가지고 있는 엄청난 수의 세포들 때문에, 우리는 수년 동안 그러한 화합물을 소비하는 데 (C) 해로운 결과를 보지 못할 수도 있다. 그리고 비록 이런 일이 당신에게 일어난다고 해도, 아직 그것을 알지 못한다.

26 ② 제시문에 따르면 다른 코끼리들이 죽어가고 있는 늙은 수컷 코끼리를 돕거나, 사냥꾼이 쏜 총에 맞은 부상당한 동료 코끼리를 돕는 것이 자주 목격되었다고 서술하고 있다. 그

러므로 빈칸에는 ②의 'compassion for their fellows(그들의 동료들에 대한 동정심)'가 들어갈 말로 가장 적절하다.

오답풀이
① 부상에 대한 자가 치료
③ 자손을 위한 가족 간의 연대
④ 그들의 포식 동물을 속이기 위한 기술
⑤ 야생에서 먹이를 구하기 위한 협력

- solely : 오로지, 단지
- claw : 발톱, 집게발
- bull elephant : 수컷 코끼리
- ton one's feet : 서 있는 상태로
- trunk : (코끼리의) 코
- tusk : 엄니, 상아
- strenuously : 강하게, 심하게
- comrade : 동무, 동료, 친구
- gunshot : 발포, 총소리
- work in concert : 협력하다
- companion : 동료, 동지, 벗
- gigantic : 거대한, 굉장히 큰
- stick : 집어넣다
- self-treatment : 자가 치료
- compassion : 연민, 동정심
- family ties : 가족 연대
- offspring : 자식, 자손, 새끼
- deceiving : 속이는, 기만하는
- predator : 포식자, 포식 동물
- collaboration : 협력, 협조, 제휴

해석

관찰자들은 야생 동물들이 단지 '이빨과 발톱'만으로 사는 것이 아니라 그들의 동료들에 대한 동정심을 자주 나타낸다는 것을 여러 차례 발견했다. 한 때, 늙은 수컷 코끼리가 죽어가고 있을 때, 인간 관찰자들은 그의 모든 가족이 그 코끼리를 다시 일어서게 하기 위해 온갖 시도를 다했다고 언급했다. 우선, 그들은 자기 코와 엄니를 그 코끼리 밑에 넣으려고 시도했다. 그때 그 늙은 녀석을 일으켜 세우려고 너무 세게 잡아당기다가 그 과정에서 어떤 놈은 자신의 엄니를 부러뜨렸다. 늙은 친구에 대한 그들의 걱정은 자신들의 안위보다 훨씬 더 컸다. 코끼리들은 총소리를 무서워하면서도 사냥꾼이 쏜 동지를 도우러 오는 것이 또한 관찰되었다. 다른 코끼리들은 부상당한 동료가 다시 걷도록 일으켜 세우기 위해 협력한다. 그들은 상처를 입은 코끼리의 어느 한 쪽을 밀착시키고 걸으면서, 그들의 거대한 몸 사이로 친구를 이동시키려고 협력한다. 코끼리

들은 또한 부상당한 친구에게 먹이를 주고 힘을 내도록 하기 위해 그들의 입에 풀을 집어넣는 것을 목격했다.

27 ① 제시문에 따르면 차에 탄 앞 좌석 승객이 대게 운전자들보다 더 불안해한다고 했으므로, 사람들이 두려움을 이겨내도록 도와주는 요인이 통제되고 있음을 보여준다. 그러므로 빈칸에는 ①의 'being in control(통제되고 있다)'이 들어갈 말로 가장 적절하다.

오답풀이

② 지켜보기
③ 좋은 일을 회상하기
④ 친구와 함께 하기
⑤ 적절한 훈련과 연습

어휘

- factor : 요소, 요인
- withstand : 견뎌내다, 이겨내다
- reveal : 드러내다, 폭로하다
- aircrew : 항공기 승무원
- theater of operation : 작전 구역, 전투 지역
- sign up : 참가하다, 가입하다
- enlisted man : 사병, 지원병
- single-handed : 혼자의, 단독의
- heavy bomber crew : 중폭격기 승무원
- reluctance : 싫음, 마지못해 함, 꺼림
- casualty : 사상자, 피해자 cf) casualty rate : 사상률
- dreadful : 끔찍한, 지독한
- companion : 동료, 친구, 벗
- proper : 적당한, 타당한

해석

사람들이 두려움을 이겨내도록 도와주는 요인이 통제되고 있다. 예를 들어, 차에 탄 앞 좌석 승객은 대게 운전자들보다 더 불안해한다. 미군에 대한 연구에서 이러한 사실이 밝혀졌는데, 1944년 6월 유럽의 작전 구역에 있던 승무원에게 "다시 한 번 전투비행에 참가할 생각이 있느냐?"고 물었을 때이다. 조종사들은 항상 다른 사병들(39~51%) 이상으로 "네, 꼭 그러겠습니다"(51~84%)라고 답했고, 전투기 조종사들은 폭격기 조종사(51~74%)보다 단독 비행(84%)이 많았다. 중폭격기 승무원들은 그들이 더 많은 임무를 수행할수록 점점 더 꺼리는 모습을 보였는데, 그 이유는 어렵지 않게 찾을 수 있다. 사상자율(70% 이상이 6개월 후 작전 중 전사 또는 실종, 17.5%가 작전 중 부상 또는 상해)이 끔찍했다.

28 ② 빈칸 앞의 'capability(능력)'는 우리 자신의 아이들을 설계하고 인류 자체를 일종의 공예품으로 만들 수 있는 생명공

학이나 유전공학의 능력을 의미한다. 그러므로 빈칸에는 ②의 'to alter nature in fundamental ways(근본적인 방법으로 자연을 변화시키다)'가 들어갈 말로 가장 적절하다.

오답풀이

① 과학을 미학적으로 이용하다
③ 변형이 거의 없는 재료를 생산하다
④ 복잡한 시스템에서 숨겨진 결함을 감지하고 찾아내다
⑤ 외부와 내부의 위험으로부터 생명을 지키다

어휘

- contemporary : 동시대의, 당대의, 현대의
- ethical : 도덕적인, 윤리적인
- address : 고심하다, 다루다
- emerging : 신흥의, 신생의, 최근 생겨난
- genetic engineering : 유전공학
- prospect : 가능성, 가망성, 예상
- humanity : 인류, 인간
- artifact : 인공물, 공예품
- at a crossroads : 기로에 서 있는, 갈림길에 서 있는
- relinquish : 포기하다, 내주다
- biotechnology : 생명공학
- prohibit : 금하다, 금지하다
- genie : (램프 속의) 정령, 요정
- long-range : 장거리를 가는, 장기적인
- humility : 겸손, 겸허

해석

몇몇 현대 기술은 인류가 이전에 결코 다루지 않았던 종류의 문제인, 새롭고 심각한 윤리적 문제를 여는 것처럼 보인다. 예를 들어 유전공학의 새로운 기술은 우리 자신의 아이들을 설계하고 인류 자체를 일종의 공예품으로 만들 수 있는 가능성이 있다. 일부 저술가들은 이러한 가능성을 환영하는 듯하지만, 다른 작가들은 우리가 그러한 용감한 새로운 세계를 창조할 수 있게 해줄 지식을 얻을 기회를 포기해야 하는 기로에 서 있다고 믿는다. 다른 이들은 우리가 생명공학이나 유전공학이 인간에게 어떻게 사용될 것인지에 대해 어떤 용도는 허용하지만 다른 용도는 금지시키는 합리적인 제한을 둘 수 있다고 믿는다. 식물과 일부 동물 종(種)의 유전자 공학은 이미 널리 사용되고 있으며, 이 특별한 램프 속 요정을 다시 병에 넣는 것은 이미 불가능할 수도 있다. Hans Jonas는 우리에게 근본적인 방법으로 자연을 변화시킬 수 있는 능력을 부여한 이러한 기술들은 '장기적인 책임감'과 무엇보다도 겸허함을 가지고 접근해야 한다고 믿는다.

29 ③ 빈칸의 앞 문장에서 짧은 시간 동안에도 감정 표현이 덜한 사람의 기분이 감정 표현이 많은 사람의 기분을 닮아 갔는

데, 장시간의 접촉에 감정 이동이 더 많을 거라는 것은 이해하기 쉽다는 내용이다. 그러므로 빈칸에는 ③의 'can be even more infectious with prolonged contact(장시간의 접촉으로 훨씬 더 많이 옮겨갈 수 있다)'가 들어갈 말로 가장 적절하다.

오답풀이
① 최적 기능을 위해 가장 잘 관리될 수 있다.
② 외부 자극과는 무관하게 작동할 수 있다.
④ 사회 문화적 규범에 의해 영향을 받는다.
⑤ 모든 창조 과정과 관련이 있다.

어휘
• calm : 조용한, 침착한
• previously : 미리, 사전에
• spoil : 망치다, 못쓰게 만들다
• grouch : 불평이 많은 사람
• verbal : 언어[말]의, 구두의
• volunteer : 자원봉사자, 지원자
• identify : 확인하다, 알아보다
• exposure : 노출, 폭로
• optimal : 최적의, 최상의
• independently : 독립하여, 자주적으로
• external : 외부의, 밖의
• stimuli : stimulus(자극, 격려)의 복수
• infectious : 전염되는, 옮기 쉬운
• prolonged : 오래 계속되는, 장기적인
• norm : 표준, 규범

해석
조용한 사람 곁에 있을 때 마음이 더 평화로워지거나, 또는 이전에 불평이 많은 사람과 만나서 유쾌한 기분을 망쳤던 사례들을 틀림없이 기억할 수 있다. 연구원들은 이러한 과정은 빨리 일어나며 있다 해도 언어적 의사소통이 그다지 필요하지 않다는 것을 입증했다. 한 연구에서, 두 명의 지원자가 그들의 기분을 확인하는 조사를 마쳤다. 그 후 그들은 조용히 앉아서 2분 동안 서로 마주보고, 연구원이 방으로 돌아오기를 기다렸다. 끝날 무렵에 그들은 감정 상태를 확인하는 또 다른 조사를 마쳤다. 시간이 흘러, 짧은 노출에도 감정 표현이 덜한 사람의 기분은 감정 표현이 많은 사람의 기분을 닮아 갔다. 어떻게 감정이 장시간의 접촉으로 훨씬 더 많이 옮겨갈 수 있는지 이해하기란 쉽다. 불과 몇 달 만에, 데이트하는 연인들과 대학 룸메이트들의 감정적인 반응은 훨씬 더 비슷해진다.

30 ② 빈칸의 다음 문장에서 언어 사용과 관련된 자극이 두뇌 발달의 분발을 더욱 촉진시킨다고 하였고, 제시문의 마지막 문장에서 언어 사용은 단순히 우리가 의사소통을 할 수 있

다는 것뿐만 아니라, 우리가 외부 세계를 인식하는 방식에 심각한 영향을 미친다고 하였다. 그러므로 빈칸에는 ②의 'to memorize events much more precisely(사건을 훨씬 더 정확하게 기억하다)'가 들어갈 말로 가장 적절하다.

오답풀이
① 자연에 대한 호기심을 표현하다
③ 우리의 지각 경험을 다른 사람들과 공유하다
④ 우리 주변의 동물들과 의사소통하다
⑤ 창의적인 생각을 행동으로 옮기다

어휘
• stimulation : 자극, 격려
• associated with : ~와 관련된
• facilitate : 가능[용이]하게 하다, 촉진하다
• spurt : 분출, 분발, 용솟음침
• apparatus : 기구, 기관, 장치 cf) vocal apparatus 발성기관
• sign language : 수화(手話)
• tiny : 아주 작은
• fraction : 부분, 일부
• comparative : 비교의, 비교적, 비교를 통한
• accelerate : 가속화되다, 속도를 높이다
• obvious : 분명한, 명백한
• merely : 그저, 단지, 한낱
• profoundly : 깊이, 극심하게, 심오하게
• perceive : 인지하다, 깨닫다
• precisely : 바로, 꼭, 정확히
• perceptual : 지각의, 지각이 있는

해석
언어 사용은 우리가 사건을 훨씬 더 정확하게 기억할 수 있도록 해준다는 많은 증거가 있는데, 이는 언어 사용과 관련된 자극이 두뇌 발달의 분발을 더욱 촉진시키기 때문이다. 인간의 가족 환경에서 침팬지들을 양육함으로써 그들에게 언어 사용을 가르치려는 시도가 확대되어 왔다. 침팬지들은 말을 하기 위한 발성기관이 없기 때문에, 미국의 수화를 사용하여 교육을 받았다. 침팬지들에게 생의 처음 5년 동안 몇 백 단어까지 가르치는 것이 가능한 것으로 입증되었는데, 이것은 인간의 아이들이 성취하는 극히 일부분이다. 인간과 침팬지의 비교 능력은 첫 번째 생일과 두 번째 생일 사이에 아이들 사이에서 언어가 발달하는 시점까지 다소 유사하며, 그 이후 우리의 정신 발달은 침팬지의 정신 발달보다 훨씬 더 가속화된다. 연관점은 언어 사용을 배우기 전에 그 시기에 대한 기억이 거의 없다는 것이다. 언어 사용은 단순히 우리가 의사소통을 할 수 있다는 것뿐만 아니라, 우리가 외부 세계를 인식하는 방식에 심각한 영향을 미친다는 점은 분명하다.

31 ⑤ 글 (C)에서 일반적인 보고서는 슈퍼마켓에서 가장 잘 팔리는 제품을 식별할 수 있으나, 글 (B)에서 데이터 마이닝이나 비즈니스 인텔리전스의 도움을 받은 보고서는 이뿐만 아니라 그 제품이 최고인 이유를 설명할 수 있다고 하였다. 그러므로 글 (C) 다음에 글 (B)가 이어져야 한다. 또한 글 (A)에서 '왜'를 아는 이러한 능력이란 글 (B)에서 그 제품이 최고인 이유를 의미하므로, 글 (A) 앞에 글 (B)가 와야 한다. 그러므로 주어진 글 다음에 (C) – (B) – (A)의 순서로 이어져야 한다.

어휘

- profitable : 수익성이 있는, 이득이 되는
- advanced : 발전된, 진보된, 고급[상급]의
- analytical method : 분석 기법
- encompass : 포함[포괄]하다, 망라하다
- data mining : 데이터 마이닝(대규모 자료를 토대로 새로운 정보를 찾아내는 것)
- business intelligence : 비즈니스 인텔리전스(기업 정보 수집 활동)
- empower : 권한을 주다[부여하다], 할 수 있게 하다
- strategic : 전략상 중요한, 전략적인
- capitalize : 자본화하다, 투자[출자]하다 cf) capitalize on ~을 이용[활용]하다
- newfound : 새로 발견된
- statistical : 통계학상의, 통계에 근거한
- visualization : 눈에 보이게 함, 시각화
- neural : 신경의 cf) neural network 신경망
- uncover : 알아내다, 발견하다

해석

> 오늘날 많은 수익성 있는 사업의 성공 비결은 고급 분석 기법을 사용한 데이터 처리 능력에 있다. 정보관리 업무는 단순히 데이터를 저장하는 것 이상을 포괄한다. 그것은 또한 새로운 형태의 비즈니스 인텔리전스를 이용하여 데이터를 처리함으로써 '데이터 마이닝' 또는 정보 획득을 취급한다.

(C) 이런 이유로, 조직은 데이터 마이닝 기법(통계 분석, 시각화 및 신경망의 도움을 받아)에 투자하여 숨겨진 패턴을 알아내고 새로운 지식을 발견하며 결과적으로 현재의 비즈니스 상황에 대한 더 많은 통찰력을 얻을 필요가 있다. 예를 들어, 일반적인 보고서는 슈퍼마켓에서 가장 잘 팔리는 제품을 식별할 수 있다.

(B) 그러나 데이터 마이닝이나 비즈니스 인텔리전스의 도움을 받은 보고서는 슈퍼마켓에서 가장 잘 팔리는 제품을 식별할 수 있을 뿐만 아니라 그 제품이 최고인 이유를 설명할

수 있다.

(A) 그러므로 '왜'를 아는 이러한 능력은 조직이 필요한 전략적 변화를 만들 수 있도록 힘을 실어줄 것이다. 예를 들어, 조직은 고객과 보다 강력한 일대일 관계를 구축함으로써 새로 발견된 지식을 활용해야만 한다.

32 ③ 주어진 글 다음에는 관심 부족의 사례에 대해 설명한 글 (B)가 와야 한다. 글 (B) 다음에는 관심 부족에 대한 캐나다의 전술을 설명한 글 (C)가 와야 한다. 마지막으로는 캐나다가 미국의 관심을 끄는 데 성공했고, 결국 미국의 고위급 협상 참여를 유도했다고 설명한 글 (A)가 와야 한다. 그러므로 주어진 글 다음에 (B) – (C) – (A)의 순서로 이어져야 한다.

어휘

- Free Trade Agreement : 자유무역협정
- negotiation : 협상, 교섭
- statement : 성명, 진술, 발언
- significant : 중요한, 의미 있는
- provoke : 일으키다, 유발하다
- diplomatic : 외교의, 외교적인
- ally : 동맹국, 연합국
- participation : 참여, 참가
- enhance : 높이다, 향상시키다, 강화하다
- manifest : 드러내다, 나타내다
- entrust : 맡기다, 위임[위탁]하다
- official : 공무원, 관리
- authority : 관헌, 당국
- tactic : 전략, 작전, 전술
- stall : (교묘하게) 시간을 벌다

해석

> 캐나다-미국 자유무역협정의 사례에서 보듯, 캐나다는 협상에서 캐나다의 국력을 증가시키기 위해 미국 정치 지도자들의 관심을 얻는 것이 중요했다. 강자의 관심 부족은 상대방을 특별히 강력하거나 비중 있게 생각하지 않는다는 발언인 경우가 많다.

(B) 그러한 관심 부족은 여러 면에서 나타나겠지만, 그것은 거의 항상 자국의 정치적 지도부에 대한 권한과 접근성이 제한된 비교적 하급 관리들에게 협상을 맡김으로써 입증된다.

(C) 캐나다는 이번 협상에서 이 문제에 직면했다. 관심을 끌기 위한 전술로는 협상에서 시간을 벌거나 발을 빼는 것이 포함될 수 있다. 캐나다와 미국의 자유무역협정에서 캐나다는 미국이 그 협상을 심각하게 받아들이지 않고 있다고 느끼자 퇴장했다.

(A) 이 조치는 오랜 동맹국인 두 나라 사이의 외교적 위기를 유발했고 미국의 관심을 끄는 데 성공했으며, 이는 미국의 고위급 협상 참여로 이어졌다. 캐나다는 역사적으로 강한 양국 관계를 바탕으로 국력을 키웠다.

33 ④ 제시문은 '법'이라는 용어가 다양한 의미로 사용되어 왔음을 보여주고 있다. 주어진 글에서 법은 사회 행동의 규범이나 기준을 집행하는 수단으로 사용된 것이므로, 전통적인 사회에서 흔히 볼 수 있는 비공식적인 절차에서부터 현대 사회의 전형적인 공식적 법체계에 이르기까지 모든 조직화된 사회에서 작용하는 법의 형태를 설명한 ④에 위치하는 것이 가장 적절하다.

어휘

• alternative : 대안적인, 대체의
• enforce : 집행[시행]하다, 강요하다
• norm : 규범, 기준, 표준
• descriptive : 서술하는, 기술적인
• obvious : 분명한, 명확한
• thermodynamics : 열역학
• employ : 고용하다, 쓰다[이용하다]
• predictable : 예측[예견]할 수 있는
• inevitable : 불가피한, 필연적인
• assertion : 주장, 단언
• uncover : 알아내다, 밝혀내다
• underlie : 기초[토대]가 되다, 근간을 이루다
• ranging from A to B : 범위가 A에서 B까지 이르다
• by contrast : 그에 반해서, 대조적으로
• specifically : 구체적으로, 분명히
• distinctive : 구별이 있는, 독특한, 특수한
• institution : 기관, 단체, 협회

해석

그러나 대체 용도로는 일반적으로 법을 사회 행동의 규범이나 기준을 집행하는 수단으로 다룬다.

'법'이라는 용어는 매우 다양한 의미로 사용되어 왔다. 우선, 과학적 법칙이나 기술적 법칙이라고 불리는 것이 있다. 이것들은 자연 또는 사회 생활에서 발견되는 규칙적이거나 필연적인 행동 패턴을 묘사한다. (①) 가장 분명한 예는 자연과학에서 찾을 수 있는데, 가령 물리학자들에 의해 발전된 운동법칙과 열역학이 있다. (②) 그러나 이러한 법 개념은 예측 가능하고, 심지어 필연적인 사회 행동 양식을 강조하기 위한 시도로 사회 이론가들에 의해서도 이용되어 왔다. (③) 이것은 마르크스가 역사적이고 사회적인 발전 '법칙'을 밝혀냈다는 엥겔스의 주장과 경제이론의 근간인 이른바 수요와 공급의 '법

칙'에서 볼 수 있다. (④) 따라서 사회학자들은 전통적인 사회에서 흔히 볼 수 있는 비공식적인 절차에서부터 현대 사회의 전형적인 공식적 법체계에 이르기까지 모든 조직화된 사회에서 작용하는 법의 형태를 보아 왔다. (⑤) 이와는 대조적으로, 정치 이론가들은 법을 다른 사회적 규칙이나 규범과는 분명히 분리되어 있고 현대 사회에서나 찾아볼 수 있는 독특한 사회 기관으로 보고, 법을 좀 더 구체적으로 이해하는 경향이 있었다.

34 ④ 제시문은 항생제의 남용으로 인한 부작용을 소개한 글이다. 주어진 글은 항생제의 효능이 듣지 않는 박테리아에 대해 언급하고 있으므로, 항생제 내성에 대해 언급한 ④에 위치하는 것이 가장 적절하다.

어휘

• antibiotics : 항생제, 항생물질
• efficacy : 효과, 효능
• render : 되게 하다, 만들다
• initially : 처음에, 당초에
• infection : 감염, 전염병
• godsend : 뜻밖의[하늘이 준] 선물
• drastically : 과감하게, 획기적으로, 대폭
• life expectancy : 기대수명
• fix : 해결책
• side effect : 부작용
• digestion : 소화, 소화력
• invasive : 급속히 퍼지는, 침습성의
• antibiotic resistance : 항생제 내성
• population : 개체군, 개체 수
• in a matter of years : 불과 몇 년 사이에, 수년 안에
• staphylococci : 포도상구균

해석

또 다른 예기치 못한 결과는 항생제의 효능을 부여하여 그들을 쓸모없게 만드는 메커니즘을 극복한 박테리아의 능력이다.

처음에 기적의 약처럼 보인 항생제는 한때 널리 보급되어 세균 감염뿐만 아니라 일반적인 감기부터 두통까지 모든 것에 사용되었다. (①) 실제로 항생제는 의약품을 획기적으로 개선시키고 20세기 동안 기대수명의 증대에 크게 기여한 신의 선물이었다. (②) 많은 기술적 해결책과 마찬가지로, 항생제의 긍정적인 이점과 함께 부정적인 부작용이 나타났다. (③) 항생제는 인체에 유익한 많은 박테리아를 죽일 수 있는데, 가령 침습성 박테리아와 함께 소화를 촉진하는 박테리아도 죽일 수 있다. (④) 처음 실험실에서 호기심으로 본 항생제 내성

은 항생제에 노출된 박테리아 개체군 사이에서 일반화되었다. (⑤) 페니실린의 도입 후 불과 몇 년 만에, 페니실린을 파괴하는 포도상구균이 페니실린의 초기 사용이 많았던 병원에서 나타났다.

35 ③ 제시문은 인간보다 훨씬 정교하게 주변 환경에서 일어나는 것을 감지하고 반응하며 살아가는 생물들에 대해 설명하고 있다. 그러나 ③은 땅에 뿌리를 박고 있어 제대로 주변 환경에 적응할 수 없는 수동적 식물에 대해 설명하고 있으므로 전체적인 글의 흐름과 어울리지 않는다.

> 어휘

- inertly : 비활동적으로, 둔하게
- inhabitant : 서식 동물, 어떤 장소에 살고 있는 생물
- pasture : 초원, 목초지
- Hellenes : 그리스인
- perceive : 감지[인지]하다, 지각하다
- sophistication : 교양, 세련, 정교
- surpass : 능가하다, 뛰어넘다
- sundew plant : 끈끈이주걱(식충 식물)
- grasp : 꽉 잡다, 움켜 잡다
- infallible : 틀림없는, 어김없는, 확실한
- accuracy : 정확, 정확도
- prey : 먹이, 사냥감, 희생자
- parasitical : 기생의
- slight : 약간의, 조금의, 경미한
- odor : 냄새, 악취
- victim : 피해자, 제물, 먹이
- obstacle : 장애, 장애물
- crawl : 기다, 기어가다
- unfavorable : 호의적이 아닌, 불리한
- nectar : 꿀, 과일즙
- stem : 줄기
- sophisticated : 지적인, 수준 높은
- enlist : 모집하다, 응모하다, 협력[찬성]하다
- herbivorous : 초식의, 초식성의

> 해석

기존에 비활동적으로 움직이는 것과 달리, 초원의 서식 생물, 즉 고대 그리스인들이 보탄이라고 부르는 것은 인간보다 훨씬 정교하게 그들의 환경에서 일어나고 있는 것을 감지하고 반응할 수 있는 것처럼 보인다. ① 끈끈이주걱 식물은 먹이가 있는 곳을 향해 올바른 방향으로 움직이면서, 어김없이 정확하게 파리를 붙잡을 것이다. ② 어떤 기생 식물들은 먹이 냄새의 경미한 흔적도 알아챌 수 있으며, 모든 장애물을 극복하고 그 방향으로 기어갈 것이다. ③ 식물은 땅에 뿌리를 박고 있어

서 어떤 것이 필요할 때 또는 상황이 불리하게 변할 때 들어서 움직일 수 없기 때문에 곤란에 처한다. ④ 식물은 어느 개미가 자기 꿀을 훔치지 알고 있는 것 같아서, 이 개미들이 가까이 있을 때는 닫히고, 개미가 올라가지 못하도록 줄기에 충분한 이슬이 맺혀 있을 때는 열린다. ⑤ 더 수준 높은 아카시아 나무는 실제로 다른 곤충과 초식동물들로부터 보호하는 대가로 꿀로 보상하는 특정 개미들의 보호 서비스에 협력한다.

36 ④ 제시문은 기본적으로 위치나 규모와 같은 지리적 개념에 의존하는 교통지리학에 대해 설명하고 있다. 그러므로 개인적이고 체계적인 교통수단 덕택에 관광 산업이 발달하게 되었다고 관광 산업의 내용을 다룬 ④는 전체적인 글의 흐름과 어울리지 않는다.

> 어휘

- geography : 지리, 지리학
- evolve : 진화하다, 발전하다
- inherently : 선천적으로, 본질적으로
- facilitate : 가능하게[용이하게] 하다
- regional : 지방의, 지역의
- considerable : 상당한, 많은
- scope : 범위, 영역, 여유, 여지
- factor : 요소, 요인
- constrain : 제한[제약]하다

> 해석

교통지리학은 경제지리로부터 발전한 지리학의 한 주요 분야이다. 물론, 관광과 마찬가지로 교통도 장소를 연결하고 상품과 사람들의 이동을 가능하게 하기 때문에 본질적으로 지리학적이다. ① 교통지리학은 기본적으로 위치나 규모와 같은 지리적 개념에 의존한다. ② 예를 들어, 위치는 특정 위치로부터 또는 특정 위치로의 이동이 가능한지의 여부 및 해당 이동이 어떻게 발생하는지를 포함한 이동 패턴을 형성한다. ③ 교통망은 현지의 지역적 규모로 존재하며, 현대 세계에서 점차 글로벌 시스템으로 연결되고 있다. ④ 훨씬 더 빠른 개인적이고 체계적인 교통수단 덕분에, 오후 드라이브, 주간 여행, 야간 숙박과 주말은 관광 산업뿐만 아니라 관광객들에게도 상당한 여유를 더했다. ⑤ 게다가 물리적 장소와 인적 장소 모두 교통수단을 허용하거나 제한하는 지리적 요인이 많다.

37 ⑤ 제시문에서 생물학자인 Garrett Hardin은 땅, 물, 공기 등에 재산권이 있다면 공장에서부터 시끄러운 음악에 이르기까지 모든 것에 의해 야기되는 외적인 것을 피할 수 있다고 보고 있다. 즉, 그것들을 사적으로 소유한다면 환경적 피해를 막을 수 있다는 것이다. 그러므로 (A)에는 'prevented(막다)', (B)에는 'privately(사적으로)'가 들어갈 말로 적절하다.

	(A)		(B)
①	야기하다	……	독점적으로
②	야기하다	……	상업적으로
③	밝히다	……	흔히
④	막다	……	공적으로

어휘

- dump : 버리다 cf) dump A into B A를 B에 버리다
- sewage : 하수, 오물 cf) sewage disposal 하수 처리
- purchase : 구입하다, 사다
- septic : 썩은, 부패한 cf) septic system 오수정화 시스템
- disposal : 처리, 처분
- fraction : 부분, 일부
- internalize : 내면화하다, 받아들이다
- incentive : 자극, 유인, 동기
- prohibit : 금하다, 금지하다, ~하지 못하게 하다
- biologist : 생물학자
- assign : 맡기다, 할당하다
- property right : 재산권
- externality : 외부성, 외부 효과
- poaching : 불법 침입, 침해, 침범
- well-defined : 잘 정의된, 명확한, 분명한
- open-access : 개방 접근의
- exclusively : 배타적으로, 독점적으로
- commercially : 상업적으로, 영리적으로
- disclose : 밝히다, 폭로하다, 드러내다
- commonly : 흔히, 보통

해석

폐기물을 처리하고 보관하기 위해 오수정화 시스템을 구입하기보다는 공공 호수에 하수를 버리는 가구를 생각해 보자. 이 '직선관' 처리 방식은 수상 스포츠와 식수원으로서의 호수의 매력을 손상시킨다. 비록 하수를 버리는 사회적 비용이 오수정화 시스템의 비용보다 더 크지만, 버리는 피해의 전체 중 일부만을 부담하기 때문에 개인 가구의 버리는 비용은 크지 않다. 만약 호수 지역이 하수를 버리는 가구에 속해 있다면, 그 가구는 버리는 것으로 인한 전체 사회적 비용을 받아들이고 오수정화 시스템에 투자하게 될 것이다. 만약 호수 지역이 그밖의 누군가에 속해 있다면, 그 사람은 버리는 것을 금하고 주의 깊게 감시할 동기를 얻을 것이다. 생물학자인 Garrett Hardin은 땅, 물, 공기에 재산권을 할당함으로써 사회는 공장에서부터 시끄러운 음악에 이르기까지 모든 것에 의해 야기되는 외적인 것을 피할 수 있을 것이라고 느꼈다. 그의 논지의 증거로서, 남의 영역에 대한 침해는 재산권이 명확하고 엄격하게 시행되는 국가들보다 재산권이 약한 국가들에서 훨씬 더

큰 문제이다.

↓

Garrett Hardin에 따르면, 그 지역들을 (B) 사적으로 소유한다면, 호수 같은 개방 접근 지역에 대한 환경적 피해를 (A) 막을 수 있을 것이라고 한다.

[38~39]

어휘

- divorce : 분리하다, 단절시키다 cf) divorce A from B A와 B를 분리하다
- intertwine : 얽히다, 엮이다.
- inevitably : 필연적으로, 불가피하게
- dominant : 우세한, 지배적인
- ratio : 비, 비율
- appropriate : 적절한, 타당한
- metaphor : 은유, 비유
- impel : 강요하다, 재촉하다, 추진하다
- tremendous : 거대한, 엄청난
- subject to : ~을 받다[당하다]
- predator : 포식자, 포식 동물
- rein : 고삐
- gallop : 전속력, 질주
- beforehand : 사전에, 미리
- boldness : 대담, 뱃심, 배짱
- slave : 노예, 종속
- channel : 쏟다, 돌리다, 전환하다
- rationality : 순리성, 합리성
- optimal : 최적의, 최상의
- tame : 길들이다, 다스리다
- harness : 마구를 채우다[씌우다], 이용[활용]하다
- suppression : 진압, 억제

해석

우리는 감정과 생각을 분리할 수 없다. 그 둘은 완전히 얽혀 있다. 그러나 필연적으로 (a) 우세한 요소가 있는데, 어떤 사람들은 분명 다른 사람들보다 감정에 더 지배된다. 우리가 찾는 것은 알맞은 비율과 균형이며, 가장 효과적인 행동으로 이어지는 것이다. 고대 그리스인들은 이것에 대해 적절한 비유로 기수와 말을 들었다.
말은 끊임없이 우리를 움직이도록 (b) 재촉하는 감정적인 본성이다. 이 말은 엄청난 에너지와 힘을 가지고 있지만, 기수가 없으면 인도할 수 없다. 그것은 야생적이고 포식자의 영향을 받으며 계속해서 문제를 일으킨다. 기수는 우리의 사고

력 자체이다. 훈련과 연습을 통해 고삐를 잡고 말을 인도하여, 이 강력한 동물 에너지를 (c) 생산적인 것으로 변화시킨다. 다른 한쪽이 없는 것은 쓸모가 없다. 기수 없이는 지시된 움직임이나 목적도 없다. 말이 없으면 에너지도 힘도 없다. 대부분의 사람들은 말이 우세하고, 기수는 약하다. 어떤 사람들은 기수가 너무 강하고 고삐를 너무 꽉 잡아서 가끔 동물들이 질주하는 것을 (d) 기꺼이 한다(→ 꺼린다). 말과 기수는 함께 일해야만 한다. 이것은 (e) 미리 우리 행동을 고려한다는 것을 의미하며, 우리는 결정을 내리기 전에 어떤 상황에 대해 가능한 한 많은 생각을 한다. 그러나 일단 무엇을 할지 결정하게 되면, 고삐를 풀고 대담함과 모험정신을 가지고 행동에 들어간다. 이 에너지의 노예가 되는 대신에, 우리는 그것을 전환한다. 그것이 순리의 본질이다.

38 ① 제시문에서 감정과 생각을 각각 말과 기수로 비유하여, 감정과 생각은 분리할 수 없고 우리가 찾는 것은 알맞은 비율과 균형이며 가장 효과적인 행동으로 이어지는 것이라고 하였다. 그러므로 ①의 'necessity of finding the optimal balance of thinking and emotion(생각과 감정의 최적 균형을 찾는 필요성)'이 윗글의 주제로 가장 적절하다.

오답풀이
② 야생동물을 길들이고 이용하는 전통적 기술
③ 정서적 억압이 육체적 건강에 미치는 영향
④ 경마에서 이기기 위한 올바른 기술을 터득하는 어려움
⑤ 스포츠에서 철학의 중요성에 대한 고대 그리스의 개념들

39 ④ 어떤 사람들은 기수가 너무 강하고 고삐를 너무 꽉 잡아서 가끔 동물들이 질주하는 것을 '기꺼이 한다'가 아니고 '꺼린다'고 해야 문맥상 적절하다. 그러므로 'willing'을 'unwilling'으로 고쳐 써야 옳다.

오답풀이
① (a) 우세한
② (b) 재촉하는
③ (c) 생산적인
⑤ (e) 미리

[40~41]

어휘
• observer : 관찰자, 목격자, 참관인
• feature : 특종[특집]으로 하다, 대서특필하다
• enhancement : 향상, 증대, 강화 cf) human enhancement 인간 증강(사람의 인지와 몸의 성능을 높이기 위한 기술)
• article : 글, 기사

• be fit with : ~와 맞다, 설비[장착]하다
• state-of-the-art : 최신 기술의, 최첨단의
• bionic : 생체공학적인
• prosthetic : 보철의, 인공기관의
• outperform : 더 나은 결과를 내다, 능가하다
• limb : (하나의) 팔[다리]
• norm : 규격, 규범, 일반적인 것
• editorial : 편집의, 사설의
• out of the equation : 상황에서 벗어난[분리된]
• diagnosis : 진단, 판단
• aliment : 병, 질병
• appropriate : 적절한, 타당한
• recommendation : 추천, 권고
• dystopia : 디스토피아(反 유토피아), 반이상향
• cyborg : 사이보그, 인조인간
• practitioner : (전문직 종사자)의사, 변호사
• accessible : 접근 가능한, 이용 가능한
• disabled person : 장애인, 불구자
• equal treatment : 평등한 대우
• foretell : 예언하다, 예견하다
• calm : 진정시키다, 가라앉히다
• outdated : 구식의, 시대에 뒤떨어진
• trigger : 촉발시키다, 작동시키다
• sophisticated : 정교한, 세련된

해석
어제 발행된 '옵저버' 잡지에서는 9월 런던에서 열리는 FutureFest 축제를 앞두고 인간 증강에 관한 두 작품을 특집으로 다루고 있다. 이 기사에는 왼손 없이 태어난 스위스 남성인 Bertolt Meyer가 최근 최첨단 생체공학(스마트폰으로 조종)을 장착했다는 글과 Nick Bostrom과 Andy Miah와 같은 인간 증강 주제와 관련된 유명 저자들의 인용문도 포함되어 있다. 현재 Meyer와 같은 인공기관은 그것이 없는 사람들 사이에서 정상적인 인간의 기능을 회복하는 데 이용된다. 그러나 그러한 장치들은 속도, 힘, 행동 통제 등의 측면에서 결국 '자연적인' 팔다리를 능가할 정도로 점점 더 (A) 정교해짐에 따라 "이 장치들 중 하나를 다는 것이 일반적인 일이 될까?"라고 Meyer가 묻는다. 또한 '옵저버' 사설의 작가가 걱정하는 것처럼, "이 기술과 기기들이 너무 똑똑해져서 인간이 그 상황에서 모두 벗어날 수 있게 되면 어떻게 될까?" 예를 들어, 만약 우리가 적절한 치료 권고뿐만 아니라 질병에 대한 진단을 받기 위해 단지 인간 의사가 아닌 스마트폰으로 눈을 돌릴 수 있다면 어떨까? 그러한 제안은 사람들이 구직 시장(경쟁력 있는 스포츠 포함)과 다른 맥락에서 경쟁력을 유지하려면 좋든 싫든 '사이보그'가 되라는 압력을 받는 디스토피아의 미래에 대한 두려움을 (B) 촉발시킬 수 있고, 혹은 더 성능 좋은 기계에

의해 점차 쓸모없게 되며, 실생활에서 인간의 상호작용은 줄어들고(일반적인 전문직 종사자들뿐만 아니라, 슈퍼마켓 계산대의 직원을 대체하는 기계 등), 지금보다 이용 가능성이 떨어지게 된다(인간 의사를 보기 위해 상당한 프리미엄을 지불해야 한다고 생각한다).

40 ② 제시문은 '옵저버' 잡지에 실린 인간 증강에 대한 특집 기사를 토대로, '자연적인' 팔다리를 능가하는 인공기관의 탄생과 인간 증강 기술의 발달로 인한 사회적 문제점에 대해 서술하고 있다. 그러므로 ②의 "Human Enhancement Technologies: Blessing or Curse?(인간 증강 기술: 행복인가, 저주인가?)"가 윗글의 제목으로 가장 적절하다.

> **오답풀이**
>
> ① 기계가 사람을 대체할 수 있는 곳과 그럴 수 없는 곳
> ③ 장애인 그리고 동등한 대우를 받을 권리
> ④ 인공지능: 과학적 사실 대 허구
> ⑤ 미래 기술을 예견하는 과학 소설

41 ⑤ (A) 문맥상 인간 증강 기술의 발달로 인공기관은 '자연적인' 팔다리를 능가할 정도로 점점 더 정교해진다는 의미이므로, 'sophisticated(정교한)'가 들어갈 말로 적절하다.
(B) '자연적인' 팔다리를 능가하는 인공기관의 발달로 사람들이 경쟁력을 유지하려면 좋든 싫든 '사이보그'가 되어야 하고, 이는 디스토피아의 미래에 대한 두려움을 불러일으킬 수 있다. 그러므로 빈칸 (B)에는 'trigger(촉발시키다)'가 들어갈 말로 적절하다.

> **오답풀이**
>
> | | (A) | | (B) |
> |---|---|---|---|
> | ① | 비싼 | …… | 진정시키다 |
> | ② | 비싼 | …… | 반영하다 |
> | ③ | 구식의 | …… | 촉발시키다 |
> | ④ | 정교한 | …… | 진정시키다 |

[42~43]

> **어휘**
>
> • therapy : 치료, 요법
> • in the midst of : ~중에, ~가운데
> • purchase : 구입하다, 구매하다
> • barely : 겨우, 간신히
> • renovation : 수선, 수리
> • crash : 충돌하다, 추락하다
> • develop : (병이) 생기다, 걸리다
> • depressed : 우울한, 침울한

• tortured : 지독히 고통스러운, 괴로운
• distracting : 마음을 산만하게 하는, 주의를 딴 데 돌리는
• cognitive : 인식의, 인지의
• behavioral therapy : 행동요법
• emphasis : 강조, 역점, 주안점
• mindfulness : 염두, 유념, 마음 챙김
• panic : 극심한 공포, 공황
• scenario : 시나리오, 각본 cf) in the worst-case scenario 최악의 경우에는
• get stuck : 꼼짝 못하게 되다, 수렁에 빠지다
• come up with : 찾아내다, 내놓다
• urge : 욕구, 충동
• provider : 제공자, 부양자
• profound : 깊은, 심오한
• confusion : 혼란, 혼동, 당혹
• get in the way of : 방해되다
• session : 시즌, 회기
• take action : 조치를 취하다

> **해석**

마리오가 치료를 받으러 왔을 때, 그는 걱정거리가 많다고 설명했다. 그는 최근에 결혼을 했고 수리에 필요한 돈만 간신히 남겨둔 채, 평생 저축한 돈을 투자해야 하는 비싼 집을 구입하는 중이었다. "내가 좋은 사람과 결혼했나? 내가 미쳐가고 있는가? 내 마음이 통할까? 나는 건망증이 심한 것 같아. 내가 탄 마이애미로 가는 비행기가 추락하면 어떡하지? 아버지도 할아버지처럼 파킨슨병에 걸릴까?" 걱정거리는 (a) 끝이 없었고, 마리오도 걱정이 많을수록 더 우울하다는 것을 알았다. 괴로운 마음을 달래기 위해, 그는 식사를 하며 (b) 마음을 딴 데 돌리는 데 시간을 보냈다.

마음의 다스림과 수용에 중점을 둔 인지 행동 요법의 과정을 거치면서, 마리오는 공황 상태에 빠진 자신의 감정에 당황하지 않는 법을 배우기 시작했다. 그는 최악의 상황에서 살게 될 거라는 마음에 (c) 빠져 있기 보다는 정신적인 과정으로서 그의 근심을 일깨울 수 있게 되었다. 그는 스스로에게 "이것이 생산적인가, 비생산적인가?"라고 묻는 연습을 했다. 만약 걱정이 생산적이라면, 그는 실행 계획을 내놓았다. 만일 비생산적이라면, 몸과 마음의 감정과 생각을 인지하고 현시점으로 돌아가는 연습을 했다. 그가 긴장하여 달고 짠 음식을 먹고 싶은 충동을 느꼈을 때, 그는 자신의 감정을 의미 있는 것으로 보고, 자신의 감정을 가라앉히는 쪽을 택했다.

그의 걱정 뒤에는 무엇이 숨어 있었을까? 그는 부양자로서 봉사하고, 안전하고 사랑스러운 가정을 이루며, 아버지를 보호하는 것을 매우 (d) 소중히 여겼다. 비록 그의 감정과의 관계 즉, 너무 많은 것을 느끼고 그의 감정을 이해하지 못하는 것에 대한 깊은 두려움과 혼란이 그의 감정을 받아들이고 배우려

는 의지를 방해하지만, 그의 감정은 그에게 중요하다는 것을 (e) 부정했다(→ 인정했다). 지난 시즌 동안, "내게 문젯거리가 있기 때문에 기분이 좋아. 나는 아내에게 우리의 어려움에 대해 이야기할 수 있고, 금전적인 문제를 해결하기 위한 조치를 취할 수 있으며, 내가 얼마나 걱정하는지 아빠에게 보여줄 수 있어. 그 맛은 내 마음속에서 달달하게 느껴져."라고 그는 말했다.

42 ④ 본문 중에 그가 긴장하여 달고 짠 음식을 먹고 싶은 충동을 느꼈을 때, 자신의 감정을 가라앉히는 쪽을 택했다고 서술되어 있다. 즉, 달고 짠 음식을 먹고 싶은 마음을 달랜 것이므로, "단것과 짠 음식을 먹고 싶어 하는 충동을 이겨내는 데 결국 실패했다."는 ④의 설명은 윗글의 내용과 일치하지 않는다.

43 ⑤ 마리오가 자기 감정을 이해하지 못하는 것에 대한 깊은 두려움과 혼란이 그의 감정을 받아들이고 배우려는 의지를 방해하지만 감정에 충실하다는 의미이므로, ⑤의 'denied(부정했다)'는 'admitted(인정했다)' 등으로 바꿔야 한다.

[44~45]

어휘

• canary : 카나리아
• niece : 조카딸, 질녀 ↔ nephew 조카
• blossom : 꽃을 피우다
• tiny : 아주 작은
• sip : 홀짝거리다, 조금씩 마시다
• beverage : 음료, 마실 것
• retire : 자리를 뜨다, 물러나다, 잠자리에 들다
• flow through : 통과하다, 뚫다
• peck at : …을 주둥이로 쪼다
• desperate : 필사적인, 극단적인
• fury : 분노, 격분
• collapse : 무너지다, 쓰러지다, 드러눕다
• exhaustion : 탈진, 기진맥진
• unconscious : 의식을 잃은, 무의식적인
• loyalty : 충성심
• determination : 결정, 결심
• sacrifice : 희생, 제물
• cozily : 아늑하게, 오붓이
• startle : 깜짝 놀라게 하다
• odd : 이상한, 특이한
• tap : 톡톡 두드리다[치다]

• windblown : 바람에 날린, 바람에 부딪치는
• persistently : 끈질기게, 줄기차게
• chirp : 짹짹거리다, 지저귀다

해석

(A) 카나리아 Bibs는 옆집에 조카딸이 사는 노부인과 함께 살았고 그녀가 괜찮은지 확인하기 위해 매일 밤 살폈다. 노부인과 작은 새 사이에는 따뜻하고 달콤한 우정이 꽃을 피웠다. 매일 아침 식사 때, 그들은 토스트를 나눠 먹었고 Bibs는 그 부인이 마시는 음료라면 무엇이든 홀짝거렸다. 비가 내리는 어느 날 밤, 이모 집의 전등이 켜져 있고 모든 것이 괜찮다고 생각한 조카딸은 이모 집으로 건너가지 않고 그날 밤 남편과 함께 잠자리에 들었다.

(D) 그 부부가 불 옆에서 오붓하게 휴식을 취하고 있을 때, 그들은 창문을 두드리는 이상한 소리에 깜짝 놀랐다. 처음에 그들은 그것이 바람에 부딪치는 나뭇가지 소리라고 짐작했지만, 두드리는 소리가 점차 커지고 줄기차게 계속되었고, 이어서 이상한 울음소리가 들려왔다. 마침내 조카딸은 창가로 가서 커튼을 젖히고 창문을 사납게 두드리며 짹짹거리던 Bibs를 발견했다.

(B) 그 작은 노란 새는 이모네 집에서 탈출하여 폭풍우를 뚫고 옆집으로 날아갔다. 그곳에서 그 새는 필사적으로 사납게 창문을 쪼아대다 기진맥진하여 쓰러졌고 그들의 눈앞에서 죽었다. 매우 놀란 조카딸과 그녀의 남편은 이모네 집으로 달려갔다.

(C) 그들은 그 노부인이 피투성이가 된 채 의식을 잃고 바닥에 쓰러져 있는 것을 발견했다. 그녀는 미끄러져 넘어졌고, 탁자 모서리에 머리를 부딪쳤다. 그녀의 조카딸은 그녀를 급히 병원으로 데려갔다. 자신의 목숨을 희생해서까지 도움을 청한 작은 새의 충성심과 결단력 때문에, 그 부인은 목숨을 구했다.

44 ④ (A) 카나리아 Bibs가 옆집에 조카딸이 사는 노부인과 함께 삶
(D) 조카딸이 창문을 사납게 두드리며 짹짹거리던 Bibs를 발견함
(B) 매우 놀란 조카딸과 그녀의 남편이 이모네 집으로 달려감
(C) 피투성이가 된 채 의식을 잃고 바닥에 쓰러져 있는 이모를 발견한 후 병원으로 데려가 목숨을 구함

45 ⑤ 글 (D)를 보면, 처음에는 바람에 부딪치는 나뭇가지 소리라고 짐작했지만 조카딸이 창가로 가서 커튼을 젖혀 확인해 본 결과 Bibs가 창문을 사납게 두드리고 있다는 사실을 알았다. 그러므로 "조카딸 집의 창문에 나뭇가지가 부딪쳐 소리가 났다."는 ⑤의 설명은 윗글의 내용과 다르다.

정답 및 해설

사관학교 10개년 영어 ▼

2019학년도 기출문제 정답 및 해설

🖉 제2교시 **영어영역(공통)**

01 ⑤	02 ②	03 ②	04 ④	05 ①	06 ②
07 ③	08 ②	09 ①	10 ①	11 ④	12 ①
13 ②	14 ④	15 ⑤	16 ③	17 ④	18 ⑤
19 ④	20 ③	21 ④	22 ②	23 ⑤	24 ⑤
25 ③	26 ①	27 ①	28 ③	29 ①	30 ⑤
31 ③	32 ⑤	33 ②	34 ④	35 ③	36 ④
37 ②	38 ②	39 ②	40 ②	41 ①	42 ⑤
43 ⑤	44 ③	45 ⑤			

01 ⑤ 화성은 몇 개의 위성이 있냐는 Smith 선생님의 질문에 Sunny가 한 개라고 틀린 답을 말하자, 선생님이 화성에는 두 개의 위성이 있다고 Sunny에게 말했다.

오답풀이
① Smith 선생님은 학생들이 태양계에 대해서 다시 배워야만 한다고 생각하지 않는다.
② Sunny는 행성들과 위성들에 대해 매우 흥미있어 한다.
③ Sunny는 Smith 선생님의 질문에 왜 답을 해야 하는지 이해하지 못한다.
④ Sunny는 Smith 선생님의 첫 번째 질문에 정확한 답을 한다.

어휘
• solar system : 태양계
• and stuff : …같은 (시시한) 것

해석
Ms. Smith : 좋아요, 학생 여러분, 이번 시간에는 태양계에 대해서 다시 알아볼게요!
Sunny : 오, Smith 선생님, 그걸 해야 하나요? 지난 수업 시간에 했는데, 전 행성들과 위성 등등, 너무 지루해요.
Ms. Smith : 그렇다면 Sunny, 넌 몇 가지 질문에 답할 수 있겠구나. 그것들 모두를 맞히면 네가 원하는 것을 공부하도록 하자. 괜찮지?
Sunny : 예, 좋습니다! Smith 선생님. 최고예요! 뭐든 물어 보세요.
Ms. Smith : 첫 번째 질문, 화성은 몇 개의 위성이 있니?

Sunny : 쉬운 문제네요! 하나죠.
Ms. Smith : 미안하구나. Sunny, 첫 번째 문제부터 틀렸구나. 두 개란다.
Sunny : 아우, 제가 그걸 어떻게 알아요? 그곳에 가본 적이 없는데!

02 ② **첫 번째 빈칸** : 거리가 꽤 멀다고 했으므로 그곳에 가는 방법을 궁금해 하는 내용이 들어가야 한다. 그러므로 그곳에 어떻게 가야 할지 모르겠어(I'm not sure how to get there.)라는 b의 내용이 적절하다.
두 번째 빈칸 : 값이 싸지는 않지만 더 편할 거라고 말한 내용을 보아 선택할 수 있는 교통수단은 택시이다. 그러므로 택시를 탈 수도 있어(We could grab a taxi.)라는 a의 내용이 적절하다.
세 번째 빈칸 : 택시를 탈만한 돈의 여유가 없어서 버스를 타기로 결정했으므로, 마침 저기 버스가 한 대 온다(There's one right there.)라는 c의 내용이 적절하다.

어휘
• starve : 굶주리다, 허기지다
• transit pass : 환승권
• all the way : 줄곧, 내내
• cheap : 값싼, 돈이 적게 드는
• hop a bus : 버스를 타다
• grab : 붙잡다, 움켜잡다

해석
Julie : 배가 고프구나. 강 하류에 맛있는 치킨을 파는 집들이 많아.
Rachel : 좋은 생각이야. 그런데 여기서 꽤 멀지 않니? 그곳에 어떻게 가야 할지 모르겠어.
Julie : 음, 지하철이 있네. 나는 환승권이 있어. 너도 있니?
Rachel : 아니 없어. 게다가 온종일 뛰어다녔더니 발이 아파. 지하철역까지도 계속 걸어가야 하잖아.
Julie : 택시를 탈 수도 있어. 값이 싸지는 않지만, 더 편할 거야.
Rachel : 오, 안 돼. 그 정도 돈은 없어.
Julie : 그러면 버스를 타야 할 것 같아. 마침 저기 버스가 한 대 온다.

352

03 ② Dan과 Paul이 이빨들처럼 보이는 잎이 있는 독특한 식물
과 고약한 냄새가 나는 꽃들을 감상하는 장면이므로, 식물
원에서(at a botanical garden) 나누는 대화임을 알 수 있다.

어휘

• scary : 무서운, 겁나는
• unique : 독특한, 특유의
• grow up : 성장하다, 철이 들다
• haunted : 귀신[유령]이 나오는, 겁에 질린
• botanical : 식물의
• cosmetics : 화장품
• aquarium : 수족관

해석

Dan : 건너편에 있는 저것 좀 봐! 저런 것 본 적 있니?
Paul : 글쎄, 물론 TV에서는 봤겠지만, 그 식물을 내 눈으로 직
접 보니 좀 무서워 보여. 그것은 이빨을 가지고 있는 것 같아.
Dan : 응, 그래. 하지만 그건 이빨이 아니야. 그저 특별한 잎일
뿐이야. 그건 이곳의 가장 독특한 식물들 중 하나지.
Paul : 그래, 그러면 좀 더 가까이서 보자.
Dan : 좋아. 근데, 그거 알아? 지금 와서 생각해 보니, 냄새가
너무 고약하면, 나는 그냥 갈 거야. 아침을 배불리 먹어서 토
하고 싶지 않아.
Paul : 철 좀 들어라! 자연스러운 거야! 일부 꽃들은 냄새가 고
약하지.
Dan : 네 마음대로 해. 나는 코를 막을 테니까.

04 ④ 아이언 맨 2는 좋지 못했다는 John의 말에 Nick도 수긍하
는 한편, 그래도 3편은 괜찮았다고 말하고 있다. 그러므로
두 사람이 아이언 맨 2가 훌륭했다는 데 동의했다(The two
people agree that Iron Man 2 was excellent.)는 ④의 설명
은 윗글의 내용과 일치하지 않는다.

오답풀이

① 두 사람은 지난 밤에 함께 영화를 보았다.
② Nick은 속편이 원편보다 더 못하다는 John의 생각에 동의
하지 않는다.
③ John은 어벤저스 2편이 1편보다 훌륭하다는 것을 인정했다.
⑤ John은 앤트맨 2편이 1편만큼이나 좋은 영화라는 Nick의
생각을 인정했다.

어휘

• meet expectation : 기대에 응하다, 기대에 미치다
• sequel : 속편
• original : 원편(1편), 원작
• have a good point : 좋은 지적이다, 네 말이 그 말이다
• make a generalization : 일반화하다, 속단하다, 지레짐작하다

해석

Nick : 지난 밤에 우리가 본 영화는 정말 재미있었어. 진짜 끝내
줬어!
John : 정말? 내 기대에는 미치지 못했어. 속편들은 원편 만큼
훌륭하지 않아.
Nick : 아니, 나는 그렇게 생각하지 않아. 어벤저스 2편이 1편
만큼 좋았다고 생각해.
John : 좋아, 인정할게. 그렇다면 아이언 맨 영화는 어때? 아
이언 맨 2는 좋지 못했어.
Nick : 네 말이 맞을 수도 있어. 그러나 다른 아이언 맨 속편인
3편은 훌륭했어!
John : 맞아, 그건 사실이야. 좋은 지적이야.
Nick : 그리고 앤트맨 2는? 해! 1편만큼이나 좋았고, 어쩜 더
좋지 않니?
John : 그래, 맞아. 속단하기 전에 생각을 좀 더 해봐야 해.

05 ① 의사가 환자의 수술 일정을 잡기 전에 확실히 하기 위해
한 가지 조치가 더 남았다고 했으므로, 빈칸에는 ①의 "We
should do another test. (검사를 하나 더 해야 합니다.)"가
들어갈 말로 적절하다.

오답풀이

② 나는 건강 보험을 신청하려 하는데요.
③ 나는 직원과 점심을 먹으러 가려고요.
④ 배가 아픈데 어떻게 해야죠?
⑤ 걱정하지 마세요, 열은 높지 않아요.

어휘

• pain : 아픔, 고통, 통증
• stomach : 위, 복부, 배, 속
• surgery : 수술
• to be certain : 확실하게 말하자면, 확실히
• apply for : ~에 지원하다
• health insurance : 건강 보험
• stomachache : 위통, 복통, 배탈

해석

의사 : 어디가 아프세요?
환자 : 음, 배가 아파서요. 오른쪽 여기 아래요.
의사 : 여기 누워 보세요. [잠시 멈춤] 이렇게 누르면 아픈가요?
환자 : 으윽, 예! 아주 아파요. 다시 안 그러시면 좋겠어요.
의사 : 자, 체온을 한 번 재 봅시다. 음, 예상했던 대로 열이 꽤
높네요.
환자 : 예상했던 대로요? 선생님은 뭐가 문제인지 이미 알고
계셨나요?
의사 : 무슨 문제인지 확신합니다. 수술이 필요하다고 생각하

지만, 확실히 해두기 위해 수술 일정을 잡기 전에 한 가지 조치를 더 하려고요. 검사를 하나 더 해야 합니다.

06 ② Lisa가 식당을 새로 개업하면서 멕시코 요리와 베트남 요리 둘 중 하나로 좁혀졌다고 말하자, Suzy가 은행에서 대출을 받기 전에 결정하라고 조언하고 있다. 그러므로 "Lisa와 John은 식당을 개업할 예정이지만, 요리에 관해 최종 결정을 하지 못했다. (Lisa and John will open a restaurant, but haven't made a final decision on the cuisine.)"는 ②의 설명은 옳다.

오답풀이

① Suzy는 식당을 개업할 예정이라 훌륭한 요리사를 구하고 있다.

③ Lisa와 Suzy는 오늘밤 식당에서 어떤 종류의 음식을 먹을 것인지 정하고 있다.

④ Suzy는 Lisa가 식당에 필요한 대출을 받기 위해 Lisa와 함께 은행에 갈 것이다.

⑤ Suzy는 Lisa가 새로 여는 식당이 성공할 거라고 확신하지만, Lisa는 그렇지 않다.

어휘

• cuisine : 요리, 요리법

• narrow down to : …으로 좁히다

• particularly : 특히, 특별히

• competition : 경쟁, 시합, 대회

• unusual : 드문, 색다른

• make up one's minds : 결정[결심]하다

• loan : 대출, 융자

• make a decision : 결정하다

• confident : 자신감 있는, 확신하는

해석

Lisa : John과 나는 식당을 개업할 예정이야!

Suzy : 꽤 대담하네. 내가 듣기로 개업 첫 해에 50%의 식당이 문을 닫는데.

Lisa : 한 번 믿어봐. 우리는 요리한지가 오래 돼서, 유명한 맛집이 될 거라고 생각해.

Suzy : 어떤 종류의 요리를 준비할 생각이야?

Lisa : 멕시코 요리나 베트남 요리로 좁혀졌어.

Suzy : 와우, 꽤 다른 스타일의 요리네. 그 두 가지 요리를 특히 생각한 이유가 있니?

Lisa : 멕시코 요리가 훨씬 인기 있지만, 경쟁이 치열해서. 베트남 요리가 오히려 특색이 있지만, 한편으로는 사람들이 그 요리에 친숙하지 않아.

Suzy : 아무튼, 은행에서 대출을 받기 전에 결정을 해야 할 거야.

07 ③ 제시문에서 간과하는 정보도 있고 해결책이 명확하지 않은 경우 직관이 길잡이가 되어야 하며, 최선의 결정은 명백한 선택을 가리키는 양질의 자료와 옳은 결정을 내렸다고 확신하는 직감이라고 서술하고 있다. 그러므로 "자료를 선정하고 결정을 내릴 때 직관을 동원하라."는 ③의 설명이 필자가 주장하는 바로 가장 적절하다.

오답풀이

① 반론을 제기할 때 타당한 근거를 제시하라.

② 연구 주제와 무관한 정보를 과감하게 버리라.

④ 객관적인 자료를 바탕으로 합리적인 결정을 내리라.

⑤ 자료 수집 과정에서 정보의 양보다 질을 중요시하라.

어휘

• render : 만들다[하다], 주다[제공하다]

• intuition : 직감, 직관

• regardless of : …에 상관없이[구애받지 않고]

• direction : 방향, 목적

• sift through : 꼼꼼하게 살펴 추려내다

• weed out : 잡초를 뽑다, 제거하다

• garbage : 쓰레기, 잡동사니

• obvious : 분명한, 명백한

• gut feeling : 직감, 육감

해석

모든 결정이 완벽한 자료로부터 내려지는 것은 아니다. 비록 최선의 해결책을 제시하기 위해 모든 자료를 활용하는 것이 중요하지만, 때때로 간과하는 정보도 있고 그 해결책이 명확하지 않은 경우도 있다. 이와 같은 경우에, 당신의 직관이 길잡이가 되어야 한다. 이 말인 즉, 스스로 신념을 가지고 그 자료가 어떤 방향을 가리키는지에 상관없이 사실이라고 믿는 것을 청취하는 것이다. 의사를 결정하는 과정에 있으며 잡동사니를 제거하고 양질의 정보만을 모으기 위해 인터넷을 꼼꼼히 살펴볼 때, 모든 정보에 관해 어떻게 느끼는지 스스로 자문하는 것을 잊지 마라. 이것은 매우 중요하다. 최선의 결정은 명백한 선택을 가리키는 양질의 자료를 결합한 것과 "당신은 옳은 결정을 했어."라고 말하는 직감이다.

08 ② 마지막 문장에 서술된 "우리는 모든 장애물을 발전의 초석으로 삼아야 한다."는 압둘 바하의 말처럼 고난을 디딤돌로 삼아야 한다는 내용이므로 ②의 "Adversity can lead to achievement. (고난이 성취로 이어질 수 있다)"가 윗글이 시사하는 바로 가장 적절하다.

오답풀이

① 교육을 더 받을수록, 더 문명화 된다.

③ 남에게 대접받고자 하는 대로 남을 대접하라.

④ 협력이 기적을 이룬다.

⑤ 뛰기 전에 둘러보라.

어휘

- right away : 즉각, 즉시, 곧바로
- patience : 참을성, 인내심
- seemingly : 외견상으로, 겉보기에는
- spiritual : 정신적인, 종교적인
- affliction : 고통, 고통의 원인
- deprivation : 박탈, 면직
- blessings in disguise : 전화위복, 변장한 축복
- purified : 정제한, 정화한
- ennoble : 고귀[고상]하게 하다, 기품을 주다
- Confucius : 공자
- gem : 보석, 보배
- polish : 광택을 내다, 윤을 내다
- friction : 마찰, 충돌, 불화
- quote : 인용문[구]
- illustrate : 삽화를 쓰다, 설명하다
- stumbling block : 장애물, 걸림돌
- stepping stone : 초석, 디딤돌
- adversity : 고난, 역경

해석

당장 처리할 수 없거나 지금까지 처리하지 못한 어려움들이 있다. 바꿀 수 없는 것을 참아내는 인내심을 기억하는 것은 물론 외관상 불가능해 보이는 상황에 적응하는 다른 방법들도 있다. 많은 정신적 지도자들은 고통, 시련, 괴로움, 박탈을 내적 정신력이 자극되고, 정화되고, 고귀해지는 "변장한 축복"으로 여긴다. 공자는 "보석은 연마 없이 광이 날 수 없고, 시련 없이 완벽해지는 사람은 없다"고 말한 반면, 헬렌 켈러는 "나의 장애에 대해 신께 감사한다. 왜냐하면, 시련을 통해 나 자신과 나의 일과 하나님을 찾았다."라고 말했다. 만일 시련을 올바르게 이용한다면, 우리의 인생에서 실패, 시험, 그리고 고난은 우리의 영혼을 정화시키고 우리의 성격을 강화시키는 수단이 될 수 있다. 압둘 바하의 인용문이 이것을 특히 잘 설명한다. "우리는 모든 장애물을 발전의 초석으로 삼아야 한다."

09 ① 윗글에 따르면 공공기관과 민간기관이 기존의 서식 채우기 요건을 대폭 줄이거나, 택시 운전사가 어느 길로 갈지 물어보지 않고 가장 좋은 길을 선택해 알아서 가주거나, 친구와 식사 약속을 잡을 때 미리 장소를 제안하는 것을 사람들이 선호한다. 그러므로 윗글의 요지는 ①의 "사람들은 선택의 부담이 줄어드는 것을 더 좋아한다."이다.

어휘

- public official : 공무원
- register : 등록하다, 기재하다, 기록하다
- immensely : 굉장히, 대단하게
- frustrate : 헛되게 하다, 좌절시키다
- be better off : 더 낫다
- institution : 기관, 단체, 협회
- form-filling : 서식 채우기
- deem : 여기다, 생각하다
- considerate : 사려 깊은, 배려하는

해석

웹사이트에서 "다시 묻지 마세요."라는 대화상자에 체크하라고 하면, 많은 사람들은 응당 그 상자에 체크한다. 만일 공무원이나 의사가 똑같은 질문의 많은 서식을 작성하고 다양한 종류의 선택사항을 기재하라고 한다면, 여러분은 엄청난 좌절감을 느낄 수 있고 적어도 그 선택들 중 일부가 여러분들을 위해 만든 것임을 바랄 수도 있다. 공공기관과 민간기관이 기존의 서식 채우기 요건을 대폭 줄인다면 사람들은 더 좋아할 것이다. 그리고 택시 운전사가 낯선 도시에서 어떤 길로 가고 싶은지 선택하라고 한다면, 여러분은 그가 물어보지 않고 가장 좋다고 생각하는 길을 선택해주기를 바랄지도 모른다. 어떤 친구와 점심이나 저녁을 먹을 때, 그 친구에게 장소를 선택하라고 하기보다는 장소를 제안하는 것이 가장 사려 깊다.

10 ① 윗글에 따르면 금으로 예술 작품을 만들어도 실패할 수 있는 이유는 예술 작품에 미적 요소가 수반되어야 하기 때문이다. 또한 마지막 문장에서 기술이 예술의 미적 요소들을 전달할 수 있도록 충분히 발달되지 않는다면 그 작품의 가치는 줄어든다고 하였으므로, ①의 "기술적 요소에 미학적 요소를 더해야 예술 작품의 가치가 높아진다."가 윗글의 요지로 가장 적절하다.

어휘

- evaluate : 평가하다, 감정하다
- entirely : 전적으로, 완전히, 전부
- realism : 사실주의
- involve : 관련시키다, 연루시키다
- crafted item : 공예품
- awe : 경외하게 하다
- give credit for : ~의 공로를 인정하다
- go into : 투입되다, 쓰이다
- aesthetic : 미적인, 미학적인
- get across : 전달되다, 이해되다

해석

기술이 전부라고 생각하는 사람들이 있는데 그들은 예술 작품을 전적으로 관련 기술의 양으로만 평가한다. 그런 사람들은 대상을 사실적으로 그리는 것과 관련된 기술 때문에 회화에서

사실주의에 관심이 더 많다. 그들은 또한 공예품에 보통 더 관심이 많으며 그 물품을 만드는 데 연관된 기술에 경외심을 갖는다. 물론 우리는 예술작품을 만드는 데 투입된 많은 요소들의 공로를 인정해야 하지만, 그 요소들과 미적 요소 사이에는 차이가 있다. 우리는 노력, 기법, 기술, 재료, 크기, 그리고 작업하는데 걸리는 시간에 대한 공로를 인정해 줄 수 있다. 예술의 가치는 그러한 특성에 의해 평가되어서는 안 된다. 아무리 열심히 예술작품을 만들려고 해도, 미적으로 실패할 수도 있다. 금으로 작품을 만들 수도 있지만, 그거 또한 미적으로 실패할 수 있다. 형편없는 예술에서 규모가 큰 형편없는 예술보다 더 안 좋은 것은 없다. 결국 성공하지 못한 하나의 예술 작품에 수년 동안 작업한 것이 얼마나 수치스러운가. 만일 기술이 예술의 미적 요소들을 전달할 수 있도록 충분히 발달되지 않는다면, 그 작품의 가치는 줄어든다.

11 ④ 윗글의 마지막 부분에서 지식은 다차원성이 풍부해서 엄청난 양의 콘텐츠, 문맥, 경험을 내포하고 있으며, 이러한 세 가지 요인들 모두가 지식을 분배시키는 것을 매우 어렵게 만든다고 서술되어 있다. 그러므로 ④의 'characteristics of knowledge that make its transfer difficult (지식의 전파를 어렵게 만드는 지식의 특성)'이 윗글의 주제로 가장 적절하다.

오답풀이

① 전통적 문화 지식의 보호
② 지식과 문맥 사이의 밀접한 관계
③ 지식의 원천으로써 경험의 중요성
⑤ 정보기술을 이용한 손쉬운 지식 분배

어휘

• transfer : 이동, 전송, 전파
• tremendous : 거대한, 엄청난
• publicity : 언론의 관심[주목]
• sticky : 끈적끈적한, 달라붙는
• ever-changing : 늘 변화하는, 변화무쌍한
• irrelevant : 무관한, 상관없는
• discard : 버리다, 폐기하다
• rightful : 적법한, 정당한
• steward : 승무원, 관리인, 집사
• multi-dimensionality : 다차원성
• distribute : 나누어주다, 분배하다, 유통하다

해석

지식 전파는 집단들과 개인들 사이에서 지식의 흐름이 가능하도록 고안된 그룹웨어 및 네트워킹 도구들의 발전과 함께 최근에 엄청난 관심을 받았다. 그러한 도구의 목표는 궁극적으로 공유된 기억과 이해이다. 사실, 지식은 '접착력이 있고', 살

아있고, 풍부하기 때문에 이러한 목표는 성취하기 어렵다. 그것은 의미를 부여하는 문맥에 매우 밀접하게 연관되어 있기 때문에 '접착력'이 있다. 문맥이 없다면 지식은 단지 정보일 뿐이기 때문이다. 지식은 늘 변하고 성장함에 따라 지속적으로 주의를 기울여야 한다는 점에서 살아있다고 생각될 수 있다. 그것은 또한 사라지고, 시대에 뒤떨어지거나, 무관하게 되고, 폐기되어야 하는데, 누가 정당한 관리인인가? 마지막으로, 지식은 다차원성이 풍부해서 엄청난 양의 콘텐츠, 문맥, 경험을 내포하고 있다. 이러한 세 가지 요인들 모두가 지식을 분배시키는 것을 매우 어렵게 만든다.

12 ① 윗글에서 항공 화물은 비싼 물품이 많고, 운송 방법이 훨씬 복잡하며, 항공 화물의 90%가 대부분의 범죄가 발생하는 밤에 선적되므로 도난에 취약하다고 서술하고 있다. 그러므로 ①의 'factors that make air cargo more vulnerable to theft (항공 화물을 도난에 더욱 취약하게 만드는 요인들)'이 윗글의 주제로 가장 적절하다.

오답풀이

② 항공 여객 보안 검색의 문제점
③ 항공 화물 운송의 장점과 문제점
④ 항공 화물 배달 서비스의 짧은 역사
⑤ 다양한 화물 운송 방법

어휘

• air cargo : 항공 화물
• freight-carrying : 화물 운반
• method : 방법, 수단
• potential : 가능성이 있는, 잠재적인
• shipment : 수송, 운송
• loading dock : 짐 싣는 곳, 하역장
• along the way : 그 과정에서
• be exposed to : …에 노출되다
• handler : 취급[처리]하는 사람
• unlit : 불을 켜지 않은
• to and from : 왕복으로
• vulnerable : 취약한, 연약한
• screening : 검사, 심사
• drawback : 결점, 문제점

해석

다수의 특별한 보안 문제들이 항공 화물을 운송하는 것과 연관이 있다. 항공 화물은 종종 다른 화물 운송 방법으로 선적된 것보다 더 비싼 물품들을 포함하고 있기 때문에, 손실 가능성이 더 크다. 또한 손실이 발생한 곳을 확인하기가 더 어렵다. 다른 운송 방법에서 물품들은 간단하게 픽업, 이동, 그리고 하역장으로 배송된다. 항공 화물의 이동은 훨씬 더 복잡하다. 즉,

화물은 처음에 화물 터미널에서 비행 터미널로 옮겨졌다가 선적하기 전에 화물 항공기에 적재되는 데, 그 과정에서 도난 가능성이 생긴다. 화물을 여객기에 실을 때, 여객 터미널로 가야 하고 새로운 취급자에게 노출되기 때문에 위험이 증가한다. 많은 공항에서, 카트가 불이 꺼진 통로를 따라 왕복으로 화물을 운반해야하기 때문에 도난당할 기회가 더 많아진다. 더욱이 항공 화물의 90%가 대부분의 범죄가 발생하는 시기인 밤에 선적된다.

13 ② 윗글에 따르면 검치호랑이, 마스토돈, 거대한 털북숭이 코뿔소 등 인류가 자신보다 몇 배나 큰 포유동물들을 사냥하고 지구의 지배자가 될 수 있었던 것은 인류의 협력을 이끌어 낸 언어의 힘 때문이라고 서술하고 있다. 그러므로 ②의 'Language: A Basis of Cooperative Human Power (언어: 인간을 협동적으로 만드는 힘의 근원)'이 윗글의 제목으로 가장 적절하다.

오답풀이

① 언어 장벽을 무너뜨리기: 힘든 작업
③ 고대에서 현대에 이르는 언어의 변화
④ 동물과의 의사소통, 동물 언어의 이해
⑤ 언어가 어떻게 시작되었나?: 인류의 진화에서 몸짓과 말하기

어휘

• arresting : 시선을 사로잡는, 아주 매력적인
• formidable : 가공할, 어마어마한
• stroke of genius : 천재적 솜씨
• trial-and-error : 시행착오
• coordinate : 조직화하다, 편성하다, 조정하다
• negotiated : 협의된, 합의된
• algae : 조류, 해조, 말무리
• far-reaching : 광범위한, 원대한
• archaeologist : 고고학자
• cliff : 절벽
• remains : 유적, 유물, 잔해
• herds : 무리, 떼
• stampede : (동물 등이) 우르르 몰다
• paleolithic : 구석기 시대의
• fossil : 화석
• ingenuity : 창의력, 독창성
• shed light on : …을 밝히다, 해명하다
• saber-tooth tiger : 검치호랑이
• mastodon : (코끼리와 비슷한 고생물) 마스토돈
• wooly : 털이 뒤덮인, 털북숭이의
• rhinoceros : 코뿔소

• extinct : 멸종된, 소멸된
• habitat : 서식지

해석

정말로 인간에 관해 매력적인 것은 단 하나의 언어를 말하는 인류가 천국에 너무나 가까이 다가가서 신이 위협을 느낀 바벨탑 이야기에 잘 나타나 있다. 공용어는 지역 사회의 구성원을 어마어마한 집단 권력을 가진 정보 공유 네트워크에 연결한다. 천재적 솜씨, 행운의 사고, 그리고 현재나 과거의 누군가에 의해 축적된 시행착오의 지혜로 누구든 혜택을 볼 수 있다. 또한 사람들은 팀별로 일할 수 있고, 그들의 노력은 합의된 계약에 의해 조정된다. 그 결과, 호모 사피엔스는 청록색 조류와 지렁이처럼 지구를 광범위하게 변화시켰던 종(種)이다. 고고학자들은 프랑스의 절벽 밑바닥에서 만 마리의 야생마의 뼈를 발견했는데, 그것은 17,000년 전 구석기 시대의 사냥꾼 무리에 의해 절벽 꼭대기로 몰린 동물들의 유해이다. 고대의 협력과 공유된 창의성으로 만들어진 화석들은 왜 검치호랑이, 마스토돈, 거대한 털북숭이 코뿔소, 그리고 수십 마리의 다른 큰 포유동물들이 현대 인류가 그 동물들의 서식지에 도착했을 무렵에 멸종되었는지 밝혀 줄지도 모른다. 우리 조상들은 분명히 그 동물들을 전멸시켰다.

14 ④ 윗글의 마지막 부분에서 영업직의 현지 채용은 적절히 훈련받은 직원의 유용성에 영향을 받으며, 다국적 기업들은 현지에서 모집된 인력들을 훈련시키기 위해 관례상 본사로 보낸다고 서술되어 있다. 그러므로 ④의 'Education: One Vital Consideration for Foreign Businesses (교육: 해외 업무를 위한 주요 고려사항)'이 윗글의 주제로 가장 적절하다.

오답풀이

① 사회이동의 수단으로서의 교육
② 교육의 배경과 경제 상황
③ 교육과 직업 구조의 추세
⑤ 교육받은 노동력: 경제 성장의 원동력

어휘

• assess : 재다, 평가하다
• literacy rate : 식자율(국민 중 글을 아는 사람들의 비율)
• enrollment : 등록, 기재, 입학
• qualitative : 질적인
• emphases : (emphasis의 복수형) 강조, 역점, 주안점
• facility : 시설, 기관
• trainee : 연습생, 실습생, 훈련생
• take into account : ~을 고려하다, 참작하다
• illiteracy : 문맹, 무식
• availability : 유효성, 유용성, 효용
• routinely : 일상적으로, 관례대로

• headquarter : 본사, 본부
• occupational : 직업의, 직업과 관련된
• driving force : 추진력, 원동력
• vital : 필수적인, 중요한, 중대한

해석

공식적이든 비공식적이든, 교육은 문화의 전수와 공유에 중요한 역할을 한다. 한 문화의 교육 수준은 이차적인 데이터 출처에서 이용할 수 있는 정보인 식자율과 중등 또는 고등교육의 입학률을 보고 평가할 수 있다. 다국적 기업들은 교육의 질적 측면, 즉 특정 기술에 대한 강조와 제공되는 교육의 전반적인 수준에 대해 알 필요가 있다. 예를 들어, 한국과 일본은 과학, 특히 공학을 서구 나라들보다 훨씬 더 강조한다. 교육 수준은 다양한 사업 기능에 영향을 미칠 것이다. 생산 시설을 위한 훈련 프로그램은 훈련생들의 교육 배경을 고려해야 할 것이다. 예를 들어, 높은 수준의 문맹은 인쇄된 설명서보다 시각적 보조 기구를 이용해야 한다는 것을 시사한다. 영업직의 현지 채용은 적절히 훈련받은 직원의 유용성에 영향을 받을 것이다. 몇몇 경우에, 다국적 기업들은 현지에서 모집된 인력들을 훈련시키기 위해 관례상 본사로 보낸다.

15 ⑤ 위의 도표에서 2007–2011년 그리고 2012–2016년 사이의 세계 무기 구매 비중의 차이가 가장 적었던 나라는 터키가 아니라 알제리이므로 ⑤의 설명은 윗글의 내용과 일치하지 않는다.

어휘

• purchase : 구입, 구매
• account for : (부분ㆍ비율을) 차지하다

해석

위의 도표는 2007–2011년과 2012–2016년의 두 기간 동안에 걸쳐 7개국의 세계 무기 구매 비중을 보여준다. ① 2012–2016년의 기간 동안 인도는 세계 무기 수입의 가장 큰 비중을 차지했으며, 사우디아라비아, 아랍에미리트(UAE), 중국, 알제리, 터키, 호주 등이 그 뒤를 이었다. ② 2007–2011년의 기간과 비교해서 인도, 사우디아라비아, 아랍에미리트, 터키의 세계 무기 수입 비중은 2012~2016년의 기간에 증가했다. ③ 반면에 2012–2016년의 기간 동안 중국, 알제리, 호주의 세계 무기 수입 비중은 전년 대비 감소했다. ④ 특히 중국의 세계 무기 수입 비중은 두 기간 사이에 5.5%에서 4.5%로 가장 많이 감소했다. ⑤ 2007–2011년 그리고 2012–2016년 사이의 세계 무기 구매 비중의 차이는 사우디아라비아가 가장 컸고, 터키가 가장 작았다.

16 ③ 본문에 따르면 Bertolt Brecht는 1차 세계대전에 참전한 후, 연극 'Drums in the Night'로 성공을 거두었다. 그러므로 1

차 세계대전 이전에 연극 'Drums in the Night'로 성공을 거두었다는 ③의 설명은 옳지 못하다.

어휘

• staging : 상연, 연출
• implication : 영향, 함축, 암시
• flee from : …에서 달아나다
• investigate : 조사하다, 수사하다
• Communist : 공산주의자, 공산당원
• theater company : 극단

해석

Bertolt Brecht는 20세기 연극에 중대한 영향을 미쳤다. 그는 관객들로 하여금 그의 연극의 도덕적, 정치적 의미에 대해 생각해보도록 하는 목적을 달성하기 위해 독특한 연출 및 다른 연기 방식을 이용하여 새로운 양식의 연극을 탐구했다. Brecht는 독일 아우크스부르크에서 태어났고, 뮌헨과 베를린 대학에서 의학과 철학을 공부했다. 1차 세계대전에 참전한 후, 그는 연극 'Drums in the Night'로 성공을 거두었다. 1920년대와 1930년대 초반에 걸쳐 그는 보다 많은 희곡을 썼다. 1933년에 Brecht와 그의 아내는 히틀러가 집권한 후 독일로부터 도망칠 수밖에 없었다. Brecht는 결국 미국에 도착했지만, 그곳에서 공산주의 이념을 가지고 있다는 이유로 수사를 받았다. 그는 미국을 떠나 1947년 동베를린으로 돌아왔고, 그곳에서 세계적으로 유명한 극단인 베르너 앙상블을 설립했다.

17 ④ ①, ②, ③, ⑤의 'he'는 George McClellan 장군을 가리키며, ④의 'he'는 링컨 대통령을 가리킨다.

어휘

• at the height of : …의 절정에, …이 한창일 때에
• the Civil War : (미국) 남북전쟁
• Secretary of War : 육군 장관
• battle side house : 전투
• urgent : 긴급한, 시급한
• parlor : 응접실, 객실, 거실
• maid : 하녀, 가정부
• unacceptable : 용납할 수 없는, 인정할 수 없는
• dismiss : 해고하다, 전역시키다, 퇴임시키다
• dirt : 먼지, 때, 흙
• bloodshed : 유혈 사태, 참사, 학살

해석

남북전쟁이 한창일 때에, 몇 가지 긴박한 문제로 링컨 대통령과 육군 장관은 George McClellan 장군의 전장 옆 주택을 방문했다. ① 그가 집에 없었기 때문에, 그들은 응접실에서 기다렸다. 장군이 마침내 집으로 돌아왔을 때, 그는 방문객들이

있는 것을 보았지만 그들을 알아보지 못했다. 대신에 그는 곧장 자기 방으로 갔다. ② 그가 곧 나올 거라고 생각하며, 그들은 그를 기다렸다. 한 시간 뒤에, 아직 그가 나타나지 않자, 그들은 가정부를 보내 알아봐 달라고 했다. 잠시 후 그녀는 돌아와서 "대통령님, 죄송하지만 장군은 저에게 ③ 그가 매우 피곤해서 잠자리에 들었다고 전해달라고 부탁했습니다."라고 말했다. 육군 장군은 충격을 받고 "각하, 이건 도저히 용납할 수 없습니다. 즉시 그를 장군의 직위에서 물러나게 해야 합니다!"라고 말했다. 링컨은 잠시 생각했고, ④ 그는 "아니, 나는 그를 퇴임시키지 않겠네. 그는 훌륭한 장군일세. 그는 전투에서 이기고 있네. 만약 ⑤ 그가 이 유혈사태를 단축시킬 수 있다면, 나는 그의 말을 붙잡고, 그의 부츠에 묻은 먼지를 한 시간 동안이라도 털 걸세."라고 말했다.

18 ⑤ 'which' 이하가 완전한 문장이고 앞부분에 'So + 형용사 + 동사 + 주어'의 도치구문이 사용됐으므로, 'so'와 호응을 이루는 접속사 'that'을 사용해야 한다.

> **오답풀이**

① 'potentially(잠재적으로)'가 be 동사 뒤에 위치했으므로 올바르게 사용되었다.

② 앞의 'others'를 수식하기 위해 능동의 의미를 지닌 현재분사 'undergoing'을 사용한 것은 적절하다.

③ 동사 'make'의 목적어인 'to think~' 이하가 길므로 이를 대신하기 위해 가목적어 'it'을 사용한 것은 적절하다.

④ 'in similar fashion ~ objects'는 삽입구에 해당하며, 이를 생략하면 'The workings of the body can be examined and ~'의 수동태 문장이 된다.

> **어휘**

• given : …을 고려해 볼 때
• dominance : 우월, 우세, 지배
• naturalistic : 자연주의적인, 자연을 모방하는
• grasp : 움켜잡다, 이해하다, 파악하다
• victim : 피해자, 희생자, 환자
• transplant : 이식, 이식된 장기[조직]
• undergo : 겪다, 경험하다
• cosmetic surgery : 성형 수술
• surgeon : 외과의, 외과 전문의
• reconstruct : 재건하다, 복원하다, 재구성하다
• commonplace : 아주 흔한, 상습적인
• component : 요소, 부품
• up to a point : 어느 정도
• take apart : 분해하다, 해체하다
• reassemble : 재조립하다, 다시 모으다
• in fashion : …방식으로

• malfunction : 고장, 기능 불량
• diagnose : 진단하다, 진찰하다
• remedy : 치료하다, 고치다, 보수하다

> **해석**

인체의 자연주의적인 관점에 대한 서양 문화의 우월성을 고려해 볼 때, 문화에서 인체의 개념은 잠재적으로 이해하기 어렵다. 사고 피해자, 이식 환자 그리고 성형수술을 받는 사람들의 인체는 외과의사에 의해 글자그대로 물리적으로 매일 복원된다. 이러한 상습적인 행위가 비교적 쉽게 인체를 기계로 생각하게 한다. 기계와 마찬가지로 인체는 어느 정도 분해되어 재조립할 수 있는 부품을 가지고 있다. 인체에 대한 작업은 물품처럼 다른 기계와 비슷한 방식으로 검사되고 고장은 진단되고 수리된다. 말 그대로 프랑켄슈타인 박사에 의해 만들어진 Mary Shelley의 괴물은 인체와 같은 기계의 발상에서 나온 고전적인 작업이다. 인체에 관한 이런 사고방식들이 너무나 친숙해서 우리 중 일부는 인체의 사회 구조적인 생각들과 문화에서의 인체에 대한 생각들이 터무니없는 것처럼 보일 수도 있다.

19 ④ 'respond to' 다음에 전치사 'to'의 목적어에 해당하는 명사 상당어구가 와야 하는데 'in a very different manner'라는 부사구가 왔으므로, 전치사 'to'의 목적어를 주어로 사용한 수동태 형태인 'be responded to'가 되어야 한다.

> **오답풀이**

① 'where'는 앞의 'many areas'를 선행사로 하는 관계부사로 바르게 사용되었으며, '전치사 + 관계대명사'의 형태인 'in which'로 바꿔 쓸 수 있다.

② 앞의 명사절 'what they say'가 주어에 해당하므로, 3인칭 단수 형태의 be 동사인 'is'를 사용한 것은 적절하다.

③ 'when' 다음에 '주어 + be동사'의 형태인 'it is'가 생략되고, be 동사의 보어로 형용사인 'possible'을 사용한 것이므로 올바르다.

⑤ A and B의 병치 구조에서 앞의 'to come into'에 맞추어 'to start'를 사용해야 하나, to 부정사의 병치에서 뒤에 나온 'to'는 생략이 가능하므로 원형동사의 형태인 'start'를 사용한 것은 올바르다.

> **어휘**

• adolescence : 사춘기, 청소년기
• rebellion : 반란, 반항
• strive : 힘쓰다, 노력하다, 투쟁하다
• liver : 간
• garbage : 쓰레기, 찌꺼기
• decent : 괜찮은, 제대로 된

해석

사춘기는 반항의 시기이자 독립을 투쟁하는 시기이다. 결과적으로 아이들은 당신의 의견에 동의하지 않거나 당신과 똑같은 방식으로 상황을 보려고 하지 않는 많은 영역이 있을 것이다. 기억해라. 그들이 말하는 것은 그들이 말하는 방법만큼 중요하지 않다. 만일 그들이 가족 정책과 처우에 동의할 수 없다는 의사를 전달하면, 분명하게 그들의 말에 귀를 기울이고 가능하면 긍정적으로 응답하려고 노력해라. "저는 더 많은 시간을 전화하는데 보낼 수 있어야 한다고 생각해요. 하루에 15분은 부족해요. 저는 숙제를 모두 했고 성적도 좋아요"라고 부모에게 합리적으로 말하는 아이는 전화할 시간이 부족하다고 소리를 지르며 화를 내기 시작하는 아이와 아주 다른 방식으로 응답해야 한다. 한 십대 아이가 월요일 밤마다 간을 먹는 것을 좋아하지 않는다고 엄마에게 말하는 것은 수용되어야 한다. 그러나 그가 월요일 저녁에 부엌으로 들어와 이 '쓰레기'를 먹지 않을 테니 어머니가 '제대로 된' 요리를 배우는 편이 더 낫다고 위협하기 시작하는 것은 절대로 용납될 수 없다.

20 ③ (A) 앞의 'no matter how'가 양보의 부사절을 이끌어 주어와 동사가 도치된 형태로, 사물인 'the task'가 주어이므로 감정동사 'exhaust'는 현재분사의 형태인 'exhausting'이 되어야 한다.
   (B) 'energy to'와 'focus on' 다음에 목적어가 없으므로 관계대명사를 사용해야 하는데, 선행사가 없으므로 선행사를 포함하는 관계대명사 'what'이 적절하다.
   (C) 접속사 'as'가 이끄는 부사절로, 앞의 'other laws'가 주어이므로 be 동사는 복수 형태인 'are'를 사용해야 옳다.

어휘

• at hand : 가까운 장래에, 머지않아
• exhaust : 기진맥진하게 하다, 지치게 하다
• stand a chance of : …의 가능성이 있다
• attraction : 끌어당기는 힘, 인력
• magnifying glass : 확대경, 돋보기
• manifest : 나타내다, 표현하다
• ups and downs : 기복, 흥망성쇠, 새옹지마
• mishap : 작은 사고[불행]
• vibration : 울림, 진동

해석

당신이 인생에서 무언가가 일어나기를 원한다면, 당신은 그것에 집중할 필요가 있다. 집중하지 않고, 여러분이 성취하고자 하는 것을 믿지 않는다면, 여러분은 가까운 장래에 그 일을 성취할 수 없다. 아무리 그 일이 힘들어 보일지라도, 이러한 집중의 법칙은 당신에게 포기하지 말 것을 상기시켜 준다. 계속해서 믿고 그것에 집중함으로써, 여러분은 원하는 결과를 이

룰 수 있는 가능성이 더 높아진다. 에너지와 인력의 법칙을 통해, 여러분이 에너지를 쏟고 집중한 것에 여러분의 인생을 인도할 것이다. 태양 에너지를 모으는 데 사용된 돋보기는 불을 지필 수 있다. 사고와 믿음에 집중된 에너지를 통해 여러분은 원하는 것을 표현할 수 있다. 새옹지마의 법칙과 같은 다른 법칙들이 당신 뒤에서 작동하는 것처럼, 여러분은 계속해서 고난, 투쟁, 그리고 불행과 마주할 것이다. 당신은 집중하는 모든 것에 힘과 생명을 불어넣는다. 집중을 통해 울림이 증가되기 때문에 당신은 원하는 것에 마술을 부린다.

21 ④ (A) 뒤에 '주어 + 동사 + 목적어' 형태의 완벽한 문장이 왔으므로, 'efficient'는 동사 'could have harvested'를 수식하기 위해 부사의 형태인 'efficiently'를 사용해야 한다.
   (B) 주어인 'a family'를 수식하기 위한 형용사절이므로 'that worked'를 사용해야 하며, 본동사는 'would have been ~'이다.
   (C) 앞의 명사 'time'을 수식하기 위해 'to 부정사'의 형용사적 용법에 해당하는 'to harvest'를 사용해야 한다.

어휘

• hunter-gatherer : 수렵채집인
• semi-settled : 반정착의
• nomadic : 유목의, 방랑의
• shelter : 주거지, 거주지
• cereal grain : 곡물
• archaeologist : 고고학자
• flint-blade : 돌칼
• sickle : 낫
• efficient : 능률적인, 효율적인
• prehistoric : 선사시대의
• quantity : 양, 수량, 분량
• be reluctant to : ~을 주저하다, 망설이다, 꺼리다
• unguarded : 무방비의, 보호하지 않은

해석

비록 임시로 또는 계절에 따라 여러 주거지 사이를 이동하는 유목민의 생활보다 수렵채집인들이 더 먼저 반정착 생활을 시작했지만, 곡물을 저장할 수 있는 능력으로 인해 사람들이 한 장소에 머무르게 되었다. 1960년대에 시행된 실험이 그 이유를 보여준다. 한 고고학자가 돌칼 낫을 사용해서 선사시대의 가족이 얼마나 효율적으로 터키의 일부 지역에서 여전히 재배되는 곡식을 수확할 수 있었는지를 보여주었다. 한 시간에 그는 2파운드 이상의 곡식을 모았는데, 이것은 3주 동안 매일 8시간을 일한 가족이 식구 모두에게 일 년 동안 매일 1파운드의 곡식을 제공할 만큼 충분히 수확했다는 것을 의미한다. 하지만 이것은 그 가족이 야생곡물을 수확하기 위한 최적기를 놓

치지 않도록 야생곡물 근처에 머물렀다는 걸 뜻한다. 그리고 많은 양의 낟알을 수확했다면, 그들은 무방비 상태로 두는 것을 꺼렸을 것이다.

22 ② 윗글은 종군기자의 파견이 옳은 정책인지 아닌지를 다룬 글로, 종군기자들이 전쟁 상황을 객관적으로 정확하게 보도해야 하는데, 취재 대상과 너무 친해지거나 함께 생활함으로써 동질감을 갖게 되면 과연 객관적인 보도가 가능한지를 우려하고 있다. 그러므로 ②의 'gaining(얻다)'은 'losing(잃다)'으로 고쳐 써야 한다.

어휘

- embed : (종군 기자 등을) 파견하다
- ground-breaking : 신기원을 이룬, 획기적인
- controversial : 논란이 많은, 논란의 여지가 있는
- charge : ~를 비난하다
- troop : 병력, 군대, 부대
- identify with : ~와 동일시하다[동질감을 갖다]
- phenomenon : 현상
- Stockholm Syndrome : 스톡홀름 증후군
- hostage : 인질, 볼모
- empathize with : …에 마음으로부터 공감하다
- captor : 포획자, 체포자
- advocate : 지지하다, 옹호하다
- up close and personal : 밀착취재
- portray : 그리다, 묘사하다, 보여주다
- footage : 장면, 화면

해석

획기적이었지만, 종군기자를 파견하는 것은 ① 논란이 많은 정책임에 틀림없다. 일부 비평가들은 파견된 종군기자들이 군대나 임무를 위험에 빠뜨릴 수도 있다고 비난했다. 다른 사람들은 기자들이 취재 대상과 '너무 친해지고', 함께 생활하거나 보호를 받는 사람들과 자연스럽게 보다 직접적으로 동질감을 갖게 되면, 그들에 대한 객관성을 ② 얻을(→ 잃을) 거라고 걱정했다. 이 현상은 인질들이 인질범들과 공감하게 되는 스톡홀름 증후군과 관련이 있다. 그럼에도 불구하고, 종군기자 파견을 옹호하는 사람들은 그것이 몇 가지 이점이 있다고 주장한다. 그것은 '밀착취재'를 제공하고 기자들로 하여금 군대처럼 전쟁을 경험하도록 ③ 허용함으로써, 전쟁을 수행하는 사람들의 노력을 묘사할 수 있게 해준다. 그것은 다른 방법으로는 불가능한 전탱터와 전쟁 사건에 대한 ④ 직접적인 접근을 제공한다. 생생한 화면과 '실시간 보도'는 ⑤ 현실적인 '역사의 첫 장면'을 제공하고 전쟁을 일어난 그대로 기록한다.

23 ⑤ 지구상에는 물이 너무나 풍부하기 때문에 금성과 화성 같

은 태양계의 다른 행성들도 응당 물이 풍부할거라고 여긴다. 그러므로 ⑤의 'scarce(부족한)'은 'ample(풍부한)'으로 고쳐 써야 옳다.

어휘

- liquid : 액체의, 액체 상태의
- perception : 지각, 인지, 인식
- vivid : 생생한, 활발한
- canal : 운하, 수로
- swamp : 늪, 습지
- planetary : 행성의
- presuppose : 예상하다, 추정하다
- polar cap : (화성의) 극관
- ice sheet : 빙상, 판빙, 대륙 빙하
- overgrown version : 확장판
- rainforest : 열대우림

해석

가장 맘에 드는 해변의 끝에 서서 밖을 쳐다보라. 당신은 우주가 제공하는 가장 특이한 광경 중의 하나인 엄청난 양의 물을 보고 있다. 지구의 대양들을 ① 독특한 현상으로 인식한 것은 최근의 일이다. 공상과학 소설을 읽는 사람들은 '화성의 운하'와 '금성의 늪'에 대한 생생한 기억을 떠올릴 것이다. 25년 전만 해도 우리 이웃 행성의 특성에 관한 최선의 과학적 추측은 많은 양의 물이 ② 존재한다고 추정했다. 화성의 경우, 하얀 극관들은 물이 액체가 되기에는 온도가 너무 차가울 수 있다는 것을 보여주었고, 그 결과 물이 빙상에 ③ 갇혀 있다고 생각했다. 금성의 경우, 구름층으로 인해 그 표면을 볼 수는 없지만, 그 행성을 아마존 우림의 확장판으로 ④ 상상하는 것을 막지는 못했다. 두 가지 사례에서, 이웃행성들에 대한 우리의 견해는 지구상에는 물이 너무나 풍부해서 태양계 안의 다른 모든 곳에서도 물이 ⑤ 부족할(→ 풍부할) 것이라는 기대감에 의해 형성되었다.

24 ⑤ (A) 복잡한 자료들을 훨씬 더 간단한 순서로 한다고 했으므로, 처리하는 차원의 수를 늘리는 것이 아니라 줄이는 것이다. 그러므로 'reduce(줄이다)'가 문맥상 적절하다.

(B) 연대기적 감각을 만들어 한 방향으로 움직이게 하려면 그 이야기를 부정하는 것이 아니라 도입해야 한다. 그러므로 'imposing(도입하다)'가 문맥상 적절하다.

(C) 진실된 일련의 사건들을 회상하는 것이 아니라 전보다 솔직하게 보이게 하는 재구성된 사건을 회상한다고 하였으므로, 문맥상 'straightforward(솔직한)'이 들어갈 낱말로 적절하다.

어휘

- make sense : ~을 이해하다

- attach to : …에 붙이다, …에 부여하다
- drive : 충동, 욕구
- reduce : 줄이다, 축소하다
- dimension : 차원
- narrative : 묘사, 기술, 서술, 이야기
- causality : 인과 관계
- randomness : 무작위, 임의성
- deny : 거부하다, 부인[부정]하다
- impose : 도입[시행]하다, 부가하다
- chronology : 연대기, 연대표
- perpetuate : 영구화하다, 영속시키다
- straightforward : 간단한, 쉬운, 솔직한

해석

Black Swan이라는 훌륭한 책의 저자인 Nassim Taleb에 따르면, 정보 저장에 부가되는 비용들이 있기 때문에 우리는 주위에 있는 모든 정보들을 이해하려고 노력한다. 그래서 정보를 더 정돈되게 만들수록, 마음속에 저장하기가 쉽고 비용도 적게 든다. 이것은 우리가 더 정돈되고 더 임의적이지 않은 정보를 선호한다는 것을 의미한다. 우리는 처리하는 차원의 수를 (A) 줄이려고 하는 욕구가 있어서, 이것을 행하는 방법으로 복잡한 자료들을 훨씬 더 간단한 순서로 두려고 한다. Taleb는 이것이 서술의 목적일 뿐만 아니라 인과관계라고 생각한다. 우리는 세상의 복잡성과 임의성을 처리하기 위해 가만히 있기 보다는 설명하고 이해할 수 있도록 인과관계를 사건 탓으로 돌리려고 한다. 또한, 서술을 (B) 도입하는 목적은 연대기적 감각을 만들어, 둘 모두를 한 방향으로 움직이게 한다. 서술은 스토리에 적합하고, 그 이야기가 영속화시킨 인과관계의 요구사항을 충족시키는 사실들을 회상하는 경향이 있다. 그러면 우리는 진실된 일련의 사건들을 회상하는 것이 아니라 인과성을 전보다 훨씬 더 (C) 솔직한 것처럼 보이게 하는 재구성된 사건을 회상한다.

25 ③ (A) 군 간병인들은 그 자체로 영웅이지만 접속사 'but'에 의해 그렇지 않다는 내용이 와야 하므로, 'unrecognized (인정받지 못하다)'가 문맥에 맞는 낱말로 적절하다.
   (B) 군인들은 조국을 위해 희생했기 때문에 명예, 보상, 혜택을 받을 자격이 있다. 그러므로 'rightly(정당하게)'가 문맥에 맞는 낱말로 적절하다.
   (C) 군 간병인들은 명예나 보상은 거의 없다고 하였으나, 'Yet(그럼에도 불구하고)'이 왔으므로 군 간병인들의 가치는 아주 높다는 의미가 되어야 한다. 그러므로 'enormous(엄청난)'이 문맥에 맞는 낱말로 적절하다.

어휘

- veteran : 베테랑, 참전 용사, 재향 군인

- military caregiver : 군 간병인[돌봄이]
- award : 상, 보상
- recognition : 인정, 승인
- accolade : 포상, 칭찬
- deserve : ~을 받을 만하다[자격이 있다]
- the disabled : 장애인, 불구자
- incidental : 우연한, 부수적인
- enormous : 거대한, 엄청난
- insignificant : 대수롭지 않은, 사소한, 하찮은
- render : 주다, 제공하다, 부여하다

해석

부상당하고, 병들고, 다친 현역 군인들과 참전 용사들 옆에는 이들을 돌보는 사람들이 있는데, '군 간병인'이라고 칭한다. 군 간병인들은 그 자체로 영웅이지만, 그들의 노력은 종종 (A) 인정받지 못한다. 그들의 부양 책임감은 전투가 끝난 후 몇 달 내지 몇 년 동안 지속되기 때문에, 그들은 전쟁의 그늘에서 봉사한다. 조국을 위해 희생한 군인들은 군복무를 인정받아 종종 명예, 보상, 그리고 혜택을 받는데, 그들이 (B) 정당하게 받을 자격이 있는 포상과 기회이다. 그러나 군 간병인들은 장애인들이 걷고 먹는 것을 도우며, 상처를 치료해 주거나 진료 예약을 잡아주지만, 명예나 보상은 거의 없다. 이러한 군 간병인들은 부수적인 사람들로, 오직 그들이 보살핌을 제공하는 사람들에 대한 관심의 결과로써만 정책적 주목을 받아왔다. 그럼에도 불구하고 그들의 가치는 (C) 엄청나다. 군 간병인들은 그들이 사랑하는 사람들뿐만 아니라 사회에도 또한 도움을 주고 있다. 그들이 제공하는 도움은 정부와 사회에 의료비를 줄이도록 돕는다.

26 ① 해외 특파원들이 방송 보도의 트렌드 변화에 따라 해외지사의 폐쇄와 국제 뉴스 보도 등의 축소되어 설 자리를 잃고 있다는 내용이므로, 빈칸에는 ①의 'an endangered species (멸종위기에 처한 종)'이 들어갈 말로 가장 적절하다.

오답풀이

② 아마추어 대사
③ 이국적인 생각의 원천
④ 특히 싫어하는 인물
⑤ 비밀전쟁의 이야기꾼

어휘

- foreign correspondent : 해외 특파원[통신원]
- apply to : ~에 적용되다
- overseas bureau : 해외 지사
- coverage : 보도, 방송
- reverse : 뒤바꾸다, 역전시키다

- by a wide margin : 너끈히, 여유 있게, 큰 차이로
- workload : 업무량, 작업량
- ambassador : 대사, 사절
- exotic : 외국의, 이국적인

해석

몇몇 역사가들은 해외 특파원, 즉 나라 밖의 사건들을 취재하는 기자가 멸종위기에 처한 종이라고 단언한다. 이런 표현은 특히 전통적인 대중 매체 특파원들에게 적용된다. 1980년 이래로 미국 방송국들은 해외지사의 대부분을 폐쇄했고 국제 뉴스 보도를 축소했다. 2001년 9월 11일의 테러도 이라크 전쟁도 이러한 추세를 바꾸지 못했다. 예를 들어 2007년을 살펴보면, 방송국의 텔레비전 뉴스를 모니터하는 Tyndall Report는 이라크 전쟁이 언급할 필요도 없이 그 해의 뉴스였지만, 2001년 이후 그 방송국의 해외 지사들은 업무량이 가장 적다는 것을 발견했다. 경제적인 압력, 지구촌 독립, 기술 혁신, 그리고 대중들의 무관심이 외신들이 보도되고 소비되는 방식을 변화시켰다.

27 ① 환경을 보존하는 데 인구가 중요한 문제라고 말하지만, 사실 미국의 인구 증가가 세상에 미친 영향이 개발도상국의 전체 인구가 세상에 미친 영향과 동일하다고 했으므로, 환경을 보전하는 데 정작 중요한 것은 '세상을 대하는 우리의 방법(our way of dealing with the world)'이다.

오답풀이

② 복지 문제에 대한 우리의 관점
③ 개발도상국에 대한 인도주의적 지원
④ 빈곤과 폭력을 끝내는 방법
⑤ 경제적 평등의 정도를 측정하는 방법

어휘

- rural : 시골의, 지방의
- counterpart : 상대, 상대방
- inappropriate : 부적절한, 부적합한
- justifiable : 정당한, 타당한
- humanitarian : 인도주의적인, 인도주의의
- put an end to : …을 끝내다, 그만두게 하다
- poverty : 빈곤, 가난
- violence : 폭행, 폭력

해석

만일 당신이 미국과 같은 나라에 산다면, 환경을 보존하는 데 인구가 중요한 문제라고 말하기 쉽다. 하지만 좀 더 깊게 생각해보면, 소비와 우리가 사용하는 기술의 종류 또한 미래의 세계를 위한 무대를 꾸미는 데 매우 중요하다는 것을 빠르게 이해할 수 있다. 예를 들어, 브라질 또는 인도네시아의 시골에

사는 사람들은 대부분의 개발도상국 사람들처럼, 미국 사람들의 소비 수준의 약 40분의 1로 살아간다. 2차 세계대전의 종전 이후 미국의 인구가 1억 3천 5백만 명이 증가했다는 것을 고려하면, 미국의 추가 인구가 세계에 끼친 영향은 - 소비 수준, 오염 수준, 스스로를 파괴할 수도 있는 부적절한 기술들의 사용 수준의 관점에서 - 42억만 명인 개발도상국의 전체 인구가 세계에 끼친 영향과 거의 동등하다. 인구가 유일한 요인이라고 말하는 것은 타당하지 못하다. 정말로 중요한 것은 우리가 세상을 대하는 방법이다.

28 ③ 다른 사람의 성격을 파악할 때 그 사람이 친근한지, 신뢰할 수 있는지, 감정적인지, 주도적인지 등등 그 사람의 인상을 보게 된다는 것이므로, 빈칸에는 ③의 'how we perceive other people (타인을 인지하는 법)'이 들어갈 말로 가장 적절하다.

오답풀이

① 우리의 성격을 형성하는 법
② 잘못된 정보를 선별하는 것
④ 인과 관계에 대해 추론하는 것
⑤ 우리의 성격에 적합한 직업을 구하는 것

어휘

- personality : 성격, 인격, 개성
- extract : 뽑다, 추출하다
- attribute : 속성, 특성
- trustworthy : 신뢰할 수 있는, 믿을 수 있는
- dominant : 우세한, 지배적인, 주도적인
- dispositional : 기질의, 기분의
- inference : 추론
- stereotype : 고정 관념, 정형화된 생각
- be saturated with : …에 흠뻑 젖어들다, …으로 가득 차 있다
- happy-go-lucky : 태평스러운, 낙천적인
- aggressive : 공격적인, 적극적인
- awkward : 어색한, 서투른
- greedy : 탐욕스러운, 욕심 많은
- perceiver : 지각[인지]하는 사람
- sort out : 선별하다, 분류하다
- causality : 인과 관계

해석

성격 특징은 자신을 정의하는 법뿐만 아니라, 타인을 인지하는 법도 중요하다. 사회심리학자들은 우리가 다른 사람의 인상을 파악할 때, 그들이 어떻게 보이고 행동하는지, 즉 친근한지, 신뢰할 수 있는지, 감정적인지, 주도적인지 등등으로부터 그들의 성격 특성에 대한 정보를 얻으려 한다는 사실을 보여주었다. 인상 파악이란 다른 사람의 성격에 대한 '기질적 추

론'으로 알려진 것을 만드는 모든 것이다. 마찬가지로, 우리가 특정한 사회 집단에 대해 갖고 있는 고정관념은 성격적 특성으로 가득 차 있다. 정확하든 부정확하든, 이러한 고정관념들은 집단 구성원들의 성격 묘사를 나타내는데, 이를테면 낙천적이든, 공격적이든, 사회적으로 서툴든, 탐욕스럽든지 간에 말이다. 다시 한 번 말하자면, 성격 특징들은 그것들이 사람들의 중요한 핵심 측면들이기 때문에 우리에게 사회적 인지자로서 중요하다.

29 ① 윗글에서 수세기 동안 혼자 일하는 예술가는 거의 없었으며 심지어 르네상스의 천재 예술가도 보조 예술가들이 일하는 작업장을 운영했다고 서술되어 있다. 따라서 오늘날의 일부 유명한 예술가들도 그러하다는 내용이 빈칸에 와야 하므로, ①의 'employ other artists to realize their ideas (자신들의 생각을 실현시키기 위해 다른 예술가들을 고용하다)'가 들어갈 말로 가장 적절하다.

오답풀이

② 체제의 범위 내에서 일하다.
③ 논란을 불러일으킬 작품을 원하다.
④ 수많은 단계적 해결책을 얻다.
⑤ 재정적 지원을 후원자에게 의존하다.

어휘

• elevate : 승진[승격]시키다, 높이다[증가시키다]
• liberal art : 교양 과목
• popularize : 대중화하다, 보급하다
• controversial : 논란이 많은, 논란의 여지가 있는
• promote : 촉진시키다, 고취시키다
• staff : 직원으로 일하다
• assistant : 보조, 조수
• confines : 한계, 범위
• incite : 선동하다, 조장하다
• controversy : 논란
• patron : 후원자, 보호자

해석

교양과목으로서 그들의 전문성을 높이기 위한 르네상스 예술가들의 노력 덕분에, 서양 세계는 매우 개인적인 것을 표현하기 위해 자신만의 예술을 창조하는 고독한 개인의 생각을 대중화시켜왔다. 19세기와 20세기에 예술가들은 자신의 작품 모양과 내용을 개별적으로 결정하고, 자기표현의 새로운 형태를 찾는 과정에서 종종 매우 논란이 되었던 예술을 만드는 일이 더 흔해졌다. 이것은 오늘날에도 여전히 사실이다. 그러나 이전 수세기 동안, 혼자 일하는 예술가는 거의 없었다. 심지어 창조적인 천재성을 고취시켰던 르네상스 예술가들도 주인의 디자인을 예술 작품으로 바꾸는 것과 관련된 대부분의 일을

수행했던 보조 예술가들이 일하는 작업장을 운영했다. 심지어 오늘날 Jeft Koons와 같은 일부 유명한 예술가들조차 자신들의 생각을 실현시키기 위해 다른 예술가들을 고용한다.

30 ⑤ 아리스토텔레스적인 정신으로 행동하는 것은 플라톤이나 헤라클레이토스를 읽는 것을 거부함으로써가 아니라 그들의 장점을 이해하고 약점을 비판함으로써 이루어진다. 그러므로 빈칸에는 ⑤의 'intelligent departures from even the most accomplished authorities (가장 뛰어난 권위들로부터 똑똑한 출발들)'이 들어갈 말로 가장 적절하다.

오답풀이

① 훈련을 통해 함께 일할 기회
② 정치학, 윤리학, 문학 같은 인문학의 명예
③ 철학자들에 의해 공유된 가치에 기반한 주요 관계
④ 개개인의 특징에 관해 만들어진 일반화

어휘

• antiquity : 고대, 아주 오래됨, 유물
• comprehensive : 포괄적인, 종합적인
• range over : 다루다, 아우르다, 섭렵하다
• problematic : 문제가 많은
• legacy : 유산, 유물
• inhibit : 억제[저해]하다, 못하게 하다
• irreverence : 불경, 불손
• vital : 필수적인, 생명유지와 관련된
• successor : 후계자, 계승자
• paradoxically : 역설적으로
• critique : 비평한 글, 평론
• appreciation : 감상, 공감
• allow for : …을 위해 감안하다, …을 고려[참작]하다
• discipline : 규율, 훈련
• humanities : 인문학

해석

고대의 모든 사상가들 중에서, 아마도 아리스토텔레스가 가장 종합적이었는데, 그의 작품은 가령 물리학, 정치학, 그리고 윤리학과 같은 지식 전반을 다루었다. 그러나 아리스토텔레스의 방대한 업적은 문제가 많은 유산을 남겼다. 우리 자신의 이익을 위해 너무나 영리한 아리스토텔레스와 같은 작가들이 있다. 그렇게 많은 말을 하고서도, 그들은 마지막 말을 한 것처럼 보인다. 그들의 천재성 때문에 후계자들의 창작활동에 필수적인 불손함은 억제된다. 역설적으로, 아리스토텔레스는 그를 가장 존경하는 사람들이 그처럼 행동하는 것을 막을지도 모른다. 플라톤이나 헤라클레이토스를 읽는 것을 거부함으로써가 아니라, 그들 장점의 공감을 바탕으로 일부 약점에 중요한 비판들을 제기함으로써, 그는 단지 그 앞에 축적된 많은 지

식을 의심하여 위대해졌다. 정말로 아리스토텔레스적인 정신으로 행동하는 것은 가장 뛰어난 권위들로부터 똑똑한 출발들을 창작하는 것을 의미할 지도 모른다.

31 ③ 주어진 글에서 학급 크기의 선호에 대해 설명하고 있고, 글 (B)에서는 15명 정도의 작은 학급에 대해 그리고 글 (C)에서는 30명 정도의 큰 학급에 대해 설명하고 있다. 그런데 글 (C)가 대조의 부사구인 'On the other hand(반면에)'로 시작되므로 글 (B) 다음에 위치해야 한다. 그리고 글 (A)가 첨가의 접속부사인 'Furthermore(게다가)'로 시작되고 그 내용이 규모가 큰 학급과 관련된 것이므로 글 (C) 다음에 와야 한다. 따라서 (B) – (C) – (A)의 순으로 글이 배열되는 것이 적절하다.

어휘

• discipline : 규율, 훈육
• doze : 깜빡 잠이 들다, 졸다
• daydreaming : 낮잠
• makeup work : 보충 수업

해석

학부모들과 일반대중에게, 학급의 크기는 학교의 질에 관한 "리트머스 테스트"처럼 보인다. 학급 크기가 작은 학교는 학급 크기가 큰 학교보다 더 좋은 것으로 인식된다. 조사에 따르면 학부모들은 학교 안전을 제외한 다른 무엇보다도 학급 규모에 더 관심을 보인다.

(B) 결국, 교사가 한 반에 15명 정도의 학생만 있으면, 교사가 각 학생에게 개별적 관심을 기울일 수 있는 가능성이 훨씬 더 많다. 아무도 방치되지 않을 것이며, 아무도 스스로 앞으로 나올 필요도 없다.

(C) 반면에, 30명 정도 규모의 학급 교사들은 학생 각자를 개별 지도할 수 없다. 선생님들은 채점해야 할 산더미 같은 시험지, 계산해야 할 성적, 결석한 학생들을 위한 보충 수업, 부모님들과의 연락, 답해야 할 이메일들이 있다.

(A) 게다가, 훈육은 훨씬 더 어렵다. 예를 들어, 학생들은 선생님 모르게 교실에서 졸지도 모르며, 확실히 선생님은 낮잠의 흔적이 있는 모든 학생들을 지적할 수도 없다.

32 ⑤ 글 (C)의 'this rate(이 속도)'는 주어진 글에서의 'the rate'를 가리키고, 글 (B)의 'That concern(그런 우려)'은 글 (C)의 'concern'을 가리킨다. 그리고 글 (A)의 'If this happens(이런 상황이 일어나면)'은 글 (B)의 'a chronic battle(고질적인 싸움)'을 의미한다. 그러므로 (C) – (B) – (A)의 순으로 글이 배열되는 것이 적절하다.

어휘

• get over : ~을 극복[처리]하다
• frustration : 불만, 좌절
• picky : 까다로운, 별스러운
• chronic : 만성적인, 고질적인
• obvious : 분명한, 명확한

해석

먹는 것이 한 살배기 아이에게는 여전히 즐겁지만, 어린이의 생활에서 더 이상 주된 관심사는 아니다. 아이들의 음식에 대한 욕구는 대게 그들의 활동 수준과 그들의 키와 몸무게의 성장 속도에 의해 결정된다.

(C) 이 속도가 2년차에는 현저히 떨어지기 때문에, 많은 어린이들이 실제로 8–10개월 때보다 5–18개월 때 더 적게 먹는다. 예상했던 대로 이것은 아이들의 몸집이 더 크고 나이가 많을수록 분명히 더 많이 먹어야 한다고 느끼는 많은 부모들을 크게 걱정시키고 있다.

(B) 그런 우려는 종종 아이들이 더 많이 먹도록 부모들을 강요하게 한다. 부모들이 강요하고 아이들이 저항할 때, 어느 음식부터 먼저 시작할 것인가의 문제보다 관련된 모든 이들에게 더 중요한 고질적인 싸움이 시작된다.

(A) 이런 상황이 일어나면 모든 사람이 패자가 된다. 부모들은 아이들이 먹는 방식에 대한 불만을 결코 극복하지 못하기 때문에 패자가 되고, 아이들은 음식에 까다롭거나 까탈스러워지며 또는 고질적인 과식자가 되기 때문에 패자가 된다.

33 ② 주어진 문장에서 'That'은 박테리아 감염과 불쾌함의 주요 원인이 되었던 '속옷'이므로, 해당 문장은 ②에 들어가는 것이 적절하다.

어휘

• prompt : 촉발하다, 유도하다
• chemical-repelling : 화학물질 탈취
• biological : 생물학적인
• casualty : 사상자, 피해자
• infection : 감염, 전염병
• tiny : 아주 적은
• nanoparticle : 나노 입자
• fiber : 섬유
• fabric : 직물, 천
• repel : 격퇴하다, 물리치다, 제거하다
• virtually : 사실상, 거의
• undergarment : 속옷

- stuff : 것, 물건, 물질
- wearer : 입는 사람, 착용자

해석

그것은 군대로 하여금 생물학 무기들로부터 군인들을 보호하기 위해 개발했던 화학물질 제거 기술을 티셔츠와 속옷에 적용하도록 유도했다.

1991년 걸프전 당시 사막의 폭풍 작전으로 가장 많은 사상자가 박테리아 감염으로 발생했다는 사실을 누가 알겠는가? 전투 중인 군인들은 설령 그들이 갈아입을 깨끗한 속옷을 가지고 있다 하더라도, 항상 새 속옷으로 갈아입을 수 있는 사치를 누릴 수 있는 것은 아니다. (①) 뜨거운 사막 환경에서 매일 입는 속옷은 박테리아 감염과 불쾌함의 주요 원인이 되었다. (②) 속옷은 마이크로파 에너지를 이용함으로써 아주 작은 '나노 입자들'을 속옷 천의 섬유와 결합시켜 제조된다. (③) 그런 다음 기름, 물, 박테리아 및 기타 물질을 제거하는 화학물질이 나노 입자와 결합된다. (④) 그 결과 거의 아무 것도 달라붙지 않기 때문에, 때가 타기가 아주 어려운 속옷이 되었다. (⑤) 그리고 박테리아가 결코 생기지 않기 때문에, 그 물질로 만들어진 속옷은 세탁하지 않고 착용자의 건강에 무리를 주지 않으면서 몇 주 동안 입을 수 있다.

34 ④ 주어진 문장이 역접의 접속 부사 'However(그러나)'로 시작되므로, 이전의 문장은 이와 반대되는 내용이 서술되어야 한다. 즉, 주어진 문장이 사유재산권을 적극적으로 인정하는 사회에서조차 용납할 수 없는 경우를 언급하고 있으므로, 소유주가 자기 재산을 자기 마음대로 처리하겠다고 말한 다음인 ④에 위치하는 것이 가장 적절하다.

어휘

- private property right : 사유재산권
- mixture : 혼합물, 혼합체
- organizational : 조직의
- consequently : 결과적으로
- sacred : 성스러운, 종교적인, 신성시되는
- restoration : 복원, 부활, 회복
- formidable : 가공할, 어마어마한
- inevitable : 불가피한, 필연적인
- wetland : 습지
- filling : 매립
- draining : 배수
- altering : 변경, 개조
- ecological : 생태계의, 생태학의
- betterment : 향상, 개선, 개량

해석

그러나 사유재산권은 이 문제에 관해 강경론을 펼치는 사회에서조차 신성시되지 못한다.

조망 수준의 복원은 거의 항상 공공 재산(특히 물과 관련된)과 조직 및 개인 재산의 혼합을 내포하고 있다. (①) 결과적으로 조망 방법의 강력한 장벽은 환경 보호와 재산권 사이의 불가피한 충돌이다. (②) 작은 습지를 가진 개인 소유주는 습지를 주로 매립, 배수, 개조하는 것이 불법이라는 말을 들었을 때 화를 낼 가능성이 높다. (③) 소유주는 가끔씩 이 재산은 사적인 것이므로, "내가 원하는 대로 내 재산을 처리하겠다."라고 말한다. (④) 각 개인은 사유지에서뿐만 아니라, 타인과 함께 하는 더 큰 생태계에서 산다. (⑤) 그래서 핵심 질문인 즉, 개인, 조직 혹은 국가적 행동과 태도는 인간의 다른 종과 다른 종들의 개선을 위해 어느 정도까지 수정되어야 하는가이다.

35 ③ 윗글은 재능 있는 아이들이 이상과 현실의 큰 차이 때문에 결국 사회에 잘 적응하지 못하고 중도하차하게 된다는 내용이므로, 같은 나이 또래의 사회적 혹은 행동적 기준을 따른다는 ③의 설명은 이와 배치되므로 글 전체의 흐름과 관계가 없다.

어휘

- extreme : 극도의, 극심한
- sensitivity : 감성, 감수성, 세심함
- mediocrity : 보통, 평범
- greed : 탐욕, 욕심
- corruption : 타락, 부패
- hypocrisy : 위선
- flaw : 결함, 흠, 결점
- disillusioned : 환멸을 느낀
- conform : 따르다, 순응하다
- norm : 표준, 기준
- what's the point? : 무슨 소용이지?
- underachieve : 자기 능력 이하의 성적을 내다
- drop out of : ～에서 중도하차하다, 낙오하다

해석

극도의 감정적인 감수성과 이상주의를 지닌 재능 있는 아이들은 상황이 어떻고 어떠해야만 하는지 사이에서 종종 큰 차이를 발견한다. 그들의 가정에서, 학교에서, 지역공동체에서, 그리고 더 큰 세계에서 말이다. ① 예리한 정신과 날카로운 사고와 추론 능력 때문에, 그들은 평범, 탐욕, 가난, 타락, 폭력, 학대, 공해, 위선, 그리고 사회의 다른 결점들을 잘 알고 있다는

사실을 스스로 깨닫는다. ② 그들은 아무도 신경 쓰지 않거나 이러한 문제들은 결코 고쳐질 수 없다는 사실에 낙담하고 환멸을 느낀다. ③ 그들은 같은 나이 또래의 사회적 혹은 행동적 기준들을 따르기 위해 안도감을 느끼고 신속하게 행동할 지도 모른다. ④ "무슨 소용이지?"라는 태도 때문에, 지적으로 재능 있는 많은 젊은이들이 학교에서 능력 이하의 성적을 내거나, 일부는 고등학교, 대학교, 심지어 사회에서도 중도하차 한다. ⑤ 그들은 사회적 위선이나 그들을 불편하게 하는 사회의 다른 측면을 다룰 필요가 없는 삶이나 직업을 찾을지도 모른다.

36 ④ 윗글은 동물들이 인간과 마찬가지로 문화를 가지고 있는지에 대해 학자들 간의 논쟁 대상이며 계속해서 흥미로운 연구 분야가 된다고 서술하고 있으므로, 동물들의 법적 지위에 대해 서술한 ④의 내용은 윗글의 전체 흐름과 관계가 없다.

어휘

- mounting : 증가하는
- squarely : 꼭, 똑바로, 정확하게
- ongoing : 계속 진행 중인
- debate : 토론, 논쟁
- sufficiency : 충분한 양, 충분함
- ecological : 생태계의, 생태학의
- genetic : 유전적인
- explanation : 설명, 해명
- rule out : 제외시키다, 배제하다
- nonhuman animals : (인간이 아닌) 일반 동물
- legal status : 법적 지위
- fundamental : 근본적인

해석

일부 동물들이 도구를 사용하고, 도덕적인 규범에 의해서 살아가고, 복잡한 의사소통 체계를 사용하고, 문화를 가지고 있다는 과학적인 증거가 많아지고 있다. ① 이러한 연구 결과는 인간과 다른 동물들 사이의 차이는 종(種)이 아니라 정도의 차이라고 예측하는 찰스 다윈의 진화론에 정확하게 들어맞는다. ② 그럼에도 불구하고 동물들 간의 문화에 대한 본성과 증거의 충분함에 대한 논쟁이 계속되고 있다. ③ 일부 학자들은 동물행동에 대한 생태학적, 유전적 설명이 모든 사례에서 배재되었다고 확신하지 않는 반면에, 다른 학자들은 인간이 아닌 동물을 배제하는 방식으로 문화를 정의한다. ④ 인간이 아닌 동물의 법적 지위를 이해하기 위해서는 법체계가 어떻게 작용하는지에 대한 근본적인 이해가 필요하다. ⑤ 새로운 발견과 중요한 진보가 주기적으로 나타나면서 미해결된 논쟁은 이것을 능동적이고 흥미 있는 연구 분야로 만든다.

37 ② 관리자가 직원들에게 업무 지시를 내릴 때 너무 구체적이고 명확한 지시를 하게 되면 직원들의 창의력이 제약을 받으므로, (B) 추상의 수준을 조절함으로써 직원들이 그들의 (A) 창의력을 보여 줄 기회를 제공할 수 있다. 그러므로 빈 칸 (A)에는 'creativity(창의력)', (B)에는 'abstraction(추상)'이 들어갈 말로 가장 적절하다.

어휘

- employee : 종업원, 직원
- concrete : 사실에 근거한, 구체적인
- assignment : 과제, 임무
- propose : 제안하다
- overview : 개요, 개관
- embark on : ~에 착수하다
- benchmark : 기준(점)
- assess : 재다, 가늠하다, 평가[사정]하다
- criteria : 규준, 표준, 기준
- ambiguous : 막연한, 모호한
- opportunity : 기회
- instruction for an assignment : 업무 지시
- abstraction : 관념, 추상적 개념
- enthusiasm : 열광, 열정
- frequency : 빈도, 빈발

해석

직원들의 계획 기법들을 시험하고 싶어 하는 새로운 관리자에 대해 생각해 보라. 그녀는 어떤 특정 프로젝트에 대한 계획서를 개발하라고 요구할 수도 있다. 그 과제를 설명하기 위해서 매우 구체적인 특정 언어를 사용할 수도 있다. "나는 당신이 제의받은 프로젝트에 대해 5페이지짜리 계획을 개발하기를 바랍니다. 먼저, 도입부에 프로젝트 개요를 포함시켜야만 합니다. 둘째, 우리가 왜 이 프로젝트에 착수했는지에 대한 분석을 강조하는 섹션을 원합니다. 셋째, 보고서에 솔루션 섹션을 원합니다. 마지막으로 제의 받은 솔루션의 성공 여부를 평가하기 위한 기준과 벤치마크에 대한 설명을 원합니다." 이 요청은 매우 구체적인 특정 언어를 사용하지만, 관리자의 요구에 부합하는가? 사업 제안서의 길이와 형식을 개략적으로 제시함으로써, 매니저는 자신이 원하는 바를 분명히 명시하고, 그렇게 함으로써 직원들의 계획 능력을 평가할 기회를 줄이게 된다. 그녀는 요구를 더 모호하게 할 수도 있었다. 즉, "이 프로젝트의 제안서를 개발해 주세요. 여러분의 창의력을 제한하고 싶지 않기 때문에, 너무 많은 것을 말하고 싶지 않아요." 비록 이 언어가 더 추상적이지만, 그것은 매니저에게 각각의 직원들이 어떻게 생각하고 계획하는지에 대한 더 나은 통찰력을 제공할 수도 있다.

↓

367

직원들의 계획기법을 평가할 때, 관리자는 업무 지시에서 (B) <u>추상</u>의 수준을 조절함으로써 직원들이 그들의 (A) <u>창의력</u>을 보여주는 기회를 제공할 수 있다.

[38~39]

어휘

- greatness : 거대함, 중요
- countless : 무수한, 셀 수 없이 많은
- absurd : 불합리한, 모순된
- innovative : 획기적인
- come up with : 생산하다, 제시[제안]하다, 찾아내다
- ridiculous : 말도 안 되는, 터무니없는
- distasteful : 불쾌한, 혐오스러운
- imaginable : 상상할 수 있는
- emergency : 비상
- parachute : 낙하산
- conceive : 상상하다, 생각해내다
- evacuation : 피난, 대피
- extreme : 극도의, 지나친
- breakthrough : 돌파구, 혁신
- beverage : 음료
- infinite : 무한한
- prematurely : 조급하게, 시기상조로
- blossom : 꽃이 피다, 개화하다
- brainstorming : 브레인스토밍, 창조적 집단 사고
- intention : 의도
- suspend : 유예하다, 연기[유보]하다
- judgement : 판단, 판결

해석

당신은 소위 나쁜 생각이 그 속에 언제 위대한 씨앗을 품고 있을 지 결코 알지 못한다. 우리는 업무에서 그런 상황을 수없이 보아왔다. 나쁜, 심지어 불합리한 아이디어가 제시되고, 몇 분 내에 그것은 혁신적인 사고의 훌륭한 본보기로 바뀌었다. 우리는 참여자들에게 상상할 수 있는 최악의, 가장 터무니없는, 심지어 불쾌한 생각을 떠올리게 하는 효과적인 아이디어 생성 방법을 사용하는데 후에 그런 생각들은 훌륭한 아이디어로 전환되거나 바뀐다.

"우리 모두 창문 밖으로 뛰어내린다면 어떨까?"라는 극단적인 예를 생각해 보라. 이러한 나쁜 생각에서, 여러분은 높은 도시 빌딩에서 근무하는 사람들을 위해 혁신적인 비상 개인 낙하산 제품을 개발할 수도 있다. 혹은 화재 시 높은 층에서의 향상된 피난 과정을 생각해보라. 새로운 '팀 행글라이딩' 극한

스포츠 행사. 사람들이 무리지어 새 음료를 마신 후에 날 수 있는 혁신적인 광고 개념. 방 안에 있는 모든 사람이 창문 밖으로 뛰어내려야 한다는 나쁜 생각으로부터 수많은 다른 가능성들이 생겨날 수 있다. 즉, 나쁜 생각 속에 들어있는 위대한 생각이 꽃을 피우기 전에 조급하게 폐기되지만 않는다면, 그래서 어떤 생각이 모든 것을 보여줄 수 있는 공정한 기회를 지닐 때까지 <u>판단을 유보해라</u>.

38 ② 윗글은 나쁜 생각도 혁신적인 사고의 훌륭한 본보기로 전환될 수 있으며, 나쁜 생각으로부터 수많은 다른 가능성이 생겨날 수 있다고 설명하고 있다. 그러므로 ②의 'Bad Ideas Can Lead to Big Ideas (나쁜 생각이 큰 생각을 이룰 수 있다)'가 윗글의 제목으로 가장 적절하다.

 오답풀이

① 창의적인 광고가 영감을 줄 것이다.
③ 왜 창조적 집단 사고를 하지 않는가?
④ 좋은 의도도 나쁜 결과를 가져올 수 있다.
⑤ 혼자 일 때 아니면 함께 일 때 사람들이 더 창의적인가?

39 ③ 꽃을 피우기 전에 조급하게 폐기되지만 않는다면 평범한 생각도 훌륭한 생각으로 전환될 수 있으므로, 그 때가 무르익을 때까지 기다리라는 내용이다. 그러므로 빈칸에는 ③의 'suspend judgment (판단을 유보해라)'가 들어갈 말로 가장 적절하다.

오답풀이

① 실수를 찾아라
② 전통을 따르라
④ 악행을 처벌하라
⑤ 낮잠을 줄여라

[40~41]

어휘

- politically correct : 정치적으로 정당한, 차별적인 언어 사용을 피하는
- proponent : 지지자, 제창자
- rid A of B : B에서 A를 제거하다[없애다]
- discriminatory : 차별적인
- offend : 기분 상하게 하다, 범죄를 저지르다
- handicap : 장애, 불리한 조건
- equipment : 장비, 설비
- secondary : 이차적인, 부차적인
- substitution : 대리, 대용

- ridicule : 조롱하다, 비웃다
- satirize : 풍자하다, 꼬집다
- overcompensate : 과대[과잉] 보상을 하다
- political agenda : 정치적 선전
- sexist language : 성차별적인 언어
- directive : 지시, 지휘, 명령
- broader : (폭이) 넓은
- foster : 조성하다, 발전시키다
- equity : 공평, 공정
- merely : 그저, 단지
- hoped-for : 기대된, 원하는
- pros and cons : 장단점, 갑론을박, 찬반양론
- necessity : 필요, 필수품

해석

우리의 관심을 끄는 언어능력의 한 예로 '차별이 적은 언어', 즉 PC 언어라는 용어에 대해 생각해 보자. 그 용어의 지지자들은 차이와 장애를 언급하는 식으로 사람들을 불쾌하게 할 수 있는 모든 단어나 구를 우리 언어에서 제거함으로써 마음속에서 차별적인 생각을 없앨 수 있다고 주장한다. 캘리포니아에 있는 LA 카운티에서는 문화적 민감성 때문에, 1차 및 2차 하드 디스크 드라이브를 지칭하는 용어가 일반적으로 사용되지만, 컴퓨터 장비에 관한 '마스터' 및 '슬레이브'라는 용어의 사용을 중지하도록 공급업체에 요청했다. 가령 'policeman'을 대신한 'police officer'는 그러한 직위가 남성과 여성 모두에 의해 유지된다는 것을 강조하기 위해 의도되었다. (A) 그러나 PC 언어를 사용하는 것과 PC가 되는 것은 부정적인 것으로 보였고, 심지어 그 언어들이 다른 사람들의 민감성을 과잉 보상하기 때문에 조롱과 풍자까지 받았다. PC 언어가 상당히 조롱받기 쉬운 이유 중 하나는 그것의 정치적 의제가 큰 사회 문화적 기관과 항상 연결되어 있는 것은 아니기 때문이다. (B) 예를 들어 남성과 여성 사이에 동등한 관계를 만들기 위한 노력의 일환으로 우리가 직장에서 성차별적인 언어를 없앨 필요가 있다고 말하지만, 이러한 지시가 성 임금 평등 그리고 승진과 출세의 동등한 기회를 조성하는 폭넓은 의제와 연결되지 않는다면, 단순히 직장에서 성차별적인 언어를 없애는 것만으로 기대했던 효과를 창출하지 못할 수도 있다.

40 ③ 차별이 적은 PC 언어 사용을 지지하는 사람들은 차이와 장애를 언급하는 말을 제거함으로써 차별적인 생각을 없앨 수 있다고 주장하는 반면, 그것의 사용을 부정적으로 보는 사람들은 다른 사람들의 민감성을 과잉 보상하기 때문에 조롱과 풍자의 대상이 된다고 말하고 있다. 그러므로 ③의 'pros and cons of using politically correct language (차별이 적은 언어 사용에 대한 찬반양론)'이 윗글의 주제로 가

장 적절하다.

오답풀이

① 차별이 적은 언어 사용을 지지하는 배경
② 사회 발전이 언어 변화에 미치는 영향
④ 남성과 여성의 언어 사용 차이
⑤ 정확한 표현으로 정확한 생각을 구사할 필요성

41 ① (A) 첫 번째 단락에서는 차별이 적은 PC 언어 사용을 지지하는 견해에 대해 서술하고 있고, 두 번째 단락부터는 이의 사용을 부정적으로 보는 견해에 대해 서술하고 있다. 그러므로 역접의 접속부사 'however(그러나)'가 들어갈 연결어구로 적절하다.
　(B) PC 언어가 조롱받기 쉬운 이유에 대해 직장에서의 성차별적 언어 사용을 예로 들어 설명하고 있다. 그러므로 'For example(예를 들면)'이 들어갈 연결어구로 적절하다.

[42~43]

어휘

- automatically : 자동적으로
- sibling : 형제자매
- immigration authority : 이민 당국
- suspect : 의심하다, 용의자
- imposter : 남의 이름을 사칭하는 사람
- suspicion : 혐의, 불신
- residency : 거주
- genetic : 유전의
- donor : 기증자, 헌혈자
- recipient : 수령인, 수취인
- fragment : 조각, 파편
- fingerprinting : 지문
- laboratory : 실험실
- indicate : 나타내다, 보여주다
- evidence : 증거, 흔적

해석

한 소년이 가나 출신의 부모로부터 태어났다. 그 소년은 영국에서 태어났기 때문에 자동적으로 영국시민이었다. 어렸을 때 그의 어머니와 두 명의 누이들과 한 명의 남동생을 남겨두고, 그의 아버지와 살기 위해서 가나로 돌아왔다. 몇 년 후 그는 엄마와 형제 자매들과 살기 위해 영국으로 돌아왔다. 여기에서 이야기가 (a) 복잡해진다. 이민국은 그 소년이 사기꾼이라고 의심했고, 그가 관련이 없는 아이이거나 그 아이의 엄마의

조카라고 생각했다. 의심에 근거해서. 그 소년의 거주 신청은 (b) 거부되었다. 그 소년의 가족은 그가 태어난 나라에서 살 수 있도록 그의 정체성을 확립하기 위해 싸웠다. 첫 번째 의료 테스트는 혈액형뿐만 아니라 장기 기증자와 수혜자를 일치시키기 위해 일반적으로 사용되는 유전자 표지를 사용했다. 결과는 그 소년이 그의 어머니라고 주장하는 여성과 밀접한 관련이 있다는 것을 (c) 확인했지만. 그 테스트는 그녀가 그의 어머니인지 이모인지 구별할 수 없었다.

가족들은 레스터 대학의 과학자인 Alec Jeffreys에게 도움을 청했다. 그들은 Jeffreys의 연구실에서 개발된 기술인 DNA 지문 감식이 아이의 신원을 확인할 수 있는지 물었다. 하지만, 엄마의 언니들과 소년의 아버지는 테스트를 받을 수 없었다. 이러한 문제에도 불구하고, Jeffreys는 이 사건을 맡는 데 동의했다. 그는 소년과 그가 소년의 형제자매라고 믿었던 아이들 그리고 어머니라고 주장하는 여자로부터 혈액 샘플을 채취했다. DNA 지문으로 알려진 밴드의 패턴은 소년의 신원을 확인하기 위해 분석되었다. 샘플들이 모두 아버지와 관련된 DNA 조각을 (d) 공유했기 때문에. 소년이 그의 형제자매들과 같은 아버지를 가지고 있다는 것을 보여주는 결과가 나왔다. 가장 중요한 질문은 그 소년과 그의 '어머니'가 연관되어 있는지 여부였다.

Jeffreys는 그 여성의 DNA 조각 25개가 그 소년의 것과 일치한다는 것을 발견했고, 그녀가 실제로 그 소년의 엄마라는 것을 보여주었다. 이 증거에 직면하여, 이민국은 그들의 입장을 (e) 유지해야(→ 변경해야)만 했다. 당국은 그 소년이 그의 가족과 함께 영국에서 살도록 허락했다.

42 ⑤ 본문에서 엄마의 이모와 소년의 아버지는 혈액 샘플을 받을 수 없었다고 서술되어 있으므로, 'Alec Jeffreys는 소년의 아버지의 혈액 샘플을 받았다.'는 ⑤의 설명은 윗글의 내용과 일치하지 않는다.

43 ⑤ 소년의 신원 회복을 위한 DNA 검사 결과 소년과 가족들의 DNA가 일치했으므로, 그 소년의 거주 신청을 거부했던 이민 당국은 입장을 '유지하는(maintain)' 것이 아니라 '바꿔야 (change)' 했다.

[44~45]

어휘

• embarrassed : 창피한, 쑥스러운

• horrify : 무서워하다, 몸서리치다

• ridiculous : 조롱하는, 비웃는

• novice : 초보자, 애송이

• sibling : 형제자매

• patient : 참을성 있는

• discomfort : 불편

• hunch : 구부리다

• erase : 지우다, 삭제하다

• crouch over : ~위로 몸을 구부리다

• stick out : 툭 튀어나오다, 내밀다

• absurd : 불합리한, 모순된

• adopt : 채택하다, 도입하다

• humiliate : 창피를 주다, 망신을 주다

• shame : 수치심

해석

(A) 여름이었고 Mary는 14살이었다. 그녀의 가족 모두는 주말마다 강가에서 수상스키를 타고, 수영을 하며 즐거운 시간을 보냈다. 하지만 Mary는 오빠, 언니들처럼 스키를 탈 수 없었다. 그녀는 너무 부끄러워서 시도조차 할 수 없었다. (a) 그녀는 우스꽝스럽게 보이고, 숙련되고 경험 많은 형제들 옆에 있는 것이 초보자처럼 보인다는 생각에 충격을 받았다. 어느 날 그녀는 엄마에게 이것에 대해 모두 말했다.

(C) Mary는 스키를 타는 사람들이 물 밖으로 처음 몸을 일으킬 때, 엉덩이를 뒤로 뺀 채, 완전히 우스꽝스러운 자세로 스키 위에서 몸을 웅크리기 시작했다고 설명했다. 그리고 어느 맑은 주말이면 강에는 많은 사람들이 있었다. 그들 중 몇몇은 남자 아이였고, 그들 모두는 (d) 그녀가 수치스러운 자세를 취하면 보게 될 것이다. Mary는 엄마에게 이런 수치심을 무릅쓰고 싶지 않다고 말했다.

(D) 이 대화가 끝난 직후인 어느 목요일 날, Mary의 어머니는 점심 식사 후 퇴근하고 집으로 돌아왔다. Mary는 왜 엄마가 집에 있는지 이해하지 못했지만. 엄마는 그녀에게 보트 트레일러를 차에 연결시키는 것을 도와달라고 말했다. 그녀의 어머니는 무언가를 제안하고 있었고, Mary는 (e) 그녀의 제안을 받아들여야 했다. 그녀가 무슨 일이 일어났는지 알기 전에, Mary와 엄마는 보트에 있었고, 잔잔한 물 위에 따뜻한 햇살이 비치는 강으로 향했다. 목요일이었기 때문에 주변에 다른 사람은 아무도 없었다. 아무도 Mary가 우스꽝스럽게 보이는 것을 보지 못했다.

(B) 그날, Mary는 스키를 배웠다. 그녀의 어머니는 참을성이 있었고 신중했다. 스키 타는 것은 Mary가 생각했던 것만큼 어렵지 않았고, 보는 사람이 없어서 (b) 그녀는 스키 위에서 몸을 구부리는 것에 대해 불편함을 느끼지 않았다. 오후가 지날 무렵, 그녀는 스키에 더 꼿꼿이 섰다. 다음 주말 강 여행 때 (c) 그녀의 당혹감은 엄마의 자상한 행동으로 지워진 채, Mary가 그녀의 형제자매들과 함께 행복하게 스키를 타는 것을 보게 될 것이다.

44 ③ 글 (A)의 마지막 문장에서 Mary가 창피해서 수상스키를 타
    지 못하는 것에 대해 엄마에게 말했고, 이에 대한 내용이
    글 (C)에 서술되어 있다. 그리고 글 (D)의 'this talk'가 글 (C)
    에 해당하므로 글 (C) 다음에 글 (D)가 와야 한다. 마지막으
    로 글 (B)는 Mary가 엄마의 도움을 받아 결국 수상스키를
    배워 행복하게 스키를 타는 장면을 묘사하고 있으므로 마
    지막에 위치해야 한다. 따라서 글의 흐름상 (C) – (D) – (B)
    의 순으로 배열되어야 한다.

45 ⑤ (e)는 Mary의 엄마를 가리키고, (a), (b), (c), (d)는 모두 Mary
    를 지칭한다.

2018학년도 기출문제 정답 및 해설

제2교시 **영어영역(공통)**

01 ⑤	02 ③	03 ③	04 ⑤	05 ①	06 ④
07 ③	08 ④	09 ③	10 ③	11 ⑤	12 ③
13 ①	14 ①	15 ②	16 ②	17 ④	18 ②
19 ②	20 ②	21 ①	22 ⑤	23 ⑤	24 ①
25 ①	26 ④	27 ⑤	28 ④	29 ④	30 ①
31 ⑤	32 ②	33 ④	34 ②	35 ③	36 ①
37 ①	38 ⑤	39 ②	40 ②	41 ④	42 ③
43 ④	44 ④	45 ⑤			

01 ⑤ Joanne가 발레 공연을 보러 가자는 말에 Jimmy가 발레를 몹시 싫어해서 보러 가고 싶지 않다고 답변했다. 그러므로 Jimmy가 발레 팬(Jimmy is a fan of the ballet.)이라는 ⑤의 설명은 옳지 못하다.

오답풀이

① Joanne는 이번 주말 캠핑하는 것에 흥미가 없다.
② 지난 주말에는 비가 내렸다.
③ 텐트가 전혀 방수가 되지 않는다.
④ 이번 주말의 날씨는 좋을 것으로 예상된다.

어휘

• soak : 담그다, 흠뻑 적시다
• leak : 새다, 누설[유출]하다
• forecast : 예측, 예보
• fair enough : 괜찮다, 좋다
• ballet performance : 발레 공연
• waterproof : 방수(防水)의

해석

Jimmy : 이번 주말에 캠핑 갑시다.
Joanne : 또요! 지난 주말에 갔다가 비만 잔뜩 맞았잖아요.
Jimmy : 그렇죠. 텐트가 조금 새서. 그렇지만 이번 주 일기예보에 따르면 하늘에 구름 한 점 없는데요.
Joanne : 그냥 연극이나 다른 문화생활을 할 순 없나요?
Jimmy : 괜찮죠. 지난 주말에는 내가 원하는 걸 했으니까, 이번엔 당신이 계획을 세워 보세요. 뭘 하고 싶으세요?

Joanne : 마을 문화 센터에서 멋진 발레 공연을 한다고 들었어요. 맘에 들 거예요.
Jimmy : 미안하지만, 발레를 보러 가고 싶지는 않아요! 발레는 정말 싫어요. 다른 건 없나요?

02 ③ **첫 번째 빈칸** : 학교가 너무 멀어서 아이가 걸어가는 걸 싫어한다는 말에 근처에 좋은 학교가 있다고 했으므로, 그 학교는 단지 한 블록 떨어져 있다(It's just a block away.)는 c의 부연 설명이 적절하다.

두 번째 빈칸 : 공공요금이 어떤지를 묻는 질문에 건물이 최신식이고 에너지가 효율적이라고 말했으므로, 공공요금이 아주 적당하다(They're very affordable.)는 d의 부연 설명이 적절하다.

세 번째 빈칸 : 좀 더 조용한 곳에 살고 싶다는 말에 아이가 없는 한 젊은 부부와 노부모 몇몇이 살고 있다고 했으므로, 전혀 소음이 없을 거라는(It shouldn't be noisy at all.) b의 부연 설명이 적절하다.

오답풀이

a. 아무것도 구할 수가 없어요.

어휘

• concerns : 걱정, 염려, 관심사
• utilities : 유용성, 공공요금
• energy-efficient : 연료 효율이 좋은, 연비가 좋은
• affordable : 줄 수 있는, (가격이) 알맞은, 적당한

해석

Janet : 이 아파트가 정말 맘에 들지만, 걱정거리가 좀 있어요. 우선, 제게 어린 아이가 있는데 학교가 너무 멀어서 걸어가는 걸 싫어해요.
Dave : 충분히 이해합니다. 이 근처에 좋은 학교가 있어요. 그 학교는 단지 한 블록 떨어져 있어요.
Janet : 공공요금은 어떤가요? 사실 쓸 돈이 그렇게 많지는 않아요.
Dave : 이 건물은 아주 최신식이고 에너지도 효율적이에요. 공공요금은 아주 적당합니다.
Janet : 오, 안심이네요. 그리고 이웃들은 어떻습니까? 좀 더 조용한 곳에 살고 싶어서요.
Dave : 현재 아이가 없는 한 젊은 부부와 노부부 몇이 이

건물에 살고 있어요. <u>전혀 소음이 없을 거예요.</u>

Janet : 좋네요! 이곳이 적당할 것 같아요.

03 ③ 오늘 이용 가능한 차가 있느냐는 물음에 선호하는 차종을 물었고 연비가 좋은 소형차 종류를 희망한다고 하였으므로, 다음 대화가 이루어진 장소는 자동차 대여점(at a rental agency)이다.

오답풀이

① 주유소에서
② 자동차 수리점에서
④ 여행사에서
⑤ 보험회사에서

어휘

• site : 위치, 장소, 지역
• short notice : 촉박한 통보
  cf. at short notice : 예고 없이, 촉박하게
• compact : 소형의, 간편한, 작은
• get a good mileage : 주행거리가 길다, 연비가 좋다
• extra insurance : 추가 보험
• recommend : 권하다, 추천하다
• contract : 계약, 약정
• drop it off : 갖다 놓다, 내려주다
• rental agency : 대여점
• insurance : 보험, 보험업[금]

해석

Aaron : 좋은 아침입니다. 오늘 이용 가능한 차가 있나요. 낮 동안에 시내에 있다가 밤 비행기로 출발하려고요, 그리고 몇 몇 지역을 방문하고 싶어서요.

Krista : 음, 촉박하지만 몇 가지 선택 사항이 있긴 합니다. 선호하시는 차가 있나요?

Aaron : 사실, 연비가 좋은 소형차 종류를 희망합니다.

Krista : 문제없습니다. 맘에 드실 차가 있습니다. 추가 보험을 원하세요? 추천 드립니다.

Aaron : 그럼요. 안전한 게 낫죠.

Krista : 좋습니다. 면허증 좀 보여주시고요, 계약서를 준비할 게요. 반납하실 때 연료를 가득 채울지 확인해 주세요.

Aaron : 알겠습니다. 오늘 저녁쯤에 가져다 드릴게요.

04 ⑤ Bill이 결혼기념일 선물로 강아지를 선물하지만, Diane은 비용부담과 책임 때문에 강아지 키우는 것을 망설인다. Bill이 강아지를 책임질 거라고 약속했고 또한 강아지가 너무 귀여워서 Bill과 Diane은 강아지를 키우기로 한다(Bill and Diane are going to keep the dog).

오답풀이

① Bill은 작년에 결혼기념일을 잊어버렸다.
② Diane는 결혼기념일 선물로 Bill에게 애완동물을 사주었다.
③ Diane 강아지를 키우는 일이 식은 죽 먹기라고 생각한다.
④ Bill은 요즘 집에서 일하지 않는다.

어휘

• wedding anniversary : 결혼기념일
• Oh my lord : 신이시여!, 맙소사!
• puppy : 강아지
• absolutely : 전적으로, 틀림없이
• adorable : 사랑스러운, 귀여운
• bond with : ~와 관계를 맺다[유대를 형성하다]
• snuggle : 바싹 파고들다, 달라붙다
• awfully : 정말, 몹시
• cute : 귀여운, 앙증맞은
• have a point : 일가견이 있다, 일리가 있다
• a piece of cake : 식은 죽 먹기, 누워서 떡 먹기

해석

Bill : 여보, 오늘 우리 첫 번째 결혼기념일이라. 특별한 걸 준비했어. 맘에 들 거야. 한 번 열어 봐.

Diane : 맙소사, 강아지네! 우리는 강아지를 키울 수 없어. 그걸 키우는데 돈이 너무 많이 들고, 큰 책임이 필요해.

Bill : 실제로 그렇게 돈이 많이 들지는 않을 거야. 그리고 요즘 내가 집에서 일을 하니까 강아지 돌보기가 쉬워. 당신은 아무것도 할 게 없어.

Diane : 확실해? 당신이 강아지를 전부 책임질 거라고 약속하지?

Bill : 물론이지. 게다가 쟤를 봐봐! 너무 귀엽지 않아. 이미 당신하고 친해진 거 같은데. 당신에게 딱 달라붙어 다니잖아.

Diane : 솔직히 너무 귀엽네. 당신 말이 일리가 있네. 한 번 키워보자.

05 ① 고속도로를 이용하지 않고 시내로 가는 것에 대해 승객이 의구심을 품었지만, 택시 기사님이 여유 있게 목적지에 도착했으므로 승객은 사과와 함께 택시 기사님을 인정하는 긍정적인 행위가 있어야 한다. 그러므로 빈칸에 들어갈 말로는 ①의 "Here's the fare and a well-earned tip.(여기 요금과 충분한 팁이 있어요.)"가 적절하다.

오답풀이

② 제시간에 도착하지 못할 것 같아요.
③ 지하철을 탔어야 했나 봐요.
④ 그냥 고속도로로 갑시다.
⑤ 잔소리가 불편하네요.

• bother : 괴롭히다, 귀찮게 하다

• construction : 건설[건축] 공사

• clog : 막다, 막히다

• destination : 목적지, 도착지

• with time to spare : 여유 있게

• apology : 사과[사죄]하다

• skepticism : 회의론, 의구심

• well-earned : 충분한, 당연한

• supervisor : 감독관, 관리자, 통제자

택시 기사 : 어서 오세요. 어디로 모실까요?

승객 : 마을을 지나 Smythe 빌딩으로요. 서둘러 주세요.

택시 기사 : 걱정 마세요. 이 시각에는 교통이 막히지 않아요.

[5분 후]

승객 : 귀찮게 해서 죄송합니다만, 왜 고속도로를 이용하지 않고 시내로 가시나요? 저는 꼭 40분 안에 회의에 가야합니다.

택시 기사 : 고속도로를 막게 하는 큰 공사가 있어서요. 저는 모든 지름길을 잘 알고 있습니다. 제 시간에 도착할 거예요.

승객 : 알겠습니다. 그러길 바랄게요.

[25분 후]

택시 기사 : 여유 있게 목적지에 도착했습니다. 선생님.

승객 : 의구심을 품은 것에 사과드릴게요. 여기 요금과 충분한 팁이 있습니다.

06　④ 위의 대화 내용에서 Tim은 혼자서도 집안일을 잘 할 수 있고, 새 직장의 보수도 나쁘지 않다고 걱정하는 부모님을 안심시키고 있다. 그러므로 Tim은 이사 중이며 독립이 준비되었다고 생각한다(Tim is moving away and thinks he is prepared for his independence).

① Tim은 부모님을 보살피기 위해 집으로 돌아 왔다.

② Tim의 부모님은 그를 보살피기 위해 정기적으로 Tim을 방문하기로 결정했다.

③ Tim의 아버지는 Tim이 오래간만에 집에 돌아와서 행복했다.

⑤ Tim은 대학에 다니지만 여전히 부모님의 도움을 필요로 한다.

• nest : 집, 보금자리

• on one's own : 혼자서, 혼자 힘으로, 단독으로

• laundry : 세탁물

• independence : 독립, 자립

• after a long absence : 오래간만에

아버지 : 드디어 첫째가 혼자 힘으로 집을 떠나 이사한다니 믿을 수가 없구나.

Tim : 걱정하지 마세요, 아빠. 아빠와 엄마는 저 없이도 잘 지내실 거예요. 겨우 두 시간 거리라, 언제든지 보실 수 있어요.

아버지 : 우린 걱정되지 않는단다. 얘야. 너 혼자 힘으로 빨래, 아파트 청소, 세금 납부를 할 수 있을지가 걱정이란다.

Tim : 사실, 빨래를 여기로 가져와서 아빠가 해주고, 엄마가 제 집에 와서 청소해 주고, 아빠가 세금을 내줬으면 좋겠어요.

아버지 : 농담하니. 너는 독립한 젊은이란다. 이게 독립이라는 거야.

Tim : 물론 농담이죠. 저 혼자서도 집안일을 잘 할 수 있어요. 게다가, 새 직장 보수가 나쁘지 않아요. 아무 걱정하지 마세요.

07　③ ①, ②, ④, ⑤는 모두 대학의 총장(the president)을 가리키고, ③은 캠퍼스를 방문한 부자(a very wealthy man)를 가리킨다.

• financial difficulties : 재정 곤란, 재정적 궁핍

• academic standard : 학업[학문] 수준

• exceptionally : 예외적으로, 유난히, 월등히

• designated : 지정된, 지명[임명]된

• attired : 복장의, 복장을 한

• donation : 기부, 기증

• enclose : 에워[둘러]싸다, 동봉하다

• humility : 겸손, 겸허

• be fitted for : ~에 적합하다[알맞다]

• purse strings : 돈줄, 경제권

J. F. Cowan 박사는 학업 수준이 월등히 높았음에도 불구하고 재정적 어려움을 겪고 있는 작은 대학에 관한 이야기를 전했다. 어느 날 한 부자가 캠퍼스에 와서 벽에 그림을 그리고 있는 ① 백발의 노인을 발견하고는 총장을 어디서 찾을 수 있는지 물었다. 그 화가는 캠퍼스에 있는 어떤 집을 가리켰고 ② 그는 총장을 정오에 그곳에서 만날 수 있을 거라고 확신했다. 지정된 시각에 그 방문객이 총장실의 문을 두드리자 아까와 다른 복장을 하고 있지만, ③ 그가 캠퍼스에서 말을 나눴던 바로 그 동일인이 문을 열어 주었다. 방문객은 ④ 화가인 총장의 점심 초대에 응했고, 대학이 필요로 하는 것에 관한 여러 질문을 하고는 약간의 기부금을 보내겠다고 말했다. 이틀 후 5만 달러의 수표가 동봉된 편지가 도착했다. 대학 총장으로서 ⑤ 그의 직위에 적합했지만, 작업복을 입고 필요한 일을 하며 그리 오만하지 않은 한 남자의 겸손함이 그 부자의 지갑 끈을 열었다.

08 ④ 윗글은 올림픽 경기가 시작되었을 무렵 로마의 정복 활동과 영토 확장에 대해 설명하고 있다. 그러므로 그리스의 스포츠 성향과 구성에 대해 설명한 ④의 내용은 윗글의 전체 흐름과 연관성이 부족하다.

[어휘]

- surround : 둘러싸다, 에워싸다
- tribe : 부족, 종족
- athletic : 육상의, 운동의
- settle into : 틀[윤곽]이 잡히다, 자리 잡다
- predictable : 예측[예견]할 수 있는
- hostile : 적대적인, 적군의
- administrative officials : 행정 관료
- dominate : 지배[군림]하다, 우월하다
- imperial : 제국의, 황제의
- individualistic : 개인[이기]주의적인
- geared : (~에 맞도록) 설계된[구성된]
- participant : 참가자, 참여자
- rim : 가장자리, 테두리

[해석]

기원전 776년에 첫 번째 올림픽 승자가 기록되었을 때, 로마는 전쟁 부족들로 둘러싸인 단순한 농촌 지역이었다. ① 기원전 500년 경, 올림픽 경기 프로그램이 고정적이고 예측 가능한 형태로 자리 잡을 때, 로마인들은 북쪽의 적대적 이웃인 에트루리아인의 통치에 반기를 들었다. ② 2세기 동안 로마 군대는 이탈리아의 모든 행정 관료, 언어, 문화를 지배했다. ③ 그 때 시칠리아, 카르타고, 그리스의 제국 정복을 시작했다. ④ 더욱이 그리스의 스포츠와 경기들은 지나치게 개인적이어서, 관중의 호응보다는 참가자들 위주로 구성되었다. ⑤ 기원전 1세기가 끝날 무렵 로마 제국은 지중해 전역을 점령하였는데, 영국의 북부, 유럽 다뉴브, 동쪽의 카스피 해까지 넓혔다.

09 ③ 윗글은 조직 내에 축적된 데이터가 비즈니스에 미치는 영향을 파악하기보다 그저 실적 수치를 확인하는 기능으로만 사용되는 것이 문제라고 꼬집고 있으므로, 인간 행동과 관련된 데이터를 이해하는 것이 마케터들과 사회 과학자들의 오랜 기술이라는 ③의 설명은 윗글의 전체 흐름과 연관성이 부족하다.

[어휘]

- huge : 거대한, 엄청난
- step back : 뒷걸음치다, 한 걸음 물러나 생각하다
- long-standing : 오래된
- analysis : 분석, 분석 연구
- uncover : 알아내다, 적발하다
- measure performance : 성능을 측정하다, 실적을 계량하다

- method : 방법, 체계성
- relevance : 적절, 타당성, 관련

[해석]

크고 작은 대부분의 조직들이 지금 데이터로 가득 차 있다는 사실은 나쁜 것이 아니다. ① 사실, 그것은 결코 이전에 생각하지 못했던 통찰력과 지식을 획득할 수 있는 엄청난 사업 기회이다. ② 그러나 문제는 대부분의 조직들이 그 데이터를 어떻게 탐구하고 이해해야 하는지 한 걸음 물러나 생각하지 않는다는 것이다. ③ 인간 행동과 관련된 데이터를 이해하는 것은 마케터들과 사회 과학자들의 오랜 기술이다. ④ 새로운 통찰력을 알아내기 위해 고안된 분석 과정은 혼란스럽고 실적 계량에 이용된 분석 과정과 혼합된다. ⑤ 분석 방법이 실제로 비즈니스에 영향을 미치는지에 대한 관심이 부족하다. 즉, 비즈니스 결과와 관련이 있기보다 여전히 수치를 확인하는 손쉬운 기능으로써의 측정에 지나친 초점을 맞추고 있다.

10 ③ ③의 'what'은 앞의 본동사 'think'의 목적어로써 명사절을 이끄는 완벽한 문장이 와야 하므로 'that'으로 바꿔 써야 옳다. 'think'는 목적어로써 A, B or C의 문장을 이끌고 있는데, A는 'that positive affect ~', B는 'that positive emotions ~', 그리고 C는 'that, because ~'이다.

[어휘]

- depression : 우울(증), 침울
- disorder : 무질서, 혼란
- no less : 역시, 마찬가지로
- fascinating : 매우 흥미로운, 매력적인
- positive affect : 긍정적 감정
- misconception : 오해, 오인
- distort : 비틀다, 왜곡시키다
- disrupt : 방해하다, 지장을 주다
- in one's own right : 자기 능력으로, 독자적으로

[해석]

수년간 심리학은 우울, 슬픔, 분노, 긴장 그리고 걱정과 같은 부정적 감정 혹은 부정적 영향에 관한 연구에 관심을 돌렸다. 놀랄 것도 없이, 심리학자들은 부정적 감정이나 영향들이 종종 심리적 혼란을 가져오거나 심리적 혼란이 있음을 알려주기 때문에 그것들을 흥미롭다고 생각했다. 그러나 긍정적 감정에 존재하는 많은 상식적 오해들 때문에 긍정적 감정들도 역시 매우 흥미롭다. 예를 들면 긍정적 감정은 일반적인 성질상 올바르고 실질적인 사고를 왜곡시키거나 방해하며, 긍정적인 감정들은 왠지 '단순'하며 혹은 이런 감정들은 오래가지 못하기 때문에 장시간 영향을 미칠 수 없다고 생각하는 경향이 있다. 연구 결과에 따르면 위와 같은 결과는 나타나지 않았지만, 거기에 도달하는 데는 어느 정도 시간이 걸렸다. 비교적 최근에

심리학자들은 긍정적인 감정들이 독자적으로 귀중한 것으로 보일 수 있다는 사실을 깨닫고 그것들을 연구하기 시작했다.

11 ⑤ ⑤의 과거분사 'written'은 해당 문장이 주절에 해당되므로 본동사의 형태로 쓰여야 한다. 또한 편지가 파피루스 위에 쓰여지는 것이므로 수동의 의미를 지니고, 시제는 과거에 복수이므로 'were written'으로 고쳐 써야 옳다.

어휘

• mount : 끼우다, 고정시키다
• stylus : 바늘, 철필
• wax tablet : 밀랍을 칠한 서지판, 납판
• recipient : 받는 사람, 수령인[수취인]
• deliver : 배달하다, 데리고 가다
• erase : 지우다, 없애다

해석

고대 로마에서 가까운 거리에서 보내진 메시지들은 빠른 답변이 기대되기 때문에 책처럼 접힌 목재 틀에 끼워진 납판에 철필로 적힌다. 현대적 시각으로 보면 목재 틀로 둘러싸인 평평한 필기 면이 있는 이 납판은 태블릿 컴퓨터와 특히 비슷해 보인다. 수신자의 응답이 동일한 납판 위에 새겨질 수 있으며, 그것을 전달했던 배달원이 발신자에게 곧바로 되 가져갈 수 있다. 그 납판은 철필의 평평한 끝으로 유색 납을 매끄럽게 하여 지우거나 재사용될 수 있다. 도시 내에서 이것은 누군가에게 질문을 빠르게 보내고 한 두 시간 내에 답변을 얻는 손쉬운 방법이었다. 보다 먼 거리에 보내진 편지들은 파피루스에 적혔는데, 더 비싸지만 더 가볍고 따라서 전달에 더 적합했다. 한 장의 파피루스는 보통 폭이 약 6인치 높이가 10인치여서 짧은 서신용으로도 충분했다.

12 ③ (A) 본동사는 앞의 'can end'이므로 'are'는 올 수 없고, to 부정사의 부사적 용법 중 결과에 해당하는 'to be'가 사용되어 '~해서 그 결과 ~하다'의 의미를 갖는다.
(B) 'a brilliant book'을 선행사로 하는 관계사가 와야 하는데, 뒤의 종속절이 완벽한 문장이므로 관계부사 'where'를 사용하거나 또는 전치사 + 관계대명사인 'in which'를 사용해야 한다.
(C) 본동사 'find'의 목적어가 'to throw ~'로 길어서 가목적어 'it'을 대용하고 진목적어 'to throw ~'를 뒤로 후치시킨 문장이다.

어휘

• commodity : 상품, 물품
• junk : 쓸모없는 물건, 폐물, 쓰레기
• bygone : 지나간, 옛날의, 구시대의
• be disposed of : 처리되다

• literally : 그야말로, 문자[말] 그대로
• supposed : 소위, 이른바
• snap up : 덥석 사다, 잡아채다
• vintage : 고전적인, 전통 있는, 클래식의
• tumble drier : 회전식 건조기
• symbolic : 상징적인, 상징하는

해석

개인용 컴퓨터는 일상 용품이라고 생각될 수 있다. 그것은 '과거의 물건'인 쓰레기로 생을 마감하는데, 그야말로 쓰레기로 버려지거나, 재판매되거나, 누군가에게 건네지거나, 보이지 않는 어딘가에 보관되는 등 어떤 식으로든 처리된다. Christine Finn (2001)은 컴퓨터 쓰레기에 관한 훌륭한 책을 저술했는데, 그 책에서 그녀는 컴퓨터들이 처리되는 방법, 즉 재사용할 수 있는 부품을 떼어든 혹은 골동품 컴퓨터 수집가에 의해 수집되든지 간에 소위 PC의 생애가 끝날 때까지 일어나는 모든 활동들을 보여준다. 우리 세대의 사람들은 컴퓨터를 쓰레기로 생각하는 걸 좋아하지 않는데, 왜냐하면 우리에게 컴퓨터는 여전히 새로운 물건이기 때문이다. 예를 들어 나는 회전식 건조기보다 컴퓨터를 버리는 것이 훨씬 더 어렵다고 생각하며, 20년 된 자동차보다 20년 된 컴퓨터에서 훨씬 더 많은 상징적 가치를 볼 수 있다.

13 ① (A) 흰 생쥐가 백마로 변신된 것이므로, 수동의 의미를 지닌 과거분사 'transformed'를 사용해야 한다.
(B) 'for a caterpillar'는 전치사구이고, 뒤의 동사 'turn'이 주어로 사용되기 위해서는 to 부정사의 명사적 용법에 해당하는 'to turn'이 와야 한다.
(C) 뒷 문장의 본동사인 'surprise'의 대상이 나비가 애벌레로 변하는 것이므로, 앞 문장을 대신하는 'it'을 주어로 사용해야 한다.

어휘

• fairy story : 요정 이야기, 동화
• profoundly : 심오하게, 매우
• unrealistic : 비현실적인, 비사실적인
• biological : 생물학의, 생물체의
• transition : 변이, 변화, 변천
• virtually : 사실상, 거의, 가상으로
• rule out : 제외시키다, 배제하다
• caterpillar : 애벌레
• gene : 유전자
• tadpole : 올챙이

해석

동화는 개구리가 왕자로 변신하거나, 호박이 흰 생쥐에서 변신한 백마가 끄는 마차로 변하는 이야기로 가득하다. 그러한

공상은 매우 비현실적이다. 생물학적 이유에서가 아니라 수학적 이유로 일어날 수가 없다. 그러한 변이는 사실상 불가능한데, 실제적인 목적 때문에 그것들을 배제할 수 있다는 것을 의미한다. 그러나 애벌레 때문에 나비로 변화는 것은 문제가 되지 않는다. 즉, 그 일은 항상 일어났고, 그 규칙들은 자연의 선택에 따라 세월이 지나면서 축적되어 왔다. 그리고 비록 나비가 애벌레로 변화는 것을 본적이 없다고 하더라도, 그것이 개구리가 왕자로 변화는 것과 똑같이 우리를 놀라게 하지는 않는다. 개구리는 왕자가 되기 위한 유전자를 갖고 있지 않다. 그러나 개구리는 올챙이가 될 유전자를 갖고 있다.

14 ① 윗글은 일부 종교들이 철학적 신념과 정치적 해석을 통해 사회적 변화를 억제하는 경향이 있다고 설명하고 있다. 예를 들어 운명론에 근거한 힌두교는 현 상황을 바꿀 수 없는 것으로 받아들이게 하는 효과를 가져왔고, 무슬림 지도자들은 새로운 가치와 행동의 도입에 강한 반대 입장을 보인다고 하였으므로 빈칸에 들어갈 말로는 ①의 'conservative(보수적인)'이 가장 적절하다.

오답풀이
② 민주적인
③ 공정한
④ 지적인
⑤ 고무하는

어휘
• status quo : 현재 상태[상황], 현상(現狀)
• keep in line : 규칙을 지키게 하다, 정렬하게 하다
• supernatural sanction : 초자연적인 제재
• relieving : 보조하는, 보조용의
• conviction : 유죄 선고[판결]
• interpretation : 해석, 이해, 설명
• inhibit : 억제[저해]하다, 금하다
• orthodox : 정통의, 전통적인
• fatalistic : 운명론적인, 숙명적인
• bring about : 야기하다, 초래하다
• initiative : 계획, 추진력, 주도권
• conservative : 보수적인
  cf. conservative force : 보수 세력
• impartial : 편파적이 아닌, 공정한

해석
종교의 다양한 기능들을 조사함으로써, 종교가 사회 내에서 <u>보수</u> 세력임을 알 수 있다. 일반적인 의미에서 종교는 초자연적인 제재를 통해 사람들이 규칙을 지키게 하고, 사회적 갈등을 해소하고, 불행한 사건을 해명함으로써 현 상황을 유지한다. 더욱이 일부 주요 세계 종교들은 철학적 신념과 정치적 해

석을 통해 사회적 변화를 억제하는 경향이 있다. 예를 들어 현재의 삶의 조건이 과거의 삶의 행위에 의해 결정된다는 생각에 근거한 정통 힌두교 신념은 신자들이 너무 운명론적이어서 그들의 현 상황을 바꿀 수 없는 것으로 받아들이게 하는 효과를 가져왔다. 그러한 세계관은 큰 혁명이나 변화를 위한 작은 계획조차 야기하지 않을 것 같다. 마찬가지로 일부 무슬림 지도자들은 특히 서구 세계로부터 새로운 가치와 행동의 도입에 강한 반대 입장을 보였다.

15 ② 윗글에 따르면 서로 다른 두 위치에서 발생하는 소리의 크기를 식별할 수 있는 능력만으로도 자신의 위치를 파악할 수 있다고 한다. 단, 각 음원이 각자의 위치에 대한 명확한 신호를 보낸다는 전제 조건이 뒤따른다. 그러므로 빈칸에 들어갈 말로는 ②의 'provide unambiguous cues to position(명확한 위치 신호를 보내다)'이다.

오답풀이
① 더 오랫동안 경계를 유지하다
③ 위치 선정을 방해하다
④ 방해 단계를 더 높이다
⑤ 청각 기능을 약화시키다

어휘
• square : 정사각형의, 제곱[평방]의
• road crew : 도로 작업단, 현장 요원
• jackhammer : 착암기, 휴대용 압축 드릴
• adjacent : 인접한, 가까운
• street vendor : 가두 판매소, 노점상, 행상
• jingle : 징글, 딸랑, 쨍그랑
• wander : 방황하다, 배회하다, 헤매다
• work out : ~을 계산[산출]하다
• gauge : 측정하다, 추정하다
• triangulate : 삼각으로 만들다, 삼각 측량을 하다
• accuracy : 정확, 정확도
• discriminate : 식별[구별]하다, 차별하다
• provided : ~이라는 조건으로, 만약 ~ 이라면
• source of sound : 음원
• alert : 경계, 경보
• unambiguous : 모호하지 않은, 분명한, 명료한
• hinder : 저해[방해]하다, ~하지 못하게 하다
• positional awareness : 위치 선정
• distraction : 방해, 혼란, 산란
• diminish : 줄이다, 감소하다, 약화시키다
• auditory : 청각의

해석
당신이 커다란 정사각형 필드에 서 있다고 생각해 보라. 필드

한 쪽 편에서 소음을 내는 현장 요원이 착암기로 보수 작업을 하고 있다. 필드의 인접한 곳에서 푸드 카트 노점상이 큰 소리로 연신 종을 울리고 있다. 눈을 감은 채 필드를 돌아다닐 수 있고, 소리의 크기를 측정함으로써 현장 요원 또는 푸드 카트로부터의 거리를 계산할 수 있다. 둘 사이의 거리를 알면 단지 소리의 크기를 식별하는 능력만으로도 필드에서 당신의 위치를 정확하게 삼각 측량하는 것이 가능하다. 이 사례에서 더욱 흥미로운 것은 서로 다른 두 위치에서 두 음원이 <u>명확한 위치 신호를 보낸다는</u> 기본 원칙만 이해하고 있다면, 결코 필드에서 전에 가본 적이 없는 위치에서 조차 당신의 위치를 파악할 수 있다는 것이다.

16 ② 윗글에 따르면 음성 언어보다 비언어적 메시지가 오해의 소지가 더 크므로, 아무런 의도가 없을 때도 문화가 다른 두 사람이 대화를 나눌 때 불쾌감을 주고받을 수 있다. 그러므로 빈칸에 들어갈 말로는 ②의 'might give or take offense when none is intended(아무런 의도가 없을 때도 불쾌감을 주고받을 수 있다.)'가 가장 적절하다.

오답풀이

① 더 주의 깊게 언어적 메시지에 초점을 맞춰야 한다.
③ 상대방의 의도를 분명하게 함으로써 의사소통을 끝낼 수도 있다.
④ 말로 서로의 감정을 명확하게 전달할 것이다.
⑤ 서로 간에 의사소통이 더 잘 될 것이다.

어휘

• nonverbal : 말로 할 수 없는, 비언어적인
• inherently : 타고나서, 본질적으로, 선천적으로
• convention : 관습, 관례
• arbitrary : 임의적인, 제멋대로인, 자의적인
• converse : 대화[이야기]를 나누다
• offense : 모욕, 불쾌, 화
• clarity : 명확하게 하다, 분명히 말하다

해석

말과 마찬가지로 대부분의 비언어적 의사소통의 형태도 상징적인 행동들이다. 즉, 특정 신체 동작이나 거리는 본질적으로 어떤 메시지를 전달하지 않지만 단지 관습이나 공통적인 이해 때문에 어떤 메시지를 전달한다. 많은 비언어적 의사소통이 자의적이고 관습적이기 때문에, 사람들이 비언어적 메시지에 대한 동일한 의미를 공유하지 못할 때 즉, 사람들이 다른 관습을 익혀왔을 때 오해의 소지가 더 크다. 아마도 오해의 소지는 음성 언어보다 비언어적 메시지가 훨씬 더 크다. 문화가 다른 두 사람이 대화를 나눌 때, 일반적으로 둘 다 상대방의 언어를 이해하지 못한다는 것을 알고 있으므로 적어도 각자는 자기 자신의 무지를 알고 있다. 그러나 둘 다 비언어적 메시지를 이

해한다고 생각할 가능성이 더 크므로, 그들은 <u>아무런 의도가 없을 때도 불쾌감을 주고받을 수 있다.</u>

17 ④ 윗글에서 스트레스의 원인이 무엇이든 쉽고 빠르게 해결될 수 없으므로, 배우자와 함께 상의하여 공동으로 대처하는 것이 중요하다고 설명하고 있다. 그러므로 빈칸에 들어갈 속담으로는 ④의 "A problem shared is a problem halved(고통을 나누면 반이 된다.)"가 가장 적절하다.

오답풀이

① 요리사가 너무 많으면 스프를 망친다. → 사공이 많으면 배가 산으로 간다.
② 솜씨 없는 일꾼이 연장만 나무란다.
③ 옆에 없으면 더 애틋해지는 법이다.
⑤ 죽은 영웅보다 살아 있는 겁쟁이가 더 낫다. → 위험할 때는 도망가는 것이 상책이다.

어휘

• irritable : 짜증을 내는, 화가 난
• short-tempered : 성급한, 성을 잘 내는
• in the heat of the moment : 발끈하여, 그만 흥분해서
• relieve : 없애[덜어] 주다, 경감하다
• tackle : 태클하다, 씨름하다, 솔직하게 말하다[따지다]
• reassuring : 안심시키는, 걱정[불안감]을 없애 주는
• broth : 수프, 죽

해석

사람들은 스트레스를 받을 때 다르게 반응한다. 그들은 먹고 자기가 어렵다. 짜증을 내고 성질을 부린다. 그들은 말하지 않아도 될 것을 순간 화가 나서 말할 지도 모른다. 부부가 스트레스를 받으면 다르게 반응하기 때문에, 한 배우자가 다른 배우자보다 훨씬 더 영향을 받아서 관계가 틀어질 수도 있다. 해답은 스트레스의 근원을 확인하고 어떻게 해야 할지를 알아보는 것이다. 우선 스트레스를 받고 있다는 사실과 스트레스가 관계에 문제가 될 수 있다는 사실을 인정해야만 한다. 그런 다음 함께 앉아 그 문제를 논의하라. 그것만으로도 일부 스트레스를 덜어주기에 종종 충분하다. 스트레스의 원인이 무엇이든 쉽고 빠르게 해결될 가능성은 없으며, 그것을 꼭 인식하고 그것에 대처할 몇몇 종류의 계획을 세우는 것이 불안감을 없애 주는 일이다. 더욱 중요한 것은 배우자와 함께 앉아서 스트레스에 관해 이야기를 나눔으로써 그것을 해결하기 위해 함께 대처할 수 있다. "<u>고통을 나누면 반이 된다.</u>"는 속담에는 많은 진리가 있다.

18 ② 윗글에서 필자는 백만장자가 되고 싶다면 우선 '천 달러를 가진 사람'이 되어야 하고, 천 달러를 모으게 되면 다음으로 '만 달러를 가진 사람'이 되어야 한다고 주장하고 있다.

그러므로 윗글이 시사하는 바는 ②의 "Each person must walk before he or she can run. (사람은 달릴 수 있기 전에 걸어야만 한다.)"이다.

오답풀이

① 긍정적인 생각은 빚에서 벗어날 수 있다.

③ 정말 열심히 일한다면, 단기간에 부자가 될 것이다.

④ 직장을 그만두기 전에 여러 행동 방침을 개발해야 한다.

⑤ 삶의 질은 과거의 경험을 어떻게 무효화 시키느냐에 달려 있다.

어휘

- seminar : 세미나
- mismanagement : 그릇된 처리[관리], 실수, 실패
- neutralize : 무효화[상쇄] 시키다, 중화시키다
- leap into : 뛰어 오르다, 비약하다
- affluence : 풍족, 풍부, 부
- decade : 10년
- frustration : 좌절, 실패
- thousandaire : 천 달러를 가진 사람
- get out of debt : 빚을 갚다[청산하다]

해석

아주 종종 사람들은 세미나 후 내게 다가와 재정 목표를 결정했다고 말한다. 그게 뭔지 물어보면, 그들은 내 년 혹은 2년 내에 백만장자나 억만장자가 되기로 결심했다고 말한다. 거의 모든 경우 이런 사람들은 돈이 아예 없거나 거의 없는 사람들이다. 그들은 종종 30대 또는 40대이며 평생 재무적 관리가 잘못된 이들이다. 그럼에도 불구하고 그들은 과거의 모든 경험을 무시한 채 아무런 준비 없이, 자산도 없이, 어떻게 그것을 얻을지에 관한 명확한 생각도 없이 어떻게든 부자가 될 수 있다고 생각한다. 그들은 자기들이 해야 할 일은 행복한 생각을 하는 것뿐이며 수십 년 간의 좌절과 실패를 극복하기 위해 필요한 모든 것을 마술처럼 불러일으킬 것이라고 믿는다. 사람들이 가능한 빨리 백만장자가 되고 싶다고 말할 때, 나는 우선 '천 달러를 가진 사람'이 되라고 말한다. 그들이 용케 천 달러를 모으고 빚을 갚으면, '만 달러를 가진 사람' 등등이 될 수 있다.

19 ② 윗글의 마지막 줄에서 교과과정 및 교과서를 학습 계획 및 지침의 안내서로 활용해야 하지만, 그것이 전부는 아니라는 것을 기억하라고 하였으므로, 필자는 교사가 교과과정과 교과서에 전적으로 의존해서는 안 된다고 주장하고 있다.

어휘

- pre-service teacher : 교생, 예비 교사
- subject matter : 주제, 소재

- jurisdiction : 관할권, 관할 구역
- department of education : 교육부, 교육청
- mandate : 명령[지시, 지정]하다, 권한을 주다
- stepping stone : 징검돌, 디딤돌, 발판
- assess : 재다[가늠하다], 평가하다
- align with : ~에 맞추어 조정하다[공조하다]
- solely : 오로지, 단지, 단독으로
- instruction : 설명, 지시, 가르침

해석

예비 교사들이 갖는 가장 큰 두려움 중의 몇몇은 그들이 무엇을 가르쳐야 하고 수업할 주제를 충분히 알고 있는지의 여부이다. 관할 교육청은 준수해야 할 교과과정을 지정해 줄 것이다. 교과과정을 교사가 가르쳐야 하고 학생들이 배워야 할 정보의 디딤돌로 여겨라. 교과과정의 학습 결과를 따라야 하지만, 교과과정 문서에는 학생들을 가르치는 방법이나 평가 방법을 밝히지 않고 있다. 교과과정에 덧붙여, 관할 지역 학생들의 학습 비전에 맞추어 승인받은 교과서가 있다. 최고의 교사들은 오로지 교과과정이나 교과서에만 의존하지 않고 학생의 관심사를 토대로 일부 영역을 확장할 것이다. 교과과정 및 교과서를 학습 계획 및 지침의 안내서로 활용해야 하지만, 그것이 전부는 아니라는 것을 기억해라.

20 ② (A) 앞 문장에서 관광산업이 선진국에서 후진국으로 부와 투자를 옮기는 효과적인 수단처럼 보인다고 하였으므로, 이것은 부의 재분배를 의미한다. 그러므로 빈칸 (A)에는 'redistribution(재분배)'이 들어갈 말로 적절하다.

(B) 후진국의 관광 산업에 대한 선진국의 투자는 후진국들로부터 이익을 착취하고, 잠재적으로 후진국이 관광 산업에 투자한 선진국과 기업에 의존하게 하는 것이다. 그러므로 빈칸 (B)에는 'exploitation and dependency (착취와 의존)'가 들어갈 말로 적절하다.

오답풀이

	(A)	(B)
①	집중	착취와 의존
③	불균형	번영과 안전
④	재분배	번영과 안전
⑤	불균형	협력과 개발

어휘

- domestically : 가정적으로, 국내에서, 국내 문제에 관해서
- transfer : 옮기다, 이동하다
- expenditure : 지출, 경비, 비용
- tourist-generating : 관광객을 발생[유발]시키는
- facility : 시설, 기관
- net retention : 순 보유액

• more often than not : 자주, 대개

• profit : 이익, 수익, 이윤

• divert : 전환시키다, 우회시키다

• concentration : 집중

• exploitation : 착취, 개발

• dependency : 의존, 종속

• redistribution : 재분배, 재배급

• prosperity : 번성, 번영, 번창

• security : 보안, 방위, 안전

• collaboration : 공동 작업[연구], 협력

해석

국제적으로나 국내적으로나, 관광산업은 더 부유하고 개발된 국가 또는 지역에서 개발이 덜 된 가난한 지역으로 부와 투자를 옮기는 효과적인 수단처럼 보인다. 이론상 이러한 부의 (A) 재분배는 목적지에서 관광객들의 지출의 결과로 그리고 관광 시설에서 관광객을 유발시키는 좀 더 부유한 국가들의 투자 결과로써 발생한다. 후자의 경우, 선진국들은 원직적으로 관광 산업에 투자함으로써 후진국들의 경제 성장 및 개발을 지원한다. 그러나 여행자 지출의 순 보유액은 한 목적지에서 다른 목적지에 이르기까지 꽤 다양하지만, 반면에 관광 시설에 대한 해외 투자는 대개 (B) 착취와 의존으로 이어질지 모른다고 오랫동안 인식되어 왔다. 이것은 주로 후진국들로부터 전환된 이익으로 보일 수 있으며, 잠재적으로 그들은 투자 국가와 기업에 종속하게 된다.

21
① (A) 우리의 기억 속에 저장된 지식은 좋아하는 것과 싫어하는 것에 관한 개개인의 기호에 관한 지식인데, 다음 행에서 좋아하는 수프를 예로 들어 이를 설명하고 있으므로 빈칸 (A)에는 'for example(예를 들어)'이 들어갈 말로 가장 적절하다.

(B) 전에 많은 종류의 수프를 먹어본 경험이 있기 때문에 어떤 수프를 좋아하는지 기억하는 것처럼 좋아하는 친구, 가수, 축구 팀, 색깔, 책, TV 프로그램도 마찬가지라는 것이다. 그러므로 빈칸 (B)에는 'Similarly(마찬가지로)'가 들어갈 말로 가장 적절하다.

오답풀이

	(A)	(B)
②	예를 들면	따라서
③	그와 반대로	마찬가지로
④	그와 반대로	그와 달리
⑤	바꾸어 말하면	따라서

어휘

• egg drop : 계란탕, 계란 수프

• extensive : 광범위한, 포괄적인

• contrast : 대조, 대비

• on the contrary : 그와 반대로

해석

우리가 기억 속에 저장해 온 일종의 개인적 지식은 좋아하는 것과 싫어하는 것에 관한 지식이다. 이것은 개개인의 기호에 따른 극히 개인적인 종류의 지식이다. (A) 예를 들어, 가장 좋아하는 종류의 수프를 물어보면 당신은 보르시치, 치킨 누들 또는 계란 수프라고 말할 지도 모른다. 전에 많은 종류의 수프를 먹어본 적이 있기 때문에 답을 알고 있으며, 어떤 수프를 가장 좋아하는지 기억한다. 그 기억을 토대로, 아마도 집이나 식당에서 반복해서 그 수프를 주문한다. (B) 마찬가지로, 가장 친한 친구가 누구이고, 좋아하는 가수가 누구이며, 가장 좋아하는 축구 팀이 어느 팀인지 뿐만 아니라 좋아하는 색깔이나 책 또는 TV 프로그램이 무엇인지 쉽게 말할 수 있다. 과거에 직접적으로 광범위한 경험을 했기 때문에 이 모든 것을 기억하며, 가장 즐거움을 주는 것이 어느 것인지 결정하기 위해 다양한 경험들과 쉽게 비교하고 대조할 수 있다.

22
⑤ 코끼리는 인간의 전투에서 효과적이지 못했다고 했으므로, 암컷 코끼리가 새끼들이 다치고 짓밟혀 운다면 즉각 모든 군대 의무를 수행하는 것이 아니라 거부 또는 무시하고 구출에 돌입할 것이다. 그러므로 ⑤의 'assume(책임 · 의무를 맡다, 수행하다)'은 'refuse(거부하다)' 또는 'ignore(무시하다)' 등으로 고쳐 써야 옳다.

어휘

• domesticated animal : 가축

• terrify : 무섭게[겁먹게] 하다

• elaborately : 공들여, 애써서, 정교하게

• ornament : 장식품, 장신구

• headpiece : 투구, 헬멧

• clanging bell : 땡 소리 나는 종

• fermented : 발효된

• fierce : 사나운, 맹렬한

• bombard : (폭격, 공격, 비난) 퍼붓다, 쏟다 붓다

• retreat : 후퇴[철수/퇴각]하다

• inflict : 가하다, 안기다

• assume : 추정하다, 맡다

• rescue : 구하다, 구출하다

• offspring : 자식, 새끼

• trample : 짓밟다, 밟아 뭉개다

해석

길들인 짐승은 고대 전쟁에서 무기와 장비로 자주 활용된다. 그리스인들은 코끼리를 전쟁 장비로 종종 이용했다. 주로 적에게 겁을 줄 의도로, 코끼리는 투구와 소리 나는 종과 같은

장신구로 공들여 장식되었다. 코끼리들은 가끔 발효된 포도주를 마셨고, 그것은 맹렬한 행동을 하도록 자극했다. 그러나 전선에서 코끼리를 이용하는 것은 전쟁 동물로써의 실제적 이용보다 아마도 힘의 과시를 위한 것이었다. 코끼리는 전투적인 인간 전쟁에서 효과적이지 못했는데, 만일 화살 공격을 받으면 코끼리는 돌아서서 퇴각하여 적보다는 아군에 더 많은 피해를 입혔다. 더욱이 암컷 코끼리는 새끼와 떨어지면 싸움을 거부하고, 새끼들이 다치고 짓밟혀 운다면 즉각 모든 군대 의무를 <u>수행하고</u> 구출에 돌입할 것이다.

23 ⑤ 윗글에 따르면 고객 만족도가 수익성의 핵심 열쇠라는 오랜 가정에 소비자들의 경험적 데이터가 대치되는 것이 아니라 일치하고 부합하는 것이므로, ⑤의 'contradicting'은 'consistent with' 또는 'in line with' 등으로 고쳐 써야 옳다.

어휘

• firm : 회사
• novelty item : 신상품
• pet rock : 애완용 돌
• regulation : 규정, 규제, 단속
• profit-oriented : 이익[수익] 지향의
• profitability : 수익성, 이윤율
• appliance : 기기, 가전제품
• watchdog organization : 감시 기구[단체]
• empirical : 경험적인, 실증적인
• contradict : 부정[부인]하다, 반박하다
• long-held : 오랫동안 간직해 온
• assumption : 추정, 가정, 전제

해석

자본주의 사회에서 회사는 이익을 창출하기 위해 존재한다. 만일 회사 제품이 소비자에게 한번 구입하고 마는 제품(예 : 애완용 돌과 같은 신상품)으로 비춰지거나, 성능 수준이 규제 대상이 아니며, 단지 제한적으로만 상호 의사소통 채널이 소비자에게 열려 있다면, 고객 만족도는 순전히 수익 지향적인 회사에서는 중요한 목표가 아닐 것이다. 그러나 이러한 조건에 부합하는 제조사는 거의 없다. 대부분의 제조사는 재구매가 지속적인 수익 창출에 필수적이라고 생각한다. 구매 주기가 긴 제품(예 : 주요 가전 제품, 자동차) 조차, 만족도는 입소문과 소비자 연합처럼 지속적으로 만족도 보고서를 추적하는 수많은 감독 기관의 활동 때문에 중요하다. 이제는 더욱 활용 가능성이 높으며, 만족도, 품질 및 다른 척도에 영향을 미치는 경험적 데이터는 고객 만족도가 수익성의 핵심 열쇠라는 오랜 가정과 <u>모순된다</u>.

24 ① 윗글에서 건설적인 비판은 부정적인 공격보다 더 큰 진전을 가져다준다고 하였으므로, 윗글의 제목으로는 ①의 'Keep Your Criticism Positive(비판을 긍정적으로 하라.)가 가장 적절하다.

오답풀이

② 왜 비판을 받아들이기가 어려운가.
③ 성장을 위해 부정적인 비판을 수용하라.
④ 공치사인지 알아내는 방법
⑤ 부정적인 피드백의 제공 가치

어휘

• constructive : 건설적인, 구조적인
• stylish : 유행을 따른, 멋진, 우아한
• barber : 이발사
• compliment : 칭찬, 찬사
  cf. empty compliment : 공치사
• tastefulness : 멋있음, 세련됨
• attire : 의복, 복장, 옷차림
• legitimate : 합법적인, 타당한
• conform : 따르다, 순응하다
• turn up : 나타나다, 찾게 되다

해석

심리 언어학자들은 어떤 사람이 부정적인 것을 이해하는 데 걸리는 시간의 약 3분의 2의 시간으로 긍정적인 말을 이해한다는 사실을 알아냈다. 인생의 유일한 목적이 그들이 원하는 바를 하도록 남에게 동기를 부여하는 일이라고 할지라도, 건설적인 비판은 부정적인 공격보다 더 큰 진전을 가져다 줄 것이다. 만일 누군가가 반은 옳고 반은 틀린 상태로 무언가를 끝냈다면, 그가 제대로 작동하는 기술을 지속적으로 이용하기만 한다면 완제품이 얼마나 훌륭할지를 강조하라. 누군가의 옷이 멋지고 우아하지만, 머리카락은 장님 이발사가 자른 것처럼 보인다면 그의 옷차림의 세련됨을 칭찬하라. 반면에 그의 외모를 바꿀 타당한 필요성을 느낀다면, 자신의 헤어스타일을 자신의 옷 스타일에 맞추면 훨씬 더 보기 좋을 것이라고 제안해라. 비판이 아닌 해결책을 제시하라 그리고 다른 사람들에게 힌트를 얻을 수 있는 기회를 제공하라. 그들이 그렇게 하지 않는다면, 당신은 그들이 그렇게 할 때까지 늘 비판하게 된다.

25 ① 윗글에 따르면 사람들은 거짓말을 하고 있을 때 무의식적으로 다리를 떨거나 단추 혹은 장신구를 만지작거리면서 언성을 높이는 등 일관성이 없는 비언어적 행동들을 보인다고 설명하고 있다. 그러므로 윗글의 제목으로는 ①의 'Patterns of Behavior That Reveal Deception(거짓임을 드러내는 행동 패턴들)'이 가장 적절하다.

정답 및 해설

오답풀이

② 속임수를 쓰는 심리적인 요인들

③ 비언어적 메시지의 일반적 특징

④ 속임수에서 벗어나는 강한 유대감 형성하기

⑤ 사람들의 진실 또는 거짓에 대한 부정확한 평가

어휘

• unconsciously : 무심코, 무의식적으로

• inconsistency : 불일치, 모순, 일관성이 없음

• nonverbal : 말로 할 수 없는, 비언어적인

• contradict : 모순되다, 상반되다

• aloof : 초연한, 무관심한

• jewelry : 보석류, 장신구

• perception : 지각, 인식, 통찰력

• courtroom testimony : 법정 증거

• stereotypically : 진부하게, 틀에 박혀서

• deceptive : 기만적인, 현혹하는

• trigger : 방아쇠를 당기다, 촉발[작동]시키다

• suspicion : 혐의, 의심

• familiarity : 친근함, 익숙함

• inaccurate : 부정확한, 오류가 있는

• assessment : 평가, 사정

해석

사람들은 무의식적으로 일관성이 없는 비언어적 행동을 통해 거짓말을 하고 있다는 신호를 보낸다. 거짓말을 하고 있는 누군가를 잡아본 적이 있다면, 대화의 후반부 진술이 처음의 진술과 상반되거나 아마도 그 사람의 몸짓이 말할 때의 단어들과 모순되는 것처럼 보였다는 것을 알아차렸을지도 모른다. 그 사람은 조용하고 초연하게 행동했지만, 동시에 자신의 발을 떨거나 단추 혹은 장신구를 만지작거리면서 언성을 높여 말하고 있었을지도 모른다. 법정 증거에 관한 사람들의 생각을 조사해 보면 틀에 박힌 기만적 행동이 반드시 의심을 불러일으키는 것은 아니지만, 일관성이 없는 비언어적 행동은 동반되는 특정 행동에 관계없이 빈번히 속임수로 판명된다. 연구에 따르면 한 개인의 전형적인 비언어적 행동에 익숙해지면 속임수를 보다 쉽게 발견할 수 있다고 한다. 특히 사람들은 상대방의 진실된 행동에 대한 이전의 경험이 있을 때 상대방이 진실을 말하고 있는지 혹은 거짓말을 하고 있는지 더 잘 알 수 있다.

26 ④ 윗글은 사람마다 다른 스포츠의 의미에 대해 설명하고 있는데, 주어진 글에서 'different meanings(서로 다른 의미)'와 ④의 'As an example of these differing meanings(이러한 서로 다른 의미의 예로써)~'가 서로 호응하므로 주어진 글은 ④에 들어가는 것이 가장 적절하다.

어휘

• periphery : 주변, 주변부

• context-dependent : 문맥 의존, 문맥 종속

• ballroom dancing : 사교춤

• define : 정의하다, 규정하다

• competitive : 경쟁적인, 경쟁을 하는

• spectator : 구경꾼, 관중

• diversion : 바꾸기, 전환

• vicarious : 대리의, 간접적인

해석

> 그러나 똑같은 스포츠가 다른 집단의 사람들에게 서로 다른 의미를 가질 수 있다.

교육과 더불어, 스포츠는 함께 공유하는 핵심적 의미를 지니고 있으며 주변부의 부가적인 의미는 문맥에 따라 매우 다르다. (①) 바꾸어 말하면, 우리들 대부분은 스포츠가 무엇인지 공통적으로 이해하고 있지만, 여전히 스포츠는 다른 사람들에게 다른 것을 의미할 수 있다. (②) 일반적으로 우리는 축구를 스포츠라고 알고 있지만 사교춤은 그렇지 않다. 자동차 경주는 스포츠지만, 차로 출근하는 것은 그렇지 않다. 바다에서 보트를 항해하는 것은 스포츠지만, 유조선을 타고 항해하는 것은 아니다. (③) 그 단어가 사용될 때마다 스포츠가 의미하는 것을 정의할 필요는 없다. (④) 이러한 서로 다른 의미의 예로써 테니스란 스포츠를 생각해 보자. (⑤) 전문 테니스 선수에게 테니스는 직업이지만, 아무리 경쟁적일지라도 동호회 선수에게 테니스는 근본적으로 취미이며, 윔블던 대회 관중에게 테니스는 일시적인 기분 전환이나 모든 것을 소비하는 대리 열정일지도 모른다.

27 ⑤ 보모가 자신의 새끼를 갖지 않는 이유를 물었으므로 ⑤에는 이에 해당하는 답변이 와야 한다. 주어진 글이 이에 대한 답변으로, 보모가 자신의 새끼를 갖지 않는 이유는 둥지가 부족하거나 먹이가 충분하지 않을 수도 있기 때문이다. 그러므로 주어진 글은 ⑤에 들어가는 것이 가장 적절하다.

어휘

• habitat : 서식지, 산지

• breeder : 번식하는 동물, 사육자

• strike out on one's own : 스스로 독립하다

• track down : ~을 찾아내다

• nutritious : 영양분이 많은, 영양가가 높은

• surrogate : 대리의, 대용의

• (baby) sitter : 보모, 애기 보는 사람

• take turns : ~을 교대로 하다, 번갈아 하다

- nonbreeding : 비번식
- altruism : 이타주의, 이타심
- tie up in : ∼에 묶어 두다
- sibling : 형제자매, 동기
- marginal : 가장자리의, 변두리의
- hold off : 연기하다, 미루다

해석

안전하고 전부 점령된 서식지에서, 둥지가 부족하거나 혹은 어떤 특정 해에 새로 번식한 동물이 스스로 독립할 정도로 먹을 수 있는 먹이가 충분하지 않을 수도 있다.

플라밍고, 펭귄, 타조, 기린, 돌고래, 악어 등 많은 종들이 어린 새끼를 잠시 다른 어미의 품에 맡겨둔다. 이 때문에 부모는 가족을 부양하기 위해 가장 영양가가 높은 먹이를 찾을 여유가 생긴다. (①) 어린 새끼를 돌보는 대리 부모는 누구인가? (②) 그 보모는 무작위로 교대하는 부모일 수도 있고 부모와 관계있는 비번식자일 수도 있다. (③) 이타주의처럼 보일 수도 있지만, 보모는 단순히 자신이 돌보고 있는 어린 조카 또는 형제자매에 묶여 있는 자신의 유전자를 증진시키는 것뿐이다. (④) 그들의 목표가 자기 유전자를 발전시키는 것이라면, 왜 자신의 새끼를 갖지 않는가? (⑤) 강제로 변두리 둥지로 쫓겨나기 보다는 1년을 연기할 수도 있고, 그 사이에 더 나은 부모가 될 기술들을 배울 수도 있다.

28 ④ 윗글의 마지막 문장에서 소비가 개인과 집단에 어떤 영향을 미치는지 연구하지 않고 우리가 인간을 이해한다고 진정으로 말할 수 없다고 하였으므로, "인간을 이해하기 위해서는 소비에 대한 연구가 반드시 필요하다."는 ④의 내용이 윗글의 요지로 가장 적절하다.

어휘

- expose : 드러내다, 폭로하다, 노출하다
- consumption : 소비, 소모
- engage in : ∼에 종사하다, ∼에 관여하다
- be overtaken by : ∼에 압도되다, 추월당하다

해석

일상생활에서 사람들은 소비의 여러 측면에 반복적으로 노출된다. 광고, 기차 여행, 식료품 쇼핑, TV 시청, 음악 청취, 인터넷 서핑, 의류 쇼핑, 책 읽기는 모두 사람들이 소비하는 사례들이다. 사람이 관여하는 거의 모든 행동은 직 · 간접적으로 소비와 관련이 있다. 크리스마스와 같은 전통적인 휴일조차도 요즘에는 주로 소비에 관한 것이다. 원래 종교적인 휴일이었던 것이 산타클로스가 선물을 배달하는 가장 전형적인 사례로 소비의 측면이 부각되었다. 근본적으로 소비가 인간의 일상생활의 일부라는 사실을 피할 방법은 없다. 따라서 소비가 개인과 집단에 어떤 영향을 미치는지 연구하지 않고 우리가 인간을 이해한다고 진정으로 말할 수 없다.

29 ④ 윗글에 따르면 배경지식이 없는 예술가가 자신의 문화적 경험에서 벗어난 이야기를 전달하려고 할 때 삽화들을 통해 이야기를 잘못 전달할 위험에 빠질 수 있다고 하였다. 그러므로 "배경지식이 부족하면 타문화권 이야기의 삽화를 정확하게 그리기 어렵다."는 ④의 내용이 윗글의 요지로 가장 적절하다.

어휘

- complication : 문제, 합병증
- realm : 영역, 범위
- misrepresent : 잘못 전하다[표현하다]
- imitate : 모방하다, 흉내 내다
- extract : 발췌하다, 추출하다, 뽑다
- authentic : 진본[진품]인, 진짜인
- accurately : 정확하게, 정밀하게
- depict : 그리다, 묘사하다

해석

한 예술가가 자신의 문화적 경험의 범위에서 벗어난 이야기를 설명하려고 할 때 문제들이 발생한다. 만일 그 예술가가 특정 영역에 배경지식이 거의 없고 연구를 철저히 조사할 의지가 아예 없거나 할 수 없는 경우, 특히 어떤 시도가 '본래의' 스타일을 모방하도록 만들어진다면, 삽화들을 통해 이야기를 잘못 전달할 위험에 빠질 수 있다. 외부인이 자신들이 추출할 전반적인 상황을 이해하지 못하고 세부 사항을 효과적으로 추출하는 것은 매우 어렵다. 그것은 할 수 없다는 말이 아니다. 예를 들어, 에드 영은 그가 다른 문화권의 전통 이야기를 위해 만든 작품에서 정확한 세부 사항에 주의를 기울이는 것으로 유명하다. 예를 들어 Kimiko Kajikawa가 쓴 「쓰나미」에서, 영은 19세기 중반 일본의 의복, 헤어스타일 및 건축물의 특성을 정확하게 묘사하고 있다.

30 ① 윗글은 최초의 유료 입장 경기, 프로 선수 최초의 보증 계약, 최초의 유료 시청 경기 등 스포츠 마케팅의 출현 배경과 사례 등을 서술하고 있다. 그러므로 ①의 'the emergence and expansion of sports marketing(스포츠 마케팅의 출현과 확장)'이 윗글의 주제로 가장 적절하다.

오답풀이

② 스포츠 마케팅 활동을 위한 효과적인 예산 책정
③ 스포츠 마케팅에 영향을 미치는 사회적 변화
④ 스포츠 마케팅에 관한 오해
⑤ 스포츠 후원의 어두운 측면

- athletic : 운동(경기)의, 육상의
- admission : 입장료, 입학금
- organizer : 조직자, 창시자, 주최자
- endorsement : 지지, 보증[홍보]
- partner with : ~와 협력[제휴]하다.
- pay-per-view : 유료 시청제
- take on : ~와 대전[대결]하다
- closed-circuit : 폐쇄 회로, 유선 채널
- capitalize : 자본화하다, 출자하다
- debut : 데뷔, 첫 출연[출전]
- advertiser : 광고주
- emergence : 출현, 발생
- budgeting : 예산
- misconception : 오해, 오인

해석

스포츠 마케팅은 새로운 것이 아니다. 유료 입장을 요구했던 최초의 운동 경기는 1858년 뉴욕의 롱 아일랜드에서 열렸던 야구 경기로, 관중들은 50센트의 돈을 지불했다. 스포츠 주최자들은 곧 스포츠 경기와 프로 선수의 재정적 잠재력을 깨달았다. 골퍼 Gene Sarazen은 1923년 윌슨 스포츠 용품과 보증 계약을 체결했다. 최초의 계약은 평균 여행 경비를 합산하여 연간 6,000달러였다. 1949년에 Babe Didrikson Zaharias는 윌슨 스포츠 용품과 1년에 10만 달러에 달하는 최초의 의미 있는 여성 보증 계약을 체결했다. 코카콜라는 1928년 하계 올림픽과 제휴한 후 지금까지도 후원사로 남아있다. 최초의 유료 시청 경기는 권투 시합이었는데, 1975년 필리핀에서 조 프레이저를 상대로 한 무하마드 알리의 "마닐라의 스릴라"였다. 그 시합은 276개의 유선 채널로 방송되었다. 스포츠의 인기를 토대로 출자한 ESPN은 1979년에 데뷔하여 광고주에게 목표 시장에 도달할 수 있는 새로운 방법을 제안했다. 오늘날 많은 고등학교와 대학에서 스포츠 마케팅 프로그램을 제공한다.

31 ⑤ 윗글은 전쟁에서의 선전전이 상당수 날조되었지만, 사람이 계속해서 싸움을 하도록 유도함으로써 정치적 사안을 국민에게 파는데 효과적이었다고 설명하고 있다. 그러므로 ⑤의 'the application of advertising to political matters(정치 문제의 광고 적용)'이 윗글의 주제로 가장 적절하다.

오답풀이

① 다른 문화권에서의 다른 광고 방법들
② 선전으로 야기된 정치적 · 사회적 갈등
③ 광고 선전의 영향력 증가
④ 광고와 선전의 차이점

- manufacturer : 제조사[자], 생산 회사
- apply to : ~에 적용되다
- evident : 분명한, 눈에 띄는
- propaganda : 선전, 선동
- appalling : 끔찍한, 소름끼치는
- atrocity : 잔혹, 포악, 극악
- solely : 오로지, 단지, 단독으로
- agenda : 의제, 안건, 사안

해석

금세기 초에, 광고에 대한 관심이 커지면서 광고의 잠재력을 볼 수 있는 사람이 제조업자들만은 아니었다. 정치인들 또한 '제품을 파는 방법'이 자신의 아이디어를 파는데 적용될 수 있다는 사실을 깨달았을 때 광고에 관심을 갖게 되었다. 이것은 제1차 세계 대전 동안 선전전이 사람들이 계속 싸움을 하도록 유도하는 도구로 사용되었을 때 특히 두드러졌다. 예를 들어 영국인과 미국인은, 가령 적군 병사들로 비누를 제조하는 것과 같은 독일인의 소름끼치는 행동에 관한 소문을 퍼트렸다. 이것은 사람들이 그러한 무자비한 국가가 전쟁에서 승리하도록 하면 안 된다는 사실을 이해하고 계속해서 싸울 가치가 있다고 생각하도록 하기 위함이다. 소위 '잔혹한 이야기'가 대부분 사용되었고, 일부는 정말 사실적 요소를 포함하고 있지만, 상당수가 오로지 영국과 미국 정부의 이익을 위해서 날조되었다. 그럼에도 불구하고 그것들은 정치적 사안을 국민에게 파는데 효과적이었던 것으로 나타났다.

32 ③ Romain Rolland가 16세기 이탈리아 유화에 관한 논문으로 취득한 학위는 박사학위가 아니라 석사학위(a master's degree)이다.

- tribute : 공헌, 기여
- lofty : 고상한, 숭고한
- gravitate : 인력에 끌리다[움직이다]
- doctorate : 박사 학위[과정]
- a master's degree : 석사학위
- thesis : 학위 논문, 논지
- resign : 사임[퇴임]하다, 물러나다

해석

Romain Rolland는 1915년에 그의 문학 작품인 숭고한 이상주의에 대한 기여로 노벨 문학상을 수상한 프랑스 극작가이자 소설가 및 미술 사학자였다. 그는 1866년에 Nièvre의 Clamecy에서 태어났다. 우수한 학생이었던 그는 École Normale Supérieure에 입학하여, 그곳에서 예술과 음악에 이끌리기 전

에 철학을 공부했다. 1889년에 졸업한 후, 그는 이탈리아의 르네상스 걸작을 연구하면서 수년간을 이탈리아에서 보냈다. 프랑스로 돌아오고 나서, Rolland는 1895년에 초기 유럽 오페라에 관한 연구로 박사학위를 받았다. 같은 해 그는 16세기 이탈리아 유화에 관한 석사 논문 학위를 취득했다. 그는 1912년까지 대학 과정에서 가르쳤고, 자신의 직위를 사임한 후 글쓰기에 전념했다. 그의 가장 위대한 문학 작품은 희곡 형태로 나왔다. 그는 극장이 신체적으로나 지적으로 대중들에게 환영을 받아야한다고 굳게 믿었다. 그는 관객들에게 프랑스의 혁명 역사를 상기시키는 희곡들을 선호했다.

33 ④ 위의 도표에서 보면 매년 일본에서 세 번째로 많은 자동차가 판매되지만, 2013년에 그곳에서 판매된 자동차 대수는 같은 해에 중국에서 판매된 자동차 대수의 약 4분의 1이었다.

어휘
• vehicle : 차량, 탈 것
• the largest economies : 경제 대국
• consistently : 계속해서, 지속적으로

해석
위의 그래프는 2009년과 2013년 사이에 5대 경제 대국에서 각각 판매된 자동차 대수를 나타낸다. ① 5년 동안 매년 중국은 미국을 계속해서 앞서며, 가장 큰 자동차 판매량을 보여주었다. ② 중국에서 판매된 자동차 대수는 2009년에 1,400만대 언저리에서 2013년에 2,100만대 이상으로 매년 꾸준히 증가했다. ③ 중국과 미국에서 판매된 자동차 대수의 격차는 2009년에는 300만대 이상, 2013년에는 500만대 이상이었다. ④ 매년 일본에서 세 번째로 많은 자동차가 판매되지만, 2013년에 그곳에서 판매된 자동차 대수는 같은 해에 중국에서 판매된 자동차 대수의 3분의 1이었다. ⑤ 매년 4번째로 많은 자동차가 독일에서 판매되었으나, 그 나라에서 판매된 자동차 대수는 5년 중에 어떤 해에도 400만대에 이르지 못했고, 프랑스는 매년 최소 자동차 판매량을 보였다.

34 ② 윗글은 크기와 같은 물리적인 조건이 변해도 대상의 속성이 일정하게 지각되는 현상인 지각 항등성을 설명한 글이다. 주어진 글이 친구가 다가올 때 커지는 사례를 예로 들고 있으므로 커지는 것에 대한 지각 항등성을 설명한 (B)가 와야 하고, 다음으로 자동차가 멀어질 때 작아지는 것에 대한 지각 항등성을 설명한 (A)가 와야 한다. 그리고 (B)와 (A)의 두 가지 예가 지각 항등성의 사례들이므로 (C)가 마지막에 위치한다.

어휘
• move off : 떠나다, 출발하다
• perception : 지각, 자각, 인식
• retinal : 망막의
• expansion : 확대, 확장, 팽창
• indication : 암시, 지표, 표시
• perceptual constancy : 지각 항등성
• depth plane : 깊이 기준면

해석
친구가 당신을 향해 달려오고 있는 것을 본다. 그가 다가올수록 점점 커진다. 그러나 그가 실제로 성장하는 것이 아니라, 친구가 점점 가까워지고 있다는 사실을 당신은 알고 있다.

(B) 이것은 당신의 기억 속에 사람들의 크기를 숙지하고 있고, 사람들이 그렇게 빨리 크기를 바꾸지 못한다는 사실을 알고 있기 때문이다. 사실, 망막의 이미지는 확장하고 있으며, 그 확장 속도는 친구의 경우처럼 대상이 얼마나 빨리 다가오고 있는가에 대한 표시이다.

(A) 마찬가지로, 자동차가 지나가거나 멀어질 때, 그것은 점점 작아진다. 그러나 크기에 대한 인식은 망막 이미지의 크기 변화로부터 예상되는 것과 크게 다르지 않다고 한다.

(C) 이것들이 지각 항등성의 사례들이다. 기본적으로 우리는 자동차가 멀어지거나 또는 한 사람이 가까이 다가오는 것을 경험한다. 우리는 크기가 변하는 우리 자신의 모습을 걱정하지 않는다. 우리는 깊이 면에서 움직임을 주는 것으로 정보를 해석한다.

35 ⑤ 윗글은 타인을 지도하면서 스스로도 발전할 수 있는 값진 결과를 얻을 수 있다고 설명하고 있다. (C)에서는 지도하기 전의(Before we coach) 학습 과정을, (B)에서는 지도한 후의(After coaching) 학습 과정을 설명하고 있고, (A)에서는 이러한 학습의 순환이 지도 관계 전체를 통해서 되풀이 된다고 설명하고 있다.

어휘
• genuine : 진짜의, 진정한, 진실한
• intention : 의도, 의사, 의향
• spurs ~ on to : 자극하여[격려하여] ~하게 하다
• inculcate : 되풀이하여 가르치다[이해시키다]
• competency : 능숙함, 능력, 기능
• session : 시간, 기간
• hands-on : 직접 해 보는, 실천하는, 실질적인
• reflect on : ~을 반성하다, 되돌아보다

사람들을 지도하면서 얻는 가장 값진 결과들 중의 하나는 지도하는 과정 속에서 스스로를 또한 발전시킬 수 있다는 것이다. 우리를 격려하여 스스로를 변화시키는 것은 타인을 성장시키기 위한 진정한 열정과 의도이다.

(C) 다른 사람들을 발전시키기 위해, 우리는 먼저 스스로를 발전시켜야 한다. 그리고 지속적으로 다른 사람을 변화시키기 위해서, 우리는 스스로를 지속적으로 변화시킬 수밖에 없다. 지도하기에 앞서, 우리는 배우고, 준비하며, 어떻게 효과적으로 지도할 수 있는지 되돌아본다.

(B) 지도 기간 동안에, 우리는 직접적인 경험을 얻고 지도 기술과 기교를 연습한다. 지도 후에 우리는 대화를 통해 무슨 일이 있었으며, 무엇이 잘 되었고, 무엇이 잘못 되었는지, 그리고 어떻게 다음번에 우리가 더 잘 할 수 있는지 반성한다.

(A) 이러한 학습의 순환은 지도 관계 전체를 통해 반복적으로 되풀이 된다. 우리가 더 많은 사람을 지도할수록, 우리를 도와 줄 여러 방면의 전문적이고 개인적인 삶 속에서 지도를 통해 지식과 기술 그리고 능력들을 되풀이하여 가르친다.

36 ① (A) 담배 라이터, 콘택트 렌즈, 시계와 카메라조차 그냥 쓰고 버린다고 하였고, 앞에 부정어 'less'가 있으므로 빈칸에는 'durable(내구성이 있는, 오래 가는)'을 사용하는 것이 적절하다.

② (B) 의류와 액세서리처럼 유행이 지나면 수명을 다하여 쓸모가 없어지는 제품을 의미하므로, 빈칸에는 'expires(만료되다, 끝나다)'를 사용하는 것이 적절하다.

③ (C) 개인 용품에 대한 감정이 시간이 지남에 따라 줄어드는 것이므로, 빈칸에는 'attachment(애착)'을 사용하는 것이 적절하다.

어휘

- economy : 절약, 검약
- thrift : 절약, 검소
- durable : 내구성이 있는, 오래 가는
- fragile : 부서지기[손상되기] 쉬운
- be meant to do : ~하지 않으면 안 된다
- be disposed of : ~을 없애다[처리하다], 폐기되다
- throwaways : 그냥 쓰고 버리는
- perishable : 잘 상하는, 부패하기 쉬운, 수명을 다하는
- expire : 만료되다, 만기가 되다, 끝나다
- prevail : 만연하다, 팽배하다
- attachment : 애착, 믿음, 부속

- aversion : 혐오, 싫음

해석

과거에는 절약과 검소가 당시의 도리였다. 아무리 하찮아 보일지라도 아무 것도 버리지 않았다. 구입한 모든 제품은 중요했으며 모든 달러는 저축할 가치가 있었다. 오늘날, 제품들은 (A) 내구성이 부족하여 버리지 않으면 안 된다. 담배 라이터, 콘택트 렌즈, 시계와 카메라조차그냥 쓰고 버려진다. 마찬가지로, 의류 및 액세서리도 일단 유행이 지나면 쓸모가 (B) 없어진다는 점에서 수명을 다한다. 새로운 쇼핑 트렌드와 관련하여 이것은 노소를 막론하고 물건들이 빠르고 쉽게 폐기되는 세상에서 생활하는데 소비자들이 점점 익숙해진다는 것을 의미하며, 신제품들은 그것들을 교체하기 위해 구매된다. 삶의 속도가 꾸준히 증가함에 따라 버려지는 제품들의 수요가 더욱 증가하고 있다. 개인 용품에 대한 정서적인 (C) 애착은 시간이 지남에 따라 줄어들고 있으며, 그것은 더 많은 제품에 대한 더 많은 수요가 있음을 의미한다.

37 ① 윗글에 따르면 개인적인 특성과 같은 (A) 분명치 않은 정보에 대해 답변하는 첫 번째 그룹의 학생들이 과정상의 특정 단계와 같은 간단한 질문에 답변하는 다른 그룹의 학생들보다 답변이 (B) 늦는 경향이 있었다. 그러므로 빈칸 (A)에는 'abstract(추상적인)', (B)에는 'postpone(늦다, 미루다)'이 들어갈 말로 가장 적절하다.

오답풀이

	(A)	(B)
②	추상적인	강조하다
③	양적인	미루다
④	실질적인	과장하다
⑤	실질적인	강조하다

어휘

- questionnaire : 설문지, 질문서
- mundane : 재미없는, 일상적인
- imply : 의미하다, 암시[시사]하다
- intangible : 만질 수 없는, 막연한, 분명치 않은
- bank teller : 은행 직원
- initial deposit : 초입금
- to a great extent : 대부분은, 매우
- postpone : 연기하다, 미루다, 늦추다
- quantitative : 양적인, 양적으로

해석

한 심리학적 연구에서, 조사원들은 두 그룹의 학생들에게 설문지를 작성하여 전자 메일로 응답하도록 요청했다. 모든 질문은 은행 계좌 개설과 같은 몇 가지 일상적인 업무와 관련이

있었다. 그러나 두 그룹은 질문에 대답하기 위한 다른 지시를 받았다. 첫 번째 그룹의 학생들은 개인적인 특성, 예를 들면 어떤 부류의 사람이 은행 계좌를 가지고 있는지와 같은 몇 가지 분명치 않은 정보에 관해 어떤 활동 의미가 있는가를 기술해야 했다. 두 번째 그룹은 과정상의 특정 단계 즉, 은행 출납원에게 말하고, 양식을 작성하고, 초기 입금을 하는 등에 대해 간단하게 기술했다. 두 그룹의 응답 시간에는 상당한 차이가 있음이 입증되었다. 첫 번째 그룹의 학생들은 답변이 늦는 경향이 있었고, 실제로 일부는 과제를 전혀 완수하지 못했다. 대조적으로 두 번째 그룹의 학생들은 업무의 방법, 시기 및 장소에 초점을 맞추어 첫 번째 그룹보다 더 빨리 과제를 완수했다.

↓

연구에 따르면, 더 (A) 추상적인 용어의 사고를 요하는 과제를 받은 첫 번째 그룹은 다른 그룹의 학생들보다 대부분 답변이 (B) 늦는 것으로 나타났다.

[38~39]

- ecological : 생태계의, 생태학의
- ecosystem : 생태계
- susceptible : 민감한, 예민한
- ill-health : 나쁜 건강, 건강 악화
- hypothermia : 저체온증
- organism : 유기체, 생물
- vector : (병균의) 매개 곤충, 매개체
- tropical : 열대 지방의, 열대의
- mosquito : 모기
- reproduction rate : 증식률, 번식률
- micro-organism : 미생물
- invertebrate : 무척추 동물
- transmit : 전송하다, 송신하다
- infectious agent : 감염원, 감염체
- hygiene : 위생
- combat : 싸우다, 전투하다

해석

인간의 건강에 대한 생태학적 접근은 인간을 보다 광대한 생태계의 일부로 여긴다. 질병 생태학자들은 인간과 그들이 살고 있는 환경과의 상호작용에 초점을 맞추고, 장소에 따른 건강과 질병의 패턴을 기술하고 설명하는 것을 돕는다. 인간은 다소 건강 악화에 민감한 다양한 방식으로 그들의 환경과 상호작용한다. 예를 들어, 추운 날씨에 너무 오래 동안 외부에 머무르는 것은 저체온 즉, 위험할 정도로 낮은 체온 상태를 야

기할 수 있고, 혹은 태양에 너무 많이 노출되면 피부암의 발병을 촉진시킬 수도 있다. (A) 그러나, 모든 인과관계가 직접적인 것은 아니다. 질병 생태학이 질병 패턴을 설명하는데 유용한 주된 방법 중의 하나는 어떻게 특정 환경이 질병을 유발하는 유기체나 그것들을 옮기는 매개 곤충이 살 수 있는 곳에 영향을 미치는지 생각해 보는 것이다. (B) 예를 들어, 대다수 질병은 연중 따뜻한 온도로 인해 모기와 같은 매개 곤충이 번식할 수 있는 열대 기후에 국한된다. 온난한 기온은 또한 바이러스 및 박테리아와 같은 미생물뿐만 아니라 이들을 전염시키는 무척추 동물의 번식률을 높여 사람들 간의 질병 전파를 더욱 빠르게 한다. 사람과 병원균 사이의 관계를 분석하는 것은 질병 생태학자의 첫 번째 관심사 중 하나였으며 오늘날에도 질병 생태학의 핵심적인 부분으로 남아있다.

38 ⑤ 윗글의 마지막 줄에서 사람과 병원균 사이의 관계를 분석하는 것은 질병 생태학자의 첫 번째 관심사 중 하나였으며 오늘날에도 질병 생태학의 핵심적인 부분으로 남아있다고 설명하고 있다. 그러므로 ⑤의 'Disease Ecologists' Concerns: Environment and Human Diseases(질병 생태학자들의 관심사 : 환경과 인간의 질병)'이 윗글의 제목으로 가장 적절하다.

오답풀이

① 질병 퇴치를 위한 효과적인 위생 습관
② 과학 분야로서의 질병 생태학의 기원
③ 전형적인 질병 유발 생물의 진화
④ 환경 변화가 질병의 확산에 미치는 영향

39 ② (A) 앞 문장에서 인간과 환경과의 상호작용을 예로 들어 추우면 저체온에 걸리고 햇볕에 오래 쬐면 피부암에 걸릴 수 있다고 했으나, 이 모든 인과관계가 직접적인 것은 아니라고 부정하고 있으므로 (A)에는 역접의 접속부사 'However(그러나)'가 들어가는 것이 가장 적절하다.

(B) 특정 환경이 질병을 유발하는 매개체에 어떻게 영향을 미치는지 그 사례들을 다음 문장에서 열거하고 있으므로 (B)에는 'For example(예를 들면)'이 들어가는 것이 가장 적절하다.

[40~41]

- citadel : 성채, 요새
- terrace : 계단식 논[밭], 다랑이
- purposeful : 목적의식이 있는, 결단력 있는
- proximity : 가까움, 근접, 접근성

- rainforest : 열대 우림
- geography : 지리학, 지리, 지형
- prize : 소중히 여기다, 높이 평가하다
- exotic : 외국의, 이국적인
- healing herb : 약초, 향초
- tribe : 부족, 종족
- guinea pig : 기니피그
- quinoa : 퀴노아(명아주속의 일년초)
- take into account : ~을 고려하다[참작하다]
- habitat : 거주지, 서식지
- endangered species : 멸종위기 종

해석

Machu Picchu는 그 요새 아래 2,000피트에 위치한 Urubamba 강으로 둘러싸여 있다. 이 강은 자연이 그들에게 신성했기 때문만은 아니라 자연이 가져다주는 이점들 때문에 잉카 사람들에게 신성한 것으로 여겨졌다. 그것은 Machu Picchu가 위치한 산 주위를 구부러지고 일부 농경지는 강 하류까지 내내 이어진다. Machu Picchu의 위치에서 강을 항해할 수는 없지만, 더 멀리 강 하류에서 보트를 타고 아마존 강과 대서양까지 항해하여 사람과 물품을 이동시키는 것이 가능하다. 이것은 사람들이 Machu Picchu로 직접 항해하는 것을 피할 목적이었지만 여전히 비교적 가까운 (A) 운송 경로를 제공한다.

열대 우림과의 접근성은 분명히 Machu Picchu 지형의 또 다른 이점이었다. 열대 우림은 다른 생산품들 중에서 다채로운 조류 깃털, 나비, 코카나무 잎, 이국적인 과일과 채소 그리고 치료용 허브와 같은 잉카제국이 소중하게 여기는 희귀한 생산품의 원천이었다. 잉카 사람들은 감자, 기니피그, 보석, 퀴노아 그리고 금과 같이 그들에게 없는 것들을 위해 열대 우림의 부족들과 이들 생산품을 교환하였고 그것들을 종교 의식에 사용하곤 했다. Machu Picchu를 건설할 때, 잉카 사람들은 (B) 무역으로 열대 우림에 가까운 혜택을 고려했음에 틀림없다.

40 ② 윗글에서 운송과 무역을 하는데 열대 우림과의 접근성은 분명히 Machu Picchu 지형의 또 다른 이점이었다고 설명하고 있다. 그러므로 윗글이 시사하는 바는 "Machu Picchu 건설에 있어, 잉카 사람들은 그들의 주변 지형을 고려하였다"는 ②의 설명이다.

오답풀이

① 문자가 없어서, Machu Picchu가 어떻게 건설되었는지 잉카 사람들에게 기록으로 남아있지 않다.
③ Machu Picchu 관광 산업의 미래를 위해 대화 노력이 필요하다.
④ Machu Picchu는 일부 멸종위기 종에 안정된 서식처를 제공하는 열대우림에 자리해 있다.

⑤ 대서양에서 직접 오는 운송로가 없어서 잉카 문명의 개발이 늦어졌다.

41 ④ (A) 아마존 강과 대서양까지 항해하여 사람과 물품을 이동시키는 경로를 제공하는 것이므로, 빈칸 (B)에는 'transportation(운송)'이 들어갈 말로 가장 적절하다.
(B) 잉카제국에서 생산되는 희귀한 물품을 열대 우림의 다른 부족과 교환하는 것이므로, 빈칸 (B)에는 'trading(무역)'이 들어갈 말로 가장 적절하다.

[42~43]

어휘

- colleague : 동료, 동업자
- commission : 의뢰[주문]하다
- national anthem : 국가(國歌)
- fascinating : 대단히 흥미로운, 매력적인
- misstep : 실수, 실책
- alley : 골목, 통로, 복도
- take a bad turn : 악화하다
- arrangement : 편곡
- silly : 어리석은, 바보 같은
- arranger : 편곡자
- be called to task : 나무람을 듣다, 질책[책망]을 받다
- dismissal : 면직, 해고
- relentless : 무정한, 가차[사정] 없는, 인정사정 없는
- subtly : 민감하게, 예민하게
- redirect : 전가하다, 전용하다
- orchestration : 관현악 편곡
- expertise : 전문 지식[기술]
- swallow : 삼키다, 넘기다
- bait : 미끼
- presence of mind : 침착성, 태연자약
- intimidate : 겁을 주다, 위협하다
- unimaginative : 상상력이 부족한
- dictator : 독재자
- piercing gaze : 뚫어져라 쳐다봄
- insecurity : 불안(감), 불안정
- straightforwardly : 노골적으로, 단도직입적으로

해석

제2차 세계 대전 중에, 작곡가 드미트리 쇼스타코비치와 그의 동료 몇 명은 러시아의 통치자 조셉 스탈린과의 미팅에 소집되었는데, 그는 새로운 국가(國歌)를 작곡하도록 의뢰했다. 쇼스타코비치는 스탈린과의 만남이 (A) 몹시 무서웠다고 들었

다. 한 번의 실수로 어두운 복도로 끌려갈 수도 있었다. 그는 목구멍이 타들어갈 때까지 빤히 내려다 볼 것이다. 그리고 스탈린과의 만남이 종종 그러했듯이, 이번 만남도 나쁜 쪽으로 흘러갔다. 그 통치자는 형편없는 편곡을 이유로 작곡가 중 한 명을 비판하기 시작했다. 어리석게도 겁을 먹고, 그 남자는 형편없이 일 한 편곡자를 고용했다고 인정했다. 그는 몇 개의 무덤을 파고 있었다. 분명히 형편없는 편곡자도 질책을 받을 수 있다. 그 작곡자는 (B) 고용에 책임이 있었고, 그 또한 실수를 책임져야 했다. 그러면 쇼스타코비치를 포함한 다른 작곡가들은 어떤가? 스탈린은 일단 두려움의 냄새를 맡으면 인정사정이 없었다.

쇼스타코비치는 충분히 들었다. 그는 대개 명령을 따르는 편곡자를 나무라는 것은 어리석다고 말했다. 그런 다음 그는 작곡가가 직접 관현악 작곡을 해야 할지 아닌지 다른 주제로 대화의 방향을 미묘하게 바꿨다. 그 문제에 대해 스탈린은 어떻게 생각했을까? 항상 자신의 전문성을 입증하기를 열망했던 그는 미끼를 물었다. 위험한 순간이 지나갔다.

쇼스타코비치는 여러 면에서 침착성을 유지했다. 첫째, 스탈린이 그를 위협하는 대신에, 그는 자신을 그처럼 작고, 뚱뚱하고, 못생기고, 상상력이 부족한 남자처럼 보이도록 했다. 그래서 독재자의 유명한 날카로운 시선은 그저 자신의 (C) 불안감을 나타내는 속임수였다. 둘째, 쇼스타코비치는 스탈린을 똑바로 쳐다보고 보통 때처럼 단도직입적으로 이야기했다. 그의 행동과 목소리로, 그 작곡가는 자신이 위협받고 있지 않음을 보여주었다.

42 ③ (A) 다음 문장에서 한 번의 실수로 어두운 복도로 끌려갈 수도 있고, 목구멍이 쬐일 때까지 빤히 내려다 볼 수도 있다고 했으므로, 빈칸 (A)에는 'terrifying(몹시 무서워하는)'이 들어갈 말로 가장 적절하다.

(B) 그 작곡자도 형편없는 편곡자를 이용한 것에 대한 책임이 있으므로, 빈칸 (B)에는 'hire(고용)'이 들어갈 말로 가장 적절하다.

(C) 쇼스타코비치가 스탈린처럼 작고, 뚱뚱하고, 못생기고, 상상력이 부족한 남자처럼 보이도록 했다고 했으므로, 빈칸 (C)에는 'insecurity(불안감)'이 들어갈 말로 가장 적절하다.

43 ④ 윗글에 따르면 스탈린은 항상 자신의 전문성을 입증하기를 열망했다고 했으므로, 스탈린은 자신이 전문적 지식을 지녔음을 입증하는 것을 원하지 않았다는 ④의 설명은 적절하지 않다.

[44~45]

어휘

• backpacking : 배낭여행
• atop : 꼭대기에, 맨 위에
• inactive volcano : 휴화산
• trek : 트래킹, 오지 여행
• figure : 생각[판단]하다, 계산하다
• breathless : 숨이 가쁜, 숨이 찬
• sympathetic : 동정적인, 동정어린
• steep : 가파른, 경사진
• majestic : 장엄한, 위풍당당한
• make it all the way : 끝까지 가다, 끝까지 해내다

해석

(A) Don이 25살이었을 때, 그는 동남아시아로 배낭여행을 떠났다. 3주 동안, 그는 Bukittinggi라고 불리는 아름다운 마을에 잠깐 들렸다가, 인도네시아 주위를 여행했다. 게스트하우스에서 그는 스웨덴에서 온 멋진 친구인 Stephen을 만났는데, 그는 (a) 그가 휴화산 꼭대기의 인근 호수를 탐험할 것을 권했다.

(D) (e) 그의 조언에 따라, Don은 그곳까지 버스를 타고 갔다. 그렇게 가깝지 않았고, 오히려 가파르고 바람이 불며 다소 위험한 길을 4시간 가까이 올라갔다. 꼭대기의 경치가 장관이었기 때문에 그것은 가치가 있었다. 한때 화산의 입구였던 산 정상에 엄청나게 장엄한 호수가 있었다. Stephen에 따르면, 그것은 주위를 둘러보는데 약 2시간이 걸리는 아름다운 산책로로 둘러싸여 있다.

(B) (b) 그가 호수 주위로 트레킹을 시작할 때, Don은 산을 내려가는 마지막 버스가 오후 5시에 떠난다는 사실을 알고 있었고, 그래서 그때까지는 틀림없이 버스 정류장으로 돌아와야만 했다. 오후 1시가 되었을 때, 그는 호수 주위를 끝까지 간 다음 산 아래로 내려갈 마지막 버스를 제 때 타러 가기에 남은 시간이 충분하다고 생각했다. 정말 멋진 하이킹이었다. 그러나 오후 4시 무렵, (c) 그는 호수 주변 중간쯤 어딘가에 있다는 사실을 깨달았다.

(C) 그는 왔던 길을 되돌아 내려가기로 결심했다. 버스 정류장 근처에 갔을 때, 마지막 버스가 (d) 그를 두고 가버리는 것을 보았다. 숨이 차서, 그는 산을 걸어 내려가는 것밖에 선택의 여지가 없었고 어떤 친절한 이가 그를 데리러 오기를 희망했다. 그는 어떤 차량이 오기 전까지 몇 시간을 걸었다. 다행히 멋있는 인도네시아 신사가 도움을 주려고 멈췄다. 그는 그 상황을 매우 안타까워했고 Don을 그의 게스트하우스까지 태워다 주겠다고 말했다. Don은 말로 표현할 수 없을 만큼 감사했다.

44 ④ (A) 게스트하우스에서 만난 Stephen이 휴화산 꼭대기의 인
     근 호수를 탐험할 것을 권한다.
     (D) Stephen의 조언에 따라 휴화산의 꼭대기까지 버스를
     타고 4시간 가까이 올라간다.
     (B) 호수 주위를 트래킹한 후 산 아래로 내려갈 마지막 버
     스를 타기 위해 버스 정류장으로 돌아간다.
     (C) 너무 늦어 마지막 버스를 놓쳤으나, 인도네시아 신사의
     도움으로 게스트하우스에 무사히 도착한다.

45 ⑤ (e)의 'his'는 Don이 휴화산 꼭대기의 인근 호수를 탐험할
     것을 조언한 Stephen이다. 나머지 (a), (b), (c), (d)는 모두
     Don을 가리킨다.

2017학년도 기출문제 정답 및 해설

제2교시 영어영역(공통)

01 ⑤	02 ③	03 ②	04 ⑤	05 ①	06 ②
07 ⑤	08 ④	09 ④	10 ③	11 ⑤	12 ④
13 ①	14 ①	15 ②	16 ①	17 ②	18 ①
19 ③	20 ③	21 ①	22 ④	23 ⑤	24 ③
25 ④	26 ⑤	27 ③	28 ①	29 ②	30 ④
31 ③	32 ④	33 ③	34 ③	35 ④	36 ③
37 ①	38 ②	39 ②	40 ④	41 ⑤	42 ②
43 ①	44 ⑤	45 ⑤			

01　⑤ Dave는 밥을 좋아한다고 했지만, Rachel이 밥은 훌륭한 에너지원이나 칼로리가 높아서 생선으로 조금 바꿔보라고 충고했다. 그러므로 Dave는 건강한 식단을 위해 밥을 더 먹기보다는 줄여야 한다.

【오답풀이】
① Rachel은 체육관 강사이다.
② Dave는 수분 섭취를 잘 하고 있다.
③ 균형 잡힌 식단에는 몇 가지 음식 종류가 포함된다.
④ 일부 지방은 건강한 식단에 중요하다.
⑤ Dave는 밥을 더 먹어야 한다.

【어휘】
• gym : 체육관
• nutritional : 영양상의
• get in shape : 좋은 몸 상태(몸매)를 유지하다
• fluid : 유체, 액체
• hydration : 수화(水和) (작용), 수분 섭취, 식수
• a balanced diet : 균형 잡힌 식단(식사)
• grain : 곡물, 낱알
• a gym instructor : 체육관 강사
• well-hydrated : 수분을 잘 섭취한

【해석】
Rachel : 안녕, Dave. 체육관에 온 걸 환영해. 운동을 시작할 준비가 되었니?
Dave : 좋은 아침이에요, Rachel. 저기, 시작하기 전에, 좋은

몸 상태를 유지하는 데 도움이 될 영양상의 조언 좀 해주실래요?
Rachel : 그래. 오늘 아침에 물은 충분히 마셨니?
Dave : 물론입니다. 지난 수업시간에 수분 섭취가 얼마나 중요한지 말씀해 주셨어요.
Rachel : 잘했어! 다음으로, 균형 잡힌 식사를 하고 있니? 빵과 쌀 같은 곡물, 유익한 지방과 기름 그리고 충분한 과일과 야채가 포함돼야 해.
Dave : 오, 저는 밥을 좋아해요! 와, 저는 어떤 지방들은 우리 몸에 좋다는 사실을 몰랐네요.
Rachel : 물론이지! 유익한 지방은 생선에 들어 있고 균형 잡힌 식단에 꼭 필요해. 또 밥은 훌륭한 에너지원이지만, 칼로리가 높아. 나중에 밥을 조금 생선으로 바꿔봐.

02　③ • 첫 번째 빈칸 : 앞 문장에서 Empire State Building을 추천하고 있으므로, 고층 건물에 대해 언급한 'c'가 와야 한다.
• 두 번째 빈칸 : 앞 문장에서 Yankees 상점을 추천하고 있으므로, 야구 기념품을 언급한 'a'가 와야 한다.
• 세 번째 빈칸 : 앞 문장에서 뉴욕 공공 도서관을 추천하고 있고 뒤 문장에서 서둘러야겠다고 말하고 있으므로, 문 닫는 시간을 언급한 'b'가 와야 한다.

【어휘】
• don't have a clue : 전혀 모르다, 짐작도 못하다
• tourist site : 관광지, 관광 명소
• around that corner : 코앞에, 목전에
• recommend : 추천하다, 권하다
• souvenir : 기념품, 선물
• skyscraper : 고층 건물, 마천루
• hair salon : 미장원, 미용실

【해석】
Ben : 안녕하세요, 부인. 길을 잃으셨나 봐요. 도와드릴까요?
Susan : 오, 맞아요. 매우 감사해요! 뉴욕이 처음이라 어디로 가야 할지 전혀 모르겠어요.
Ben : 도움이 되어 저도 기뻐요. 운 좋게도, 코앞에 유명한 관광 명소가 있어요. Empire State Building은 방문하셨나요? 그 건물은 최초의 고층건물 중 하나였어요.
Susan : 아직요, 하지만 반드시 그럴 계획이에요! 그밖에 어디

를 방문해야 하죠?

Ben : 스포츠를 좋아하신다면, 5번가로 향해서 36번가에 있는 Yankees 상점 쪽으로 가보세요. 사람들은 거기서 야구 기념품을 사요.

Susan : 좋아요! 저는 책 읽는 것도 좋아해요. 어디 추천 좀 해주시겠어요?

Ben : 저기, 뉴욕 공공 도서관은 막 지나친 저곳, 42번가에 있어요. 오후 6시에 문을 닫는다는 것만 꼭 알아두세요.

Susan : 오, 서둘러야겠네요. 모든 걸 조언해 줘서 너무 고마워요.

> a. 사람들은 거기서 야구 기념품을 사요.
> b. 오후 6시에 문을 닫는다는 것만 꼭 알아두세요.
> c. 그 건물은 최초의 고층건물 중 하나였어요.
> d. 그것은 유명한 미용실이에요.

03 ② 딸기와 사과의 구입 경로에 대해 대화를 나누고 있고, 마지막 Steven의 말에서 딸기와 사과의 가격과 밭의 위치 등을 설명하고 있으므로 '과수원(orchard)'에서 나누고 있는 대화임을 짐작할 수 있다.

오답풀이

① 화원에서
③ 비닐하우스에서
④ 식료품점에서
⑤ 과일 가공 공장에서

어휘

• that depends : 확실히 알 수 없다, 사정[형편]에 따라 다르다
• definitely : 분명히, 틀림없이
• recipe : 조리법, 요리법
• plot : 작은 구획의 땅, 작은 토지[지구]
• stream : 개울, 시내
• florist's : 화원
• orchard : 과수원
• fruit processing plant : 과일 가공 공장

해석

Laura : 와, 여기 밭은 정말 아름답네! 오, 저것들은 정말 신선해 보여. 직접 좀 구하고 싶은데! 그것들을 어디서 보았니?

Steven : 글쎄, 정확히 모르겠네. 딸기를 말하는 거야 아니면 사과를 말하는 거야?

Laura : 둘 다 어때? 딸기는 정말 내가 좋아하는 과일이지만, 사과 파이 만드는 것도 좋아해. 우리 할머니 요리법은 고향에서 유명해.

Steven : 좋아! 내가 따는 거를 도와주면 파이를 좀 나눠줄 수

있니?

Laura : 물론이지. 어쨌든 그것들이 어디서 났고 얼마니?

Steven : 음, 딸기는 킬로그램 당 1달러였고 밭은 개울 옆 저쪽에 있어. 사과는 킬로그램 당 2달러였고 남쪽 들판에서 볼 수 있지. 가자!

04 ⑤ 고장 난 휴대 전화를 제조사에 보내고 임시로 대체품을 받거나 지점을 방문해 기사로부터 바로 수리를 받을 수 있다는 Sam의 말에, Joe는 빨리 수리하고 싶어서 San Pedro 매장으로 오전 10시에 잠시 들린다고 했다. 그러므로 "Joe wants to visit the store in the morning.(Joe는 아침에 그 매장을 방문하기를 원한다.)"는 ⑤의 설명이 위의 대화 내용과 일치한다.

오답풀이

① Joe는 고장 난 휴대 전화기를 수리하러 온 고객이며, 전자 제품 매장에서 근무하는지는 알 수 없다.
② 휴대 전화기의 액정이 고장 난 것이며, 전화기가 켜지지 않을지는 알 수 없다.
③ 그 전화기의 보증기간이 아직 만료되지 않았다.
④ Joe는 직접 매장에 가서 빨리 수리하기를 원했다.

어휘

• customer service department : 고객 서비스 부서
• cellphone : 이동 전화, 휴대 전화
• faulty : 흠[결함]이 있는, 잘못된
• purchase : 구입, 구매, 매입
• warranty : 보증, 품질 보증서
• manufacturer : 제조사, 생산 회사
• replacement : 교체(품), 대체(물)
• technician : 기술자, 기사
• branch : 지사, 지점, 분점
• drop by : 잠깐 들르다, 불시에 찾아가다
• expire : 만료되다, 끝나다

해석

[전화벨이 울린다.]

Sam : 안녕하세요. Big 전자 고객 서비스 부입니다. 저는 Sam 입니다. 무엇을 도와드릴까요?

Joe : 안녕하세요. 저는 Joe Lee입니다. 최근에 귀사의 휴대 전화를 하나 샀는데 액정이 망가졌어요.

Sam : 죄송합니다. 고객님. 구매한 날짜와 장소를 말씀해 주시겠어요?

Joe : 그럼요. 2주 전에 구입했고, 7월 3일입니다. 장소는 LA 지점 중의 하나이고, San Pedro Street에 위치한 큰 매장이었어요.

Sam : 알겠습니다. 고객님. 고객님의 전화기는 아직 보증기간

이 남아 있습니다. 장치를 제조사에 보내고 대체품을 받으실 수 있습니다. 아니면 지점을 방문하시면 저희 기사님 중 한 분이 수리해 드릴 수 있습니다.

Joe : 음, 빨리 수리하고 싶은데요. San Pedro 매장으로 오전 10시에 잠시 들릴 수 있을 것 같아요.

Sam : 알겠습니다. 고객님. 그들에게 미리 전화해서 고객님이 약 1시간 내에 방문하신다고 전해놓겠습니다.

05 ① 소셜미디어 사이트에 비즈니스 페이지를 만들어 홍보하는 것이 사업을 빨리 알리는 검증된 방법이라는 Tom의 조언에 Emma가 감사하다고 했으므로, 빈칸에는 그걸 만들 수 있도록 도움을 요청하는 ①의 부탁의 말이 이어지는 것이 대화의 흐름상 자연스럽다.

오답풀이

② 하지만 가격이 비싸서 정말 걱정이에요. → 온라인 마케팅이 TV 광고보다 저렴하다고 했으므로 틀린 내용이다.

③ 좋습니다. 한번 해보죠. 제 블로그가 비즈니스 페이지와 연결되어 있어요. → 블로그조차 없다고 했으므로 틀린 내용이다.

④ 그러나 제 생각엔 TV에 광고하는 게 더 낫겠어요. 가격이 더 싸요. → 온라인 마케팅이 TV 광고보다 저렴하다고 했으므로 틀린 내용이다.

⑤ 하지만 이 방법이 정말 효과적일지 걱정이에요. 너무 위험한 것 같아요. → 온라인 마케팅이 간단하지만 아주 효과적인 방법이라고 했으므로 틀린 내용이다.

어휘

• grateful : 고마워하는, 감사하는
• recipe : 조리법, 요리법
• delicious : 아주 맛있는, 냄새가 좋은
• competition : 경쟁, 시합
• blog : (인터넷의) 블로그
• strategy : 계획, 전략, 방법
• effective : 효과적인, 실질적인
• subscriber : 구독자, 가입자, 이용자, 후원자
• proven : 증명된, 검증된, 입증된
• appreciate : 감사하다, 인정하다
• give it a shot : 시도해 보다, 한번 해보다

해석

Emma : 안녕하세요, Tom. 광고업계에 계신다는 데, 맞나요? 전문적인 마케팅 조언 좀 해주시면 고맙겠습니다.

Tom : 그럼요, Emma. 정말 도와드리고 싶어요! 어떤 종류의 사업인가요?

Emma : 테이크아웃 치킨점이에요. 제 요리법이 맛있다는 건 알고 있는데, 요즘 워낙 경쟁이 치열해서요. 게다가 TV 광고는

너무 비싸요.

Tom : 알겠습니다. 온라인 마케팅은 생각해 본적이 있나요? 그것은 훨씬 더 저렴한데.

Emma : 정말요? 그렇지만 컴퓨터를 잘 사용하지 못해요. 블로그조차 없어요!

Tom : 괜찮습니다. 간단하지만 아주 효과적인 방법이에요. 소셜미디어 사이트에 비즈니스 페이지를 만들어 가입자에게 할인을 해 줄 수도 있어요. 그것은 사업을 빨리 알리는 검증된 방법이에요.

Emma : 왜! 조언 정말 감사합니다. 굉장히 좋은 생각인거 같아요! 그걸 만드는 걸 도와줄 수 있나요?

06 ② 위의 대화는 Julia가 광고를 보고 찾아온 Diana와 요리, 애완동물, 청결 등 함께 살면서 지켜야 할 몇 가지 주의사항에 대해 서로 대화를 나누고 있다. 그러므로 "Julia is searching for a roommate.(Julia는 룸메이트를 찾고 있는 중이다.)"는 ②의 설명이 가장 적절하다.

오답풀이

① Julia는 애완동물을 기르는 것에 대해 Diana의 조언을 듣고자 한다.

③ Julia와 Diana는 그들의 취미에 관해 이야기를 나누고 있다.

④ Diana는 새로운 친구를 사귀려고 하고 있다.

⑤ Diana는 구직 면접 중이다.

어휘

• respond : 대답하다, 응답하다
• first impression : 첫인상
• pet : 애완동물
• healthily : 건강하게
• affectionate : 다정한, 애정 어린
• organized : 정리된, 체계적인
• cleanliness : 위생, 청결
• absolutely : 전적으로, 틀림없이
• mess : 엉망(진창)인 상태, 지저분한 상태

해석

Julia : 안녕하세요, Diana. 제 광고에 응해줘서 고마워요.

Diana : 오, 천만에요. 그저 제 첫인상이 맘에 들면 좋겠어요.

Julia : 무척 맘에 듭니다. 하지만, 우리가 함께 살려면 몇 가지 꼭 알아둬야 할 게 있어요. 우선 요리를 할 수 있나요? 그리고 애완동물이 있나요?

Diana : 예, 할 수 있어요. 저는 건강하게 살려고 노력해요. 그리고 고양이 한 마리가 있지만, 조용하고 훈련이 잘 되서 아주 다정해요.

Julia : 그거 괜찮네요. 저는 애완동물은 없지만 개보다는 고양이를 더 좋아해요. 다음으로, 정리를 잘 하는 분인가요? 저는

청결이 정말 중요하다고 생각해요.

Diana : 저도요. 엉망진창인 걸 정말 싫어해요.

07 ⑤ ①, ②, ③, ④의 그는 호수에서 수영을 하고, Kline에게 살아있는 가장 위대한 수학자 5명이 누구냐고 질문하는 Wiener를 가리킨다. 반면에 ⑤의 그는 Wiener의 질문에 4명의 이름을 빠르게 대답한 Kline를 가리킨다.

어휘

- mathematician : 수학자
- adjacent : 인접한, 가까운
- cottage : 오두막집, 작은 별장, 산장
- dock : 부두, 선착장
- keep company : ~의 곁에 있어 주다, 친구가 되어 주다
- paddle : 노를 젓다, (작은 배를 노를 저으며) 타다
- rowboat : 보트, 노 젓는 배
- carry on a conversation : 대화를 계속하다
- steadfastly : 확고부동하게, 단호히
- progress : 나아가다, 진행하다
- puffing and gasping : 숨을 헐떡거리는
- bleat out : 힘없는 소리로 이야기하다
- tick off : ~에 체크 표시를 하다
- splutter : (화가 나거나 당황해서) 식식거리며[더듬거리며] 말하다
- delicate : 미묘한, 교묘한, 신중한, 사려 깊은

해석

J. R. Kline는 다른 수학자들에 관한 이야기를 하기 좋아했다. Norbert Wiener에 관한 다음의 이야기를 가장 좋아했다. 어느 여름날, Kline 가족과 Wiener 가족은 New Hampshire의 호수에 인접한 오두막집에 있었다. Wiener는 ① 그의 선착장에서 호수의 중앙에 있는 작은 섬까지 수영하는 버릇이 있었다. 수영 중에 Kline는 곁에서 보트를 저으며 따라갔고, 그리고 그들은 Wiener가 ② 그의 목표를 향해 나아가고 있는 동안 계속해서 대화를 나누곤 했다. Wiener는 ③ 그가 작은 땅덩어리를 향해 숨을 헐떡거리고 있을 때조차도, 항상 대화의 주도권을 쥐려고 노력했다. 그러던 어느 날 수영이 거의 끝날 무렵, ④ 그는 "Kline, 살아있는 가장 위대한 수학자 5명은 누구일까?"라고 힘없는 소리로 물었다. 조용히 Kline는 "재미있는 질문이네. 어디보자."라고 대답했다. ⑤ 그는 4명의 이름(그들 중 'Wiener'의 이름은 없음)을 빠르게 체크했다. "알았어, 알았어, 가자."라고 Wiener가 식식거리며 말했다. 교묘한 유머로 Kline는 다섯 번째 이름을 말하는 것을 회피했다.

08 ④ 윗글은 만성적인 스트레스에 의해 유발되는 코티솔 수치의 증가로 식욕 증가, 복부 지방, 심장 질환, 당뇨병, 암 등과 같은 부정적 영향에 대해 설명하고 있다. 그런데 운동으로 인한 코티솔 수치의 증가는 면역 기능, 기억력, 그리고 체중 감량에 유익하다는 ④의 설명은 글의 전체 흐름과 상반되는 주제이므로 어울리지 않는다.

어휘

- sustain : 지탱하다, 유지하다
- cortisol : 코티솔(부산 피질에서 생성되는 스테로이드 호르몬의 일종)
- trigger : 촉발시키다, 유발시키다
- chronic : 만성적인, 만성 질환을 앓고 있는
- appetite : 식욕, 욕구
- craving : 갈망, 열망
- refuel : 연료를 채우다, 재충전하다
- stressor : 스트레스 요인
- elevate : 높이다, 증가시키다
- accumulate : 쌓다, 축적하다
- stress-induced : 스트레스가 유발된
- abdominal : 복부의, 배의
- immune : 면역성이 있는, 면역이 된
- be associated with : ~와 관련[연관]되다
- diabetes : 당뇨병
- cancer : 암

해석

과학적인 연구에 따르면 지속적인 높은 수치의 코티솔은 만성적인 스트레스에 의해 유발되는데, 장기간의 건강에 부정적인 영향을 미친다는 사실을 분명히 보여준다. ① 이러한 영향들 중에는 식욕 증가와 특정 음식에 대한 갈망이 있다. ② 왜냐하면 코티솔의 역할 중의 하나는 스트레스 요인에 반응한 후 인체가 스스로 재충전하도록 독려하기 때문인데, 높아진 코티솔 수치는 식욕을 증가시킨다. ③ 게다가 이런 스트레스로 유발된 식욕의 결과로 축적되는 지방의 종류는 일반적으로 다음 스트레스에 대응하기 위해 복부에 위치한다. ④ 운동은 코티솔 수치를 증가시키지만, 이런 단기간의 증가는 면역 기능, 기억력, 그리고 체중 감량에 유익하다. ⑤ 복부 지방의 주요 문제는 이런 유형의 지방이 또한 심장 질환, 당뇨병, 그리고 암과 매우 관련이 높다는 것이다.

09 ④ 윗글은 마지막 문장에서 설명한 것처럼, 어떠한 보충제도 인지 기능을 향상시키지 못했고, 종합 비타민의 복용이 치매의 치료에 아무런 효과가 없다는 연구 사실을 밝히고 있다. 그런데 아무런 효과가 없다는 내용과 달리, ④에서는 눈에 띄는 몇 가지가 있다고 반대로 설명하고 있으므로, 전체적인 글의 흐름과 어울리지 않는다.

- evaluate : 평가하다, 감정하다
- efficacy : 효과, 효능, 효험
- multivitamin : 종합 비타민
- cognitive : 인식의, 인지의
- decline : 감소, 하락, 쇠퇴
- elderly male : 남성 노인
- placebo : 플라시보, 속임약, 위약
- overall : 종합적인, 전체의
- verbal : 말의, 언어의, 구두의
- well-nourished : 영양 상태가 좋은
- supplementation : 보충함, 보충하는 것
- fatty acid : 지방산
- impairment : 장애, 결함, 손상
- moderate : 보통의, 중간의
- dementia : 치매
- optimal : 최적의, 최선의, 최상의
- stand out : 두드러지다, 눈에 쉽게 띄다
- intake : 섭취(량), 복용, 흡입
- treatment : 치료, 처치, 대우
- indicate : 가리키다, 지적하다, 나타내다, 보여주다

【해석】

한 연구는 5,947명의 노년층 남성들을 상대로 일일 종합 비타민의 효능이 인지 능력의 쇠퇴를 막을 수 있는지 평가했다. ① 12년간의 추적 끝에, 전반적인 인지 수행 능력과 언어 기억 능력에 있어서 종합 비타민 복용 그룹과 위약 복용 그룹 사이에 별다른 차이가 없었다. ② 연구원들은 영양 상태가 좋은 노년층 인구의 종합 비타민 보충제의 복용이 인지 능력의 쇠퇴를 막지 못했다고 결론을 내렸다. ③ 이런 결론은 가벼운 인지 장애 또는 보통의 가벼운 치매가 있는 사람에게 종합 비타민, 비타민 B, 비타민 E와 C, 그리고 오메가-3 지방산의 보충을 평가했던 몇몇 다른 연구들의 검토에서 더욱 지지를 받았다. ④ 모든 비타민들이 최상의 건강과 뇌 기능을 위해 필요했지만, 건강한 뇌를 위하여 무엇보다도 꼭 필요한 눈에 띄는 몇 가지가 있다. ⑤ 어떠한 보충제도 인지 기능을 향상시키지 못했고, 종합 비타민의 복용이 치매의 치료에 아무런 효과가 없다고 지적했다.

10 ③ 윗글의 마지막 문장에서 정상적인 수면 시간 동안 먹은 쥐들이 정상적인 식사 시간에 먹은 쥐들보다 학습 능력이 떨어진다고 설명하고 있다. 그러므로 쥐들의 실험을 통해 정상적인 수면 시간에 음식을 먹는 것이 인지 능력을 약화시킬 수 있음을 시사하고 있다.

- condition : 길들이다, 훈련시키다
- normal-schedule : 정상적인 일정
- peer : 또래, 친구, 동년배
- odd : 별난, 이상한, 특이한
- scary : 무서운, 겁나는
- misaligned : 어긋난, 정렬이 안 된
- severe : 엄한, 심각한
- deficit : 적자, 결손, 부족액
- previously : 미리, 사전에, 이전에
- jet lag : 시차증
- strengthening : 강화, 보강
- neural connection : 신경망

【해석】

한 실험에서, 두 무리의 쥐들은 어떤 특정 위치에서 두려움을 느끼도록 훈련받았고, 나중에 연구원들은 그 쥐들이 두려움을 나타내는지 보기 위해 그 위치로 돌려놓았다. 흥미롭게도 식사 일정이 정상적인 수면 시간으로 옮겨진 쥐들은 정상적인 일정의 쥐들보다 무서운 상황 속에서 두려움을 덜 느꼈는데, 비정상적인 식사와 수면 일정이 무서운 상황에 대한 동물의 기억에 영향을 미쳤음을 암시한 것이다. "일정이 어긋난 쥐들은 그 쥐들이 받은 훈련을 회상하는 데 심각한 결손을 보였다."고 Colwell이 말했다. 그의 연구 팀은 이전에 시차증이 인간과 쥐에 관한 연구 둘 다에서 기억력에 유사한 영향을 미친다는 사실을 발견했다. 그 연구들은 또한 뇌에서 학습의 척도인 신경 연결의 강화를 측정했다. 놀랄 것도 없이, 그들은 정상적인 수면 시간 동안 먹은 쥐들이 정상적인 식사 시간에 먹은 쥐들보다 덜 빠르게 배운다는 사실을 발견했다.

11 ⑤ increasing → increased

that절 이하에서 동명사 'dying'이 이끄는 'dying~stains'까지가 주어부에 해당되므로, 이어서 종속절 전체의 동사가 와야 한다. 종속절의 동사는 주절의 동사와 시제를 일치시켜 'increased'로 고쳐 써야 옳다.

【오답풀이】

① 앞의 'The textile'을 선행사로 하고, 'called'의 목적어로써 사물을 나타내는 목적격 관계대명사 'which'를 사용한 것은 문법상 적절하다.

② 앞의 'The origin'이 주어에 해당되므로, be 동사의 3인칭 단수 현재의 형태인 'is'를 사용한 것은 적합하다.

③ 부사 'quickly'는 앞의 동사 'went through'를 수식하고, 생략해도 문장 전체에 영향을 주지 않으므로 'quickly'를 사용한 것은 아무런 문제가 없다.

④ 글의 내용상 '너무 ~해서 ~하다'는 'so~that' 구문으로 사

용되었으므로, 문법적으로 이상이 없다.

어휘

- cotton cloth : 무명, 면직물
- sturdy : 튼튼한, 견고한
- textile : 직물, 옷감
- weaver : 직공, 방직공
- immigrant : 이민자, 이주민
- tailor : 재단사, 양복장이
- canvas : 캔버스 천, 화폭
- covered wagon : 포장마차
- stitch : 바느질하다, 꿰매다, 깁다
- stiff : 뻣뻣한, 뻑뻑한
- in demand : 수요가 많은
- denim : 데님(청바지를 만드는 데 쓰이는 보통 푸른색의 질긴 면직물)
- dye : 염색하다
- neutral-colored : 중간색의, 무채색의
- minimize : 최소화하다, 축소하다
- stain : 얼룩, 자국
- popularity : 인기

해석

청바지가 바지이기 전에, jean은 튼튼한 작업복을 만드는 데 사용했던 면직물이었다. 그 옷감은 이탈리아의 Genoa에서 생산되었는데, 프랑스 방직공들이 'jeans'란 단어의 어원인 Genes라고 불렀다. 하지만 청바지의 기원은 사실 미국으로 이민 온 재단사인 Levi Strauss의 이야기이다. 그가 1850년대 골드러시 동안 San Francisco에 도착했을 때, 그는 천막과 포장마차를 위한 캔버스 천을 팔았다. 현명한 관찰자로 그는 광부들이 바지를 빨리 갈아입는다는 사실을 알아차렸고, 그래서 Strauss는 캔버스 천 조각으로 바지를 만들었다. 비록 무겁고 뻣뻣했지만, 그 바지는 아주 잘 버텨서 Strauss는 재단사로서 일감이 많았다. 1860년대에, 그는 캔버스 천을 데님으로 교체했다. 그리고 Strauss는 흙 얼룩을 최소화하기 위해 무채색 데님 바지를 검푸른 색으로 염색하는 것이 매우 인기가 높음을 알았다.

12 ④ supported → are supported

해당 문장에서 'many of our beliefs'가 주어부이고, 동사는 수와 시제 그리고 태 등을 핵심 주어인 'many'에 일치시켜야 한다. 따라서 복수의 현재시제 그리고 태는 '우리들 믿음의 상당수가' 지지를 받는 것이므로 수동태를 사용해야 한다. 그러므로 'supported'를 'are supported'로 고쳐 써야 옳다.

오답풀이

① cause는 '~을 야기하다[초래하다]'는 뜻으로, cause + 목적어 + 목적보어(to 부정사)의 5형식 문장을 이끈다. 그러므로 목적보어인 'to question'을 사용한 것은 적절하다.

② 'them'은 앞의 'beliefs'를 받는 지시대명사로 옳게 사용되었다.

③ 문장의 주어인 'You'와 목적어가 동일인이므로, 재귀대명사 'yourself'를 사용한 것은 문법상 아무런 문제가 없다.

⑤ 뒤에 나오는 동사 'have believed'의 목적어가 없고 선행사도 없으므로, 선행사를 포함한 관계대명사 'what'을 사용한 것은 아무런 문제가 없다.

어휘

- trigger : 촉발시키다, 유발시키다
- reference : 참조, 참고
- cognitive table : 인지 도표
- absolute : 절대적인, 완전한, 순
- certainty : 확실한 것, 확실성
- work out (일이) 잘 풀리다, 좋게 진행되다
- obviously : 확실히, 분명히
- tremendously : 엄청나게, 굉장히
- empower : 권한을 주다, 할 수 있게 하다
- validity : 유효성, 타당성
- blindly : 맹목적으로, 무턱대고
- scrutinize : 세심히 파고들다, 면밀히 조사[검토]하다
- unconsciously : 무의식적으로, 무심코
- presupposition : 예상, 상정, 추정

해석

새로운 경험은 우리의 믿음에 의문을 야기할 경우에만 변화를 촉발시킨다. 기억하라, 우리가 무언가를 믿을 때마다 어떤 식으로든 우리는 그것에 더 이상 의문을 갖지 않는다. 우리가 우리의 믿음에 솔직하게 의문을 갖기 시작하는 순간, 우리는 더 이상 그 믿음에 대해 전혀 확신을 느끼지 못한다. 우리는 인지 테이블의 참고 다리를 흔들기 시작할 것이고, 결과적으로 절대적인 확실성 대한 우리의 감정을 상실하기 시작한다. 어떤 일을 하는데 당신의 능력을 의심해 본 적이 있는가? 어떻게 했는가? 여러분은 아마도 자신에게 "일이 잘 안 되면 어떡하지?"와 같은 쓸데없는 질문을 했을 것이다. 그러나 만일 우리가 단지 맹목적으로 받아들였을지 모를 믿음에 대한 타당성을 조사하는 데 그 질문들을 사용한다면 그것들은 분명히 엄청난 힘이 될 수 있다. 사실 우리들 믿음의 상당수가 그 당시 질문하지 못했던 다른 질문들로부터 받아 온 정보에 의해 지지를 받았다. 만일 그것들을 면밀히 조사한다면, 우리가 수년 동안 무의식적으로 믿어왔던 것이 잘못된 예상을 근거로 했을지도 모른다는 사실을 발견할 수도 있다.

13 ① (A) how / what

'how'는 의문부사이고 'what'은 의문대명사인데, 뒤에 완전한 문장이 왔으므로 의문부사 'how'를 사용하는 것이 적절하다.

(B) do / are

앞의 문장 내용과 동일한 내용이 반복될 때, '~도 또한 그렇다'의 의미로 'so + 동사 + 주어'의 도치구문을 사용한다. 앞 문장의 동사가 일반 동사 'differ'이므로 대동사 'do'를 사용하는 것이 적절하다.

(C) Understanding / Understand

뒤의 be 동사 'is'가 문장 전체의 동사이고 앞 문장 전체가 주어부이므로, 동명사 'Understanding'을 사용하는 것이 적절하다.

어휘

- verbally : 말로, 구두로, 언어적으로
- nonverbally : 말로 할 수 없이, 비언어적으로
- take it for granted ~을 당연한 것으로 여기다
- adulthood : 성인, 성년
- hesitate : 주저하다, 망설이다
- when it comes to : ~에 대해서라면, ~에 관해서라면
- mistakenly : 잘못하여, 실수로
- appreciate : 인정하다, 고마워하다

해석

가장 넓은 의미에서의 의사소통은 언어적으로(언어를 통한) 그리고 비언어적으로 둘 다 동시에 일어난다. 하지만 비언어적 행동이 중요함에도 불구하고, 우리는 흔히 그것들을 당연한 것으로 여긴다. 비록 비언어적 메시지와 신호를 보내고 받는 방법에 관해 공식적인 훈련을 받지는 않지만, 성인이 될 때쯤 그것에 매우 능숙해져서 무의식적으로 그리고 저절로 그렇게 행동한다. 비언어적 행동들은 다른 언어들만큼이나 많다. 구두 언어가 나라마다 다른 것처럼, 비언어적 언어도 또한 그렇다. 구두 언어 간의 차이점을 알고 있기 때문에, 우리는 다른 언어들을 이해하는데 도움이 되는 사전과 다른 자원을 활용하는 것을 망설이지 않는다. 그러나 비언어적 언어에 관해서라면, 흔히 우리의 의사소통 체계가 비언어적으로 모두 똑같을 거라고 잘못 가정한다. 비언어적 행동에 관한 문화적 차이를 이해하는 것은 의사소통의 문화적 차이를 진정으로 인정하는 과정의 첫 단계이다.

14 ① (A) sending / sent

하수관을 통해 배설물을 하수 처리 공장으로 보내는 것이므로, 능동의 의미인 현재분사 'sending'을 사용하는 것이 적절하다.

(B) where / which

앞의 'industrial-commercial cities'를 선행사로 하는 관계사가 와야 하는 데, 뒤에 완전한 문장이 왔으므로 장소를 나타내는 관계부사 'where'를 사용하는 것이 적절하다.

(C) build / built

앞의 'most cities'를 공통 주어로 하고 등위 접속사 'and'에 의해 연결되는 'A and B'의 구조이므로, 앞의 동사 'created'에 맞추어 과거시제의 동사 'built'를 사용하는 것이 적절하다.

어휘

- water-based toilet : 수세식 화장실
- extensive : 아주 넓은, 대규모의
- sewage pipe : 하수[배출]관
- outflow : 흘러나옴, 유출, 분출
- sewage processing plant : 하수 처리 공장
- cholera : 콜레라
- outbreak : 발생, 발발
- devastate : 완전히 파괴하다, 휩쓸다
- urban population : 도시 인구
- industrial-commercial : 상공업의
- untreated : 처리되지 않은, 치료를 받지 않는
- human waste : 사람의 배설물
- dump : 버리다, 비우다
- contaminate : 오염시키다
- ground water : 지하수
- water supply : 상수도
- out break : 발생, 발발
- faecal-contaminated : 배설물로 오염된
- reservoir : 저수지, 급수장
- filter out : ~을 걸러내다

해석

선진 세계에서 19세기 중반부터 수세식 화장실의 폭넓은 사용은 하수 처리 공장으로 배설물을 보내는 하수관의 광범위한 연결 시스템이 도시에 건설되었다는 것을 의미했다. 이 시스템은 19세기 초 성장하는 상공업 도시의 많은 도시민을 휩쓸었던 콜레라의 발생을 해결하는 데 일조했는데, 그곳에서 처리되지 않은 사람의 배설물은 단지 인근 지역의 강에 버려지고 지하수와 지역 상수를 오염시켰다. 비록 질병의 발생과 배설물로 오염된 상수도 사이의 관계를 구축하는 데 시간이 걸렸지만, 선진 세계의 대부분의 도시들은 저수지로부터 광범위한 상수도 시스템을 구축했고 건물에 화장실의 수가 증가하는 흐름에 맞추어 별도의 하수 시스템을 건설했는데, 그것은 유해한 물질을 걸러내는 하수 처리 시스템의 발전을 가져왔다.

정답 및 해설

15　② 제조 식품의 생산자들이 농부들에 비해 유리한 점은 감자 칩의 생산에서 보듯 아무 설탕이나 기름 혹은 녹말 등의 재료를 가격에 따라 대체하여 사용할 수 있기 때문이다. 그러므로 빈칸에는 ②의 'substitution(대체)'이 들어가는 것이 적합하다.

【오답풀이】

① integration(통합)

③ conservation(보존)

④ simplification(단순화)

⑤ overconsumption(과소비)

【어휘】

• manufactured food : 생산 식품, 제조 식품

• have an advantage over : ~보다 유리하다

• flexibility : 구부리기 쉬움, 유연성

• ingredient : 재료, 원료, 성분

• source : 얻다, 공급자를 찾다

• sweetener : 감미료

• derive from : ~에서 유래하다, 파생하다

• sugarcane plant : 사탕수수 농장

• starch : 탄수화물, 녹말 (가루)

• wheat : 밀

• grain : 곡물, 낟알

• illustrate : 설명하다, 도해[삽화]를 넣다

• disadvantaged : 불리한, 불우한

• within : (특정한 기간) 이내에

• agrofood : 농식품

【해석】

제조 식품의 생산자들은 그들이 농장 생산량을 구매하고 어떤 재료를 사용하고 어디서 구할지에 대해 유연성이 있기 때문에 농부보다 유리하다. 예를 들어, 제조 식품은 감미료를 필요로 하지만, 반드시 사탕수수 농장에서 나온 설탕일 필요는 없다. 기름을 필요로 하지만, 꼭 옥수수로부터 나온 기름일 필요는 없다. 녹말을 필요로 하지만, 감자나 밀 혹은 많은 다른 곡식들로부터 얻을 수 있다. 감자 칩의 생산은 이런 대체 효과의 좋은 예를 보여준다. 즉, 생산자는 생산 시기에 가장 값이 싼 아무 기름에나 칩을 튀길 수 있다. 이것은 왜 농부들이 흔히 농식품 체계에서 불리한 위치에 있는지를 설명한다.

16　① 윗글은 이식된 칩을 이용하여 쥐들의 기억력을 재생시키는 실험 과정에 대해 설명하고 있다. 윗글의 마지막 문장에서 이 기술을 사용하여 쥐들의 기억력이 완전히 회복될 수 있었다고 했으므로, ①의 'long-term memory regeneration(장기간의 기억 재생)'이 빈칸에 들어갈 말로 적합하다.

【오답풀이】

② 기억 용량의 증가

③ 선별적 기억의 왜곡

④ 외상 기억의 삭제

⑤ 메모리 변환 속도의 강화

【어휘】

• implant : 심다, 이식하다

• hippocampus : (대뇌 측두엽의) 해마

• transform : 변형시키다, 변환시키다

• an extended period of time : 장기간 동안

• remove : 제거하다, 없애다

• section : 부분, 부문, 구획

• reload : 재장전하다, 다시 집어넣다

• artificially : 인위적으로, 인공적으로

• regeneration : 재생, 갱생, 부활

• memory capacity : 기억 용량

• selective : 선택적인, 선별적인

• distortion : 왜곡, 곡해, 일그러짐

• deletion : 삭제, 말소

• traumatic : 외상 기억

• enhancement : 강화, 증대, 상승

【해석】

Theodore Berger는 쥐들의 손상된 해마 부위를 대체하기 위해 이식된 칩을 이용함으로써 장기간의 기억 재생에 성공을 거두었다. Southern California 대학의 Berger와 그의 팀은 장기간 동안 이 동물들의 해마 속에 저장되어 있던 컴퓨터 코드 메모리로 기록하고 변환시키는 데 성공했다. 그들은 쥐들이 기억 작업을 수행하도록 했다. 그리고 나서 다운로드하고 그 작업 메모리를 디지털 코드로 변환시켰다. 나중에 그들은 이 메모리들이 있었던 쥐들의 해마 부분을 제거하고 특별한 컴퓨터 칩으로 뇌의 일부를 대체했는데, 그들은 인공적으로 저장된 메모리를 다시 집어넣었다. 그들은 이 기술을 사용하여 쥐들의 기억력이 완전히 회복될 수 있음을 알아냈다.

17　② 윗글은 외국인들이 적어도 두 가지 이유에 있어서 암암리에 질병의 확산 가능성을 암시하는 대상이 되고 있다고 설명하고 있다. 그러므로 빈칸에는 병의 전염성과 관련된 ②의 'to pose the threat of infection(전염병의 위협이 되는)'이 들어가는 것이 적합하다.

【오답풀이】

① 현지 주민들을 고립시키는

③ 새로운 기술을 전파하는

④ 지역 경제에 해로운

⑤ 현지 위생 기준에 부합된

어휘

- foreign-ness : 외래성, 외국풍, 이질성
- implicitly : 암암리에, 함축적으로, 내재하여
- exotic : 외국의, 이국적인
- exposure : 노출, 폭로
- germ : 세균, 미생물
- contagious : 전염성의, 전염되는
- introduce : (어떤 지역에 동물·식물·질병을 처음으로) 전하다[들여오다]
- outsider : 국외자, 외부인, 이방인
- be ignorant of : ~을 모르다
- norm : 표준, 규범
- barrier : 장벽, 장애물
- transmission : 전염, 전파, 전송
- pertaining to : ~에 관계된[속하는]
- hygiene : 위생
- food-preparation : 취사, 음식 준비
- violate : 위반하다, 어기다
- outgroup : 외집단
- status : 신분, 지위
- perceive : 감지하다, 인지하다, 여기다
- isolate : 격리하다, 고립시키다
- infection : 감염, 전염병
- novel : 새로운, 신기한, 참신한

해석

왜 '외래성'에 대한 주관적 의미가 암암리에 질병의 확산 가능성을 암시하는지 적어도 두 가지 이유가 있다. 첫째, 역사적으로 외국 사람들과의 접촉은 외부 세균들에 대한 노출을 증가시켰고, 그 세균들이 현지 주민들에게 전해졌을 때 특히 전염되는 경향이 있었다. 둘째, 외부인들은 흔히 세균 전염의 장벽 역할을 했던 현지의 행동 규범(예를 들면, 위생과 취사와 관계된 규범)을 잘 모른다. 결과적으로, 그들은 이런 규범들을 더욱 위반하기 쉬울 것이고, 그로 인해 현지 주민 내부의 세균 전염의 위험성을 증가시킨다. 따라서 외부 집단이라는 신분에 의해 암시되는 다른 위험들 외에, 사람들은 주관적으로 외국인이 암암리에 전염병의 위협이 된다고 판단하게 된다.

18 ① 윗글은 프랑스인보다 더 프랑스 사람다운 Josephine Baker와 유태인 태생으로 영국의 보수당 총수가 된 Benjamin Disraeli를 통해 이주한 나라의 문화에 적응한 사례를 보여주고 있다. 그러므로 빈칸에는 이방인으로서 이주한 나라의 문화에 적응하는 방법에 대해 설명한 ①의 'how deeply you prefer their tastes and customs to your own(얼마나 깊이 그들의 취향과 관습을 자신의 것보다 선

호하는지)'이 들어가는 것이 적합하다.

오답풀이

② 당신이 얼마나 오해를 받고 있는 지 불평하지 않는 것
③ 당신이 뚜렷한 취향, 의견, 경험들을 소유하고 있다는 것
④ 당신이 숭고하고 너그러운 행동을 하려고 얼마나 열심인 지
⑤ 자신의 정체를 기꺼이 밝히는 것

어휘

- revue : 익살극, 시사 풍자극
- exoticism : 이국정서, 이국풍
- sensation : 돌풍, 선풍, 센세이션
- seduce : 꾀다, 유혹하다
- for good : 영원히, 영구히
- stylish : 유행을 따른, 멋진, 우아한
- seductive : 유혹[매혹/고혹]적인
- adopt : 쓰다, 채택하다, 입양하다
- feature : 특색, 특징
- provincial : 주의, 지방의
- Conservative Party : 보수당
- turn it to advantage : 이용하다
- distinct : 뚜렷한, 분명한
- noble : 숭고한, 고귀한
- charitable : 자선을 베푸는, 너그러운
- deed : 행위, 행동
- disclose : 밝히다, 폭로하다, 드러내다
- identity : 신원, 신분, 정체

해석

1925년에 모두가 흑인으로 구성된 익살극의 일부로 Josephine Baker가 파리로 이동했을 때, 그녀의 이국정서는 하룻밤에 선풍적인 인기를 끌었다. 그러나 Baker는 그녀에 대한 프랑스인들의 관심이 다른 누군가에게 매우 빠르게 전달되는 것을 느꼈다. 그들을 영원히 유혹하기 위해, 그녀는 프랑스어를 배웠고 프랑스어로 노래를 부르기 시작했다. 그녀는 마치 미국의 생활방식보다 프랑스의 생활방식을 더 좋아한다고 말하듯이, 멋진 프랑스 여인처럼 옷을 입고 행동하기 시작했다. 국가들도 사람들과 마찬가지인데, 국가들은 다른 관습에 위협을 느낀다. 이방인이 자신들의 방식에 적응하는 것을 보는 것은 어떤 민족에게는 종종 매우 매혹적이다. Benjamin Disraeli는 영국에서 태어나 평생 동안 살았지만, 그는 태생이 유태인이었고 외모가 이국적이었으며 영국 지방에서는 그를 이방인으로 생각했다. 그러나 그의 태도와 취향은 영국인보다 더 영국적이었고, 이것은 그의 매력의 일부였으며 보수당의 당수가 됨으로써 입증하였다. 당신이 이방인이라면, 얼마나 깊이 그들의 취향과 관습을 자신의 것보다 선호하는지 그 집단에게 보여주는 식으로 그것을 이용해라.

19 ③ 글의 서두에 보호자 역할과 개인의 역할에 균형을 유지해야만 한다고 서술되어 있고, 마지막 문장에서도 육아가 자기희생을 필요로 하지만, 당신과 가족을 위한 건강한 균형을 얻으려고 노력해야 한다고 서술되어 있다. 그러므로 "부모는 자녀 양육과 자신의 삶 사이에서 균형을 잡아야 한다."는 ③의 내용이 필자가 주장하는 바이다.

어휘

- caregiver : 돌보는 사람, 보호자
- sacrifice : 희생하다
- socialize with : ~와 사귀다[교제하다]
- stimulated : 고무된, 자극된
- maintain : 유지하다, 지탱하다
- adulthood : 성인, 성년
- martyr : 순교자
- parenthood : 부모임, 어버이임
- shell : 껍데기, 겉모습
- parenting : 육아
- strive for : ~을 얻으려고 노력하다

해석

가족의 모든 구성원은 전체 가족의 일부이자 개인이다. 부모로써, 필요에 따라 보호자 역할과 개인의 역할에 균형을 유지해야만 한다. 만일 성인들과 교제하지 않고, 지적으로 자극을 받지 못하고, 혹은 건강한 신체와 정신을 유지하지 못한 채 가족에게 모든 시간과 에너지를 희생한다면, 가족 전체가 고생할 것이다. 기억하라. 당신은 자녀들에게 어른의 모델이다. 즉, 순교자를 어버이의 모델로 삼지 마라. 공허하고 자기희생적인 모습이 그들이 보기를 원하는 롤 모델은 아니다. 물론 매일같이 모두가 완벽하게 만족하기는 힘들지만, 불가능한 것은 아니다. 육아가 보통 어느 정도의 자기희생을 필요로 하지만, 당신과 가족을 위한 건강한 균형을 얻으려고 노력해야 한다.

20 ③ (A) hide
다음 문장에서 어떤 개념의 한 측면에 집중하도록 하면서 다른 측면의 개념에 집중하지 못하게 할 수 있다는 의미는 '한 측면만 보고 다른 측면은 보지 못한다.'는 뜻이므로 'hide(숨기다)'가 들어가는 것이 가장 적합하다.
(B) preoccupied with
상대방과의 논쟁을 상호 이해가 아닌 싸움이라는 측면에서 볼 때는 협력적인 면을 찾을 수 없다고 했으므로, 싸움에 몰두한다는 의미인 'preoccupied with(집착하는)'가 들어가는 것이 가장 적합하다.

오답풀이

① 숨기다 ...... 무관심한
② 폭로하다 ...... 열중한
③ 숨기다 ...... 집착하는
④ 폭로하다 ...... 집착하는
⑤ 영향을 미치다 ...... 무관심한

어휘

- systematicity : 조직성
- in terms of : ~면에서, ~에 관하여
- metaphorical : 은유의, 비유의
- be inconsistent with : ~와 일치하지 않다, 상반되다, 모순되다
- metaphor : 은유, 비유
- in the midst of : ~중에, ~가운데의
- opponent : 상대, 반대자
- lose sight of : ~을 잃다, 안보이다
- cooperative : 협력[협동]하는
- commodity : 상품, 물품, 원자재
- reveal : 드러내다, 폭로하다
- preoccupied with : ~에 집착하는

해석

우리가 어떤 개념의 한 측면을 다른 측면(예를 들면, 주장의 한 측면을 싸움이라는 측면에서 이해하는 것)에서 이해하도록 하는 바로 그 조직성은 그 개념의 다른 측면을 필연적으로 (A) 숨길 것이다. 우리가 어떤 개념의 한 측면(예를 들어 논쟁의 전투적 측면)에 집중하도록 하면서, 비유적 개념은 그 비유와 일치하지 않는 다른 측면의 개념에 집중하지 못하게 할 수 있다. 예를 들면 열띤 논쟁 중에, 우리가 상대편의 입장을 공격하고 우리 자신의 입장을 방어하려고 할 때, 논쟁의 협력적인 측면을 보지 못할 수도 있다. 당신과 논쟁하는 누군가가 상호간의 이해를 달성하려는 노력으로 그 사람의 시간과 귀중한 물품을 제공하면 보일 수 있다. 그러나 우리가 싸움이라는 측면에 (B) 집착할 때, 우리는 흔히 협력적인 측면을 보지 못한다.

21 ① (A) On the other hand
앞에서는 긍정적인(positive) 신체 이미지에 대해 설명하고 있고, 뒤에서는 상반되는 내용인 부정적인(negative) 신체 이미지에 대해 설명하고 있으므로, 'On the other hand(한 편으로, 반면에)'가 들어가는 것이 적합하다.
(B) therefore
"긍정적인 신체 이미지를 만드는 것은 결코 끝나지 않는 과정이다."라는 말은 한 때는 부정적인 신체 이미지를 가질 수도 있고 다른 한 때는 긍정적인 신체 이미지를 가질 수도 있다고 말한 앞 문장의 결과에 해당되므로, 'therefore(따라서)'가 들어가는 것이 적합하다.

어휘

- body image : 신체상, 신체 이미지
- be involved in : ~에 개입되다, 관계되다
- athletic activity : 체육[운동] 활동
- positive : 긍정적인, 낙관적인
- confidence : 자신(감), 신뢰, 비밀
- thoughtless : 무심한, 경솔한, 부주의한
- evolve : 발전하다, 진전하다
- adjust : 조정[조절]하다, 적응하다
- mature : 성숙한, 분별 있는

해석

신체 이미지는 하룻밤에 만들어지지 않는다. 오히려 시간이 지나면서 천천히 발달하며, 많은 것들이 그것에 영향을 미친다. 예를 들면 수년간 스포츠를 하고 체육 활동에 참여하는 것은 그 사람의 신체와 체력에 자신감을 줌으로써 긍정적인 신체 이미지를 만드는데 도움을 줄 수 있다. (A) 반면에, 신체에 관해 무심하고 불친절한 평을 듣는 것은 신체 이미지에 장기간의 부정적인 영향을 미칠 수 있다. 더욱이 신체 이미지는 평생에 걸쳐 계속해서 발전하고 변한다. 대부분의 사람들은 육체적으로, 정신적으로, 감성적으로 나이가 들고 성숙함에 따라 그들의 신체 이미지를 조절한다. 당신은 한 때는 부정적인 신체 이미지를 가질 수도 있고 다른 한 때는 긍정적인 신체 이미지를 가질 수도 있다. (B) 따라서 긍정적인 신체 이미지를 만드는 것은 결코 끝나지 않는 과정이다.

22 ④ emerge → immerge

ADHD에 걸린 아이들의 뇌는 정상적인 아이들보다 상당히 느린 속도로 발달하지만, 다행히도 사춘기가 끝날 무렵에 전두엽의 크기가 정상이 된다고 했으므로, 아이들의 행동 장애가 거의 같은 시기에 'emerge(나타나는)'것이 아니라 '사라진다(immerge)'고 해야 옳다.

어휘

- the National Institute of Mental Health : 국립정신건강연구원
- uncover : 알아내다, 밝혀내다
- deficit : 적자, 결손, 장애
- ADHD : 주의력 결핍 및 과잉 행동 장애(Attention Deficit Hyperactivity Disorder)
- disorder : 장애, 이상
- turn out : ~인 것으로 드러나다[밝혀지다]
- developmental problem : 발달 장애
- significantly : 상당히, 크게
- lag : 지연, 지체, 뒤떨어짐
- obvious : 분명한, 명확한
- prefrontal cortex : (뇌의) 전전두엽 피질

- literally : 문자[말] 그대로
- muscle : 근육, 근력, 힘
- tempting : 유혹하는, 구미가 당기는, 솔깃한
- stimuli : 자극(제)(stimulus의 복수형)
- adolescence : 사춘기, 청소년기
- frontal lobes : 전두엽
- coincidence : 우연의 일치, 동시 발생
- behavioral problem : 행동 장애
- emerge : 나타나다, 출현하다
- developmental lag : 발달 지체[지연]
- counter : 반박[논박]하다, 대응하다
- urge : 욕구, 충동
- compulsion : 강박, 강제, 충동
- marshmallow : 마시멜로

해석

2007년 11월에, 국립정신건강연구원과 McGill 대학 출신의 연구 팀이 ADHD 뇌의 특정 장애를 밝혀냈다고 발표했다. 그 장애는 주로 발달상의 장애인 것으로 드러났는데, 종종 ADHD에 걸린 아이들의 뇌는 정상적인 아이들보다 상당히 느린 속도로 발달한다. 이러한 지체는 전전두엽 피질에서 가장 분명하게 나타났는데, 아이들이 말 그대로 구미가 당기는 자극을 참는 데 필요한 정신 근육이 부족한 것을 의미했다. 하지만 다행인 것은 뇌가 항상 '느린 시작'으로부터 회복한다는 것이다. 사춘기가 끝날 무렵에, 이 아이들의 전두엽은 정상적인 크기에 이른다. 아이들의 행동 장애가 거의 같은 시기에 나타나기(→ 사라지기) 시작하는 것은 우연의 일치가 아니다. 발달 장애를 가지고 있던 아이들은 마침내 그들의 욕구와 충동에 대응할 수 있었다. 아이들은 구미가 당기는 마시멜로를 보고도 기다리는 편이 더 낫다고 결정할 수 있다.

23 ⑤ up-to-date → out-of-date

제1차 세계대전 동안 항공과 참호 전투의 등장으로 군인과 예술가들의 협업을 통한 위장 전투복의 기술이 발전했다고 설명하고 있으므로, 전쟁 초기에 입었던 전통적인 군복은 'up-to-date(최신식)'이 아니라 'out-of-date(구식)'으로 보이기 시작했다가 옳다.

어휘

- military : 군사의, 무력의
- represent : 대표[대신]하다, 나타내다
- loyalty : 충성심
- camouflage : 위장, 변장, 속임수
- bring up : (화제를) 꺼내다, 불러일으키다
- lawmaker : 입법자
- emergency : 비상사태, 위급한 상황

- war-spending bill : 전쟁 예산
- fund : 자금[기금]을 대다
- troop : 병력, 군대, 부대
- evidently : 분명히, 명확히
- muddy : 진창인, 진흙투성이인
- mountainous terrain : 산악 지형
- emergence : 출현, 등장, 발생
- aerial : 항공기에 의한, 공중의
- trench : 참호, 도랑
- warfare : 전투, 전쟁
- give rise to : 낳다, 일으키다
- strategy : 전략, 계획
- fruitful : 생산적인, 유익한
- collaboration : 공동 작업, 협력, 협업
- concealing : 은폐
- coloration : (생물의) 천연색
- launch : 시작하다, 착수하다
- bullet : 총알, 탄환
- all directions : 사방(팔방)에서
- up-to-date : 최신의, 최신식의
- downright : 순전한, 완전한

해석

옷이 사람을 만든다고 하는데, 군대보다 이 말이 사실인 곳은 없다. 군복은 충성심부터 직함과 계급에 이르는 모든 것을 나타낸다. 그리고 위장에 관한 한, 그것은 삶과 죽음의 문제이다. - 여러 가지 것들 중에서, 아프가니스탄에 주둔한 병력을 위한 70,000벌의 새 군복에 쓰일 1,060억 달러의 긴급 전쟁 예산을 통과시킬 준비를 하면서 어떤 쟁점이 미국 입법자에 의해 부각되었다. 분명히 그 나라의 진흙투성이의 산악 지형은 바그다드와 같은 먼지투성이의 사막 도시를 위해 설계된 '보편적인 위장 패턴'과 어울리지 않는다. 제1차 세계대전 동안 항공과 참호 전투의 등장은 위장 전투복의 전략과 기술을 낳았고, 군인들, 예술가들 그리고 Abbot Thayer와 같은 자연주의자들 사이에서 생산적인 협업을 일으켰는데, 그가 1909년에 저술한 「동물 왕국의 은폐색」은 새롭게 창설된 미군 위장 디자이너들의 부대에게 필독서가 되었다. 군인들은 사방에서 날아오는 폭탄과 총알을 피해야만 했으므로, 전쟁 초기에 입었던 전통적이고 영광스러운 군복은 아주 위험하지는 않지만, 최신식(→ 구식)으로 보이기 시작했다.

24 ③ 글의 서두에서 한 사람의 행복을 다른 사람과 비교하는 것은 무의미하며, 행복은 사람마다 다르게 경험되는 별개의 것을 의미한다고 했으므로, ③의 "Happiness Is Tailored to Each Person(행복은 개개인에 맞게 재단된다.)"가 윗글의

제목으로 가장 적절하다.

오답풀이

① 자기만족의 함정에 빠지지 마라.
② 주관성은 객관성에서 온다.
④ 타인의 시각으로 네 자신을 평가하라.
⑤ 더 많은 것을 이룰수록, 더 행복해질 것이다.

어휘

- when it comes to : ~에 대해서[관해서]라면, ~에 관한 한
- comparison : 비교, 비유
- phenomenon : 현상
- disparity : 차이, 격차
- requirement : 필요(한 것), 필요조건, 요건
- look over : 대충 훑어보다, 살펴보다
- simply put : 간단히 말해서
- direct path : 직통로
- appreciate : 인정하다, 감사하다
- purport : 주장하다, 칭하다
- in relation to : ~에 관하여, ~와 비교하여
- clarity : 명확하게 하다, 분명히 말하다
- priority : 우선 사항, 우선권
- tailor : 맞추다, 조정하다
- assess : 재다, 평가하다

해석

행복에 관해서라면, 비교가 된다 하더라도 거의 도움이 되지 않는다. 행복은 주관적인 현상이다. 즉, 모든 사람에게 다르게 경험되며 사람 각자마다 별개의 것을 의미한다. 갑에게는 약이 되는 것이 을에게는 독이 된다는 속담처럼, 우리의 욕구와 욕망은 다양해서 어떤 사람에게 행복한 것이 다른 사람에게는 똑같은 영향을 주지 않을 수도 있다. 비록 우리들 대부분이 개인적인 필요조건의 차이를 알지만, 이웃들이 소유하고 있는 것을 보고 우리도 또한 그것이 필요하다고 생각하면서 울타리 너머 함정에 빠지기 쉽다. 간단히 말해서, 이것은 부질없으며 대개 불행의 지름길이다. 가장 행복한 사람들은 그들이 소유한 것에 감사하며 그들이 덜 가진 것에 그다지 관심을 갖지 않는다고 연구에서 보여준다. 행복에 관한 장기간의 연구는 그것을 분명히 보여주는데, 행복한 사람들은 다른 사람들과 비교하여 자신을 판단하기보다는 그들에게 중요한 것이 무엇인지 명확히 하고 나서 그들이 우선적으로 달성하고 완수하려는 것에 집중한다.

25 ④ 글의 서두에서 나트륨의 주요 공급원인 소금을 과잉 섭취하게 되면 뇌졸중이나 심근경색의 원인이 될 뿐만 아니라 지나친 나트륨의 섭취는 뼈에도 또한 해롭다고 서술되어 있다. 그러므로 윗글의 제목으로 ④의 'Bone Weakening:

Another Threat of Excessive Sodium Intake(뼈의 약화 : 과다한 나트륨 섭취로 인한 또 다른 위협)'이 가장 적절하다.

오답풀이

① 노화가 골다공증에 미치는 중대한 영향
② 체중 감량과 뼈의 약화와의 관계
③ 소변을 통한 나트륨의 비정상적인 배출 원인
⑤ 균형 잡힌 칼슘 : 건강한 심장의 새로운 지름길

어휘

- sodium : 나트륨
- cardiovascular disease : 심장혈관계 질병, 심장 혈관 질환
- stroke : 뇌졸증
- heart attack : 심근경색, 심장마비
- intake : 섭취, 흡입
- calcium : 칼슘
- urination : 배뇨, 방뇨, 용변
- trigger : 촉발[유발]시키다, 작동시키다
- osteoclast : 파골 세포, 용골 세포
- reduction : 축소, 감소, 쇠퇴
- diet : 식단, 식습관, 다이어트
- bone–thinning disease : 골다공증
- osteoporosis : 골다공증
- hip bone density : 골반뼈 밀도
- urinary : 소변[오줌]의, 비뇨기의
- excretion : 배설, 배출, 분비
- excessive : 과다한, 지나친
- shortcut : 지름길, 손쉬운 방법

해석

많은 사람들이 나트륨의 주요 공급원인 소금을 과잉 섭취하면 뇌졸중 또는 심근경색을 포함한 심장 혈관 질환의 중요한 원인이 된다고 알고 있다. 하지만 지나친 나트륨 섭취는 또한 뼈에도 해롭다는 사실을 알고 있는 사람들은 많지 않다. 배뇨를 통해 인체가 빼앗기는 칼슘의 양은 섭취하는 소금의 양에 따라 증가한다. 혈중 칼슘 수치가 낮아 유발되는 파골 세포는 칼슘을 혈중에 방출하기 위해 뼈를 파괴하며, 잠재적으로 뼈의 부피 감소의 원인이 된다. 그래서 고염도의 식단은 골다공증으로 알려진 뼈가 야위는 질환 같은 원치 않는 부작용이 생길 수 있다. 예를 들면 2009년 노인 여성에 관한 연구에 따르면, 그 연구를 시작한 시점에서 2년간에 걸친 골반뼈 밀도의 손실은 24시간 동안 소변의 나트륨 배출과 관련되어 있으며, 골소실과의 관계는 칼슘 섭취의 관계만큼이나 강했음을 보여준다. 다른 연구에서는 나트륨 섭취를 줄이는 것이 칼슘의 균형을 유지하는 데 도움이 되며, 소금을 적게 먹는 것이 노화로 인해 뼈에서 칼슘이 빠져나가는 것을 늦출 수 있다고 제안했다.

26 ⑤ 스웨덴 영화감독인 Ingmar Bergman은 감독 초기에는 출연진과 제작진과의 잦은 마찰로 불화가 심했지만, 스웨덴에서 가장 훌륭한 촬영감독, 편집자, 미술 감독, 그리고 배우들과 한 팀이 된 후 그런 불화가 줄어들고 출연진과 제작진에 맡기게 되었다는 내용이다. 그러므로 주어진 글은 ⑤에 위치하는 것이 가장 적합하다.

어휘

- rein : 고삐, 통제
- bring to life : ~에 활기[생기]를 불어넣다
- film director : 영화감독
- overwhelm : 압도하다, 제압하다, 괴롭히다, 위축시키다
- frustration : 불만, 좌절감
- demanding : 부담이 큰, 힘든
- immense : 엄청난, 어마어마한
- scold : 야단치다, 꾸짖다
- cast : 출연자들, 배역진
- crew : 승무원, 제작진
- stew : 생각하다, 마음 졸이다
- resentment : 분함, 억울함, 분개
- dictatorial : 독재의, 군림하는
- obedient : 순종의, 복종의
- automaton : 자동 장치, 작은 로봇
- put together : 조립하다, 준비하다

해석

그것은 명령의 고삐를 느슨하게 했다. Max von Sydow와 같은 배우들과 함께, 그는 마음속에 있던 것을 단지 제안하고 위대한 배우가 그의 생각에 활력을 불어넣는 것을 지켜볼 수 있었다.

그의 경력 초기에, 위대한 스웨덴 영화감독인 Ingmar Bergman은 자주 불만으로 가득했다. (①) 그는 본인이 만들고 싶었던 영화에 대한 비전이 있었지만, 감독이 되는 일은 너무 부담이 크고 압박이 엄청나서 소리치며 명령하거나 자기가 원하는 대로 하지 않는다고 공격을 퍼부으며 그의 출연진과 제작진들을 질책하곤 했다. (②) 어떤 이들은 그의 독단적인 태도에 분개하며 마음을 졸였고, 다른 이들은 순종적인 자동기계가 되었다. (③) 거의 모든 새 영화에서 Bergman은 새로운 출연진과 제작진과 시작해야만 했고, 이것은 단지 상황을 더욱 안 좋게 만들었다. (④) 그러나 마침내 그의 높은 수준을 함께 하고 그가 신뢰하는 스웨덴에서 가장 훌륭한 촬영감독, 편집자, 미술 감독, 그리고 배우들과 한 팀이 되었다. (⑤) 위대한 통제는 이제 놓아버리는 것에서 나올 수 있었다.

27 ③ 주어진 문장이 'Yet(그러나)'으로 시작하므로 앞 문장과 반대되는 내용에 위치해야 한다. 그러므로 지구촌 경제에 활기를 불어넣는 국제무역이 합당하며 가치가 있다는 내용과 미국이 멕시코의 토마토 수입을 제한한 사례가 상반되므로 그 사이인 ③에 위치하는 것이 가장 적절하다.

어휘

- restrict : 제한하다, 한정하다
- firm : 상사, 상회, 회사
- contribute to : ~에 기여하다, 공헌하다
- volume : 용적, 용량, 부피
- fuel : 연료를 공급하다, ~에 활기를 불어넣다
- theoretically : 이론상, 이론적으로
- interstate trade : 주간무역
- every bit as ~ as : ~와 똑같은 ~의, 한 치도 틀림없이 ~인
- logical : 논리적인, 타당한, 당연한
- undercut : ~보다 저가로 팔다[공급하다]
- domestic : 국내의, 가정의
- trade agreement : 무역 협정
- eliminate : 제거하다, 없애다

해석

> 그러나 국가들은 여러 가지 이유로 특정 상품의 수입을 제한하려는 경향이 있다.

다른 나라에 있는 상사들과 사업을 하는 크고 작은 회사들의 수가 점차 증가하고 있다. 몇몇 회사들은 외국에 있는 상사에 물건을 팔고, 다른 회사들은 자기 나라에 수입하기 위해 세계로부터 물품을 구매한다. (①) 그들이 국경을 넘어 제품을 구매하든 또는 판매하든 간에, 이러한 사업들 모두 지구촌 경제에 활기를 불어넣는 국제 무역의 크기에 기여하고 있다. (②) 이론상으로 국제 무역은 가령 California와 Washington 사이의 주간 무역과 마찬가지로 합당하며 가치가 있다. (③) 예를 들어 2000년대 초반에, 미국은 국내산 토마토 가격보다 더 저가로 팔고 있다는 이유로 멕시코의 토마토 수입을 제한했다. (④) 그러한 제한에도 불구하고, 국제 무역은 제2차 세계대전 이후 꾸준히 증가해 왔다. (⑤) 많은 산업 국가들이 국가 간의 사업상 문제들을 제거하고 저개발 국가들이 세계 무역에 참여하는 데 도움이 되도록 무역 협정에 서명해 왔다.

28 ① 윗글에 따르면 비판적으로 듣고 읽는 기술은 비판적인 질문을 중심으로 만들어지며, 비판적인 질문은 비판적인 사고를 위한 자극과 방향을 제시한다고 설명하고 있다. 그러므로 ①의 "비판적인 질문은 비판적인 사고를 하는 데 필요하다."가 윗글의 요지로 가장 적절하다.

어휘

- evaluation : 평가, 감정
- build around : ~를 중심으로 만들다
- identify : 확인하다, 동일시하다
- be consistent with : ~와 일관되다, ~와 일치하다
- stimulus : 자극(제), 고무, 격려
- continual : 지속적인, 끊임없는
- ongoing : 계속 진행 중인

해석

비판적으로 듣고 읽기 – 즉, 듣고 읽는 것에 대한 체계적인 평가로 반응하기– 는 일련의 기술과 태도를 필요로 한다. 이러한 기술과 태도는 연관성 있는 일련의 비판적 질문을 중심으로 만들어진다. 우리가 그것들을 하나씩 배울 것이지만, 우리의 목표는 활용 가능한 최선의 결정을 확인하는데 그것들을 같이 이용할 수 있다는 것이다. 우리는 그것들을 당신이 해야 할 일들에 대한 목록으로 표현할 수 있지만, 질문 체계는 호기심, 궁금증 그리고 비판적 사고에 필요한 지적인 모험 정신과 더욱 일치한다. 신중히 생각하는 것은 항상 끝나지 않은 계획이며, 결코 도달하지 못할 결과를 구하는 이야기와 같다. 비판적인 질문은 비판적인 사고를 위한 자극과 방향을 제시한다. 그것들은 우리를 끊임없이 계속 진행 중인 더 나은 견해, 결정, 혹은 판단을 향해 앞으로 나아가도록 할 것이다.

29 ② 윗글의 마지막 부분에서 효과적인 공간 사고의 많은 측면이 문화적인 요인에 달려 있고 이것은 결과적으로 인지적 보편성의 한계를 암시한다고 설명하고 있으므로, ②의 "인간의 공간적 사고에는 인지적 보편성의 한계가 있다."가 윗글의 요지로 가장 적절하다.

어휘

- spatial cognition : 공간 인지
- fundamental : 기본적인, 근본적인, 본질적인
- requirement : 필요조건, 요건
- species : 종(種)
- territory : 지역, 영토, 영역
- home base : 본거지, 주둔지
- reasoning : 추리, 추론
- centrality : 중심성, 구심성
- metaphor : 은유, 비유
- domain : 영역, 지역, 범위
- intuition : 직관력, 직감
- perception : 지각, 인식
- unspectacular : 흥미진진하지 않은, 특별하지 않은
- city-dweller : 도시 거주자

[해석]

공간 인지는 고정된 영역이나 주거지가 있는 움직이는 모든 종(種)에게 기본적인 디자인 요건이다. 그리고 의심의 여지없이 그것은 인간의 사고와 추론에 중심적인 역할을 수행한다. 실제로 중심성에 대한 증거는 우리 모두의 주변에 있는데, 공간 비유가 여러 다른 지역에 사용되는 우리의 언어 속에 그리고 기억 속의 장소에 대한 특별한 역할 속에 있다. 공간이 우리의 본성에 기초한 기본적인 직관이라는 생각은 적어도 Kant로 거슬러 올라가며, 공간 인식이 인지적 보편성에 의해 통제된다는 생각은 현대의 인지 과학에 많은 정보를 제공한다. 그러나 어떤 면에서 인간의 공간 인지는 수수께끼이다. 첫 번째로, 그것은 특별하지 않다는 것이다. 즉, 우리는 어떤 종(種)과 달리 벌, 비둘기, 박쥐 또는 돌고래들과 비교하여 우리의 방식을 찾는 데에 능숙하다. 두 번째로, 인간의 공간 인지는 분명히 가변적이라는 것이다. 즉, 사냥꾼, 선원 그리고 택시 운전수는 평범한 도시 거주자들과 다른 리그에 있다. 이것은 효과적인 공간 사고의 많은 측면이 문화적인 요인에 달려 있다는 것을 암시하며, 이것은 결과적으로 이 영역에서 인지적 보편성의 한계를 암시한다.

30 ④ 윗글에서 경험이 부족한 초보 작가들이 흔히 하는 실수는 자신의 생각과 의도를 제대로 전달하지 못하는 이유가 모호하고 미숙한 생각 때문이 아니라 부족한 어휘력 때문이라고 생각하는 데 있다고 설명하고 있다. 그러므로 ④의 'beginning writer' mistake of confusing unclear ideas with a lack of words(불분명한 생각과 부족한 어휘를 혼동하는 초보 작가의 실수)'가 윗글의 주제로 가장 적절하다.

[오답풀이]

① 일부 작가들이 그들의 작품에 진실하지 못한 이유
② 체계적으로 아이디어를 개발하는 법을 학생들에게 훈련시키는 방법
③ 한 편의 작품을 효과적으로 쓰는데 풍부한 어휘의 중요성
⑤ 그것을 표현할 만한 충분한 어휘 없이 분명한 생각을 이해하는 어려움

[어휘]

• inexperienced : 경험이 부족한, 미숙한
• have a grasp on : ～을 이해하다
• utter : 말하다, 발언하다
• claim : 주장, 요구
• deliberate : 고의의, 의도[계획]적인
• liar : 거짓말쟁이
• confuse : 혼란시키다, 혼동하다
• intuitive sense : 직관, 직감
• precisely : 바로, 꼭, 정확히

• be stuck for : (대답 따위)에 궁하다, (말이) 막히다
• vague : 모호한, 희미한
• unformed : 형성되지 않은, 미숙한, 미발달의
• concrete : 구체적인, 사실에 근거한
• unclear : 불분명한, 불확실한

[해석]

경험이 부족한 작가들은 종종 단어보다 자신의 생각을 더 확실히 이해한다고 생각하는 실수를 저지른다. 그들은 "나는 말하고 싶은 것을 알고 있지만, 꼭 맞는 단어를 찾을 수가 없어."라고 자주 불평한다. 이러한 주장은 대개 사실이 아니며, 초보 작가가 의도된 거짓말쟁이라서가 아니라 그들이 그것이 무엇인지 이미 정확히 알고 있다는 잘못된 인식을 가지고 무언가를 말하려고 하는 그들의 직관을 혼동하고 있기 때문이다. 어떤 작가가 단어들이 막혔을 때, 그 문제는 단지 단어만의 문제는 아니다. 경험이 부족한 작가들은 그들이 정말로 필요한 것이 좀 더 분명한 생각과 의도일 때 풍부한 어휘가 필요하다고 생각할 수도 있다. 단어들이 막혔다는 것은 누군가 전달하고 싶어 하는 생각이 여전히 모호하고, 미숙하며, 탁하고, 혼란스럽다는 것을 나타낸다. 마침내 구체적인 의미를 찾게 되면, 동시에 그것을 표현할 알맞은 단어들을 찾게 될 것이다.

31 ③ 당구를 예로 들어, 당구는 땀을 흘리는 육체적인 노력이 없다는 점에서 진정한 스포츠가 아니라는 사람들과 손과 눈의 훌륭한 조화가 필요하며 항상 부상의 가능성이 있다는 점에서 스포츠라고 생각하는 사람들 사이에 "스포츠의 정의가 무엇인가?"에 대한 논란의 대상이 된다. 그러므로 ③의 'dispute over the defining criteria for sports(스포츠의 기준을 정하는 논쟁)'이 윗글의 주제로 가장 적절하다.

[오답풀이]

① 스포츠에 속하는 여가 활동
② 인기가 높은 경쟁 활동
④ 스포츠가 인간의 정신 건강에 미치는 영향
⑤ 당구를 스포츠로 정의하는 특징들

[어휘]

• seemingly : 외견상으로, 겉보기에
• define : 정의하다, 규정하다
• armchair athlete : 운동을 즐기는 선수, 운동 관람을 좋아하는 사람
• vigorous : 활발한, 격렬한
• competitive : 경쟁을 하는, 경쟁력이 있는
• shuffleboard : 셔플보드(판 위에 원반들을 얹어 놓고 긴 막대를 이용하여 숫자판 쪽으로 밀면서 하는 게임)
• bring up : (화제를) 꺼내다, 불러일으키다
• controversy : 논란, 논쟁

• dispute : 반박하다, 이의를 제기하다, 논란을 벌이다
• first and foremost : 다른 무엇보다도 더, 맨 처음에
• physical exertion : 격렬한 신체 운동, 육체적 노력
• break a sweat : 열심히 땀을 흘리다, 열심히 노력하다
• criteria : 표준, 기준, 규준
• decent : 상당한, 훌륭한, 고상한
• coordination : 합동, 조화, 조직
• ever-present : 항상 존재하는
• sustaining : 지탱하는, 유지하는
• specification : 설명서, 사양
• doubter : 의심하는 사람, 의혹을 품은 사람
• embedded : 구체화된, 포함된, 속한

해석

"스포츠에 관한 정의가 무엇인가?"라는 외관상 단순한 질문이 프로선수와 운동을 즐기는 사람 사이에서 수년간 논쟁과 대화의 주제였다. 야구, 미식축구 그리고 축구와 같이 격렬하고 매우 경쟁적인 활동들이 진정한 스포츠라는 것에는 의심의 여지가 없어 보이지만, 다트, 체스 그리고 셔플보드와 같은 다른 활동들이 꺼내지면 논쟁의 중심에 있음을 발견한다. 만일 당구를 스포츠가 아니라고 하면, 그것은 정확히 무엇인가? 당구가 스포츠라고 반박하는 사람들은 당구가 간단한 여가 활동이라고 응답할 것이다. 그들은 계속해서 진정한 스포츠는 다른 무엇보다도 육체적인 노력의 형태를 필요로 한다고 주장할 것이다. 더욱 중요한 점은, 만일 어떤 선수가 열심히 땀을 흘리지 않는다면, 그 사람이 하고 있는 것은 스포츠가 아니다. 그것을 초월한 더욱 중요한 기준은 손과 눈의 훌륭한 조화가 필요하며 항상 부상의 가능성이 존재한다는 것이다. 당구는 단지 그런 사양들 중 하나(손과 눈의 조화)에만 부합되므로, 따라서 의혹을 품은 사람들에게 그것은 진정한 스포츠가 아니다.

32 ④ Warhol로 분장한 Midgette는 예술에 관해 아무것도 몰랐기 때문에, 학생들의 질문에 대한 답변은 Warhol처럼 짧고 수수께끼 같았다고 했으므로, "예술에 조예가 깊은 사람을 골라 대신 강연하게 했다."는 ④의 내용은 윗글과 일치하지 않는다.

어휘

• lecture : 강의, 강연
• impersonate : 가장하다, 흉내 내다, 분장하다
• tan : 햇볕에 타다, 햇볕에 그을리다
• part : 반쯤, 어느 정도
• resemble : 닮다, 비슷하다
• in the least : 조금도 ~ 않은
• enigmatic : 수수께끼 같은, 불가사의한
• impersonation : 의인화, 분장, 흉내 내기

• icon : 아이콘, 우상, 성상

어휘

1967년에 Andy Warhol은 여러 대학에서 강연 요청을 받았다. 그는 특히 자신의 예술에 관해 말하기를 꺼려했다. "말 할 것이 적을수록, 더욱 완벽해진다."라고 그는 느꼈다. 그러나 돈은 필요했고, 그래서 Warhol은 항상 거절하기는 어려웠다. 해결 방법은 간단했다. 그는 Allen Midgette라는 배우에게 그를 흉내 내도록 부탁했다. Midgette는 검은 머리에, 피부는 그을리고, 반은 Cherokee Indian 출신이었다. 그는 조금도 Warhol을 닮지 않았다. 그러나 Warhol과 친구들은 그의 얼굴에 분칠을 하고, 갈색 머리에 실버 스프레이를 뿌리고, 검은 안경을 주고, Warhol의 옷을 입혔다. Midgette는 예술에 관해 아무것도 몰랐기 때문에, 학생들의 질문에 대한 답변은 Warhol처럼 짧고 수수께끼 같은 경향이 있었다. 그 흉내는 성공적이었다. Warhol은 우상이 되었을지 모르지만, 가끔 더 짙은 안경을 쓰고, 심지어 그의 얼굴조차 세세한 면까지 친숙하지 않았기 때문에, 아무도 그를 정말로 알아보지 못했다.

33 ③ TV는 Z세대뿐만 아니라 Silent 세대에게도 가장 인기 있는 여가 활동이 아니므로, "TV는 Z세대를 제외한 모든 세대에게 가장 인기 있는 여가 활동이었다."는 ③의 설명은 위의 도표의 내용과 일치하지 않는다. Silent 세대에게 가장 인기 있는 여가 활동은 독서이며, Z세대의 4분의 1 미만(23%)이 가장 좋아하는 여가 활동으로 TV를 선택했다는 내용은 옳다.

어휘

• generational : 세대의, 세대 간의
• participation percentage : 참여율
• recreational : 레크리에이션의, 오락의, 여가의
• pursuit : 추구하는 것, 일, 활동, 취미
• millennials : 밀레니얼 세대(1980년대에서 2000년대 사이에 태어난 세대)
• counterpart : 상대, 대응 관계의 사람[것]
• visibly : 눈에 띄게, 분명히
• a quarter : 4분의 1
• baby boomer : 베이비 붐 세대인 사람(2차 세계대전 이후 1946년부터 1964년 사이에 태어난 세대)

해석

위의 도표는 세 가지 인기 있는 여가 미디어 활동의 세대 간 참여율을 나타낸다. ① 세 가지 여가 활동 중 음악은 Z세대에게 가장 인기 있는 여가 활동인 반면에, 독서는 Silent 세대에게 가장 인기가 있다. ② 여가 시간을 독서를 하며 보내는 밀레니얼 세대의 비율은 다른 세대들보다 눈에 띄게 적었다. ③ TV는 Z세대를 제외한 모든 세대에게 가장 인기 있는 여가 활동이었는데, Z세대의 4분의 1 미만이 가장 좋아하는 여가 활동

으로 TV를 선택했다. ④ X 세대, 베이비 붐 세대, 그리고 Silent 세대에게 음악은 독서보다 인기가 덜 했다. ⑤ 가장 젊은 세대보다 독서를 더 많이 하는 두 세대는 베이비 붐 세대와 Silent 세대이다.

34 ③ (B) : 주어진 글의 '처리 방법(approach)'에 대한 설명이 글 (B)의 '이러한 국부 조직의 처리 방법(This local systems approach)~'으로 이어지므로, 주어진 글 다음에 글 (B)가 와야 한다.

(C) : 글 (B)가 부정문으로 끝났으므로, 화제 전환을 나타내는 접속 부사 'Instead(대신에)'로 시작하는 글 (C)가 글 (B) 다음에 와야 한다.

(A) : 글 (C)에서 인체는 하부 조직의 통합체라고 했으므로, 하부 조직에 미치는 생리학적 영향에 대해 설명한 글 (A)가 글 (C) 다음에 와야 한다.

어휘
- emergence : 출현, 등장, 발생
- medical speciality : 의학 전문가
- organ system : 장기 조직
- tissue : (세포들로 이루어진) 조직
- physiological effect : 생리학적 영향
- subsystem : 하부[하위] 조직
- integration : 통합
- therapy : 치료, 요법
- broad-ranging : 광범위한, 넓은 범위의
- treatment : 치료, 처치
- give way to : ~로 바뀌다, 대체되다
- integrative : 통합적인, 완전하게 하는
- methodology : 방법론
- biochemistry : 생화학, 생리
- anatomy : 해부학
- genetics : 유전학
- immunology : 면역학
- multiple : 다수의, 다중의, 다양한, 복합적인
- molecular : 분자의, 분자로 된
- cellular : 세포의

해석

20세기 의학은 의학 전문가의 출현과 질병 치료를 위한 장기 조직의 처리 방법에 중점을 두는 것이 특징이다.

(B) 이러한 국부 조직의 처리 방법은 이제 의학 관리 대신 통합 방법론으로 대체되고 있다. 아픈 환자는 생화학 문제나 해부학 문제 또는 유전학 문제나 면역학 문제를 나타내는

것이 아니다.

(C) 대신에, 각 개인은 건강과 질병을 결정하기 위해 복합적인 방법으로 상호작용하는 다양한 분자적, 세포적, 유전적, 환경적 그리고 사회적 영향의 산물이다. 인체는 하부 조직의 통합체이다.

(A) 하나의 조직과 장기의 변화는 다른 하부 조직에 생리학적 영향을 미칠 수 있다. 통합은 또한 치료가 광범위한 영향을 미칠 수 있다는 것을 의미한다. 예를 들면, 한 조직에서 질병의 치료는 다른 조직에 복잡한 영향을 미칠 수도 있다.

35 ④ (C) : 주어진 글이 '임계값 규칙'에 대한 정의이므로, 그에 대한 사례를 들어 설명한 글 (C)가 주어진 글 다음에 와야 한다.

(A) : '임계값 규칙'과 대조되는 규칙인 '개인 기준'에 대한 설명이 이어져야 하므로, 역접의 접속 부사 'Conversely(반대로)'로 시작하는 글 (A)가 글 (C) 다음에 와야 한다.

(B) : '임계 규칙'과 '개인 기준'에 대한 내용을 요약정리하고, 그 규칙들 모두가 우리의 생활에 체계를 준다고 결론을 내고 있으므로, 마지막에 위치하는 것이 적절하다.

어휘
- intense : 극심한, 강렬한
- pain : 고통, 아픔, 통증
- threshold rule : 임계값 규칙
- conversely : 정반대로, 역으로
- personal standard : 개인 기준
- be willing to : 기꺼이[흔쾌히] ~하다
- be phrased with : ~로 표현되다
- structure : 구조, 체계, 짜임새
- violate : 위반하다, 어기다, 침해하다

해석

그것들을 위반하면, 그 가능성을 고려조차 해보지 않은 극심한 고통을 주는 특정 규칙들이 있다.

(C) 예를 들어 "당신이 결코 하지 않는 것이 무엇이냐?"고 묻는다면, 임계값 규칙을 답할 것이다. 당신이 결코 위반하지 않을 규칙을 내게 말할 것이다. 왜? 그것에 너무 많은 고통이 연결되어 있기 때문이다.

(A) 반대로, 위반하기를 원하지 않는 규칙이 있다. 이 규칙은 개인 기준이라고 부른다. 만일 그 규칙을 위반한다면, 기분은 좋지 않겠지만, 그 이유에 따라서는 단기간에 그 규칙들을 흔쾌히 위반한다. 이 두 규칙들 사이의 차이점은 흔

히 'must'와 'should'란 단어들로 표현된다.

(B) 우리가 해야만 하는 특정한 것들이 있고, 하지 말아야 할 특정한 것들이 있으며, 결코 하지 말아야 할 특정한 것들과 항상 해야만 하는 특정한 것들이 있다. 'must'와 'must never' 규칙들은 임계 규칙들이며, 'should'와 'should never' 규칙들은 개인 기준 규칙들이다. 그 규칙들 모두가 우리의 생활에 체계를 준다.

36 ③ (A) : 어깨 너머로 소금을 뿌리는 의식은 악령을 쫓아내기 위한 미신이므로, 'repel(쫓아내다)'이 들어갈 말로 적절하다.

(B) : 마음이 불확실하다는 것은 만족스러운 것이 아니라 불편한 것이므로, 'uncomfortable(불편한)'이 들어갈 말로 적절하다.

(C) : 어떤 상황에 대한 통제력이란 안전한 것을 의미하는데, 역접의 접속 부사 'otherwise(그와 달리)'가 사용되었으므로, 의미가 반대되는 어휘인 'unsettling(불안한)'이 들어갈 말로 적절하다.

어휘

- ritual : 의식, 의례
- on a daily basis : 매일
- ward off : ~을 피하다, 막다, 물리치다
- repel : 물리치다, 쫓아내다
- superstition : 미신
- anthropologist : 인류학자
- perceive : 감지하다, 인지하다
- uncertainty : 불확실성, 반신반의
- cognitive gap : 인지 격차
- appease : 달래다, 위로하다
- blind : 눈이 멀게 만들다, 안 보이게 만들다
- silly : 어리석은, 바보 같은
- nonbeliever : 비(非)신자, 믿음이 결여된 사람
- secure : 안전한, 확실한
- unsettling : 동요시키는, 불안하게 만드는

해석

오늘날의 현대 사회에서조차, 많은 사람들이 아직도 매일 의식을 행하고 있다. 그들은 액운을 피하기 위해 나무를 두드리거나 악령을 (A) 쫓아내기 위해 어깨 너머로 소금을 뿌린다. 모든 문화에는 미신이 있고, 이제 인류학자들과 심리학자들은 이유를 안다고 생각한다. 그 이유는 뇌가 항상 우리가 인식한 중요한 사건들의 원인을 찾으려고 작동하기 때문이다. 설명할 수 없는 이상한 일이 일어날 때, 우리의 마음은 불확실성으로 (B) 불편해진다. 하지만 이러한 인지 격차를 쓸모 있는 어떤 설명으로든 채우며, 미신은 불가사의한 사건을 설명하기 위한

간단한 방법을 제공한다. 그들은 나무속에 사는 혼령들이 위로를 받아야만 하거나, 혹은 소금을 뿌리는 것이 악귀를 보이지 않게 한다고 믿는다. 미신은 그것들을 공유하지 못하는 비(非)신자들에게는 어리석어 보일 수도 있다. 반대로 믿는 사람들에게 그러한 의식은 (C) 불안한 것과 달리 상황에 대한 어떤 통제력을 제공하고 있다.

37 ① 윗글은 푸른 눈을 가진 학생들과 갈색 눈을 가진 학생들의 학습 동기 부여 실험에서, 선생님이 학생들의 '자기 이미지(자아상)'를 어떻게 설정하느냐에 따라 학생들의 학습 의욕과 동기 그리고 학업 성취도 등에 중요한 영향을 미칠 수 있음을 보여주고 있다. 그러므로 (A)에는 'self-images(자아상)', (B)에는 'academic achievement(학업 성취도)'가 들어가는 것이 적절하다.

오답풀이

② 자아상 ······ 직업 선택
③ 전통적인 가치관 ······ 정신적 행복
④ 전통적인 가치관 ······ 학업 성취도
⑤ 선입관 ······ 직업 선택

어휘

- partake : 먹다[마시다], 참가하다
- aptitude : 적성, 소질
- uncertified : 보증되지 않은, 검증되지 않은
- monitor : 모니터하다, 감시하다, 관찰하다
- drastically : 과감하게, 급격하게
- self-image : 자아상, 자기 이미지
- academic achievement : 학업 성취도
- psychological wellbeing : 정신적 행복, 심리적 안정
- prejudice : 선입관, 편견

해석

30년 전 미국에서 한 초등학생 집단에게 시행된 흥미로운 실험이 있다. 그 실험에 참여했던 선생님은 학생들에게 말했다. "최근의 연구에 따르면, 푸른 눈을 가진 아이들이 갈색 눈을 가진 아이들보다 학업 적성이 더 높았데요." 학생들에게 조금은 검증되지 않은 정보를 말한 후, 그녀는 아이들에게 자기 눈의 색을 카드에 적어 목에 걸라고 했다. 아이들은 일주일 동안 관찰되었고 그 결과는 다음과 같았다. 갈색 눈을 가진 아이들의 학습 동기는 떨어졌고, 푸른 눈의 아이들은 성적이 급격히 좋아졌다. 그 다음에 선생님은 학생들에게 "그 실험이 틀렸다는 보고가 있었어요. 사실은 갈색 눈의 아이들은 푸른 눈의 아이들보다 성적이 더 좋았데요."라고 말했다. 결과는 어땠을까? 이번에는 갈색 눈을 가진 아이들의 성적은 우수했고 푸른 눈을 가진 아이들의 학습 의욕은 떨어졌다.

↓

위의 실험에 따르면, 선생님에 의해 계획된 (A) 자아상은 학생들의 (B) 학업 성취도를 결정할 수 있다.

[38~39]

어휘

- print : 활자, 인쇄
- literacy : 글을 읽고 쓸 줄 아는 능력
- a focal point : 초점
- subsequent : 이후의, 다음의, 차후의
- socioeconomic status : 사회 경제적 지위
- parenting style : 양육 방법
- parental : 부모의, 어버이의
- directional : 지향성의, 방향의
- causality : 인과 관계, 상호 관계
- disentangle : 구분하다, 풀다, 끄르다
- genetic make-up : 유전자 구성, 유전적 기질
- biological parent : 생물학적인 부모, 생모, 친부모
- enthusiasm : 열정, 열광
- willingness : 기꺼이 하기, 자진해서 하기
- behavioral : 행동의, 행동에 관한
- minimal relative : 최소한의 관계
- in part : 부분적으로, 어느 정도
- endowment : 기부, (타고난) 자질[재능], 천성
- confound : 혼동 요인
- thus far : 지금껏, 여태껏, 이제까지는
- given : 주어진, 특정한, 감안하면, 고려해 볼 때
- inherently : 선천적으로, 타고나서
- social intelligence : 사회지능
- unwilling : 꺼리는, 싫어하는, 마지못해 하는

해석

많은 아이들에게 활자와의 첫 번째 경험은 가정에서 발생한다. 읽고 쓰는 능력의 개발은 함께 독서하는 가정 활동에 중점을 둔 가족의 아이들에게는 유리하다. (A) 하지만, 초기의 읽고 쓰는 경험이 아이들의 차후 언어와 활자 능력에 영향을 미친다는 정확한 메커니즘에 관한 연구는 거의 없다. 문화적인 믿음, 사회경제적 지위, 육아 방식 그리고 부모의 신뢰를 포함한 다양한 요인들이 아이들의 독서 개발에 영향을 미칠 수도 있다. 더욱이 이런 요인들 중에 방향적인 인과 관계를 확립하기란 어렵다.

아이들의 유전자 구성에 관한 영향과 생물학적 부모의 유전자 구성에 관한 영향을 구분하기란 또한 어렵다. 비록 부모의 동기부여, 열정, 그리고 독서에 대한 의지는 자녀들에게 행동상

의 영향을 미치지만, 부모의 영향은 아이 자신의 욕구와 필요에 비해 상대적으로 아주 작다. 자녀들에게 책을 많이 읽어주는 부모는 아이들이 독서에 흥미가 있다는 사실에 주로 반응한 것일 수도 있다. 적어도 부분적으로, 그러한 영향은 유전적으로 결정된다. (B) 마찬가지로, 자녀들에게 책을 거의 읽어 주지 않는 부모는 아이들의 관심이 부족하거나 혹은 유전적으로 부모와 아이들 둘 다 독서와 관련된 행동이 지루하거나 어렵다는 사실에 반응한 것일 수도 있다. 아이들의 유전적인 자질은 부모가 아이들과 어떻게 상호 작용하는가에 강하게 영향을 미친다. 부모의 행동과 가족의 유전자 구성의 혼동 요인을 감안하면, 부모와 자식이 함께 독서하는 실험은 가정환경이 독서와 관련된 능력에 영향을 미칠 수 있는 아마도 지금껏 가장 명백한 증거일 것이다.

38 ② 윗글은 아이들이 읽고 쓰는 능력을 발전시키는 데 영향을 미치는 다양한 요인들 중 유전적 요인과 가정환경과에 대해 설명하고 있다. 그러므로 ②의 "What Influences Children's Literacy Development?(아이들의 읽고 쓰는 능력의 발전에 영향을 주는 것은 무언인가?)"이 윗글의 제목으로 가장 적절하다.

오답풀이

① 아이들은 천성적으로 훌륭한 독자이다.
③ 읽고 쓰는 능력과 문화적인 믿음 사이의 관계
④ 가정환경에 의해 결정되는 사회 지능
⑤ 아이들이 독서를 싫어하는 이유는 무엇인가?

39 ② (A) However
앞 문장에서는 '아이들에게는 유리하다'고 긍정문이 사용되었고, 다음 문장에서는 부정어 'little'과 함께 '정확한 메커니즘에 관한 연구는 거의 없다'고 부정문이 사용되었으므로, 역접의 접속사 'However(하지만)'을 사용하는 것이 가장 적절하다.

(B) Similarly
앞 문장의 '자녀들에게 책을 많이 읽어주는 부모'와 뒤 문장의 '자녀들에게 책을 거의 읽어 주지 않는 부모' 모두 동일하게 유전적인 영향과 관련이 있다는 내용이므로, 동일성을 나타내는 부사 'Similarly(마찬가지로)'를 사용하는 것이 적절하다.

[40~41]

어휘

- unhelpful : 도움이 안 되는, 쓸모없는
- fatal : 치명적인, 운명의, 피할 수 없는

- Stockdale paradox : 스톡데일 패러독스(비관적인 현실을 냉정하게 받아들이는 한편, 앞으로는 잘될 것이라는 굳은 신념으로 냉혹한 현실을 이겨내는 합리적인 낙관주의)
- torture : 고문하다, 몹시 괴롭히다
- predicament : 곤경, 궁지
- ordeal : 시련, 불쾌한 경험[일]
- paradox : 역설, 모순
- remarkable : 놀랄 만한, 주목할 만한
- optimistic : 낙관적인, 낙천적인
- prisonmate : 감방[감옥] 동료
- Easter : 부활절
- broken heart : 상심, 실망, 비탄
- confront : 닥치다, 직면하다, 맞서다
- ostrich : 타조, 현실도피주의자
- self-delusion : 자기기만
- preclude : 못하게 하다, 불가능하게 하다
- negativity : 부정적[비관적] 성향, 부정성, 음성
- unconditional : 무조건적인, 무제한의
- devotion : 헌신, 전념

해석

Jim Collins가 「좋은 기업을 넘어 위대한 기업으로」에서 지적한 것처럼, (A) 비현실적인 낙관론과 상황을 있는 그대로 보지 못하는 것은 아무런 도움이 되지 못할뿐더러 치명적일 수 있다. 그는 미군 장교인 James Stockdale의 이름을 따서, 이것을 스톡데일 패러독스라고 불렀다. Stockdale은 베트남 전쟁 동안 8년 간 포로로 잡혀있었다. 그는 수없이 고문을 당했고 아내를 살아서 다시 볼 수 있으리란 확신이 없었다. 비록 Stockdale은 곤경에 처한걸 알았지만, 그것을 견뎌내고 시련에서 살아남아 인생의 경험담으로 사용하려는 희망을 결코 놓지 않았다. 그리고 여기에 모순이 있다.

Stockdael은 알 수 없는 상황 속에서도 분명한 신념이 있었지만, 그는 살아서 그곳을 나가지 못한 대부분의 수용소 동료들이 항상 낙관적이었던 것에 주목했다. "그들은 '크리스마스까지는 나가게 될 거야.'라고 말했던 사람들이었다. 그리고 크리스마스가 왔고, 크리스마스가 지나갔다. 그다음 그들은 '부활절까지는 나가게 될 거야.'라고 말했다. 그리고 부활절이 왔고, 부활절이 지나갔다. 그 다음에는 추수감사절이었고, 그리고 다시 크리스마스가 되었다. 그들은 상심하다 병으로 죽었다." 낙관론자들이 실패한 것은 현 상황에 맞서는 것이었다. 그들은 모래에 머리를 박고 어려움이 지나가기를 바라는 타조(현실도피주의자)의 접근법을 (B) 선호했다. 자기기만으로 잠깐 동안은 마음이 더 편했을 수는 있지만, 결국 현실에 맞닥뜨리게 되었을 때, 너무 엄청나서 감당할 수가 없었다.

물론 그러한 근거 없는 낙관론으로 인해 그 상황에서 Stockdale

이 정확히 실행했던, 최선을 다한 조치를 취하지 못했다.

40 ④ (A) unrealistic optimism

Stockdale이 베트남 전쟁 중에 포로로 붙잡혔을 때, 낙관적이었던 수용소 동료들이 석방될 거라는 막연한 기대감에 상심하다 병으로 죽은 것은 상황을 있는 그대로 보지 못한 '비현실적 낙관론(unrealistic optimism)' 때문이었다.

(B) preferred

석방될 거라는 막연한 기대감에 상심하다 병으로 죽은 수용소 동료들처럼 낙관론자들은 모래에 머리를 박고 어려움이 지나가기를 바라는 타조처럼 현실도피주의적인 방법을 '선호했다(preferred).

오답풀이

	(A)		(B)
①	비이성적인 부정성	……	비판했다
②	비이성적인 부정성	……	선호했다
③	비현실적인 낙관론	……	거절했다
④	비현실적인 낙관론	……	선호했다
⑤	무조건적인 헌신	……	거절했다

41 ⑤ 윗글에 따르면 낙관적이었던 수용소 동료들이 석방될 거라는 막연한 기대감에 상심하다 병으로 죽은 것과는 달리, Stockdale은 시련을 견디려 최선을 다했다고 설명하고 있다. 그러므로 "수용소 동료들에게 곧 풀려날 것이라는 희망을 불어 넣어주었다."는 ⑤의 설명은 윗글의 내용과 일치하지 않는다.

[42~43]

어휘

- application : 지원, 적용, 응용
- civilianisation : 민간화
- escalate : 확대시키다, 증가시키다
- prominence : 저명, 탁월, 명성
- internal armed conflict : 내전
- war fighter : 전투원, 전사
- civilian : 시민, 민간인
- removal : 제거, 철폐
- hostilities : 교전, 군사 행동
- outsource : 아웃소싱하다, 외부에 위탁하다
- contractor : 계약자, 도급업자, 하청업자
- private military : 사설 군대, 용병, 사병
- security firm : 보안 회사
- tactical : 작전의, 전술의, 전략적인

- treaty : 조약, 협정
- monopoly : 독점, 전매, 전유물
- emergence : 출현, 등장, 발생
- transnational : 초국가적인, 다국적의
- reduction : 축소, 감소, 쇠퇴
- expansion : 확대, 확장, 팽창
- battlespace : 전투 공간, 전장
- encompass : 포함하다, 망라하다, 아우르다
- territory : 지역, 영토, 영역
- downsize : 줄이다, 축소하다
- budget : 예산, 비용
- augment : 늘리다, 증가시키다
- flexible : 신축성 있는, 유연한, 휘기 쉬운
- military strength : 병력
- recruit : 모집하다, 뽑다, 채용[고용]하다
- maintenance : 유지, 지속
- foxhole : 참호
- expertise : 전문 지식[기술]
- discharge : 면하게 하다, 해고하다, 제대시키다
- urgent : 긴급한, 시급한
- resolution : 해결, 결심, 결의안
- intervention : 조정, 중재
- involvement : 관련, 연루, 포함, 참여
- sector : 부문, 분야, 구역, 지역

해석

무력 분쟁에 관한 법 적용에 영향을 미쳐 온 것은 현대전에서 민간화의 확대 경향이다. 이러한 경향은 전투원들의 대다수가 민간인들인 내전의 확대와 민간인 중심 지역으로 교전 행위의 (A) 이동 등 여러 과정에서 발생하고 있다. 게다가 현대식 군대는 지원과 핵심 기능도 사설 군대나 보안 회사처럼 일부가 군사 작전의 역할로 고용된 하도급자에게 점차 위탁되고 있다. Westphalia 조약 이후로 3세기 반이 지났고, 국가는 국제 관계에서 중요한 역할을 하고 있으며, 영향력과 군대에 관한 독점권을 보유해 왔다. 초국가적인 무력 집단의 등장, 비국제적인 무력 분쟁의 증가 그리고 전 영토를 망라한 전장의 (B) 확대는 모두가 민간인들이 지금보다 더 분쟁에 개입된다는 것을 뜻했다. 군대 또한 규모를 줄이고 예산을 삭감하라는 압력을 받고 있다. 이러한 경향의 일부로, 민간 하도급자와 용병들은 지속적인 변화 요구에 따라 병력을 유지하기 위해 용이하고 유연한 방법으로 점차 방위군을 늘리는데 이용되고 있다. 더욱이 전쟁 무기와 장비들이 더욱 기술적으로 발전되면서, 기본적인 유지와 지원 기능을 제공하기 위해 때때로 '공장에서 참호까지' 민간인들이 (C) 채용되었다. 민간인들은 최신의 기술적인 전문 지식에 접근하는데 용이하며 비용이 적게 든다. 즉, 그들

은 필요에 따라 고용될 수 있고, 더 이상 필요성이 시급하지 않으면 해고될 수 있다.

42 ② 윗글은 사실 군대나 보안 회사로 군사 작전의 위탁과 '공장에서 참호까지' 민간인들의 채용 등 현대전에서의 민간화의 확대 경향에 대해 서술하고 있다. 그러므로 ②의 'civilian involvement in a variety of military affairs(여러 군사 문제에 민간인의 참여)'가 윗글의 주제로 가장 적절하다.

오답풀이

① 군사 개입 없는 분쟁 해결
③ 국가 안전을 위한 군사력의 유지
④ 사설 부문과 공공 부문 간의 경쟁
⑤ 군사적인 기술 발달이 민간인들에게 얼마나 유익한가?

43 ① (A) shift
현대전에서 민간화의 확대 경향은 민간인들의 내전 확대와 민간인 중심 지역으로 교전 행위가 '이동(shift)'하는 과정에서 발생하고 있다.

(B) expansion
민간인들이 분쟁에 더 개입하게 된 원인은 초국가적인 무력 집단의 등장, 비국제적인 무력 분쟁의 증가와 전 영토를 망라한 전장의 (B) '확대(expansion)'이다.

(C) recruited
현대전에서 민간화 확대 경향에 따라 민간인들은 기본적인 유지와 지원 기능을 제공하기 위해 '공장에서 참호까지' '채용(recruited)'되고 있다.

오답풀이

② 이동	……	축소	……	배제된
③ 이동	……	축소	……	채용된
④ 제거	……	확대	……	배제된
⑤ 제거	……	축소	……	배제된

[44~45]

어휘

- sneak : 살금살금[몰래] 가다, 몰래 도망치다
- toilet tank : 화장실 수조
- lecture : 강연, 설교, 훈계, 잔소리
- good defense : 선방
- disappoint : 실망시키다, 낙담시키다
- priest : 신부, 목사, 성직자
- take responsibility for : ~을 책임지다
- a guilty party : 죄인[가해자] 측

• notify : 알리다, 통지하다

• disgrace : 망신, 수치, 불명예

• regret : 후회하다, 유감스럽게 생각하다

• involvement : 관련, 연루, 포함, 참여

• embarrass : 당황하게 하다, 난처하게 하다

• get kicked out : 쫓겨나다

• scowl : 노려[쏘아]보다, 얼굴을 찌푸리다

• confront with : ~와 대면시키다

• yell : 소리치다, 고함치다

• scream : 비명을 지르다, 악을 쓰다

• misdeed : 비행, 악행

• firm hand : 확고한 통제[훈육]

• confess : 자백[고백]하다, 시인[인정]하다

해석

(A) 어느 여름날 고등학교에 다닐 때, Colin은 교회 캠프에 참가했고 안 좋은 영향을 끼치는 새로운 친구들 몇 명을 사귀었다. 그들은 맥주를 사러 캠프 밖으로 몰래 나가자고 (a) 그에게 말했고, 그러고 나서 맥주를 차갑게 보관하려고 화장실 수조 중 하나에 숨겼다. 그들은 아무도 찾지 못할 거라고 생각했다. 그러나 틀렸다.

(D) 캠프 책임자는 맥주가 발견되었다는 사실을 그들에게 대면시키기 위해 소년들 모두를 집합시켰다. 목사님은 고함을 치거나 악을 쓰지 않았다. (e) 그는 죄가 있는 사람들은 일어나서 남자답게 행동하고 잘못된 행동에 대해 책임을 지라고 요구했다. Colin Powell은 유년 시절 내내 엄마의 단호한 훈육을 받은 터라, 맨 처음으로 곧장 나왔다. "목사님, 제가 그랬어요."라고 Colin이 시인했다.

(C) 그의 정직함 때문에, 다른 두 소년들 또한 죄를 인정했다. 부모님들 모두에게 이 사실을 알렸고, 소년들은 불명예스럽게 집으로 돌아갔다. 기차를 탄 Colin은 (d) 그가 했던 일에 관해 생각했고 함께 한 것을 후회했다. 그와 부모님에게 얼마나 민망한 일인가! 교회 캠프에서 쫓겨난 일은 결코 상상할 수 없는 일이었다. 기차에서 집으로 천천히 걸어오다. Colin은 문 앞에서 얼굴을 찌푸리고 계시는 어머니를 만났다.

(B) 그는 어머니가 신뢰와 책임감에 관해 (b) 그에게 훈계를 할 때, 그의 행동에 변명의 여지가 없다는 것을 알기에 말 없이 서 있었다. 그 다음에 아들이 얼마나 실망스러웠는지 아버지가 Colin에게 말씀하실 차례였다. 가족의 대화가 고조되는 가운데, 성 Margaret 교회의 성직자인 Weeden 목사님이 Colin의 부모님에게 전화를 걸어 어떻게 아들이 남자답게 일어나서 (c) 그의 행동에 책임을 졌는지에 관해 이야기를 전부 했다. 그 가족은 Colin이 올바르게 행동한 것을 자랑스러워했다.

44 ⑤ (A) : 교회 캠프에 참가했다가 맥주를 사서 화장실 수조에 숨긴다.

(D) : 캠프 책임자가 맥주를 발견하고 Colin이 맨 처음 죄를 시인한다.

(C) : 캠프에서 쫓겨나 집으로 돌아오며 후회한다.

(B) : 부모님이 훈계하던 중에 사건의 전말에 대한 목사님의 전화를 받고 Colin의 올바른 행동을 자랑스러워한다.

45 ⑤ 죄가 있는 사람들은 일어나서 남자답게 행동하고 잘못된 행동에 대해 책임을 지라고 요구한 사람은 목사님이므로, (e)의 그는 목사님이다. (a), (b), (c), (d)는 모두 Colin을 가리킨다.

2016학년도 기출문제 정답 및 해설

✏ 제2교시 영어영역(공통)

01 ③	02 ①	03 ①	04 ②	05 ⑤	06 ④
07 ③	08 ③	09 ④	10 ⑤	11 ③	12 ④
13 ①	14 ⑤	15 ③	16 ④	17 ②	18 ②
19 ⑤	20 ②	21 ④	22 ⑤	23 ①	24 ②
25 ②	26 ⑤	27 ②	28 ①	29 ⑤	30 ③
31 ②	32 ③	33 ③	34 ①	35 ④	36 ⑤
37 ①	38 ④	39 ①	40 ④	41 ③	42 ①
43 ②	44 ②	45 ②			

01 ③ Mrs. Sanders는 딸의 남자 친구를 만난 적이 없고, 그를 만난 Mr. Sanders를 통해 그 남자 애가 어땠는지 됨됨이를 물어보고 있다. 위의 대화 내용으로 보면 Mrs. Sanders가 남자 애를 싫어한다고 말한 적이 없으며, 사실이 아니다.

어휘

• at first glance : 첫눈에, 처음에는
• decent : 괜찮은, 제대로 된, 예의 바른
• skeptical : 의심 많은, 회의적인

해석

Mr. Sanders : 오늘 바이올린 수업에서 우리 딸을 데리러 갔을 때 누구를 만났는지 당신은 생각도 못 할 거야!
Mrs. Sanders : 애 그만 태우고, 누군데?
Mr. Sanders : 우리 딸 첫 남자 친구. 걔가 벌써 데이트를 한다는 게 믿을 수가 없어.
Mrs. Sanders : 맙소사! 우리 딸 다 컸네. 그렇지? 그 남자 친구는 어떤 것 같아?
Mr. Sanders : 내가 아빠잖아, 물론 첫 눈에 차지는 않아. 우리 소중한 딸한테 딱히 만족스러운 사람은 없지.
Mrs. Sanders : 그러지 말구! 객관적으로 말해 봐. 그 남자 어땠어?
Mr. Sanders : 솔직히, 잠깐 얘기해 봤는데, 꽤 괜찮은 남자 애 같았어. 아직도 걔에 대해 궁금한 게 많아.

02 ① 위의 대화 내용에서 Tom이 찾고자 하는 도서에 대해 알고 있는 정보는 제목뿐이다. 그러므로 도서 검색 컴퓨터에 입력해야 할 첫 빈칸의 내용은 책의 '제목(title)'임을 알 수 있다. 두 번째 빈칸에는 다음 줄에서 저쪽 계단으로 가야 한다고 알려주고 있으므로, '층(floor)'에 관한 정보를 제공하며, 세 번째 빈칸에는 다음 줄에 각 책장의 번호를 확인해 보라고 했으므로, '서가(shelf)' 위치에 대한 정보를 제공한다.

어휘

• librarian : (도서관) 사서
• digit : 숫자, 손[발]가락

해석

사서 : 안녕하세요. 무엇을 도와 드릴까요?
Tom : 솔직히, 전 도서관이 처음이에요. "Bob's Big Barbecue"라는 책을 찾아야 하는데, 누가 그 책을 썼는지 몰라요.
사서 : 괜찮습니다. 우선 여기 컴퓨터에 그 책의 제목을 입력하면, 숫자들을 보여줄 거예요. 첫 번째 숫자는 몇 층인지를 알려주는데, 저쪽 계단으로 가야 한다고 보여주고 있네요.
Tom : 다음 숫자들은요?
사서 : 그 숫자들은 서가 위치를 알려주는데, 맞는 숫자 범위를 찾을 때까지 각 서가 번호들을 확인해 보세요.
Tom : 도와주셔서 정말 감사합니다.

03 ① 본문 중에 동물의 발을 의미하는 'paw'라는 단어를 사용한 것과 "상처를 핥지(lick) 않도록 머리에 큰 플라스틱 고깔모자를 써야 한다"는 내용으로 미루어, 위의 대화가 이루어진 장소는 '동물 병원(Veterinary Clinic)'임을 알 수 있다.

오답풀이

② Dentist's Office(치과 의원)
③ Pharmacy(약국)
④ Medical Supply Center(의료 지원 센터)
⑤ Hospital Information Desk(병원 안내 데스크)

어휘

• surgery : 수술, 진료
• limp : 절뚝거리다
• paw : (동물의) 발
• cone : 원뿔, 고깔모자

• veterinary : 수의과의

• pharmacy : 약국, 조제실

해석

Mr. Gupta : Mia를 치료하러 데려와서 기쁘네요. 좋은 소식은 Mia가 괜찮을 거라는 것이고, 나쁜 소식은 부상으로 수술이 필요하다는 거예요.

Susan : 그게 걱정이에요. 사고 이후로 몹시 절뚝거려서 뒷발이 완전히 낫지 않았을 거예요.

Mr. Gupta : 불행히도, 맞습니다. 뒷다리의 뼈가 부러져서 수술이 필요해요.

Susan : 하지만 수술 후에는 괜찮겠지요?

Mr. Gupta : 수술 후에는 집에서 몇 주간 회복해야 하고, 상처를 핥지 않도록 머리에 큰 플라스틱 고깔모자를 써야 할 거예요. 하지만 그 이후엔 100% 회복될 겁니다.

Susan : 천만 다행이네요!

04 ② 위 글의 대화내용을 보면 Steve는 밖에서 텐트를 치고 자고 싶어 하지만, Dean은 이런저런 이유를 들어 밖에서 자는 것을 불평한다. 결국 Dean이 방값을 내는 조건으로 Steve가 양보하게 되므로 ②의 "Dean은 밖에서 자는 걸 좋아하지 않는다.(Dean isn't fond of sleeping outdoors.)"가 옳은 내용이다.

오답풀이

① Dean wants to set up the tent near the water.(Dean은 물가 근처에 텐트를 치고 싶어 한다.) → Steve가 물가 근처에 텐트를 치고 싶어 한다.

③ Steve and Dean are going to sleep in the tent.(Steve와 Dean은 텐트에서 잘 것이다.) → Steve와 Dean은 호텔에서 잘 것이다.

④ Steve is afraid of wild animals.(Steve는 야생동물을 겁낸다.) → Dean이 야생동물을 겁낸다.

⑤ Steve will pay for the accommodation.(Steve가 숙박비를 낼 것이다.) → Dean이 숙박비를 낼 것이다.

어휘

• stalk : 몰래 접근하다. 활보하다

• accommodation : 숙소, 거처

해석

Steve : 와, 정말 멋진 곳이구나! 여기서 평생 살고 싶다. 그래서 텐트를 어디에 설치할까?

Dean : 정말 밖에서 자고 싶어? 길 바로 밑에 적당한 호텔이 있는데.

Steve : 에이, 저기 물가는 어때? 바닥이 평평하고 괜찮아 보이는데.

Dean : 글쎄. 그늘이 없고 태양 바로 밑이잖아.

Steve : 그럼, 약간 뒤 저 나무 아래는 어때?

Dean : 거긴 더 안 좋아. 주위에 벌레가 많고 밤에는 야생동물이 돌아다니는 곳에서 가까워.

Steve : 애처럼 구는구나! 알았어. 내가 포기할게. 대신 방값은 네가 내야 해.

Dean : 상관없어. 밖에서 자는 것만 아니라면.

05 ⑤ 은행 지점장은 대출 신청자가 아이스크림 가게의 개업 장소를 잘못 선택한 것 때문에 사업의 성공 가능성을 확신할 수 없다고 하였으므로, 빈칸에 들어갈 내용은 ⑤의 "죄송합니다만, 고객님의 대출 신청을 처리해 드릴 수가 없습니다.(We're sorry, but we will not be able to process your loan application.)"가 적절하다.

오답풀이

① It sounds like a great idea and we wish you luck.(좋은 아이디어이며 행운을 빕니다.) → 은행 지점장은 대출 신청자의 아이스크림 사업에 대해 계속해서 부정적이었다.

② Please fill out these forms to begin your loan application.(대출 신청을 위해 이 서류들을 작성해 주세요.) → 이미 은행에서는 대출 신청자의 소기업 대출 신청서를 재검토한 상황이다.

③ We look forward to a long and healthy business relationship.(장기적으로 건전한 사업 관계가 유지되기를 바랍니다.) → 은행 지점장은 대출 신청자의 사업적인 성공 가능성에 대해 회의적이므로, 장기적인 사업 관계를 논의할 필요가 없다.

④ We're pleased to tell you that you've been approved for the loan.(대출이 승인 되었습니다.) → 아이스크림 가게의 개업 장소를 잘못 선택한 것 때문에 대출 승인을 기대하기 어렵다.

어휘

• bank manager : 은행 지점장

• loan applicant : 대출 신청자

• loan : 대출, 융자

• application : 지원, 신청

• fool-proof : 실패할 염려가 없는, 바보라도 해낼, 손쉬운

• desirability : 바람직함

• viable : 실행 가능한, 성공할 수 있는

해석

은행 지점장 : 고객님의 소기업 대출 신청을 재검토했지만, 사업 계획이 성공 가능한지 전혀 납득할 수가 없어서요.

대출 신청자 : 무슨 말씀이세요? 그 사업은 실패할 염려가 없어요. 누구나 아이스크림을 좋아하고, 그곳에는 수백 마일 내

에 다른 아이스크림 가게도 없어요.

은행 지점장 : 상품의 기대치가 문제가 아닙니다.

대출 신청자 : 이해할 수가 없네요. 제 경험 부족이 문제인가요? 약속했다시피, 아이스크림에 관해 알아야 할 모든 걸 배웠어요.

은행 지점장 : 아니요, 정말 문제는 위치입니다. 연중 겨울인 알래스카의 작은 마을에 개업 준비를 하셨어요. 아이스크림 가게가 그런 곳에서 성공할 사업이라고 생각하기 어렵네요. 죄송합니다만, 고객님의 대출 신청을 처리해 드릴 수가 없습니다.

06 ④ Donna는 주문한 물품이 제때 모두 오지 않아 불만을 제기했고, Sam은 죄송하다는 사과의 말과 함께 그 문제점을 신속하게 처리하겠다고 약속하여 Donna은 감사해 했다. 그러므로 위 글의 상황을 올바르게 표현한 문장은 ④의 "Sam은 그 문제를 해결하려고 노력했고 고객은 만족했다.(Sam will try to solve the problem and make his customer happy.)"가 알맞다.

(오답풀이)

① Donna was completely satisfied with Sam's delivery service.(Donna는 Sam의 배달 서비스에 매우 만족했다.) → Donna는 주문한 물품이 제때 모두 오지 않아서 Sam에게 불만을 제기했다.

② Donna regrets that Sam has ignored her complaints for weeks.(Donna는 Sam이 몇 주 동안 그녀의 불만사항을 무시한 것을 유감스러워 한다.) → Sam은 Donna의 불만사항을 무시하지 않고 바로 처리했다.)

③ The order was properly filled so there is nothing Sam can do.(주문이 올바르게 처리되어 Sam이 할 수 있는 게 없다.) → 주문이 올바르게 처리되지 않아서 Sam이 그 원인을 찾아 바로잡았다.

⑤ Donna is planning to cancel her order with Sam's Office Supplies.(Donna는 Sam의 사무용품점에 한 주문을 취소할 계획이다.) → Donna는 Sam이 불만사항을 신속히 처리한 것에 대해 감사했으므로, 주문 취소를 예상할 수 없다.

(어휘)

• office supply : 사무용품

• shipment : 선적, 수송품, 적하물

• get to the bottom of : ~의 원인을 밝히다

• ship out : (배편으로) 보내다

(해석)

Sam : Sam의 사무용품점입니다. 무엇을 도와드릴까요?

Donna : 한 달 전에 A4 용지 10박스를 주문하려고 전화했는데, 그 때 1주일이면 배달된다고 말씀하셨어요.

Sam : 물론이죠, 주문 사항은 지역에 따라 1주일 이내에 배달하는 것을 보증합니다. 무슨 문제가 있습니까?

Donna : 물품이 2주 늦게 도착했을 뿐만 아니라 반 밖에 배달이 되지 않아서, 아직도 나머지 반을 기다리고 있어요.

Sam : 대단히 죄송합니다. 저희 기록에는 10박스 모두가 배달된 것으로 나타나지만, 문제점을 찾아서 나머지 5박스를 바로 보내드리겠습니다.

Donna : 감사합니다. 그리고 다시는 이런 일이 없도록 해주세요.

07 ③ ①, ②, ④, ⑤는 모두 운동선수인 Misty May-Treanor와 Kerri Walsh를 가리키며, ③의 'them'은 'Misty May-Treanor와 Kerri Walsh'를 주어로 하는 'wanting'의 목적어로, 자원봉사자들(volunteers)을 가리킨다.

(어휘)

• volunteer : 자원봉사자, 지원자

• retrieve : 회수하다, 검색하다

• rake : 갈퀴로 긁다[모으다]

• literally : 문자[말] 그대로, 그야말로

• wave to : ~을 향해 손을 흔들다

• mandatory : 법에 정해진, 의무적인

• autograph : 사인

(해석)

Misty May-Treanor와 Kerri Walsh는 위대한 운동선수이자, 위대한 사람들이다. 2008년 베이징 올림픽 비치발리볼 준결승전에서, ① 그들은 매우 뛰어난 브라질 팀에게 패했다. 경기 후 그들은 브라질 팀원들과 악수를 하고 "고맙다."고 말했다. 그러고 나서 ② 그들은 볼을 회수하고 모래를 고른 많고 많은 자원봉사자들과 악수를 했다. 경외심에 Mike Celizic 기자가 다음과 같이 썼다. "그들은 경기장을 떠날 때 뒤에 남아있던 몇몇 자원봉사자들을 말 그대로 쫓아 다녔고, ③ 그들이 자기들의 노력이 얼마나 감사받을 일인지 모른 채 떠나기를 원치 않았다." ④ 그들은 또한 팬들에게 손을 흔들고 의무적인 약물 검사 후 돌아오겠다고 약속했다. 그들은 돌아 왔고, 많고 많은 팬들에게 사진을 찍기 위해 포즈를 취하고 사인을 해 주었다. 그리고 물론, 팬들은 ⑤ 그들과 악수를 해서 정말로 고마워했다.

08 ③ 제시문은 MSG의 안전성에 대해 글루타민산염 협회가 주장하는 근거들을 서술하고 있으므로, MSG에 대한 ③의 부정적인 내용은 위 글의 통일성을 깨뜨리는 문장으로 볼 수 있다.

(어휘)

• concentrate : 집중하다, 농축하다

- sodium : 나트륨
- extract : 뽑다, 추출하다
- beet : 근대, 사탕무
- liberate : 해방시키다, 자유롭게 하다
- protein : 단백질
- fraction : 부분, 일부, 분수
- deaden : 줄이다, 죽이다
- proportion : 부분, 비율
- constitute : 구성하다[이루다], ~이 되다

해석

MSG는 본래 해초, 사탕무, 곡식에서 추출된 나트륨 농축물이다. ① 글루타민산염 협회는 MSG가 매우 안전하다고 주장한다. ② 그들은 MSG가 식품 단백질을 섭취할 때 체내에 분해되는 글루타민산염과 다르지 않고, 식품에 첨가된 MSG가 대부분의 식품에 본래 포함된 글루타민산염에 비해 소량일 뿐이라고 주장한다. ③ 여러 같은 이유로, 많은 요리사들이 MSG를 싫어하며, 음식의 맛을 떨어뜨리거나 저급한 식품에 보충하기 위해 너무 자주 사용된다고 믿고 있다. ④ 예를 들면, 대부분의 요리법들은 고기 1파운드당 MSG 반 스푼을 필요로 한다. ⑤ 이 비율에 따라, 닭고기에 사용된 MSG는 이미 닭고기에 존재하는 글루타민산염의 10% 이하가 됐을 것이다.

09 ④ 글의 서두에서 유머가 광고에 자주 이용되는 핵심 도구임을 명시하고, 다음 행부터 유머가 광고에 미치는 긍정적인 효과들에 대해 설명하고 있다. 그러나 ④의 경우 유머가 매우 비효과적이며 심지어 역효과를 낳는다고 위의 주제와 상반되는 내용을 서술함으로써 글의 통일성을 깨뜨리고 있다.

어휘

- typically : 보통, 일반적으로, 전형적으로
- persuasive : 설득력 있는
- on behalf of : ~을 대신하여, ~을 대표하여
- identifiable : 인식 가능한, 알아볼 수 있는
- on a daily basis : 매일
- intentional : 의도적인, 고의의
- tactic : 전략, 전술
- intent : 주목, 집중, 의지, 목적
- strategic : 전략적인
- infrequently : 드물게, 어쩌다
- prevalent : 널리 퍼져 있는, 일반적인
- counterproductive : 역효과를 낳는
- first world countries : 제1세계 국가, 선진국

해석

전통적인 광고는 보통 유명한 스폰서들을 대신하여 대중매체

를 통해 소비자들에게 전달되는 설득력 있고 공적인 커뮤니케이션으로 정의되며, 그리고 유머가 자주 이용되는 핵심 도구이다. ① 대부분의 소비자들이 매일 수많은 광고에 노출되기 때문에, 유머러스한 광고는 의도적인 유머를 접하는 가장 흔한 방법일 것이다. ② 광고주들은 유머를 메시지 전략으로 이용하는데, 다양한 전략적 목적을 달성하기 위해 광고의 잠재성을 강화시키려는 의도이다. ③ 유머는 현대식 광고 초기에는 오히려 드물게 사용되었다. 그러나 조사원들은 유머가 당대의 광고들, 특히 방송 매체에서 널리 이용되었음을 확인했다. ④ 유머가 매우 비효과적이며 심지어 역효과를 낳는다고 광고 산업 전반에 인식되었다. ⑤ 비록 이것이 가장 산업화된 선진국에서는 보통 당연하지만, 유머는 동양보다 서양 광고에서 더 자주 볼 수 있다.

10 ⑤ 제시문은 공공 장소이든 가사 공간이든 모든 생활 공간에서 사생활과 사회생활이 둘 다 반영된 특징들을 찾을 수 있다고 했으므로, ⑤의 "생활 공간에는 사생활과 사회생활에 대한 필요가 반영된다."를 위 글의 요지로 볼 수 있다.

어휘

- potentially : 잠재적으로, 어쩌면
- ubiquitous : 어디에나 있는, 아주 흔한
- architectural : 건축학의
- obligatory : 의무적인, 의무감에서
- prop : 지주, 버팀목, 받침대
- prevalence : 유행, 보급
- region : 지방, 지역
- penetrate : 뚫고 들어가다, 관통하다

해석

대부분의 사람들은 어쩌면 서로 상반된 바람을 가진다. 즉, 하나는 사회생활을 위해 다른 사람에게 시간을 내는 것이고, 다른 하나는 사생활을 가지는 것이다. 어떤 이들은 더 많은 사생활을 바라며, 다른 사람들은 더 많은 사회생활을 바란다. 만일 공공 장소나 가사 공간 수준의 환경을 생각한다면, 이런 두 바람이 반영된 특징들을 볼 수 있다. 서구 사회에서 문은 어디에나 있는 건축학적 특징이며, 커튼은 거의 집안의 중추적 필수품이다. 열고 닫는 것이 가능한 문과 커튼은 사용 가능함을 표시하는 장치이다. Goffman은 가정 환경과 공공 환경 모두에서 뒤쪽(사적) 영역과 앞쪽(공공) 영역의 유행에 관심을 가졌다. 침실, 목욕탕 그리고 가끔 부엌을 포함한 집 안에서 뒤쪽 영역은 아주 친밀한 사람만이 허락 없이 들어올 수 있는 영역이다. 앞 영역은 공공에게 개방되어 있다.

11 ③ "~many antibiotics don't have the same effect that they once ③ were."란 문장에서 that절 이하의 they는 앞의

many antibiotics를 받는 대명사이고, "많은 항생제들이 옛날에 영향을 미친 것과 똑같은 영향을 미치지 못하다"는 뜻이므로, once 다음의 동사도 be 동사가 아닌 앞의 have의 과거형 'had' 또는 대동사 'did'를 사용해야만 한다.

어휘

• antibiotic 항생제
• blunt 둔화시키다, 약화시키다
• complication 합병증
• infection 감염, 전염병
• outwit ~보다 한 수 앞서다, 선수치다, 허점을 찌르다
• spur 원동력이 되다, 자극하다
• evolutionary 진화의, 점진적인
• microbe 미생물
• purge 제거[숙청]하다, 몰아내다

해석

질병을 유발하는 박테리아에 대한 항생제의 승리는 현대 의학의 가장 위대한 성공 이야기 중의 하나이다. 이런 약들이 2차 세계대전 시기에 처음으로 널리 사용되면서, 수많은 생명을 구하고 무서운 질병과 전염병으로부터 심각한 합병증들을 약화시켰다. 그러나 널리 사용된 지 50년 이상이 지난 후, 많은 항생제들은 옛날과 똑같은 효능을 보지 못했다. 시간이 지나면서 어떤 박테리아는 항생제의 효능을 무색케 진화했다. 만연한 항생제의 사용은 점차 더 강력한 약에도 생존하도록 박테리아의 변형을 촉진시켰다. 항생제의 저항력이 미생물을 이롭게 하는 동안 인류는 두 가지 커다란 문제에 직면했다. 즉, 인체에서 전염병을 몰아내기가 더욱 어려워졌다는 것과 병원에서 감염될 위험이 더 높아졌다는 것이다.

12 ④ 인터뷰를 하는 사람이 읽기 위해 멈춘 것이 아니라 읽기를 중단한 것이므로 ④의 'to read'는 'reading'으로 고쳐 써야 옳다.

• stop + to 부정사 : ~하기 위해 (걸음을) 멈추다
• stop + 동명사 : ~를 그만두다[중단하다]

어휘

• primacy effect : 초두성 효과
• murky : 어두운, 흐린
• recency effect : 신근성 효과

해석

설문조사에서 응답 문항이 시각적으로 주어질 때, 응답자들이 대개 목록의 처음부터 시작하여 순서대로 남은 문항들을 처리한다고 보는 것이 합리적이다. 따라서 초두성 효과는 규칙성

이 있어 보인다. 응답자들은 목록의 처음 문항들을 마지막 문항보다 더 선호한다. 그러나 인터뷰하는 사람이 응답자에게 응답 문항들을 읽어준다면 그 장면은 약간 모호해 진다. 설문 조사자들은 질문지를 빨리 읽게 되고 응답자들은 보통 다음 문항으로 넘어가기에 앞서 첫 번째 문항을 판단할 시간이 없을 것이다. 응답자들은 마지막 문항부터 시작할 가능성이 높은데, 인터뷰하는 사람들이 읽기를 중단했을 때 그 문항이 기억 속에 남아있기 때문이다. 결과적으로 질문이 응답자에게 큰 소리로 제시되었을 때 신근성 효과 − 목록의 마지막에 있는 문항들을 선택하는 경향 −를 기대하게 한다.

13 ① (A) : 해당 문장의 주어가 'The reward(보상)'이므로, 단수 형태인 'was'를 사용해야 한다.
   (B) : 해당 문장의 종속절은 "scoring is relatively infrequent (in the sport)"를 의미하므로, 'sports'를 선행사로 하는 'in which(전치사 + 관계대명사)'의 형태가 되어야 한다.
   (C) : 전치사 'without'의 목적어이므로 동명사 형태이고, 골이 선수에 의해 득점되는 것이므로 수동태 형태인 'being scored'를 사용해야 한다.

어휘

• tremendous : 굉장한, 엄청난
• feat : 위업, 솜씨
• bowler : (크리켓의) 투수, 볼링선수
• successive : 연속적인, 잇따른
• scorer : 득점자, 기록원
• proceed : 진행, 과정
• surface : 수면으로 올라오다, 표면화되다

해석

"해트트릭"은 원래 연속 투구로 세 명의 타자를 아웃시킨 투수의 엄청난 활약을 묘사하는 데 사용된 영국의 크리켓 용어였다. 많은 크리켓 클럽에서 이 업적에 대한 보상은 새로운 모자였다. 다른 클럽들은 그들의 영웅을 팬들 사이에서 "모자 넘기기"를 하고 득점 선수에게 넘김으로써 경의를 표했다. 그 용어는 득점이 상대적으로 적게 나는 다른 스포츠로 퍼졌고 − "해트트릭"은 또한 축구에서 세골을 넣은 활약을 묘사하는 데에도 사용됐다. 내셔널 하키 리그의 Belinda Lerner에 따르면, 그 표현은 하키에서 1900년대 초에 나타났다. "하키에서 그 용어의 실제 의미에 약간의 혼동이 있다. 오늘날 '진짜' 해트트릭은 경기에서 다른 선수에 의해 득점된 골이 없이 한 선수가 연속 세 골을 넣었을 때를 말한다."

14 ⑤ (A) : 'whether A or B(A 아니면 B)' 즉, 양자 선택의 구문이므로 'whether'를 사용해야 한다.

(B) : 감각을 안내하는 것이 아니라 감각에 의해 안내되는 것이므로 수동태 형태의 'guided'를 사용해야 한다.

(C) : that절의 주어가 'force'이고 3인칭 단수 형태의 동사 'influences'를 사용해야 한다.

어휘

- barren 소득[결실] 없는, 척박한
- primarily 주로
- apparently 듣자[보아] 하니, 분명히
- vague 막연한, 모호한

해석

우리 대부분은 우리가 주도하는 삶을 선택한다. 비록 우리는 그것을 알지 못하지만, 매일 행복하거나 불행하거나, 건강하거나 아프거나, 창의적이거나 무능하거나를 결정하는 선택을 한다. 우리는 이런 선택의 대부분을 무의식 단계에서 결정하며, 과거에 우리에게 무슨 일이 있었으며 앞으로 우리에게 어떤 일이 일어날지 주로 감각에 의해 안내된다. 분명하게도 이런 자동적인 의사결정 과정은 우리가 계속해서 선택하고 있다는 사실을 숨기려 한다. 시간이 지나면서 삶의 새로운 매 순간마다 선택하고 있다는 의식을 잃어버린다. 그 결과 막연한 외부의 힘 – 운명, 숙명 또는 행운 –이 우리가 어떻게 살지, 우리가 무엇을 할지, 그리고 때로는 우리가 어떻게 죽을지에 영향을 미친다고 믿게 된다.

15 ③ 위의 제시문에서 이상적인 용광로는 각 개인들의 독특함을 기존의 시스템에 맞추기 위해 개인적인 희생을 요구하며, 그 결과는 독특한 특징들이 희석된 동일(homogeneous) 제품이라고 했으므로 빈칸에 들어갈 말로는 ③의 '동일함(sameness)'이 적절하다.

어휘

- melting pot 용광로, 도가니, 융합
- uniqueness 독특성
- blend 섞다, 혼합하다
- ingredient 재료, 성분, 구성 요소
- homogeneous 동종의, 동질의
- dilute 희석하다, 묽게 하다
- metaphor 은유, 비유

해석

사회에 대한 용광로 관점은 호소력이 있는데, 그것은 누구든지 열심히 노력하면 성공할 수 있다고 제시하기 때문이다. 그러나 어느 순간 이런 형태의 평등이 차이와 다양성을 제거하는 것임을 깨달아야 한다. 보통 이상적인 용광로는 각 개인들의 독특함을 기존의 시스템에 맞추기 위해 개인적인 희생을 필요로 한다. 성공하기 위한 유일한 방법은 적어도 사회적으로 용인되는 방식(유명한 갱스터가 되는 것이 아니라) 내에서 자신의 문화적 배경을 포기한 채 꼭 들어맞는 개발 방식을 요구한다. 우리는 용광로에 대한 아이디어를 다른 요소들과 혼합하는 방식으로 이용했지만, 이런 용광로의 결과가 독특한 특징들이 희석된 동일 제품이라는 것을 깨달아야 한다. 간단히 말하면, 용광로 비유는 동일함에 대한 욕구를 반영한다.

16 ④ 위의 제시문에 따르면 대부분의 사람들이 시간을 물리적인 의미에서 실제로 존재한다고 믿으며, 시간은 감지할 수 없는 것일지는 모르지만 명백히 만질 수 있는 결과물로 여긴다. 그러므로 ④의 "외부 세계에 객관적으로 존재한다(is objectively embedded in the external world)"가 빈 칸의 내용으로 알맞다.

오답풀이

① passes with its own driving force(자체 추진력으로 움직인다.)

② cannot be perceived physically(물리적으로 상상할 수 없다.)

③ is not dealt with in the field of physics(물리학 분야에서 다루지 않는다.)

⑤ is an imaginary construct of human experience(인간 경험의 상상물이다.)

어휘

- dimension 차원, 크기, 규모
- conceive 상상하다, 마음속으로 품다
- theoretical 이론적인, 이론상
- empirical 경험에 의한, 실증적인
- primitive 원초, 원시
- term 칭하다, 일컫다
- on this account 이런 이유로, 이것 때문에
- imperceptible 감지[지각]할 수 없는
- manifest 명백한, 분명한
- tangible 만질 수 있는, 분명히 실재하는
- duration 지속, 기간
- embed 박다, 끼워 넣다

해석

시간은 세상과 우리의 위치를 이해하는 데 중요하고 필수적인 차원을 더한다. 시간이 존재하지 않는 경험 세계를 상상하기란 거의 불가능하다. 결국, 사건은 시간 속에서 발생한다. 이것은 물리학자들이 공간과 함께 시간을 이론적이고 경험적인 원초로 취급하는 결과를 낳았다. 시간이 어떤 수준에서 우주의 물리적 구조의 일부이고, 물리적으로 실재한다는 관점은 내가 시간에 관한 보편적 관점이라고 명명한 것과 일치한다. 대부분의 사람들은 이런 시간의 관점에서 '진정한' 시간을 물

리적인 의미에서 실제로 존재하는 시간이라고 믿는다. 즉, 이런 이유로 시간은 우리가 거주하는 환경을 지배하는 물리적인 법칙을 반영함으로써, <u>외부 세계에 객관적으로 존재한다.</u> 시간은 "감지할 수 없는" 것일지는 모르지만, 그럼에도 불구하고 실제하며 명백히 만질 수 있는 결과물이다. 시간의 "통로" 없이 아무 것도 연속될 수 없고 따라서 지속을 경험할 수 없다.

17   ② 위의 제시문에서 큰 꿈과 야망을 실현하기 위해서는 작은 것부터 천천히 단계를 밟아 실천해 나가는 단편적인 전략이 중요하다고 말하고 있다. 그러므로 ②의 '작은 첫 걸음을 내딛는 것(taking that small first step)'이 빈 칸의 내용으로 적절하다.

> **오답풀이**

① getting help from others(다른 사람들에게 도움을 청하는 것)
③ looking back into the past(과거를 돌아보는 것)
④ sharing our desires with someone(누군가와 욕망을 나누는 것)
⑤ sacrificing ourselves for a good cause(대의를 위해 희생하는 것)

> **어휘**

• vastness : 광대, 넓음
• tedious : 지루한, 싫증나는
• in terms of : ~면에서, ~에 관하여
• piecemeal : 조금씩 하는, 단편적인
• first bite : 첫술
• second bite : 두 번째 기회
• immeasurable : 헤아릴 수 없는, 측정할 수 없는
• magnitude : 규모, 중요도
• overwhelm : 압도하다, 제압하다
• realizable : 실현 가능한
• therapeutic : 치료상의, 치료법의
• for a good cause : 대의[명분]를 위해, 좋은 일을 위해

> **해석**

우리들 대부분이 직면한 문제는 큰 꿈과 야망을 가지고 있다는 것이다. 꿈의 감정과 원대한 욕망에 사로잡혀, 우리는 그것들을 성취하기 위해 보통 필요로 하는 작고 지루한 단계에 집중하기가 매우 어렵다. 우리는 커다란 도약이라는 측면에서 성공을 생각한다. 그러나 자연과 마찬가지로 사회에서 크기와 안정성에 관한 모든 것은 천천히 성장한다. 단편적인 전략은 우리의 당연한 조바심에 완벽한 교정수단이다. 즉, 그것은 첫 번째 도약에서 작고 당면한 것에 집중하고, 이 후 두 번째 도약에서 어디서 어떻게 궁극적인 목표에 좀 더 가까워질 수 있

는 지 집중하게 한다. 그것은 과정이란 측면에서 계속 연결된 단계와 행동으로 생각하게 하며, 아무리 작더라도 측정할 수 없는 심리적 이점들이 또한 있다. 욕망의 거대함이 너무나 자주 우리를 압도한다. 작은 첫걸음이 그것들을 실현할 수 있게 해준다. 행동보다 나은 치료는 없다.

18   ② 보통 근심(anxiety)은 부정적인 요소이나, 위의 제시문에서는 근심이 불쾌한 상황을 알려주며, 무엇인가를 행하도록 경고하며, 공격받을 위험에 처했을 경우 대처할 수 있도록 해준다고 그 긍정적 요소에 대해 설명하고 있다. 그러므로 글의 서두에서 빈칸에 들어갈 내용은 ②의 "생존과 안락함에 도움을 주다(helps keep you alive and comfortable)"가 적절하다.

> **오답풀이**

① instills a sense of responsibility in you(책임감을 불어넣다)
③ makes you tolerate all kinds of insults(온갖 모욕을 참아내다)
④ prevents you from pursuing your desires(욕망을 쫓지 않게 하다)
⑤ inhibits clear thinking in stressful situations(스트레스 상황에서 명확한 사고를 억제하다)

> **어휘**

• anxiety : 근심, 걱정
• obnoxious : 아주 불쾌한, 몹시 기분 나쁜
• watchful : 지켜보는, 신경 쓰는
• vigilant : 바짝 경계하는, 조금도 방심하지 않는
• panicked : 공황[공포] 상태에 빠진
• instill : 스며들게 하다, 서서히 주입시키다[불어넣다]
• inhibit : ~하지 못하게 하다, 억제[저해]하다

> **해석**

믿거나 말거나 근심은 <u>당신의 생존과 안락함에 도움을 준다.</u> 우리는 욕망, 선호, 목표를 가지고 태어나고 커왔는데, 아무런 근심이 없고 욕망을 성취하는데 완전히 관심이 없다면 온갖 불쾌한 것들을 견디고 그것들로부터 벗어나거나 탈출하기 위해 아무 것도 하지 않을 것이다. 근본적으로 근심은 불쾌한 상황 – 욕망에 상반되는 것을 의미함 –이 일어나고 있거나 일어날 것을 알려주며 무엇인가를 행하는 편이 낫겠다고 경고하는 불편한 감정과 행동 경향이다. 따라서 공격받을 위험에 처해 있고 다치지 않기를 바란다면, 도망가기, 공격자와 싸우기, 경찰 부르기 등 몇 가지 가능한 행동들을 선택해야 한다. 그러나 아무런 관심, 관망, 근심, 긴장, 주의, 경계, 공포가 없다면 아마 이런 행동들 중 아무 것도 하지 않을 것이다. 공격의 위험을 인지하지만, 아무 것도 하지 않을 것이다.

19 ⑤ 위 글은 인공지능이 복잡한 문제 해결에 뛰어난 능력을 보이지만, 설명서에 없어서 탐색 공간에서 그 해답을 찾을 수 없는 문제들에 직면했을 때 한계가 있다고 비판한다. 이것은 본문의 마지막 문장에서 "인공지능 시스템은 보통 창조 활동이라 부르는 지능의 기초적인 측면을 거의 수행할 수 없다."는 내용으로 단언된다. 그러므로 필자가 주장하는 위 글의 요지는 ⑤의 "인공지능은 창의성 결여라는 한계를 극복하지 못하고 있다."임을 알 수 있다.

어휘

- correspond : 부합하다
- autonomous : 자주적인, 자율적인
- intelligent agent : 지능형 에이전트(요원, 동작주, 행위자)
- criticism : 비판론
- specification : 설명서, 사양
- flexible : 잘 구부러지는, 유연한, 신축성 있는
- at best : 기껏해야, 잘해야, 끽해야
- perspective : 관점, 시각, 원근
- constraint : 제약, 제한, 통제

해석

처음 시작부터 인공지능 연구의 주요 초점은 항상 문제 해결에 쟁점을 두고 있었다. 이런 관점에서 보면, 지능은 로봇팔의 정확한 자율 동작에서 자연스러운 언어 문장의 이해까지 복잡한 문제를 해결하는 능력과 일치한다. 전형적인 설정은 문제를 해결할 공간을 탐색하는 것이며, 그 공간에서 지능형 기기가 최선의 선택을 찾아낸다. 인공지능의 문제 해결 방식에 대한 가장 흔한 비판은 설명서에 없는 상황들을 처리하는 능력에 한계가 있다는 것이다. 탐색 공간은 유연하고 복잡하며 적응력이 뛰어난 시스템처럼 보이지만, 보통 엄격히 규정된다. 탐색 공간에 만족스러운 해답이 없는 문제와 직면했을 때, 인공 지능 시스템은 그 해답이 관점 변화, 통제 완화, 새로운 기호 추가 등의 가장 단순한 연산을 통해 성취할 수 있을 때조차도 기껏해야 탐색 공간에 존재하는 가장 적게 실패할 결과를 단순히 돌려준다. 바꾸어 말하면, 그러한 시스템은 보통 창조 활동이라 부르는 지능의 기초적인 측면을 거의 수행할 수 없다.

20 ② (A) : 위의 내용은 정신과 육체는 서로 별개의 것이 아니라 '유기적(organic)'으로 연관되어 있다고 본다.
    (B) : 위의 내용은 인간의 정신은 육체와의 연관성에 '근거를 두고(grounded in)' 있다고 본다.

해석

- emerge : 모습을 드러내다, 나타나다
- aesthetic : 미적인, 심미적
- sensorimotor : 감각운동의

- implication : 함축, 암시, 영향[결과]
- dualism : 이원론, 이중성
- provocative : 도발적인, 화를 돋우려는
- objectionable : 불쾌한, 무례한
- come to grips with : ~와 마주치다, 직면하다, 씨름하다
- far-reaching : 지대한 영향을 가져올
- rethink : 다시 생각하다, 재고하다
- at odds with : ~와 불화하여
- inherit : 상속받다, 물려받다

해석

우리가 "정신"이라고 부르는 것과 "육체"라고 부르는 것은 둘이 아니라 오히려 하나의 (A) 유기적 과정이며, 우리의 모든 의미, 사상, 언어는 심미적 차원에서 이런 구체화된 행동으로 나타난다. 그런 심미적 차원들 중에서도 으뜸은 성질, 심상, 감각운동성 처리 양식 그리고 감정이다. 적어도 과거 30년 동안, 학자들과 연구자들은 많은 훈련을 통해 정신과 의미 구현을 위한 논거와 증거를 축적했다. 그러나 그들의 연구 결과는 대중 의식에 진입하지 못했고, 정신/육체 이원론의 부정은 아직도 대부분의 사람들이 불쾌하고 심지어 위협적이라고 느낄 매우 도발적인 주장이다. 구현을 위해 씨름하는 것은 당신이 마주하게 될 가장 심오한 철학적 작업 중의 하나이다. 모든 측면의 인간 정신이 어떤 환경에서 특정한 형태의 육체적 연관성에 (B) 근거한다고 인정하는 것은 우리가 누구이고 무엇인지 지대한 영향을 가져올 재고를 요구하며, 어떤 면에서 우리가 물려받은 서양 철학과 종교적인 전통의 상당수와 커다란 불화가 된다.

21 ④ (A) : 군사 지도자들이 직면한 곤경을 적이 정보를 노출시키려 하지 않는 것과 이질적인 문화라는 병렬 구조로 설명하고 있으므로, 앞뒤의 문장이 '첨가(in addition)'로 연결되는 것이 적절하다.
    (B) : 난공불락의 적에 대한 유일한 해결책을 다음 문장에서 취사용 불의 수를 파악하는 것으로 설명하고 있으므로, 앞뒤의 문장이 '예시(for example)'로 연결되는 것이 적절하다.

어휘

- predicament : 곤경, 궁지
- disclose : 폭로하다, 드러내다
- alien : 이국의, 외계의, 이질적인
- peculiar : 이상한, 특이한
- impenetrable : 들어갈[관통할] 수 없는, 눈앞이 안 보이는
- scrutinize : 세심히 살피다, 면밀히 조사하다
- strategist : 전략가

해석

초기 전쟁의 역사에서, 군사 지도자들은 다음과 같은 곤경에 직면했다. 어떤 전쟁이든 그 성공은 상대편에 관해 가능한 많이 알아내는 능력에 달려 있다. – 상대편의 목적, 상대편의 강점과 약점. 그러나 적은 결코 이런 정보를 노출시키려 하지 않을 것이다. (A) 게다가, 적은 독특한 사고방식과 행동양식을 가진 이질적인 문화에서 왔다. 어떤 장군이 적장의 속셈이 무엇인지 정말로 알 수가 없었다. 외부에서 적은 난공불락의 신비로운 존재로 보였다. 그리고 아직 상대편에 대한 이해가 부족한 장군은 어둠 속에서 움직였다. 유일한 해결책은 내부에서 무슨 일이 일어나고 있는 지 외부에 나타는 표시를 통해 적을 세심히 살피는 것이었다. (B) 예를 들면, 전략가는 적의 진지에서 취사용 불과 그 수의 시간에 따른 변화를 센다. 그것은 적군의 규모를 알려준다.

22 ⑤ (A) : 뒤의 문장에서 '섬세한 과정(delicate process)'이라고 했으므로, '미세하게(slightly)'가 알맞다.

(B) : 스톱 모션 촬영술은 눈을 속여 움직이는 것처럼 보이게 하는 것이라고 했으므로, 찰흙 모형이 '움직이는(moving)' 것처럼 보인다가 알맞다.

(C) : 스톱 모션 촬영은 미세한 잔상이 없어서 피사체가 갑자기 움직이는 것처럼 보이므로, 컴퓨터 애니메이션으로 프레임을 '흐릿하게(blurry)' 처리하여 사실적인 움직임을 표현할 수 있다.

어휘

- clay : 점토, 찰흙
- dinosaur : 공룡
- considerably : 많이, 상당히
- slightly : 약간, 조금, 미세한
- delicate : 연약한, 섬세한
- blur : 희미한[흐릿한] 것
- jerky : 갑자기 움직이는, 변덕스러운

해석

스톱 모션 촬영술은 눈을 속여 움직이는 것처럼 보이게 하는 것이다. 스틸 사진은 찰흙 모형 공룡과 같은 물체로 만든다. 그 물체는 (A) 조금씩 움직이며 또 다른 사직이 찍힌다. 이런 섬세한 과정은 수천 번 반복된다. 사진 또는 프레임이 초당 24 프레임의 모션 픽처 카메라의 속도로 보여지면, 찰흙 모형은 (B) 움직이는 것처럼 보인다. 스톱 모션 촬영의 큰 문제점은 "잔상"이 없다는 것이다. 만일 거리를 따라 뛰어가는 사람을 촬영한다면, 각 프레임마다 약간의 잔상이 남을 것이다. 비록 관객들은 알아채지 못하지만, 잔상은 움직임을 부드럽고 사실적으로 만든다. 스톱 모션 촬영에서 뛰어가는 피사체는 갑자기 움직이는 것처럼 보인다. 이런 문제는 컴퓨터 애니메이션

으로 해결되었고, 사실적인 움직임을 표현하기 위해 프레임을 (C) 흐릿하게 만드는 데 사용될 수 있다.

23 ① (A) : 헤드셋이 달린 휴대폰은 시간을 절약하기 위한 도구이므로, 전화를 하는 동시에 통근하는 것이 '허용(allow)'된다.

(B) : 사람들 대다수가 개인적으로 스스로를 위한 시간이 갈수록 줄어든다고 느끼므로, 시간은 진정으로 '귀중한(precious)' 상품이 되었다.

(C) : 종일 일에 '묶여있다(bound)'는 말과 반대되는 말이 와야 하므로, 처음에는 '해방(liberation)'의 도구였다는 문장이 되어야 적절하다.

어휘

- in a matter of seconds : 순식간에
- commodity : 상품, 물품, 원자재
- around the clock : 24시간 내내, 밤낮으로, 종일
- nomadic : 유목의, 방랑의
- herald : 예고하다, 알리다
- constraint : 제약, 제한, 통제
- liberation : 해방, 석방
- crunch : 으드득[뽀드득], 중대 상황, 부족 사태
- juggle : 저글링하다, 곡예하듯 하다, 효율적으로 조직하다

해석

현대 기술은 무수히 많은 시간 절약 기기들을 제공한다. 헤드셋이 달린 휴대폰은 친구나 동료와 전화로 얘기하면서 동시에 출퇴근 시간과 싸우도록 한다. 컴퓨터는 손으로 하면 몇 개월이 걸릴지 모르는 계산을 순식간에 수행할 수 있다. 그럼에도 불구하고 우리들 대부분은 시간이 충분하지 않다고 불평한다. 조사에 따르면 사람들 대다수가 개인적으로 스스로를 위한 시간이 갈수록 줄어든다고 느낀다. 시간은 진정으로 귀중한 상품이 되었다. 한 국가의 조사에서는 51%의 성인 응답자가 많은 돈보다는 많은 시간을 가질 것으로 나타났다. 일부 문제는 현대 사회에서 일이 집까지 따라오는 데 있다. 그래서 사람들은 처음에는 해방의 도구로 여겼던 유목민과 같은 도구들 – 휴대폰, 태블릿, 무선 이메일 –에 의해 종일 일에 묶여있다는 사실을 알았다. 이러한 시간 부족을 해결하기 위해 더욱 많은 사람들이 일, 가족 그리고 가사 책임의 균형을 잡으려 잠을 줄이고 있다.

24 ② 위의 제시문에서 위기는 자본주의에서 불균형이 확대될 때 합리성을 회복시키는 기능을 하므로, 불가피할 뿐만 아니라 필연적인 것으로 설명하고 있다. 그러므로 ②의 "자본주의에서 위기의 필요성(Necessity of Crises in Capitalism)"이 위 글의 제목으로 알맞다.

놀이로 인한 피해)

① Destructive Nature of Crises(위기의 파괴적 성질)

③ Avoiding Crises in a Capitalist System(자본주의 체제에서 위기 모면)

④ Competition: Driving Force of Capitalism(경쟁 : 자본주의의 원동력)

⑤ Capitalism: Way Out of Crises and Chaos(자본주의 : 위기와 혼란의 탈출구)

어휘

• explanatory : 이유를 밝히는, 설명하기 위한

• inherent : 내재하는, 고유의

• contradiction : 모순, 반박

• impose : 도입[시행]하다, 부과하다, 강요하다

• collapse : 붕괴, 실패, 쇠약

• rationality : 합리성, 순리성, 도리를 알고 있음

• undermine : 약화시키다

• irrational : 비이성적인, 비논리적인

• rationaliser : 합리화 도구

• crucial : 중대한, 결정적인

• agentive : 행위의, 동작주를 나타내는

해석

자본주의 비판이론의 설명에 따르면, 위기는 자본주의에 내재된 모순이 불균형 즉, 현재의 시스템이 기능을 유지하기 위해 반드시 필요한 균형(예를 들면 수요와 공급 사이에서)의 상실을 초래할 때 발생한다. 위기는 불가피할 뿐만 아니라 필연적인데, 불균형이 확대될 때 사람들이 붕괴와 혼란의 상황에서 질서를 확립해야만 하기 때문이다. 위기는 합리화 기능, 즉 그것이 약화되었을 때 합리성을 회복시키는 기능을 한다고 말할 수 있다. Harvey의 말에 따르면, 위기는 "항상 불안정한 자본주의의 비이성적인 합리화 도구"이다. 위기는 객관적이며 조직적인 측면이 있지만 또한 필수적이고 정말로 중요한 주관적 측면도 있는데, 그것은 행위적이며 전략적이다. 위기 속에서 사람들은 어떻게 대응할지 그리고 균형과 합리성을 회복시킬 것으로 기대되는 특정한 행동 또는 정책을 추구하기 위해 어떠한 전략을 개발할지 결정해야만 한다.

25 ② 위의 제시문의 마지막 문장에서 아이가 단지 시간을 보내기 위해서 노는 것은 아니며, 아이가 놀이로 선택하는 것은 내적인 과정, 욕망, 문제, 불안이 동기가 된다고 했으므로, ②의 '놀이 : 아이들의 내적 자아의 표현(Play: Expression of Children's Inner Self)'가 위 글의 제목으로 알맞다.

① Harm Caused by Children's Violent Play(아이들의 난폭한

③ Importance of Restricting Children's Play(아이들 놀이 제한의 중요성)

④ How to Raise Physically Healthy Children(육체적으로 건강하게 아이들을 기르는 방법)

⑤ Children's Play: Means of Making Friends(아이들의 놀이 : 친구 사귀기의 수단)

어휘

• spontaneously : 자발적으로, 즉흥적으로

• while away the time : 시간[여가]를 보내다

• violent : 폭력적인, 난폭한

해석

"아이들의 놀이는 스포츠가 아니라 가장 중요한 행위로 여겨야 한다."고 16세기의 수필가 Montaigne가 기술했다. 아이를 이해하고 싶다면, 아이의 놀이를 이해할 필요가 있다. 현대 심리학의 창시자 Freud는 놀이를 아이가 자신을 표현하는 수단으로 여겼다. 그는 또한 아이들이 놀이를 통해 자기의 생각과 감정을 얼마나 많이 그리고 얼마나 잘 표현하는지 주목했다. 아이의 놀이로부터 아이가 세상을 어떻게 보며 해석하는지 – 아이가 바라는 게 무엇인지, 아이의 걱정과 문제가 무엇인지 – 이해할 수 있다. 아이를 관찰하는 어른이 그렇다고 생각할지 모르지만, 아이가 단지 시간을 보내기 위해 즉흥적으로 노는 것은 아니다. 아이가 일부 빈 시간을 채우기 위해 놀이에 빠져 있을 때조차도, 아이가 놀이로 선택하는 것은 내적인 과정, 욕망, 문제, 불안이 동기가 된다.

26 ⑤ 위대한 카리스마 있는 지도자 모델의 한 가지 중대한 결점은 인간은 반드시 죽는다는 것이므로, 글의 흐름으로 보아 "모든 지도자가 죽는다."는 명제에 해당하는 주어진 문장을 ⑤에 삽입하는 것이 적절하다.

어휘

• charismatic : 카리스마가 있는, 독실한

• secondary : 이차[부차]적인, 부수적인

• institution : 기관, 단체, 협회

• buy : (특히 사실 같지 않은 것을) 믿다

• analogy : 유추, 비유

• flaw : 결함, 결점, 흠

• transcend : 초월하다

• mortality : 죽음을 피할 수 없음, 사망

• first and foremost : 다른 무엇보다도 더

그리고 이것은 영원히 사라지지 않을 것이며 – 지금도, 22세기에도, 천년이 지난 후에도 : 모든 지도자는 죽는다.

카리스마 있는 지도자 모델을 보면, 세상이 정확히 반대 방향으로 가고 있다는 생각이 든다. 21세기를 보라. 거의 전 세계가 민주주의를 향해 움직였다. (①) 민주주의의 본질은 단일 지도자에 대한 과도한 의존을 피하는 것이며 그 과정에 주된 초점을 맞추는 것이다. (②) 아마 지난 세기 가장 위대한 단일 지도자였던 Churchill조차도 국가와 그 과정에 이차적인 존재였고, 2차 세계대전 말에 집무실에서 쫓겨났다. (③) Hitler, Stalin, Mussolini – 이들은 그들이 소속된 조직보다 그리 중요치 않다는 사실을 이해하지 못했던 카리스마 있는 지도자들이었다. (④) 민주주의로의 이동과 회사 발전 사이의 유사성을 믿지 않더라도, 위대한 카리스마 있는 지도자 모델은 한 가지 중대한 결점이 있다. (⑤) 인간은 반드시 죽는다는 이런 불변의 현실을 초월하기 위해, 무엇보다도 한명의 위대한 카리스마 있는 지도자 대신 조직의 특성을 쌓는데 초점을 맞추어야 한다.

27 ② 주어진 문장에서 이 단계(this stage)란 현 회의에서 주요 의제들이 논의되기에 앞서 결정과 약속이 이미 정해진 '이전의 만남'을 의미하므로, 이 단계에서 반대와 혼동이 있다면 다음의 만남이 결실을 보기 어렵다는 것이다. 그러므로 주어진 문장은 글의 흐름상 ②에 삽입되는 것이 적절하다.

어휘

• ensuing : 다음의, 뒤이어 일어나는, 결과로서 따르는
• encounter : 접촉, 만남, 대면
• commitment : 약속, 전념, 헌신
• transaction : 거래, 매매, 처리 과정
• party : (소송·계약 등의) 당사자
• implication : 영향[결과], 함축, 암시
• minutes of meeting : 회의록
• at the outset : 처음에, 처음부터
• agenda : 의제, 안건
• ensure : 보장하다
• forthcoming : 다가오는, 곧 있을, 마련된
• circulate : 순환하다, 유포하다
• cognitive : 인식의, 인지의

만약 이 단계에서 반대와 혼동이 있다면, 다음의 만남이 결실을 보기 어려울 것이다.

많은 개인 간의 거래에서 한 번의 만남은 이전의 만남에서 정해진 결정과 체결된 약속에 영향을 받는다. (①) 다시 말해 모든 당사자가 이전의 협의에서 발생한 주요 쟁점들에 동의하고 지금의 논의를 위해 이 결과들을 확정짓는 것이 중요하다. (②) 이 문제는 회의록이 작성되는 많은 비즈니스 상황에서 공식적으로 해결된다. (③) 현 회의에서 주요 의제들이 논의되기에 앞서, 이전의 회의록이 검토되고 처음부터 의견이 일치된다. (④) 이런 절차는 모든 참가자들이 이전에 이루었던 것에 동의함을 보장하고, 따라서 곧 있을 회의에서 공통된 참조 기준이 된다. (⑤) 게다가 의제는 대개 회의 전에 돌려지며, 본질적으로 이것은 개인들이 논의될 주요 영역에 대해 스스로 준비하도록 인식의 틀이 된다.

28 ① 제시문의 마지막 문장에서 로봇 공학이 사회 전반에 미치는 파급효과(ripple effect)에 대해 설명하고 있으므로, 위 글의 시사하는 바는 ①의 "로봇 공학은 전쟁에서 사회 전반에 영향을 미칠 혁명을 초래한다.(Robotics is bringing about a revolution in warfare whose effects reach far into society.)"이다.

오답풀이

② Unmanned systems are the only way to save human soldiers from the battlefield.(무인 시스템은 전장에서 병사를 구할 유일한 방법이다.)
③ Robotics, which is developing rapidly, will eventually bring an end to warfare.(빠르게 발전하고 있는 로봇 공학은 결국 전쟁을 종식시킬 것이다.)
④ There will be little change in the way wars are fought.(전쟁에서 싸우는 방식에는 거의 변화가 없을 것이다.)
⑤ Governments must make robotics investment a priority.(정부는 로봇 공학에 최우선적으로 투자해야 한다.)

어휘

• unmanned : 무인의
• machine gun : 기관총
• robotics : 로봇 공학
• identity : 신원, 신분, 정체, 독자성
• monopoly : 독점, 전매
• ripple : 잔물결[파문]을 일으키다
• substantially : 상당히, 많이, 주로, 대체로

해석

역사학자들이 이 시대를 볼 때, 우리가 다른 형태의 혁명, 즉 원자폭탄의 발명과 같은 전쟁 혁명에 처해 있다고 결론을 내릴 것이다. 그러나 훨씬 더 큰 문제일 수 있는데, 무인 시스템이 단지 전투 '방법'에만 영향을 미치는 것이 아니라, 가장 기초적인 수준에서 싸울 '대상'에 영향을 미치기 때문이다. 전쟁에서 이전의 모든 혁명이라고 하는 것은 기관총이든 원자폭탄이든 더 빨리, 더 멀리 쏘거나 또는 더 큰 폭발을 내는 시스템에 대한 것이다. 그것은 물론 로봇 공학이라고 하지만, 병사의 경험뿐만 아니라 병사의 정체성마저 바꿔버린다. 달리 말하면 전투에 관한 인류의 5천 년간의 독점이 우리 일생에서 무너져 내리는 것이다. 시간이 흘러 외부에 파급되는 효과는 인간의 발전, 우리 사회, 법, 도덕 등의 방향을 상당히 변화시킬 것이다.

29 ⑤ 위의 제시문에서 말 또는 이론이 아니라 실제로 일어나는 행동의 결과, 즉 '실체적 진실(effective truth)'이 중요하다고 했으므로, 위의 글이 시사하는 바는 ⑤의 "의사소통은 다른 사람들에게 영향력이 있을 때에만 효과적이다.(Communication is effective only when it has the power to influence others.)"이다.

오답풀이

① It is important to remain consistent in applying your principles.(원칙을 적용하는데 일관성을 가지는 것이 중요하다.)

② The search for truth through actions has proven to be difficult.(행동으로 진리를 탐색하는 것은 어려운 것으로 입증됐다.)

③ People interpret others' words according to their own preconceptions.(사람들은 타인의 말을 선입견을 가지고 해석한다.)

④ Good speakers focus not only on their message but on their presentation.(훌륭한 연설가는 메시지뿐만 아니라 프레젠테이션에도 초점을 맞춘다.)

어휘

• barometer : 기압계, 지표
• self-indulgent : 제멋대로 하는, 방종한
• alter : 바꾸다, 변경하다
• proven : 입증된, 증명된
• preconception : 선입견, 선입관, 예상

해석

"문제는 사람들이 말하고 의도하는 것이 아니라 행동의 결과이다." 이것을 Machiavelli는 "실체적 진실 – 진정한 진실이라

고 불렀는데, 바꾸어 말하면 말 또는 이론이 아니라 실제로 일어나는 것이다. 똑같은 지표를 의사소통의 시도에 적용해 볼 수 있다. 만일 어떤 이가 혁명적이라고 생각하는 무언가를 말하고 쓰며 세상을 바꾸고 인류를 발전시킬 것이라고 희망하지만, 결국 아무도 실질적으로 영향을 받지 않는다면, 그것은 전혀 혁명적이거나 진보적이지 않다. 원인에 다가가지 못하고 바라는 결과를 낳지 못하는 의사소통은 그저 사람들이 자신의 목소리를 사랑하는 자기만족의 이야기일 뿐이다. 그들이 쓰고 말한 실체적 진실에는 아무런 변화가 없다. 사람들에게 다가가 그들의 견해를 바꾸는 능력은 중대한 일이다.

30 ③ 위의 제시문은 중세에서 현재까지 종교가 경제에 미치는 영향을 여러 예를 들어 설명하고 있다. 그러므로 ③의 '경제에 미친 종교의 중대한 영향(significant impact of religion on economy)'이 위 글의 주제로 적절하다.

오답풀이

① how economic boom supports religion(경제적 호황이 종교를 지원하는 방법)

② geographical features of religious centres(종교 중심지의 지리적 특성)

④ pilgrimage as the heart of religious activity(종교 활동의 중심 성지순례)

⑤ why different religions exist in different regions(각기 다른 지역에 서로 다른 종교가 존재하는 이유)

어휘

• money-lender : 대부업자, 고리대금업자
• Prophet : 마호메트, 선지자[예언자]
• borrower : 채무자, 대출자
• prohibit : 금하다, 금지하다
• pilgrim : 순례자
• holy site : 신성한 지역, 성지
• caste : 카스트, 계급, 계층
• prescribe : 처방하다, 규정[지시]하다
• birthright : 생득권
• suitability : 적당, 적합, 어울림
• pilgrimage : 순례, 성지 참배

해석

종교는 상업에 강한 영향을 미칠 수 있다. 예를 들면 중세 유럽에서 기독교는 이자를 받는 대부업을 강하게 반대했는데, 유대인들은 이런 종교적 계율에 얽매이지 않았기 때문에 대부업자의 역할을 맡았다. 최근까지도 무슬림에서 은행 기관들이 발달하지 못했는데, 마호메트가 채무자로부터 이자 받는 것을 금했기 때문이다. 반면에 종교적 순례자들에 의해 막대한 돈이 성지에 흘러들었다. 성지순례는 사우디아라비아의 Mecca,

프랑스의 Lourdes, 그리고 인도의 Banaras와 같은 종교 중심
지의 경제에 중요한 역할을 했다. 종교는 사람의 고용에도 강
한 영향을 미치는데, 특히 힌두 사회에서는 카스트 제도가 적
성이 아닌 생득권에 의해 특정한 의무와 직업을 규정한다.

31 ② 위의 제시문은 우리 자신의 능력을 평가하는 것은 상대적
    일 수밖에 없으며, 타인과의 비교, 특히 충분히 밀접한 관
    계가 있는 사람들과의 비교를 통해 판단하게 된다고 설명
    하고 있다. 그러므로 ②의 '자기평가에 있어 관련 비교의
    역할(role of relevant comparison in self-evaluation)'이 위
    글의 주제로 적절하다.

   오답풀이

   ① damaging effects of over-focusing on competition(지나치
      게 집중된 경쟁의 폐해)
   ③ importance of having high self-esteem(높은 자존감의 소
      유의 중요성)
   ④ development of a competitive spirit(경쟁 정신의 계발)
   ⑤ sports as a measure of self-worth(자기 가치의 척도로서
      스포츠)

   어휘

   • self-esteem : 자존심, 자부심, 자긍심
   • derive from : ~에서 유래하다, 파생되다, 비롯되다
   • ample : 충분한, 풍부한
   • relevant : 관련 있는, 적절한
   • overall : 전체의, 종합적인
   • over-focusing : 과초점
   • dimension : 차원, 치수, 크기, 규모, 범위, 관점

   해석

   아마도 우리 자신에 관해 생각한 가장 중요한 차원은 자존감
   의 수준을 평가하는 것이다. 우리가 세계적으로 자신에 관해
   인정받는 정도는 우리가 어떻게 행동하느냐, 특히 다른 사람
   과 어떻게 행동하느냐에 영향을 미친다. 우리 자신에 대한 평
   가는 어느 정도 다른 사람들과의 비교에 달려 있다. 예를 들면
   특별한 능력을 판단하는데 있어 우리의 판단은 정말로 상대적
   일 수밖에 없다. 즉, 어떤 테니스 선수나 음악가 그리고 요리
   사가 얼마나 뛰어난지에 대한 질문은 다른 사람의 성적에서
   비롯된 크기를 참고해야만 의미가 있을 수 있다. 관련 있는 사
   람들과 우리 스스로를 비교할 기회를 찾는다는 증거는 충분하
   다. 관계란 전체적인 규모에 관해서 의미 있는 비교를 위해
   우리와 충분히 밀접한 사람들을 의미한다. 예를 들면 지역 테
   니스 클럽은 국제 챔피언십 경기보다 테니스 기술에 관해 더
   많은 의미 있는 비교를 제공한다.

32 ③ 본문의 중간에 "특히 소설은 너무 길고, 너무나 형이상학적

상상들로 가득하며, 너무나 분명하게도 독자들이 단지 재
미와 즐거움을 위해 읽는 것이 아니라 도덕적 교훈을 배우
기를 갈망한다."고 되어 있으므로 ③의 내용과 일치하지 않
는다.

어휘

• adequate : 충분한, 적당한
• canon : 규범, 기준, 법규 목록
• absurd : 우스꽝스러운, 터무니없는
• trivial : 사소한, 하찮은
• preacherly : 설교적인
• oppositionist : 야당 당원
• mystifying : 어리둥절한, 혼란스러운
• genre : 장르
• abrupt : 돌연한, 갑작스런
• bizarre : 기이한, 특이한
• metaphysical : 형이상학의, 철학적인
• manifestly : 명백히, 분명하게
• parody : 패러디하다, 풍자하다
• pretension : 허세, 가식, 주장
• crave : 갈망하다, 열망하다

해석

올바른 영어 번역이 존재했던 세기 동안, 러시아 소설과 연극
작품 목록은 평판과 확실한 '색조'를 얻었다. 그것은 진지하고
(비극적이거나 엉뚱하기는 했지만 절대 가볍거나 사소하지 않
은), 약간은 설교적이며, 종종은 정치적 저항자이고, 빈번하게
는 돌발적이고 특이한 시작과 결말을 가진 혼란스러운 장르로
여겨졌다. 특히 소설은 너무 길고, 너무나 형이상학적 상상들로
가득하며, 너무나 분명하게도 독자들이 단지 재미와 즐거움을
위해 읽는 것이 아니라 도덕적 교훈을 배우기를 갈망한다. 이
책들은 가식을 풍자할 때조차도 선과 악에 빠져있다. 만일 희
극이라면 피를 얼음처럼 차갑게 할 반전이 결말 가까이에 있
다. 러시아 문학의 등장인물들은 돈, 경력, 사회에서의 성공 그
자체, 트로피를 받을 만한 아내와 남편, 교외의 집 대신 다른
얻기 어려운 것들을 갈망한다.

33 ③ 도표를 보면 막대그래프에서 2013년에 불에 탄 헥타르의
    숫자는 2012년도에 비해 세배가 아니라 약 두 배 정도임을
    알 수 있다. 그러므로 도표와 ③의 내용이 일치하지 않는다.

   어휘

   • significant : 중요한, 의미심장한, 커다란
   • spike : 뾰족한 것
   • substantial : 상당한, 크고 튼튼한
   • fluctuation : 변동, 파동, 오르내림
   • correlation : 연관성, 상관관계

해석

위의 그래프는 2003년에서 2013년 사이에 캐나다에서 불에 탄 숲의 면적과 산불의 횟수를 나타낸다. ① 이 시기에 불에 탄 헥타르의 숫자는 세 개의 큰 뾰족한 (막대)그래프로 2004년과 2010년에는 3백만 이상이며, 2013년에는 4백만 이상이다. ② 또한 2009년에는 불에 탄 숲의 면적이 1백만 헥타르 미만으로 상당히 감소했다. ③ 이 시기에 불에 탄 헥타르의 숫자는 2013년에 가장 컸으며, 전년도에 비해 세 배 이상이 되었다. ④ 산불의 횟수는 큰 변동 폭을 보이는데, 2006년에는 거의 1만 건으로 높았다가 2011년에는 5,000건 미만으로 떨어졌다. ⑤ 전체적으로 한 해 동안 불에 탄 숲의 면적과 산불의 횟수와는 지속적인 상관관계가 없다.

34 ① (주어진 글) 살충제는 환경오염 때문에 비난을 받는다.
→ (A) 곤충은 살충제의 빈번한 사용으로 저항력이 강해진다.
→ (C) 이런 문제로 해충 관리 방법은 복잡해지고, 관리자도 강도 높은 훈련을 받는다.
→ (B) 따라서 살충제를 안전하고 효과적으로 사용해야 한다.

어휘

- pesticide : 살충제, 농약
- pest : 해충, 유해 동물
- scrutinize : 세심히 살피다, 면밀히 조사하다
- physiological : 생리학상의, 생리적인
- publicly-sensitive : 대중에[여론에] 민감한
- supervise : 감독[지휘]하다, 지도하다

해석

살충제는 식량 생산과 공공 건강을 위해 해충 관리 전략의 중요한 구성요소이다. 그런 중요성에도 불구하고, 이 화학물질은 환경오염 때문에 종종 비난을 받는다.

(A) 사실 우리 사회에서 흔히 사용되는 다른 화학물질보다 더 면밀히 조사되는 것은 없다. 더욱이 곤충은 살충제의 빈번한 사용으로 저항력이 강해진다.

(B) 따라서 살충제를 안전하고 효과적으로 사용하기 위해, 살충제를 어떤 특정 조건에서 사용해야 하는지 알아야 할뿐만 아니라, 또한 생물학적, 생리학적, 환경적 결과들을 이해해야만 한다.

(C) 이런 모든 문제들은 해충 관리를 과거의 단순한 작업에서 오늘날 대중에게 민감한 복잡한 작업으로 변화시켰다. 현대의 해충 관리 방법을 개발하고 감독하는 사람들은 여러 지역에서 살충제의 용법에 관해 강도 높게 훈련을 받아야만 한다.

35 ④ (주어진 글) 차 밑에서 겁에 질린 강아지를 발견한다.
→ (C) 강아지를 구하고 깊은 유대감이 생긴다.
→ (A) 출장을 가기 위해 친구에게 맡긴 강아지가 없어진다.
→ (B) 포스터를 붙여 강아지를 되찾는다.

어휘

- a dog person : 강아지를 좋아하는 사람, 강아지 애호가
- pathetic : 불쌍한, 가엾은
- fur : 털, 모피
- cower : 몸을 숙이다, 웅크리다
- scared : 무서워하는, 겁먹은
- scour : 샅샅이 뒤지다, 문질러 닦다
- drastically : 과감하게, 철저하게
- crawl : 기어가다
- snatch : 와락 붙잡다, 잡아채다
- snuggle : 바싹 파고들다, 달라붙다

해석

나는 결코 강아지 애호가가 아니다. 나는 개들을 싫어한다고 말할 수 있다. 그것은 내 차 밑에서 웅크리고 있던 가엾은 털 뭉치를 발견하기 전까지의 일이었다. 그것은 겁에 질린 작은 강아지였다. 마치 일주일 내내 먹지 못하고 씻지 않은 것처럼 보였다.

(A) 나는 다음날 출장을 가야했지만 그 강아지는 너무 약해서 홀로 남겨둘 수가 없었고, 그래서 강아지를 돌봐달라고 친구에게 부탁했다. 내가 돌아왔을 때 강아지를 데리러 달려갔지만 꼭 '탈출한' 것처럼 보였다. 나는 밤새도록 동네를 샅샅이 뒤졌지만 빈손으로 돌아왔다.

(B) 나는 강아지에 대한 설명과 전화번호가 있는 포스터를 만들었고, 그것을 동네방네 붙였다. 그러나 일주일이 지나도록 아무런 소식이 없었다. 그러다 마침내 전화가 울렸다. 강아지는 내게 돌아왔고 우리는 그이후로 떨어진 적이 없다. 두말할 필요 없이 개에 대한 내 감정은 철저하게 바뀌었다.

(C) 그 강아지는 너무 겁을 먹어서 밖으로 꺼낼 수가 없었고, 그래서 나는 그곳 밑으로 기어들어가 와락 붙잡았다. 바로 그때 그런 일이 생겼다. 그 강아지는 내게 와락 안겼다. 그 순간부터 유대감이 생겼다. 그 강아지는 내 것이며, 내 책임이며, 나의 가장 친한 친구였다.

36 ⑤ 위의 제시문에 따르면 외부 온도나 활동량의 증가로 체온이 올라가면 땀을 통해 몸의 열을 식히고, 주변 온도가 내려가면 체온이 떨어지지 않도록 몸의 열이 방출되는 것을 막거나 더 많은 일조량을 확보하도록 해야 한다. 그러므로

몸의 열이 방출되는 것을 '촉진시키는(accelerate)' 것이 아니라 '방지해야(avoid)' 한다.

어휘

• physiological : 생리학상의, 생리적인
• incoming radiation : 일조량, 일사량
• deem : 여기다, 간주하다
• sophisticated : 세련된, 정교한, 교양 있는
• perception : 지각, 자각, 통찰력
• fever : 열, 흥분
• evaporative cooling : 증발 냉각
• perspiration : 땀, 땀 흘리기
• decreased : 줄어든, 감소된
• humidity : 습도, 습기
• ambient : 주위의, 주변의
• provision : 공급, 제공, 준비
• accelerate : 가속화하다, 촉진하다
• solar radiation : 태양 복사

해석

생리적인 편안함은 상대적으로 생리적인 스트레스에서 ① 벗어난 상황에서 경험할 수 있는 감각이다. 이런 편안함은 정교한 도구에 의해 ② 쾌적하다고 여길 특정한 범위의 온도, 일조량, 습도, 풍속 내에 존재한다. 편안함을 측정하는 데 사용되는 이 정교한 도구가 바로 인체이다. 몸의 체온이 바람직한 범위 내에서 유지되는 한 자각은 편안함 쪽이다. 불편함은 환경적 조건이 이런 내부 조건을 지탱하는 한계를 ③ 넘어설 때 발생한다. 외부의 기온이 상승하거나, 증가된 활동 또는 열이 내부 온도를 상승시킬 때 피부의 표면에 증발 냉각(땀)이 더해진 몸의 열을 제거하기 위해 증가한다. 빨라진 공기 속도 또는 낮아진 습도는 증발 냉각의 이득을 증가시킴으로써 상승한 온도로 인한 스트레스를 ④ 줄일 수 있다. 반대로 주변의 온도가 떨어지면, 몸의 열이 방출되는 것을 ⑤ 촉진시키거나 더 많은 일조량을 확보하도록 대비해야만 한다.

37 ① 위의 제시문은 버빗 원숭이들의 '먹이 전환(switching food)' 행동을 예로 들어, 사람들도 주위의 동료 집단과 동일화 되는 '사회적 순응(social conformity)'의 행동 특성을 갖고 있음을 단적으로 설명하고 있다.

어휘

• lunchroom : 구내식당, 간이식당
• vervet monkey : 버빗 원숭이(긴꼬리원숭이의 일종)
• tint : 물들이다, 염색하다
• aloe : 알로에
• tribe : 부족, 종족, 무리
• peer : 또래, 동료, 동등한 사람
• peer pressure : 동료 집단으로부터 받는 사회적 압력
• conformity : 따름, 순응
• abundance : 풍부, 많음

해석

많은 십대들은 학교 구내식당에서 모두와 동등하기를 바란다. "생각하는 것만큼 우리는 특별하지 않다."고 원숭이의 행동을 연구한 Erica van de Waal이 말했다. "동물에게서 우리 행동의 많은 근원을 찾을 수 있다." 그녀의 연구팀은 야생에서 무리지어 살고 있는 109마리의 버빗 원숭이에게 분홍색 또는 푸른색으로 물들인 먹이를 주었다. 각 무리에게 한 색깔은 맛이 없게 알로에로 물들였지만, 처음 몇 번의 끼니일 뿐이다. 맛이 정상으로 돌아온 후에도 원숭이들은 맛이 없다고 생각한 색깔을 먹지 않으려 했다. 그리고 나서 푸른색을 먹는 몇몇 원숭이들이 분홍색을 먹는 무리로 갔고 분홍색을 먹는 몇몇 원숭이들은 푸른색을 먹는 원숭이 무리로 갔다. 그것은 연구원들이 동료간 압력 행사를 목격한 때였다. 분홍색 먹이를 먹은 원숭이들 구역으로 옮긴 푸른색 먹이를 먹은 원숭이들은 전에 분홍색 먹이를 피했음에도 불구하고 색을 바꾸었다. 분홍색 먹이를 먹은 원숭이들도 또한 푸른색 먹이 지역으로 옮겼을 때 색을 바꿨다. 그 원숭이들은 다른 원숭이들 모두가 먹는 것을 먹었다.

> 버빗 원숭이들의 (A) 먹이 전환 행동은 새 무리에서 (B) 사회적 순응의 결과로 생각된다.

[38~39]

38 ④ 위의 제시문은 우리 주변에서 일어나는 많은 불행한 사고들이 무의식적인 의도에서 비롯되는 경우가 많다고 프로이드의 견해를 들어 설명하고 있다. 그러므로 ④의 '사고 속에 숨겨진 무의식적인 의도(Unconscious Intention Hidden in Accidents)'가 위 글의 제목으로 알맞다.

오답풀이

① How to Avoid Accidents(사고를 피하는 방법)
② Resistance to Undesirable Urges(원치 않는 충동에 저항)
③ Good Intention Matters More than Result(결과 보다 중요한 좋은 의도)
⑤ Unconscious Desire for Safety and Comfort(안전과 편안을 위한 무의식적인 욕구)

39 ① 프로이드의 견해에 따르면 환자가 의사와의 정기 진료 약속을 잊어버렸다고 말하는 것은 그 의사가 환자에게 병에 관한 안 좋은 이야기를 할 거라는 것을 무의식적으로 의

식하기 때문에 환자에게는 의사와의 만남을 '방해하려는 (hinder)' 무의식적인 의도가 있다고 여긴다.

어휘

• irreplaceable : 대체[대신]할 수 없는, 귀중한
• statue : 조각상
• shatter : 산산이 부서지다, 산산조각 나다
• stem from : ～에서 생겨나다[기인하다]
• prized : 소중한
• deliberate : 고의의, 의도적인
• uncover : 알아내다, 적발하다
• reckless : 무모한, 신중하지 못한
• self-inflicted : 자초한
• urge : 욕구, 충동

해석

친구와 언쟁을 벌이던 중 그 친구의 소중한 조각상을 "실수로" 떨어뜨린다고 가정해보자. 그 조각상은 수리할 수 없게 산산조각이 나버린다. 일부러 그런 것이 아니라고 말하며 사과한다. 그러나 이것이 정말 실수일까? 프로이드의 견해에 따르면, 많은 명백한 사고들이 사실 무의식적인 충동에 기인한 의도된 행동이다. 프로이드는 친구의 소중한 물품을 깨뜨렸을 때 친구를 다치게 하려는 무의식적인 욕망을 표출한 것이라고 주장할 수도 있다. 실수로 정기 진료 약속을 잊어버렸다고 말하는 고객은 프로이드가 '저항'이라 부르는 것을 보여준 것일 수도 있다. 의식적으로 고객들은 그 약속을 단순히 기억하지 못하는 것이라고 믿는다. 거기에는 무의식적으로 위협적인 무의식 요소를 거의 알아낼 치료사를 방해하려는 의도된 노력이 있었다. 비슷하게 난폭 운전자들은 자해의 무의식적 욕망을 충족시키기 위해 사고를 저지를 수도 있다. 프로이드파 심리학자들에게, 많은 불행한 사건들은 사람들이 의도하지 않는다는 의미가 아니라, 의식적으로 그것을 의도하지 않는다는 의미의 사고이다.

[40~41]

40 ④ (d)의 'him'은 Rimbaud가 자기 작품의 복사본과 쪽지를 보낸 출판업자 Paul Demeny이고, 나머지 (a), (b), (c), (e)는 모두 Rimbaud 본인 자신이다.

41 ③ 위의 제시문에는 Rimbaud가 십대 때에 가장 최근에 쓴 시를 보여주고 싶어서, 그의 예전 Georges Izambard 선생님을 교문 밖에서 서성거리며 매일 기다렸다는 내용이 있지만, "그가 선생님으로부터 시에 관한 자신만의 독특한 비전을 획득했는지(He acquired his own unique vision for poetry from his teacher.)"의 여부는 설명된 바가 없어 알

수 없다.

오답풀이

① He worked in fields unrelated to literature as an adult. (그는 어른이 돼서 문학과 관련 없는 분야에서 일했다.)
② He wanted to be a poet as a teenager. (그는 십대 때에 시인이 되고 싶었다.)
④ He hoped his poems would be published. (그는 시가 출판되기를 희망했다.)
⑤ His poetic images were based on a conflict of senses or thoughts. (그의 시적 이미지들은 심상과 사상의 충돌에 근거했다.)

어휘

• in later life : 만년에
• anarchist : 무정부주의자
• palely : 창백하게, 파랗게 질려
• hang around : 기다리다, 서성거리다
• verse : 운문, 시
• accompany : 동반하다, 동행하다
• visionary : 선지자
• boundless : 끝없는, 한없는
• systematize : 체계화[조직화]하다
• disorganization : 해체, 분열, 혼란
• grapple : 붙잡고 싸우다, 고심하다
• derange : 어지럽히다, 미치게 하다, 발광시키다
• novel : 새로운, 신기한, 참신한
• jostle : 거칠게 밀치다[떠밀다]

해석

만년에 Arthur Rimbaud는 무정부주의자이자, 사업가이자, 무기상이자, 금융업자이자 탐험가였다. 그러나 십대에 (a) 그가 되고 싶었던 것은 오로지 시인이었다. 1871년 5월에 16살이었던 Rimbaud는 두 장의 편지를 썼고, 한 장은 (b) 그의 예전 선생님이신 Georges Izambard에게, 그리고 한 장은 감명을 주기를 간절히 바랬던 출판업자 Paul Demeny에게 썼다. Rimbaud는 파랗게 질려 교문 밖에서 서성거리며 Izambard 선생님을 매일 기다렸고, 가장 최근에 쓴 시를 그 젊은 교수에게 보여주고 싶어 했다. 그는 또한 작품 사본을 Demeny에게 보냈고, (c) 그가 자기 시에 관해 말하려는 내용이 적힌 쪽지를 함께 보내 출판하고 싶다는 강한 암시를 주었다. Demeny에게 보낸 쪽지에서, Rimbaud는 새 시집에 대한 비전을 제시했다. "시는 스스로를 선지자로 만든다", "모든 감각의 길고 끝없이 조직화된 해체를 통해서"라고 Rimbaud는 (d) 그에게 설교를 늘어놓았다. Rimbaud는 오직 그것만이 "향기, 소리, 색깔, 고뇌하는 사고와 같은 모든 것을 포함할" 언어를 창조할 수 있다고 주장했다. (e) 그의 시적 프로그램은 전통적인 인지 순서

를 뒤엎고, 습관적으로 사용한 시각, 청각, 후각, 촉각, 미각을 뒤섞고, 새로운 조합으로 재배치하는 것이다. 심상과 심상이 부딪히고, 사상과 사상이 씨름할 때 신선하고, 생동감 있고, 때로는 충격적인 이미지들이 만들어진다.

[42~43]

42 ① 위의 제시문은 공통된 관심사를 가진 사람들끼리 어울리려는 성향에 의해 사회 연결망이 형성되며, 구체적으로 사람들은 세 가지 방법에 의해 그런 사회 연결망을 선택한다고 설명하고 있다. 그러므로 위 글은 어떻게 사회 연결망이 형성되었는지 ①의 '사회 연결망을 형성하는 방법(how we shape our social networks)'이 그 주제로 적절하다.

오답풀이

② how online social networks affect our life(온라인 사회 연결망이 우리 삶에 미치는 영향)

③ tips for restoring damaged social networks(손상된 사회 연결망을 회복시키는 요령)

④ dangers of diversifying your social networks(다양한 사회 연결망의 위험성)

⑤ necessity of social networks in finding a job(구직 활동에 사회 연결망의 필요성)

43 ② 앞의 문장에서 닮은 사람들끼리 어울리려는 의식적인 또는 무의식적인 성향이며, 우리의 관심과 역사와 꿈을 공유할 사람들을 찾아 나선다고 했으므로 '유유상종'에 해당하는 ②의 "날개가 같은 새들이 함께 모인다(Birds of a feather flock together)."는 속담이 빈칸의 내용으로 적합하다.

오답풀이

① Familiarity breeds contempt. (친하면 무례해지기 쉽다.)

③ Too many cooks spoil the broth. (요리사가 너무 많으면 수프를 망친다.)

④ Don't judge a book by its cover. (표지만 보고 책을 판단하지 마라.)

⑤ A rolling stone gathers no moss. (구르는 돌에는 이끼가 끼지 않는다.)

어휘

• homophily : 동종애
• hide-and-seek : 숨바꼭질
• densely : 밀집하여, 빽빽이
• groom : 신랑
• bridesmaid : 신부 들러리
• mingle with : ~와 섞다
• astonish : 깜짝 놀라게 하다

• embed : 박다, 끼워 넣다
• conducive : ~에 좋은, 도움이 되는
• diversify : 다각[다양]화하다
• broth : 수프, 죽

해석

인간은 의도적으로 사회 연결망을 항상 만들거나 재형성한다. 이것에 관한 주요 예시가 바로 '동종애'(문자 그대로 비슷한 것을 좋아함을 뜻함)인데, 닮은 사람들끼리 어울리려는 의식적인 또는 무의식적인 성향이다. 우표 수집가이든, 커피 마시는 사람이든, 번지 점프하는 사람이든 간에 사실은 우리의 관심과 역사와 꿈을 공유할 사람을 찾아 나선다는 것이다. 속담에 따르면 "유유상종"이다.

그러나 우리는 또한 세 가지의 중요한 방법으로 연결망 구조를 선택한다. 첫 번째는 얼마나 많은 사람들과 연결되어 있는가를 결정하는 것이다. 체커 게임을 같이 할 한 사람을 원하는가 아니면 숨바꼭질을 할 여러 사람을 원하는가? 미친 삼촌과 계속해서 연락하고 싶은가? 두 번째로 우리 친구들이나 가족과 얼마나 밀접하게 서로 연락하느냐에 영향을 미친다. 결혼식에서 신랑의 대학 룸메이트를 신부 들러리 옆에 앉혀야 하는가? 모든 친구들이 서로 만날 수 있도록 파티를 열어야만 하는가? 사업 파트너를 소개해야만 하는가? 그리고 세 번째로 우리가 얼마나 사회 연결망의 중심에 있는가를 통제한다. 파티의 달인으로 그 방의 중심에서 모두와 섞여있는가 아니면 가장자리에 머물러 있는가?

이런 다양한 선택들은 우리가 소속된 전 연결망에 깜짝 놀랄만한 다양한 구조를 형성한다. 그리고 이런 선택의 다양성은 사회 연결망 속에서 우리들 각자를 특별한 위치에 놓는다. 물론 이따금 이런 구조적 특징들은 선택의 문제만은 아니다. 즉, 다소 친구 사귀기에 좋은 곳에서 살 수도 있고, 대가족이나 소가족에서 태어날 수도 있다. 그러나 이런 사회 연결망에 노출될 때조차도, 그것들은 여전히 우리의 삶을 통제한다.

[44~45]

44 ② → (C) 종이에 이름이 적힌 사람은 그것을 고른 사람이 선물을 사주도록 되어 있는 가족 전통에 대해 소개한다.
→ (B) 종이가 접혀 있었기 때문에 몰래 선물을 준비했고, 누구로부터 선물을 받을지 궁금해 하며 크리스마스 날을 기다렸다.
→ (D) 그런데, 동생 Joe가 모든 종이에 자기 이름을 적어서 다른 식구들 모두가 Joe에게 줄 선물을 사도록 사건을 꾸몄다.

정답 및 해설

45 ② 종이에 이름이 적힌 사람은 그것을 고른 사람이 선물을 사주도록 되어 있는데, 가족들 모두가 Joe에게 줄 선물을 샀으므로, 동생 Joe가 그 종이들 모두에 자기 이름을 적었음을 유추할 수 있다.

오답풀이

① he'd saved enough money to buy a present(선물을 살 충분한 돈을 구한 것)

③ he'd been proud of this unique tradition of our family(우리 가족의 이런 특별한 전통을 자랑스러워 한 것)

④ he'd properly finished what he had been expected to do(하려고 했던 일을 제대로 끝마친 것)

⑤ he'd wanted to give a gift to every member of our family(우리 가족 모두에게 선물을 주고 싶었던 것)

어휘

• costly : 많은 돈[비용]이 드는

• fold up : 접다, 포개다, 녹초가 되다

• purchase : 구입하다, 사다

해석

(A) 우리가 어렸을 때, 형제들과 나는 부모님으로부터 크리스마스 선물을 받았다. 보통 어머니와 아버지는 우리 각자에게 매우 비싼 선물 하나와 조금 덜 비싼 선물 몇 개를 주셨다. 그러나 이것이 크리스마스 때에 우리 집에서 벌어진 유일한 선물주기는 아니다.

(B) 종이들이 접혀있기 때문에, 아무도 자기가 선택한 사람의 이름을 말할 수 없었다. 또한 아무도 그들이 선택했던 사람의 이름을 다른 누군가에게 말하지 않았다. 이런 식으로 우리 가족의 식구들은 가족 개인에게 줄 무언가를 몰래 샀다. 우리는 누구로부터 선물을 받을지 궁금해 하며, 정말로 크리스마스 날을 학수고대했다.

(C) 우리 가족에게는 또한 특별한 전통이 있었다. 매년 11월경에 작은 종잇조각에 각자의 이름을 적고, 그 종잇조각을 접어 모자 안에 넣었다. 다음에 한 사람 한 사람씩 종잇조각을 골랐다. 종이에 이름이 적힌 사람은 그것을 고른 사람이 선물을 사주도록 되어 있었다.

(D) 그러다 어느 해 예상치 못했던 일이 벌어졌다. 크리스마스 날에 "비밀 선물"을 나눠 줄 시간이 왔을 때, 부모님과 형 그리고 나는 모두 내 동생 Joe에게 줄 선물을 샀다는 사실을 알고 충격을 받았다. 그때서야 Joe가 종잇조각을 준비한 사람이었고, 그것들 모두에 자기 이름을 적었음을 깨달았다.

2015학년도 기출문제 정답 및 해설

제2교시 영어영역(공통)

01 ①	02 ②	03 ④	04 ①	05 ⑤	06 ①
07 ③	08 ③	09 ②	10 ②	11 ⑤	12 ⑤
13 ④	14 ②	15 ③	16 ①	17 ⑤	18 ②
19 ③	20 ②	21 ①	22 ①	23 ⑤	24 ④
25 ④	26 ④	27 ③	28 ⑤	29 ③	30 ⑤
31 ⑤	32 ③	33 ⑤	34 ③	35 ④	36 ②
37 ①	38 ②	39 ③	40 ④	41 ③	42 ⑤
43 ④	44 ④	45 ①			

01 ① 대화가 이루어지고 있는 장소를 묻는 문제이다. 'wearing a uniform and serving your nation(제복을 입고 나라를 위해 일하는)'과 'Air Force brochures(공군 안내 책자)'라는 내용을 통해 'at a military recruitment center(군 채용 센터에서)' 대화하고 있음을 알 수 있다.

오답풀이

② 병영 식당에서
③ 사관생도 생활관에서
④ 항공관제탑에서
⑤ 전쟁기념관에서

어휘

• recommend : 추천하다
• branch : 분과, 부서
• appreciate : 감사하다
• traverse : 횡단하다, 돌아다니다
• brochure : 책자

해석

Captain Sim : 그러면 내가 어떻게 도와주면 되겠습니까?
Sonya : 잘 모르겠습니다. 저는 삶에서 제가 하고 싶은 것을 찾으려고 노력해왔고, 한 친구가 저에게 여기를 가보라고 권했습니다.
Captain Sim : 현명한 결정이네요. 우리는 본인과 같은 유망한 젊은이에게 제안할 훌륭한 직업 선택 사항을 가지고 있습니다. 어떤 병과를 생각하고 있습니까?

Sonya : 전혀 모르겠습니다. 조언을 해주시면 감사하겠습니다.
Captain Sim : 글쎄, 제복을 입고 나라를 위해 일하는 자랑스러운 본인의 모습을 눈을 감고 상상해 보십시오. 본인이 높은 바다를 항해하고 광활한 하늘로 날아오르거나 이국적인 외국을 돌아다니는 모습이 보입니까?
Sonya : 음... 비행은 멋질 것 같습니다.
Captain Sim : 그러면, 공군 안내 책자를 보여주겠습니다.

02 ② 대화의 내용과 일치하지 않는 것을 고르는 문제이다. 남편의 승진으로 스웨덴으로 이사를 가야 하는 상황에서 Perez 부인이 "I'd have to resign from work.(내가 일을 그만두어야 하겠네요.)"라고 말한 것을 통해 현재 직장을 다니고 있음을 알 수 있다. 따라서 'Mrs. Perez is currently unemployed.(Perez 부인은 현재 실직 상태이다)'는 대화와 일치하지 않는다.

오답풀이

① Perez 씨가 전근을 받아들이면 승진될 것이다.
③ Perez 부인은 스웨덴어를 구사하지 못한다.
④ Perez 씨가 그 일을 얻으면 더 많은 돈을 벌 것이다.
⑤ Perez 부인은 스웨덴으로 가는 것을 망설인다.

어휘

• promotion : 승진, 진급
• transfer : 옮기다, 이동하다
• resign : 사직하다, 물러나다
• hesitant : 주저하는, 망설이는

해석

Mr. Perez : 잠깐 할 이야기가 있는데.
Mrs. Perez : 그래요, 여보. 무슨 일이에요?
Mr. Perez : 오늘 승진 제안을 받았어. 좋은 기회이고 신이 나긴 하는데. 몇 년 동안 스웨덴으로 옮겨야 한다는 얘기야.
Mrs. Perez : 왜! 그런데... 잘 모르겠어요. 내가 일을 그만두어야 하겠네요. 게다가 거기서 어떻게 새 일자리를 구할 수 있을까요? 난 스웨덴어도 모르는데요.
Mr. Perez : 그건 걱정 안 해도 돼. 승진에 당신이 일을 하지 않아도 될 정도로 급여를 많이 올려준다는 사항이 포함되어 있거든.

Mrs. Perez : 우리가 집과 친구들을 그렇게 오랫동안 정말로 떠날 수 있을까요? 이 문제는 정말로 생각해봐야만 하겠네요.

03 ④ 빈칸에 들어갈 적절한 표현을 보기에서 골라 순서대로 연결하는 문제이다. 첫 번째 빈칸에는 전화한 지 3일 만에 수리 기사가 방문했다는 말에 대한 응답으로 사과의 말이 들어가는 것이 적절하다. 따라서 'd. I do apologize. (정말 죄송합니다)'가 들어가야 한다. 두 번째 빈칸의 앞에서 Frank가 고장 난 부분을 빠르게 고치겠다고 하였으므로 두 번째 빈칸에는 어떤 부분이 문제인지 물어보는 말이 들어가야 한다. 따라서 'a. What seems to be the problem?(어디가 문제인가요?)'이 들어가야 한다. 세 번째 빈칸에는 Mrs. won이 말한 문제점을 듣고 그에 따른 반응을 나타내는 표현이 들어가야 하는데, 빈칸 뒤에서 Frank가 빠르게 처리할 수 있다고 말했기 때문에 'c. That should be a simple fix.(간단하게 고칠 수 있겠네요)'가 들어가는 것이 적절하다.

어휘

- heat wave : 무더위
- fix : 해결책
- leak : 새다
- in no time : 곧, 당장에
- melt : 녹다

해석

Mrs. Won : 와주셔서 정말 감사해요. 드디어! 제가 3일 동안 계속 전화를 했거든요!
Frank : 정말 죄송합니다. 그런데 무더위 때문에, 시내에 사는 모든 사람들이 에어컨 정비를 받길 원하는 것 같아요.
Mrs. Won : 충분히 이해해요. 하지만, 저희 가족과 저는 더워서 못 견디고 있어요.
Frank : 자, 그럼 에어컨을 고쳐서 가능한 빨리 고객님과 가족분들이 시원하도록 하겠습니다. 어디가 문제인가요?
Mrs. Won : 에어컨을 켜면, 따뜻한 바람만 나와요.
Frank : 간단하게 고칠 수 있겠네요. 프레온 가스를 충전하기만 하면 될 것 같아요. 만약에 새는 곳이 전혀 없다면, 당장 처리할 수 있어요.
Mrs. Won : 좋아요. 하지만 서둘러주세요. 제가 녹아내릴지도 몰라요.

04 ① 두 사람의 관계를 묻는 문제이다. 회사로부터 고발을 당한 여자가 법정에 출두하게 된 상황에서 통화를 하는 상대는 변호사일 가능성이 높다. 따라서 여자와 남자의 관계는 'client – attorney(고객 – 변호사)'이다.

오답풀이

② 판사 – 피의자
③ 범인 – 피해자
④ 경찰관 – 용의자
⑤ 고용주 – 피고용인

어휘

- in need of : ~을 필요로 하고
- arrest : 체포하다
- steal from : ~의 것을 훔치다
- leave out : 빼다
- pay back : 갚다, 돌려주다
- represent : 대표하다, 변호하다
- in a court of law : 재판소, 법원

해석

Woman : 제가 곤란한 상황이고 당신의 도움이 필요해서 전화했어요.
Man : 무엇을 도와드릴까요?
Woman : 회사의 것을 훔쳤다고 상사가 저를 신고해서 저는 체포되었어요. 지금 경찰은 제가 법정에 가야 할 거라고 말하거든요.
Man : 저에게 자초지종을 말씀하시고 어떤 것도 빠뜨리면 안 됩니다.
Woman : 정확히 저는 그렇게 하지 않았어요. 큰 오해였어요. 저는 그저 돈을 빌렸을 뿐이라고요. 그 돈을 갚으려고 했어요.
Man : 이제 걱정 마세요. 제가 이 문제를 처리하겠습니다. 하지만 만약에 제가 당신을 법원에서 제대로 변호하게 된다면, 우리는 만나서 이것에 대해 이야기를 나누어야 합니다.

05 ⑤ 빈칸에 들어갈 알맞은 응답을 고르는 문제로, 교사와 학부모가 상담을 하는 내용이다. 교사가 학생의 문제점을 설명하지만, 학부모가 전혀 알지 못하는 상황이므로 빈칸에는 'Please talk with him, because if he doesn't improve, he could fail the class.(만약에 Sam이 나아지지 않으면 낙제할 수 있기 때문에 Sam과 이야기를 해보세요)'가 들어가는 것이 적절하다.

오답풀이

① 만약 다시 그렇게 한다면, 그는 정학을 당할 수 있다.
② 나는 그의 학교 성적이 현재의 수준을 계속해서 유지하길 바란다.
③ 학기가 진행될수록 Sam은 지속적으로 향상되고 있다.
④ 처음부터 학습에 흥미가 없었기 때문에, 그를 포기했다.

어휘

- hear from : ~에게서 연락을 받다
- distracted : 주의가 산만한
- term : 학기
- distant : 서먹서먹한, 냉담한

해석

Sam's Teacher : 오늘 학교로 와 주셔서 감사합니다. 전화로 말씀드렸다시피, Sam이 조금 걱정이 되어서요.

Sam's Dad : 선생님께 연락을 받고 놀랐습니다. Sam이 무슨 잘못을 했나요?

Sam's Teacher : 아뇨, 전혀 아니에요. 그저 Sam이 최근에 주의가 산만해져서 집중을 잘 하지 못하는 것 같아요. 이번 학기를 시작할 때, Sam은 우수한 학생들 중에 한 명이었어요. 하지만 최근에 숙제도 늦게 해오고 성적이 떨어지고 있고, 학급 친구들과도 멀어진 것 같아요. 집에 무슨 일이 있나요?

Sam's Dad : 그것 참 이상하네요. 저는 Sam이 학교에서 잘하고 있다고 늘 생각했거든요. 어떤 문제가 있는지 전혀 모르겠습니다. 사실 가정생활은 좋았거든요.

Sam's Teacher : <u>만약에 Sam이 나아지지 않으면 낙제할 수 있기 때문에 Sam과 이야기를 해보세요.</u>

06 ① 대화의 상황을 가장 잘 묘사하고 있는 선택지를 고르는 문제이다. 'When are Mom and Dad coming back from their trip?'을 통해 Bobby의 부모님이 여행 중이어서 할아버지가 Bobby를 돌보고 있다는 것을 알 수 있다. 따라서 정답은 'Grandpa is looking after Bobby. (할아버지는 Bobby를 돌보는 중이다)'이다.

오답풀이

② Bobby의 부모님은 늦은 시간까지 일하는 중이다.
③ Bobby는 스마트폰 게임을 하고 있다.
④ Bobby와 할아버지는 함께 여행 중이다.
⑤ 할아버지는 Bobby와 함께 밖에서 놀고 싶지 않다.

어휘

- sunrise : 일출
- sunset : 일몰, 해질녘
- entertain : 즐겁게 하다

해석

Bobby : 할아버지, 심심해요. 할아버지 스마트폰으로 게임해도 돼요?

Grandpa : 그런 게임들은 그저 시간과 에너지 낭비일 뿐이야. 밖에 나가서 노는 게 어떠니? 날이 좋구나.

Bobby : 하지만 나가서 할 게 아무것도 없어요. 엄마와 아빠는 여행에서 언제 다시 돌아오세요?

Grandpa : 전 세계를 일주하고 온다는구나. 내가 어렸을 때, 난 해 뜰 때부터 해질녘까지 밖에서 놀았단다. 스마트폰이나 비디오 게임 없이 즐겁게 보낼 방법들을 항상 찾았지. 우리가 일주일을 더 함께 보내야 하니까, 우리 스스로 재미있을 방법들을 몇 가지 찾아보자꾸나.

Bobby : 저와 함께 나가서 놀아주실래요?

Grandpa : 그러고 싶구나. 나가자.

07 ③ ③은 Piaget가 유모를 공격했다고 생각한 남자이고, 나머지는 Piaget를 가리킨다.

어휘

- fabricate : 조작하다, 왜곡하다
- convince : 납득시키다, 확신시키다
- no less person than : 다름 아닌 바로
- personage : 저명인사
- psychologist : 심리학자
- frequently : 자주
- early childhood : 유아기
- vivid : 생생한
- nanny : 유모
- leap : 뛰다, 뛰어오르다
- bush : 덤불, 관목숲
- in an attempt to : ~하기 위하여, ~하려는 시도로
- kidnap : 납치[유괴]하다
- struggle : 싸우다, 투쟁하다
- fight off : ~와 싸워 물리치다
- inflict : 가하다, 입히다
- scratch : 긁힌 상처, 생채기
- frightening : 무서운
- exquisitely : 절묘하게
- detailed : 상세한
- recall : 기억해내다, 상기하다
- subsequently : 그 후에, 나중에
- take place : 일어나다, 발생하다
- write to : ~에게 편지를 보내다
- confess : 고백하다, 인정하다
- make up : (이야기 등을) 지어내다

해석

기억은 쉽게 왜곡될 수 있기 때문에 사람들은 전혀 일어나지 않았던 현실의 어떤 일을 확신하게 된다. 한 가지 유명한 예를 다름 아닌 저명한 스위스의 심리학자 Jean Piaget에게서 찾을 수 있다. <u>그의</u> 일생 동안, Piaget는 유아기 때 있었던 일에 대

정답 및 해설

한 생생한 기억을 자주 말했다. 어느 날, 유모가 그를 유모차에 태워서 길 아래로 걸어가는 동안, 어떤 남자가 Piaget를 유괴하려고 숲에서 뛰쳐나왔다. 그 남자는 유모와 싸웠고, 그가 그녀의 얼굴에 상처를 입히기 전까지 유모가 그를 잘 물리쳤다. 무서운 사건에 대한 Piaget의 기억은 낱낱이 자세했다. 그는 그 장면에서 그 사람들의 얼굴과 경찰의 제복과 유모의 얼굴에 난 상처들과 공격을 받은 정확한 장소를 기억해냈다. 그렇지만 Piaget와 그의 가족이 나중에 알게 되었듯이, 그 사건은 전혀 일어난 적이 없었다. 몇 년 후, 유모는 Piaget의 부모에게 편지를 보냈고, 상처를 포함하여 전부 다 지어낸 이야기였다고 고백했다.

08 ③ 이 글이 전반적으로 관습에 얽매이지 말자는 주장을 하고 있는데 반해, 'Following social conventions forms the basic ground-work for building a safe and stable society.(사회적 관습을 따르는 것은 안전하고 안정된 사회를 구축하기 위한 기본적인 토대를 형성한다)'는 사회적 관습을 따라야 한다는 내용으로, 글의 주제와 상반된다.

어휘

- Muhammad Ali : 무하마드 알리(미국의 권투 선수, 전(前) 헤비급 세계 챔피언)
- refuse : 거절하다, 거부하다
- run counter : ~을 거스르다, 상충되다
- unconventional : 관습에 얽매이지 않은, 색다른
- exactly : 정확하게
- legendary : 전설적인
- boxer : 복서, 권투 선수
- conform : 따르다, ~을 일치시키다
- code : 암호, (사회적) 관례[규칙]
- price : (치러야 할) 대가, 가격
- pay for : 대가를 지불하다, (손해 따위를) 입다
- blindly : 맹목적으로
- individuality : 개성, 특성
- authentically : 확실하게
- convention : 관습
- stable : 안정적인
- ground-work : 기초, 기본 원리
- imitate : 모방하다, 흉내 내다
- peculiarity : 특성, 별난 태도
- authentic : 진정한, 진짜인
- attention : 주의, 배려
- extraordinary : 기이한, 비범한

해석

무하마드 알리는 평범한 방법으로 권투를 하기를 거부했다. 거의 모든 방법에서 알리의 방식은 그 당시의 복싱 기술에 상충되었지만, 이러한 색다른 방식은 바로 그를 전설적인 복서로 만들었다. 어린아이와 청소년일 때, 우리는 사회적 가치와 다르게 행동할 것을 배우면서, 행동의 특정 규칙과 일을 하는 방법들을 배운다. 하지만 맹목적으로 순응할 경우 더 큰 대가를 치르게 된다. 즉, 우리는 우리의 개성과 진정으로 우리 자신의 것들을 하는 방법에서 온 능력을 잃는다. 사회적 관습을 따르는 것은 안전하고 안정된 사회를 구축하기 위한 기본적인 토대를 형성한다. 진정으로 관습에 얽매이지 않는 방법은 누구도 모방하지 않고 당신 자신의 리듬에 맞춰 맞서 싸우고 움직이는 것이다. 만약 당신의 특이한 점이 충분히 진정성을 지니고 있다면, 그것은 당신에게 배려와 존중을 가져다 줄 것이다 — 관습에 얽매이지 않고 비범한 것에 대해 군중들이 늘 지니는 성질의 것.

09 ② 대인 관계 기술이 미숙한 청소년들의 문자 메시지 사용에 대한 우려를 담고 있는 글이다. 성인의 경우 처음 문자 메시지를 이용할 때 이미 안정적인 사회적 존재였던 것에 비해, 어린이들은 그렇지 않기 때문에 문자 메시지에 지나치게 의존해서는 안 된다는 것이다. ② 'Besides, their ability to have a face-to-face conversation dramatically declines after extensive reliance on text messages.(게다가, 문자 메시지에 지나치게 의존한 이후로 얼굴을 마주보고 하는 대화를 하는 그들의 능력이 극적으로 감소한다)'는 문자 메시지로 인해 성인들의 의사소통 능력이 감소했다는 것으로, 글 전체 흐름에 맞지 않는다.

어휘

- developmental psychologist : 발달 심리학자
- texting : 휴대 전화로 문자 메시지 주고받기
- interpersonal skill : 대인 관계 기술
- reliance : 의존
- overly : 지나치게, 과도하게
- reason : 판단하다, 추론하다
- prevent : 막다, 방해하다
- acquire : 습득하다, 배우다
- sufficient : 충분한

해석

청소년들은 대인 관계 기술이 아직 제대로 형성되지 않았기 때문에 문자 메시지의 영향을 연구하는 발달 심리학자들은 청소년들에 대해 특히 걱정한다. 어린이들과 달리, 대부분의 성인들이 처음으로 문자 메시지가 가능한 휴대용 모바일 기기를 그들의 손에 쥐었을 때, 그들은 이미 안정적인 사회적 존재였

다. 게다가, 문자 메시지에 지나치게 의존한 이후로 얼굴을 마주보고 대화를 하는 그들의 능력이 극적으로 감소한다. 하지만, MIT대학 대인 관계 개발 연구원인 Sherry Turkle에 따르면, 어린이들의 경우에 그렇지 않다. 그녀는 어린이들이 의사소통을 하기 위하여 문자 메시지에 지나치게 의존한다면 얼굴을 마주보고 하는 대화 기술을 발달시키지 못할 것이라고 믿는다. 생각하고 판단하고 성찰하는 기술들은 언어적 의사소통에서 충분한 경험 없이 습득되기 어렵기 때문에 이것은 또한 그들이 이러한 기술들을 배우는 것을 막을지도 모른다.

10 ② 'In social science terms, television constructed the frame of meaning with which audiences and decision-makers came to understand Katrina.(사회 과학 측면에서, 텔레비전은 시청자와 의사 결정자가 카트리나를 이해하도록 하는 의미의 틀을 구성했다)'에서 알 수 있듯이, 텔레비전 보도를 통해 자연재해를 이해하는 전체적인 틀을 제공받는다는 내용임을 파악할 수 있다.

어휘

• accompaniment : 수반되는 것, 반주
• continuous : 지속적인, 계속되는
• 24/7 : 하루 24시간 1주 7일 동안, 언제나
• coverage : (신문, 텔레비전, 라디오의) 보도
• construct : 구성하다, 건설하다
• frame : (이론, 사상 등의) 틀
• audience : 시청자
• decision-maker : 의사 결정자
• storm : 폭풍(우)
• slightly : 약간, 조금
• come through : 전해지다, 들어오다
• victim : 희생자
• electrical power : 전력
• appliance : 가전제품, 기기
• confirm : 확인하다, 입증하다
• context : 맥락

해석

카트리나는 (하루 24시간) 지속적인 텔레비전 보도가 수반된, 미국을 강타한 첫 번째 허리케인이었다. 사회 과학적 측면에서, 텔레비전은 시청자와 의사 결정자가 카트리나를 이해하도록 하는 의미의 틀을 구성했다. 해안을 따라 어떤 경우에, 카트리나와 관련된 개인적인 경험이 도움이 되었을지도 모른다. 만약 당신이 도핀섬이나 빌럭시 만, 세인트루이스 또는 버번 스트리트의 한 술집 안에 있다면, 그 폭풍우는 조금 달랐을 것이다. 하지만, 우리 대부분에게 그 폭풍우의 실제는 텔레비전 방송국을 통해 전해진다. 전력을 잃은 '희생자'

의 경우, 그것이 다시 공급되면 커피포트와 텔레비전이 첫 번째 다시 작동되는 가전제품이 되었을 것이기 때문에 그들 자신의 경험은 매체에 의해 제공된 정보의 맥락 안에서 이해되고 확인된다.

11 ⑤ 'Your communication takes on defensive strategies are designed to protect yourself.'에서 주어는 'Your communication'이고, 동사는 'takes on'이다. 'are designed to protect yourself'는 선행사 'defensive strategies'를 수식하고 있기 때문에 'strategies'와 'are' 사이에 주격 관계대명사 'which'가 생략되어 있음을 알 수 있다. 참고로 주격 관계대명사는 생략할 수 없으나 '주격 관계대명사 + be동사'는 생략 가능하다. 따라서 'are designed'를 'which are designed' 또는 'designed'로 바꿔야 한다.

어휘

• communication : 의사소통
• present : 보여주다, 나타내다
• involve : 수반하다, 관련시키다
• reject : 거부하다, 거절하다
• climate : 기후, 분위기
• on the basis of : ~을 기반으로, ~에 근거하여
• feel secure : 안심하다
• defensive : 방어적인
• strategy : 전략
• insist : 고집하다, 주장하다
• shoot down : 비난하다
• comment : 발언, 의견
• ridicule : 비웃다, 놀리다
• figure out : 이해하다, 알아내다
• publicly : 공개적으로, 공공연하게
• sarcasm : 빈정댐, 비꼬는 말
• take on : 나타내다, 띠다

해석

의사소통은 당신 자신과 당신의 역할, 상황과 다른 사람들이 거부할지도 모를 그 밖의 것들을 그들에게 보여주는 것을 의미하기 때문에, 다른 사람들과의 의사소통에는 일종의 위험이 수반된다. 의사소통 분위기는 주어진 상황에서 당신에게 얼마나 많은 위험이 수반되는지를 당신이 예측하는 것의 중요한 부분이다. 당신은 자신이 얼마나 안전한지에 대한 판단에 근거하여 행동한다. 만약 안심할 수 없다면, 당신은 방어적인 전략들을 사용할 것이다. 아마도 당신은 교사가 학생들이 솔직하게 문제들을 논의함으로써 참여해야 한다고 계속 주장하면서도, 학생들이 그렇게 할 때 교사가 그들의 의견을 비난하거나 그들을 비웃는 교실 상황에 있어본 적이 있을 것이다. 공개

적으로 비꼬는 말에 타도되는 것은 기분이 좋은 일이 아니라는 것을 당신이 생각해내는 데 그리 오랜 시간이 걸리지 않는다. 당신은 그 분위기가 안전하지 않다는 것을 빠르게 알게 된다. 당신의 의사소통은 자신을 보호하도록 되어 있는 방어적인 전략들을 띠게 된다.

12 ⑤ 'But Galileo, whom people consider the father of the experimental method, to praise Copernicus precisely for what he did; for staying with his belief.'에서 주어는 'Galileo'이고, 'whom people consider the father of the experimental method'는 삽입된 구문으로 선행사 'Galileo'를 수식하고 있다. 문장의 동사가 없는 구조이므로 'to praise'를 'praised'로 바꿔야 한다.

어휘

- quest : 탐구, 탐색
- triumph : 큰 업적, 승리
- agony : 극도의 고통, 괴로움
- go hand in hand : 관련되다, 함께 가다
- planetary : 행성의
- far from : 전혀[결코] ~이 아닌
- definitely : 명확하게, 분명히
- heliocentric : 태양을 중심으로 하는
- proposition : 제안, 명제
- supplement : 보충하다
- in nature : 사실상
- handiwork : 일, 작품
- readily : 손쉽게
- prediction : 예측, 예견
- geometrical : 기하학적
- simplicity : 단순성
- bold : 대담한, 선명한
- cling to : ~을 고수하다
- shake one's head : 고개를 젓다

해석

과학의 탐구는 많은 업적과 함께 극심한 고통을 보여 왔다. 이 둘은 늘 떨어질 수 없는 관계였고 과학을 위한 신념의 역할을 동일하게 잘 입증했다. 주요한 첫 번째 업적은 행성의 순서에 대한 코페르니쿠스의 개요였다. 그는 태양중심설을 전혀 명확하게 입증하지 않았다. 하지만 그는 물리적인 증거가 부족한 부분을 사실상 그의 신념으로 보완했다. 자연이 창조주의 작품이라는 신념을 바탕으로, 그는 자연은 단순하다는 결론을 손쉽게 내렸다. 행성에 대한 그의 가설은 프톨레마이오스가 했던 것보다 행성의 움직임에 대해 더 나은 예측을 제시하지 않았다. 가장 눈길을 끄는 코페르니쿠스의 증거는 행성의 새

로운 배열에 대한 기하학적 단순성에서 찾을 수 있었다. 그것은 대담한 견해였고, 사람들이 믿지 못하여 고개를 내젓긴 했지만 그는 그것을 고수했다. 하지만 실험법의 아버지로 여겨지는 갈릴레오는 코페르니쿠스가 했던 것을 확실히 칭찬했다. 그가 신념을 지켰기 때문이다.

13 ④ (A)의 경우 'obstacles' 뒤에 온 'to'가 전치사이므로 뒤에 (동)명사가 와야 하기 때문에, increasing이 적절하다. (B)는 'whose extra energy storage could reduce the battery's weight by 15 percent'에서 'the battery's weight'가 목적어에 해당하기 때문에 수동태가 아닌 능동태의 동사 표현인 'reduce'가 와야 한다. (C)의 경우, 문장 내에서 타동사의 주어와 목적어가 일치하는 경우 목적어를 재귀대명사로 표현하는 재귀용법이 적용되므로 'themselves'를 선택해야 한다.

어휘

- obstacle to : ~에 대한 장애(물)
- emerge : 떠오르다, 나타나다
- concept : 개념
- electricity : 전기
- draw attention : 관심을 끌다
- potential : 가능성이 있는, 잠재적인
- breakthrough : 돌파구
- experiment : 실험하다
- prototype : 원형, 견본, 시제품
- reduce : 줄이다
- ultimately : 궁극적으로, 결국
- efficiency : 효율(성)
- lithium-ion battery : 리튬이온전지

해석

하이브리드 자동차의 범위를 늘리는 것의 가장 큰 장애물 중에 하나는 바로 건전지의 무게이다. 더 강력한 건전지는 더 먼 거리로 차량을 움직이게 하지만, 또한 무게가 더 많이 나간다. 차량의 문과 보닛 등에 전기를 비축할 수 있는, 새롭게 알려진 하이브리드 자동차의 설계 개념은 이러한 문제를 해결하는 데 가능성 있는 돌파구로 관심을 끌고 있다. 몇몇 연구원들은 이미 에너지를 저장하는 트렁크 플로어를 지닌 견본 전기 자동차를 가지고 실험을 하기 시작했는데, 여분의 에너지 저장은 건전지의 무게를 15퍼센트까지 줄일 수 있다. 궁극적으로, 만약 이러한 새로운 기술이 현재의 리튬이온전지의 효율성을 지닌다면, 이러한 종류의 차량은 지붕이나 문과 같이 건전지가 적용되지 않는 부분에 차량 자체를 80마일 정도 움직이도록 하기에 충분한 전기를 저장할 수 있다.

14 ② (A)의 경우, 'a comprehensive case describing the operational activities in a steel company'에서 'case'와 'describing' 사이에 'which was'가 생략되었다고 볼 수 있으며, 'describing' 뒤에 'the operational activities'의 목적어가 있으므로 수동이 아닌 능동으로 표현해야 한다. (B)의 경우 'only 29 percent of the others'의 동사 자리에 쓰인 대동사를 찾아야 하는데, 'but'을 사이로 앞 절에 쓰인 동사가 일반 동사이므로 대동사는 시제에 맞춰 'did'를 선택해야 한다. (C)는 'these participants interpreted the case's priorities in terms of the activities and goals of the functional areas to which the executives were attached'가 완전한 절에 해당하므로 동격의 'that'이 적절하다. 관계대명사 'which'의 경우 뒤이어 오는 절이 주어 혹은 목적어가 빠진 불완전한 절이어야 하는 반면, 동격의 that은 '포괄적(추상적) 의미의 명사 + that + 앞 명사의 내용을 구체적으로 설명해주는 완전한 절'과 같은 구조를 지닌다.

어휘

- represent : 나타내다, 보여주다
- classic study : 고전 연구
- perception : 인지, 통찰력
- executive : 경영진, 이사
- accounting : 회계
- miscellaneous : 여러 가지 종류의
- company president : 회사 사장
- rate : 평가하다, 여기다
- give priority to : ~을 우선으로 하다, 중점을 두다
- finding : 결과
- lead to : ~로 이어지다, ~을 초래하다
- participant : 참가자
- interpret : 이해하다, 설명하다
- in terms of : ~의 관점에서, ~면에서

해석

다음은 인지에 관한 고전 연구를 보여준다. 중간 관리직 스물세 명은 한 제강 회사의 운영 활동을 서술한 포괄적인 사례를 읽어야 했다. 스물세 명의 경영진들 중에 여섯 명은 판매, 다섯 명은 생산, 네 명은 회계, 그리고 여덟 명은 다른 여러 부서에서 일하고 있었다. 그 사례를 읽고 난 후, 경영진들은 각각 새로 취임한 회사 사장이 처음으로 처리해야 하는 문제를 판별해야 했다. 판매부 경영진들의 83퍼센트는 판매가 가장 중요하다고 여겼지만, 나머지 부서의 경영진들 중 29퍼센트만이 그렇게 생각했다. 유사하게 생산부 경영진은 생산 영역을 우선시하였고, 회계부는 회계 문제에 중점을 두었다. 이러한 결과를 통해 참가자들은 자신들이 속해 있는 부서의 기능 영역의 활동과 목표의 관점에서 사례의 우선 사항들을 이해했다는 결론을 얻었다.

15 ③ 이 글은 학습에 방해가 되는 요소로 집중력의 부재를 언급하고 있으며, 'indecision(망설임)'은 정신 집중의 적이라고 하였다. 따라서 망설임을 시간 낭비이며 공부에 대한 부정적인 태도를 유지시킨다고 볼 수 있으므로 'eliminate(없애다, 제거하다)'는 문맥상 어울리지 않는다.

오답풀이

① enhance : 높이다, 향상시키다
② low : 낮은
④ preoccupied : (생각 · 걱정이) 뇌리를 사로잡힌
⑤ constructive : 건설적인

어휘

- take place : 생기다, 일어나다
- concentrate : 집중하다
- intelligence : 지능
- indecision : 망설임
- interfere with : ~을 방해하다, ~에 지장을 주다

해석

만약 당신이 배우고 있는 것에 세심하게 집중하지 않는다면 전혀 학습되지 않는다. 정신 집중은 기본적으로 사고하는 것이다. 정신 집중은 정신적이고 육체적인 과제를 하는 당신의 능력을 향상시킬 수 있다. 따라서 학교에서 실패를 많이 하는 이유는 낮은 지능보다 형편없는 집중력 때문이다. 연구원들은 정신 집중의 한 가지 적은 주저하는 것이라고 덧붙인다. 언제 공부하고 어느 과목을 먼저 공부할지를 망설이는 것은 시간 낭비일 뿐만 아니라, 공부하는 측면에 부정적인 태도를 없애는(→ 유지하는) 확실한 방법이다. 개인적인 문제들 또한 정신 집중에 지장을 준다. 만약 개인적인 문제들에 몰두하고 있다면, 당신은 지능을 충분히 이용하지 못할 것이다. 당신의 문제에 어느 정도 건설적인 조치를 취하고 나면 당신은 잘 배우거나 수행할 수 있는 더 나은 상태에 있을 것이다.

16 ① 텔레비전을 시청하거나 음식을 먹는 것은 그 순간에 행복감을 주는 효과는 있지만, 그 이외에 추가적, 부가적인 효과는 없다는 내용이므로 빈칸에 들어갈 말로 가장 적절한 것은 'additive(부가적인)'이다.

오답풀이

② 감소하는
③ 일시적인
④ 즉각적인
⑤ 피할 수 있는

<어휘>

- psychological : 심리적인
- linear : 일차원적인, 직선 모양의
- systematic : 조직적인, 체계적인
- relation : 관계, 관련
- around the clock : 24시간 내내, 계속
- cease : 중단되다, ~하지 않게 되다
- be rewarding : 보람이 있다
- the same is true of : ~에서도 마찬가지다
- relaxation : 휴식
- in small doses : 조금씩
- tend to : (~하는) 경향이 있다
- daily life : 일상생활
- diminishing returns : 수확체감(생산 요소 투입이 일정 수준을 넘으면 투입에 따르는 한계 생산성이 상대적으로 줄어드는 현상)

<해석>

행동의 심리적인 효과는 일차원적이지 않지만, 우리가 하는 다른 모든 것들과의 체계적인 관계에 따라 달라진다. 예를 들어, 음식이 즐거움의 원천일지라도 우리는 24시간 내내 음식을 먹으면서 행복할 수 없다. 식사는 우리의 행복의 수준을 높이지만, 우리가 깨어 있는 시간의 약 5퍼센트 정도를 음식을 먹으면서 보낼 때뿐이다. 만약 우리가 식사를 하면서 그날을 온전히 다 보냈다면, 음식은 곧 가치가 사라질 것이다. 삶에서 대부분의 다른 좋은 것들도 마찬가지다. 휴식 삼아 조금씩 텔레비전을 시청하는 것은 일상생활의 질을 향상시킬 수 있지만, 그 효과는 부가적이지 않다. 수확체감점에 빠르게 도달한다.

17 ⑤ 'National Geographic magazine has come to be one of the primary means by which people in the United States receive information and images of the world outside their own borders.(내셔널 지오그래픽 매거진은 미국에 있는 사람들이 국경 너머 바깥세상의 정보와 이미지를 접하는 주요한 수단 중에 하나가 되어 왔다)'를 통해 내셔널 지오그래픽 매거진이 미국인들이 다른 국가들, 특히 제3세계 국가들에 대한 다양한 이야기들을 접할 수 있게 하는 역할을 해오고 있다는 것을 알 수 있다. 따라서 빈칸에 들어가기에 적절한 표현은 'different cultures from their own(그들 자신들과 다른 문화)'이다.

<오답풀이>

① 그들 자신의 전통
② 지역 경제 문제
③ 환경 운동

④ 근로 조건의 현실

<어휘>

- over the course of : ~ 동안
- primary : 주요한
- border : 국경(경계)지역
- cover : 보도하다, 취재하다, ~을 다루다
- a range of : 다양한
- geographic : 지리적인
- wonder : 경이로운 것, 기적
- account : 설명, 계좌
- exploration : 탐험, 탐사
- ice cap : 만년설
- portion : 일부
- photograph : 사진
- exotic : 이국적인, 색다른
- travelogue : 여행 관련 방송, 여행기
- faraway : 멀리 떨어진, 먼
- marvel : 놀라다

<해석>

지난 세기 동안, 내셔널 지오그래픽 매거진은 미국에 있는 사람들이 국경 너머 바깥세상의 정보와 이미지를 접하는 주요한 수단 중에 하나가 되어 왔다. 내셔널 지오그래픽이 다양한 주제 ― 미국의 지리적이고 문화적으로 놀라운 것들, 야생 동물과 자연의 이야기들, 그리고 우주 탐사와 해양, 극지의 만년설에 관한 설명 ― 를 다루긴 하지만, 글과 사진의 상당 부분은 제3세계의 민족과 문화의 특이하고 색다른 이미지 위주로 이루어져 있다. 내셔널 지오그래픽은 멀리 떨어진 곳의 사람들과 장소의 이야기와 사진들을 가지고 돌아오도록 스태프들을 먼 곳으로 다녀오게 하기 때문에, 여행 관련 방송의 오랜 전통을 이어가고 있다. 독자들이 그들의 집안에서 개인적으로 사진과 이야기들을 보고 놀라는 동안, 내셔널 지오그래픽은 그들 자신들과 다른 문화를 접하도록 사람들을 끌어들인다.

18 ② 제품 생산비와 판매 가격을 동시에 낮추어야 할 경우 어떤 방법이 바람직한가에 관한 글로, 이 글에 따르면 응답자들은 기존의 '익숙한 사회적 가치(familiar social values)'를 우선 고려한다고 볼 수 있다.

<오답풀이>

① 곧 있을 선거
③ 최대 생산성
④ 국가 경쟁력
⑤ 새로운 기술의 발전

어휘

- lower : 낮추다, 내리다
- production cost : 생산비
- material : 재료, 원료
- machinery : 기계
- output : 생산량
- profit : 수익, 이윤
- desirable : 바람직한
- scarcely : 거의 ~않다
- either of : ~중 어느 한쪽
- vote for : ~에 (찬성) 투표하다
- cruelly : 잔인하게, 몹시
- exploit : 착취하다
- labor : 노동
- pollutant : 오염물질
- depend on : ~을 확신하다, 신뢰하다
- patent : 특허권을 얻다
- respondent : 응답자
- take ~ into account : ~을 고려하다, 참작하다

해석

경쟁사 다섯 곳이 모두 생산비와 그들이 생산하는 모든 표준 제품의 판매 가격을 낮추려 한다고 가정해 보자. 한 회사는 근로자의 급여를 삭감함으로써 그렇게 한다. 한 회사는 근로자들에게 더 오랜 시간 근무를 하도록 하면서 그렇게 한다. 한 회사는 더 가난한 나라로부터 일부 원료를 더 싼 값에 구입하면서 그렇게 한다. 한 회사는 몇몇 근로자들을 로봇으로 대체함으로써 그렇게 한다. 한 회사는 누구에게도 피해를 주지 않고 — 생산량, 수익, 일자리 혹은 급여의 손실 없이 — 근로 시간을 단축하게 하는 것을 가능하게 하는 일부 기계의 개선을 생각해 냄으로써 그렇게 한다. 어떤 변화가 가장 바람직한지를 물어보라. 그러면 거의 아무도 처음 둘 중에 어느 것도 말하지 않을 것이다. 비록 조건부일지라도, 나머지 세 가지 각각의 방법을 뽑을 것이다. 해외 공급이 잔인하게 착취된 노동에 의해서 혹은 오염물질 폐기물을 발생시키면서 생산되었는가? 로봇으로 대체된 근로자들이 다른 일자리를 찾는 것을 확신할 수 있겠는가? 개선된 기계를 발명한 사람이 특허를 받아서 다른 회사들과 근로자들이 그것의 이익을 공유할 수 없는가? 응답자들은 결국 문제를 고찰할 때 익숙한 사회적 가치를 고려한다.

19 ③ 이 글은 면접과 시험에 통과하여 회사에 취직되었음을 알리는 내용이다. 따라서 이 글의 목적으로 가장 적절한 것은 'to offer Ms. Hart a position at the ACME Consulting Firm(ACME 컨설팅 회사에서 Hart 씨를 채용하기 위하여)'

이다.

오답풀이

① ACME 컨설팅 회사에 지원하도록 Hart 씨를 격려하기 위하여
② 인턴십 과정을 완료한 Hart 씨를 축하하기 위하여
④ Hart 씨에게 곧 있을 계약 갱신을 알려주려고
⑤ 입사 지원이 거절되었다는 것을 Hart 씨에게 통보하려고

어휘

- completion : 완료, 완성
- screen : 선별하다, 심사하다
- applicant : 지원자
- extremely : 매우, 대단히
- resume : 이력서
- unpaid : 무보수의, 무급의
- salary : 급여, 월급
- including : ~을 포함하여
- transfer : 옮기다, 전근가다
- no later than : 늦어도 ~까지는

해석

Hart 씨에게

백여 명의 지원자들을 선별하는 작업을 마치고 나서, 우리가 귀하의 이력서와 인터뷰, 그리고 시험 결과에 크게 감동을 받았다는 사실을 알려드리게 되어서 기쁩니다. 따라서 귀하는 ACME 컨설팅 회사에서 현재 충원하고 있는 다섯 가지 직책 중 하나에 선발되었습니다. 이를 받아들이기로 결정한다면, 귀하는 6개월 동안 무급 인턴사원 프로그램에 즉시 참여하게 될 것입니다. 성공적으로 완수하면, 귀하는 모든 기본적인 수당을 포함하여 월급을 받는 정규직 사원으로 발령이 날 것입니다. 전국의 많은 지점들 중에 한 곳으로 이동을 하거나 이곳 시내에 있는 본사에서 근무할 기회가 주어질 수도 있습니다. Hart 씨, 축하드립니다! 늦어도 이달 말까지는 결정을 내려서 저희에게 알려주시길 바랍니다.

ACME 컨설팅 회사 인사부

Cheryl Smith 드림

20 ② 'DNA characters are copied with an exactness (DNA의 특징들은 정확하게 복제된다)'를 통해 유전자가 복제되는 정확도가 상당하다는 것을 알 수 있으므로 (A)에는 'immense(엄청난, 굉장한)'이 들어가는 것이 적절하다. 'those bodies take active steps to preserve and propagate those same DNA messages(신체는 동일한 DNA 메시지를 유지하고 유전시키기 위하여 적극적인 조치를 취한다)'를 통해 (B)에는 'reproduce(복제하다)'가 들어가는 것이 적절하다는 것을 알 수 있다.

'Therefore(그러므로)'가 들어가는 것이 적절하다.

어휘

- transition : 이행, 전환
- alternate energy : 대체 에너지
- scarcity : 부족, 결핍
- fossil fuel : 화석 연료
- for decades : 수십 년 동안
- continually : 지속적으로, 끊임없이
- identify : 확인하다
- reserve : 비축, 보유
- economically : 경제적으로
- deem : 여기다, 간주하다
- access : 이용하다, 접근하다
- extract : 추출하다
- methane : 메탄, 천연가스의 주성분
- combine : 합치다
- humanity : 인류, 인간
- to date : 지금까지
- fraction : 부분, 일부
- severe : 심각한
- concerted effort : 일치단결, 혼신의 노력
- on the other hand : 반면에
- nevertheless : 그럼에도 불구하고
- on the contrary : 그와는 반대로
- in the same way : 같은 방법으로

해석

화석 연료의 부족이 대체 에너지로의 전환의 동기가 될 수는 없다. 수십 년 동안, 에너지 생산자들은 지속적으로 새로운 화석 연료 보유고를 확인해 왔고, 이전에 접근하기에 너무 어렵다고 여겨졌던 매장지로부터 경제적인 관점에서 석유와 가스를 끌어내기 위하여 기술을 발전시켜 왔다. 예를 들어, 일본은 최근 바다 속 수산화물층으로부터 메탄을 추출할 수 있었는데, 이는 지구상의 화석 연료를 다 합친 것보다 두 배 이상 많은 탄소를 함유한 것으로 보인다고 발표했다. 이것은 인류가 지금까지 화석 연료의 극히 일부만을 사용해 왔다는 것을 의미한다. 비록 우리가 그렇게 적은 양의 화석 연료를 이용해 왔음에도 불구하고, 지구는 이미 심각한 온난화 문제를 겪어오고 있다. 만약 우리가 에너지 공급을 위하여 계속해서 화석 연료에 크게 의존한다면, 실질적인 화석 연료 공급의 압박을 받기 훨씬 오래전에, 이미 기후 변화와 관련된 피해는 매우 심각해질 것이다. 그러므로, 살기 좋고 건강에 좋은 기후를 유지하기 위하여 대체 에너지를 위한 운동에 혼신의 노력을 기울여야 한다.

어휘

- gene : 유전자
- encode : 암호로 바꾸다, 부호화하다
- recode : 재부호화
- decode : 해독하다
- accuracy : 정확(도)
- exactness : 정확성
- rival : ~에 비할 만하다, 필적하다
- occasional : 가끔의
- combination : 조합
- numerous : 수많은
- obviously : 분명히
- automatically : 자동적으로
- propagate : 전하다, 유전시키다
- survival : 생존
- immense : 엄청난, 굉장한
- remove : 제거하다
- moderate : 알맞은, 보통의
- insignificant : 사소한, 하찮은
- reproduce : 복사[복제]하다

해석

유전자는 순수한 정보 — 의미의 어떠한 변화도 없이, 부호화하고 재부호화하고 해독할 수 있는 정보이다. 순수한 정보는 그대로 복제될 수 있고, 복제의 정확도는 굉장하다. 사실상, DNA의 특징들은 현대 공학자들이 할 수 있는 어떤 것에 비할 수 있을 정도로 정확하게 복제된다. 그것들은 세대를 이어 복제되는데, 아주 가끔 일치하지 않는 부분을 내놓는 실수가 있기도 하다. 이러한 불일치 중에 세상에서 더 다양해진 암호로 된 이러한 조합들은 분명히 그리고 자동적으로 신체 내에서 해독되고 작용될 때 신체가 동일한 DNA 메시지를 유지하고 유전시키기 위하여 적극적인 조치를 취하게 하는 것이 될 것이다. 우리는 — 그리고 모든 살아 있는 것들을 의미하는 — 프로그래밍을 했던 데이터베이스를 복제하기 위하여 프로그램을 짜 넣은 생존 기계이다. 현재 다원설은 순수 코드의 단계에서 생존자들의 생존인 것으로 보인다.

21 ① 빈칸에 들어갈 알맞은 연결사를 선택하는 문제로, 앞뒤 내용을 논리적으로 파악해야 한다. 이 글은 화석 연료의 부족으로 대체 에너지를 찾는 일에 크게 노력해야 한다는 내용의 글이다. 최근 경제적 관점에서 기술을 발전시켜 석유와 가스를 끌어내고 있다는 내용 뒤에 구체적으로 일본의 예를 들어 설명하고 있으므로 (A)에는 'For example(예를 들어)'가 들어가야 한다. 그리고 마지막 문장은 앞서 한 이야기의 결론에 해당하는 내용이 언급되고 있으므로 (B)에는

22 ① 'It is crucial that plants can sense light and respond to it. Plants need to locate light sources and grow towards them.(식물이 빛을 감지하고 그것에 반응을 보일 수 있는 것은 매우 중요하다. 식물은 광원을 찾아내서 그쪽을 향해 자라야만 한다)'을 통해 빛에 대한 노출을 극대화해야 한다는 것을 알 수 있다. 따라서 (A)에는 'maximize(극대화시키다)'가 쓰이는 것이 적절하다. 'Plants live in a changing environment, with day and night changes, seasonal changes, weather changes, and habitat changes.(식물은 낮과 밤이 변하고 계절이 바뀌고 날씨가 변하며 서식지가 바뀌는, 변화하는 환경에서 산다)'를 통해 식물이 융통성 있는 습성을 지녀야 한다는 것을 알 수 있으므로 (B)에는 'flexible(적응성 있는, 유연한)'이 적절하다. 'Photosynthesis has to be modified continually to cope with changing illumination,(광합성은 빛의 변화에 대응하기 위하여 끊임없이 적응해야만 한다)'을 통해 식물이 한낮에 빛의 세기에 따라 변화를 겪는다는 것을 알 수 있으므로, (C)에는 'variation(변화)'가 쓰이는 것이 적절하다.

어휘

• dependent upon : ~에 의존하는
• photosynthesize : 광합성하다
• crucial : 매우 중대[중요]한
• respond to : ~에 대응하다
• light source : 광원
• ensure : ~을 확실하게 하다
• habitat : 서식지
• photosynthesis : 광합성
• modify : 수정하다
• continually : 지속적으로
• cope with : ~에 대처[대응]하다
• illumination : 빛
• at midday : 정오에
• temporarily : 일시적으로
• block out : 차단하다, 가리다
• lead to : ~로 이어지다, 초래하다
• intensity : 강도, 세기
• flexible : 적응성 있는, 유연한
• variation : 변화
• maximize : 극대화하다
• constancy : 불변(성)
• minimize : 최소화하다
• rigid : 엄격한, 경직된

해석

식물의 자가 영양의 본성은 스스로를 빛에 매우 의존하게 만드는데, 광합성을 할 수 없는 식물종은 많지 않다. 따라서 식물이 빛을 감지하고 그것에 반응을 보일 수 있는 것은 매우 중요하다. 식물은 광원을 찾아내서 그쪽을 향해 자라야만 한다. 그러고 나서 광합성 기관에 대한 빛의 노출을 극대화시키는 올바른 방법으로 잎들이 적응하는지를 식물은 확실하게 해 둘 필요가 있다. 하지만 식물들이 빛을 감지하여 얻는 것보다 더 자세한 정보가 있다. 식물은 낮과 밤이 변하고 계절이 바뀌고 날씨가 변하며 서식지가 바뀌는, 변화하는 환경에서 산다. 이것은 식물이 그들의 환경을 볼 수 있어야 하고 이러한 변화들에 대응하기 위하여 아주 유연한 습성을 지녀야 한다는 것을 의미한다. 심지어 광합성은 빛의 변화에 대응하기 위하여 끊임없이 적응해야만 한다. 태양은 한낮에 가장 밝아야 하지만, 일시적으로 태양을 가리는 구름이 없는 날은 많지 않다. 이는 식물이 처리할 수 있는 빛의 세기에 큰 변화를 초래한다.

23 ⑤ 'in other words, when people behave to get rewards(다시 말해, 사람들이 보상을 얻기 위하여 행동을 할 때)'를 통해 행동이 보상을 받기 위한 수단이 된다는 것을 알 수 있으므로, (A)에는 'instrumental(수단이 되는)'이 들어가야 한다. (B) 뒤의 내용을 통해 어떠한 행동에 대한 보상을 하는 이유는 그 행동을 지속하기를 바라기 때문이라는 것을 알 수 있다. 따라서 (B)에는 'persist(계속하다, 지속하다)'가 알맞다. 제시된 예의 내용을 보면 보상이 없더라도 아이들이 지속적으로 공부하기를 원한다는 것을 알 수 있으므로, (C)에는 'terminated (끝난, 종료된)'이 적절하다.

어휘

• rewards : 보상
• monetary : 화폐의, 금전의
• in other words : 다시 말해서
• last : 계속되다, 이어지다
• forthcoming : 다가오는, 마련된
• report card : 성적표
• enthusiastic : 열중해 있는
• irrelevant : 관계가 없는, 무의미한
• instrumental : 수단[도구]이 되는
• persist : 계속하다, 지속하다
• cease : 중단하다
• terminated : 끝난, 종료된
• initiate : 시작하다

해석

일단 사람들을 통제하기 위하여 보상을 이용하기 시작했다면, 당신은 쉽게 돌아갈 수 없다. 행동이 금전적인 보상의 수단이

될 때 — 다시 말해, 사람들이 보상을 얻기 위하여 행동을 할 때 — 그러한 행동들은 보상이 마련되어 있는 동안만 지속될 것이다. 어떤 경우에 괜찮을 수 있지만, 대부분의 경우에 우리가 보상하는 행위는 보상이 중단된 후에도 오랫동안 우리가 지속하기를 바라는 것이다. 예를 들어, 만약 당신이 공부하는 것에 대해 아이들에게 보상을 제시한다면 — 성적표에 기재된 'A' 점수에 1달러씩을 — 당신은 보상 제도가 종료된 후에도 아이들이 계속해서 열심히 공부를 하기를 원할 것이다. 하지만 만약 보상을 받으려고 공부를 한다면, 보상이 더 이상 없을 때 그들은 공부를 하지 않을 가능성이 높아진다.

24 ④ 이 글에 따르면 칫솔을 사용하여 이를 닦는 것은 단순히 개인의 위생을 위해서뿐만 아니라, 자기 관리의 개념과 스스로 질서를 확립하고 규칙을 발전시키는 것과 연결된다. 더불어 칫솔이 산업 혁명으로 천천히 자연스럽게 나아가도록 하는 역할을 했다고 하였으므로, 이 글의 제목으로 가장 적절한 것은 'Role of the Toothbrush in Developing an Industrial Workforce(산업 노동력 개발에서의 칫솔의 역할)'이다.

오답풀이

① 아나폴리스 : 위대한 고고학의 매력
② 영어에서 '칫솔'의 출현
③ 치과 산업에 끼친 칫솔의 영향
⑤ 산업 혁명에 의해 초래된 경제적 변화들

어휘

• be accustomed to : ~에 익숙하다
• ritual : 의식
• preserve : 지키다, 보호하다
• gum : 잇몸
• benefit : 혜택, 이익
• archaeologist : 고고학자
• remains : 유적, 나머지
• be eager for : ~을 열망하다
• floss : 치실을 사용하다
• numerous : 수많은
• hygiene : 위생
• discipline : 규율
• comb : 빗
• orderly : 질서 있는
• ease : ~을 편하게 하다
• instrumental : 주된 역할을 하는

해석

우리는 매일 이를 닦는 것에 익숙하다. 우리는 그것이 우리의 치아와 잇몸을 보호하고 우리가 미소를 짓도록 하는 건강한

의식이라고 알고 있다. 그것의 이점은 사회적일 뿐만 아니라 개인적이다. 하지만 18세기 아나폴리스 — 새로운 계층의 사람들이 일자리를 찾으려고 애썼던 곳 — 의 유적들을 가지고 일하는 고고학자들은 어떻게, 그리고 왜 우리가 모두 이렇게 양치질을 하고 치실을 사용하고 신경을 쓰는지에 대한 새로운 관점을 제시해 왔다. Mark Leone와 그의 도시 고고학자팀은 아나폴리스의 도로 아래에서 수많은 칫솔을 발견했다. 18세기 칫솔은 개인위생에 대한 새로운 강조와 자기 관리하는 개인의 개념을 제시한다. 근로자들이 제시간에 도착해서 일을 하도록 하는 것은 중요하며, 그들은 규율을 발전시켜야만 한다. 따라서 산업 사회는 양치질과 사람들이 그들 스스로 질서를 잘 지키도록 하는 빗이나 시계와 같은 많은 다른 것들을 중요시한다. 칫솔은 산업혁명으로 자연스럽게 넘어가도록 하는 데 주된 역할을 했던 것으로 드러났다.

25 ④ 다이어트 음료에 대한 터무니없는 확신으로 방어 호르몬 분비의 감소를 간과하고 있다는 점을 지적하는 내용이므로, 이 글의 제목으로 가장 적절한 것은 'Disruptive Effect of Diet Drinks on Protective Hormones(방어 호르몬에 지장을 주는 다이어트 음료의 효과)'이다.

오답풀이

① 탄산음료 중독 예방과 치료
② 다이어트 음료에 들어가는 대용 설탕의 유행
③ 탄산음료 시장에 대한 소비자의 최근 선호도
⑤ 설탕 과다 섭취에 뇌가 대응하는 방식

어휘

• correlation : 연관성, 상관관계
• consumption : 소비, 섭취
• undesirable : 바람직하지 않은
• superficial : 피상적인
• unfounded : 근거 없는
• point out : 지적하다, 언급하다
• normally : 보통, 일반적으로
• intake : 섭취
• show up : 나타나다
• protective : 방어적인

해석

연구자들은 수년간 다이어트 음료 섭취와 좋지 않은 건강 사이의 연관성에 주목해 왔다. 하지만 많은 사람들은 이러한 바람직하지 않은 연관성이 이미 건강하지 않거나 뚱뚱한 사람들이 다이어트 탄산음료를 마시는 경향이 있다는 사실 때문이라고 믿을 뿐이다. 그러나 Purdue 대학교의 Susan Swithers 교수는 이러한 피상적인 행동에 관한 설명은 다이어트 음료에 대한 터무니없는 확신으로 야기된 건강 문제들을 설명하지 않

는다고 주장한다. 그녀는 일반적으로 몸이 당분에 반응할 때, 몸은 칼로리와 당분의 증가된 섭취에 스스로 준비하기 위하여 필요한 호르몬을 분비한다고 지적한다. "당신이 다이어트 탄산음료를 마실 때 일어난 일은 당신이 단맛을 느끼는 것이다 — 하지만 칼로리와 당분이 드러나지 않는다."라고 Swithers는 덧붙였다. 따라서 그녀는 만약 이러한 비정상적인 상황이 오랜 시간 동안 일어난다면, 실제로 진짜 설탕을 섭취할 때, 사람들의 뇌와 신체는 더 이상 방어 호르몬을 분비하지 않는 것에 익숙해질지도 모른다고 경고한다.

26 ④ 주어진 문장의, 역접을 나타내는 연결사 'even so(그렇다 하더라도)'를 염두에 두고 지문을 읽어야 한다. 주어진 문장은 현대의 일기 예보를 긍정적으로 보고 있으므로 이 문장의 앞에서 일기 예보의 한계점을 언급하는 것이 적절하다. 따라서 주어진 문장은 ④에 들어가야 한다.

어휘

- fuse : 융합하다, 결합되다
- property : 재산
- increasingly : 점점, 더욱 더
- meteorologist : 기상학자
- imperfect : 불완전한
- inaccurate : 부정확한
- skillfully : 능숙하게
- at the rate of : ~의 비율[속도]로
- ensemble forecasting : 종합적 분석에 기반을 둔 기상예보

해석

그렇다 하더라도, 현대의 일기 예보는 현대의 기상학과 모든 과학의 위대한 성과들 중 하나이다.

현대의 일기 예보는 오늘날 축적된 인간의 통찰력으로 만들어진 첨단 컴퓨터와 결합된다. 더불어, 1993년 3월의 '세기의 폭풍'과 2012년 10월의 슈퍼스톰 Sandy와 같이 점점 더 정확한 예측을 통해서 그것들은 생명을 구하고 재산을 보호한다. (①) 종합적 분석에 기반을 둔 기상 예보는 훨씬 더 나은 예보에 의거하여 기상학자들이 많은 '다른 사람의 의견'을 얻을 수 있도록 한다. (②) 하지만 예보가 얼마나 좋게 되는지에 있어서 한계가 있다. (③) 불완전한 자료와 대기가 어떻게 작용하는지에 관한 불완전한 지식, 연산능력의 한계, 그리고 심지어 카오스 이론은 부정확한 예보의 원인이 된다. (④) 능숙하게 날씨를 예보하는 우리의 능력은 향후 10년마다 약 하루 정도 더 빠른 속도로 향상되어 왔다. (⑤) 그것은 종합적 분석에 기반을 둔 기상 예보와 같은 새로운 기술을 통해서 당신의 일생 동안 계속해서 개선될 것이다.

27 ③ 앞서 말한 내용과 다르거나 반대되는 말을 도입할 때 쓰이는 연결사인 'rather(오히려, 차라리)'에 주목해야 한다. 주어진 문장은 'we are not moving towards a cultural rainbow(문화적 다채로움을 지향하고 있지 않다)'와 반대되는 내용으로, 'the rise of an increasingly homogenized popular culture(동질화된 인기 있는 문화의 성공)'이라고 언급되어 있다. 따라서 그에 대한 구체적인 예시 앞에 오는 것이 적절하므로 ③에 들어가야 한다.

어휘

- globalization : 세계화
- alike : 비슷한
- unfortunately : 유감스럽게도
- move toward : ~쪽으로 가다, ~을 지향하다
- reflect : 반영하다
- diversity : 다양성
- increasingly : 점점 더
- homogenized : 동질화된
- interpretation : 해석, 설명
- inhabitant : 주민, 사람
- proponent : 지지자
- norm : 기준
- vulnerable : 취약한
- popular culture : 대중문화

해석

오히려, 우리는 서양의 '문화산업'에 의해 건네진 점점 더 동질화된 인기 있는 문화의 성공을 목격하고 있다.

세계화는 전 세계 사람들을 더 비슷하게 하는가 아니면 더 다르게 만드는가? 이것은 문화적 세계화에 관한 논제에서 가장 자주 제기되는 질문이다. (①) 어떤 그룹의 사람들은 유감스럽게도 전자가 사실일 것이라고 주장한다. (②) 그들은 우리가 세계의 기존 문화들의 다양성을 반영하는 문화적 다채로움을 지향하지 않고 있다고 말한다. (③) 해석에 대한 증거로 이들은 나이키 운동화를 신고 있는 아마존 인디언들, 양키 야구 모자를 구입하는 사하라 사막 남부 지방의 주민들, 그리고 라말라 도심에서 시카고 불스가 쓰여 있는 운동복 상의를 자랑스럽게 드러내 보이는 팔레스타인의 젊은이들을 지적한다. (④) '세계의 미국화'와 같이 영미의 가치와 소비재의 확산을 언급하면서, 이러한 문화적 동질화 이론의 지지자들은 서양의 기준과 생활양식이 더 취약한 문화를 압도하고 있다고 주장한다. (⑤) '문화 제국주의'의 이러한 힘에 저항하기 위하여 몇몇 나라들이 진지하게 시도해오고 있지만, 미국 대중문화의 확산은 막을 수 없어 보인다.

28 ⑤ 'But few took his ideas seriously at that time; he seemed to be somewhat out of touch with the world.(하지만 그 당시에 그의 견해는 거의 진지하게 받아들여지지 않았다. 그는 세상과의 접촉을 끊은 것 같았다)'의 내용으로 보아, 그 당시 Adams의 사상은 크게 공감을 얻지 못했을 것이다.

오답풀이

① 'the American colonies, he believed, should one day win complete independence from England and establish a government based on the writings of the English philosopher John Locke.(그는 언젠가 미국의 식민지들이 영국으로부터 완전한 독립을 쟁취하고 영국의 철학자 John Locke의 저서를 바탕으로 정부를 수립해야 한다고 믿었다)'를 통해 John Locke의 영향을 받았음을 알 수 있다.

② 'Adams had inherited a brewery from his father, but he did not care about business.(Adams는 그의 아버지로부터 양조장을 물려받았지만, 그는 사업에 관심을 가지지 않았다)'를 통해 알 수 있다.

③ 'he spent his time writing articles on the ideas of Locke and the need for independence.(그는 Locke의 생각과 독립의 필요성에 관한 기사를 쓰면서 시간을 보냈다)'고 언급되어 있다.

④ 'He was an excellent writer, good enough to get his articles published.(그가 쓴 글들을 출판할 정도로 그는 충분히 훌륭한 작가였다)'고 언급되어 있다.

어휘

- colonial-era : 식민지 시대
- colony : 식민지
- independence : 독립
- based on : ~을 근거하여
- philosopher : 철학자
- reflect : 반영하다
- citizen : 시민, 국민
- inherit : 이어받다, 물려받다
- brewery : 양조장, 맥주공장
- care about : ~에 관심을 가지다
- go into bankruptcy : 파산하다
- seriously : 진지하게
- out of touch with : ~와 접촉하지 않고
- sink into : 빠져들다, 가라앉다
- depression : 우울증
- self-appointed : 자기 혼자 정한

해석

젊었을 때, 보스턴 식민지 시절의 Samuel Adams(1722~1803)는 꿈을 키웠다. 그는 언젠가 미국의 식민지들이 영국으로부터 완전한 독립을 쟁취하고, 영국의 철학자 John Locke의 저서를 바탕으로 정부를 수립해야 한다고 믿었다. Locke에 따르면, 정부는 국민의 의지를 반영해야 한다. 그렇게 하지 않았던 정부는 존재의 이유를 잃었다. Adams는 그의 아버지로부터 양조장을 물려받았지만, 그는 사업에 관심을 가지지 않았다. 양조장이 파산하는 동안, 그는 Locke의 생각과 독립의 필요성에 관한 기사를 쓰면서 시간을 보냈다. 그가 쓴 글들이 출판되기에 충분할 정도로 그는 훌륭한 작가였다. 하지만 그 당시에 그의 견해는 거의 진지하게 받아들여지지 않았다. 그는 세상과의 접촉을 끊은 것 같았다. 스스로에게 약속한 임무가 절망적이었기 때문에 Adams는 우울증 증세를 보이기 시작했다.

29 ③ 첫 번째 문장에서 'people have better learning outcomes when they taken handwritten notes, rather than typed ones.(사람들이 타이핑하는 것보다 손으로 필기를 할 때 더 나은 학습 결과를 얻는다)'라고 제시된 것처럼, 손글씨는 타이핑보다 빠르지 않기 때문에 강의를 들으면서 무엇을 적어야 할지를 선택하기 위하여 집중을 하게 되고, 그 결과 더 나은 점수를 얻게 된다. 따라서 이 글이 의미하는 바를 가장 잘 나타낸 것은 'Handwriting note-taking is recommended for better academic performance.(손글씨 필기는 더 나은 학문적 성과를 위해 권장된다)'이다.

오답풀이

① 키보드로 필기를 하는 것은 실제 내용에 대한 기억을 더 잘하게 한다.

② 손글씨 필기의 우월성에 대한 증거는 전혀 없다.

④ 지필로 필기를 하는 것은 일반적으로 더 완벽하고 상세한 필기로 이어진다.

⑤ 휴대용 컴퓨터로 말한 그대로 필기하는 것은 일반적으로 더 높은 시험 점수를 보장한다.

어휘

- conduct : 실시하다, 수행하다
- outcome : 결과
- word-for-word : 문자 그대로
- relatively : 비교적, 상대적으로
- copious : 방대한
- inferior : 하위의, 하등한
- retrieval : 검색, 회수
- transcription : 필기, 글로 옮김
- selectivity : 선택

해석

Mueller와 Oppenheimer가 수행한 최근의 연구는 사람들이 타이핑하는 것보다 손으로 필기를 할 때 더 나은 학습 결과를 얻는다는 새로운 증거를 강조한다. 연구원들은 손으로 필기를 하는 사람들은 비교적 간결하게 필기를 하는 반면에 휴대용 노트북을 이용하는 사람들은 공부할 때 일반적으로 길게 말한 그대로 필기를 하는 것을 관찰했다. 시험 점수로 밝혀졌듯이, 그들은 더 방대하고 상세한 필기가 사실과 개념 이해에 대한 형편없는 검색으로 이어졌다는 사실에 면밀한 주의를 기울였다. 키보드는 정확히 말한 그대로 글로 옮기기에 충분히 빠르기 때문에 노트북 컴퓨터에 필기를 하는 사람들은 무엇을 타이핑할지를 선택할 필요가 없었다. 반면에, 손으로 필기를 하는 사람들은 손글씨가 빠르지 않기 때문에 무엇을 적어야 할지를 선택하기 위해서 더 주의 깊게 정보를 처리해야만 했다. 이러한 초기의 선택은 강의 자료를 장기간 더 잘 이해하려는 이유로 여겨진다.

30　⑤ 이 글은 창의성을 향상시키기 위하여 근로자들 사이의 사회적 네트워크가 중요함을 강조하는 내용이므로, 이 글의 주제로 가장 적합한 것은 'value of supportive social networks for enhancing creativity(창의성을 향상시키는 데 힘이 되는 사회적 네트워크의 가치)'이다.

오답풀이

① 강한 협력 관계가 창의성에 미치는 해로운 영향
② 혜택을 못 받는 사람들을 지원하기 위한 사회적 네트워크의 필요성
③ 직장 내에서 개성 존중의 중요성
④ 창의적인 결과물을 지나치게 강조하는 것에 대한 우려

어휘

• expertise : 전문지식
• consequently : 그 결과, 따라서
• facilitate : 가능하게 하다, 촉진하다
• creativity : 창의성
• workplace : 직장
• colleague : 동료
• enhance : 향상시키다
• supervisor : 관리자
• foster : 촉진하다, 발전시키다
• consideration : 이해, 배려

해석

전문지식의 분야와 수준에 변화를 주면서 개인에 대한 근로자의 접촉을 증가시키기 때문에 사회적 네트워크는 특히 중요해지고 있다. 그 결과로써 협력 관계, 특히 약한 협력 관계의 발

전을 촉진시키는 것은 창의성에 긍정적인 영향을 끼칠 것이다. 직장 내에서 동료들로부터 얻는 정보적 지지와 정서적 지지는 더 높은 수준의 창의성과 관련이 있다는 것 또한 분명하다. 그러므로 창의성을 계발시키는 것에 관심이 있는 관리자들(혹은 지도자들)은 근로자들 사이의 강한 유대 관계를 장려해야 한다. 마지막으로, 창의적인 동료들의 존재는 지도자들이 창의성을 향상시키기 위한 그들 자신의 노력의 영향력을 깨닫는 데 필요하다. 개별 근로자들은 창의적인 동료들과 있을 때, 관리자의 피드백에 대한 반응으로 가장 높은 수준의 창의성을 발휘한다. 분명히, 개인의 창의성을 촉진하는 것은 그 개인뿐만 아니라 그들의 사회적 상황에 대한 이해를 필요로 한다.

31　⑤ 로마 제국이 멸망하면서 고전 라틴어도 함께 소멸되었으나, 라틴어가 천 년 후에 다시 사용되기 시작했으며 되살아난 용어들 중에 대표적인 예로 'satellite'를 언급하고 있다. 따라서 이 글의 주제로 가장 적합한 것은 'evolution of the meaning of the word satellite ('satellite'라는 단어의 의미의 변화)'이다.

오답풀이

① 목성 주변 위성들의 발견
② 로마 제국의 흥망성쇠
③ 격식을 갖춘 말로 고전 라틴어의 부활
④ 로마 시민들을 위한 무장한 경호원의 필요성

어휘

• hub : 중심지, 중추
• civilization : 문명
• economic unrest : 경제 불안
• a series of : 일련의
• cease to be : 없어지다, 죽다
• commerce : 무역, 상업
• armed : 무장한, 무기를 갖춘
• satellite : 위성, 추종자
• tongue : 혀, 언어
• medieval : 중세의
• Jupiter : 목성
• courtier : 조신, 신하
• revolve : 돌다, 회전하다
• encircle : 둘러싸다
• heavenly : 하늘의

해석

수천 년이 넘는 기간 동안, 로마는 서양 문화의 중심지였다. 그러나 결국 로마 제국의 생명은 경제 불안과 정부의 급격한 변화에 위협을 받았다. 어떠한 주요 인사도 추종자로 알려진

무장한 경호원들 없이 감히 그 수도의 거리를 걸어 다닐 수 없는 상황에 이르렀다. 로마 제국이 멸망했을 때, 고전 라틴어는 더 이상 상업과 과학의 언어가 아니었다. 하지만 10세기 후에 학식 있는 사람들이 고대의 언어를 다시 가져왔고 가장 격식을 갖춘 언어로 사용했다. 되살아난 용어들 중에 'satellite'가 있는데, 중세의 통치자들이 그들의 개인 경호원들에게 사용했던 표현이다. Johannes Kepler가 목성 주변을 돌고 있는 이상한 물체에 관하여 들었을 때, 그는 왕을 둘러싸고 있는 경호원들과 신하들을 떠올렸다. 그래서 1611년에 Kepler는 그것들을 'satellite'라고 이름 붙였고, 곧 그 용어는 주요 행성 주변을 회전하는 하늘의 모든 물체에 적용되었다.

32 ③ 'deeds do not lie. You must also apply this logic to yourself.(행동은 거짓말을 하지 않는다. 당신은 또한 이러한 논리를 스스로에게 적용시켜야 한다)'와 마지막 문장인 'People will judge you by what you do, not what you say.(사람들은 당신이 말하는 것이 아니라 당신이 행동하는 것을 보고 당신을 판단할 것이다)'를 통해 말보다 행동으로 자신의 가치를 증명하기 위하여 노력해야 한다는 내용임을 알 수 있다. 따라서 이 글이 시사하는 바로 가장 적절한 것은 'Actions speak louder than words.(말보다 행동이 중요하다)'이다.

오답풀이

① 잘 생각해보고 행동하라.

② 남에게 대접받고자 하는 대로 남을 대접하라.

④ 펜은 칼보다 강하다.

⑤ 제비 한 마리가 왔다고 해서 여름이 온 것은 아니다(작은 조짐 하나를 너무 심각하게 확대 해석하지 마라).

어휘

• brilliance : 뛰어남, 재기
• warfare : 전쟁, 전투
• eloquence : 웅변
• battlefield : 전쟁터
• general : 장군
• troop : 부대
• defeat : 패배
• ruthless : 무자비한, 냉혹한
• deed : 행위, 행동
• logic : 논리
• brag : 자랑하다, 허풍떨다

해석

탁월한 전투는 아무리 많은 설득이나 회의도 전쟁터에서의 실패를 해명하는 데 소용이 없다는 것이다. 장군은 그의 부대를 패배로 이끌었고, 목숨이 바쳐졌고, 그리고 역사가 그를 평가

할 것이다. 당신은 사람들을 그들의 행동의 결과들과 보이거나 평가될 수 있는 행동들, 그리고 그들이 목표를 달성하기 위하여 취했던 조치들로 판단하면서 이러한 냉혹한 기준을 당신의 일상에 적용하기 위하여 애써야 한다. 사람들이 스스로에 관하여 이야기하는 것은 중요하지 않다. 사람들은 어떠한 말도 할 것이다. 그들이 해왔던 것을 보라. 행동은 거짓말을 하지 않는다. 당신은 또한 이러한 논리를 스스로에게 적용시켜야 한다. 떠벌리는 것을 멈추고 당신의 노고에 대한 성과로 당신의 가치를 증명하라. 사람들은 당신이 말하는 것이 아니라 당신이 행동하는 것을 보고 당신을 판단할 것이다.

33 ⑤ 도표에 따르면 2005년부터 2008년까지 45세에서 63세 사이의 경우, 남성의 9%, 여성의 22%가 우울증 치료제를 처방받았으므로, 여성이 남성보다 두 배 이상 많이 처방을 받았다는 것을 알 수 있다. 따라서 'In the period 2005-2008, for those 45-64 years old, over twice as many males took prescription antidepressant medication as females.'는 도표의 내용과 일치하지 않는다.

어휘

• prescription : 처방
• antidepressant : 우울증 치료제, 항우울제
• medication : 약, 약물
• time frame : 기간, 시간
• significant : 중요한, 상당한
• respectively : 각각
• moderate : 알맞은, 적당한
• in contrast : 반대로
• drastic : 급격한

해석

위의 표는 성별과 연령에 따라 1988년부터 1994년까지와 2005년부터 2008년에 걸쳐 "지난달에 당신은 우울증 치료제를 처방받았나요?"라는 질문에 그렇다고 대답한 미국인의 비율을 보여준다. 두 기간의 성별과 연령대 전체에 걸쳐 우울증 치료제 처방이 전반적으로 증가하였다. 연령이 높은 두 부류의 남성의 경우 2%에서 9%, 그리고 2%에서 10%로 각각 크게 증가하였지만, 18세에서 44세 사이의 남성들은 1%에서 4%로 다소 약간 증가하였다. 반면에, 세 부류의 모든 여성들은 18세에서 44세 사이의 경우 10%, 45세에서 64세 사이의 경우 17%, 그리고 가장 나이가 많은 그룹의 경우 13%로 더 급격한 증가를 보였다. 남성은 가장 나이가 많은 그룹에서 가장 큰 증가를 보인 반면에, 여성들의 경우 45세에서 64세 사이의 연령대의 경우에 크게 증가하였다. 2005년부터 2008년까지의 기간 동안 45세에서 64세의 경우, 여성보다 두 배 이상 많은 남성들이 우울증 치료제를 처방받았다.

34 ③ 모든 사람들이 예술적으로 동일한 판단을 내리는 것은 아니지만 일반적으로 누구나 느끼기에 좋은 결합과 그렇지 않은 결합이 있다는 내용의 (B)가 오고, 음악으로 비슷한 예를 언급한 (C)가 이어지고 나서 마지막으로 미술과 관련된 예를 든 (A)가 연결되는 것이 자연스럽다.

어휘

• characteristic : 특질, 특징
• appreciation : 감상
• combination : 조합, 결합
• universally : 일반적으로
• discord : 불협화음
• geometrical : 기하학적
• arrangement : 배열
• displeasing : 불쾌한
• harmonize : 조화를 이루다

해석

아름다워지기 위하여 사물은 평범한 사람이 느끼는 감상력을 불러일으키는 어떠한 특징을 지녀야 한다. 모두가 동일하게 예술적 판단을 지니고 있지 않으며, 혹은 적어도 그것이 모두에게 똑같이 계발되지 않는다는 것은 사실이다.

(B) 하지만, 일반적으로 화음이라고 불리는 소리의 특정 결합과 불협화음이라고 불리는 그 밖의 것들이 있다. 기분 좋게 여겨지는 색깔의 특정 조합과 불쾌한 다른 것들이 있다.

(C) 마찬가지로 아름다운 특정 기하학적 형태나 공간 배치가 있지만, 불쾌한 것들도 있다. 음악가들은 어떤 음색이 조화를 이룰 것인지, 그리고 그렇지 않을 것인지를 알고 있다.

(A) 음악 교육을 받지 않은 사람은 그러한 지식을 갖출 수 없지만, 그는 음색을 듣고 그것의 조화를 인식한다. 색채 화가는 색깔을 가지고 만족스러운 효과를 거두는 방법을 알고 있다. 비록 그들이 그의 일을 평가할 수 있을지라도 그는 다른 사람들이 가지고 있지 않은 이러한 지식을 얻는다.

35 ④ 출근길에 발생한 자전거 사고의 상황을 시간 순서대로 연결해야 한다. 주어진 글에서 John이 중심을 잃고 넘어졌으므로, 그 순간 휴대 전화가 파손되는 것을 막으려고 팔을 치켜들어 얼굴이 땅에 먼저 닿았다는 내용의 (C)가 이어져야 한다. 이어서 몸보다는 마음의 고통을 크게 느낀 John이 주위를 둘러보고 얼굴에 묻은 흙을 털어내는 내용의 (A)가 연결되어야 한다. 마지막으로 회사에 도착하고 나서야 얼굴에 큰 상처가 났다는 것을 알고 병원에 가서 치료를 받았다는 내용의 (B)가 이어지는 것이 적절하다.

어휘

• split second : 아주 짧은 순간
• instinct : 본능
• at the cost of : ~을 희생하여
• pavement : 포장도로
• embarrassing : 당황스러운, 난처한
• tumble : 굴러 떨어짐
• witness : 목격자
• severely : 심하게
• bandage : 붕대를 감다

해석

어느 날 John이 자전거를 타고 출근을 하고 있을 때, 그의 휴대 전화가 울리기 시작했다. 그는 주머니에 있는 휴대 전화를 꺼내려고 오른손을 뻗으면서 왼손으로 브레이크를 잡았다. 그는 중심을 잃었고 자전거 앞쪽으로 넘어졌다.

(C) 그 짧은 순간, 그는 본능적으로 자신의 신체적 건강을 희생하여 휴대 전화가 파손되는 것을 막았다. 휴대 전화가 도로에 부딪치는 것을 막기 위하여 그는 팔을 치켜들었는데, 대신에 얼굴이 먼저 땅에 떨어지면서 충격을 덜 받았다.

(A) John은 고통을 많이 느끼지는 않았지만, 그의 자아는 상처를 입었다. 그는 재빨리 몸을 폈고 아무도 자신이 굴러 떨어지는 모습을 보지 않았는지를 확인하려고 주위를 둘러봤다. 다행스럽게도 목격자는 없었다. 그는 얼굴에 묻은 흙을 털어내고 가던 길로 돌아갔다.

(B) 회사에 도착한 후에, John은 자신의 얼굴이 심하게 긁혀서 뺨에 크게 베인 상처가 났다는 것을 알게 되었다. 그는 서둘러 병원으로 달려갔는데, 병원에서 붕대를 감고 몇 바늘 꿰맸다. 크게 다치지 않았지만, 가족에게 그 사고를 설명하는 데 그는 여전히 창피했다.

36 ② 두려움, 분노, 조바심, 자만심, 사랑, 애착 등 감정의 변화는 상황을 파악하는 방식에 영향을 끼치기 때문에 감정의 영향력을 인정하고 그에 따른 반응을 제한하거나 보완해서 현실을 있는 그대로 직시해야 한다는 내용의 글이다. 따라서 필자가 주장하는 바로 가장 적절한 것은 '현실을 바로 보려면 감정에 휘둘리지 말라'이다.

어휘

• overestimate : 과대평가하다
• passively : 수동적으로
• impatience : 성급함, 조바심
• cut off : 차단하다, 방해하다
• overconfidence : 과신, 자만심
• particularly : 특히

• affection : 애정, 애착

• blind : ~을 보이지 않게 하다, ~을 알 수 없게 하다

• treacherous : 믿을 수 없는, 배신하는

• gradation : 단계적 변화

• color : 영향을 끼치다

• inevitable : 불가피한, 피할 수 없는

• compensate for : 보상하다

• wary : 경계하는, 조심하는

• exaggerate : 과장하다

해석

두려움으로 인해 당신은 문제를 과대평가하고 너무 소극적으로 행동하게 될 것이다. 분노와 조바심은 당신이 선택할 수 있는 것을 차단시키는 경솔한 행동으로 당신을 끌어들일 것이다. 성공의 결과, 특히 자만심으로 인해 당신은 도에 넘게 행동할 것이다. 사랑과 애착은 분명히 당신 편인 사람들의 믿을 수 없는 행동을 당신이 보지 못하게 할 것이다. 심지어 이러한 감정의 가장 미묘한 변화는 당신이 어떤 일들을 보는 방식에 영향을 끼칠 수 있다. 유일한 해결책은 감정의 영향력은 불가피하다는 것을 알고, 그것이 일어나고 있을 때 그것을 깨닫고 보완하는 것이다. 성공을 거둘 때, 각별히 조심하라. 화가 날 때, 어떤 행동도 하지 마라. 두려울 때, 직면한 위험을 당신이 과장할 것임을 알아라. 감정적 반응을 제한하거나 보완할수록, 당신은 그것을 있는 그대로 더 가까이서 보게 될 것이다.

37 ① 새로운 화석을 찾고자 위험을 무릅쓰고 몇백 년 동안 종족 갈등이 이어져 오던 두 종족을 설득할 수 있었던 것은 Zeray Alemseged 박사의 'perseverance(인내)' 덕분이다. 연구 결과, 기존에 밝혀졌던 것보다 더 늦게 인류의 조상들이 나무 타기 능력을 포기했다는 것을 알 수 있었다고 하였으므로 (B)에는 'abandoned(포기한)'가 들어가야 한다.

어휘

• remarkable : 놀랄만한

• contribution : 기여, 공헌

• anthropology : 인류학

• Ph.D. : 박사학위

• isolated : 외딴, 고립된

• optimal : 최적의

• fossil : 화석

• tribal conflict : 종족 갈등

• give up : 포기하다

• convince : 납득시키다, 설득하다

• fossilized : 화석화된

• skeleton : 해골

• shoulder blade : 어깨뼈

• intact : 손상되지 않은

• paper-thin : 종잇장같이 얇은

• climber : 잘 기어오르는 동물

• considerably : 상당히, 많이

• evidence : 증거

• generosity : 관대함

• abandoned : 포기한

• perseverance : 인내

• acquired : 획득한

• improved : 향상된

• creativity : 창의성

해석

Zeray Alemseged 박사는 인류학 분야에 크게 공헌하였다. 에티오피아 국립 박물관에서 근무한 경험에서 영감을 받은 Alemseged는 박사 과정을 밟으려고 파리 대학을 다녔다. 에티오피아로 돌아온 후, 그는 새로운 화석을 찾기 위한 최적의 장소로 외딴 지역을 목표로 정했다. 일하기에 너무 위험할 정도로 몇백 년 동안 이어져 온 종족 갈등 때문에, 다른 과학자들은 이러한 지역을 피했었지만, 그는 자신을 그곳에서 일하도록 허락해 줄 양쪽 종족들을 설득하는 것을 포기하지 않았다. Alemseged와 그의 팀은 마침내 330만 년 된 여자 아기의 화석화된 뼈를 발견했다. 거의 손상되지 않은 어깨뼈가 포함되어 있었는데, 지금까지 종잇장같이 얇게 화석화된 뼈를 발견한 적이 전혀 없었다. 이 어깨뼈의 모양에 근거하여, Alemseged와 그의 동료들은 한 연구를 발표했다. 330만 년 전 오스트랄로피테쿠스 아파렌시스는 잘 기어 올라갈 수 있는 종이었는데, 이는 많은 연구자들이 이전에 제안했던 것보다 상당히 더 늦게 우리의 조상들이 나무 타기를 포기했던 것을 의미한다는 내용의 연구였다.

↓

Zeray Alemseged 박사의 인내 덕분에, 다른 연구원들이 주장했었던 것보다 상당히 더 늦게 인류의 조상들이 나무 타기 능력을 포기했다는 증거를 찾음으로써 그는 인류학의 발전에 크게 기여해 왔다.

[38~39]

38 ② 'he openly acknowledged his error by good-naturedly shaking his fist at the piano(그는 피아노를 향해 부드럽게 주먹을 흔들면서 공개적으로 그의 실수를 인정했다)'와 'do not allow your mistakes to interrupt your performance(실수가 당신의 연주를 방해하지 않도록 하라)'에서 알 수 있듯이, 실수를 하더라도 그것을 있는 그대로 받아들이고 계속 이어서 연주를 하라는 내용이므로 빈칸에는 'get on with the show(그 공연을 잘 해나가라)'가

들어가야 한다. 'get on with'는 '~을 해 나가다, ~와 잘 지내다'라는 뜻이다.

오답풀이

① 짧은 시간 동안 나가라
③ 화가 나서 주먹을 휘둘러라
④ 처음부터 다시 시작하라
⑤ 연주할 다른 곡을 선택하라

어휘

- recital : 연주회
- the late : 고인이 된
- deliver a performance : 연주하다
- luminous : 빛을 발하는
- virtuoso : 거장, 명연주자
- audibly : 들릴 정도로
- acknowledge : 인정하다
- good-naturedly : 온화하게, 부드럽게
- evoke : 불러일으키다
- interrupt : 방해하다, 중단시키다
- blunder : 실수
- err : 실수를 범하다

해석

내가 들어봤던 가장 감동적인 피아노 연주회 중에 하나는 고(故) Rudolf Serkin이 베토벤의 '발트슈타인 소나타'와 슈베르트의 '방랑자 환상곡'을 명쾌하게 연주했던 것이다. 슈베르트의 작품으로 구성된 거장의 연속 공연들 중에 하나를 하는 동안, Serkin의 손가락이 들릴 정도로 뒤엉켰다. 명백한 실수에도 불구하고, Serkin은 당황하지 않고 계속 연주를 했다. 연주를 마치고 의자에서 일어났을 때, 그는 피아노를 향해 부드럽게 주먹을 흔들면서 공개적으로 그의 실수를 인정했다. 난처한 상황이 될 수도 있었던 분위기에서 재치 있는 행동으로 Serkin은 청중으로부터 웃음을 자아낼 수 있었다. 말할 필요도 없이, 청중은 전반적으로 훌륭한 공연에 감동받았다. 내가 들어본 적 있는 다른 음악가들이 연주한 많은 다른 '완벽한' 것보다 더 드러내 보이고 더 아름다운 전무후무한 연주였다. 교훈은 분명하다. 전반적으로 좋은 연주를 하라. 그러면 당신은 하나 혹은 둘, 심지어 분명한 한 가지 실수도 용서받을 것이다. 오히려, 실수가 당신의 연주를 방해하지 않도록 하라. Serkin의 청중이 그의 실수를 잡아내려는 목적으로 연주회에 참석하지 않았던 것처럼, 당신이 실수를 저지르는 모습을 보려는 목적으로 청중이 모였을 가능성은 거의 없다. 그리고 만약 당신이 연주를 하는 동안 정말 실수를 범한다면, 실수를 받아들이고 그 공연을 잘해 나가라.

③ 'Despite the apparent mistake, Serkin wouldn't have this

bother him, and went on playing.(명백한 실수에도 불구하고, Serkin은 당황하지 않고 계속 연주를 했다)'에서 알 수 있듯이, Serkin이 실수를 했지만 그 순간 연주를 중단하지 않았으므로 ③은 이 글의 내용과 일치하지 않는다.

오답풀이

① 'the late Rudolf Serkin, who delivered a luminous performance of the Beethoven Waldstein Sonata and the Schubert Wanderer Fantasy.(고(故) Rudolf Serkin이 베토벤의 '발트슈타인 소나타'와 슈베르트의 '방랑자 환상곡'을 명쾌하게 연주했다)'를 통해 알 수 있다.
② 'Despite the apparent mistake, Serkin wouldn't have this bother him, and went on playing.(명백한 실수에도 불구하고, Serkin은 당황하지 않고 계속 연주를 했다)'는 내용에서 그가 연주 중에 실수를 저질렀음을 알 수 있다.
④ 'Serkin was able to evoke laughter from the audience with his witty action.(재치 있는 행동으로 Serkin은 청중으로부터 웃음을 자아낼 수 있었다)'는 내용으로 보아 실수를 재치 있게 인정했음을 알 수 있다.
⑤ 'the audience were moved by the lovely performance as a whole.(청중은 전반적으로 훌륭한 공연에 감동받았다)'는 내용으로 보아, 작은 실수에도 불구하고 청중이 감동을 받았다는 것을 알 수 있다.

[40~41]

40 ④ (d)는 무대 위로 올라온 지원자 관객이다. 나머지는 Montemagno를 가리킨다.

해석

나는 관객을 사로잡는 신나는 방법들을 만들어내는 의사소통을 항상 찾는다. 젊은 이탈리아인 사업가이자 텔레비전 방송 진행자인 Marco Montemagno보다 더 소품을 사용하는 사람을 나는 거의 본 적이 없다.

Montemagno는 인터넷을 받아들이고 우려하지 않아도 되는 이유를 이탈리아인에게 제시하면서 인터넷 문화를 주제로 자주 언급한다. 그는 로마와 밀라노, 베니스와 같은 곳에서 3천 명 정도 되는 많은 사람들 앞에서 발표한다. 대부분의 관객들이 인터넷을 사용하는 데 초보자이기 때문에, (당신이 이탈리아어를 안다고 가정하고) (a) 그는 모든 사람들이 이해할 수 있는 언어를 사용한다. 그가 만든 슬라이드는 아주 간단하고 시각적이다. 그는 종종 사진과 애니메이션, 그리고 비디오를 사용한다. 하지만 Montemagno가 다수의 발표자와 정말로 다른 점은 믿을 수 없을 정도로 많은 (b) 그의 소품들과 실례이다.

발표의 일부 중에, Montemagno는 관객에게 무대 위로 올라

와서 그와 함께 해달라고 요청할 것이다. 예를 들어, (c) 그는 지원자에게 무대 위에서 티셔츠를 접어달라고 부탁한다. 대부분의 사람들처럼, 그 지원자는 약 20초 정도의 시간이 걸려서 평범한 방법으로 그 셔츠를 접을 것이다. (d) 그가 다 했을 때, 관중은 5초 내에 셔츠를 접는 방법이 나오는 인기 있는 유튜브 비디오를 본다. 그리고 나서 Montemagno는 관객이 환호성을 지를 때 그것을 재현한다. (e) 그의 요점은 인터넷이 깊이 있고 지적인 수준으로 알려줄 수 있지만, 그것은 또한 가장 재미없는 일을 더 쉽게 만들 수도 있다는 것이다.

41 ③ 'He presents to groups as large as three thousand people in places(3천 명 정도 되는 많은 사람들 앞에서 발표한다)'와 'he uses language that everyone can understand (well, assuming you know Italian)[(당신이 이탈리아어를 안다고 가정하고) 모든 사람들이 이해할 수 있는 언어를 사용한다)]'을 통해 그가 영어가 아니라 이탈리아어로 발표를 한다는 것을 알 수 있다. 따라서 'He makes presentations to very large groups in English.(그는 많은 사람들 앞에서 영어로 발표한다)'는 이 글의 내용과 일치하지 않는다.

오답풀이

① 그는 사업에 종사하며 텔레비전 프로그램을 진행한다. : 'a young Italian entrepreneur and television host, Marco Montemagno(젊은 이탈리아인 사업가이자 텔레비전 방송 진행자인 Marco Montemagno)'라고 소개한 것을 통해 그가 사업가이고 방송 프로그램의 진행자임을 알 수 있다.

② 그는 인터넷을 두려워하지 않도록 관중들을 격려한다. : 'showing Italians why the Internet should be embraced and not feared(인터넷을 받아들이고 우려하지 않아도 되는 이유를 이탈리아인에게 제시한다)'를 통해 알 수 있다.

④ 그는 소품들과 다른 시각적 자료를 발표에 활용한다. : 'His slides are very simple and visual(그가 만든 슬라이드는 아주 간단하고 시각적이다)'과 'his unbelievable number of props(믿을 수 없을 정도로 많은 그의 소품들)'를 통해 파악할 수 있다.

⑤ 그는 발표를 하면서 관중의 참여를 포함시킨다. : 'In parts of his presentation, Montemagno will ask for his audience to join him onstage.(발표 중에, Montemagno는 관중에게 무대 위로 올라와서 그와 함께 해달라고 요청할 것이다)'를 통해 그가 관중의 참여를 유도한다는 것을 알 수 있다.

어휘

• engage : 사로잡다, 끌다
• entrepreneur : 사업가
• prop : 소품, 소도구

• employ : 쓰다, 이용하다
• majority of : 다수의
• conventional : 평범한
• duplicate : 재현하다, 복사하다
• instruct : 가르치다, 알려주다
• mundane : 재미없는

[42~43]

42 ⑤ 주어진 글 (A)에서 어떤 귀족이 하이든에게 찾아와서 작곡 수업을 받고 싶다고 이야기했으므로, (A)에는 수업을 시작하는 부분이 제시된 (D)가 이어져야 한다. (D)에서 귀족이 4중주곡을 검토해 보자는 제안을 했으므로 여기에는 작품을 자세히 살펴보는 (C)가 이어져야 한다. (C)에서 귀족이 하이든에게 조음을 한 이유를 밝히라고 했지만, 이에 대해 명쾌한 대답을 하지 못한 하이든이 귀족에게 그 작품을 다시 써 볼 것을 제안하는 (B)가 이어지는 것이 자연스럽다.

어휘

• aspect : 양상, 측면
• pupil : 학생, 제자
• beloved : (대단히) 사랑하는, 연인
• nobleman : 귀족
• fondness : 애정, 기호
• composition : 작곡
• objection : 이의, 반대
• modulation : 변조, 전조
• progression : (선율, 화성의) 진행
• set to work : 일에 착수하다
• composer : 작곡가
• persist : 집요하게 계속되다, 고집하다
• patience : 인내심
• deserve : ~을 받을 만하다
• farewell : 작별(인사)
• show somebody the door : ~에게 나가라고 하다, 쫓아내다

해석

(A) 하이든은 전반적으로 런던을 즐거워했지만, 그가 몹시 사랑하는 비엔나로 돌아갔을 때 그가 두고 오지 않을 이유가 전혀 없는 제자와 비슷한 사람이 한 명 있었다. 어느 날 한 귀족이 그를 방문했고, 음악에 대한 애정을 표현하면서 그가 하이든에게 수업 당 1파운드를 주고 작곡 수업을 몇 번 받고 싶다고 말했다.

(D) 하이든은 동의했고 그들이 수업을 시작할 때 요청했다. "이의가 없으면, 지금 당장 합시다." 그는 하이든의 4중주곡 중 하나를 주머니에서 꺼내면서 말했다. "첫 번째 수업

으로 먼저 이 4중주곡을 살펴보고 나서 작곡의 모든 규칙에 상반되는 몇 가지 조음과 일부 선율의 진행에 대한 이유를 말해주시오."

(C) 하이든은 이러한 제안에 어떠한 반대도 하지 않았다. 그러고 나서 그들은 그 음악을 검토해보기 시작했다. 몇 군데에서 어떤 것들이 발견되었고, 왜 이렇게 저렇게 했는지 질문을 받았을 때, 하이든은 좋은 효과를 얻기 위해서 그렇게 썼다고 말할 뿐이었다. 하지만 그 귀족은 그러한 이유에 만족하지 않았고 만약 작곡가가 자신에게 변경한 것에 대한 더 나은 이유를 제시하지 않는다면, 그것들은 아무 소용이 없다고 단언했다.

(B) 그러자 하이든은 그 제자에게 그의 취향대로 그 음악을 다시 써보라고 제안했다. 하지만 그는 계속해서 하이든의 작곡 선택에 관하여 질문을 하면서도 이렇게 하길 거절했다. 마침내, 하이든은 이러한 고상한 비평가를 참을 수 없었고, 다음과 같이 말했다. "저를 가르칠 만큼 좋은 사람이 바로 대공이라는 걸 알고 있습니다. 대공처럼 그러한 명인으로 존경을 받을 만하지 않기 때문에, 저는 대공의 가르침을 원하지 않습니다. 제가 작별을 고해야겠습니다." 그리고 그 귀족에게 떠나라고 했다.

43 ④ 어떤 귀족이 하이든에게 작곡 수업을 받고 싶다고 했지만, 수업을 받고자 하는 것보다 하이든의 작품을 비평하려는 의도가 더 컸기 때문에, 하이든에게 그 귀족은 제자나 친구가 아닌 그저 혹평가였을 뿐이었다. 따라서 이 글의 제목으로 가장 적절한 것은 'Not a Good Pupil, But a Harsh Critic(좋은 벗이 아니라, 혹평가)'이다.

오답풀이

① 돈으로 인내심을 산다
② 음악을 살펴보는 즐거움
③ 가장 아름다운 런던의 기억
⑤ 도전적인 질문으로부터 얻은 영감

[44~45]

44 ④ 'Arctic sea ice that was previously considered permanent is now rapidly disappearing(이전에 영구적이라고 여겨졌던 북극해 빙하는 현재 급속도로 사라지고 있다)'과 'scientists expect water temperatures to rise even more, causing the melting ice to disappear at an ever-increasing rate(계속 증가하는 비율로 녹고 있는 얼음을 사라지게 하면서 수온이 훨씬 더 상승할 것이라고 과학자들은 예상한다)'를 통해 지구 온난화 현상이 심화되고 있음을 알 수 있다. 따라서 이 글의 제목으로 가장 적절한 것은 'Vicious Circle of Global Warming and Arctic Ice Melt(지구 온난화와 북극 빙

하가 소실되는 악순환)'이다.

오답풀이

① 북극 빙하 소실과 방지를 위한 계획 세우기
② 지구 온난화를 관찰하는 과학적 방법들
③ 육지와 바다에서 태양 광선의 효과의 차이
⑤ 지구 온난화로 인한 원양항해의 변화들

어휘

• chunk : 덩어리
• float : 떠다니다
• milestone : 중요한[획기적인] 사건
• floating ice : 유빙, 부빙
• the Northwest Passage : 북서항로(유럽에서 서북으로 항해하여 태평양과 아시아에 이르는 항로)
• atmosphere : 대기
• reflect : 반사하다
• absorb : 흡수하다
• direct sunlight : 직사광선
• expect : 예상하다
• solid : 단단한
• vulnerable : 영향받기 쉬운
• defenseless : 무방비의

45 ① (A)의 앞뒤 문장에서 북극 지방의 빙하가 빠른 속도로 사라지고 있고, 얼음 덩어리가 외해에서 녹고 있다고 한 것으로 보아, 캐나다와 알래스카 지역의 해안 빙하 역시 소실되고 있다는 내용이 되어야 하므로, (A)에는 'brittle(부서지기 쉬운, 불안정한)'이 들어가야 한다. 빈칸 (B) 앞의 북극해에 해빙이 적었고 2005년에는 사상 최저치를 기록했다는 내용과 (B) 뒤의 북극해 빙하가 현재 급격하게 소실되고 있다는 내용을 통해, (B)의 문장은 기존에는 북극해의 빙하가 영원할 것이라고 착각했다는 내용이 되어야 하므로, (B)에는 'permanent(영구적인, 영속적인)'가 들어가야 한다.

해석

지구 온난화를 방지하기 위한 많은 환경친화적 움직임에도 불구하고 북극지방의 빙하가 이전에 본 적 없는 속도로 서서히 사라지고 있다. 빙하가 녹는 것은 캐나다와 알래스카 지역의 해안 빙하가 상당히 불안정해진 상태로 이어진다. 그 빙하는 큰 덩어리로 쉽게 떨어져 나가고 (빙하분리로 알려진 과정) 외해에서 녹는다.

빙하가 대서양에 떠다니기 때문에 북극해에 해빙이 더 적게 있다. 2005년 8월 15일에 북극 지방의 해빙이 사상 최저치를 기록했지만, 북극은 2007년 여름에 또 다른 중요한 사건을 목격하게 된다. 8월에 북서항로에는 유빙이 거의 없었다. 1972년에 기록하기 시작한 이후로 배가 다니도록 그 항로가 완전히

개방되었던 첫 번째 시기였다.

이전에 영구적이라고 여겨졌던 북극해 빙하는 현재 급속도로 사라지고 있다. 전 세계의 온도를 낮게 유지하는 데 빙하가 중요한 역할을 하기 때문에 이러한 빙하의 소실을 진지하게 주목해야 한다. 해빙은 대기로 투사되는 태양 광선의 80퍼센트를 반사하는 반면, 해수는 90퍼센트를 흡수한다. 녹고 있는 얼음이 더 많은 바다를 직사광선에 노출시키기 때문에, 계속 증가하는 비율로 녹고 있는 얼음을 사라지게 하면서 수온이 훨씬 더 상승할 것이라고 과학자들은 예상한다.